D1744719

# Intermediate Spanish

## Course Book

**Berlitz Publishing**
New York Munich Singapore

INTERMEDIATE SPANISH



Contacting the Editors
Every effort has been made to provide accurate information in this publication, but changes are inevitable. The publisher cannot be responsible for any resulting loss, inconvenience or injury. We would appreciate it if readers would call our attention to any errors or outdated information by contacting Berlitz Publishing, 193 Morris Avenue, Springfield, NJ 07081, USA. Fax: 1-908-206-1103, email: comments@berlitzbooks.com



Printed in China, April 2008

Text: Rosa María Martín, Phil Turk
Editors: Inés Greenberger, Saskia Gorospe Rombouts, Mercedes Roffé, Sheryl Olinsky Borg, Juergen Lorenz, Lorraine Sova, Francesca Onofri, Angela Malovich Castro, Diane Gigantino
Production Editor: Joyce Gaskin, Elvira Ortiz
Production: Steve Maher, Wee Design Group, Molly Pike Riccardi, Kent Wilkinson
Audio Producer: Paul Ruben Productions
Cover Design: Claudia Petrilli
Interior Design: Max Crandall
Art Director: Barbara Rusin
Production Director: Helen Breen
Production: Lyndall Culbertson, Elizabeth Onorato, Laura Shatz
Opener Illustrations: Andy Levine
Illustrations: David Chen, Lyndall Culbertson, Mona Daly, Daniel Dumont, Annie Gusman, Fanny Mellet Berry, Dan Potash, Chris Reed, George Thompson, Kurt Vargo
Maps: MAGELLAN Geographix, Parrot Graphics
Cover Photos: © Authors Image/Robert Harding; © rubberball/age fotostock; © digitalsport-photoagency, 2006 Used under license from Shutterstock, Inc.; © 2007 Jupiterimages Corporation

# Contents

# Unit 4

# Unit 5

# Unit 6

Unit 1 is about your home and your daily routine. When you have completed this unit, you will know how to:

- describe your home
- describe your daily routine

# Hablar de tu casa 1

## Word Bank

| | |
|---|---|
| afuera | *outside* |
| las afueras | *suburbs* |
| al lado de | *next to* |
| alquilar | *to rent* |
| aparte | *separate* |
| arriba | *upstairs* |
| el ascensor | *elevator* |
| el barrio | *neighborhood, district* |
| la bañera | *bathtub* |
| el baño | *bathroom* |
| la casa | *house* |
| claro que | *of course* |
| la cocina | *kitchen* |
| el comedor | *dining room* |
| comer | *to eat* |
| cómodo/a | *comfortable* |
| completamente | *completely* |
| el cuarto de baño | *bathroom* |
| dar a | *to look on to, to lead on to* |
| el desván | *attic* |
| doble | *double* |
| el dormitorio | *bedroom* |
| la ducha | *shower* |
| encontrarse | *to meet, to be found* |
| la escalera | *staircase, stairs* |
| espacioso/a | *spacious* |
| el estudio | *study* |
| el garaje | *garage* |
| general | *general* |
| la habitación | *room* |
| el inmueble | *apartment building* |
| el jardín | *garden* |
| jugar | *to play* |
| el lavabo | *wash basin* |
| más bajo | *lower down* |
| Me encanta . . . | *I love . . .* |
| el piso | *floor, apartment* |
| por eso | *therefore* |
| por lo menos | *at least* |
| por supuesto | *of course* |
| preparar | *to prepare* |
| la sala de estar | *living room* |
| secar (la ropa) | *to dry (clothes)* |
| sentarse | *to sit down* |
| el sitio | *place, room (to)* |
| el sótano | *basement, cellar* |
| el techo | *roof* |
| la terraza | *terrace, balcony* |
| todo | *everything* |
| ver | *to see* |
| el vestíbulo | *entrance hall* |

# Se alquila casa

## Renting a house

RECORDING

**1.** ***Listen to Sra. Gutiérrez speaking to her friend Sra. Molina about her new house.***

RECORDING

## 2.

*Listen to the conversation again and say if the following statements about the conversation are true or false. Then correct the false statements.*

1. La Sra. Gutiérrez vive en un piso.
2. La casa de la Sra. Gutiérrez es muy nueva.
3. La familia Gutiérrez come en la sala de estar.
4. La cocina está al lado de la sala de estar.
5. La casa tiene cuatro dormitorios.
6. En la casa hay dos cuartos de baño.
7. La casa tiene una terraza.
8. El garaje es pequeño.

RECORDING

## 3.

*Now listen to some people talking about the houses or apartments they live in. Check off the places you hear in the house or apartment.*

| sala de estar | cocina | comedor | cuarto de baño | dormitorio | terraza | jardín |
|---|---|---|---|---|---|---|
| 1. | | | | | | |
| 2. | | | | | | |
| 3. | | | | | | |

RECORDING

**4.** *Three clients who want to buy or rent an apartment telephone a real estate agency. Match the ad to the client. Say which ad belongs to each conversation.*

**Barrio Las Condes**
*¡Oportunidad!*
Piso en edificio moderno con una gran sala de estar, dos dormitorios y cocina pequeña. Cerca del metro.
**Propiedades Maravilla**

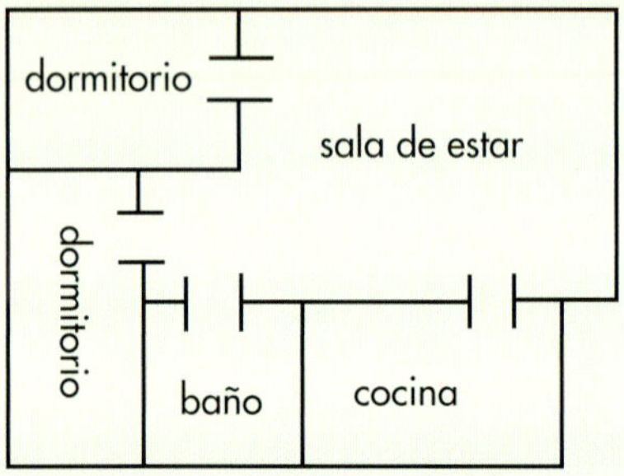


**a.** ________

**Mar de Plata**
*En el Centro*
Piso moderno y bonito en décimo piso.
Un dormitorio, sala de estar, comedor, baño y cocina.
**Corredores Sarmiento**

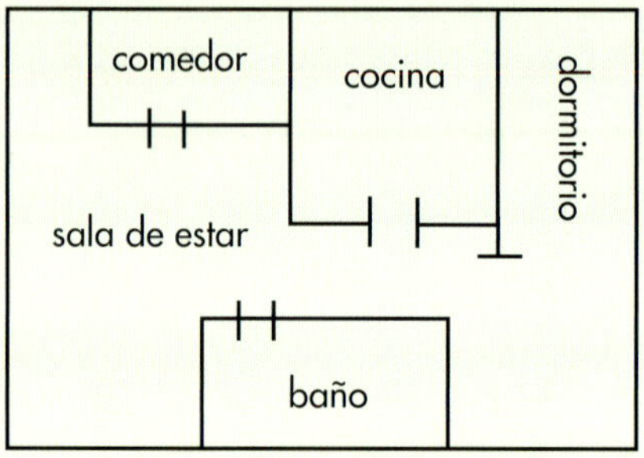


**b.** ________

**Lo mejor de Bailén**
Enorme piso de 5 dormitorios, sala de estar, pieza de estudio, dos baños, comedor y garaje doble. Excelente zona escolar.
**Dos estrellas, S.A.**

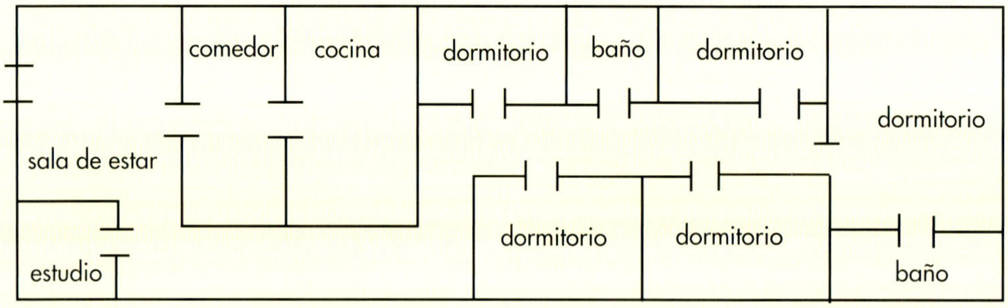


**c.** ________

*Now repeat the part of each of the clients.*

5. *You are making notes for a real estate agent about the sort of house or apartment you would like to buy. Draw a simple layout plan and then write a description of it in Spanish.*

## Your turn

*You are having dinner with a friend who is very interested in your new house. Tell him about it: the rooms it has, where they are, their size, if you have a garage or garden. How much can you say about it?*

*You want to buy an apartment in a Spanish shore resort. Can you remember the questions that you want to ask the real estate agent?*

## Close-up

*If you want to express yourself a little more strongly and say you absolutely love something, use* **me encanta** *instead of* **me gusta***:*

| | |
|---|---|
| **Me encanta esta casa.** | *I love this house.* |
| **A ella le encantan estas habitaciones.** | *She loves these rooms.* |

*Don't use this expression for people, however. Use* **quiero***:*

| | |
|---|---|
| **Quiero mucho a Jaime.** | *I love Jaime very much.* |

# La casa nueva

## *Describing your new house*

## Word Bank

| | | | |
|---|---|---|---|
| la almohada | *pillow* | la manta | *blanket* |
| el aparador | *cabinet* | maravilloso | *wonderful* |
| el armario | *wardrobe* | la mesita de café | *coffee table* |
| el azulejo | *tile* | necesitar | *to need* |
| la baldosa | *floor tile* | no funciona | *doesn't work* |
| bonito/a | *pretty, nice* | la pantalla | *screen* |
| la butaca | *armchair* | la pared | *wall* |
| la cortina | *curtain/drape* | la persiana | *blind* |
| el descuento | *discount, reduction* | por ciento | *percent* |
| el dinero | *money* | por lo general | *usually, generally* |
| el espejo | *mirror* | ¡Qué suerte tienes! | *You're so lucky!* |
| estar roto/a | *to be broken* | la sábana | *sheet* |
| hermoso/a | *beautiful* | el sofá | *sofa* |
| la lámpara | *lamp* | el televisor | *television set* |
| la luz | *light* | todos los días | *every day* |

RECORDING

1. ***Sra. Gutiérrez shows her new house to her friend Sra. Molina. She has bought a lot of new furniture and is eager to show it off. Listen to the entire conversation.***

RECORDING

## 2.

*Listen to the dialog again. Match the furniture to the room it is in.*

| | la sala de estar | el comedor | el estudio | los dormitorios | el cuarto de baño | el pasillo |
|---|---|---|---|---|---|---|
| el aparador | | | | | | |
| las butacas | | | | | | |
| el escritorio | | | | | | |
| la lámpara | | | | | | |
| los azulejos | | | | | | |
| la alfombra | | | | | | |
| la mesa grande | | | | | | |
| las camas | | | | | | |
| el sofá | | | | | | |
| el televisor | | | | | | |
| la mesita de café | | | | | | |
| las cortinas | | | | | | |
| las sillas | | | | | | |

RECORDING

## 3.

1. *Listen to this advertisement for the furniture store* **Muebles Mendoza**. *First, try repeating the ad to see how well you would do as a salesperson in Spanish. Then write down what furniture the store has on sale, what reductions they offer, and how long the sale will last.*
2. *Carmen dreams about her wedding and the furniture she wants for her apartment. What furnishings does Carmen want, and where does she want them to be placed? Now dream along with Carmen, repeating what she says.*
3. *Alfredo and his wife, Merche, are talking about the furniture they are going to buy for their new apartment. Listen to them, then write down what they need. Why does Alfredo have second thoughts?*

## 4.

*You've bought an apartment. Make a list of furniture you'll need for each room.*

## 5.

*Word Jumble. Find the eight hidden words.*

| | | | | | | | |
|---|---|---|---|---|---|---|---|
| C | S | I | M | E | I | A | T |
| E | O | V | D | P | C | A | C |
| U | F | R | R | A | O | M | A |
| S | A | A | T | I | S | E | M |
| I | L | U | D | I | F | T | A |
| L | B | D | E | L | N | A | R |
| L | A | M | P | A | R | A | E |
| A | P | A | R | A | D | O | R |
| A | L | F | O | M | B | R | A |

### Did You Know?

The vast majority of city-dwellers in both Spain and Latin America live in apartment buildings. These can be buildings from three to fifteen or more floors. There are a number of residential developments in the outer suburbs, but they cost considerably more to buy or rent.

RECORDING

## 6.

*Listen to Alonso, who is describing what his family is doing at their new house. Then match the person to the activity.*

Jaime Clara Jorge Isabel

a. ____________________

b. ____________________

c. ____________________

d. ____________________

## Your turn

RECORDING

*You are completely refurnishing your apartment and discussing with a friend the furnishings you need to buy for each room. Complete the dialog.*

| | |
|---|---|
| *Amiga:* | Bueno, ¿qué quieres comprar para la sala de estar? |
| *Usted:* | *Say you want some red curtains and a coffee table.* |
| *Amiga:* | ¿Y para el comedor? |
| *Usted:* | *A new mirror.* |
| *Amiga:* | Y, ¿qué necesitas para los dormitorios? |
| *Usted:* | *Say that the children want a television set and that you want a big wardrobe.* |
| *Amiga:* | ¿Necesitas algo en el cuarto de baño? |
| *Usted:* | *Say you'd like some pretty tiles on the walls.* |

**7.** *Imagine that you are asked what various members of your family or friends are doing at this moment. Using any of the verbs you have learned, describe aloud what you think at least five of them are doing and then write the descriptions down on paper.*

*Example:* Juan está tomando una cerveza.

## Close up

*In this unit you have encountered the present continuous tense, which tells you what is happening, what you are doing. It works very similarly to the corresponding English ("to be" + the "-ing" ending of the verb). In Spanish you use the present tense of* **estar** *and the ending* **-ando** *with* **-ar** *verbs and* **-iendo** *with others.*

| | | |
|---|---|---|
| hablar | **Estoy hablando** con mi amigo. | *I'm talking to my friend.* |
| comer | **Estamos comiendo**. | *We're eating.* |
| vivir | **Están viviendo** en Guadalajara. | *They are living in Guadalajara.* |

# La vida de todos los días

*Talking about your daily routine*

## Word Bank

| | | | |
|---|---|---|---|
| a las tres de la mañana | *at 3 o'clock in the morning* | lavarse | *to wash* |
| a veces | *sometimes* | levantarse | *to get up* |
| acostarse | *to go to bed* | nunca | *never* |
| almorzar | *to have lunch* | el ordernador/ la computadora | *computer* |
| alrededor de | *around* | pasar | *to spend (time)* |
| desayunar | *to have breakfast* | el patio | *yard* |
| describir | *to describe* | por la mañana | *in the morning* |
| despertarse | *to wake up* | el recreo | *recess, playtime* |
| los dientes | *teeth* | la rutina diaria | *daily routine* |
| dormir | *to sleep* | salir de casa | *to leave home* |
| dormirse | *to fall asleep* | siempre | *always* |
| ducharse | *to shower* | soler | *to be accustomed to* |
| empezar | *to begin* | tarde | *late* |
| en seguida | *at once* | temprano | *early* |
| generalmente | *generally, usually* | venir | *to come* |
| irse | *to go off, to leave* | | |

RECORDING

**1.** ***Listen to Isabel, who is a secretary, describing her daily routine. Repeat what she says.***

RECORDING

**2.** ***Answer the questions about Isabel's routine aloud and then write your answers down.***

1. ¿A qué hora se despierta Isabel?
2. ¿Se ducha todas las mañanas?
3. ¿Qué hace antes de salir de casa?
4. ¿Adónde se va?
5. ¿A qué hora vuelve a casa a almorzar?
6. ¿Qué suele hacer después de almorzar?
7. ¿Qué hace cuando llega a casa por la tarde?
8. ¿A qué hora se acuesta su hija?
9. ¿Cuándo se duerme Isabel?
10. ¿Qué piensa de su familia?

RECORDING

## 3.

*Listen to these three dialogs, then write in the box who does which of the actions mentioned. Note that some actions may be performed by more than one of the children.*

| |
|---|
| 1. |
| 2. |
| 3. |
| 4. |
| 5. |
| 6. |
| 7. |
| 8. |

1. ¿Quién se despierta a las 8:45?
2. ¿Quién se ducha?
3. ¿Quién juega con sus compañeros?
4. ¿Quién almuerza en casa?
5. ¿Quién no vuelve a casa a almorzar?
6. ¿Quién juega en la calle?
7. ¿Quién se acuesta generalmente a las doce?
8. ¿Quién se acuesta a veces muy tarde?

RECORDING

## 4.

*Listen to the employees of Jugofruta talking about their workday. Then repeat what Paco, Pili, and Rosa said. On the timesheets, put the name of the employee next to the hours worked. The first one has been done for you.*

| NOMBRE | HORA DE ENTRADA | HORA DE SALIDA | PAUSA PARA COMER | | HORAS EN TOTAL |
|---|---|---|---|---|---|
| *Paco* | *8:30* | *6 de la tarde* | ✔ *sí una hora* | *no* | *8 1/2 horas* |
| | | | | | |
| | | | | | |
| | | | | | |

## 5.

*You are taking part in a survey about how people spend their day. Answer these questions aloud and then write your answers down.*

1. ¿A qué hora se despierta usted?
2. ¿Se levanta usted temprano o tarde?
3. Por la mañana, ¿se ducha, se baña o se lava?
4. ¿A qué hora se va al trabajo o al colegio?
5. ¿Dónde almuerza?
6. ¿A qué hora vuelve a casa?
7. ¿Juega usted al béisbol o a otro deporte?
8. ¿Cuándo se acuesta?
9. ¿Se duerme en seguida?

## 6.

*Now you ask the questions but address two people, one of whom answers on behalf of both. You need to change the forms of the questions and answers as follows:*

*Example:* ¿A qué hora se despiertan ustedes?
Nos despertamos a las siete.

## Your turn

*You are in a conversation with someone and the topic is their daily routine. Ask the person you are speaking with as many questions about his/her daily routine that come to mind.*

*Write a paragraph to a friend giving an account of your usual workday routine.*

## Pronunciation

RECORDING

*In this unit you were introduced to a number of stem-changing verbs, where the vowel sound changes from* **o** *to* **ue** *or* **e** *to* **ie**. *This change from a single vowel to two vowels is called a diphthong. Practice saying the following forms of the verbs* **volver** *(to return) and* **pensar** *(to think):*

**volver:** **vuelvo, vuelves, vuelve, volvemos, vuelven**
**pensar:** **pienso, piensas, piensa, pensamos, piensan**

*Many Spanish words contain a diphthong. For example:*

*With* **ue: puerta, Puerto Rico, nueve, pues, bueno, escuela.**
*With* **ie: siete, diez, bien, siempre, tiempo.**

# Close up

## *Reflexive Verbs*

*In this unit you have encountered some verbs like* **levantarse** *(to get up), which are called "reflexive" verbs because you do the action to yourself. There are many more reflexive verbs in Spanish than in English. The "reflexive pronoun"* **se***, as you see, is attached to the infinitive, but comes off and usually precedes the verb when it is in its conjugated form. You also adjust it depending on the person (myself, yourself, and so on). Here is the complete present tense of* **levantarse.**

| | |
|---|---|
| **me levanto** | **nos levantamos** |
| **te levantas** | **os levantáis*** |
| **se levanta** | **se levantan** |

*Other reflexive verbs you have used are:* **despertarse** *(to wake up),* **lavarse** *(to wash),* **ducharse** *(to shower),* **bañarse** *(to take a bath),* **irse** *(to go away, to leave),* **acostarse** *(to go to bed), and* **dormirse** *(to fall asleep).*

*You have also encountered some verbs like* **almorzar** *(to have lunch), where the* **o** *before the ending changes to* **ue***, and* **despertarse** *(to wake up), where the* **e** *changes to* **ie***. These verbs are called "stem-changing" verbs. The changes occur in the singular and the third person plural forms.*

| | |
|---|---|
| **almuerzo** | **almorzamos** |
| **almuerzas** | **almorzáis** |
| **almuerza** | **almuerzan** |

| | |
|---|---|
| **me despierto** | **nos despertamos** |
| **te despiertas** | **os despertáis** |
| **se despierta** | **se despiertan** |

*In the verb* **jugar** *(to play), the* **u** *changes to* **ue** *in the same places.*

| | |
|---|---|
| **juego** | **jugamos** |
| **juegas** | **jugáis** |
| **juega** | **juegan** |

*The **vosotros** form designates the second person plural and is mostly used in Spain.

# Checkpoints

***Can you . . . ?*** ***Yes*** ***No***

- *describe your house or apartment* . . . . . . . . . . . . . . . . . . . . . . . . . ❑ . . . . . . ❑
  Mi apartamento está en el quinto piso. Tiene cinco habitaciones.
- *describe the main living room* . . . . . . . . . . . . . . . . . . . . . . . . . . . . . ❑ . . . . . . ❑
  Hay un sofá y tres butacas.
- *tell a real estate agent what sort of house/apartment you would like* . . . . . . . . . . . . . . . . . . . . . . . . . . . . . . . . . . ❑ . . . . . . ❑
  Quiero una casa en las afueras.
- *say what accommodations you need* . . . . . . . . . . . . . . . . . . . . . . . . . ❑ . . . . . . ❑
  Como somos cinco en la familia, necesitamos un apartamento grande.
- *tell where you would or would not like to live* . . . . . . . . . . . . . . . . . . ❑ . . . . . . ❑
  Tiene que estar cerca del metro.
- *say how your house/apartment is furnished* . . . . . . . . . . . . . . . . . . . ❑ . . . . . . ❑
  El cuarto de baño tiene azulejos hasta el techo.
- *say what furniture you need to buy and why* . . . . . . . . . . . . . . . . . . . ❑ . . . . . . ❑
  El espejo del vestíbulo es muy pequeño.
- *talk about your daily routine* . . . . . . . . . . . . . . . . . . . . . . . . . . . . . . . . ❑ . . . . . . ❑
  Me despierto a las siete, me levanto . . .
- *talk about someone else's daily routine* . . . . . . . . . . . . . . . . . . . . . . . ❑ . . . . . . ❑
  Mi hija vuelve del colegio a las cinco.
- *say what you or someone else is doing* . . . . . . . . . . . . . . . . . . . . . . . . ❑ . . . . . . ❑
  Jaime está jugando en la sala de estar.

## Learning tips

*If you have trouble remembering the meaning of certain words use this following tip to help you. If you reverse the change we have talked about in the Pronunciation section,* **ue** *back to* **o** *and* **ie** *back to* **e**, *you can often arrive at the meaning of a word you don't know, by comparing it with an English or French word. Think of* **Puerto** *(Puerto Rico), and revert to* **porto** *which means "port," and similarly* **puerta**, *which means "door." Also, think of the French word for "door," which is* **porte**. *What about* **huerto** *(horticulture!),* **muerto** *(mortuary?),* **tiempo** *(things temporary or temporal). Respectively, these words mean "garden," "dead," and "time."*

## Do you want to learn more?

*Read as much Spanish as you can find—newspapers, advertising brochures, and so on. Read a little at a time, and don't worry about bits you don't understand: concentrate on getting the gist of it. Once you know what the subject is, you'll be able to guess the meanings of many new words from their context. Keep a note of words that are the same or similar in Spanish and English—but look in your dictionary to check that the meaning is the same.*

Unit 2 is about eating out in a restaurant. When you have completed this unit, you will know how to:

- say what you eat
- say what you like and don't like to eat
- make comparisons

# ¡Buen provecho! 2

## Word Bank

| | |
|---|---|
| ¿Adónde? | *Where to?* |
| el aperitivo | *appetizer* |
| cariño | *darling, dear* |
| la carta | *the "à la carte" menu* |
| cenar | *to have dinner* |
| chino/a | *Chinese* |
| la comida | *food* |
| ¿Cuál? | *Which one?* |
| el cumpleaños | *birthday* |
| decidir | *to decide* |
| escoger | *to choose* |
| la idea | *idea* |
| invitar | *to invite* |
| oye (fam.), oiga | *listen* |
| ¡Siéntense! | *Sit down! (plural)* |
| típico/a | *typical* |

# ¡Que aproveche!

## *Eating out*

RECORDING

**1.** ***Listen to Miguel and Pepa talking about how they are going to celebrate Pepa's birthday. Then listen to Miguel and Eduardo talking. Repeat what Miguel says in both dialogs.***

| | |
|---|---|
| ¿Por qué no invitamos a . . . ? | *Why don't we invite . . . ?* |
| Buena idea. | *Good idea.* |
| Es igual. | *I don't care.* |
| decidir adónde ir | *to decide where to go* |
| ¡Cómo no! | *Of course!* |
| ¿Podemos ir a otro sitio? | *Can we go somewhere else?* |
| De acuerdo. | *Agreed, OK.* |

RECORDING

**2.** ***Listen to both dialogs again. All these statements are false. Can you correct them? Say the correct version aloud. Then write it down on paper. Say the answer aloud.***

1. Mañana es el cumpleaños de Miguel.
2. Pepa quiere invitar a sus amigos Eduardo y Teresa a cenar en su casa.
3. La Casona es un restaurante chino.
4. Pepa prefiere ir al restaurante chino.
5. Eduardo no quiere ir al restaurante con Miguel y Pepa.
6. A Eduardo y a Teresa les encanta la comida china.
7. Eduardo no quiere ir a La Casona.
8. Deciden cenar a las ocho.

RECORDING

**3.** *Miguel telephones the* **La Casona** *restaurant. Listen to the dialog. Then answer the following questions.*

1. ¿Para qué día reserva Miguel una mesa?
2. ¿Para cuántas personas?
3. ¿En qué parte del restaurante?
4. ¿Para qué hora?
5. ¿A nombre de quién?

## Did You Know?

*The title of this unit,* **¡Buen provecho!** *is what Spanish speakers say as they start their meal. It is the equivalent of the French "Bon appétit" or the English "Enjoy your meal." An alternative form is* **¡Que aproveche!** *It basically means "Enjoy!"*

RECORDING

**4.** *Listen to the following phone conversations as clients reserve tables. Imagine you are the host/hostess of a restaurant taking customers' reservations. Write down their requests. To give you a start, one item is written in for each column.*

RECORDING

5. *The foursome go into the restaurant and are greeted by the waiter. What three questions does the waiter ask Miguel? What choices of dishes are there? What does the waiter recommend?*

RECORDING

6. *Listen to the following radio advertisements for different restaurants. Can you match up the speciality dish or occasion with the name of the restaurant?*

| | |
|---|---|
| 1. Casa Rodrigo | a. Cocina francesa |
| 2. Casa Luigi | b. Cocina mexicana |
| 3. Restaurante París | c. Aniversario/cumpleaños |
| 4. Restaurante Cancún | d. Comida tradicional española |
| 5. Casa Marisol | e. Paella |
| 6. Las Rocas | f. Pizzas |

## Your turn

RECORDING

*Record a message on your Mexican friends' answering machine, saying that it is your birthday tomorrow and you would like them to join you for dinner. Then as a backup, write a note to leave in their mailbox.*

### Did You Know?

In Spain, the two main meals are taken somewhat later than in most other countries. Lunch may be taken at 1:30 P.M., but many people do not eat until 2:30 or 3:00, especially in the south. Shops and offices are often closed from 1:30 to 4:30. Dinner is also taken correspondingly late. Few restaurants outside of tourist areas serve dinner before 9:00 P.M. In Latin America, meals tend to be later than in the U.S., but not as late as in Spain.

RECORDING

7. *Can you phone to book a table? Listen to the recording and try completing the conversation.*

| | |
|---|---|
| *Recepcionista:* | Restaurante El Puchero. ¿Dígame? |
| *Usted:* | *Say you'd like to have dinner in the restaurant and you want to book a table.* |
| *Recepcionista:* | Sí, ¿para cuántas personas? |
| *Usted:* | *Six.* |
| *Recepcionista:* | ¿Para cuándo? |
| *Usted:* | *For tomorrow.* |
| *Recepcionista:* | ¿Para qué hora? |
| *Usted:* | *For 9:30.* |
| *Recepcionista:* | Muy bien. |
| *Usted:* | *Ask if you can have a table on the terrace.* |
| *Recepcionista:* | Sí, claro. Hasta mañana. |

## Close up

*When you use two verbs together, as in "I want to invite" or "she prefers to go," the second verb is normally in the infinitive form:*

Pepa **quiere invitar** a sus amigos Eduardo y Teresa.

*Pepa wants to invite her friends Eduardo and Teresa.*

| | |
|---|---|
| Teresa no **puede decidir.** | *Teresa can't decide.* |
| **Pensamos ir** al restaurante chino. | *We're thinking of going to the Chinese restaurant.* |

*Sometimes you need the preposition* **a** *between the two verbs:*

¿Por qué no los invitamos **a** cenar?

*Why don't we invite them to have dinner?*

# Tengo hambre

*Ordering a meal*

## Word Bank

| | |
|---|---|
| a la plancha | *grilled* |
| ambos/as | *both* |
| bien hecho/a | *well cooked* |
| el bistec | *steak* |
| el bonito | *tuna* |
| caliente | *hot, warm* |
| el/la camarero/a | *waiter/waitress* |
| la chuleta | *chop* |
| el cocido | *a kind of stew* |
| la ensalada mixta | *mixed salad* |
| la ensaladilla rusa | *Russian salad* |
| los entremeses | *hors d'oeuvres, appetizers* |
| estar de régimen | *to be on a diet* |
| el flan | *a kind of pudding* |
| frito/a | *fried* |
| el jarro | *jug, carafe* |
| ligero/a | *light* |
| manchego/a | *from* La Mancha |
| los melocotones en almíbar | *peaches in syrup* |
| morirse de hambre | *to be starving* |
| las natillas | *a kind of custard* |
| la parrillada | *grilled or barbecued steak* |
| el pescado | *fish* |
| el plato | *dish, course (also a plate)* |
| el plato principal | *main course* |
| el postre | *dessert* |
| rico/a | *delicious, good (food)* |
| la sangre | *blood* |
| sobre todo | *above all, especially* |
| la sopa | *soup* |
| la sopa de cebolla | *onion soup* |
| suficiente | *sufficient, enough* |
| la tarta helada | *ice-cream cake* |
| tener hambre | *to be hungry* |
| traer | *to bring* |

RECORDING

1. ***Listen to the four diners discussing what they would like to eat. Repeat each character's part of the dialog in the pauses.***

| | |
|---|---|
| de primero/de segundo/de postre | *for first course/second course/dessert* |
| No me gusta ninguno de esos platos. | *I don't like any of those dishes.* |
| ¿Qué recomienda(s)? | *What do you recommend?* |
| Yo prefiero carne. | *I prefer meat.* |
| Yo me muero de hambre. | *I'm starving.* |
| Para empezar... | *To start with...* |

RECORDING

2. ***Listen again to the conversation and check (✓) the items in the menu that are mentioned.***

RECORDING

3. *Now listen again to Miguel ordering. Then play his part repeating what he says in the pauses.*

RECORDING

4. *Miguel and his party have finished their main course and the waiter returns to take away the dishes. He asks if they want dessert. What does each one choose for dessert?*

## Your turn

RECORDING

*Listen again to the dialog in Activity 3. Imagine you are the waiter taking the order and write down everything that is ordered.*

## Close up

*When dining out in a restaurant, you ask the waiter or waitress to bring you your food and beverage. The verb "to bring" is* **traer**. *Its present tense is irregular:*

| | |
|---|---|
| **traigo** | **traemos** |
| **traes** | **traéis** |
| **trae** | **traen** |

*The imperative/command form is* **traiga**. *This is just one of several common verbs whose command form is constructed by dropping the final* **-o** *from the first person singular and replacing it with* **-a**. *Compare the verbs* **digo/diga** *and* **oigo/oiga**.

*There are several ways of asking the waiter/waitress to bring something:*

| | |
|---|---|
| ¿Nos trae el menú, por favor? | *Will you bring us the menu, please?* |
| ¿Quiere traerme un tenedor, por favor? | *Will you bring me a fork, please?* |
| Tráigame la cuenta, por favor. | *Bring me the check, please.* |

*Note the need for an accent when you add* **me** *or other object pronouns to the command.*

*In this lesson you have met a couple of negative expressions:*

| | |
|---|---|
| **No** me gusta **ninguno** de esos platos. | *I don't like any of those dishes.* |
| **No** tengo **nada** en la terraza. | *I don't have anything on the terrace.* |

*When a negative word is used after the verb it requires* **no** *before the verb.*

# ¡Quédese con la vuelta!

*Asking for the bill*

## Word Bank

| | | | |
|---|---|---|---|
| al vapor | *steamed* | frío/a | *cold* |
| Aquí pone... | *Here it says...* | limpio/a | *clean* |
| la bandeja | *tray* | la propina | *tip* |
| la cuchara | *spoon* | el servicio | *service* |
| la cucharilla | *teaspoon* | sucio/a | *dirty* |
| el cuchillo | *knife* | la taza | *cup* |
| la cuenta | *bill, check* | el tenedor | *fork* |
| equivocado/a | *wrong* | | |

RECORDING

1. *Miguel and his party have enjoyed their meal but before they have their coffee, the restaurant becomes very busy and things go wrong. First, listen to the whole conversation, then repeat in the pauses the complaint that each of the diners makes.*

| | |
|---|---|
| ¡Mi café está frío! | *My coffee is cold!* |
| Esta taza está sucia. | *This cup is dirty.* |
| No tengo cucharilla. | *I don't have a small spoon.* |
| Lo siento. | *I'm sorry.* |

RECORDING

2. *Listen again to the conversation. Which one of these statements is true? Correct all the other false ones. There may be more than one way of doing it!*

1. Una clienta tiene una cucharilla sucia.
2. La taza de un cliente está sucia.
3. Una clienta tiene leche fría.
4. Un cliente no tiene cucharilla.
5. Una clienta quiere café solo.
6. El café de un cliente está muy caliente.

RECORDING

3. *More complaints! Listen to the customers complaining. Complete the following sentences.*

1. El tenedor de la clienta está ________.
2. La sopa no está ________.
3. La señora quiere una chuleta de ________ y no de cerdo.
4. La clienta quiere una cuchara ________.
5. El señor no tiene ________.

RECORDING

4. *Miguel, Pepa, Eduardo, and Teresa are about to leave. Miguel asks the waiter for the check. What is the mistake on it?*

## Your turn

RECORDING

*Complete the dialog by speaking during the pauses.*

| | |
|---|---|
| *Usted:* | ***Call the waitress.*** |
| *Camarera:* | En seguida. |
| *Usted:* | ***Tell her you have no fork and that your plate is dirty.*** |
| *Camarera:* | Perdone. Le traigo otros en seguida. |
| *Usted:* | ***Ask her if she can also bring you another bottle of mineral water. This one is not cold.*** |
| *Camarera:* | Por supuesto. Aquí tiene su tortilla. |
| *Usted:* | ***Say you want an omelet with onions, not potatoes!*** |
| *Camarera:* | Espere usted un momentito. Se la cambio en seguida. |
| *Usted:* | ***Ask her if she could bring the check.*** |
| *Camarera:* | Sí, un momentito. |
| *Usted:* | ***Tell her the check is wrong. It is 90 pesos, not 95!*** |
| *Camarera:* | Ah, sí, es verdad. |
| *Usted:* | ***Ask her if the service is included.*** |
| *Camarera:* | Sí, claro. |
| *Usted:* | ***Say the service is very good, here's 100 pesos and keep the change!*** |
| *Camarera:* | ¡Oh, muchísimas gracias! |

## Pronunciation

RECORDING

*Before an* **i** *or an* **e**, *the letter* **g** *is pronounced in Spanish like the "h" in the English word "hill" but with greater friction. The sound is often referred to as the "hard* **g**.*" Listen and repeat the following words:*

**escoger, agente, régimen, generoso**

*The letter* **j** *in Spanish has a sound similar to the hard* **g**. *Listen and repeat:*

**jarro, bandeja, hijo**

*Before* **a**, **o**, *or* **u** *the* **g** *in Spanish has a softer sound similar to the "g" in the English word "go." Listen and repeat:*

**hago, tengo, segundo, traiga**

## Close up

*You have already been introduced to the direct object pronouns. In this unit you will have seen several examples of the indirect object pronoun. This means "to me," "to you," and sometimes "for me," and so on.*

| | |
|---|---|
| ¿**Me** trae el menú? | *Will you bring (to) me the menu?* |
| ¿**Me** dan sus abrigos? | *Will you give me your coats?* |
| ¿Puede trael**nos** el menú? | *Can you bring (to) us the menu?* |
| ¿Puede cambiar**me** este tenedor? | *Can you change this fork (for me)?* |
| Claro, **le** cambio el tenedor en seguida. | *Of course, I'll change the fork for you at once.* |

# Checkpoints

| *Can you . . . ?* | *Yes* | *No* |
|---|---|---|
| • *ask someone what they want to do to celebrate an occasion*<br>¿Qué quieres hacer para celebrar tu cumpleaños? | ❑ | ❑ |
| • *make a suggestion, e.g., inviting someone to do something*<br>¿Por qué no invitamos a . . . y a . . . ? | ❑ | ❑ |
| • *ask someone whether they would like to go out for a meal*<br>¿Quieres ir a comer con nosotros? | ❑ | ❑ |
| • *suggest going somewhere else*<br>¿Podemos ir a otro sitio? | ❑ | ❑ |
| • *ask someone if they agree*<br>¿De acuerdo? | ❑ | ❑ |
| • *say you agree*<br>De acuerdo. | ❑ | ❑ |
| • *phone to reserve a table in a restaurant*<br>Quisiera reservar una mesa. | ❑ | ❑ |
| • *say for how many is the reservation*<br>Para seis. | ❑ | ❑ |
| • *say where you would like to sit*<br>Cerca de la ventana. | ❑ | ❑ |
| • *say that you have a table reserved in your name*<br>Tengo una mesa reservada a nombre de . . . | ❑ | ❑ |
| • *ask for the menu*<br>¿Puede traer el menú, por favor? | ❑ | ❑ |
| • *ask the waiter/waitress what he/she recommends*<br>¿Qué recomienda usted? | ❑ | ❑ |
| • *say what you prefer to eat*<br>Yo prefiero pescado. | ❑ | ❑ |
| • *order from the waiter/waitress*<br>Para mí, una merluza a la plancha. | ❑ | ❑ |

- *say how you like your food cooked* ........................ ❑ ...... ❑
  Bien hecho/a.
- *say what you are going to have for each course* ................ ❑ ...... ❑
  Para empezar, quiero una sopa.
- *make a complaint to the waiter* ............................ ❑ ...... ❑
  Este plato está sucio.
- *ask for the bill* ........................................ ❑ ...... ❑
  ¿Me trae la cuenta, por favor?
- *tip the waiter* .......................................... ❑ ...... ❑
  ¡Quédese con la vuelta!

## Learning tips

*Don't be afraid to use your knowledge of English to work out the meanings of Spanish words. There is a lot of shared vocabulary between the two languages, so why not use it? But do watch for "false friends": some words don't mean quite the same in Spanish and English. It's advisable to check in your dictionary if you're not sure.*

## Do you want to learn more?

*Many Spanish-language housekeeping magazines have cooking recipes. If you can get hold of one, see how many of the ingredients you can identify. Also, some of the products you buy may have instructions or contents listed on the package in Spanish as well as English. Next time you're buying wine or beer, watch for Spanish wines and study the labels to see how much information you can understand.*

Unit 3 is about vacations. When you have completed this unit, you will know how to:

- talk about what you like to do on vacation and where you like to go
- talk about what there is to do at a particular destination
- describe your last vacation

# De vacaciones 3

## Word Bank

| | |
|---|---|
| el aparcamiento | *parking lot* |
| aparcar | *to park* |
| el banco | *bank* |
| la caja | *cashier's window* |
| la caja de ahorros | *savings bank* |
| el cajero automático | *teller machine (ATM)* |
| la cama de matrimonio | *double bed* |
| el cheque de viajero | *traveler's check* |
| el código postal | *zip code* |
| deletrear | *to spell out* |
| los detalles | *details* |
| la dirección | *address* |
| el dólar | *dollar* |
| el equipaje | *luggage* |
| los Estados Unidos | *USA* |
| firmar | *to sign* |
| la habitación doble | *room for two* |
| libre | *free/vacant* |
| la llave | *key* |
| la maleta | *suitcase* |
| la media pensión | *bed and breakfast* |
| mientras | *while* |
| el minibar | *minibar* |
| el pasaporte | *passport* |
| por persona | *per person* |
| propio/a | *own (one's)* |
| rellenar | *to fill in* |
| la tarjeta | *card* |
| varios/as | *several* |

# Una habitación con baño...

## *Reserving a room*

RECORDING

## 1.

***The Montserrats, a North American family, arrive at the*** **Hotel Alhambra** ***in Guadalajara. They would like to stay there. Sr. Montserrat asks the receptionist if there are any vacancies. Listen to the entire dialog and then repeat what Sr. Montserrat says.***

| | |
|---|---|
| ¿Tienen habitaciones libres? | *Do you have any vacant rooms?* |
| ¿Para cuántos días? | *For how many days?* |
| una habitación con cama de matrimonio | *a room with a double bed* |
| una habitación individual | *a single room* |
| ¿Cuánto cuesta la pensión completa? | *How much is a plan that includes meals?* |
| ¿Cuánto cuesta la media pensión? | *How much is a bed and breakfast?* |
| ¿Cuál es el precio de la habitación? | *What is the price of the room?* |

RECORDING

## 2.

***Listen to the dialog again. Are the statements true or false? If false, correct them.***

1. La familia Montserrat quiere quedarse una semana.
2. Quieren tres habitaciones.
3. Sus dos hijas pueden dormir en una habitación con dos camas.
4. El hotel sólo tiene habitaciones con dos camas.
5. Hay aire acondicionado en todas las habitaciones.
6. No todas las habitaciones tienen televisor.
7. La pensión completa cuesta 400 pesos por persona por día.
8. El Sr. Montserrat toma dos habitaciones con media pensión.

RECORDING

3. *Now listen to Sr. Montserrat who is filling out a hotel registration form. Pay close attention to how he spells his name and his address and fill out the registration form.*

## Did You Know?

*The letter* **ñ** *is a separate letter in Spanish and comes after the letter* **n** *in Spanish dictionaries.*

RECORDING

4. *The receptionist gives Sr. Montserrat his room keys. Listen to the conversation and choose the correct answer from the following:*

1. La familia Montserrat tiene las habitaciones número 401, 402 y 403 / 511, 512 y 513 / 411, 412 y 413.
2. El ascensor está a la derecha / a la izquierda / todo recto.
3. La familia tiene muchas / varias / pocas maletas.
4. Para cambiar dinero hay varios bancos cerca / no hay bancos en la misma calle / hay dos bancos cerca.

RECORDING

5. *Now, let's listen to a conversation between Sr. Montserrat and a bank employee. Then see if you can answer these questions.*

1. ¿Cuántos dólares cambia?
2. ¿Qué tiene que mostrar a la empleada?
3. ¿Qué tiene que hacer en los cheques?
4. ¿Adónde tiene que ir para recibir su dinero?

| | |
|---|---|
| ¿Dónde podemos aparcar el carro (Mex.)/coche (Sp.)? | *Where can we park the car?* |
| Quisiera cambiar unos cheques de viajero. | *I'd like to cash some traveler's checks.* |
| ¿Quiere firmar aquí? | *Will you sign here?* |

## Your turn

RECORDING

*You arrive at a hotel and you wish to stay there with your family. Complete the following conversation.*

| | |
|---|---|
| *Usted:* | *Say hello and that you'd like two rooms, one double with twin beds, one single.* |
| *Recepcionista:* | Bien. ¿Para cuántas noches? |
| *Usted:* | *For two nights.* |
| *Recepcionista:* | ¿Dos habitaciones para dos noches? |
| *Usted:* | *Say yes. Ask if the rooms have baths or showers.* |

| | |
|---|---|
| *Recepcionista:* | Todas las habitaciones tienen baño, televisor, aire acondicionado y minibar. |
| *Usted:* | *Ask what is the price of the rooms.* |
| *Recepcionista:* | Son 70 euros por habitación por día. |
| *Usted:* | *Say OK and that you'll take them.* |
| *Recepcionista:* | Aquí tiene las llaves. Son las habitaciones número 505 y 506. |
| *Usted:* | *Say thanks. Ask where you can park your car.* |
| *Recepcionista:* | Puede dejarlo delante del hotel. |
| *Usted:* | *Tell them you have several suitcases. Ask where the elevator is.* |
| *Recepcionista:* | A la derecha. El joven puede llevar sus maletas a su habitación. |

## Close up

*The verb* **continuar** *(to continue) is followed by the gerund (ending in* **-ando/-iendo***), not the infinitive.* **Seguir** *(to follow) can also mean to "carry on" and is used in the same way.*

| | |
|---|---|
| Enrique continúa leyendo su libro. | *Enrique continues reading his book.* |
| Siga trabajando. | *Continue working.* |

# ¿Adónde van ustedes de vacaciones?

*Talking about going on vacation*

## Word Bank

| | | | |
|---|---|---|---|
| el aire | *air* | nadar | *to swim* |
| el año pasado | *last year* | los negocios | *business* |
| el avión | *airplane* | la playa | *beach* |
| azteca | *Aztec* | la prima | *cousin* |
| el ciclismo | *cycling* | puro/a | *pure* |
| la costa | *coast* | respirar | *to breathe* |
| dar una vuelta | *to take a tour* | subir | *to go up* |
| ir de compras | *to go shopping* | todos juntos | *all together* |
| el monumento | *monument* | las vacaciones | *vacation* |
| la montaña | *mountain* | visitar | *to visit* |

RECORDING

1. ***Listen to the conversation between the Montserrats and the Quesadas as they talk about how they plan to spend their vacations.***

| | |
|---|---|
| ¿Dónde les gusta pasar sus vacaciones? | *Where do you like to spend your vacation?* |
| Nos gusta pasar algún tiempo en la playa. | *We like to spend some time on the beach.* |
| Pensamos ir a la costa. | *We're thinking of going to the coast.* |

RECORDING

2. *Listen again to the conversation, look at the illustrations, and then say where each family is going and what they like to do.*

a.

b.

RECORDING

3. *The conversation continues. Listen to what the two families did last year and say who went where. You can answer like this:* **El Sr. Montserrat fue . . . , la Sra. Montserrat fue . . . , o ambos fueron . . . , la señora y las niñas fueron . . . , etc.**

1. ¿Quién fue a París?
2. ¿Quién fue de compras?
3. ¿Quién fue a Sevilla?
4. ¿Quién fue a Córdoba?
5. ¿Quién fue a Barcelona?
6. ¿Quién fue a Londres?
7. ¿Quién fue a Edimburgo?

## Your turn

RECORDING

*You are staying in a hotel and have made the acquaintance of the Molina family. Complete the conversation with Sra. Molina.*

| | |
|---|---|
| *Usted:* | *Ask Sra. Molina where they like to spend their holidays.* |
| *Sra. Molina:* | Generalmente nos gusta ir a la playa. |
| *Usted:* | *Ask her what they like to do there.* |
| *Sra. Molina:* | Nos gusta nadar, tomar el sol, descansar, comer, beber… |
| *Usted:* | *Ask her if they like to go to the mountains.* |
| *Sra. Molina:* | Sí, pero preferimos la playa. |
| *Usted:* | *Ask her where they went last year.* |
| *Sra. Molina:* | Fuimos a Europa. |
| *Usted:* | *Ask her if they went to Spain.* |
| *Sra. Molina:* | Por supuesto. Fuimos a España, Francia e Inglaterra. |

## Close-up

*You have used* **me gusta** *+ infinitive to say what you like to do:*

| | |
|---|---|
| ¿Qué **le gusta** hacer? | *What do you like to do?* |
| **Nos gusta** pasar algún tiempo en la playa. | *We like to spend some time on the beach.* |

*You have also used the main past tense, also called the preterite of the verb* **ir** *(to go). Here are its preterite forms.*

| | | | |
|---|---|---|---|
| **fui** | *I went* | **fuimos** | *we went* |
| **fuiste** | *you went* | **fuisteis** | *you went* |
| **fue** | *he/she went* | **fueron** | *they went* |
| **fue** | *you went* | **fueron** | *you went* |

*You have also used* **dimos una vuelta** *(we took a trip),* **visitamos** *(we visited),* **subí** *(I went up),* **tomamos** *(we took),* **tuve** *(I had),* and **visitaron** *(they visited).*

# ¡Lo pasé estupendamente!

*Having a great vacation*

## Word Bank

| | | | |
|---|---|---|---|
| alojarse | *to stay* | el Mediterráneo | *the Mediterranean* |
| el autocar | *bus, coach* | pasar | *to spend (time)* |
| bastante | *quite a lot of* | sacar fotos | *to take photos* |
| ¿Cuánto tiempo? | *How long?* | la semana | *week* |
| la foto(grafía) | *photo(graph)* | veranear | *to go on summer vacation* |
| largo/a | *long* | el viaje | *trip* |

RECORDING

**1.** ***The Montserrats and the Quesadas have been joined in the lounge by Sra. Blanes. Listen to the conversation between Sr. Quesada and Sra. Blanes.***

| | |
|---|---|
| ¿Cuánto tiempo pasó usted allí? | *How long did you spend there?* |
| ¿Dónde se alojó? | *Where did you stay?* |
| ¿Qué hizo usted? | *What did you do?* |
| ¿Qué vio usted? | *What did you see?* |
| ¿Qué le impresionó más? | *What impressed you the most?* |
| ¡Lo pasé estupendamente! | *I had a fabulous time!* |

RECORDING

## 2.

*Now answer these questions about the conversation.*

1. ¿Cuándo hizo la Sra. Blanes su viaje a España?
2. ¿Por qué fue allí?
3. ¿Cuánto tiempo pasó en Madrid?
4. En España, ¿cómo viajó?
5. ¿Dónde se alojó?
6. ¿Qué ciudades visitó?
7. ¿Qué monumentos vio?
8. ¿Qué comió?
9. ¿Dónde nadó?
10. ¿Qué ciudad la impresionó más?

## 3.

*Sra. Blanes writes a letter to a friend about her visit to Spain. Put the correct verbs in the blanks.*

| | | | |
|---|---|---|---|
| Dormí | hice | gustó | fui |
| Comí | nadé | Vi | bebí |
| visité | tomé | pasé | |

*Hace dos años ________ a España. Primero ________ a mi hijo en Madrid durante dos semanas. Luego ________ un viaje en automóvil por toda España. ¡Lo ________ estupendamente! ________ en paradores con el grupo. ________ muy bien y ________ mucho vino español. También ________ en el Mediterráneo y ________ el sol en la playa. ________ varias ciudades españolas. Me ________ mucho Sevilla, que es una ciudad muy linda.*

### Did You Know?

*A large amount of Moorish influence can be seen in the architecture of Andalucía in southern Spain, due to its occupation by the Arabs of North Africa during the eighth to the fifteenth centuries. It can be observed in* **La Alhambra***, a famous Moorish palace in Granada, and in* **La Giralda***, an original Moorish tower now part of a cathedral in Sevilla.*

*An* **alcázar** *is a fortified palace. Perhaps the most famous one is located in Toledo, in central Spain, the scene of a famous attack during the Spanish Civil War (1936–1939).*

*Spanish words beginning with* **al-** *are usually of Arabic origin, as this is the Arabic definite article.*

parador *(Sp.) state-run hotel*

## Pronunciation

RECORDING

*You have now used quite a few verbs in the preterite tense. Practice the first and third person endings, paying particular attention to the stress.*

*I did the action:*

**visité, pasé, viajé, saqué, tomé, nadé, comí, bebí.**

*He, she, or you* **(usted)** *did the action:*

**visitó, pasó, viajó, sacó, tomó, comió, bebió.**

*Now contrast the first person form of the present tense with the first person of the preterite:*

**visito/visité, paso/pasé, viajo/viajé, saco/saqué, tomo/tomé, nado/nadé, como/comí, bebo/bebí.**

*And now, contrast the third person of the present tense with the third person of the preterite:*

**visita/visitó, pasa/pasó, viaja/viajó, saca/sacó, toma/tomó, nada/nadó, come/comió, bebe/bebió.**

## Close up

*The preterite of regular verbs is formed as follows:* **-ar** *verbs have the endings* **-é**, **-aste**, **-ó**, **-amos**, **-asteis**, **-aron**; **-er** *and* **-ir** *verbs have the endings* **-í**, **-iste**, **-ió**, **-imos**, **-isteis**, **-ieron**.

*The most notable feature is the stressed ending for the first and third person singular, in contrast to the present tense.*

*Note also that it is the third person that ends in* **-o**, *not the first:* **hablo** *(present) means "I speak," whereas* **habló** *(preterite) means "he/she spoke."*

*Note that* **dar** *(to give) has an* **-er** *preterite:* **di**, **diste**, **dio**, **dimos**, **disteis**, **dieron**.

*There are some examples of another type of preterite where the first and third person endings are not stressed and the stem is often quite different from the infinitive.* **Tener** *(to have) and* **hacer** *(to do or to make) are the examples you have encountered so far:* **tener** > **tuve**, **tuviste**, **tuvo**, **tuvimos**, **tuvisteis**, **tuvieron**; **hacer** > **hice**, **hiciste**, **hizo**, **hicimos**, **hicisteis**, **hicieron** *(note the spelling adjustment to* **hice***).*

# Checkpoints

| *Can you . . . ?* | *Yes* | *No* |
| --- | --- | --- |
| • *ask in a hotel if there are any vacant rooms*<br>¿Tiene habitaciones libres? | ❑ | ❑ |
| • *say for how long you want to stay*<br>Para tres noches. | ❑ | ❑ |
| • *say what sort of rooms you need*<br>Una habitación doble con dos camas. | ❑ | ❑ |
| • *ask the price of a room in a bed and breakfast*<br>¿Cuánto cuesta la media pensión? | ❑ | ❑ |
| • *ask how much is a plan that includes meals*<br>¿Cuánto cuesta la pensión completa? | ❑ | ❑ |
| • *ask where you can park your car*<br>¿Dónde puedo aparcar el coche? | ❑ | ❑ |
| • *ask where you can change money*<br>¿Dónde se puede cambiar dinero? | ❑ | ❑ |
| • *say you would like to cash some traveler's checks*<br>Quisiera cambiar unos cheques de viajero. | ❑ | ❑ |
| • *ask someone where they like to go on vacation*<br>¿Adónde va(n) usted(es) de vacaciones? | ❑ | ❑ |
| • *say where you usually go on vacation*<br>Generalmente voy/vamos a . . . | ❑ | ❑ |
| • *say what you like to do on vacation*<br>Me/Nos gusta tomar el sol . . . | ❑ | ❑ |
| • *ask someone where they went on vacation last year*<br>¿Adónde fue usted/fueron ustedes de vacaciones el año pasado? | ❑ | ❑ |
| • *ask what they did*<br>¿Qué hizo usted/hicieron ustedes? | ❑ | ❑ |
| • *ask what they saw*<br>¿Qué vio usted/vieron ustedes? | ❑ | ❑ |

- *say where you went last year* . . . . . . . . . . . . . . . . . . . . . . . . . . . . . . . ❑ . . . . . . ❑
  El año pasado yo fui/nosotros fuimos a México.
- *say what impressed you most* . . . . . . . . . . . . . . . . . . . . . . . . . . . . . . . ❑ . . . . . . ❑
  Me/Nos impresionó más Cuernavaca.

## Learning tips

*Learning a language isn't just about words; it's also about society and culture. Everything you can find out about Spanish-speaking countries—food, cities, sport, politics, history—will make your language studies much more enjoyable, too! Why not keep a file of newspaper clippings, pictures, and other information on Spanish-speaking countries?*

## Do you want to learn more?

*If you have access to the Internet, you may be able to find travel information in Spanish as well as in English. Otherwise, Spanish or Latin American tourist offices may be able to give you some brochures in Spanish. See how much you can understand and how many of your favorite vacation pursuits you can name in Spanish.*

Unit 4 is about the weather and making plans for leisure activities. When you have completed this unit, you will know how to:

- talk about the weather
- discuss leisure activities
- make future plans

# Nos encontramos a las siete

# 4

## Word Bank

| | |
|---|---|
| agradable | *pleasant* |
| ahí | *there (by you)* |
| atlántico/a | *Atlantic* |
| chileno/a | *Chilean* |
| el cine | *movies* |
| el clima | *climate* |
| el deporte | *sport* |
| el dibujo | *drawing* |
| esquiar | *to ski* |
| excepto | *except* |
| la gente | *people* |
| el grado | *degree* |
| el invierno | *winter* |
| el otoño | *autumn* |
| llevar | *to wear* |
| el norte | *north* |
| la nube | *cloud* |
| el pico | *peak* |
| la primavera | *spring* |
| la ropa | *clothes* |
| sin nubes | *cloudless, clear* |
| situado/a | *situated* |
| el sur | *the south* |
| el teatro | *theater* |
| la temperatura | *temperature* |
| variable | *variable* |
| el verano | *summer* |

# ¿Qué tiempo hace?

## *Talking about the weather*

RECORDING

1\. ***Listen to Silvia who lives in Santander, on the northern coast of Spain. Repeat what she says about Santander and its climate.***

| | |
|---|---|
| Hace calor. | *It's hot.* |
| Hace mucho frío. | *It's very cold.* |
| Llueve mucho. | *It rains often.* |
| Nieva. | *It snows.* |
| Hace mucho sol. | *It's very sunny.* |
| Hace buen tiempo. | *The weather's fine.* |
| Hace mal tiempo. | *The weather's bad.* |
| Se puede esquiar. | *You can ski.* |
| Hay niebla. | *It's foggy.* |
| Hace mucho viento. | *It's very windy.* |

RECORDING

2\. ***Choose the correct the word or phrase to complete Silvia's comments about Santander's climate.***

1. Santander tiene un clima muy malo/frío/agradable.
2. En verano hace mucho calor/no hace mucho calor/hace frío.
3. Sólo nieva en la costa/en las montañas/en invierno.
4. Cuando llueve la gente puede ir a la playa/a las montañas/a las tiendas.
5. En las montañas en invierno se puede esquiar/tomar el sol/ir de compras.
6. No me gusta cuando hace buen tiempo/hay niebla/hace frío.
7. En Santander a veces hace viento porque está en la costa/está cerca de las montañas/está en el centro de España.

RECORDING

3. *Now listen to Rosario, a friend of Silvia's who lives in the southern Spanish city of Seville and plans on visiting Santander. She wants to know what the weather is like and what clothing she should take with her.*

RECORDING

4. *Listen to the conversation again. All these comments are false. Can you correct them?*

1. En Sevilla hace bastante frío.
2. Estamos en verano.
3. En Santander hace frío todos los días.
4. En este momento en Santander está nevando.
5. En Sevilla los hombres llevan vestidos de verano.
6. Rosario va a llevar un vestido de verano a Santander.

RECORDING

5. *Listen to the radio weather report. Match up the places with the weather forecasts for them.*

a. Los Pirineos
b. El sur
c. Las costas del Mediterráneo
d. Canarias
e. La costa norte
f. El centro de España

1. hará buen tiempo pero por la noche hará frío
2. lloverá por la mañana pero por la tarde hará sol
3. hará viento
4. nevará
5. hará 23 grados
6. cielo cubierto

## Did You Know?

*Santander is a seaside resort on the coast of the Bay of Biscay, on the Atlantic. The weather in that area is subject to more rainfall than the center, east, and south of Spain, and the climate is quite temperate by comparison. In fact, the north and northwest are often called* la España verde. *The center of Spain is called* Castilla *and this area is situated on the high* Meseta, *or tableland, and suffers extremes of hot and cold. Andalucía in the south is dry and hot, though the valley of the Guadalquivir River on which the cities of Córdoba and Seville stand is very fertile. Because of its hot climate, almost the whole of the Mediterranean coast (from the French border to Gibraltar) attracts tourists, mainly from the colder countries of northern Europe.*

## 6.

*What will the weather be like tomorrow? Look at the illustrations and fill in the blanks.*

1. Mañana en el sur del país hará bastante ________.

2. En el centro el cielo estará ________.

3. En las montañas hará frío y ________.

4. En la costa norte por la mañana ________.

5. En la costa este hará mucho ________.

6. En la capital hará ________.

## Your turn

RECORDING

*Some Chilean friends are thinking of visiting you. They call with some questions about the weather where you live and want to know the best time of year to visit. Complete the following conversation.*

| | |
|---|---|
| *Amigo:* | ¿Cuál es la mejor estación del año para ir a visitarlos? |
| *Usted:* | *Say that spring is best.* |
| *Amigo:* | ¿Por qué? |
| *Usted:* | *Because in summer it is very hot.* |
| *Amigo:* | ¿Y en otoño? |
| *Usted:* | *In autumn it is often very windy and it rains a lot.* |
| *Amigo:* | En invierno, ¿hace mucho frío? |
| *Usted:* | *Yes, and it snows!* |
| *Amigo:* | Pues es verdad que la primavera es la mejor estación. Dime, ¿qué tiempo hace ahí hoy? |
| *Usted:* | *Say that it's raining!* |

# Close up

*In this unit you have learned the most common expressions concerning the weather. Note that the verb* **hacer** *occurs in many of them:*

| | |
|---|---|
| ¿Qué tiempo hace? | *What's the weather like?* |
| Hace calor. | *It's hot.* |
| Hace mucho frío. | *It's very cold.* |
| Hace sol. | *It's sunny.* |

*In these expressions you use* **mucho** *instead of* **muy** *for "very."*

*Note also the verbs* **llover** *(to rain) and* **nevar** *(to snow). They are both stem-changing verbs:* **llueve** *(it rains),* **está lloviendo** *(it's raining),* **nieva** *(it snows), and* **está nevando** *(it's snowing).*

*In weather forecasts you have also learned some of these expressions in the future tense, which tells you what the weather will be like:*

| | |
|---|---|
| Hará mucho calor. | *It will be very hot.* |
| Hará sol. | *It will be sunny.* |
| Lloverá. | *It will rain.* |
| Nevará. | *It will snow.* |

*With* **niebla** *you use* **hay**, *not* **hace**, *and the future is* **habrá**:

Hoy hay niebla y habrá niebla también mañana.

*It's foggy today and it will be foggy tomorrow.*

# ¿Cómo pasarás tu fin de semana?

*Making plans*

## Word Bank

| | |
|---|---|
| acompañar | *to accompany* |
| bañarse | *to bathe, swim* |
| cansado/a | *tired* |
| como siempre | *as usual* |
| descansar | *to rest, relax* |
| divertirse | *to enjoy oneself, amuse oneself* |
| durante | *during* |
| emocionado/a | *excited, thrilled* |
| la excursión | *trip, excursion* |
| la fiesta | *holiday, festival* |
| el fin de semana | *weekend* |
| largo/a | *long* |
| leer | *to read* |
| limpiar | *to clean* |
| el lunes | *Monday* |
| marcharse | *to leave* |
| la misa | *mass (in church)* |
| nadar | *to swim* |
| el novio | *boyfriend* |
| pasear(se) | *to stroll, walk* |
| la película | *film, movie* |
| la piscina | *swimming pool* |
| el polideportivo | *sports complex* |
| el proyecto | *project, plan* |
| salir de | *to leave* |
| sencillo/a | *simple* |
| sentarse | *to sit down* |
| la universidad | *university* |

RECORDING

## 1.

***It's Friday and Raquel is asking Conchita how she plans to spend her weekend. Listen to their conversation.***

| | |
|---|---|
| ¿Qué vas a hacer este fin de semana? | *What are you going to do this weekend?* |
| En mis ratos libres. | *In my free time.* |

RECORDING

## 2.

***Listen again to Conchita and Raquel's conversation and fill in the blank spaces.***

1. El sábado por la mañana, Conchita ____________ de compras a la ciudad. iré/irá/irán
2. Conchita ________ unos zapatos. compraré/compraremos/comprará
3. Esteban y Conchita ____________ en un bar. comeré/comeremos/comerán
4. Los cuatro amigos ____________ en la piscina. se bañará/se bañarán/nos bañaremos
5. Si están cansados ____________ a ver la tele. se sentarán/nos sentaremos/se sentará
6. El domingo Esteban ____________ a ver el fútbol. iremos/iré/irá
7. Conchita ____________un libro o una revista. leerán/leeremos/leerá

RECORDING

## 3.

***Nícola and Juan, two Spanish teachers, are talking with a friend about their plans for a trip to South America over the Christmas vacation. Listen to their conversation.***

| | |
|---|---|
| ¿Cuándo os marcharéis? | *When will you leave?* |
| El quince de diciembre. | *The fifteenth of December.* |
| Tomaremos el avión. | *We'll take the plane.* |
| Pasaremos tres días allí. | *We'll spend three days there.* |
| ¿Cuánto tiempo os quedaréis? | *How long will you stay?* |
| ¿Cuándo tendréis que volver? | *When will you have to return?* |

### DidYouKnow?

*You, you, you, and now you! You have so far encountered three Spanish words meaning "you" (*tú*—familiar singular,* usted*—polite singular, and* ustedes*—plural). You also know the verb forms that correspond to them:* tú compras, usted compra, *and* ustedes compran *all mean "you buy." In this unit you have also learned another verb form:* iréis, os divertiréis, os quedaréis, *which corresponds to the pronoun* vosotros *("you," plural). This is the familiar plural form of* tú, *but it is used only in Spain, rarely in Latin America.*

RECORDING

## 4.

***Listen to the conversation again. This time indicate if their comments are true or false. Correct the false comments.***

1. El martes que viene, 15 de diciembre, Nícola y Juan irán de Madrid a Caracas.
2. El martes 22 de diciembre viajarán de Caracas a Buenos Aires.
3. En Buenos Aires se quedarán en casa de una tía.
4. Irán con la tía a Punta del Este antes de Navidad.
5. Volverán a Buenos Aires para tomar el avión a Bariloche.
6. El viaje de Buenos Aires a Bariloche será largo pero barato.
7. No se quedarán en Bariloche; irán en seguida a Chile.
8. Saldrán de Chile el jueves siete de enero.

## 5.

***Using the verbs in the box below, fill in the blanks in this letter Nícola has written to a friend.***

Haremos
continuaremos
bajaremos
Estaremos
tomaremos
iremos
llegaremos
nos quedaremos
Saldremos

*Estoy muy emocionada, porque durante las vacaciones de Navidad Juan y yo ________ a Sudamérica. ________ de Madrid el quince de diciembre y ________ a Río de Janeiro el día 16. Después de Río ________ nuestro viaje hasta Buenos Aires, donde ________ en casa de una tía de Juan. Desde allí ________ el autobús a Bariloche, cerca de los Andes. ________ unas excursiones en las montañas y luego ________ a Santiago, en Chile. ________ de vuelta en Madrid justo a tiempo para las clases en enero. ¡Qué viaje!*

# Your turn

RECORDING

*A friend asks you what you're planning to do for the weekend. What will you say?*

*Amigo:* ¿Cómo pasarás este fin de semana? ¿Qué harás?

*Usted:* ***Say that on Saturday morning you'll play tennis with your friends.***

*Amigo:* ¿Y después?

*Usted:* ***Say that you'll have lunch in a bar with your friends.***

*Amigo:* ¿Y por la tarde?

*Usted:* ***Say that you and your friends will go to the soccer game.***

*Amigo:* ¿Qué haréis después del fútbol?

*Usted:* ***Say that you will return home, you'll prepare a meal, and you'll watch TV.***

*Amigo:* ¿Cómo pasarás el domingo?

*Usted:* ***Say that you'll relax. You'll read the paper but you will also have to clean your apartment!***

# Close up

*To form the future tense add the endings* **-é**, **-ás**, **-á**, **-emos**, **-éis**, **-án** *to the infinitive:* **tomar** > **tomaré**, **ir** > **iré**, *and so on. A few verbs have an irregular stem:* **hacer** > **haré**; **poder** > **podré**; **querer** > **querré**; **salir** > **saldré**; **tener** > **tendré**.

*Note that:*

- *even if the stem is irregular, it still ends in* **-r-**
- *you always use the same six endings*
- *the endings are stressed*
- *you need the stress accent on all endings but* **-emos**

*Two expressions in Spanish that go along with the phrase for saying "next weekend," "next year," and so on, are:* **que viene** *or* **próximo**:

| | |
|---|---|
| el fin de semana que viene<br>el fin de semana próximo | *next weekend* |
| el año que viene<br>el año próximo | *next year* |
| el martes que viene<br>el martes próximo | *next Tuesday* |

# ¿Qué fecha es?

*Asking about days and dates*

## Word Bank

| | |
|---|---|
| arreglar | *to arrange* |
| el alpinismo | *climbing, mountaineering* |
| la bicicleta | *bicycle* |
| el boxeo | *boxing* |
| cada uno/a | *each one* |
| el campo | *the country(side)* |
| la caña de pesca | *fishing rod* |
| el ciclismo | *cycling* |
| el concierto | *concert* |
| el concurso | *contest, competition* |
| el/la deportista | *sportsman/woman; athlete* |
| el equipo | *team* |
| el espectáculo | *show, spectacle* |
| el esquí | *ski, skiing* |
| extranjero/a | *foreign* |
| el fútbol | *soccer, football* |
| el golf | *golf* |
| Italia | *Italy* |
| el monumento | *monument* |
| el museo | *museum* |
| la música | *music* |
| la ópera | *opera* |
| el paseo | *walk, ride, trip* |
| la pesca | *fishing* |
| recibir | *to receive* |
| tomar parte | *to take part* |
| el tenis | *tennis* |

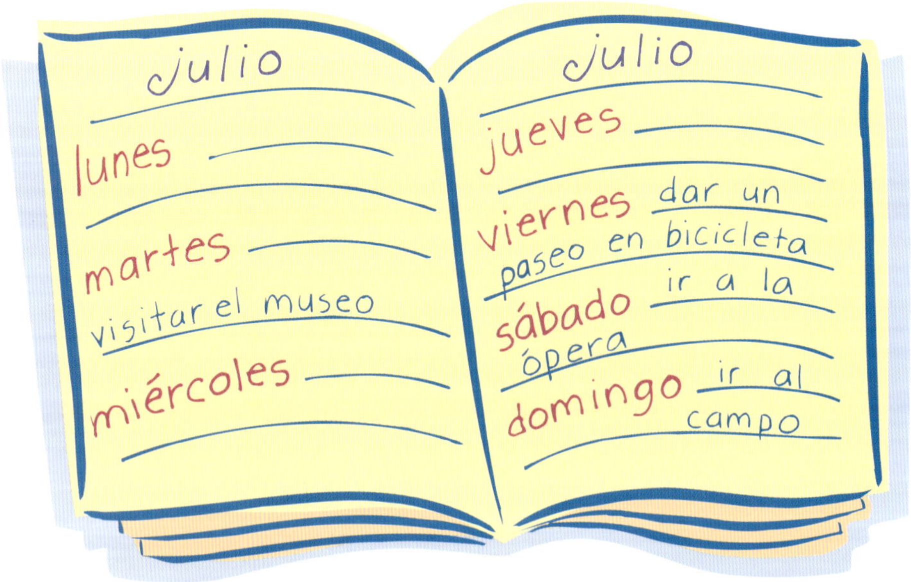

RECORDING

1. *Listen as Elena speaks with her neighbor, Sra. Notario, about her summer vacation plans.*

| | |
|---|---|
| ¿Qué fecha es hoy? | *What's the date today?* |
| Estamos a dieciocho de febrero. | *It's February 18.* |
| Desde el 18 de julio hasta el 15 de agosto. | *From July 18 to August 15.* |
| ¿Qué quieres decir? | *What do you mean?* |
| Pasaré un par de días en el campo. | *I'll spend a couple of days in the country.* |
| Me gusta ir a pescar. | *I like to go fishing.* |
| No hace tanto calor en el norte. | *It's not so hot in the north.* |

RECORDING

2. *Listen to the dialog again. Then answer the following questions.*

1. ¿Qué fecha es hoy?
2. ¿En qué mes va a tomar Elena sus vacaciones?
3. ¿En qué fecha, precisamente?
4. ¿Adónde va a ir?
5. ¿Cómo va a viajar?
6. ¿Qué harán el hermano de Elena y su mujer?
7. ¿Qué hará Elena?
8. ¿Hace más calor en el norte o en el sur de Italia?

RECORDING

3. *Now, let's listen to Antonio. He's an active sportsman, and has a really busy schedule of athletic events for the coming year. Repeat along with Antonio his activities and the dates.*

## DidYouKnow?

**La pelota** *is a game played mainly in the Basque area of Spain. It is not unlike squash and is played on a* **frontón** *as singles or doubles. The* **frontón** *consists of a side wall and a front wall, at right angles to each other, and the players have to strike the ball against the front wall and beat their opponents with the rebound. The ball may be bounced off the side wall.* **Pelota** *can be played with* **a cesta**, *a sort of scoop-like basket, which is very fast, a* **pala**, *which is a bat rather like a baseball bat, or, on a small* **frontón**, *a* **mano**, *when the ball is struck with the palm of the hand. Many bars in that area of Spain have their own* **frontón**.

RECORDING

4. *Antonio's date book is a bit mixed up. Can you put it in order? Listen again and then put the information in the correct column. Pay attention! There are two missing dates and activities. Which ones are they?*

| | | |
|---|---|---|
| 1. El 5 de enero | tomará parte | en un concurso de boxeo. |
| 2. El 14 de febrero | viajará | tres días en las montañas haciendo alpinismo. |
| 3. El 28 de marzo | dará | en un concurso de tenis. |
| 4. El 10 de mayo | recibirá | a la Argentina con su equipo de fútbol. |
| 5. El 30 de junio | irá | a unos deportistas extranjeros en su casa. |
| 6. El 12 de julio | jugará | en Francia en un concurso de ciclismo. |
| 7. El 2 de agosto | nadará | a las montañas a esquiar. |
| 8. El 13 de septiembre | pasará | un largo paseo por el campo con sus amigos. |
| 9. El 21 de noviembre | estará | a la pelota en Bilbao. |
| 10. El 28 de diciembre | tomará parte | para su equipo en el polideportivo de su ciudad. |

5. *You've marked a calendar with the birthdays of family members. Read them aloud.*

RECORDING

## Pronunciation

*You learned about stressed final vowels in the preterite tense in Unit 3. The future tense also has stressed final vowels, but with a big difference: they are always preceded by* **-r-**.

*Practice:* **volveré, tomaré, recibirá, quedaréis, vendrán.**
*Make sure you trill that* **r** *on the end of the tongue! Try some more single* **r**'s *in words that occur in this unit:*

**extranjero, siempre, sentarse, leer, miércoles, martes, viernes, largo, ópera**

*Now try the difference between single* **-r-** *and the much more strongly rolled double* **-rr-**:

**pero/perro; caro/carro; cero/cierro**

## Close up

*In this unit you have been using dates and days of the week.*

*The way to ask the date is either* **¿Qué fecha es?** *or* **¿A cuánto estamos?** *More often than not you will just reply with the date (***cinco de abril***), but you could say* **Es el cinco de abril** *or* **Estamos a cinco de abril**.

*Note:*

- *You use the cardinal number in dates, except* **el primero** *for the first of the month:* **el dos de mayo**, **el primero de junio**.
- *The number always comes before the month, followed by* **de**.
- *Days and months are spelled with a small letter:* **miércoles 5 de abril**.
- *There is no word for "on" a day or date: "on Thursday" is just* **jueves** *or* **el jueves**; *"on July 9" is* **el nueve de julio**.

*You have also used more verbs in the future tense but you can also, as in English, use* **ir a** *to indicate what you are going to do:*

**¿Qué vas a hacer? Voy a alquilar una bicicleta.**

*What are you going to do? I'm going to rent a bicycle.*

*This form is very common. In fact you have been seeing it in several units.*

# Checkpoints

***Can you . . . ?*** — ***Yes*** / ***No***

- *ask what the weather is like* ❑ ❑
  ¿Qué tiempo hace?
- *say what the weather is like* ❑ ❑
  Hace mucho calor.
- *say the seasons* ❑ ❑
  En verano...
- *say what the weather will be like tomorrow* ❑ ❑
  Mañana hará buen tiempo.
- *ask people what they are going to do in their spare time* ❑ ❑
  ¿Qué vas a hacer el sábado?
- *say what you will do/what you are going to do* ❑ ❑
  Cenaré/voy a cenar en un restaurante italiano.
- *say what you enjoy doing in your leisure time or on vacation* ❑ ❑
  Me gusta ir a la piscina.
- *talk about plans for a future vacation* ❑ ❑
  Vamos a ir a Italia.
- *say when you are going to take your vacation* ❑ ❑
  Voy a tomar mis vacaciones en julio.
- *talk about days of the week and dates* ❑ ❑
  La fiesta es el domingo tres de junio.
- *say what you will do on a given date* ❑ ❑
  El veinte de diciembre iré a Caracas.
- *say it's hotter in one place than in another* ❑ ❑
  Hace más calor en el sur que en el norte.

## Learning tips

*Don't be worried if you feel you're not making a lot of progress. The learning process is never a steady progression, and there will be times when you feel that you're not getting anywhere at all. Remind yourself that this is perfectly normal and that everyone feels this way from time to time. The important thing is to stick with it! You may even be making progress in another area without realizing it. For example, you might be trying very hard to increase your vocabulary, apparently without success; but instead, your listening comprehension improves dramatically without conscious effort.*

## Do you want to learn more?

*Look through the sports section of a Spanish-language newspaper. See how many of the sports have similar names in English and in Spanish.*

Unit 5 is about making plans to go out. When you have completed this unit, you will know how to:

- suggest going out to the movies or theater
- tell what a film or play is about
- give an opinion about a movie or play
- talk about hobbies
- say what you used to do at some point in the past

# Planes y reuniones 5

## Word Bank

| | |
|---|---|
| aburrido/a | *boring* |
| el actor | *actor* |
| la actriz | *actress* |
| clásico/a | *classical* |
| el concierto | *concert* |
| desaparecer | *to disappear* |
| el detective | *detective* |
| la discoteca | *disco* |
| las diversiones | *entertainment* |
| divertido/a | *funny, amusing* |
| durar | *to last* |
| en lugar de | *instead of* |
| la entrada | *(entry) ticket* |
| el espectáculo | *show* |
| guapo/a | *handsome, good-looking* |
| muerto/a | *dead* |
| la música | *music* |
| la obra | *work, play* |
| la ópera | *opera* |
| la orquesta | *orchestra* |
| la página | *page* |
| película | *movie, film* |
| policíaco/a | *detective movie* |
| el programa | *program* |
| el/la protagonista | *protagonist* |
| regular | *ordinary, so-so* |
| ruso/a | *Russian* |
| la tragedia | *tragedy* |
| la vida | *life* |

# ¿Por qué no vamos al cine?

## *Going to the movies*

RECORDING

**1.** ***Mari-Carmen and Tomás are talking about their plans for Saturday night. Tomás is reading the entertainment page of a newspaper. First, listen to the complete dialog, then repeat the parts in the pauses.***

| | |
|---|---|
| Ponen una nueva película. | *There's a new movie playing.* |
| ¡Será muy divertida! | *It will be very funny!* |
| ¿De qué trata? | *What's it about?* |
| ¿Qué ponen en el teatro? | *What's playing at the theater?* |
| No quedan entradas. | *There are no tickets left.* |
| Menos mal. | *What a relief!* |
| Si nos da la gana. | *If we feel like it.* |

RECORDING

**2.** ***Now, decide which of these comments are true and which are false. Correct the false comments.***

1. Hay una película vieja en el *Cine Colón.*
2. Las películas de Almodóvar son divertidas.
3. Sólo hay un cine.
4. La película policíaca termina a las once de la noche.
5. En el *Teatro Liceo* ponen una obra moderna.
6. A Tomás no le gustan las obras clásicas.
7. Hay un concierto de música española en el *Salón de Música.*
8. Todavía hay entradas para la ópera.
9. A Mari-Carmen le gusta la ópera.
10. Tomás y Mari-Carmen irán a comer antes de ir a la discoteca o al cine.

RECORDING

3. *At work on Monday, Tomás and a friend are discussing a movie. Listen to their conversation.*

RECORDING

4. *Listen to these people giving their opinions about a movie or a theatrical show that they've recently seen. Indicate with a check mark (✓) whether they liked it or not.*

1. ________ ________

2. ________ ________

3. ________ ________

4. ________ ________

5. ________ ________

6. ________ ________

7. ________ ________

8. ________ ________

## Your turn

RECORDING

*Complete this dialog with the appropriate sentences.*

| | |
|---|---|
| *Usted:* | *Suggest going to the movies or the theater.* |
| *Amiga:* | Buena idea. ¿Qué te gustaría ver? |
| *Usted:* | *Suggest a movie.* |
| *Amiga:* | Sí, quizás una película norteamericana. |
| *Usted:* | *You don't like American movies; you prefer a Spanish move.* |
| *Amiga:* | De acuerdo. |
| *Usted:* | *Ask your friend if she has the newspaper.* |
| *Amiga:* | Sí, aquí lo tienes. |
| *Usted:* | *What time does the movie start and end?* |
| *Amiga:* | Empieza a las siete y media y termina a las nueve y media. |
| *Usted:* | *Suggest that instead of going to the movie at 7:30, you go out for dinner and then go to the movie afterwards.* |
| *Amiga:* | Sí, también empieza a las diez y media. |

## Close up

**Sin** *followed by an infinitive means "without doing something":*

| | |
|---|---|
| **sin** decir nada | *without saying anything* |
| **sin** encontrar nada | *without finding anything* |

*Note that you don't need* **no** *before the verb when you use* **sin** *with a negative word such as* **nada**.

**En lugar de** *also takes an infinitive and means "instead of…":*

| | |
|---|---|
| **En lugar de** ver la película de Almodóvar. | *Instead of seeing the Almodóvar movie.* |
| **En lugar de** ir al cine. | *Instead of going to the movies.* |

*You have been meeting a few unfamiliar verb endings. Trataba (was about),* **tomaba** *(took),* **era**, **estaba** *(was, from* **ser** *and* **estar** *respectively) are examples of the imperfect past tense, which will be explained more fully in the next pages. For now just treat them as verbs in the past tense.*

# Hace años...

## *Talking about the past*

## Word Bank

| | |
|---|---|
| acordarse | *to remember* |
| el/la aficionado/a | *enthusiast* |
| las antigüedades | *antiques* |
| antiguo/a | *old, antique* |
| el árbol | *tree* |
| coleccionar | *to collect* |
| el compact-disc | *compact disc* |
| el conjunto | *group (pop)* |
| engancharse | *to get hooked* |
| la fotografía | *photography* |
| la guitarra | *guitar* |
| hacerse | *to become* |
| el interés | *pastime, hobby* |
| la máquina fotográfica | *camera* |
| la música pop | *pop music* |
| el paisaje | *landscape, countryside* |
| pintar | *to paint* |
| la pintura | *painting* |
| la porcelana | *porcelain* |
| preferido/a | *favorite* |
| el río | *river* |
| sacar fotos | *to take photos* |
| tocar | *to play (instrument)* |

RECORDING

**1.** ***Here are a few interviews with people talking about their likes and dislikes.***

| | |
|---|---|
| ¿Cuándo empezó usted a coleccionar antigüedades? | *When did you start collecting antiques?* |
| En aquel momento me enganché. | *At that moment I got hooked.* |
| Yo soy aficionada a la pintura. | *I'm a painting enthusiast.* |
| Empecé a pintar cuando tenía 20 años. | *I started painting when I was 20.* |
| Fui por primera vez a la ópera hace muchos años. | *I went to the opera for the first time many years ago.* |

RECORDING

## 2.

***Listen to the dialog again. This time match each person's name to his/her favorite interest.***

Sr. Castillo
Sra. Ponce
Pablo
Sra. Blancos
Javi
Sra. Álvarez
Felipe

## Did You Know?

*Many towns in Spain and Latin America have a flea market on Sundays. Probably the most famous one is* **El Rastro** *in the old quarter of Madrid, which attracts collectors and tourists–and pickpockets!* **La Feria de San Telmo** *in the Plaza Dorrego in Buenos Aires is also one of that city's attractions.*

RECORDING

## 3.

***Now listen again and indicate when each person began to show interest in a particular area or subject.***

| | | | |
|---|---|---|---|
| 1 | La Sra. Ponce | a | hace tres años. |
| 2 | La Sra. Blancos | b | cuando tenía 20 años. |
| 3 | Pablo | c | hace diez años. |
| 4 | El Sr. Castillo | d | hace ocho años. |
| 5 | Javi | e | cuando tenía 18 años. |
| 6 | La Sra. Álvarez | f | cuando trabajaba en Chile. |
| 7 | Felipe | g | cuando vivía en Buenos Aires. |

## 4.

*Let's see if you can complete the following sentences about these people by putting the words in their proper order. Begin each sentence with the person's name.*

1. La Sra. Ponce... años cuando empezó tenía pintar a veinte.
2. La Sra. Blancos... fotos negro sacaba y las blanco en entonces.
3. Pablo... chilenos Chile empezó trabajaba unos hace coleccionar quince a cuando en años sellos.
4. El Sr. Castillo... jarra Londres en estaba cuando una vio.
5. A Javi... tres cumpleaños compact-disc hace para sus su regalaron padres le años un.
6. La Sra. Álvarez... vez ópera madre fue primera con Buenos Aires cuando en por vivían su la a.
7. Felipe... años a guitarra aprendió ocho tocar la hace.

## 5.

*Fill in the blanks with words from the list.*

*Cuando yo tenía doce años __________ en Buenos Aires. Cada domingo por la mañana mi padre y yo __________ a la Plaza Dorrego, donde __________ un mercado de antigüedades. A veces yo __________ alguna pequeña cosa y allí __________ mi interés por las antigüedades. Ahora colecciono relojes antiguos y cuando __________ en una ciudad donde __________ un rastro, siempre lo __________. Recientemente en Madrid, __________ al Rastro un domingo por la mañana y __________ un magnífico reloj antiguo.*

había
visito
compré
vivíamos
hay
nació
fui
ibamos
estoy
compraba

## Your turn

***Write a paragraph that gives the following information.***

¿Qué interés tiene usted?

¿Hace cuánto tiempo empezó usted a practicarlo?

¿Dónde vivía cuando empezó a interesarse?

¿Cuántos años tenía?

Dé algunos detalles, por ejemplo si su interés es coleccionar sellos, ¿de qué país son?

## Close up

### *The imperfect tense*

*The imperfect tense is a past tense that is used to describe what you once did or what was going on as a background to previous events.*

| | |
|---|---|
| La película trataba de un detective. | *The movie was about a detective.* |
| Hace diez años, cuando estaba en Londres... | *Ten years ago, when I was in London...* |
| Empecé a coleccionar sellos cuando trabajaba en Chile. | *I began to collect stamps when I was working in Chile.* |
| Ibamos al teatro donde ponían muchas óperas. | *We used to go to the theater where they performed many operas.* |

*The endings are* **-aba**, **-abas**, **-aba**, **ábamos**, **-abais**, **-aban** *for* **-ar** *verbs, and* **-ía, -ías**, **-ía**, **-íamos**, **-íais**, **-ían** *for* **-er** *and* **-ir** *verbs. There are only two irregular verbs:* **ser → era**, **eras**, **era**, **éramos**, **erais**, **eran**; *and* **ir → iba**, **ibas**, **iba**, **íbamos**, **ibais**, **iban**. **Ver** *keeps the* **-e-**: **veía**, *and so on.*

**Hace** *comes before the period of time in question and means "ago."*

| | |
|---|---|
| Hace diez años. | *Ten years ago.* |
| Hace mucho tiempo. | *A long time ago.* |

# ¿Dónde vivía usted?

*Talking about the way things used to be*

## Word Bank

| | | | |
|---|---|---|---|
| el barrio | *district, neighborhood* | jubilarse | *to retire* |
| charlar | *to chat* | mientras | *while* |
| distinto/a | *different* | practicar | *to practice* |
| la diversión | *entertainment* | principalmente | *mainly* |
| el interés | *interest* | reunirse con | *to meet* |

RECORDING

1. ***Listen to Vicenta who describes what it was like living with her husband in Madrid before going to live in the country.***

| | |
|---|---|
| Yo trabajaba por las mañanas. | *I worked in the mornings.* |
| Estando libre por las tardes . . . | *Being free in the afternoons . . .* |
| Todos los sábados por la noche . . . | *Every Saturday night . . .* |

RECORDING

## 2.

*True or false? Listen to Activity 1 again and correct the false statements.*

1. En Madrid Vicenta y su marido tenían una vida muy distinta.
2. Argüelles está en el campo.
3. El marido de Vicenta trabajaba todo el día.
4. Vicenta se reunía con sus amigas por las mañanas para tomar café.
5. A su marido no le gustaba la ópera.
6. En Madrid había muchas diversiones.
7. Los domingos el marido de Vicenta pintaba la casa.
8. Cuando se jubiló su marido, Vicenta se quedó en la capital.
9. Ahora van mucho al teatro.

RECORDING

## 3.

*Listen to the dialog again. Then fill in the blanks.*

1. Cuando Vicenta y su marido ______________ en Madrid, su vida ______________ muy distinta.
2. Vicenta y su marido ______________ en el barrio de Argüelles.
3. El marido de Vicenta ______________ en el centro.
4. Vicenta sólo ______________ por las mañanas.
5. Vicenta se ______________ por las tardes con sus amigas y ______________ café en una cafetería.
6. Su marido y ella ______________ al teatro, al cine o a la ópera.
7. ______________ a algún sitio casi todos los sábados.
8. A su marido le ______________ la pintura y ______________ los domingos en el parque.
9. A veces Vicenta se ______________ en casa, a veces ______________ al parque con su marido.
10. El marido ______________ vivir en el campo y por eso ahora viven allí.

RECORDING

**4.** *Now, listen to these people talking about what they used to do for fun. Who liked to do what?*

Andrés
Julia y Pepe
Alfredo
Sra. Flores
Sr. Carmona
Sra. Alfonsín

**5.** *Sra. Moreno writes to her friend Josefa about their past. Help her by filling in the blanks. The verbs you'll need are in the box.*

Querida Josefa:

¿Te acuerdas de cuando ________ madres de niños pequeños? Tu hija Paquita ________ unos tres años y mi hijo Jorge también ________ muy pequeño. Yo ________ por las mañanas pero tú ________ no trabajar siendo madre. Después de comer ________ en el parque y ________ un paseo con los niños, que ________ juntos. ¡No ________ mucho dinero, pero ________ muy contentas!

nos reuníamos
éramos
teníamos
dábamos
tenía
preferías
estábamos
era
trabajaba
jugaban

## Your turn

RECORDING

*You're talking with the Vegas, your new neighbors. You don't know them well yet and want to find out more about them.*

| | |
|---|---|
| *Usted:* | ***Ask where they lived before coming to live here.*** |
| *Sr. Vega:* | Antes de venir a vivir aquí, vivíamos en la costa. |
| *Usted:* | ***Ask Sr. Vega what they used to do on weekends.*** |
| *Sr. Vega:* | Los fines de semana, en verano, íbamos a la playa; nos bañábamos . . . |
| *Usted:* | ***Ask Sra. Vega if she used to work downtown.*** |
| *Sra. Vega:* | Sí, tenía un trabajo que hacía por las mañanas. |
| *Usted:* | ***Ask her what interests she used to have.*** |
| *Sra. Vega:* | Los domingos iba a la costa o al campo a pintar. |
| *Usted:* | ***And what her husband used to do in his spare time.*** |
| *Sra. Vega:* | A él también le gustaba pintar en sus ratos libres. |

## Pronunciation

RECORDING

*You have encountered two examples of* **ü** *in this unit:* **antigüedades** *and* **Argüelles**. *In the combinations* **gue** *and* **gui**, *the* **u** *is silent (***paque, guitarra***) so when you need to indicate that the* **u** *is pronounced, you used the diaeresis (¨) on the* **ü**. *Look at the table below, which tells you how to write the sounds* **g** *and* **gu**, *and practice saying the examples with the recording.*

*Sound:*

| | | | |
|---|---|---|---|
| ga | diga, haga, larga | gua | agua, Guadalajara, antigua |
| gue | pague, guerra | güe | antigüedades, Argüelles |
| gui | guitarra | güi | argüir |
| go | hago, digo, largo | guo | antiguo |
| gu | algún | | |

# Close-up

*This lesson contains many more examples of the imperfect to indicate what the situation used to be, what people used to do in the past. Contrast this with the preterite, which you have already used quite a lot by now.*

Mi marido **quería** vivir en el campo, por eso **vinimos** a vivir aquí.

*My husband wanted (imperfect = was wanting) to live in the country, so we came (preterite = what we "did") to live here.*

Cuando **vivíamos** en la capital **íbamos** al teatro.

*When we lived/used to live in the capital, we went/used to go to the theater (imperfect = what we used to do, on a regular basis.)*

**Ayer fuimos al teatro.**

*Yesterday we went to the theater (preterite = that's what we did on one occasion.)*

**Antes de** *means "before", and* **después de** *means "after." When you use them with a verb, you use the infinitive:* **antes de vivir aquí** *"before living here,"* **después de comer** *"after eating, after lunch."*

# Checkpoints

| *Can you . . . ?* | *Yes* | *No* |
|---|---|---|
| • *suggest going out somewhere* ¿Por qué no vamos al teatro? | ❑ | ❑ |
| • *ask what a film or play is about* ¿De qué trata esta película? | ❑ | ❑ |
| • *say what it is about* Trata de un detective privado. | ❑ | ❑ |
| • *ask what time a show begins* ¿A qué hora empieza la obra? | ❑ | ❑ |
| • *and what time it ends* ¿A qué hora termina la película? | ❑ | ❑ |
| • *ask what's on at the movies or theater* ¿Qué ponen en el *Cine Colón*? | ❑ | ❑ |
| • *say what you would like to do* Me gustaría salir al cine. | ❑ | ❑ |
| • *ask what happened in a movie or play* ¿Qué ocurrió en la película? | ❑ | ❑ |
| • *ask someone when he or she started a hobby* ¿Cuándo empezaste a coleccionar sellos? | ❑ | ❑ |
| • *state how long ago something happened* Hace cinco años. | ❑ | ❑ |
| • *say how old you were at a given point in time* Yo tenía dieciocho años. | ❑ | ❑ |
| • *ask people what they like to do in their spare time* ¿Qué le gusta hacer en sus ratos libres? | ❑ | ❑ |
| • *say what you liked or didn't like* No me gustó la acción. | ❑ | ❑ |

- *say where you lived at the time* . . . . . . . . . . . . . . . . . . . . . . . . . . . . ❑ . . . . . . ❑
  Vivía en Valparaíso.
- *say what you used to do at some period in the past* . . . . . . . . . . . . . ❑ . . . . . . ❑
  Cuando vivíamos en Buenos Aires, íbamos mucho al teatro.
- *say "before doing something"* . . . . . . . . . . . . . . . . . . . . . . . . . . . . . ❑ . . . . . . ❑
  Antes de ir al cine . . .
- *say "after doing something"* . . . . . . . . . . . . . . . . . . . . . . . . . . . . . . ❑ . . . . . . ❑
  Después de ir al teatro . . .

## Learning tips

*Try keeping a diary in Spanish. Don't look words up and don't check the grammar. If you can't think of the right word, use the English word instead. Write as quickly as you can and don't go back to correct your writing. The point of this exercise is to learn to express yourself fluently in Spanish, not to improve your vocabulary or grammar. Try to write for a few minutes each day. After a few weeks, look back to the beginning and compare your entries with what you're writing now.*

## Do you want to learn more?

*Look through any Spanish-language newspaper or magazine you have for ads and listings for theaters, restaurants, travel agents, and so on. Think about what you would say if you were phoning to make a reservation.*

Unit 6 is about getting in shape and staying healthy. When you have completed this unit, you will know how to:

- describe how someone looks
- talk about health and fitness
- describe how you feel
- give advice about health

# ¡En forma!

# 6

## Word Bank

| | |
|---|---|
| adelgazar | *to lose weight* |
| los consejos | *advice* |
| el corazón | *heart* |
| cuidarse la salud | *to look after one's health* |
| delgado/a | *slim* |
| la dieta | *diet* |
| el ejercicio | *exercise* |
| engordar | *to put on weight, get fat* |
| la fiebre | *fever* |
| francamente | *frankly* |
| el gimnasio | *gymnasium* |
| gordo/a | *fat (adj.)* |
| la grasa | *fat (n.)* |
| correr | *to jog, go jogging* |
| mantenerse en forma | *to keep fit* |
| o sea | *or rather* |
| el pastel | *cake* |
| pesar demasiado | *to be overweight* |
| preocupar | *to worry* |
| quemar | *to burn (up)* |
| seguir | *to follow* |
| sufrir | *to suffer* |
| tratar de | *to try to* |

# Usted y su salud

## Getting in shape

RECORDING

**1.** ***Listen to Benjamín and Arturo talk about staying in shape.***

| | |
|---|---|
| ¡Cuántos años sin verte! | *Haven't seen you for years!* |
| ¡Qué bien estás de salud! | *Don't you look well!* |
| ¡Qué vida tan enérgica! | *What an energetic life!* |
| ¡Qué delgado estás! | *How slim you are!* |

RECORDING

**2.** ***Listen to the conversation again and fill in the blanks.***

1. Arturo ________ de mantenerse en forma.
2. Arturo va al gimnasio ________ ________ por ________.
3. Por la mañana hace ________ antes de ir al trabajo.
4. La vida de Arturo es muy ________.
5. Arturo es muy ________.
6. A Arturo no le gustan las ________.
7. Prefiere ________ la grasa con el ________.
8. Benjamín encuentra las ________ muy aburridas.
9. Según Arturo hay que tener ________ con la ________.
10. Si no, Benjamín podría tener ________ del ________.

RECORDING

**3.** ***Benjamín and Arturo continue talking. Listen and then repeat each of their parts.***

| | |
|---|---|
| Hay que tener cuidado con la salud. | *We have to take care of our health.* |
| Lo del corazón. | *That business of the heart.* |
| ¿Qué debería comer? | *What should I eat?* |
| A ver lo que puedo hacer. | *Let's see what I can do.* |

**4.** *All of Arturo's advice is mixed-up. See if you can put it into its proper order. What does Arturo tell Benjamín?*

1. Podrías pie a ir trabajo al.
2. Podrías continuar a autobús pie luego tomar y el.
3. Deberías bicicleta comprar quizás una.
4. Podrías bici en trabajo al ir.
5. También paseos podrías ratos sus dar unos en libres.
6. Deberías día ejercicio cada hacer.
7. Deberías . . . hora dos de hacer veces ejercicios semana media por.
8. Deberías no chocolate comer.

**5.** *Write a paragraph telling a friend how to go about losing weight. Use the verb forms* **deberías** *and* **podrías** *with expressions like "to go to the gym," "exercise," and "to buy a bike."*

Guadalajara,
2 de marzo de 2003

Querida Elena:

______________________________
______________________________
______________________________
______________________________
______________________________
______________________________
______________________________

**6.** *Complete these statements with the appropriate words.*

1. ¡Qué ________ tan enérgica!
2. ¡Qué ________ eres!
3. ¡Qué dieta tan ________!
4. ¡Qué ________ estás de salud!
5. ¿Vas a correr? ¡Qué ________!

## Your turn

RECORDING

*Your friend wants to lose weight. Tell her what she ought to do.*

| | |
|---|---|
| *Usted:* | ***Ask her if she exercises.*** |
| *Amiga:* | Muy poco. |
| *Usted:* | ***Tell her that she should walk to work.*** |
| *Amiga:* | Pero prefiero ir en coche. |
| *Usted:* | ***Suggest that she could take the bus and then walk. Or she could buy a bicycle.*** |
| *Amiga:* | Sí, es verdad, pero necesito el coche cuando voy al supermercado a comprar comida. |
| *Usted:* | ***Tell her she should not buy cake; suggest that she should eat more fruit.*** |
| *Amiga:* | Pero encuentro muy aburridas las dietas. |
| *Usted:* | ***Tell her that she could have heart problems.*** |
| *Amiga:* | ¡Ay! ¡Qué horror! Entonces debería tratar de adelgazar, ¿no? |

## Close-up

*To give advice use* **debería** *"ought to" or "should" and* **podría**, *which means "could." The first and third persons singular end as illustrated and the* **tú** *form ends in* **-s**: **deberías**, **podrías**. *They are followed by the verb in the infinitive:*

| | |
|---|---|
| **Deberías** hacer más ejercicio. | *You ought to/should do more exercise.* |
| Benjamín no **debería** comer chocolate. | *Benjamin ought not to/shouldn't eat chocolate.* |
| Usted **podría** comprar una bici. | *You could buy a bike.* |

**¡Qué . . . !** *used before a noun or an adjective in an exclamation means "What a . . . !" or "How . . . !"*

| | |
|---|---|
| ¡**Qué** delgado eres! | *How slim you are!* |
| ¡**Qué** vida! | *What a life!* |

*If the noun is qualified by an adjective, you need to insert* **tan** *or* **más**:

| | |
|---|---|
| ¡Qué vida **tan** enérgica! | *What an energetic life!* |
| ¡Qué régimen **más** aburrido! | *What a boring diet!* |

# Me duele...

*Describing how you feel*

*Parts of the body*
**Las partes del cuerpo**

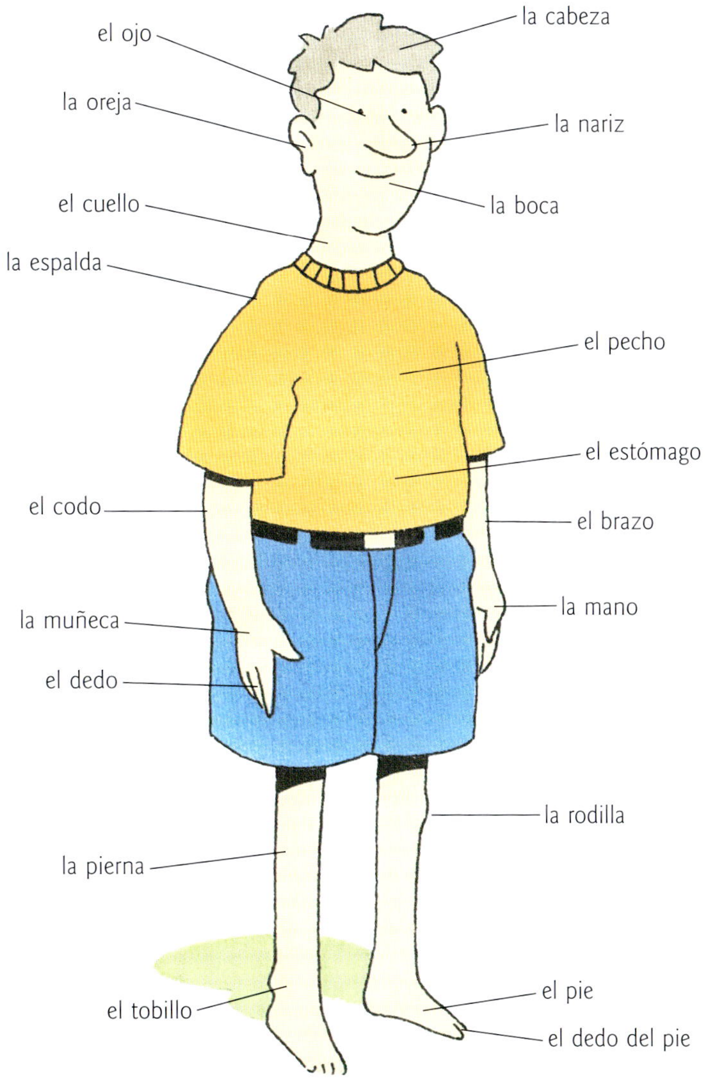

# Word Bank

| | |
|---|---|
| el agujero | *hole* |
| la aspirina | *aspirin* |
| el consultorio | *doctor's office* |
| cuidado | *be careful* |
| la diarrea | *diarrhea* |
| el dolor | *pain* |
| el dolor de estómago | *stomachache* |
| el dolor de garganta | *sore throat* |
| el empaste | *filling* |
| la gripe | *flu* |
| la inyección | *injection* |
| los mariscos | *seafood* |
| el/la médico/a | *doctor* |
| la muela | *tooth/molar* |
| las pastillas antibióticas | *antibiotic tablets* |
| la receta | *prescription* |
| reponerse | *to recover* |
| respirar | *to breathe* |
| sentirse bien/mal | *to feel well/ill* |
| la temperatura | *temperature* |
| la tos | *cough* |
| vomitar | *to vomit* |

RECORDING

**1.** ***Sra. Menéndez is explaining to the doctor why she doesn't feel well. Listen to the conversation.***

| | |
|---|---|
| ¿Qué le pasa? | *What's wrong?* |
| No me siento bien. | *I don't feel well.* |
| Me duele mucho la cabeza. | *I've got a bad headache.* |
| Me duelen los brazos. | *My arms ache.* |
| ¿Desde cuándo le duelen? | *How long have they ached/hurt?* |
| Desde hace dos o tres días. | *For two or three days.* |
| ¿Tiene usted fiebre? | *Have you got a temperature?* |
| ¡Abra la boca . . . diga ah! | *Open your mouth, say ah!* |
| No es nada grave. | *It's nothing serious.* |
| Tiene que guardar cama. | *You must stay in bed.* |

RECORDING

## 2.

***Listen again and choose the correct statements about Sra. Menéndez. Can you correct the inaccurate statements?***

1. Le duelen las muelas.
2. Le duele la cabeza.
3. Le duelen las piernas y los brazos desde hace cinco días.
4. Tiene una temperatura de 39 grados.
5. Tiene tos.
6. Puede hablar pero le duele la garganta.
7. Tiene que pasar unos días en la cama.
8. La Sra. Menéndez está muy grave.

RECORDING

## 3.

***José-María is talking with his doctor. Listen to the dialog.***

| | |
|---|---|
| ¡Enséñeme la lengua! | *Show me your tongue!* |
| Tiene una intoxicación alimenticia. | *You have food poisoning.* |
| ¡Tome dos pastillas tres veces por día! | *Take two tablets three times a day!* |
| Se repondrá dentro de unos días. | *You'll recover in a few days.* |

RECORDING

## 4.

***Imagine that you're a doctor. Check the symptoms that José-María has and cross out those he doesn't have.***

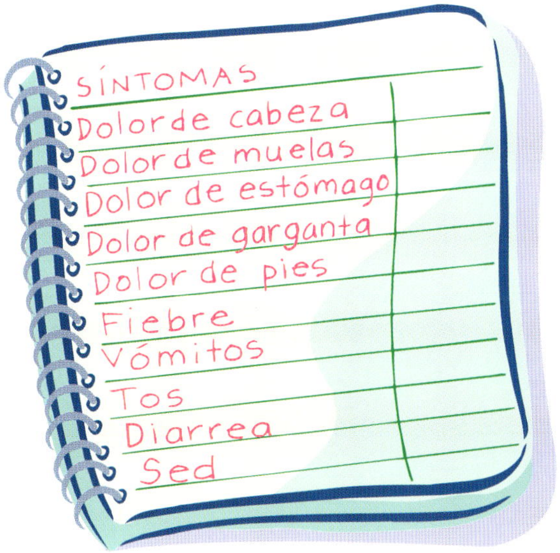

RECORDING

## 5.

*Listen again and answer the following questions.*

1. ¿Qué le pasa a José-María?
2. ¿Desde cuándo le duele el estómago?
3. ¿Tiene fiebre?
4. ¿Adónde fue el sábado por la noche?
5. ¿Qué comió?
6. ¿Por qué no está enferma Beatriz?
7. ¿Qué tiene José-María?
8. ¿Qué le recetó el médico?
9. ¿Qué tiene que hacer José-María?

RECORDING

## 6.

*Marco has a toothache. He goes to the dentist. Listen to the entire dialog.*

RECORDING

## 7.

*Choose the correct word to complete the following sentences.*

1. Marco tiene dolor de ________.
2. El dentista le pregunta dónde le ________.
3. Marco tiene un ________ ________ en su muela.
4. El dentista va a ponerle un ________ en el agujero.
5. Antes de empezar, el dentista le va a poner una ________.

## 8.

*You are on vacation and your spouse or partner is sick. Write a postcard to a friend describing the illness, which is very similar to José-María's. The answers to the questions in Activity 5 will help you.*

### Did You Know?

*In Spain and Latin America, it is usual to go to the drugstore or pharmacy for remedies for minor ills: coughs, colds, insect stings, minor sprains, and so on. The pharmacist will also sell pills, plasters, and other over-the-counter remedies.*

# Your turn

RECORDING

***You don't feel well and go to the doctor. Complete the dialog with the doctor.***

*Médica:* Buenos días. ¿Qué le pasa?

*Usted:* ***Say you don't feel well. You have a headache and stomachache.***

*Médica:* ¿Tiene usted fiebre?

*Usted:* ***Say you don't think so, but you are sick from time to time and have diarrhea.***

*Médica:* ¿Desde cuándo?

*Usted:* ***Say since 3 or 4 days ago.***

*Médica:* Vamos a ver. ¿Dónde le duele el estómago?

*Usted:* ***Say it hurts here . . . and here.***

*Médica:* ¿Qué comió usted hace tres o cuatro días?

*Usted:* ***Say you went to a restaurant on Sunday and ate some seafood.***

*Médica:* Entonces, usted tiene un poco de intoxicación alimenticia.

*Usted:* ***Ask if it is serious. Ask if you can eat anything.***

*Médica:* No es nada grave, pero coma poco y beba agua. Le daré unas pastillas y se repondrá muy pronto.

# Close up

*There are two ways to describe aches and pains in Spanish. You can say* **me duele la cabeza**, **me duelen las muelas**, *which means "my head hurts me," or "my teeth hurt me." If you are asking someone, you say* **¿te duele(n)?** *for* **tú** *and* **¿le duele(n)?** *for* **usted**, *and talking about someone else, you say* **¿le duele(n)?** *Don't forget to use* **duelen** *if what hurts is plural! The verb you are using is* **doler, (ue)**, *"to hurt" or "to ache."*

*The other way, simpler but less common, is to say* **tengo dolor de cabeza**, *and so on.* **Dolor** *is the word for "pain."*

# Me torcí el tobillo...

*Explaining an injury*

## Word Bank

| | | | |
|---|---|---|---|
| la avispa | *wasp* | el medicamento | *medicine* |
| caer | *to fall* | hacerse daño | *to hurt oneself* |
| la cocina eléctrica | *electric cooker* | hinchado/a | *swollen* |
| cortarse | *to cut oneself* | la picadura | *sting, bite* |
| la crema | *cream* | quemarse | *to burn, to get burned* |
| curar | *to cure, heal* | las tiritas | *adhesive strips* |
| la farmacia | *pharmacy* | torcerse el tobillo | *to twist one's ankle* |
| el insecto | *insect* | la venda | *bandage* |

RECORDING

**1.** ***Sra. Palanco is in the doctor's office. Listen to the conversation.***

| | |
|---|---|
| Quítese el zapato. | *Take off your shoe.* |
| ¿Dónde le duele? | *Where does it hurt?* |
| Me torcí el tobillo andando por la calle. | *I twisted my ankle walking along the street.* |
| Se ha torcido el tobillo. | *You've twisted your ankle.* |

RECORDING

**2.** ***Listen to the conversation again and fill in the blanks.***

1. A la Sra. Palanco le duelen ________ y ________ .
2. Tiene que quitarse ________ .
3. Se torció el tobillo ________ por la calle.
4. Le duele donde el pie está un poco ________ .
5. La Sra. Palanco se curará el tobillo ________ en agua fría.
6. El médico no le da ________ porque puede comprar ________ en la ________ .

RECORDING

## 3.

***Six people are buying medicine in a pharmacy. Listen and then repeat what they say.***

| | |
|---|---|
| Quisiera algo para las quemaduras de sol. | *I'd like something for a sunburn.* |
| Estaba trabajando cuando me corté el dedo. | *I was working when I cut my finger.* |
| Me hice daño en la rodilla jugando al fútbol. | *I hurt my knee playing soccer.* |

RECORDING

## 4.

***Look at the drawings and write what the people were doing when they injured themselves.***

*Example:* Una señora estaba preparando la comida cuando se quemó.

1.

2.

3.

4.

5.

6.

RECORDING

5. *Listen to this telephone conversation between Sra. Torres and the doctor's receptionist. Then repeat what Sra. Torres says.*

*Now listen as Sra. Torres calls her friend Sra. Matilde Pérez to share her problem.*

RECORDING

6. *Answer the following questions.*

1. ¿Por qué llama la Sra. Torres al médico?
2. ¿Qué hora le dan primero?
3. ¿Qué hora prefiere?
4. ¿Para qué llama a su amiga Matilde?
5. ¿Qué problema tiene?
6. ¿Qué estaba haciendo la Sra. Torres cuando se hizo daño?

## Your turn

*What would you say in the following circumstances?*

1. *You want some adhesive strips because you cut your finger when you were working in the garden.*
2. *You would like some ointment because you burned your hand while preparing a meal.*
3. *You sprained your ankle playing tennis.*
4. *You were sunbathing in the garden when an insect stung you.*
5. *You hurt your arm playing soccer.*
6. *You want your friend to "get well soon."*

RECORDING

## Pronunciation

*The consonant* **d** *is sounded rather differently from its English equivalent. Try putting your tongue against the back of your top teeth, and then say* **d, d, d, d.** *Now try these words with the tape:* **de, desde, derecha, diez, dormitorio, delgado.** *Did you notice anything about the second* **d***? It actually slipped in between the teeth of the speaker! This usually happens when the* **d** *is between two vowels. Try:* **delgado, nada, comida, cuidar, puedo, edad, ciudad, verdad.** *In the last three examples, did you notice how the same thing happens to a* **d** *at the end of a word? Lots of words end in* **-dad,** *so practice pronouncing them correctly!*

## Close up

*In this unit you have been using the gerund in the imperfect continuous tense to express what was happening. To form the imperfect continuous, use the imperfect form of* **estar** *plus the gerund:* **estaba hablando,** *"I was speaking." This tense is particularly useful when you want to emphasize what was going on when something else happened (in the preterite, of course):*

Estaba preparando la comida cuando me quemé la mano.

*I was getting the meal ready when I burned my hand.*

La Sra. Torres estaba bajando del autobús cuando se cayó.

*Sra. Torres was getting off the bus when she fell.*

*The gerund can be separated from the verb* to be *just as in English:*

Estaban en la farmacia comprando medicamentos.

*They were in the pharmacy buying medicine.*

*You can also use the gerund by itself to mean "while" or "by doing something":*

Me torcí el tobillo bajando la escalera.

*I twisted my ankle (while) coming down the stairs.*

*When you say you hurt something, remember to use a reflexive verb plus the definite article and not a possessive as in English:*

| | |
|---|---|
| Me quemé la mano. | *I burned my hand.* |
| Me la quemé. | *I burned it.* |
| José se torció el pie. | *José twisted his foot.* |
| José se lo torció. | *José twisted it.* |

# Checkpoints

| *Can you . . . ?* | *Yes* | *No* |
|---|---|---|
| • *say how healthy someone looks* <br> ¡Qué bien estás de salud! | ❑ | ❑ |
| • *ask what someone does to keep fit* <br> ¿Qué haces para mantenerte en forma? | ❑ | ❑ |
| • *say how many times you exercise* <br> Dos veces por semana. | ❑ | ❑ |
| • *say you have to take care of your health* <br> Hay que tener cuidado de la salud. | ❑ | ❑ |
| • *suggest what someone could do to look after his/her health* <br> Podrías comprar una bicicleta. | ❑ | ❑ |
| • *say what one should or should not eat or drink* <br> No deberías comer chocolates. | ❑ | ❑ |
| • *say where you have a pain* <br> Me duele el estómago. | ❑ | ❑ |
| • *say how long you've had the pain* <br> Desde hace dos días. | ❑ | ❑ |
| • *say if you have a temperature* <br> Tengo una temperatura de 39. | ❑ | ❑ |
| • *say what else is wrong with you* <br> Vomito y tengo diarrea. | ❑ | ❑ |
| • *explain how you suffered an injury* <br> Me quemé la mano. | ❑ | ❑ |
| • *say what you were doing when it happened* <br> Estaba preparando la comida cuando me quemé. | ❑ | ❑ |
| • *ask for an appointment with the doctor or dentist* <br> ¿Puede darme hora con el médico? | ❑ | ❑ |
| • *wish someone to get well soon* <br> ¡Que te mejores pronto! | ❑ | ❑ |

## Learning tips

*When you're speaking Spanish, getting the grammar and vocabulary right is important because it helps people to understand you and accept you as a competent communicator. But more important are fluency and confidence. Think about foreign speakers of English you've met. Did you keep a tally of their mistakes as they spoke? Probably not—you were concentrating on understanding the message. So don't expect Spanish speakers to notice your mistakes and try not to be self-conscious when you speak. We all make mistakes, even in our own language. But it doesn't really matter as long as we get the message across.*

## Do you want to learn more?

*Read as much Spanish as you can find—newspapers, advertising brochures, whatever. Read a little at a time, and don't worry about bits you don't understand: concentrate on getting the gist. Once you know what the subject is, you'll be able to guess the meanings of many new words from their context. Keep a note of words that are the same or similar in Spanish and English—but look in your dictionary to check that the meaning is the same.*

# 1 Extra!

## Hablar de tu casa

RECORDING

**1.** *Listen to this ad from a real estate agency. Check (✓) if the apartment in the ad has the following:*

_____ lavadero
_____ teléfono
_____ jardín
_____ 4 dormitorios
_____ baños en suite
_____ sala de recepción
_____ cocina amueblada
_____ balcón
_____ hidromasaje en la suite principal
_____ ascensor

**2.** *Conchita is writing a letter to her friend Elena, describing her new house. Read her letter and then write a paragraph describing the house or apartment in which you live.*

Querida Elena:

Me encanta mi nueva casa. En la planta baja, el salón tiene una puerta-ventana que da a la terraza y al jardín. El salón y el comedor son muy espaciosos. La cocina está muy bien. Arriba hay cuatro dormitorios y un magnífico cuarto de baño con bañera, ducha y lavabo. El dormitorio principal tiene un balcón. En el desván vamos a hacer otra habitación donde los niños puedan jugar. Tienes que venir a visitarnos.

Un abrazo de tu amiga

Conchita

## 3. *What's Rodrigo doing? Write a sentence describing each illustration.*

1. Está despertándose.

2. ____________________

3. ____________________

4. ____________________

5. ____________________

6. ____________________

7. ____________________

8. ____________________

# 2 Extra!

*¡Buen provecho!*

RECORDING

**1.** ***Listen to the recorded telephone reservations at a restaurant. Can you determine who is making them? Write the number of the corresponding conversation.***

_____ a. Una madre que prepara una fiesta para el cumpleaños de su hija de nueve años.

_____ b. Una familia que quiere celebrar el Año Nuevo.

_____ c. Dos hombres de negocios.

_____ d. Tres parejas jóvenes.

_____ e. Una pareja que celebra su aniversario de boda.

RECORDING

**2.** ***Look at the menu displayed in this busy restaurant and listen to the customers as they give their order to the waitress. Indicate the order in which the requests are taken.***

RECORDING

## 3.

***Match up the customers' complaints with the waiter's replies.***

_____ a. Sí, los plátanos están un poco pasados. ¿Le traigo una naranja o unas uvas?

_____ b. Un momentito, le pongo unas papas fritas.

_____ c. Vamos a ver... veinticuatro más cuarenta... sí, es verdad, usted tiene razón.

_____ d. Sí, señora. Voy a buscar otro en la nevera.

_____ e. Espere un momento, le traigo otro más hecho.

_____ f. Ah, sí, es verdad. Se lo cambio en seguida. De cordero, ¿no?

_____ g. Ah, sí. Perdone. La trucha era para el señor, ¿no?

## 4.

***In Spain, menus are often displayed in sections under headings, rather than as first or second courses. Can you put the following items under their correct headings?***

tortilla de jamón
fruta de la estación
consomé
solomillo de vaca
tortilla de champiñones
merluza en salsa
huevos fritos
gazpacho andaluz
chuleta de cerdo
sopa de lentejas
lomo de vaca
macedonia de frutas
pescado frito
leche frita
trucha molinera

| Sopas | Huevos | Pescados | Carnes | Postres |
|---|---|---|---|---|
| | | | | |
| | | | | |
| | | | | |

## 5.

***Read this ad about a restaurant that offers home delivery service. Complete the sentences below with the most suitable word or expression.***

CHINO VELOZ

"La verdadera comida china a domicilio" abrió sus puertas hace un año. Al mediodía, sus clientes suelen ser de oficinas. Por las noches son más variados, generalmente jóvenes. El pedido mínimo es de ocho euros, y a partir de esa cifra, se venden menús para dos personas desde diez euros, todo en menos de 30 minutos. La carta dice que se trata de platos bajos en calorías, colesterol y sodio, respetando los principios de la comida tradicional china.

1. Para el almuerzo, los clientes son generalmente *jóvenes/chinos/gente que trabaja en oficinas.*
2. Para la cena, los clientes son *más grandes / más españoles/más variados.*
3. El precio mínimo es de *10 euros/8 euros/30 euros.*
4. Tiene que esperar *más de 30 minutos/30 minutos/menos de 30 minutos.*
5. La comida que sirven tiene *mucho colesterol / pocas calorías/poca relación con la comida china.*

# 3 Extra!

## De vacaciones

RECORDING

**1.** *Listen to these radio ads for different types of vacations. Check (✓) what ad offers what.*

| | 1 | 2 | 3 | 4 | 5 | 6 |
|---|---|---|---|---|---|---|
| 8 días | | | | | | |
| hotel con desayuno | | | | | | |
| todas las visitas incluidas en el precio | | | | | | |
| todas las comidas | | | | | | |
| 17 días | | | | | | |
| pensión completa | | | | | | |
| todas las bebidas | | | | | | |
| 7 noches | | | | | | |
| crucero de 5 días | | | | | | |
| media pensión | | | | | | |

RECORDING

**2.** *You're working as a receptionist in a hotel in Mexico. Listen to the following people calling the hotel with special requests. Write the number of the dialog next to the corresponding request.*

El/la cliente . . .

_____ a. . . . quiere una cama especial para un niño.

_____ b. . . . no quiere pagar en efectivo.

_____ c. . . . quiere una habitación en la planta baja.

_____ d. . . . no quiere pagar por una habitación doble.

_____ e. . . . necesita usar el servicio de lavandería.

_____ f. . . . quiere proteger su dinero en una caja fuerte.

RECORDING

## 3.

***Listen to more guests complaining. Check (✓) what they are complaining about.***

1. a. El agua en la habitación está fría.
   b. No tienen lavabo ni ducha.

2. a. Tienen algunas almohadas, pero no las suficientes.
   b. Necesitan almohadas para todas las camas.

3. a. No se cierran bien las ventanas.
   b. Las ventanas no se abren.

4. a. Hay un problema con el funcionamiento del aire acondicionado.
   b. El aire acondicionado está puesto muy fuerte.

5. a. Necesitan jabón y champú.
   b. Hay jabón, pero no hay champú.

6. a. El cliente tiene la llave de otra habitación.
   b. El cliente tiene la llave correcta, pero no funciona.

| | |
|---|---|
| la cuna | *crib* |
| la almohada | *pillow* |

RECORDING

## 4.

***Listen to these hotel guests spelling the names of their cities. Write them down.***

## 5.

***You need to send the following faxes to a hotel in Spain. Include the following information:***

a. Para reservar habitaciones para usted y su familia o amigos, para mañana, indicando cuántas noches quiere pasar y las habitaciones que necesita.

b. Para decirle al director del hotel que usted dejó algo importante o de valor en su habitación. Indique el número de la habitación y dónde lo dejó.

# 4 Extra!

## Nos encontramos a las siete

RECORDING

**1.** *Listen to the weather forecast. Check (✓) which weather conditions are announced in each weather forecast.*

| | sol | nieve | calor | tormentas | viento | hielo | frío | lluvia | nubes |
|---|---|---|---|---|---|---|---|---|---|
| 1. | | | | | | | | | |
| 2. | | | | | | | | | |
| 3. | | | | | | | | | |
| 4. | | | | | | | | | |
| 5. | | | | | | | | | |
| 6. | | | | | | | | | |

RECORDING

**2.** *Now listen to another weather forecast and answer the following questions.*

1. Por lo general, ¿subirán o bajarán las temperaturas?
2. ¿Va a hacer sol en las montañas de España?
3. ¿Lloverá en las regiones de Cantabria y Cataluña?
4. Si está usted a más de 1.000 metros de altura en el centro de España, ¿qué tiempo hará?
5. En el sur, ¿hará más o menos frío?
6. Según el pronóstico meteorológico, ¿en qué estación del año estamos?

RECORDING

## 3.

*What will they do this weekend? Write the number of the conversation next to the corresponding statement(s).*

_____ a. Montará en bicicleta.

_____ b. Hará unas cortinas.

_____ c. Tomará el sol.

_____ d. Leerá el periódico

_____ e. Verá un partido de fútbol.

_____ f. Irá a un bar con unos amigos.

_____ g. Se bañará en un lago.

## 4.

*Yesterday or tomorrow? Tell if the event took place yesterday* (**ayer**) *or if it will take place tomorrow* (**mañana**).

1. Fuimos a la ciudad a hacer las compras.
2. Jugamos tenis en el polideportivo.
3. Iremos a Guadalajara a visitar a nuestros tíos.
4. Compré una nueva máquina fotográfica.
5. Compraré los boletos para nuestras vacaciones en Ecuador.
6. Veré el partido de fútbol en la televisión.
7. Vi un partido de pelota vasca en el frontón.
8. Manuela estuvo en Monterrey.
9. Felipe y Casilda se fueron a Bolivia.
10. Enrique va a dar una gira por el Canadá.

RECORDING

## 5.

*Your boss is announcing the company's plans for the next year. Match the dates with the corresponding events.*

| | |
|---|---|
| 1. El 2 de enero . . . | a. . . . tres directores se jubilarán. |
| 2. El 4 de febrero . . . | b. . . . la compañía se unirá con otra. |
| 3. El 10 de abril . . . | c. . . . habrá una exposición importante en la capital española. |
| 4. El 25 de mayo . . . | d. . . . unos químicos del Japón vendrán a visitar a la compañía. |
| 5. El 7 de julio . . . | e. . . . la compañía tendrá un nuevo director. |
| 6. El 31 de agosto . . . | f. . . . unos representantes de la compañía irán a los Estados Unidos. |
| 7. El 15 de octubre . . . | g. . . . la compañía tendrá un nombre nuevo. |

## 6.

*Write a paragraph of about 100–120 words describing your plans for a trip abroad. Where will you go? What will you do?*

*Example:* El nueve de agosto saldremos mi novio/a y yo para París. El diez de agosto . . .

# 5 Extra!

## Planes y reuniones

RECORDING

**1.** ***Listen to these critics reviewing a movie or play. Put a check mark (✓) if they liked it and put an "✗" if they didn't. If their opinion is not clear, put a question mark (?).***

1. ________ 4. ________

2. ________ 5. ________

3. ________ 6. ________

RECORDING

**2.** ***Listen to this interview with a famous, legendary actress. Then answer the following questions.***

1. ¿Cuándo se jubiló Camila?
2. ¿Cuántos años tenía cuando actuó en público por primera vez?
3. ¿Cuál fue su primera experiencia en el teatro profesional?
4. En aquella época, ¿actuaba siempre en un teatro?
5. ¿Qué rol desempeñaba cuando se hizo famosa?
6. ¿Hace cuánto tiempo ocurrió esto?

RECORDING

## 3.

*Listen to these people talking about their pastimes and hobbies. Match the person to his or her interest.*

¿Quién se interesa por…

_____ a. … coleccionar tarjetas de teléfono?

_____ b. … los deportes de invierno?

_____ c. … la familia real española?

_____ d. … las computadoras?

_____ e. … coser y hacer ropa?

_____ f. … los trenes antiguos?

## 4.

*Read the following article about the compact disc. Then say whether the statements that follow are true or false. Correct the false statements.*

Hace más de ciento veinte años, en 1877, Edison reprodujo por primera vez la voz humana en su fonógrafo. Entre esta fecha y la aparición del disco de vinilo, el 'elepé', en 1948, transcurrieron 71 años. De entonces a la irrupción del casete pasaron 15 años, y 34 más para que entrara en el mercado el disco compacto.

El CD entró en los mercados del Japón en noviembre de 1982, y tres meses más tarde llegaba a los consumidores europeos y norteamericanos. Las ventas superaron de inmediato todas las expectativas. Philips y Son esperaban vender más de 10 millones de discos compactos en 1985. Durante 1985 se vendieron 59 millones y al año siguiente ya sumaban 136 millones.

En los años después de 1989 las ventas del disco de vinilo de larga duración descendieron y los CD experimentaron un incremento progresivo.

1. Nadie reprodujo la voz humana antes de 1877.
2. El disco 'elepé', de vinilo, apareció 15 años más tarde.
3. El CD apareció 34 años después del disco de vinilo.
4. Los discos compactos empezaron a venderse en América en febrero de 1983.

# 6 *Extra!*

*¡En forma!*

RECORDING

**1.** ***Once a week the police department broadcasts descriptions of wanted criminals. Match the descriptions you hear with the corresponding pictures below.***

RECORDING

## 2.

*Listen to these ads about drugstore products. Match the ad to the corresponding illustration.*

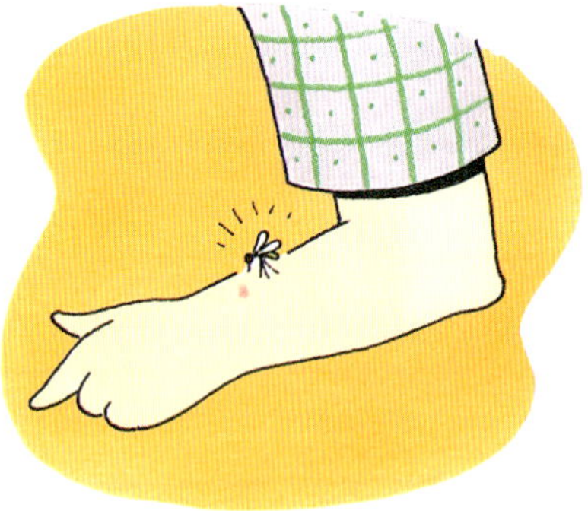

**a.** ________

**b.** ________

**c.** ________

**d.** ________

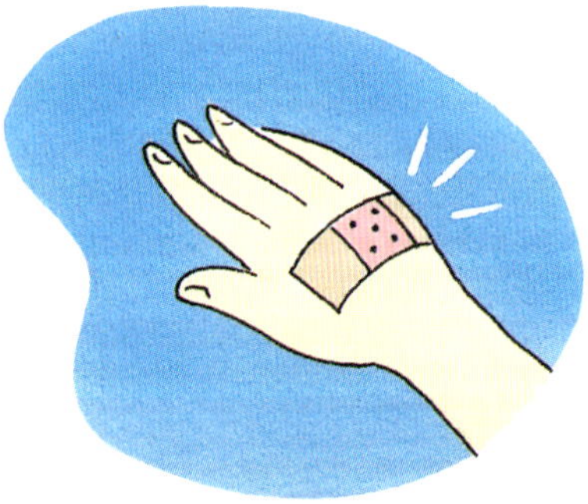

**e.** ________

**f.** ________

**g.** ________

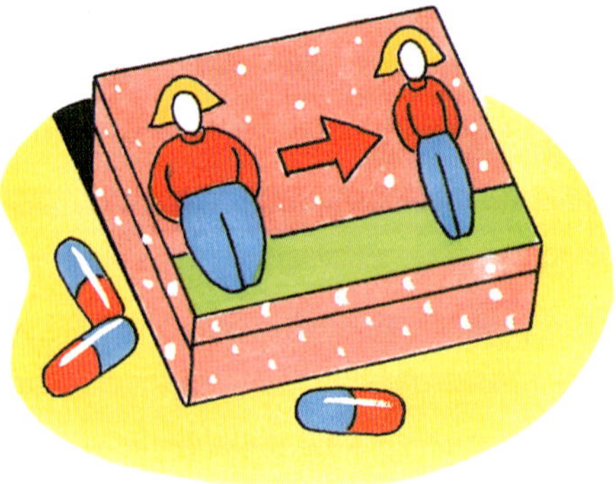

**h.** ________

## 3. *Combine elements of Column A with those of Column B to form complete sentences.*

*Example:* Estaba dando un paseo en bicicleta cuando me caí y me rompí el brazo.

| A | B |
|---|---|
| Estaba llevando una maleta ... | ... cuando me caí y me rompí el brazo. |
| Estaba dando un paseo en bicicleta ... | ... cuando me quemé la mano. |
| Estaba bailando ... | ... cuando me torcí el pie. |
| Estaba cocinando ... | ... cuando me caí y me hice daño en la rodilla. |
| Estaba jugando al tenis ... | ... cuando me tiré un músculo en la espalda. |
| Estaba corriendo por la calle ... | ... cuando tropecé y me hice daño en la pierna. |

## 4. *Your friend Julia has many health problems. Give her some advice using* **deberías** *or* **podrías.**

*Example:* Julia: Tengo dolor de cabeza.
Usted: Podrías tomar unas aspirinas. - o - Deberías ir a ver al médico.

1. Me duele el estómago.
2. Tengo unas picaduras de mosquito en la pierna.
3. Peso demasiado.
4. Me corté el dedo.
5. Tengo tos y me duele al tragar.
6. Me quemé tomando el sol en la playa.

# Test 1

## Review of Units 1–2

**1.** *Which is the odd word in the following groups?*

| | | | | |
|---|---|---|---|---|
| 1. comedor | sala de estar | cuarto de baño | cortina | cocina |
| 2. butaca | ducha | mesa | sofá | silla |
| 3. me lavo | me levanto | invito | me ducho | me acuesto |
| 4. cuchillo | cuenta | tenedor | taza | plato |
| 5. desván | sopa | trucha | ensalada | flan |

**2.** *Put these words in the correct order.*

1. ¿hora / despierta / a / usted / se / qué?
2. ¿piso / tiene / dormitorios / cuántos / su?
3. ¿el / traer / puede / favor / menú / por?
4. ¿cuchara / favor / cambiarme / esta / puede / por?
5. ¿ir / otro / a / podemos / sitio?

**3.** *Supply the questions to these answers.*

1. Hay un dormitorio grande, con cuarto de baño, y otros dos.
2. Generalmente me acuesto a las once.
3. Sí, señor. Una mesa para cuatro personas.
4. Yo le recomiendo el pescado hoy.
5. Para mí, una merluza a la plancha.

## 4. *Fill in the blanks using* **me, te, se,** *or* **nos.**

1. Isabel ________ levanta a las siete.
2. Los niños ________ duchan por la mañana.
3. Carmen, ¿dónde ________ encuentras con tus compañeras de clase?
4. Yo nunca ________ duermo antes de las doce y media.
5. Mi marido y yo ________ acostamos a las doce.

## 5. *Choose the correct verb.*

1. Los sábados Carmen y yo **(almuerzo/almorzamos)** en un restaurante.
2. Elena **(volvemos/vuelve)** a casa a la una.
3. Yo **(me despierto/nos despertamos)** a las siete.
4. Isabel y su marido **(nos acostamos/se acuestan)** a las once.
5. ¿A qué hora **(se sienta/se sientan)** ustedes a cenar?

## 6. *Fill in the blanks using the correct form of the present continous of the verb provided.*

1. Luisa ________ **(hablar)** con una amiga.
2. Nosotros ________ **(comer)** en un restaurante nuevo.
3. Alfonso y Mercedes ________ **(tomar)** una cerveza en el bar.
4. Anita ________ **(jugar)** con sus compañeros de clase.
5. ¿________ **(tú/hacer)** la tarea o ________ **(ver)** la televisión?
6. Ustedes ________ **(ayudar)** en la cocina.

## 7. *How would you . . .*

1. *. . . ask a hotel receptionist if there are any vacancies?*
2. *. . . ask where you can park your car?*
3. *. . . say you want to reserve a table for two for 8 P.M. tomorrow evening?*
4. *. . . ask for the check in a restaurant?*
5. *. . . say your spoon is dirty and ask the waiter for a clean one?*
6. *. . . explain what kind of apartment you want to a real estate agent?*

## 8. *Put this conversation in the correct order.*

_____ Lo siento. Esta noche ya tenemos una cena de cumpleaños en la terraza.

_____ Para las ocho y media, ¿de acuerdo?

_____ Estupendo, entonces, ¡hasta esta noche!

_____ Cuatro personas . . . ¿Dónde quieren sentarse?

_____ En este caso, cerca de la ventana.

_____ Sí, de acuerdo. Un momento, ¿tienen menú del día?

_____ Quisiera reservar una mesa para esta noche para cuatro.

_____ Cuatro personas, cerca de la ventana. ¿Para qué hora?

_____ ¿Tienen una mesa en la terraza?

_____ Claro. El menú del día ofrece tres platos con bebida a 12 euros, pero también pueden escoger de la carta.

# Test 2

## Review of Units 3–6

**1.** *Which is the odd word in the following groups?*

| | | | | |
|---|---|---|---|---|
| 1. primavera | otoño | verano | tiempo | invierno |
| 2. televisión | tenis | fútbol | béisbol | ciclismo |
| 3. febrero | martes | diciembre | mayo | agosto |
| 4. volveremos | nadamos | tomaremos | cruzaremos | acompañaremos |
| 5. gripe | estómago | cabeza | brazo | garganta |
| 6. acostarse | torcerse | cortarse | romperse | quemarse |

**2.** *Match the words in the first column with those in the second column.*

| | |
|---|---|
| 1. hace | a. lloviendo |
| 2. hay | b. los actores |
| 3. está | c. la mano |
| 4. me torcí | d. una bicicleta |
| 5. me quemé | e. niebla |
| 6. empieza | f. el tobillo |
| 7. no me gustaron | g. a las siete de la tarde |
| 8. alquilaré | h. mucho calor |

**3.** *Supply the questions to these answers.*

1. Aquí en Madrid hace mucho frío.
2. Sí, me gusta mucho vivir en San Sebastián.
3. El sábado iré de compras y el domingo iré a la playa con mi novio.
4. El año pasado fuimos a la Argentina a visitar a mi familia.
5. Viajaremos en autocar.
6. Mis amigos querrán ver muchos monumentos antiguos.
7. Por lo general, mi mujer y yo pasamos las vacaciones en México.
8. Tuve mis últimas vacaciones en agosto. Fui a Costa Rica.

## 4. *Write out these dates. Note that the figures below follow American English usage: first the month, followed by the date.*

1. 11/29
2. 2/2
3. 12/24
4. 4/17
5. 10/12
6. 5/30
7. 9/9

## 5. *Put these words in the correct order.*

1. verano / calor / en / aquí / mucho / hace
2. ¿semana / a / vas / este / qué / fin / hacer / de?
3. en / sencillo / de / casa / algo / prepararé / comer
4. ¿hora / empieza / qué / película / a / la?
5. ¿en / para / haces / mantenerte / qué / forma?
6. años / pintar / cinco / a / empecé / hace

## 6. *Choose the correct form of the verb.*

1. El martes que viene **(fuimos/iremos)** a Sudamérica.
2. El año pasado **(visitamos/visitaremos)** a mis primos en Venezuela.
3. Ayer **(invité/invitaré)** a mi novio a cenar.
4. Mañana por la mañana **(compré/compraré)** unos sellos en Correos.
5. El domingo que viene **(descansamos/descansaremos)** por la mañana y por la tarde **(vimos/veremos)** el fútbol en la tele.
6. El verano que viene Elena **(alquiló/alquilará)** una bicicleta.
7. El próximo 28 de marzo Antonio **(jugó/jugará)** a la pelota en Bilbao.

## 7. *Using* **deberías** *or* **podrías** *plus a phrase from the second column, provide a remedy for the problem expressed in the first column.*

| | Deberías/Podrías . . . |
|---|---|
| 1. Me duele la cabeza. | pasar unos días en la cama. |
| 2. Estoy muy gorda. | ir al cajero automático. |
| 3. Tengo fiebre. | ir a una agencia de viajes. |
| 4. Quiero ir de vacaciones a Chile. | ir a la feria de antigüedades. |
| 5. Necesito dinero. | ir al gimnasio. |
| 6. Quisiera comprar porcelana antigua. | tomar unas aspirinas. |

## 8. *Choose the correct preterite form of the verb.*

1. Cuando yo **(viví/vivía)** en Nueva York, **(fui/iba)** todos los sábados al cine.
2. Cuando Elena **(estaba/estuvo)** en Europa **(fue/iba)** todos los años a Italia, porque le **(gustaba/gustó)** mucho.
3. Cuando Enrique **(visitaba/visitó)** España, **(iba/fue)** a Sevilla por primera vez.
4. Estaba trabajando en la cocina cuando me **(cortaba/corté)** el dedo.
5. Estaba jugando al fútbol cuando me **(caí/caía)** y me **(rompí/rompía)** la pierna.

## 9. *Put this conversation in the correct order.*

_____ Me caí. ¿Es grave?

_____ Gracias, doctor. ¿Cuánto le debo?

_____ Sí, es verdad. ¿Qué estaba haciendo cuando se hizo daño?

_____ Aquí, en el pie izquierdo. Está muy hinchado.

_____ Buenos días. ¿Qué le pasa?

_____ ¿Dónde precisamente?

_____ No, no es muy grave, pero tiene que descansar unos días.

_____ ¿Y cómo ocurrió?

_____ Me duele mucho el pie.

_____ Estaba trabajando en el jardín.

## 10. *How would you . . .*

1. *. . . ask what the weather is like?*
2. *. . . ask someone what he/she is going to do on the weekend?*
3. *. . . ask when someone is going away?*
4. *. . . ask the date?*
5. *. . . suggest going to the movies?*
6. *. . . say you would like to cash some traveler's checks?*
7. *. . . ask someone where he/she went on vacation last year?*
8. *. . . ask what someone was doing when he/she hurt his/her foot?*
9. *. . . ask someone where he/she used to live?*
10. *. . . ask someone what is the matter?*

# Answer Key

## Unit 1

### Pages 2–4

**2.** 1. *false*: Vive en una casa. 2. *true* 3. *false*: Comen en el comedor. 4. *false*: Hay un comedor entre la cocina y la sala de estar. 5. *false*: Tiene tres dormitorios, el grande y otros dos para los hijos. 6. *true* 7. *true* 8. *false*: El garaje es bastante grande, es para dos coches.

**3.** 1. sala de estar, cocina, cuarto de baño y dos dormitorios; 2. sala de estar, cocina, comedor, cuatro dormitorios, terraza; 3. sala de estar, cocina, comedor, dos cuartos de baño, tres dormitorios, jardín

**4.** a. 3; b. 1; c. 2

**5.** *Answers will vary.*

*Your turn: Answers will vary.*

### Pages 6–9

**2.** la sala de estar: las butacas, la lámpara, la alfombra; el sofá, la mesita de café, las cortinas / el comedor: el aparador, la mesa grande, las sillas / el estudio: el escritorio / los dormitorios: las camas, el televisor / el cuarto de baño: los azulejos

**3.** 1. *Furniture on sale*: butacas, sofás, lámparas, alfombras, camas, armarios, mesas, sillas; 50% (cincuenta por ciento) de descuento; hasta el día diez. 2. En la sala de estar: un sofá para tres personas, tres butacas, persianas y cortinas verdes, tres lámparas, suelo de baldosas, un televisor con una gran pantalla y un vídeo; en la terraza: mesa y sillas; en el dormitorio: una cama grande, un tocador, dos armarios grandes; en el cuarto de baño: ducha con toallas de lujo. 3. *Furniture they need:* un sofá, dos butacas, cortinas nuevas, una mesa, una cama, un espejo, un televisor. *Antonio has second thoughts because it's a lot of furniture. It's expensive.*

**4.** *Answers will vary.*

**5.** *Word jumble*: butaca, cortina, sofá, lámpara, aparador, alfombra, mesita, cama, silla

**6.** a. Jaime; b. Isabel; c. Jorge; d. Clara

*Your turn:* Quiero unas cortinas rojas y una mesita de café. / Un espejo nuevo. / Los niños quieren un televisor y yo quiero un armario grande. / Quiero unos azulejos bonitos en las paredes.

**7.** *Answers will vary.*

### Pages 11–12

**2.** 1. Se despierta a las ocho. 2. Se ducha si tiene tiempo. 3. Desayuna. 4. Se va a la oficina. 5. Vuelve a la una y media. 6. Suele arreglar un poco la casa. 7. Juega un poco con su hija pequeña. 8. Su hija se acuesta a las ocho. 9. Nunca se duerme antes de las doce. 10. Piensa que es una familia bastante normal.

**3.** 1. Ángela; 2. Miguelito, Pablo; 3. Pablo; 4. Pablo; 5. Ángela; 6. Pablo; 7. Miguelito; 8. Ángela

**4.** Nombre: Pili; Hora de entrada: 9:00; Hora de salida: 1:00; Total horas: 4 / Nombre: Rosa; Hora de entrada: 3 de la tarde; Hora de salida: siete de la tarde; Total horas: 4 / Nombre: Luis; Hora de entrada: 10 de la noche; Hora de salida: 6 de la mañana; Total horas: 8

**5. / 6.** *Answers will vary.*

*Your turn: Answers will vary.*

## Unit 2

### Pages 18–21

**2.** 1. Mañana es el cumpleaños de Pepa. 2. Quieren ir a un restaurante. 3. La Casona es un restaurante típico español. 4. A Pepa le da igual. 5. Eduardo sí quiere ir. 6. A Eduardo y a Teresa no les gusta la comida china. 7. Eduardo sí quiere ir a La Casona. 8. Deciden cenar a las nueve.

**3.** 1. Para mañana. 2. Para cuatro. 3. Cerca de la ventana. 4. Para las nueve. 5. Miguel Carmona.

**4.** 1. Personas: 6; Hora: 8:30 (ocho y media); Mesa: en la terraza / 2. Personas: 2; Hora: 9:15 (nueve y cuarto) Mesa: cerca de la ventana / 3. Personas: 5; Hora: 1:00 (la una); Mesa: en el centro del restaurante / 4. Personas: 12; Hora: 11 (once de la noche); Mesa: en la terraza / 5. Personas: 3; Hora: 1:30 (una y media); Mesa: no importa dónde

**5.** 1. *Questions:* ¿Su nombre, por favor? ¿Me dan los abrigos? ¿Quieren tomar un aperitivo? 2. *Choices:* menú del día (tres platos con botella de vino incluida) o escoger de la carta. 3. *The waiter recommends*: el pescado.

**6.** 1. c; 2. f; 3. a; 4. b; 5. d; 6. e

*Your turn: Answers will vary.*

**7.** Quiero reservar una mesa para cenar. / Para seis. / Para mañana. / A las nueve y media. / ¿Tienen una mesa en la terraza?

## Pages 23–24

**2.** *Items mentioned*: Menú del día: sopa de cebolla, ensaladilla rusa, cocido, bonito, melocotones en almíbar, natillas; Menú: merluza a la plancha, chuleta de cordero, trucha a la plancha, parrillada, entremeses, sopa, ensalada.

**4.** Un flan, una tarta helada y queso manchego.

*Your turn:* una merluza a la plancha, trucha a la plancha, un bistec (bien hecho), chuletas de cordero, una sopa de cebolla, tres ensaladas mixtas (con el plato principal), un jarro del vino tinto de la casa y un jarro de vino blanco.

## Pages 26–28

**2.** 1. *false*: Una clienta no tiene cucharilla. 2. *true* 3. *false*: Un cliente tiene café frío. / Una clienta tiene café con leche y quiere café solo. 4. *false*: La esposa de un cliente no tiene cucharilla. 5. *true* 6. *false*: El café de un cliente está frío.

**3.** 1. sucio; 2. muy caliente; 3. cordero; 4. limpia; 5. cuchillo

**4.** *Mistake on the check:* Pone "cuatro ensaladas" y son tres ensaladas y una sopa.

*Your turn:* ¡Camarera! / No tengo tenedor y mi plato está sucio. / ¿Me trae otra botella de agua mineral? Ésta no está fría. / Quiero una tortilla con cebolla, no de patata. / ¿Me trae la cuenta, por favor? / La cuenta está equivocada. Son noventa pesos, no noventa y cinco. / ¿Está incluido el servicio? / El servicio es muy bueno. Tenga cien pesos y quédese con la vuelta.

# Unit 3

## Pages 34–36

**2.** 1. *false*: Quiere quedarse tres o cuatro dias. 2. *true;* 3. *true;* 4. *true;* 5. *true;* 6. *false:* Todas las habitaciones tienen televisor. 7. *true*; 8. *false:* Toma tres habitaciones con desayuno.

**3.** Nombre: Ricardo Montserrat; Dirección: 404 Cranleigh Gardens; Ciudad: Waukesha; Código postal: Wisconsin 53154

**4.** 1. 411, 412 y 413; 2. a la izquierda; 3. varias; 4. hay dos bancos cerca

**5.** 1. Cambia dos cheques de cien dólares. 2. Tiene que mostrarle su pasaporte. 3. Tiene que firmar. 4. Tiene que ir a la caja.

*Your turn*: Buenas tardes. Necesitamos dos habitaciones: una doble con dos camas y una individual. / Para dos noches. / Sí. ¿Tienen baño o ducha? / ¿Cuánto cuestan las habitaciones? / Bueno. Las tomamos. / ¿Dónde podemos aparcar el carro? / Tenemos varias maletas. ¿Dónde está el ascensor?

## Pages 38–40

**2.** a. Familia Montserrat: Les gusta la playa (nadar, tomar el sol). Piensan ir a la costa; b. Familia Quesada: Les gusta ver monumentos, descansar, respirar aire puro. Este año van a dar una vuelta por México para ver monumentos aztecas y a las montañas (respirar aire puro y hacer senderismo).

**3.** 1. La familia Montserrat fue a Paris. 2. La señora Montserrat fue de compras. 3. La señora Montserrat fue a Sevilla con sus hijas a visitar a su prima. 4. El señor fue a Córdoba a visitar a su hermano. 5. Todos juntos fueron a Barcelona. 6. Toda la familia fue a Londres. 7. La señora Montserrat y las niñas fueron en tren a Edimburgo.

*Your turn*: ¿Dónde les gusta pasar sus vacaciones, Sra. Molina? / ¿Qué les gusta hacer allí? / ¿Les gusta ir a las montañas? / ¿Adónde fueron ustedes el año pasado? / ¿Fueron a España?

## Pages 41–42

**2.** 1. Hace dos años. 2. Porque su hijo trabaja en Madrid. 3. Pasó dos semanas con su hijo y otras dos viajando por España. 4. Viajó en autocar. 5. Se alojó en hoteles. 6. Visitó Madrid, Toledo y Sevilla. 7. Vio el Alcázar de Toledo y la Giralda de Sevilla. 8. Comió paella y gazpacho. 9. Nadó en el Mediterráneo. 10. Sevilla.

**3.** fui; visité; hice; pasé; Dormí; Comí; bebí; nadé; tomé; Vi; gustó

# Unit 4

## Pages 48–50

**2.** 1. agradable; 2. no hace mucho calor; 3. en las montañas; 4. a las tiendas; 5. esquiar; 6. hay niebla; 7. está en la costa

**4.** 1. En Sevilla hace calor (ya hace 25° grados). 2. Estamos en primavera. 3. No todos los días; a veces hace frío, a veces hace calor. 4. Está lloviendo. 5. En Sevilla las mujeres llevan vestidos de verano. 6. Rosario va a llevar un abrigo a Santander.

**5.** a. 4; b. 5; c. 6; d. 3; e. 2; f. 1

**6.** 1. frío; 2. nublado; 3. nevará; 4. lloverá; 5. viento; 6. sol

*Your turn*: La mejor estación es la primavera. / Porque en

verano hace mucho calor. / En otoño a menudo hace mucho viento y llueve mucho. / Sí, ¡y nieva! / Está lloviendo.

**Pages 53–55**

**2.** 1. irá; 2. comprará; 3. comerán; 4. se bañarán; 5. se sentarán; 6. irá; 7. leerá

**4.** 1. *false*: El miércoles que viene...; 2. *true*; 3. *true*; 4. *false*: Irán con la tía a Punta del Este después de Navidad. 5. *false*: Volverán a Buenos Aires y viajarán a Bariloche en autobús. 6. *true*; 7. *false*: Harán excursiones a los Andes desde Bariloche. 8. *true*

**5.** iremos; Saldremos; llegaremos; continuaremos; nos quedaremos; tomaremos; Haremos; bajaremos; Estaremos

*Your turn*: El sábado por la mañana jugaré al tenis con unos(as) amigos(as). / Almorzaré en un bar con mis amigos(as). / Mis amigos y yo iremos al partido de fútbol. / Volveremos a casa. Prepararé algo de comer y veré la televisión. / Descansaré. Leeré el periódico pero también limpiaré mi apartamento.

**Pages 57–58**

**2.** 1. 18 (dieciocho) de febrero. 2. Va a tomarlas en julio y agosto. 3. Desde el 18 de julio hasta el 15 de agosto. 4. Va a ir con su hermano y su mujer a Italia. 5. Va a viajar en coche. 6. Irán a la ópera o a un concierto. También visitarán varios museos y monumentos. 7. Dará paseos a pie o en bicicleta. Alquilará una bici y pasará un par de días en el campo. También irá de pesca. 8. En el sur de Italia.

**4.** 1. El 5 de enero irá a las montañas a esquiar. 2. El 14 de febrero pasará tres días en las montañas haciendo alpinismo. 3. El 28 de marzo jugará a la pelota en Bilbao. 4. El 10 de mayo tomará parte en un concurso de boxeo. 5. El 30 de junio estará en Francia en un concurso de ciclismo. 6. El 12 de julio nadará para su equipo en el polideportivo de su ciudad. 7. El 2 de agosto recibirá a unos deportistas extranjeros en su casa. 8. El 13 de septiembre tomará parte en un concurso de tenis. 9. El 21 de noviembre dará un largo paseo por el campo con sus amigos. 10. El 28 de diciembre viajará a Argentina con su equipo de fútbol. *Missing dates and activities*: El 17 de abril dará un paseo en bicicleta. El 31 de octubre tendrá que estar en Portugal para un concurso de golf.

**5.** el cinco de enero; el catorce de febrero; el veintiocho de marzo; el diez de mayo; el treinta de junio; el doce de julio; el dos de agosto; el cinco de agosto; el trece de septiembre; el veintiuno de noviembre; el veintiocho de diciembre

# Unit 5

**Pages 64–66**

**2.** 1. *false*: Hay una película nueva. 2. *true*; 3. *false*: Hay más de un cine. 4. *false*: La película policíaca termina sobre las nueve o la una. 5. *false*: En el Teatro Liceo ponen una obra clásica. 6. *true*; 7. *false*: Hay un concierto de música rusa. 8. *false*: No quedan entradas para la ópera. 9. *false*: A Mari-Carmen no le gusta la ópera. 10. *true*

**4.** 1. no; 2. sí; 3. no; 4. no; 5. sí; 6. sí; 7. no; 8. sí

*Your turn*: ¿Por qué no vamos al cine/al teatro? / ¿Por qué no vamos a ver (*name of movie*)? / No me gustan las películas americanas. Prefiero una película española. / ¿Tienes el periódico? / ¿A qué hora empieza y termina la película? / En lugar de ir a las siete y media, ¿por qué no vamos a cenar y luego vemos la película?

**Pages 67–70**

**2.** Sr. Castillo: g; Sra. Ponce: b; Pablo: f; Sra. Blancos: c; Javi: e; Sra. Álvarez: d; Felipe: a

**3.** 1. b; 2. e; 3. f; 4. c; 5. a; 6. g; 7. d

**4.** 1. La Sra. Ponce empezó a pintar cuando tenía veinte años. 2. La Sra. Blancos entonces sacaba las fotos en blanco y negro. 3. Pablo empezó a coleccionar sellos chilenos cuando trabajaba en Chile hace unos quince años. 4. El Sr. Castillo vio una jarra cuando estaba en Londres. 5. A Javi hace tres años sus padres le regalaron un CD para su cumpleaños.
6. La Sra. Álvarez fue a la ópera por primera vez con su madre cuando vivían en Buenos Aires. 7. Felipe aprendió a tocar la guitarra hace ocho años.

**5.** vivíamos; íbamos; había; compraba; nació; estoy; hay; visito; fui; compré

*Your turn: Answers will vary.*

**Pages 71–74**

**2.** 1. *true*; 2. *false*: Argüelles es un barrio de Madrid. 3. *true*; 4. *false*: Vicenta se reunía con sus amigas por las tardes. 5. *false*: A los dos les gusta la ópera. 6. *true*; 7. *false*: Pintaba en los parques o en el campo. 8. *false*: Vicenta y su marido se fueron a vivir en el campo. 9. *false*: Ahora ven las obras de teatro en la televisión.

**3.** 1. vivían, era; 2. vivían; 3. trabajaba; 4. trabajaba; 5. reunía, tomaba; 6. iban; 7. Salían; 8. gustaba, pintaba; 9. quedaba, iba; 10. quería

**4.** Andrés: f; Julia y Pepe: a; Alfredo: b; Sra. Flores: d; Sr. Carmona: e; Sra. Alfonsín: c

**5.** éramos, tenía, era, trabajaba, preferías, nos reuníamos, dábamos, jugaban, teníamos, estábamos

*Your turn:* ¿Dónde vivían antes de venir aquí? / ¿Qué hacían los fines de semana? / ¿Trabajaba usted en el centro de la ciudad, señora Vega? / ¿Qué le gustaba hacer (en sus ratos libres)? ¿Y qué le gustaba hacer a su marido en sus ratos libres?

# Unit 6

### Pages 80–82

**2.** 1. trata; 2. dos veces, semana; 3. footing; 4. energética; 5. delgado; 6. dietas; 7. quemar, ejercicio; 8. dietas; 9. cuidado, salud; 10. problemas, corazón

**4.** 1. Podrías ir al trabajo a pie. 2. Podrías tomar el autobús y luego continuar a pie. 3. Quizás deberías comprar una bicicleta. 4. Podrías ir en bici al trabajo. 5. También podrías dar unos paseos en sus ratos libres. 6. Deberías hacer ejercicio cada día. 7. Deberías hacer media hora de ejercicio dos veces por semana. 8. No deberías comer chocolate.

**5.** *Answers will vary.*

**6.** 1. vida; 2. delgado; 3. aburrida; 4. bien; 5. bien

*Your turn:* ¿Haces ejercicio? / Deberías ir al trabajo a pie. / Podrías tomar el autobús y luego ir a pie. O podrías comprar una bicicleta. / No deberías comprar pasteles y deberías comer más fruta. / Podrías tener problemas del corazón.

### Pages 84–87

**2.** 1. *false*: Le duele la cabeza, y también le duelen los brazos y las piernas. 2. *true*; 3. *false*: Le duelen desde hace dos o tres días. 4. *false*: Tiene fiebre de 38 grados. 5. *true*; 6. *true*; 7. *true*; 8. *false*: No es nada grave.

**4.** *Symptoms that José María has*: dolor de estómago, vómitos, diarrea

**5.** 1. Tiene dolor de estómago. 2. Desde hace dos o tres días. 3. No. 4. Fue a cenar a un restaurante. 5. Comió mariscos. 6. Ella no comió mariscos. 7. Tiene una intoxicación alimenticia. 8. Le recetó unas pastillas antibióticas. 9. Tiene que tomar dos pastillas tres veces por día, no comer mucho y beber agua.

**7.** 1. muelas; 2. duele; 3. pequeño agujero; 4. empaste; 5. inyección

**8.** *Answers will vary.*

*Your turn:* No me siento bien. Tengo dolor de cabeza y estómago. / No, no creo, pero me siento mal de vez en cuando y tengo diarrea. / Desde hace tres o cuatro días. / Me duele aquí . . . y aquí. / Fui a un restaurante el domingo y comí mariscos. / ¿Es grave? ¿Puedo comer?

### Pages 88–90

**2.** 1. el pie, el tobillo; 2. el zapato; 3. andando; 4. hinchado; 5. bañándolo; 6. medicamentos, analgésicos, farmacia

**4.** 2. Un señor estaba leyendo en el jardín cuando le picó una avispa. 3. Un señor estaba trabajando en el jardín cuando se cortó el dedo. 4. Un señor estaba jugando al fútbol cuando se hizo daño en la rodilla. 5. Una señora estaba tomando el sol en la playa cuando se quemó. 6. Una señora estaba bajando la escalera cuando se cayó y se torció el tobillo.

**6.** 1. Porque tiene un problema con el pie y quiere hora con el médico. 2. Le dan hora esta tarde a las seis. 3. Un poco más temprano. 4. Para decirle que va a ir al médico esta tarde. 5. Le duele mucho el pie. Está muy hinchado y no puede andar. 6. Estaba bajando del autobús.

*Your turn:* 1. Quiero unas tiritas porque me corté el dedo cuando estaba trabajando en el jardín. 2. Quiero una crema (para quemaduras) porque me quemé la mano cuando estaba preparando la comida. 3. Me torcí el tobillo cuando jugaba/estaba jugando al tenis. 4. Estaba tomando el sol en el jardín cuando me picó un insecto. 5. Estaba jugando al fútbol cuando me hice daño en el brazo. 6. ¡Que te mejores pronto!

# Extra 1

### Pages A1–A2

**1.** *They have everything except:* jardín *and* hidromasaje en la suite principal

**2.** *Answers will vary.*

**3.** 2. Está lavándose la cara. 3. Se está duchando. 4. Está desayunando. 5. Está trabajando. 6. Está jugando con su hijo. 7. Está viendo la televisión. 8. Está leyendo un libro en la cama.

# Extra 2

### Pages A3–A5

**1.** a. 5; b. 4; c. 2; d. 1; e. 3

**2.** 1. gambas a la plancha; 2. sopa de tomate; 3. pescado frito; 4. chuleta de cerdo; 5. fabada asturiana; 6. frijoles; 7. entremeses; 8. huevos fritos; 9. pollo asado;

**3.** a. 4; b. 3; c. 7; d. 2; e. 1; f. 5; g. 6

**4.** *Chart*: Sopas: consomé, gazpacho andaluz, sopa de lentejas / Huevos: tortilla de jamón, tortilla de champiñones, huevos fritos / Pescados: merluza en salsa, pescado frito, trucha molinera /

Carnes: chuleta de cerdo, lomo de vaca, solomillo de vaca / Postres: macedonia de frutas, leche frita, fruta de la estación

**5.** 1. gente que trabaja en oficinas; 2. más variados; 3. 8 euros; 4. menos de 30 minutos; 5. pocas calorías

# Extra 3

## Pages A6–A7

**1.** 1. 8 días, todas las comidas, todas las bebidas; 2. 8 días, media pensión; 3. hotel con desayuno, 7 noches; 4. 17 días; 5. todas las visitas incluidas en el precio; 6. pensión completa, crucero de 5 días

**2.** a. 3; b. 5; c. 1; d. 6; e. 2; f. 4

**3.** 1. a; 2. b; 3. b; 4. a; 5. a; 6. b

**4.** 1. *Milwaukee;* 2. *Sheffield;* 3. *Maastricht;* 4. *Dublin;* 5. *Wellington;* 6. *Ottawa*

**5.** *Answers will vary.*

# Extra 4

## Pages A8–A10

**1.** 1. nieve, frío, lluvia; 2. tormenta, viento; 3. sol, calor, nubes; 4. viento, tormentas; 5. calor, lluvia; 6. frío, hielo

**2.** 1. Por lo general las temperaturas subirán. 2. Sí. 3. Sí. 4. Hará más fresco, unos 25 °C. 5. En el sur hará menos frío/más calor. 6. En verano.

**3.** a. 3; b. 4; c. 1; d. 3; e. 1; f. 4; g. 2

**4.** 1. ayer; 2. ayer; 3. mañana; 4. ayer; 5. mañana; 6. mañana; 7. ayer; 8. ayer; 9. ayer; 10. mañana

**5.** 1. b; 2. g; 3. a; 4. e; 5. f; 6. c; 7. d

**6.** *Answers will vary.*

# Extra 5

## Pages A11–A12

**1.** 1. ✓ 2. ✓ 3. ✗ 4. ✓ 5. ✗ 6. ?

**2.** 1. Se jubiló hace dos años. 2. Tenía doce años. 3. Con una tropa de actores ambulantes que viajaba por Argentina, Uruguay y Chile. 4. No siempre. A veces actuaban al aire libre en las plazas de las ciudades y pueblos. 5. El rol de Adela en "La Casa de Bernarda Alba." 6. Hace unos veinte años.

**3.** a. 1; b. 5; c. 6; d. 4; e. 2; f. 3

**4.** 1. *true*; 2. *false*: Apareció 71 años más tarde; 3. *true*; 4. *true*

# Extra 6

## Pages A13–A15

**1.** 1. e; 2. b; 3. a; 4. f; 5. c; 6. d

**2.** a. 2; b. 7; c. 6; d. 4; e. 5; f. 1; g. 3; h. 8

**3.** *Sample answers*: Estaba llevando una maleta cuando tropecé y me hice daño en una pierna. Estaba dando un paseo en bicicleta cuando me caí y me hice daño en la rodilla. Estaba bailando cuando me torcí el pie.

**4.** *Sample answers*: 1. Deberías pasar unos días en la cama. 2. Podrías comprar algo para las picaduras. 3. Deberías hacer más ejercicio. 4. Deberías comprar unas tiritas. 5. Podrías ir al médico. 6. Deberías protegerte contra el sol.

# Test 1

## Pages B1–B3

**1.** 1. cortina; 2. ducha; 3. invito; 4. cuenta; 5. desván

**2.** 1. ¿A qué hora se despierta usted? 2. ¿Cuántos dormitorios tiene su piso? 3. ¿Puede traer el menú, por favor? 4. Por favor, ¿puede cambiarme esta cuchara? 5. ¿Podemos ir a otro sitio?

**3.** 1. ¿Cuántos dormitorios tiene Ud./tienes? 2. ¿A qué hora se acuesta Ud./te acuestas (generalmente)? 3. ¿Tiene(n) una mesa para cuatro personas? 4. ¿Qué (me) recomienda? 5. ¿Qué desean/quieren?

**4.** 1. se; 2. se; 3. te; 4. me; 5. nos

**5.** 1. almorzamos; 2. vuelve; 3. me despierto; 4. se acuestan; 5. se sientan

**6.** 1. está hablando; 2. estamos comiendo; 3. están tomando; 4. está jugando; Estás haciendo, estás viendo; 5. están ayudando

**7.** 1. ¿Tiene(n) habitaciones libres? 2. ¿Dónde puedo/se puede aparcar el coche? 3. Quisiera reservar una mesa para dos para las ocho de la tarde, mañana. 4. ¿Me trae la cuenta, por favor? 5. Esta cuchara está sucia. ¿Puede cambiarla, por favor? 6. *Sample answers:* Quisiera un piso con dos/tres/etc. dormitorios, sala de estar, comedor, cuarto de baño.

**8.** 4, 7, 10, 2, 5, 8, 1, 6, 3, 9

# Test 2

## Pages B4–B7

**1.** 1. tiempo; 2. televisión; 3. martes ; 4. nadamos (*present tense: all the others are future*) 5. gripe; 6. acostarse

**2.** 1. h; 2. e; 3. a; 4. f; 5. c; 6. g; 7. b; 8. d

**3.** 1. ¿Qué tiempo hace (ahí) en Madrid? 2. ¿Te/Le gusta vivir en San Sebastián? 3. ¿Qué harás / hará usted el fin de semana ? 4. ¿Adónde fueron de vacaciones el año pasado? 5. ¿Cómo viajarán ustedes/viajaréis? 6. ¿Qué querrán ver tus/sus amigos? 7. (Por lo general) ¿Cómo pasan las vacaciones? 8. ¿Cuándo tuvo/tuviste sus/tus últimas vacaciones? ¿Qué hizo/hiciste?

**4.** 1. veintinueve de noviembre; 2. dos de febrero; 3. veinticuatro de diciembre; 4. diecisiete de abril; 5. doce de octubre; 6. treinta de mayo; 7. nueve de septiembre

**5.** 1. En verano hace mucho calor aquí. 2. ¿Qué vas a hacer este fin de semana? 3. Prepararé algo sencillo de comer en casa. 4. ¿A qué hora empieza la película? 5. ¿Qué haces para mantenerte en forma? 6. Empecé a pintar hace cinco años.

**6.** 1. iremos; 2. visitamos; 3. invité; 4. compraré; 5. descansaremos, veremos; 6. alquilará; 7. jugará

**7.** 1. Deberías/Podrías tomar unas aspirinas. 2. Deberías/Podrías ir al gimnasio. 3. Deberías pasar unos días en la cama. 4. Podrías/Deberías ir a una agencia de viajes. 5. Podrías/Deberías ir al cajero automático. 6. Deberías/Podrías ir a la feria de antigüedades.

**8.** 1. vivía, iba; 2. estaba, iba, gustaba; 3. visitó, fue; 4. me corté; 5. me caí, me rompí

**9.** 8, 10, 5, 4, 1, 3, 9, 7, 2, 6

**10.** 1. ¿Qué tiempo hace? 2. ¿Qué vas/va usted a hacer el fin de semana? 3. ¿Cuándo te marcharás/se marchará usted? 4. ¿Qué fecha es? 5. ¿Por qué no vamos al cine? 6. Quiero cambiar unos cheques de viajero. 7. ¿Dónde fuiste/fue de vacaciones el año pasado? 8. ¿Qué estabas/ estaba haciendo cuando te hiciste/se hizo daño en el pie? 9. ¿Dónde vivías/vivía? 10. ¿Qué te/le pasa?

**Provinces of Spain**

1.La Coruña
2.Lugo
3.Ovieda
4.Santander
5.Vizcaya
6.Guipúzcoa
7.Pontevedra
8.Orense
9.León
10.Palencia
11.Burgos
12.Alava
13.Navarra
14.Zamora
15.Valladolid
16.Segovia
17.Soria
18.Logroño
19.Zaragoza
20.Huesca
21.Lérida
22.Barcelona
23.Gerona
24.Salamanca
25.Ávila
26.Madrid
27.Guadalajara
28.Teruel
29.Tarragona
30.Cáceres
31.Toledo
32.Cuenca
33.Castellón
34.Badajoz
35.Ciudad Real
36.Albacete
37.Valencia
38.Huelva
39.Córdoba
40.Jaén
41.Murcia
42.Alicante
43.Cádiz
44.Sevilla
45.Málaga
46.Granada
47.Almeria
48.Baleares
49.Santa Cruz de Tenerife
50.Las Palmas

South America
Atlantic Ocean
South Pacific Ocean
South Atlantic Ocean
Tropic of Capricorn
Barranquilla
Maracaibo
Caracas
San Cristóbal
Venezuela
Ciudad Guayana
Georgetown
Paramaribo
Guyana
French Guiana (France)
Suriname
Cayenne
Medellín
Magdalena
Orinoco
Isla de Malpelo (Colombia)
Bogotá
Cali
Colombia
Boa Vista
Mitú
Macapá
Negro
Quito
Ecuador
Guayaquil
Amazon
Fonte Boa
Manaus
Santarém
Belém
São Luís
Iquitos
Fortaleza
Teresina
Piura
Marañon
Ucayali
Xingu
Tocantins
Natal
Rio Branco
Pôrto Velho
Brazil
Recife
Trujillo
Huánuco
Pôrto Nacional
São Francisco
Peru
Aracaju
Lima
Cuzco
Bolivia
Salvador
Ica
Lago Titicaca
Trinidad
Cuiabá
Brasília
Arequipa
La Paz
Cochabamba
Santa Cruz
Goiânia
Arica
Sucre
Belo Horizonte
Victória
Paraguay
Paraná
Rio de Janeiro
São Paulo
Antofagasta
Asunción
Curitiba
Chile
San Miguel de Tucumán
Resistencia
Isla San Felix (Chile)
Isla San Ambrosio (Chile)
Florianópolis
Pôrto Alegre
Córdoba
Salto
Rosario
Mendoza
Uruguay
Valparaíso
Santiago
Juan Fernández Islands (Chile)
Buenos Aires
Montevideo
Argentina
Concepción
Mar del Plata
Bahia Blanca
San Carlos de Bariloche
Puerto Montt
Comodoro Rivadavia
0 500 kilometers
0 nautical miles 500
Stanley
Falkland Islands
(administered by th U.K., claimed by Argentina)
Strait of Magellan
Punta Arenas
Ushuaia
Cape Horn
South Georgia (Falkland Islands)
0°
20°
40°
80°
60°
40°
20°

Central America
United States of America
Gulf of Mexico
Mexico
Cuba
Jamaica
Haiti
Dominican Republic
Belize
Caribbean Sea
Guatemala
Honduras
El Salvador
Nicaragua
Costa RIca
Panama

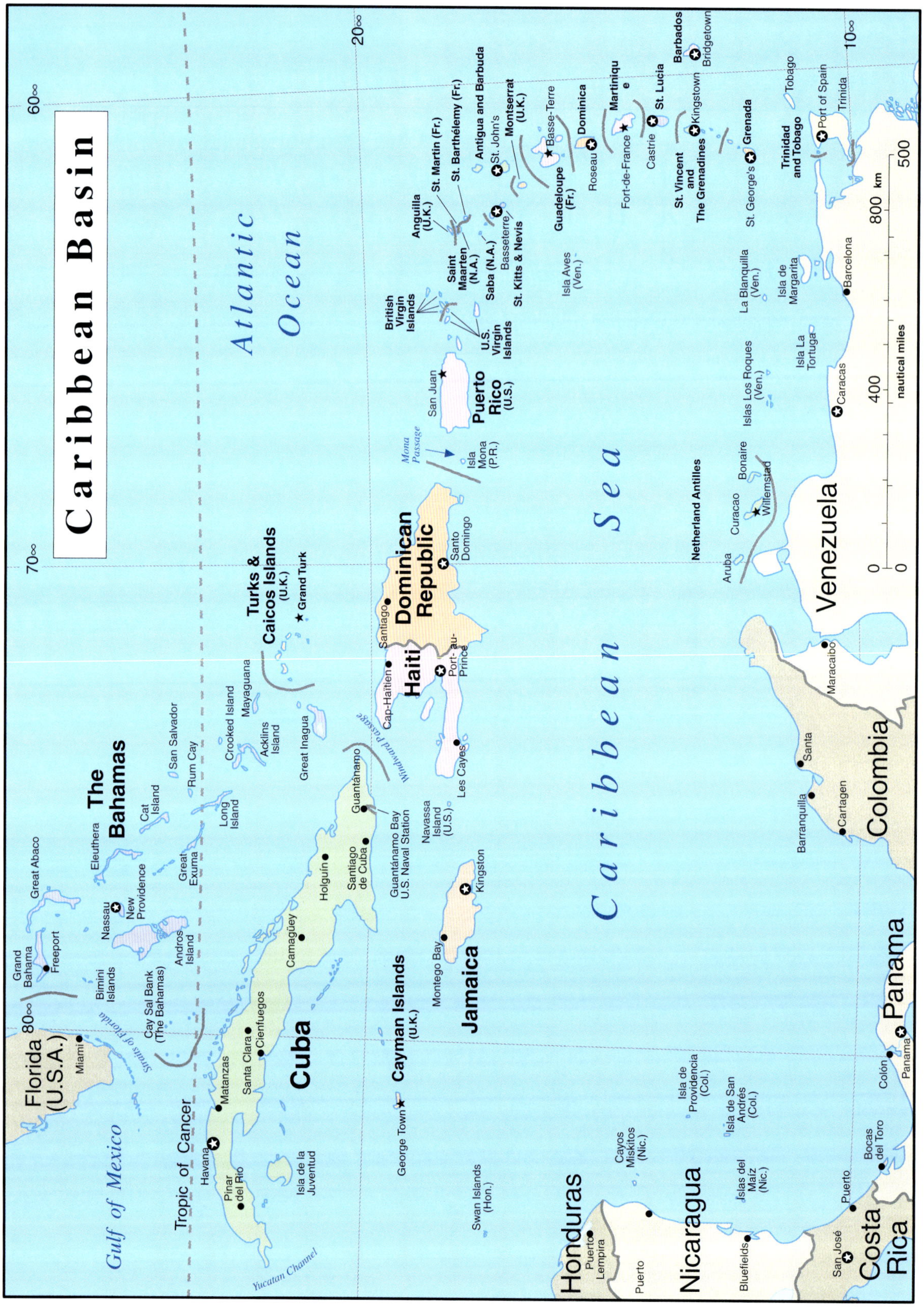

Caribbean Basin
Atlantic Ocean
Caribbean Sea
Gulf of Mexico
Tropic of Cancer
Straits of Florida
Yucatan Channel
Windward Passage
Mona Passage
80∞
70∞
60∞
20∞
10∞
Florida (U.S.A.)
Miami
The Bahamas
Grand Bahama
Freeport
Great Abaco
Bimini Islands
Nassau
New Providence
Eleuthera
Cay Sal Bank (The Bahamas)
Andros Island
Great Exuma
Cat Island
San Salvador
Rum Cay
Long Island
Crooked Island
Acklins Island
Mayaguana
Great Inagua
Turks & Caicos Islands (U.K.)
Grand Turk
Cuba
Havana
Pinar del Río
Matanzas
Santa Clara
Cienfuegos
Camagüey
Holguín
Santiago de Cuba
Guantánamo
Guantánamo Bay U.S. Naval Station
Isla de la Juventud
Cayman Islands (U.K.)
George Town
Jamaica
Montego Bay
Kingston
Navassa Island (U.S.)
Haiti
Cap-Haïtien
Port-au-Prince
Les Cayes
Dominican Republic
Santiago
Santo Domingo
Isla Mona (P.R.)
Puerto Rico (U.S.)
San Juan
U.S. Virgin Islands
British Virgin Islands
Anguilla (U.K.)
St. Martin (Fr.)
St. Barthélemy (Fr.)
Saint Maarten (N.A.)
Saba (N.A.)
St. Kitts & Nevis
Basseterre
Antigua and Barbuda
St. John's
Montserrat (U.K.)
Guadeloupe (Fr.)
Basse-Terre
Dominica
Roseau
Martinique
Fort-de-France
St. Lucia
Castrie
Barbados
Bridgetown
St. Vincent and The Grenadines
Kingstown
Grenada
St. George's
Trinidad and Tobago
Tobago
Port of Spain
Trinida
Isla Aves (Ven.)
Netherland Antilles
Aruba
Curacao
Willemstad
Bonaire
Islas Los Roques (Ven.)
La Blanquilla (Ven.)
Isla La Tortuga
Isla de Margarita
Venezuela
Maracaibo
Caracas
Barcelona
Colombia
Barranquilla
Cartagen
Santa
Panama
Colón
Panama
Costa Rica
San José
Puerto
Bocas del Toro
Nicaragua
Bluefields
Puerto
Islas del Maíz (Nic.)
Cayos Miskitos (Nic.)
Isla de Providencia (Col.)
Isla de San Andrés (Col.)
Honduras
Puerto Lempira
Swan Islands (Hon.)
0
400
800 km
0
500
nautical miles

# Notes

# Notes

Berlitz®

# Dictionary

## Spanish – English
## English – Spanish

# Diccionario

## Español – Inglés
## Inglés – Español

Berlitz Publishing
New York Munich Singapore

Edited by the Berlitz Editorial Staff

Cover photo by ID Image Direkt CD-ROM GmbH, Germany



Berlitz Publishing
193 Morris Ave.
Springfield, NJ 07081
USA

Printed in Singapore
ISBN 981-246-375-5

# Contents

# Indice

# Preface

In selecting the vocabulary and phrases for this dictionary, the editors have had the traveller's needs foremost in mind. This book will prove a useful companion to casual tourists and business travellers alike who appreciate the reassurance a small and practical dictionary can provide. It offers them—as well as beginners and students—all the basic vocabulary they will encounter and have to use, giving the key words and expressions to allow them to cope in everyday situations.

Like our successful phrase books and travel guides, these dictionaries—created with the help of a computer data bank—are designed to slip into your pocket or purse, and thus have a role as handy companions at all times.

Besides just about everything you normally find in dictionaries, there are these Berlitz bonuses:

- simplified pronunciation after each foreign-word entry, making it easy to read and enunciate words whose spelling may look forbidding
- a unique, practical glossary to simplify reading a foreign restaurant menu and to take the mystery out of complicated dishes and indecipherable names on bills of fare
- useful information on how to tell the time and how to count, on conjugating irregular verbs, commonly seen abbreviations and converting to the metric system, in addition to basic phrases.

While no dictionary of this size can pretend to completeness, we are confident this dictionary will help you get most out of your trip abroad.

Berlitz Publishing

# Prefacio

Al seleccionar las entradas de este diccionario, los redactores han tenido especialmente en cuenta las necesidades del viajero. Este diccionario, pequeño y práctico, ofrece no solo el vocabulario básico, sino también las expresiones más frecuentes del lenguaje diario. Por ello, resulta una obra indispensable para viajeros, turistas y hombres de negocios.

Al igual que nuestros conocidos manuales de conversación y guías turísticas, este diccionario ha sido ideado para llevarse encima, ya sea en el bolsillo o en un bolso de mano, asumiendo de este modo su papel de compañero disponible en todo momento.

Además de la información que de ordinario se ofrece en un diccionario, esta obra proporciona:

- Una transcripción fonética sencilla, que facilita la pronunciación sin necesidad de conocimientos específicos
- un léxico gastronómico inédito, que le permitirá "descifrar" los menús en un restaurante y acceder al secreto de los platos complicados y a los misterios de la cuenta
- Apéndices prácticos que le ayudarán a comunicar la hora y a contar, así como a utilizar los verbos irregulares, las abreviaturas más comunes y algunas expresiones útiles.

Este diccionario, pequeño, ligero y práctico, no pretende ser completo sino proporcionar a quien lo emplee un medio para enfrentarse al viaje en el extranjero.

Berlitz Publishing

# Spanish-English

# Español-Inglés

# Introduction

This dictionary has been designed to take account of your practical needs. Unnecessary linguistic information has been avoided. The entries are listed in alphabetical order regardless of whether the entry word is printed in a single word or in two or more separate words. When an entry is followed by sub-entries, such as expressions and locutions, these, too, have been listed in alphabetical order.

Each main-entry word is followed by a phonetic transcription (see guide to pronunciation). Following the transcription is the part of speech of the entry word whenever applicable. When an entry word may be used as more than one part of speech, the translations are grouped together after the respective part of speech.

Spanish feminine headwords are shown as follows:

**abonado** ... *m*, **-a** *f* subscriber
**ciudadano** ... *m*, **-a** *f* citizen
**comediante** ... *m*, **-a** *f* actor; comedian

The feminine forms of these headwords are: **abonada** (pl ~s), **ciudadana** (pl ~s), **comedianta** (pl ~s).

Whenever an entry word is repeated in sub-entries a tilde (~) is used to represent the full entry word.

An asterisk (*) in front of a verb indicates that the verb is irregular. For details you may refer to the lists of irregular verbs.

The dictionary is based on Castilian Spanish. All words and meanings of words that are exclusively Mexican have been marked as such (see list of abbreviations used in the text).

## Abbreviations

| | |
|---|---|
| *adj* | adjective |
| *adv* | adverb |
| *Am* | American |
| *art* | article |
| *conj* | conjunction |
| *f* | feminine |
| *fMe* | feminine (Mexican) |
| *fpl* | feminine plural |
| *fplMe* | feminine plural (Mexican) |
| *L.Am.* | Latin America |
| *m* | masculine |
| *Me* | Mexican |
| *mMe* | masculine (Mexican) |
| *mpl* | masculine plural |
| *mplMe* | masculine plural (Mexican) |
| *n* | noun |
| *nAm* | noun (American) |
| *num* | numeral |
| *p* | past tense |
| *pl* | plural |
| *plAm* | plural (American) |
| *pp* | past participle |
| *pr* | present tense |
| *pref* | prefix |
| *prep* | preposition |
| *pron* | pronoun |
| *v* | verb |
| *vAm* | verb (American) |
| *vMe* | verb (Mexican) |

## Guide to Pronunciation

Each main entry in this part of the dictionary is followed by a phonetic transcription which shows you how to pronounce the words. This transcription should be read as if it were English. It is based on Standard British pronunciation, though we have tried to take account of General American pronunciation also. Below, only those letters and symbols are explained which we consider likely to be ambiguous or not immediately understood.

The syllables are separated by hyphens, and stressed syllables are printed in *italics*.

Of course, the sounds of any two languages are never exactly the same, but if you follow carefully our indications, you should be able to pronounce the foreign words in such a way that you'll be understood. To make your task easier, our transcriptions occasionally simplify slightly the sound system of the language while still reflecting the essential sound differences.

### Consonants

| | |
|---|---|
| **bh** | a rather indecisive **b**, i.e. one verging on **v** |
| **dh** | like **th** in **th**is, often rather indecisive, possibly quite like **d** |
| **g** | always hard, as in **g**o |
| **g** | a **g**-sound where the tongue doesn't quite close the air passage between itself and the roof of the mouth, so that the escaping air produces audible friction; it is also on occasions pronounced as an indecisive **g** |
| **kh** | like **g**, but based on a **k**-sound; therefore hard and voiceless, like **ch** in Scottish lo**ch** |
| **l**$^{y}$ | like **lli** in mi**lli**on |
| **ñ** | as in the Spanish se**ñ**or, or like **ni** in o**ni**on |
| **r** | slightly rolled in the front of the mouth |
| **rr** | strongly rolled **r** |
| **s** | always hard, as in **s**o |

## Vowels and Diphthongs

| | |
|---|---|
| **ah** | a short version of the **a** in c**a**r, i.e. a sound between **a** in c**a**t and **u** in c**u**t |
| **igh** | as in s**igh** |
| **ou** | as in l**ou**d |

1) Raised letters (e.g. **ay**$^{oo}$, $^{y}$**ah**) should be pronounced only fleetingly.
2) Spanish vowels (i.e. not diphthongs) are pure and fairly short. Therefore, you should try to read a transcription like **oa** without moving tongue or lips while pronouncing the sound.

## Latin-American Pronunciation

Our transcriptions reflect the pronunciation of Castilian, the official language of Spain. In Latin America, two of the Castilian sounds are practically unknown:
1) **ll** as in the word ca**ll**e (which we represent by **l**$^{y}$) is usually pronounced like Spanish **y** (as in English **y**et); in the Río de la Plata region, though, both **ll** and **y** are pronounced like **s** in plea**s**ure.
2) The letters **c** (before **e** and **i**) and **z** are pronounced like **s** in **s**o instead of **th** as in **th**in.

# A

**a** (ah) *prep* to, on; at; **a las ...** at ... o'clock
**abacería** (ah-bhah-thay-*ree*-ah) *f* grocer's
**abacero** (ah-bhah-*thay*-roa) *m* grocer
**abadía** (ah-bhah-*dhee*-ah) *f* abbey
**abajo** (ah-*bhah*-khoa) *adv* downstairs; down; **hacia ~** downwards
**abandonar** (ah-bhahn-doa-*nahr*) *v* abandon
**abanico** (ah-bhah-*nee*-koa) *m* fan
**abarrotería** (ah-bhah-rroa-tay-*ree*-ah) *fMe* grocer's
**abarrotero** (ah-bhah-rroa-*tay*-roa) *mMe* grocer
**abastecimiento** (ah-bhahss-tay-thee-*m^y ayn*-toa) *m* supply
**abatido** (ah-bhah-*tee*-dhoa) *adj* down
**abecedario** (ah-bhay-thay-*dah*-r^y oa) *m* alphabet
**abedul** (ah-bhay-*dhool*) *m* birch
**abeja** (ah-*bhay*-khah) *f* bee
**abertura** (ah-bhayr-*too*-rah) *f* opening
**abeto** (ah-*bhay*-toa) *m* fir tree
**abierto** (ah-*bh^y ayr*-toa) *adj* open
**abismo** (ah-*bhee*-zmoa) *m* abyss
**ablandador** (ah-bhlahn-dah-*dhoar*) *m* water softener
**ablandar** (ah-bhlahn-*dahr*) *v* soften
**abogado** (ah-bhoa-*gah*-dhoa) *m*, **-a** *f* barrister, lawyer, attorney; solicitor; advocate
**abolir** (ah-bhoa-*leer*) *v* abolish
**abolladura** (ah-bhoa-l^y ah-*dhoo*-rah) *f* dent
**abonado** (ah-bhoa-*nah*-dhoa) *m*, **-a** *f* subscriber
**abono** (ah-*bhoa*-noa) *m* subscription
**aborto** (ah-*bhoar*-toa) *m* miscarriage; abortion
**abrazar** (ah-bhrah-*thahr*) *v* embrace; hug
**abrazo** (ah-*bhrah*-thoa) *m* hug; embrace
**abrecartas** (ah-bhray-*kahr*-tahss) *m* paper knife, *Am* letter opener
**abrelatas** (ah-bhray-*lah*-tahss) *m* tin opener, can opener *Am*
**abreviatura** (ah-bhray-bh^y ah-*too*-rah) *f* abbreviation
**abrigar** (ah-bhree-*gahr*) *v* shelter
**abrigo** (ah-*bhree*-goa) *m* coat, overcoat; **~ de pieles** fur coat
**abril** (ah-*bhreel*) April
**abrir** (ah-*bhreer*) *v* open; unlock; turn on
**abrochar** (ah-bhroa-*chahr*) *v* button
**abrupto** (ah-*bhroop*-toa) *adj* steep
**absceso** (ahbhs-*thay*-soa) *m* abscess
**absolutamente** (ahbh-soa-loo-tah-*mayn*-tay) *adv* absolutely
**absoluto** (ahbh-soa-*loo*-toa) *adj* sheer; total
**abstemio** (ahbhs-*tay*-m^y oa) *m* teetotaller
***abstenerse de** (ahbhs-tay-*nayr*-say) abstain from
**abstracto** (ahbhs-*trahk*-toa) *adj* abstract
**absurdo** (ahbh-*soor*-dhoa) *adj* absurd; foolish
**abuela** (ah-*bhway*-lah) *f* grandmother
**abuelo** (ah-*bhway*-loa) *m* grandfather, granddad; **abuelos** *mpl* grandparents *pl*
**abundancia** (ah-bhoon-*dahn*-th^y ah) *f* abundance, plenty
**abundante** (ah-bhoon-*dahn*-tay) *adj* abundant, plentiful
**aburrido** (ah-bhoo-*rree*-dhoa) *adj* boring, dull
**aburrir** (ah-bhoo-*rreer*) *v* bore, annoy
**abusar de** (ah-bhoo-*sahr*) exploit
**abuso** (ah-*bhoo*-soa) *m* misuse, abuse

**acá** (ah-*kah*) *adv* here
**acabar** (ah-kah-*bhahr*) *v* end; **acabado** finished; over
**academia** (ah-kah-*dhay*-m$^{y}$ah) *f* academy; ~ **de bellas artes** art school
**acampador** (ah-kahm-pah-*dhoar*) *m* camper
**acampar** (ah-kahm-*pahr*) *v* camp
**acantilado** (ah-kahn-tee-*lah*-dhoa) *m* cliff; *adj* steep
**acariciar** (ah-kah-ree-*th$^{y}$ahr*) *v* caress
**acaso** (ah-*kah*-soa) *adv* perhaps
**accesible** (ahk-thay-*see*-bhlay) *adj* accessible
**acceso** (ahk-*thay*-soa) *m* entrance, access; approach
**accesorio** (ahk-thay-*soa*-r$^{y}$oa) *adj* additional; **accesorios** *mpl* accessories *pl*
**accidental** (ahk-thee-dhayn-*tahl*) *adj* accidental
**accidente** (ahk-thee-*dhayn*-tay) *m* accident; ~ **aéreo** plane crash
**acción** (ahk-*th$^{y}$oan*) *f* action; deed; stock; **acciones** *fpl* stocks and shares
**acechar** (ah-thay-*chahr*) *v* watch for
**aceite** (ah-*thay*-tay) *m* oil; ~ **bronceador** suntan oil; ~ **de oliva** olive oil; ~ **lubricante** lubrication oil
**aceitoso** (ah-thay-*toa*-soa) *adj* oily
**aceituna** (ah-thay-*too*-nah) *f* olive
**acelerador** (ah-thay-lay-rah-*dhoar*) *m* accelerator
**acelerar** (ah-thay-lay-*rahr*) *v* accelerate
**acento** (ah-*thayn*-toa) *m* accent
**acentuar** (ah-thayn-*twahr*) *v* emphasize, stress
**aceptar** (ah-thayp-*tahr*) *v* accept
**acera** (ah-*thay*-rah) *f* pavement; sidewalk *Am*
**acerca de** (ah-*thayr*-kah day) about
**acercarse** (ah-thayr-*kahr*-say) *v* approach
**acero** (ah-*thay*-roa) *m* steel; ~ **inoxidable** stainless steel
***acertar** (ah-thayr-*tahr*) *v* *hit; guess right
**acidez** (ah-thee-*dhayth*) *f* acidity
**ácido** (*ah*-thee-dhoa) *m* acid
**aclamar** (ah-klah-*mahr*) *v* cheer
**aclaración** (ah-klah-rah-*th$^{y}$oan*) *f* explanation
**aclarar** (ah-klah-*rahr*) *v* clarify
**acné** (ahk-*nay*) *m* acne
**acogida** (ah-koa-*khee*-dhah) *f* reception
**acomodación** (ah-koa-moa-dhah-*th$^{y}$oan*) *f* accommodation
**acomodado** (ah-koa-moa-*dhah*-dhoa) *adj* well-to-do
**acomodador** (ah-koa-moa-dhah-*dhoar*) *m* usher
**acomodadora** (ah-koa-moa-dhah-*dhoa*-rah) *f* usherette
**acomodar** (ah-koa-moa-*dhahr*) *v* accommodate
**acompañar** (ah-koam-pah-*ñahr*) *v* accompany; conduct
**aconsejar** (ah-koan-say-*khahr*) *v* recommend, advise
***acontecer** (ah-koan-tay-*thayr*) *v* occur
**acontecimiento** (ah-koan-tay-thee-*m$^{y}$ayn*-toa) *m* event; happening, occurrence
***acordar** (ah-koar-*dhahr*) *v* agree; ***acordarse** *v* remember, recollect, recall
**acortar** (ah-koar-*tahr*) *v* shorten, reduce
***acostar** (ah-koass-*tahr*) *v* *lay down; ***acostarse** *v* *go to bed
**acostumbrado** (ah-koass-toom-*brah*-dhoa) *adj* accustomed; customary; ***estar ~ a** *be used to
**acostumbrar** (ah-koass-toom-*brahr*)

*v* accustom
***acrecentarse** (ah-kray-thayn-*tahr*-say) *v* increase
**acreditar** (ah-kray-dhee-*tahr*) *v* credit
**acreedor** (ah-kray-ay-*dhoar*) *m* creditor
**acta** (*ahk*-tah) *f* certificate; **actas** minutes
**actitud** (ahk-tee-*toodh*) *f* attitude; position
**actividad** (ahk-tee-bhee-*dhahdh*) *f* activity
**activo** (ahk-*tee*-bhoa) *adj* active
**acto** (*ahk*-toa) *m* act, deed
**actor** (ahk-*toar*) *m* actor
**actriz** (ahk-*treeth*) *f* actress
**actual** (ahk-*twahl*) *adj* present; current
**actualmente** (ahk-twahl-*mayn*-tay) *adv* now
**actuar** (ahk-*twahr*) *v* act
**acuarela** (ah-kwah-*ray*-lah) *f* watercolo(u)r
**acuerdo** (ah-*kwayr*-dhoa) *m* approval; agreement, settlement; **¡de acuerdo!** all right!, okay!; ***estar de ~ con** approve of
**acumulador** (ah-koo-moo-lah-*dhoar*) *m* battery
**acusación** (ah-koo-sah-*th$^{y}$oan*) *f* charge
**acusado** (ah-koo-*sah*-dhoa) *m*, **-a** *f* accused
**acusar** (ah-koo-*sahr*) *v* accuse; charge
**adaptador** (ah-dhahp-tah-*dhoar*) *m* adaptor
**adaptar** (ah-dhahp-*tahr*) *v* adapt; suit
**adecuado** (ah-dhay-*kwah*-dhoa) *adj* adequate; convenient, appropriate
**adelantar** (ah-dhay-lahn-*tahr*) *v* *get on; **por adelantado** in advance; **prohibido ~** no overtaking
**adelante** (ah-dhay-*lahn*-tay) *adv* ahead, onwards, forward
**adelanto** (ah-dhay-*lahn*-toa) *m* advance
**adelgazar** (ah-dhayl-gah-*thahr*) *v* lose weight
**además** (ah-dhay-*mahss*) *adv* moreover, furthermore, besides; **~ de** beyond, besides
**adentro** (ah-*dhayn*-troa) *adv* inside, in; **hacia ~** inwards
**aderezo** (ah-dhee-*ray*-thoa) *m* salad dressing
**adeudado** (ah-dhay$^{oo}$-*dhah*-dhoa) *adj* due
**adición** (ah-dhee-*th$^{y}$oan*) *f* addition
**adicional** (ah-dhee-th$^{y}$oa-*nahl*) *adj* additional
**adicionar** (ah-dhee-th$^{y}$oa-*nahr*) *v* add; count
**¡adiós!** (ah-*dh$^{y}$oass*) good-bye!
**adivinar** (ah-dhee-bhee-*nahr*) *v* guess
**adjetivo** (ahdh-khay-*tee*-bhoa) *m* adjective
**administración** (ahdh-mee-neess-trah-*th$^{y}$oan*) *f* administration; direction
**administrativo** (ahdh-mee-neess-trah-*tee*-bhoa) *adj* administrative
**admirable** (ahdh-mee-*rah*-bhlay) *adj* admirable
**admiración** (ahdh-mee-rah-*th$^{y}$oan*) *f* admiration
**admirador** (ahdh-mee-rah-*dhoar*) *m*, **-a** *f* fan
**admirar** (ahdh-mee-*rahr*) *v* admire
**admisión** (ahdh-mee-*s$^{y}$oan*) *f* admission; admittance
**admitir** (ahdh-mee-*teer*) *v* admit; acknowledge
**adolescente** (ah-dhoa-layss-*thayn*-tay) *m/f* teenager
**adonde** (ah-*dhoan*-day) *adv* where
**adoptar** (ah-dhoap-*tahr*) *v* adopt
**adorable** (ah-dhoa-*rah*-bhlay) *adj* adorable
**adorar** (ah-dhoa-*rahr*) *v* worship

**adorno** (ah-*dhoar*-noa) *m* ornament

**adquirible** (ahdh-kee-*ree*-bhlay) *adj* obtainable, available

***adquirir** (ahdh-kee-*reer*) *v* acquire; *buy

**adquisición** (ahdh-kee-see-*th$^{y}$oan*) *f* acquisition

**aduana** (ah-*dwah*-nah) *f* Customs *pl*

**adulto** (ah-*dhool*-toa) *adj* grown-up, adult; *m*, **-a** *f* grown-up, adult

**adverbio** (ahdh-*bhayr*-bh$^{y}$oa) *m* adverb

**advertencia** (ahdh-bhayr-*tayn*-th$^{y}$ah) *f* warning

**adversario** (ahdh-bhayr-*sah*-r$^{y}$oa) *m*, **-a** *f* opponent, adversary

***advertir** (ahdh-bhayr-*teer*) *v* caution, warn; notice

**aerolínea** (ah-ay-roa-*lee*-nay-ah) *f* airline

**aeropuerto** (ah-ay-roa-*pwayr*-toa) *m* airport

**aerosol** (ah-ay-roa-*soal*) *m* atomizer

**afamado** (ah-fah-*mah*-dhoa) *adj* noted

**afección** (ah-fayk-*th$^{y}$oan*) *f* affection

**afectado** (ah-fayk-*tah*-dhoa) *adj* affected

**afectar** (ah-fayk-*tahr*) *v* affect; feign

**afeitadora eléctrica** (ah-fay-tah-*dhoa*-rah ay-*layk*-tree-kah) electric razor

**afeitarse** (ah-fay-*tahr*-say) *v* shave; **máquina de afeitar** safety-razor; shaver

**afición** (ah-fee-*th$^{y}$oan*) *f* hobby

**aficionado** (ah-fee-th$^{y}$oa-*nah*-dhoa) *m* supporter

**afilar** (ah-fee-*lahr*) *v* sharpen; **afilado** sharp

**afiliado** (ah-fee-*l$^{y}$ah*-dhoa) *adj* affiliated

**afirmación** (ah-feer-mah-*th$^{y}$oan*) *f* statement

**afirmar** (ah-feer-*mahr*) *v* claim

**afirmativo** (ah-feer-mah-*tee*-bhoa) *adj* affirmative

**afligido** (ah-flee-*khee*-dhoa) *adj* sad; ***estar ~** grieve

**afluente** (ah-*flwayn*-tay) *m* tributary

**afortunado** (ah-foar-too-*nah*-dhoa) *adj* fortunate, lucky

**África** (*ah*-free-kah) *f* Africa

**África del Sur** (*ah*-free-kah dayl soor) South Africa

**africano** (ah-free-*kah*-noa) *adj* African; *m* African

**afuera** (ah-*fway*-rah) *adv* outside, outdoors; **hacia ~** outwards

**afueras** (ah-*fway*-rahss) *fpl* outskirts *pl*

**agarradero** (ah-gah-rrah-*dhay*-roa) *m* handle

**agarrar** (ah-gah-*rrahr*) *v* grasp, seize; **agarrarse** *v* *hold on

**agarre** (ah-*gah*-rray) *m* grip, grasp

**agencia** (ah-*khayn*-th$^{y}$ah) *f* agency; **~ de viajes** travel agency

**agenda** (ah-*khayn*-dah) *f* diary

**agente** (ah-*khayn*-tay) *m* agent; **~ de policía** policeman; **~ de viajes** travel agent

**ágil** (*ah*-kheel) *adj* supple

**agitación** (ah-khee-tah-*th$^{y}$oan*) *f* excitement; bustle

**agitar** (ah-khee-*tahr*) *v* stir up

**agosto** (ah-*goass*-toa) August

**agotado** (ah-goa-*tah*-dhoa) *adj* sold out

**agotar** (ah-goa-*tahr*) *v* use up

**agradable** (ah-grah-*dhah*-bhlay) *adj* agreeable; enjoyable, pleasing, pleasant; nice

***agradecer** (ah-grah-dhay-*thayr*) *v* thank

**agradecido** (ah-grah-dhay-*thee*-dhoa) *adj* grateful, thankful

**agrario** (ah-*grah*-r$^{y}$oa) *adj* agrarian

**agresivo** (ah-gray-*see*-bhoa) *adj* aggressive
**agrícola** (ah-*gree*-koa-lah) *adj* agrarian
**agricultura** (ah-gree-kool-*too*-rah) *f* agriculture
**agrio** (*ah*-gr$^y$oa) *adj* sour
**agua** (*ah*-gwah) *f* water; ~ **corriente** running water; ~ **de mar** seawater; ~ **de soda** soda-water; ~ **dulce** fresh water; ~ **helada** iced water; ~ **mineral** mineral water; ~ **potable** drinking-water
**aguacate** (ah-gwah-*kah*-tay) *m* avocado
**aguacero** (ah-gwah-*thay*-roa) *m* shower; downpour
**aguafuerte** (ah-gwah-*fwayr*-tay) *f* etching
**aguanieve** (ah-gwah-*n$^y$ay*-bhay) *f* slush
**aguantar** (ah-gwahn-*tahr*) *v* *bear
**aguardar** (ah-gwahr-*dahr*) *v* expect
**aguardiente** (ah-gwahr-*d$^y$ayn*-tay) *m* brandy; fruit-based alcoholic spirit
**agudo** (ah-*goo*-dhoa) *adj* keen; acute
**águila** (*ah*-gee-lah) *m* eagle
**aguja** (ah-*goo*-khah) *f* needle; spire; **labor de** ~ needlework
**agujero** (ah-goo-*khay*-roa) *m* hole
**ahí** (ah-*ee*) *adv* there
**ahogar** (ah-oa-*gahr*) *v* drown; **ahogarse** *v* *be drowned
**ahora** (ah-*oa*-rah) *adv* now; **de ~ en adelante** henceforth; **hasta ~** so far
**ahorrar** (ah-oa-*rrahr*) *v* save
**ahorros** (ah-*oa*-rroass) *mpl* savings *pl*; **caja de ~** savings bank
**ahuyentar** (ou-$^y$ayn-*tahr*) *v* chase away
**aire** (*igh*-ray) *m* air; sky; breath; ~ **acondicionado** air-conditioning; **cámara de ~** inner tube; ***tener aires de** look
**airear** (igh-ray-*ahr*) *v* air, ventilate
**airoso** (igh-*roa*-soa) *adj* airy
**aislado** (ighz-*lah*-dhoa) *adj* isolated
**aislador** (ighz-lah-*dhoar*) *m* insulator
**aislamiento** (ighz-lah-*m$^y$ayn*-toa) *m* isolation; insulation
**aislar** (ighz-*lahr*) *v* isolate; insulate
**ajedrez** (ah-khay-*dhrayth*) *m* chess
**ajeno** (ah-*khay*-noa) *adj* foreign
**ajetrearse** (ah-khay-tray-*ahr*-say) *v* labo(u)r
**ajo** (*ah*-khoa) *m* garlic
**ajustar** (ah-khooss-*tahr*) *v* adjust
**ala** (*ah*-lah) *f* wing
**alabar** (ah-lah-*bhahr*) *v* praise
**alambre** (ah-*lahm*-bray) *m* wire
**alargar** (ah-lahr-*gahr*) *v* lengthen; renew; hand to
**alarma** (ah-*lahr*-mah) *f* alarm; ~ **de incendio** fire alarm
**alarmante** (ah-lahr-*mahn*-tay) *adj* alarming
**alarmar** (ah-lahr-*mahr*) *v* alarm
**alba** (*ahl*-bhah) *f* dawn
**albañil** (ahl-bhah-*ñeel*) *m* bricklayer
**albaricoque** (ahl-bhah-ree-*koa*-kay) *m* apricot
**albornoz** (ahl-bhoar-*noath*) *m* bathrobe
**alboroto** (ahl-bhoa-*roa*-toa) *m* noise, racket
**álbum** (*ahl*-bhoom) *m* album
**alcachofa** (ahl-kah-*choa*-fah) *f* artichoke
**alcalde** (ahl-*kahl*-dhay) *m* mayor
**alcance** (ahl-*kahn*-thay) *m* reach, range
**alcanzable** (ahl-kahn-*thah*-bhlay) *adj* attainable
**alcanzar** (ahl-kahn-*thahr*) *v* achieve, reach
**alce** (*ahl*-thay) *m* moose
**alcohol** (ahl-*koal*) *m* alcohol; ~ **de quemar** methylated spirits

**alcohólico** (ahl-*koa*-lee-koa) *adj* alcoholic
**aldea** (ahl-*day*-ah) *f* hamlet
**alegrar** (ah-lay-*grahr*) *v* cheer up
**alegre** (ah-*lay*-gray) *adj* cheerful, merry, joyful; glad, gay
**alegría** (ah-lay-*gree*-ah) *f* gaiety; gladness
**alejar** (ah-lay-*khahr*) *v* move away
**alemán** (ah-lay-*mahn*) *adj* German; *m* German
**Alemania** (ah-lay-*mah*-n$^{y}$ah) *f* Germany
***alentar** (ah-layn-*tahr*) *v* encourage
**alergia** (ah-*layr*-kh$^{y}$ah) *f* allergy
**alérgico** (ah-*layr*-khee-koa) *adj* allergic
**alfiler** (ahl-fee-*layr*) *m* pin
**alfombra** (ahl-*foam*-brah) *f* carpet
**alfombrilla** (ahl-foam-*bree*-l$^{y}$ah) *f* rug
**alga** (*ahl*-gah) *f* alga; seaweed
**álgebra** (*ahl*-gay-bhrah) *f* algebra
**algo** (*ahl*-goa) *pron* something; *adv* somewhat
**algodón** (ahl-goa-*dhoan*) *m* cotton; cotton-wool; **de ~** cotton
**alguien** (*ahl*-g$^{y}$ayn) *pron* someone, somebody
**alguno** (ahl-*goo*-noa) *adj* any; **algunos** *adj* some; *pron* some
**alhaja** (ah-*lah*-khah) *f* gem
**aliado** (ah-*l$^{y}$ah*-dhoa) *m* associate
**alianza** (ah-*l$^{y}$ahn*-thah) *f* alliance
**alicates** (ah-lee-*kah*-tayss) *mpl* pliers *pl*
**alienado** (ah-l$^{y}$ay-*nah*-dhoa) *m* lunatic
**aliento** (ah-*l$^{y}$ayn*-toa) *m* breath
**alimentar** (ah-lee-mayn-*tahr*) *v* *feed
**alimento** (ah-lee-*mayn*-toa) *m* fare; food; **alimentos naturales** health food
**alivio** (ah-*lee*-bh$^{y}$oa) *m* relief
**alma** (*ahl*-mah) *f* soul
**almacén** (ahl-mah-*thayn*) *m* depot, warehouse, depository, store house; store; **~ de licores** off-licence; liquor store *Am*; **grandes almacenes** department store
**almacenaje** (ahl-mah-thay-*nah*-khay) *m* storage
**almacenar** (ahl-mah-thay-*nahr*) *v* store
**almeja** (ahl-*may*-khah) *f* clam
**almendra** (ahl-*mayn*-drah) *f* almond
**almirante** (ahl-mee-*rahn*-tay) *m* admiral
**almohada** (ahl-moa-*ah*-dhah) *f* pillow; **~ eléctrica** heating pad
**almohadilla** (ahl-moa-ah-*dhee*-l$^{y}$ah) *f* pad
**almohadón** (ahl-moa-ah-*dhoan*) *m* cushion; pillow
**almorzar** (ahl-moar-*thahr*) *v* have lunch; have a mid-morning snack
**almuerzo** (ahl-*mwayr*-thoa) *m* lunch, luncheon
**alojamiento** (ah-loa-khah-*m$^{y}$ayn*-toa) *m* accommodation, lodgings *pl*
**alojar** (ah-loa-*khahr*) *v* lodge
**alondra** (ah-*loan*-drah) *f* lark
**alquilar** (ahl-kee-*lahr*) *v* hire; rent, lease, *let
**alquiler** (ahl-kee-*layr*) *m* rent; **~ de coches** car hire; **de ~** for hire
**alrededor de** (ahl-ray-dhay-*dhoar* day) around, round; about
**alrededores** (ahl-ray-dhay-*dhoa*-rayss) *mpl* environment, surroundings *pl*
**altar** (ahl-*tahr*) *m* altar
**altavoz** (ahl-tah-*bhoath*) *m* loudspeaker
**alteración** (ahl-tay-rah-*th$^{y}$oan*) *f* alteration
**alterar** (ahl-tay-*rahr*) *v* alter
**alternar con** (ahl-tayr-*nahr*) mix with
**alternativa** (ahl-tayr-nah-*tee*-bhah) *f* alternative

**alternativo** (ahl-tayr-nah-*tee*-bhoa) *adj* alternate
**altiplano** (ahl-tee-*plah*-noa) *m* high plateau *pl*
**altitud** (ahl-tee-*toodh*) *f* altitude
**alto** (*ahl*-toa) *adj* high, tall; **en ~** overhead
**¡alto!** (*ahl*-toa) stop!
**altura** (ahl-*too*-rah) *f* height
**alubia** (ah-*loo*-bh$^{y}$ah) *f* kidney bean
**aludir a** (ah-loo-*dheer*) allude to
**alumbrado** (ah-loom-*brah*-dhoa) *m* lighting
**alumna** (ah-*loom*-nah) *f* schoolgirl
**alumno** (ah-*loom*-noa) *m* pupil; schoolboy
**alzar** (ahl-*thahr*) *v* raise
**allá** (ah-*l$^{y}$ah*) *adv* over there; **más ~** beyond; **más ~ de** past, beyond
**allí** (ah-*l$^{y}$ee*) *adv* there
**ama** (*ah*-mah) *f* owner; **~ de casa** housewife, homemaker; **~ de llaves** housekeeper; **~ de leche, ~ de cría** L.Am. wetnurse
**amable** (ah-*mah*-bhlay) *adj* kind, friendly
**amado** (ah-*mah*-dhoa) *adj* beloved
**amaestrar** (ah-mah-ayss-*trahr*) *v* train
**amamantar** (ah-mah-mahn-*tahr*) *v* nurse
**amanecer** (ah-mah-nay-*thayr*) *m* sunrise, daybreak
**amante** (ah-*mahn*-tay) *m/f* lover
**amapola** (ah-mah-*poa*-lah) *f* poppy
**amar** (ah-*mahr*) *v* love
**amargo** (ah-*mahr*-goa) *adj* bitter
**amarillo** (ah-mah-*ree*-l$^{y}$oa) *adj* yellow
**ámbar** (*ahm*-bahr) *m* amber
**ambicioso** (ahm-bee-*th$^{y}$oa*-soa) *adj* ambitious
**ambiental** (ahm-b$^{y}$ayn-*tahl*) *adj* environmental
**ambiente** (ahm-*b$^{y}$ayn*-tay) *m* atmosphere; **medio ~** environment
**ambiguo** (ahm-*bee*-gwoa) *adj* ambiguous
**ambos** (*ahm*-boass) *adj* both; either
**ambulancia** (ahm-boo-*lahn*-th$^{y}$ah) *f* ambulance
**ambulante** (ahm-boo-*lahn*-tay) *adj* itinerant
**amenaza** (ah-may-*nah*-thah) *f* threat
**amenazador** (ah-may-nah-thah-*dhoar*) *adj* threatening
**amenazar** (ah-may-nah-*thahr*) *v* threaten
**ameno** (ah-*may*-noa) *adj* nice
**América** (ah-*may*-ree-kah) *f* America; **~ Latina** Latin America
**americana** (ah-may-ree-*kah*-nah) *f* jacket
**americano** (ah-may-ree-*kah*-noa) *adj* American; *m* American
**amiga** (ah-*mee*-gah) *f* friend
**amígdalas** (ah-*meeg*-dhah-lahss) *fpl* tonsils *pl*
**amigdalitis** (ah-meeg-dhah-*lee*-teess) *f* tonsilitis
**amigo** (ah-*mee*-goa) *m* friend
**amistad** (ah-meess-*tahdh*) *f* friendship
**amistoso** (ah-meess-*toa*-soa) *adj* friendly
**amnistía** (ahm-neess-*tee*-ah) *f* amnesty
**amo** (*ah*-moa) *m* master
**amoníaco** (ah-moa-*nee*-ah-koa) *m* ammonia
**amontonar** (ah-moan-toa-*nahr*) *v* pile
**amor** (ah-*moar*) *m* love; darling, sweetheart
**amorío** (ah-moa-*ree*-oa) *m* affair, romance
**amoroso** (ah-moa-*roa*-soa) *adj* amorous
**amortiguador** (ah-moar-tee-gwah-*dhoar*) *m* shock absorber
**amortizar** (ah-moar-tee-*thahr*) *v* *pay off

**amotinamiento** (ah-moa-tee-nah-*m$^{y}$ayn*-toa) *m* mutiny
**ampliación** (ahm-pl$^{y}$ah-*th$^{y}$oan*) *f* enlargement; extension
**ampliar** (ahm-*pl$^{y}$ahr*) *v* enlarge; extend
**amplio** (*ahm*-pl$^{y}$oa) *adj* broad
**ampolla** (ahm-*poa*-l$^{y}$ah) *f* blister
**amueblar** (ah-mway-*bhlahr*) *v* furnish
**analfabeto** (ah-nahl-fah-*bhay*-toa) *m* illiterate
**analgésico** (ah-nahl-*khay*-see-koa) *m* painkiller
**análisis** (ah-*nah*-lee-seess) *f* analysis
**analista** (ah-nah-*leess*-tah) *m* analyst
**analizar** (ah-nah-lee-*thahr*) *v* analyse; *break down
**análogo** (ah-*nah*-loa-goa) *adj* similar
**anarquía** (ah-nahr-*kee*-ah) *f* anarchy
**anatomía** (ah-nah-toa-*mee*-ah) *f* anatomy
**anciano** (ahn-*th$^{y}$ah*-noa) *adj* aged; elderly
**ancla** (*ahng*-klah) *f* anchor
**ancho** (*ahn*-choa) *adj* broad; wide; *m* breadth
**anchoa** (ahn-*choa*-ah) *f* anchovy
**anchura** (ahn-*choo*-rah) *f* width
***andar** (ahn-*dahr*) *v* walk
**andén** (ahn-*dayn*) *m* platform
**anemia** (ah-*nay*-m$^{y}$ah) *f* anaemia
**anestesia** (ah-nayss-*tay*-s$^{y}$ah) *f* anaesthesia
**anexar** (ah-nayk-*sahr*) *v* annex
**anexo** (ah-*nayk*-soa) *m* annex, enclosure
**anfiteatro** (ahn-fee-tay-*ah*-troa) *m* amphitheater *Am*, amphitheatre; dress circle
**anfitrión** (ahn-fee-*tr$^{y}$oan*) *m* host
**ángel** (*ahng*-khayl) *m* angel
**angosto** (ahng-*goass*-toa) *adj* narrow, tight
**anguila** (ahng-*gee*-lah) *f* eel
**ángulo** (*ahng*-goo-loa) *m* angle
**angustioso** (ahng-gooss-*t$^{y}$oa*-soa) *adj* afraid
**anhelar** (ah-nay-*lahr*) *v* desire, long for
**anhelo** (ah-*nay*-loa) *m* longing
**anillo** (ah-*nee*-l$^{y}$oa) *m* ring; **~ de boda** wedding ring; **~ de esponsales** engagement ring
**animado** (ah-nee-*mah*-dhoa) *adj* crowded; lively; animated
**animal** (ah-nee-*mahl*) *m* beast, animal; **~ de presa** beast of prey; **~ doméstico** pet
**animar** (ah-nee-*mahr*) *v* encourage, inspire; animate
**ánimo** (*ah*-nee-moa) *m* mind; courage
**aniversario** (ah-nee-bhayr-*sah*-r$^{y}$oa) *m* anniversary; jubilee
**anoche** (ah-*noa*-chay) *adv* last night
**anónimo** (ah-*noa*-nee-moa) *adj* anonymous
**anormal** (ah-noar-*mahl*) *adj* abnormal
**anotación** (ah-noa-tah-*th$^{y}$oan*) *f* entry
**anotar** (ah-noa-*tahr*) *v* *write down
**ansia** (*ahn*-s$^{y}$ah) *f* anxiety
**ansioso** (ahn-*s$^{y}$oa*-soa) *adj* anxious, eager
**ante** (*ahn*-tay) *prep* in front of
**anteayer** (ahn-tay-ah-*$^{y}$ayr*) *adv* the day before yesterday
**antecedentes** (ahn-tay-thay-*dhayn*-tayss) *mpl* background
**antemano** (ahn-tay-*mah*-noa): **de ~** beforehand
**antena** (ahn-*tay*-nah) *f* aerial
**anteojos** (ahn-tay-*oa*-khoass) *mpl* glasses, spectacles
**antepasado** (ahn-tay-pah-*sah*-dhoa) *m*, **-a** *f* ancestor
**anterior** (ahn-tay-*r$^{y}$oar*) *adj* former, prior, previous
**antes** (*ahn*-tayss) *adv* before; formerly; at first; **~ de** before; **~ de que** before

**antibiótico** (ahn-tee-*bh$^y$oa*-tee-koa) *m* antibiotic
**anticipar** (ahn-tee-thee-*pahr*) *v* advance
**anticipo** (ahn-tee-*thee*-poa) *m* advance
**anticonceptivo** (ahn-tee-koan-thayp-*tee*-bhoa) *m* contraceptive
**anticongelante** (ahn-tee-koang-khay-*lahn*-tay) *m* antifreeze
**anticuado** (ahn-tee-*kwah*-dhoa) *adj* old-fashioned; ancient, out of date, quaint
**anticuario** (ahn-tee-*kwah*-r$^y$oa) *m*, **-a** *f* antique dealer
**Antigüedad** (ahn-tee-gway-*dhahdh*) *f* antiquity
**antigüedades** (ahn-tee-gway-*dhah*-dhayss) *fpl* antiquities *pl*
**antiguo** (ahn-*tee*-gwoa) *adj* ancient, antique; former
**antipatía** (ahn-tee-pah-*tee*-ah) *f* antipathy, dislike
**antipático** (ahn-tee-*pah*-tee-koa) *adj* nasty, unpleasant
**anticipado** (ahn-tee-thee-*pah*-dhoa) *adj* advance; early; **por ~** in advance
**antirrobo** (ahn-tee-*roa*-bhoa) *m* antitheft device
**antojarse** (ahn-toa-*khahr*-say) *v* fancy, *feel like
**antojo** (ahn-*toa*-khoa) *m* fad, whim
**antología** (ahn-toa-loa-*khee*-ah) *f* anthology
**antorcha** (ahn-*toar*-chah) *f* torch
**anual** (ah-*nwahl*) *adj* annual, yearly
**anuario** (ah-*nwah*-ree-oa) *m* annual
**anudar** (ah-noo-*dhahr*) *v* tie; knot
**anular** (ah-noo-*lahr*) *v* cancel
**anunciar** (ah-noon-*th$^y$ahr*) *v* announce
**anuncio** (ah-*noon*-th$^y$oa) *m* announcement; advertisement
**anzuelo** (ahn-*thway*-loa) *m* fishing hook
**añadir** (ah-ñah-*dheer*) *v* add
**año** (*ah*-ñoa) *m* year; **al ~** per annum; **~ bisiesto** leap year; **~ nuevo** New Year
**apagado** (ah-pah-*gah*-dhoa) *adj* mat
**apagar** (ah-pah-*gahr*) *v* extinguish; *put out, switch off
**aparato** (ah-pah-*rah*-toa) *m* appliance, apparatus; machine
**aparcamiento** (ah-pahr-kah-*m$^y$ayn*-toa) *m* parking; **zona de ~** parking zone
**aparcar** (ah-pahr-*kahr*) *v* park; shelve
***aparecer** (ah-pah-ray-*thayr*) *v* appear
**aparente** (ah-pah-*rayn*-tay) *adj* apparent
**aparición** (ah-pah-ree-*th$^y$oan*) *f* apparition
**apariencia** (ah-pah-*r$^y$ayn*-th$^y$ah) *f* appearance, semblance
**apartado** (ah-pahr-*tah*-dhoa) *adj* remote; *m* post office box
**apartamento** (ah-pahr-tah-*mayn*-toa) *m* suite; apartment *Am*
**apartar** (ah-pahr-*tahr*) *v* separate
**aparte** (ah-*pahr*-tay) *adv* aside; *adj* individual
**apasionado** (ah-pah-s$^y$oa-*nah*-dhoa) *adj* passionate
**apearse** (ah-pay-*ahr*-say) *v* *get off
**apelación** (ah-pay-lah-*th$^y$oan*) *f* appeal
**apelmazado** (ah-payl-mah-*thah*-dhoa) *adj* lumpy; compacted
**apellido** (ah-pay-*l$^y$ee*-dhoa) *m* family name, surname; **~ de soltera** maiden name
**apenado** (ah-pay-*nah*-dhoa) *adj* sorry, sad
**apenas** (ah-*pay*-nahss) *adv* hardly, barely, scarcely; just
**apéndice** (ah-*payn*-dee-thay) *m* appendix

**apendicitis** (ah-payn-dee-*thee*-teess) *f* appendicitis
**aperitivo** (ah-pay-ree-*tee*-bhoa) *m* aperitif, drink
**apertura** (ah-payr-*too*-rah) *f* opening
**apestar** (ah-payss-*tahr*) *v* *stink
**apetito** (ah-pay-*tee*-toa) *m* appetite
**apetitoso** (ah-pay-tee-*toa*-soa) *adj* appetizing
**apio** (*ah*-p$^y$oa) *m* celery
**aplaudir** (ah-plou-*dheer*) *v* clap
**aplauso** (ah-*plou*-soa) *m* applause
**aplazar** (ah-plah-*thahr*) *v* postpone, adjourn, *put off
**aplicación** (ah-plee-kah-*s$^y$oan*) *f* application
**aplicar** (ah-plee-*kahr*) *v* apply; **aplicarse a** apply, *be valid for
**apodo** (ah-*poa*-dhoa) *m* nickname
**apogeo** (ah-poa-*khayoa*) *m* height; zenith
***apostar** (ah-poass-*tahr*) *v* *bet
**apoyar** (ah-poa-*$^y$ahr*) *v* support; **apoyarse** *v* *lean
**apoyo** (ah-*poa*-$^y$oa) *m* support; assistance
**apreciar** (ah-pray-*th$^y$ahr*) *v* appreciate
**aprecio** (ah-*pray*-th$^y$oa) *m* appreciation
**aprender** (ah-prayn-*dayr*) *v* *learn; **aprenderse de memoria** memorize
**aprendiz** (ah-prayn-*dheeth*) *m*, **-a** *f* apprentice, trainee
**apresar** (ah-pray-*sahr*) *v* hijack
**apresurarse** (ah-pray-soo-*rahr*-say) *v* hasten, hurry
**apretado** (ah-pray-*tah*-dhoa) *adj* tight
***apretar** (ah-pray-*tahr*) *v* press; tighten
**apretón** (ah-pray-*toan*) *m* clutch; **~ de manos** handshake
**aprobación** (ah-proa-bhah-*th$^y$oan*) *f* approval
***aprobar** (ah-proa-*bhahr*) *v* approve; pass
**apropiado** (ah-proa-*p$^y$ah*-dhoa) *adj* appropriate, suitable, proper; fit
**aprovechar** (ah-proa-bhay-*chahr*) *v* profit, benefit
**aproximadamente** (ah-proak-see-mah-dhah-*mayn*-tay) *adv* about, approximately
**aproximado** (ah-proak-see-*mah*-dhoa) *adj* approximate
**aptitud** (ahp-tee-*toodh*) *f* qualification; faculty
**apto** (*ahp*-toa) *adj* suitable; ***ser ~ para** qualify
**apuesta** (ah-*pwayss*-tah) *f* bet
**apuntar** (ah-poon-*tahr*) *v* aim at; point out
**apunte** (ah-*poon*-tay) *m* note; memo; **libreta de apuntes** notebook
**aquel** (ah-*kayl*) *adj*, **-la** *f* that; **aquellos**, **aquellas** *pl* those
**aquél** (ah-*kayl*) *pron*, **-la** *f* that (one); **aquéllos** *pl* those (ones)
**aquello** *pron* that
**aquí** (ah-*kee*) *adv* here
**árabe** (*ah*-rah-bhay) *adj* Arab; *m* Arab
**Arabia Saudí** (ah-*rah*-bh$^y$ah sou-*dhee*) Saudi Arabia
**arado** (ah-*rah*-dhoa) *m* plough
**arancel** (ah-rahn-*thayl*) *m* tariff; duty
**araña** (ah-*rah*-ñah) *f* spider; **tela de ~** cobweb
**arar** (ah-*rahr*) *v* plough
**arbitrario** (ahr-bhee-*trah*-r$^y$oa) *adj* arbitrary
**árbitro** (*ahr*-bhee-troa) *m* referee; umpire; arbitrator
**árbol** (*ahr*-bhoal) *m* tree; **~ de levas** camshaft
**arbusto** (ahr-*bhooss*-toa) *m* shrub
**arca** (*ahr*-kah) *f* chest
**arcada** (ahr-*kah*-dhah) *f* arcade
**arce** (*ahr*-thay) *m* maple
**arcén** (ahr-*thayn*) *m* shoulder; hard shoulder

**arcilla** (ahr-*thee*-l$^{y}$ah) *f* clay
**arco** (*ahr*-koa) *m* arch, bow; **~ iris** rainbow
**archivo** (ahr-*chee*-bhoa) *m* archives *pl*
**arder** (ahr-*dhayr*) *v* *burn
**ardilla** (ahr-*dhee*-l$^{y}$ah) *f* squirrel
**área** (*ah*-ray-ah) *f* area; are
**arena** (ah-*ray*-nah) *f* sand
**arenoso** (ah-ray-*noa*-soa) *adj* sandy
**arenque** (ah-*rayng*-kay) *m* herring
**Argelia** (ahr-*khay*-l$^{y}$ah) *f* Algeria
**argelino** (ahr-khay-*lee*-noa) *adj* Algerian; *m* Algerian
**Argentina** (ahr-khayn-*tee*-nah) *f* Argentina
**argentino** (ahr-khayn-*tee*-noa) *adj* Argentinian; *m* Argentinian
**argumentar** (ahr-goo-mayn-*tahr*) *v* argue
**argumento** (ahr-goo-*mayn*-toa) *m* argument
**árido** (*ah*-ree-dhoa) *adj* arid
**arma** (*ahr*-mah) *f* weapon, arm
**armador** (ahr-mah-*dhoar*) *m* shipowner
**armadura** (ahr-mah-*dhoo*-rah) *f* frame; armour
**armar** (ahr-*mahr*) *v* arm
**armario** (ahr-*mah*-r$^{y}$oa) *m* cupboard; closet
**armonía** (ahr-moa-*nee*-ah) *f* harmony
**aroma** (ah-*roa*-mah) *m* aroma
**arpa** (*ahr*-pah) *f* harp
**arqueado** (ahr-kay-*ah*-dhoa) *adj* arched
**arqueología** (ahr-kay-oa-loa-*khee*-ah) *f* arch(a)eology
**arqueólogo** (ahr-kay-*oa*-loa-goa) *m*, **-a** *f* arch(a)eologist
**arquitecto** (ahr-kee-*tayk*-toa) *m* architect
**arquitectura** (ahr-kee-tayk-*too*-rah) *f* architecture
**arrancar** (ah-rrahng-*kahr*) *v* uproot, pull out; start off
**arrastrar** (ah-rrahss-*trahr*) *v* haul, drag; *draw; **arrastrarse** *v* crawl
**arrecife** (ah-rray-*thee*-fay) *m* reef
**arreglar** (ah-rray-*glahr*) *v* settle; tidy up; repair, fix; **arreglarse con** *make do with
**arreglo** (ah-*rray*-gloa) *m* arrangement; settlement; **con ~ a** in accordance with
**arrendamiento** (ah-rrayn-dah-*m$^{y}$ayn*-toa) *m* lease; **contrato de ~** lease
***arrendar** (ah-rrayn-*dahr*) *v* lease
**arrepentimiento** (ah-rray-payn-tee-*m$^{y}$ayn*-toa) *m* regret, repentance
**arrepentirse** (ah-rray-payn-*teer*-say) *v* be sorry; change one's mind; ~ de regret
**arrestar** (ah-rrayss-*tahr*) *v* arrest
**arresto** (ah-*rrayss*-toa) *m* arrest
**arriba** (ah-*rree*-bhah) *adv* above; upstairs; up
**arriesgado** (ah-rryayz-*gah*-dhoa) *adj* risky
**arriesgar** (ah-rr$^{y}$ayz-*gahr*) *v* venture, risk
**arrodillarse** (ah-rroa-dhee-*l$^{y}$ahr*-say) *v* *kneel
**arrogante** (ah-rroa-*gahn*-tay) *adj* arrogant
**arrojar** (ah-rroa-*khahr*) *v* *throw
**arroyo** (ah-*rroa*-$^{y}$oa) *m* stream, brook
**arroz** (ah-*rroath*) *m* rice
**arruga** (ah-*rroo*-gah) *f* wrinkle
**arrugar** (ah-rroo-*gahr*) *v* wrinkle
**arruinar** (ah-rrwee-*nahr*) *v* ruin; **arruinado** broke
**arte** (*ahr*-tay) *m/f* art; **artes industriales** arts and crafts; **bellas artes** fine arts
**arteria** (ahr-*tay*-r$^{y}$ah) *f* artery; **~ principal** thoroughfare
**artesanía** (ahr-tay-sah-*nee*-ah) *f* handicraft

**artesano** (ahr-tay-*sah*-noa) *m* craftsman
**articulación** (ahr-tee-koo-lah-*th$^y$oan*) *f* joint
**artículo** (ahr-*tee*-koo-loa) *m* article
**artificial** (ahr-tee-fee-*th$^y$ahl*) *adj* artificial
**artificio** (ahr-tee-*fee*-th$^y$oa) *m* artifice
**artista** (ahr-*teess*-tah) *m/f* artist
**artístico** (ahr-*teess*-tee-koa) *adj* artistic
**arzobispo** (ahr-thoa-*bheess*-poa) *m* archbishop
**asa** (*ah*-sah) *f* handle
**asamblea** (ah-sahm-*blay*-ah) *f* assembly, meeting
**asado** (ah-*sah*-doa) *adj* roasted, baked; *m* roast meat
**asalto** (ah-*sahl*-toa) *m* attack; robbery, raid; round
**asar** (ah-*sahr*) *v* roast; **~ en parrilla** roast
**asbesto** (ahdh-*bhayss*-toa) *m* asbestos
**ascensor** (ah-thayn-*soar*) *m* lift; elevator *Am*
**asco** (*ahss*-koa) *m* disgust; **me da ~** I find it disgusting; ¡qué asco! how revolting, how disgusting!
**aseado** (ah-say-*ah*-dhoa) *adj* tidy
**asegurar** (ah-say-goo-*rahr*) *v* assure, insure; **asegurarse de** ascertain
**asesinar** (ah-say-see-*nahr*) *v* murder
**asesinato** (ah-say-see-*nah*-toa) *m* murder, assassination
**asesino** (ah-say-*see*-noa) *m*, **-a** *f* murderer
**asfalto** (ahss-*fahl*-toa) *m* asphalt
**así** (ah-*see*) *adv* thus, so; **~ que** so that
**Asia** (*ah*-s$^y$ah) *f* Asia
**asiático** (ah-*s$^y$ah*-tee-koa) *adj* Asian; *m* Asian
**asiento** (ah-*s$^y$ayn*-toa) *m* seat
**asignación** (ah-seeg-nah-*th$^y$oan*) *f* allowance
**asignar** (ah-seeg-*nahr*) *v* allot; **~ a** assign to
**asilo** (ah-*see*-loa) *m* asylum
**asimismo** (ah-see-*meez*-moa) *adv* also, likewise
***asir** (ah-*seer*) *v* grip
**asistencia** (ah-seess-*tayn*-th$^y$ah) *f* attendance; assistance
**asistente** (ah-seess-*tayn*-tay) *m* assistant
**asistir** (ah-seess-*teer*) *v* assist, aid; **~ a** assist at, attend
**asma** (*ahz*-mah) *f* asthma
**asociación** (ah-soa-th$^y$ah-*th$^y$oan*) *f* association; club, society
**asociado** (ah-soa-*th$^y$ah*-dhoa) *m* associate
**asociar** (ah-soa-*th$^y$ahr*) *v* associate; **asociarse a** join
**asombrar** (ah-soam-*brahr*) *v* amaze, astonish
**asombro** (ah-*soam*-broa) *m* amazement; wonder
**asombroso** (ah-soam-*broa*-soa) *adj* astonishing
**aspecto** (ahss-*payk*-toa) *m* aspect; appearance, look; sight
**áspero** (*ahss*-pay-roa) *adj* harsh; rough
**aspiración** (ahss-pee-rah-*th$^y$oan*) *f* inhalation; aspiration
**aspirador** (ahss-pee-rah-*dhoar*) *m* vacuum cleaner; **pasar el ~** hoover, vacuum *Am*
**aspirar** (ahss-pee-*rahr*) *v* aspire; **~ a** aim at
**aspirina** (ahss-pee-*ree*-nah) *f* aspirin
**asqueroso** (ahss-kay-*roa*-soa) *adj* disgusting
**astilla** (ahss-*tee*-l$^y$ah) *f* splinter; chip
**astillero** (ahss-tee-*l$^y$ay*-roa) *m* shipyard
**astronauta** (ahss-troa-*nou*-tah) *m/f* astronaut

**astronomía** (ahss-troa-noa-*mee*-ah) *f* astronomy
**astucia** (ahss-*too*-th$^{y}$ah) *f* ruse
**astuto** (ahss-*too*-toa) *adj* cunning; clever, sly
**asunto** (ah-*soon*-toa) *m* affair, matter; concern, business; topic
**asustado** (ah-sooss-*tah*-dhoa) *adj* afraid
**asustar** (ah-sooss-*tahr*) *v* scare; **asustarse** *v* *be frightened
**atacar** (ah-tah-*kahr*) *v* attack, assault; *strike
**atadura** (ah-tah-*dhoo*-rah) *f* binding
**atajo** (ah-*tah*-khoa) *m* L.Am. short cut
**atañer** (ah-tah-*ñayr*) *v* concern
**ataque** (ah-*tah*-kay) *m* attack, fit; stroke; ~ **cardíaco** heart attack
**atar** (ah-*tahr*) *v* tie, *bind; fasten; bundle
**atareado** (ah-tah-ray-*ah*-dhoa) *adj* busy
**atardecer** (ah-*tahr-de-thayr*) *v* get dark; *m* dusk
**atasco** (ah-*tahss*-koa) *m* traffic jam
**atención** (ah-tayn-*th$^{y}$oan*) *f* attention; consideration, notice; **prestar ~** *pay attention, look out
***atender a** (ah-tayn-*dayr*) attend to, see to; nurse
**atentamente** (ah-tayn-tah-*mayn-tay*) *adv* attentively; (Yours) sincerely
**atento** (ah-*tayn*-toa) *adj* attentive; thoughtful
**ateo** (ah-*tay*-oa) *m* atheist
**aterido** (ah-tay-*ree*-dhoa) *adj* numb
**aterrador** (ah-tay-rrah-*dhoar*) *adj* terrifying
**aterrizaje** (ah-tay-rree-*thah-khay*) *m* landing; **~ forzoso, ~ de emergencia** emergency landing
**aterrizar** (ah-tay-rree-*thahr*) *v* land
**aterrorizar** (ah-tay-rroa-ree-*thahr*) *v* terrify
**Atlántico** (aht-*lahn*-tee-koa) *m* Atlantic
**atleta** (aht-*lay*-tah) *m* athlete
**atletismo** (aht-lay-*teez*-moa) *m* athletics *pl*
**atmósfera** (aht-*moass*-fay-rah) *f* atmosphere
**atómico** (ah-*toa*-mee-koa) *adj* atomic
**átomo** (*ah*-toa-moa) *m* atom
**atónito** (ah-*toa*-nee-toa) *adj* speechless
**atormentar** (ah-toar-mayn-*tahr*) *v* torment
**atornillar** (ah-toar-nee-*l$^{y}$ahr*) *v* screw
**atracar** (ah-trah-*kahr*) *v* dock
**atracción** (ah-trahk-*th$^{y}$oan*) *f* attraction
**atraco** (ah-*trah*-koa) *m* hold-up
**atractivo** (ah-trahk-*tee*-bhoa) *adj* attractive
***atraer** (ah-trah-*ayr*) *v* attract
**atrapar** (ah-trah-*pahr*) *v* ensnare; trap
**atrás** (ah-*trahss*) *adv* back
**atrasado** (ah-trah-*sah*-dhoa) *adj* overdue; delayed
**atraso** (ah-*trah*-soa) *m* backwardness; **atrasos** arrears
***atravesar** (ah-trah-bhay-*sahr*) *v* cross, pass through
**atreverse** (ah-tray-*bhayr*-say) *v* dare
**atrevido** (ah-tray-*bhee*-dhoa) *adj* daring
***atribuir a** (ah-tree-*bhweer*) assign to
**atropellar** (ah-troh-phay-l$^{y}$*ahr*) *v* knock down
**atroz** (ah-*troath*) *adj* atrocious
**atún** (ah-*toon*) *m* tuna
**audacia** (ou-*dhah*-th$^{y}$ah) *f* audacity
**audaz** (ou-*dhahth*) *adj* audacious; bold
**audible** (ou-*dhee*-bhlay) *adj* audible
**audiencia** (ou- *dh$^{y}$ayn*-th$^{y}$ah) *f* audience; court; **índice de ~** ratings

*pl*
**auditorio** (ou-dhee-*toa*-r$^y$oa) *m* audience
**aula** (*ou*-lah) *f* auditorium; lecture hall
**aumentar** (ou-mayn-*tahr*) *v* increase, raise
**aumento** (ou-*mayn*-toa) *m* increase; rise; raise *Am*
**aun** (ah-*oon*) *adv* (aún) yet; even
**aunque** (*oung*-kay) *conj* although, though
**auricular** (ou-ree kou-*lahr* ) *m* receiver; **auriculares** headphones, earphones
**aurora** (ou-*roa*-rah) *f* dawn
**ausencia** (ou-*sayn*-th$^y$ah) *f* absence
**ausente** (ou-*sayn*-tay) *adj* absent
**Australia** (ouss-*trah*-l$^y$ah) *f* Australia
**australiano** (ouss-trah-*l$^y$ah*-noa) *adj* Australian; *m* Australian
**Austria** (*ouss*-tr$^y$ah) *f* Austria
**austríaco** (ouss-*tree*-ah-koa) *adj* Austrian; *m* Austrian
**auténtico** (ou-*tayn*-tee-koa) *adj* authentic; true, original
**auto** (*ou*-toa) *m* car
**autoadhesivo** (ou-toa-ahdhea-*seeh*-boa) *adj* self-adhesive
**autobús** (ou-toa-*bhooss*) *m* coach, bus
**autocar** (ou-toa-*kahr*) *m* bus
**autocaravana** (ou-toa-kahrah-*bahna*) *f* camper van
**autoestopista** (ou-toa-ayss-toa-*peess*-tah) *m/f* hitchhiker
**automático** (ou-toa-*mah*-tee-koa) *adj* automatic
**automóvil** (ou-toa-*moa*-bheel) *m* motor-car, automobile; **~ club** automobile club
**automovilismo** (ou-toa-moa-bhee-*leez*-moa) *m* motoring
**automovilista** (ou-toa-moa-bhee-*leess*-tah) *m* motorist
**autonomía** (ou-toa-noa-*mee*-ah) *f* self-government
**autónomo** (ou-*toa*-noa-moa) *adj* independent, autonomous
**autopista** (ou-toa-*peess*-tah) *f* motorway; highway *Am*; **~ de peaje** turnpike *Am*
**autopsia** (ou-*toap*-s$^y$ah) *f* autopsy
**autor** (ou-*toar*) *m* author
**autoridad** (ou-toa-ree-*dhahdh*) *f* authority
**autoritario** (ou-toa-ree-*tah*-r$^y$oa) *adj* authoritarian
**autorización** (ou-toa-ree-thah-*th$^y$oan*) *f* authorization; permission
**autorizar** (ou-toa-ree-*thahr*) *v* allow; license
**autoservicio** (ou-toa-sayr-*bhee*-th$^y$oa) *m* self-service
**autostop: *hacer ~** (ah-*thayr* ou-toa-*stoap*) hitchhike
**auxiliar** (ouk-see-*l$^y$ahr*) *adj* auxiliary; *m/f* assistant; **~ de vuelo** stewardess, flight attendant; *v* help
**auxilio** (ouk-*see*-l$^y$oa) *m* assistance; **primeros auxilios** first aid
**avance** (ah-*bhan*-thay) *m* advance
**avalancha** (ah-bhah-*lahn*-chah) *f* avalanche
**avanzar** (ah-bhahn-*thahr*) *v* advance
**avaro** (ah-*bhah*-roa) *adj* avaricious
**ave** (*ah*-bhay) *f* bird; S.Am. chicken; **~ de presa, ~ de rapiña** bird of prey
**avefría** (ah-bhay-*free*-ah) *f* pewit
**avellana** (ah-bhay-*l$^y$ah*-nah) *f* hazelnut
**avena** (ah-*bhay*-nah) *f* oats *pl*
**avenida** (ah-bhay-*nee*-dhah) *f* avenue
**aventura** (ah-bhayn-*too*-rah) *f* adventure
***avergonzarse** (ah-bhayr-goan-*thahr*-say) *v* *be ashamed
**avería** (ah-bhay-*ree*-ah) *f* breakdown
**averiarse** (ah-bhay-*r$^y$ahr*-say) *v* *break down; **averiado** *adj* out of

order
**aversión** (ah-bhayr-*s$^{y}$oan*) *f* aversion, dislike
**avestruz** (ah-bhayss-*trooth*) *m* ostrich
**avión** (ah-*bh$^{y}$oan*) *m* aeroplane; aircraft, plane; airplane *Am*; **~ a reacción** jet; **~ turborreactor** turbojet
**avisar** (ah-bhee-*sahr*) *v* inform
**aviso** (ah-*bhee*-soa) *m* notice
**avispa** (ah-*bheess*-pah) *f* wasp
**ayer** (ah-*$^{y}$ayr*) *adv* yesterday
**ayuda** (ah-*$^{y}$oo*-dhah) *f* help; relief; **~ de cámara** valet
**ayudante** (ah-$^{y}$oo-*dhahn*-tay) *m/f* helper
**ayudar** (ah-$^{y}$oo-*dhahr*) *v* aid, help
**ayuntamiento** (ah-$^{y}$oon-tah-*m$^{y}$ayn*-toa) *m* town hall
**azada** (ah-*thah*-dhah) *f* spade
**azafata** (ah-thah-*fah*-tah) *f* hostess; stewardess
**azar** (ah-*thahr*) *m* chance, luck
**azor** (ah-*thoar*) *m* hawk
**azote** (ah-*thoa*-tay) *m* whip
**azotea** (ah-thoa-*tay*-ah) *f* flat roof; **estar mal de la ~** *colloquial* be crazy
**azúcar** (ah-*thoo*-kahr) *m/f* sugar; **terrón de ~** lump of sugar
**azucena** (ah-thoo-*thay*-nah) *f* lily
**azul** (ah-*thool*) *adj* blue
**azulejo** (ah-thoo-*lay*-khoa) *m* tile

# B

**babor** (bah-*bhoar*) *m* port
**bacalao** (bah-kah-*lah*-oa) *m* cod
**bacteria** (bahk-*tay*-r$^{y}$ah) *f* bacterium
**bache** (*bah*-chay) *m* pothole
**bahía** (bah-*ee*-ah) *f* bay
**bailar** (bigh-*lahr*) *v* dance
**baile** (*bigh*-lay) *m* dance
**baja** (*bah*-khah) *f* slump
**bajada** (bah-*khah*-dhah) *f* descent
**bajamar** (bah-khah-*mahr*) *f* low tide
**bajar** (bah-*khahr*) *v* lower; **bajarse** *v* *bend down
**bajo** (*bah*-khoa) *adj* low; short; *prep* under, below; *m* bass
**bala** (*bah*-lah) *f* bullet
**baladí** (bah-lah-*dhee*) *adj* insignificant
**balance** (bah-*lahn*-thay) *m* balance
**balanza** (bah-*lahn*-thah) *f* scales *pl*
**balbucear** (bahl-bhoo-thay-*ahr*) *v* falter
**balcón** (bahl-*koan*) *m* balcony; circle
**balde** (*bahl*-day) *m* pail, bucket
**balneario** (bahl-nay-*ah*-r$^{y}$oa) *m* spa
**ballena** (bah-*l$^{y}$ay*-nah) *f* whale
**ballet** (bah-*lay*) *m* ballet
**baloncesto** (bah-loan-*thayss*-toa) *m* basketball
**balonmano** (bah-loan-*mah*-noa) *m* handball
**bambú** (bahm-*boo*) *m* bamboo
**banca** (*bahng*-kah) *f* banking; banks *pl*; bank; Méx bench
**bancario** (bahng-*kah*- r$^{y}$oa) *adj* bank
**banco** (*bahng*-koa) *m* bank; bench
**banda** (*bahn*-dah) *f* band; gang
**bandeja** (bahn-*day*-khah) *f* tray
**bandera** (bahn-*day*-rah) *f* flag; banner
**bandido** (bahn-*dee*-dhoa) *m* bandit
**banquete** (bahng-*kay*-tay) *m* banquet
**bañador** (bah-ñah-*dhoar*) *m* swim(ming) trunks, swimsuit
**bañarse** (bah-*ñahr*-say) *v* bathe
**baño** (*bah*-ñoa) *m* bath; *mMe* bathroom; **~ turco** Turkish bath;

**calzón de ~** swim(ming) trunks; **traje de ~** swimsuit

**bar** (bahr) *m* bar; saloon, café

**baranda** (bah-*rahn*-dah) *f* banisters *pl*

**barandilla** (bah-rahn-*dee*-l$^{y}$ah) *f* rail; railing

**barato** (bah-*rah*-toa) *adj* inexpensive, cheap

**barba** (*bahr*-bhah) *f* beard

**barbacoa** (bahr-bhah-*koa*-ah) *f* barbecue

**barbero** (bahr-*bhay*-roa) *m* barber

**barbilla** (bahr-*bhee*-l$^{y}$ah) *f* chin

**barca** (*bahr*-kah) *f* boat

**barco** (*bahr*-koa) *m* boat

**barítono** (bah-*ree*-toa-noa) *m* baritone

**barman** (*bahr*-mahn) *m* bartender, barman

**barniz** (bahr-*neeth*) *m* varnish; **~ para las uñas** nail polish

**barómetro** (bah-*roa*-may-troa) *m* barometer

**barquillo** (bahr-*kee*-l$^{y}$oa) *m* waffle

**barra** (*bah*-rrah) *f* bar, rod; counter

**barrer** (bah-*rrayr*) *v* *sweep

**barrera** (bah-*rray*-rah) *f* barrier, rail; **~ de protección** crash barrier

**barril** (bah-*rreel*) *m* barrel, cask

**barrio** (*bah*-rr$^{y}$oa) *m* quarter, district; **~ bajo** slum

**barroco** (bah-*rroa*-koa) *adj* baroque

**barrote** (bah-*rroa*-tay) *m* thick bar; rung

**basar** (bah-*sahr*) *v* base

**báscula** (*bahss*-koo-lah) *f* scales, weighing machine

**base** (*bah*-say) *f* basis, base

**basílica** (bah-*see*-lee-kah) *f* basilica

**bastante** (bahss-*tahn*-tay) *adv* enough, sufficient; fairly, rather, quite

**bastar** (bahss-*tahr*) *v* suffice

**bastardo** (bahss-*tahr*-dhoa) *m* bastard

**bastón** (bahss-*toan*) *m* cane; walking stick; **bastones de esquí** ski sticks

**basura** (bah-*soo*-rah) *f* trash, rubbish, garbage; **cubo de la ~** rubbish bin

**bata** (*bah*-tah) *f* dressing gown; **~ de baño** bathrobe; **~ suelta** negligee

**batalla** (bah-*tah*-l$^{y}$ah) *f* battle

**batería** (bah-tay-*ree*-ah) *f* battery

**batido** (bah-*tee*-dhoa) *adj* well-trodden; *m* milkshake

**batidora** (bah-tee-*dhoa*-rah) *f* mixer

**batir** (bah-*teer*) *v* *beat, whip

**baúl** (bah-*ool*) *m* trunk

**bautismo** (bou-*teez*-moa) *m* baptism

**bautizar** (bou-tee-*thahr*) *v* christen, baptize

**bautizo** (bou-*tee*-thoa) *m* christening, baptism

**baya** (*bah*-$^{y}$ah) *f* berry

**bebé** (bay-*bhay*) *m* baby

**beber** (bay-*bhayr*) *v* *drink

**bebida** (bay-*bhee*-dhah) *f* drink, beverage; **~ no alcohólica** soft drink; **bebidas espirituosas** spirits

**beca** (*bay*-kah) *f* grant, scholarship

**beige** (*bay*-khay) *adj* beige

**béisbol** (*bayz*-bhoal) *m* baseball

**belga** (*bayl*-gah) *adj* Belgian; *m* Belgian

**Bélgica** (*bayl*-khee-kah) *f* Belgium

**belleza** (bay-*l$^{y}$ay*-thah) *f* beauty; **salón de ~** beauty salon

**bello** (*bay*-l$^{y}$oa) *adj* fine

**bellota** (bay-*l$^{y}$oa*-tah) *f* acorn

***bendecir** (bayn-day-*theer*) *v* bless

**bendición** (bayn-dee-*th$^{y}$oan*) *f* blessing

**beneficio** (bay-nay-*fee*-th$^{y}$oa) *m* profit, benefit

**berenjena** (bay-rayng-*khay*-nah) *f* eggplant

**berro** (*bay*-rroa) *m* watercress

**besar** (bay-*sahr*) *v* kiss

**beso** (*bay*-soa) *m* kiss

**betún** (bay-*toon*) *m* shoe polish
**biblia** (*bee*-bhl$^{y}$ah) *f* bible
**biblioteca** (bee-bhl$^{y}$oa-*tay*-kah) *f* library
**bicho** (*bee*-choa) *m* bug; creepy-crawly; creature; **¿qué ~ te ha picado?** what's eating you?
**bici** (*bee*-thee) *f*, **bicicleta** (bee-thee-*klay*-tah) *f* cycle, bicycle
**bien** (b$^{y}$ayn) *adv* well; **¡bien!** all right!; **bien … bien** either … or
**bienes** (*b$^{y}$ay*-nayss) *mpl* goods *pl*; possessions
**bienestar** (b$^{y}$ay-nayss-*tahr*) *m* ease; welfare
**bienvenida** (b$^{y}$ayn-bhay-*nee*-dhah) *f* welcome; ***dar la ~** welcome
**bienvenido** (b$^{y}$ayn-bhay-*nee*-dhoa) *adj* welcome
**biftec** (beef-*tayk*) *m* steak
**bifurcación** (bee-foor-kah-*th$^{y}$oan*) *f* fork in road
**bifurcarse** (bee-foor-*kahr*-say) *v* fork
**bigote** (bee-*goatay*) *m* moustache
**bilingüe** (bee-*leeng*-gway) *adj* bilingual
**bilis** (*bee*-leess) *f* gall, bile
**billar** (bee-*l$^{y}$ahr*) *m* billiards *pl*
**billete** (bee-*l$^{y}$ay*-tay) *m* ticket; **~ de andén** platform ticket; **~ de banco** banknote; **~ gratuito** free ticket
**biología** (b$^{y}$oa-loa-*khee*-ah) *f* biology
**biológico** (b$^{y}$oa-*loa*-khee-koa) *adj* biological
**bisagra** (bee-*sah*-grah) *f* hinge
**bizco** (*beeth*-koa) *adj* cross-eyed
**bizcocho** (beeth-*koa*-choa) *m* sponge cake
**blanco**[1] (*blahng*-koa) *adj* white; blank
**blanco**[2] (*blahng*-koa) *m* mark, target
**blando** (*blahn*-doa) *adj* soft
**blanquear** (blahng-kay-*ahr*) *v* bleach
**bloc** (bloak) *mMe* writing-pad
**bloque** (*bloa*-kay) *m* block; writing pad
**bloquear** (bloa-kay-*ahr*) *v* block
**blusa** (*bloo*-sah) *f* blouse
**bobina** (boa-*bhee*-nah) *f* spool; **~ del encendido** ignition coil
**bobo** (*boa*-bhoa) *adj* silly; foolish
**boca** (*boa*-kah) *f* mouth
**bocadillo** (boa-kah-*dhee*-l$^{y}$oa) *m* sandwich
**bocado** (boa-*kah*-dhoa) *m* bite
**bocina** (boa-*thee*-nah) *f* horn, hooter; **tocar la ~** hoot, honk *Am*
**boda** (*boa*-dhah) *f* wedding
**bodega** (boa-*dhay*-gah) *f* hold
**bofetada** (boa-fay-*tah*-dhah) *f* smack, slap
**boina** (*boi*-nah) *f* beret
**bola** (*boa*-lah) *f* ball; ball bearing; scoop; fib; **~ de nieve** snowball; **no dar pie con ~** get everything wrong
**bolera** (boa-*lay*-rah) *f* bowling alley
**boletín meteorológico** (boa-lay-*teen* may-tay-oa-roa-*loa*-khee-koa) weather forecast
**boleto** (boa-*lay*-toa) *mMe* ticket
**bolígrafo** (boa-*lee*-grah-foa) *m* ballpoint pen, Biro®
**Bolivia** (boa-*lee*-bh$^{y}$ah) *f* Bolivia
**boliviano** (boa-lee-*bh$^{y}$ah*-noa) *adj* Bolivian; *m* Bolivian
**bolsa** (*boal*-sah) *f* bag; stock market, stock exchange; purse; **~ de hielo** ice bag; **~ de papel** paper bag
**bolsillo** (boal-*see*-l$^{y}$oa) *m* pocket
**bolso** (*boal*-soa) *m* handbag; bag
**bollo** (*boa*-l$^{y}$oa) *m* bun
**bomba** (*boam*-bah) *f* pump; bomb; **~ de agua** water pump; **~ de gasolina** petrol pump; fuel pump *Am*
**bombardear** (boam-bahr-dhay-*ahr*) *v* bomb
**bombear** (boam-bay-*ahr*) *v* pump
**bomberos** (boam-*bay*-roass) *mpl* fire brigade, fire department *Am*

**bombilla** (boam-*bee*-lʸah) *f* light bulb; **~ de flash** flash bulb
**bombón** (boam-*boan*) *m* chocolate; candy *Am*
**bondad** (boan-*dahdh*) *f* goodness
**bondadoso** (boan-dah-*dhoa*-soa) *adj* good-natured, kind
**bonito** (boa-*nee*-toa) *adj* pretty; fair, nice, lovely
**boquilla** (boa-*kee*-lʸah) *f* cigarette holder
**bordado** (boar-*dhah*-dhoa) *m* embroidery
**bordar** (boar-*dhahr*) *v* embroider
**borde** (*boar*-dhay) *m* edge, border; verge, rim, brim; **~ del camino** wayside
**bordillo** (boar-*dhee*-lʸoa) *m* curb
**bordo: a ~** (ah *boar*-doa) aboard
**borracho** (boa-*rrah*-choa) *adj* drunk
**borrar** (boa-*rrahr*) *v* erase
**borrascoso** (boa-rrahss-*koa*-soa) *adj* gusty
**borrón** (boa-*rroan*) *m* blot
**bosque** (*boass*-kay) *m* wood, forest
**bosquejar** (boass-kay-*khahr*) *v* sketch
**bosquejo** (boass-*kay*-khoa) *m* sketch
**bostezar** (boass-tay-*thahr*) *v* yawn
**bota** (*boa*-tah) *f* boot; **botas de esquí** ski boots
**botadura** (boa-tah-*dhoo*-rah) *f* launching
**botánica** (boa-*tah*-nee-kah) *f* botany
**bote** (*boa*-tay) *m* row(ing) boat; **~ a motor** motorboat
**botella** (boa-*tay*-lʸah) *f* bottle
**botón** (boa-*toan*) *m* button; knob, push-button; **~ del cuello** collar stud
**botones** (boa-*toa*-nayss) *mpl* bellboy
**bóveda** (*boa*-bhay-dhah) *f* vault, arch
**boxear** (boak-say-*ahr*) *v* box
**boya** (*boa*-ʸah) *f* buoy
**braga** (*brah*-gah) *f* briefs *pl*; panties *pl*
**bragueta** (brah-*gay*-tah) *f* fly
**branquia** (*brahng*-kʸah) *f* gill
**Brasil** (brah-*seel*) *m* Brazil
**brasileño** (brah-see-*lay*-ñoa) *adj* Brazilian; *m* Brazilian
**braza** (*brah*-thah) *f* breaststroke; **~ de mariposa** butterfly stroke
**brazalete** (brah-thah-*lay*-tay) *m* bracelet; armband
**brazo** (*brah*-thoa) *m* arm; **del ~** arm-in-arm
**brea** (*bray*-ah) *f* tar
**brecha** (*bray*-chah) *f* breach
**bregar** (bray-*gahr*) *v* labo(u)r
**breve** (*bray*-bhay) *adj* brief; **en ~** soon
**brezal** (bray-*thahl*) *m* moor
**brezo** (*bray*-thoa) *m* heather
**brillante** (bree-*lʸahn*-tay) *adj* brilliant
**brillar** (bree-*lʸahr*) *v* glow, *shine
**brillo** (*bree*-lʸoa) *m* glow, gloss
**brincar** (breeng-*kahr*) *v* hop; skip
**brindar** (breen-*dahr*) *v* offer; *v* drink a toast
**brindis** (*breen*-deess) *m* toast
**brisa** (*bree*-sah) *f* breeze
**británico** (bree-*tah*-nee-koa) *adj* British; *m* Briton
**brocha** (*broa*-chah) *f* brush; **~ de afeitar** shaving brush
**broche** (*broa*-chay) *m* brooch
**broma** (*broa*-mah) *f* joke
**bronca** (*broang*-kah) *f* row
**bronce** (*broan*-thay) *m* bronze; **de ~** bronze
**bronceado** (broan-thay-*ah*-doa) *adj* tanned; *m* suntan
**bronquitis** (broang-*kee*-teess) *f* bronchitis
**brotar** (broa-*tahr*) *v* bud
**bruja** (*broo*-khah) *f* witch
**brújula** (*broo*-khoo-lah) *f* compass
**brumoso** (broo-*moa*-soa) *adj* foggy; hazy
**brutal** (broo-*tahl*) *adj* brutal
**bruto** (*broo*-toa) *adj* gross

**bucear** (boo-thay-*ahr*) *v* dive
**bueno** (*bway*-noa) *adj* good; kind; sound; **¡bueno!** well!
**buey** (bway) *m* ox
**bufanda** (boo-*fahn*-dah) *f* scarf
**buffet** (boof-*fayt*) *m* buffet
**buhardilla** (bwahr-*dee*-l$^y$ah) *f* attic
**buho** (*boo*-oa) *m* owl
**buitre** (*bwee*-tray) *m* vulture
**bujía** (boo-*khee*-ah) *f* spark(ing) plug
**Bulgaria** (bool-*gah*-r$^y$ah) *f* Bulgaria
**búlgaro** (*bool*-gah-roa) *adj* Bulgarian; *m* Bulgarian
**bulto** (*bool*-toa) *m* bulk
**bulla** (*boo*-l$^y$ah) *f* fuss
**buque** (*boo*-kay) *m* ship; vessel; **~ a motor** launch; **~ cisterna** tanker; **~ de guerra** man-of-war; **~ velero** sail(ing) boat
**burbuja** (boor-*boo*-khah) *f* bubble
**burdel** (boor-*dhayl*) *m* brothel
**burdo** (*boor*-dhoa) *adj* coarse
**burgués** (boor-*gayss*) *adj* middleclass, bourgeois
**burla** (*boor*-lah) *f* mockery
**burlarse de** (boor-*lahr*-say) mock
**burocracia** (boo-roa-*krah*-th$^y$ah) *f* bureaucracy
**burro** (*boo*-rroa) *m* donkey
**buscar** (booss-*kahr*) *v* look for; look up, *seek, search; hunt for; ***ir a ~** *get, pick up, fetch
**búsqueda** (*booss*-kay-dhah) *f* search
**busto** (*booss*-toa) *m* bust
**butaca** (boo-*tah*-kah) *f* armchair, easy chair; stall; orchestra seat *Am*
**buzón** (boo-*thoan*) *m* pillar box, letter box; mailbox *Am*

# C

**caballero** (kah-bhah-*l$^y$ay*-roa) *m* gentleman; knight
**caballitos** (kah-bhah-*l$^y$ee*-toass) *mpl* merry-go-round
**caballo** (kah-*bhah*-l$^y$oa) *m* horse; **~ de carrera** racehorse; **~ de vapor** horsepower
**cabaña** (kah-*bhah*-ñah) *f* cabin, hut
**cabaret** (kah-bhah-*rayt*) *m* cabaret
**cabecear** (kah-bhay-thay-*ahr*) *v* nod
**cabeceo** (kah-bhay-*thay*-oa) *m* nod
**cabello** (kah-*bhay*-l$^y$oa) *m* hair; **suavizante de ~** conditioner
**cabelludo** (kah-bhay-*l$^y$oo*-dhoa) *adj* hairy
**caber** (kah-*bhayr*) *v* fit; **caben tres litros** it holds three litres (*Am* liters); **cabemos todos** there's room for all of us; **no cabe duda** there's no doubt; **no me cabe en la cabeza** I just don't understand
**cabeza** (kah-*bhay*-thah) *f* head; **~ de turco** scapegoat; **dolor de ~** headache
**cabezudo** (kah-bhay-*thoo*-dhoa) *adj* headstrong, stubborn
**cabina** (kah-*bhee*-nah) *f* cabin; booth; **~ telefónica** telephone booth
**cable** (*kah*-bhlay) *m* cable
**cabo** (*kah*-bhoa) *m* cape
**cabra** (*kah*-bhrah) *f* goat
**cabritilla** (kah-bhree-*tee*-l$^y$ah) *f* kid
**cabrón** (kah-*bhroan*) *m* goat
**cacahuate** (kah-kah-*wah*-tay) *mMe* peanut
**cacahuete** (kah-kah-*way*-tay) *m* peanut
**cacerola** (kah-thay-*roa*-lah) *f*

saucepan
**cachear** (kah-chay-*ahr*) *v* search
**cachivache** (kah-chee-*bhah*-chay) *m* junk
**cada** (*kah*-dhah) *adj* every, each; **~ uno** everyone
**cadáver** (kah-*dhah*-bhayr) *m* corpse
**cadena** (kah-*dhay*-nah) *f* chain
**cadera** (kah-*dhay*-rah) *f* hip
**caducado** (kah-dhoo-*kah*-dhoa) *adj* expired
***caer** (kah-*ayr*) *v* *fall; **dejar ~** drop
**café** (kah-*fay*) *m* coffee; coffee shop
**cafeína** (kah-fay-*ee*-nah) *f* caffeine
**cafetera** (kah-fay-*tay*-rah) *f* coffee maker; coffee pot; **~ filtradora** percolator
**cafetería** (kah-fay-tay-*ree*-ah) *f* snack bar, cafeteria
**caída** (kah-*ee*-dhah) *f* fall
**caja** (*kah*-khah) *f* box; crate; pay desk; cashier *Am*; **~ de ahorros** savings bank; **~ de cartón** carton; **~ de caudales** safe, vault; **~ de cerillas** matchbox; **~ de colores** paintbox; **~ de velocidades** gearbox; **~ fuerte** safe; **~ metálica** canister
**cajero** (kah-*khay*-roa) *m* cashier; **~ automático** cash dispenser, ATM
**cajón** (kah-*khoan*) *m* drawer
**cal** (kahl) *f* lime
**calabacín** (kah-lah-bah-*theen*) *m* squash
**calamar** (kah-lah-*mahr*) *m* squid
**calambre** (kah-*lahm*-bray) *m* cramp
**calamidad** (kah-lah-mee-*dhahdh*) *f* disaster
**calcetín** (kahl-thay-*teen*) *m* sock
**calcio** (*kahl*-th$^{y}$oa) *m* calcium
**calculadora** (kahl-koo-lah-*dhoa*-rah) *f* calculator
**calcular** (kahl-koo-*lahr*) *v* reckon, calculate
**cálculo** (*kahl*-koo-loa) *m* calculation; **~ biliar** gallstone
**caldo** (*kahl*-doa) *m* stock; **~ de cultivo** breeding ground
**calefacción** (kah-lay-fahk-*th$^{y}$oan*) *f* heating
**calefactor** (kah-lay-fahk-*toar*) *m* heater
**calendario** (kah-layn-*dah*-r$^{y}$oa) *m* calendar
**calentador** (kah-layn-tah-*dhoar*) *m* heater; **~ de agua** water heater
***calentar** (kah-layn-*tahr*) *v* warm, heat
**calidad** (kah-lee-*dhahdh*) *f* quality; **de primera ~** first-class
**caliente** (kah-*l$^{y}$ayn*-tay) *adj* warm, hot
**calificado** (kah-lee-fee-*kah*-dhoa) *adj* qualified
**calina** (kah-*lee*-nah) *f* haze
**calinoso** (kah-lee-*noa*-soa) *adj* hazy
**calma** (*kahl*-mah) *f* calm
**calmante** (kahl-*mahn*-tay) *m* tranquillizer, sedative
**calmar** (kahl-*mahr*) *v* calm down; **calmarse** *v* calm down
**calor** (kah-*loar*) *m* warmth, heat
**caloría** (kah-loa-*ree*-ah) *f* calorie
**calorífero** (kah-loa-*ree*-fay-roa) *m* hotwater bottle
**calvo** (*kahl*-bhoa) *adj* bald
**calzada** (kahl-*thah*-dhah) *f* carriageway, causeway; drive
**calzado** (kahl-*thah*-dhoa) *m* footwear
**calzoncillos** (kahl-thoan-*thee*-l$^{y}$oass) *mpl* pants *pl*, briefs *pl*, drawers; shorts *plAm*
**callado** (kah-*l$^{y}$ah*-dhoa) *adj* silent, quiet
**callarse** (kah-*l$^{y}$ahr*-say) *v* *be silent
**calle** (*kah*-l$^{y}$ay) *f* street; road; **~ lateral** side street; **~ mayor** main street
**callejón** (kah-l$^{y}$ay-*khoan*) *m* alley, lane; **~ sin salida** cul-de-sac
**callo** (*kah*-l$^{y}$oa) *m* callus; corn

**cama** (*kah*-mah) *f* bed; ~ **de tijera** camp-bed; cot *Am*; **camas gemelas** twin beds; ~ **y desayuno** bed and breakfast
**cámara** (*kah*-mah-rah) *f* camera; ~ **fotográfica** camera
**camarada** (kah-mah-*rah*-dhah) *m* comrade
**camarera** (kah-mah-*ray*-rah) *f* waitress
**camarero** (kah-mah-*ray*-roa) *m* waiter; steward; **jefe de camareros** head waiter
**camarón** (kah-mah-*roan*) *m* shrimp
**cambiar** (kahm-*bʸahr*) *v* alter, change; vary; exchange, switch; ~ **de marcha** change gear
**cambio** (*kahm*-bʸoa) *m* change, variation; turn; alteration; exchange; exchange rate; **oficina de** ~ money exchange
**camello** (kah-*may*-lʸoa) *m* camel
**caminar** (kah-mee-*nahr*) *v* *go; hike
**caminata** (kah-mee-*nah*-tah) *f* walk
**camino** (kah-*mee*-noa) *m* way; road; **a mitad de** ~ halfway; **borde del** ~ roadside; ~ **de** bound for; ~ **en obras** road up; ~ **principal** main road
**camión** (kah-*mʸoan*) *m* lorry; truck *Am*
**camioneta** (kah-mʸoa-*nay*-tah) *f* van
**camisa** (kah-*mee*-sah) *f* shirt
**camiseta** (kah-mee-*say*-tah) *f* undershirt; vest
**camisón** (kah-mee-*soan*) *m* nightdress
**campamento** (kahm-pah-*mayn*-toa) *m* camp
**campana** (kahm-*pah*-nah) *f* bell
**campanario** (kahm-pah-*nah*-rʸoa) *m* steeple
**campaña** (kahm-*pah*-ñah) *f* campaign; **catre de** ~ camp bed
**campeón** (kahm-pay-*oan*) *m* champion
**campesino** (kahm-pay-*see*-noa) *m* peasant
**camping** (*kahm*-peeng) *m* camping site, camping
**campo** (*kahm*-poa) *m* countryside, country; field; ~ **de aviación** airfield; ~ **de golf** golf course; ~ **de tenis** tennis court; **día de** ~ picnic
**Canadá** (kah-nah-*dhah*) *m* Canada
**canadiense** (kah-nah-*dhʸayn*-say) *adj* Canadian; *m* Canadian
**canal** (kah-*nahl*) *m* canal; channel; **Canal de la Mancha** English Channel
**canario** (kah-*nah*-rʸoa) *m* canary
**cancelación** (kahn-thay-lah-*thʸoan*) *f* cancellation
**cancelar** (kahn-thay-*lahr*) *v* cancel
**cáncer** (*kahn*-thayr) *m* cancer
**canción** (kahn-*thʸoan*) *f* song
**cancha** (*kahn*-chah) *f* tennis court
**candado** (kahn-*dah*-dhoa) *m* padlock
**candelabro** (kahn-day-*lah*-bhroa) *m* candelabrum
**candidato** (kahn-dee-*dhah*-toa) *m* candidate
**canela** (kah-*nay*-lah) *f* cinnamon
**cangrejo** (kahng-*gray*-khoa) *m* crab
**canguro** (kahng-*goo*-roa) *m* kangaroo
**canica** (kah-*nee*-kah) *f* marble
**canoa** (kah-*noa*-ah) *f* canoe
**cansancio** (kahn-*sahn*-thʸoa) *m* fatigue
**cansar** (kahn-*sahr*) *v* tire; **cansado** tired, weary
**cantadora** (kahn-tah-*dhoa*-rah) *f* singer
**cantante** (kahn-*tahn*-tay) *m* singer
**cantar** (kahn-*tahr*) *v* *sing
**cántaro** (*kahn*-tah-roa) *m* pitcher; jug
**cantera** (kahn-*tay*-rah) *f* quarry
**cantidad** (kahn-tee-*dhahdh*) *f* amount, quantity; number; lot

**cantina** (kahn-*tee*-nah) *f* canteen; *fMe* saloon
**canto** (*kahn*-toa) *m* singing; edge
**caña** (*kah*-ñah) *f* cane; **~ de pescar** fishing rod
**cañada** (kah-*ñah*-dhah) *f* glen; gully, ravine
**cáñamo** (*kah*-ñah-moa) *m* hemp
**cañón** (kah-*ñoan*) *m* gun; gorge
**caos** (*kah*-oass) *m* chaos
**caótico** (kah-*oa*-tee-koa) *adj* chaotic
**capa** (*kah*-pah) *f* cloak, cape; layer, deposit
**capacidad** (kah-pah-thee-*dhahdh*) *f* capacity
**capaz** (kah-*pahth*) *adj* able; capable; ***ser ~ de** *be able to; qualify
**capellán** (kah-pay-*$l^y$ahn*) *m* chaplain
**capilla** (kah-*pee*-$l^y$ah) *f* chapel
**capital** (kah-pee-*tahl*) *m* capital; *adj* capital
**capitalismo** (kah-pee-tah-*leez*-moa) *m* capitalism
**capitán** (kah-pee-*tahn*) *m* captain
**capitulación** (kah-pee-too-lah-*$th^y$oan*) *f* capitulation
**capítulo** (kah-*pee*-too-loa) *m* chapter
**capó** (kah-*poa*) *m* bonnet; hood *Am*
**capricho** (kah-*pree*-choa) *m* fancy, whim
**cápsula** (*kahp*-soo-lah) *f* capsule
**captura** (kahp-*too*-rah) *f* capture
**capturar** (kahp-too-*rahr*) *v* capture
**capucha** (kah-*poo*-chah) *f* hood
**capullo** (kah-*poo*-$l^y$oa) *m* bud
**caqui** (*kah*-kee) *m* khaki
**cara** (*kah*-rah) *f* face
**caracol** (kah-rah-*koal*) *m* snail; **~ marino** winkle
**carácter** (kah-*rahk*-tayr) *m* character
**característica** (kah-rahk-tay-*reess*-tee-kah) *f* characteristic, feature; quality
**característico** (kah-rahk-tay-*reess*-tee-koa) *adj* typical, characteristic
**caracterizar** (kah-rahk-tay-ree-*thahr*) *v* characterize, mark
**caramelo** (kah-rah-*may*-loa) *m* caramel, toffee, sweet
**caravana** (kah-rah-*bhah*-nah) *f* caravan; trailer *Am*
**carbón** (kahr-*bhoan*) *m* coal; **~ de leña** charcoal
**carburador** (kahr-bhoo-rah-*dhoar*) *m* carburet(t)or
**cárcel** (*kahr*-thayl) *f* jail, gaol
**carcelero** (kahr-thay-*lay*-roa) *m* jailer
**cardenal** (kahr-dhay-*nahl*) *m* cardinal
**cardinal** (kahr-dhee-*nahl*) *adj* cardinal
**cardo** (*kahr*-dhoa) *m* thistle
***carecer** (kah-ray-*thayr*) *v* lack
**carencia** (kah-*rayn*-$th^y$ah) *f* want, shortage
**carga** (*kahr*-gah) *f* charge; cargo, freight, load; batch
**cargar** (kahr-*gahr*) *v* charge; load
**cargo** (*kahr*-goa) *m* office; freight
**caridad** (kah-ree-*dhahdh*) *f* charity
**carillón** (kah-ree-*$l^y$oan*) *m* chimes *pl*
**cariño** (kah-*ree*-ñoa) *m* affection; pet
**cariñoso** (kah-ree-*ñoa*-soa) *adj* affectionate
**carmesí** (kahr-may-*see*) *adj* crimson
**carnaval** (kahr-nah-*bhahl*) *m* carnival
**carne** (*kahr*-nay) *f* meat; flesh; **~ de cerdo** pork; **~ de gallina** goose flesh; **~ de ternera** veal; **~ de vaca** beef
**carné** (kahr-*nay*) *m* card
**carnero** (kahr-*nay*-roa) *m* mutton
**carnet** (kahr-*nayt*) *m* card; **~ de conducir** driver's license *Am*, driving licence; **~ de identidad** identity card
**carnicero** (kahr-nee-*thay*-roa) *m* butcher
**caro** (*kah*-roa) *adj* expensive, dear
**carpa** (*kahr*-pah) *f* carp

**carpintero** (kahr-peen-*tay*-roa) *m* carpenter
**carrera** (kah-*rray*-rah) *f* career; race; ~ **de caballos** horserace; **pista para carreras** racetrack
**carrete** (kah-*rray*-tay) *m* (roll of) film; ~ **de hilo** reel of thread
**carretera** (kah-rray-*tay*-rah) *f* highway
**carretilla** (kah-rray-*tee*-l$^y$ah) *f* wheelbarrow
**carril** (kah-*rreel*) *m* lane; **carril-bici** cycle lane; **carril-bus** bus lane
**carro** (*kah*-rroa) *m* cart; wagon; cartload; *Me* car
**carrocería** (kah-rroa-thay-*ree*-ah) *f* coachwork
**carroza** (kah-*rroa*-thah) *f* coach; carriage
**carta** (*kahr*-tah) *f* map; letter; menu; playing card; ~ **certificada** registered letter; ~ **de crédito** letter of credit; ~ **de recomendación** letter of recommendation; ~ **de vinos** wine list; ~ **marina** chart
**cartel** (kahr-*tayl*) *m* poster, placard
**cárter** (*kahr*-tayr) *m* crankcase
**cartera** (kahr-*tay*-rah) *f* bag; satchel; wallet
**cartero** (kahr-*tay*-roa) *m* postman; mailman
**cartón** (kahr-*toan*) *m* cardboard; carton; **de** ~ cardboard
**cartucho** (kahr-*too*-choa) *m* cartridge
**casa** (*kah*-sah) *f* house; home; **a** ~ home; **ama de** ~ housewife; ~ **de campo** cottage; ~ **de correos** post-office; ~ **del párroco** vicarage; ~ **de pisos** block of flats; apartment house *Am*; ~ **de reposo** rest home; ~ **flotante** houseboat; ~ **señorial** manor house; **en** ~ at home; indoors, indoor, home; **gobierno de la** ~ housekeeping
**casado** (kah-*sah*-doah) *adj* married; **recién** ~ newly-wed
**casarse** (kah-*sahr*-say) *v* marry
**cascada** (kahss-*kah*-dhah) *f* waterfall
**cascanueces** (kahss-kah-*nway*-thayss) *m* nutcrackers *pl*
**cáscara** (*kahss*-kah-rah) *f* shell; skin; ~ **de nuez** nutshell
**casco** (*kahss*-koa) *m* helmet; hoof
**casero** (kah-*say*-roa) *adj* homemade; homeloving; domestic
**casi** (*kah*-see) *adv* almost, nearly
**casino** (kah-*see*-noa) *m* casino
**caso** (*kah*-soa) *m* event; case; instance; ~ **de urgencia** emergency; **en** ~ **de** in case of; **en ningún** ~ by no means; **en tal** ~ then; **en todo** ~ at any rate, anyway
**caspa** (*kahss*-pah) *f* dandruff
**casquillo** (kahss-*kee*-l$^y$oa) *m* socket
**castaña** (kahss-*tah*-ñah) *f* chestnut
**castellano** (kahss-tay-*l$^y$ah*-noa) *adj* Castilian; *m* Castilian
**castigar** (kahss-tee-*gahr*) *v* punish
**castigo** (kahss-*tee*-goa) *m* penalty, punishment
**castillo** (kahss-*tee*-l$^y$oa) *m* castle
**casto** (*kahss*-toa) *adj* chaste; pure
**castor** (kahss-*toar*) *m* beaver
**casualidad** (kah-swah-lee-*dhahdh*) *f* chance; coincidence; **por** ~ by chance
**catacumba** (kah-tah-*koom*-bah) *f* catacomb
**catálogo** (kah-*tah*-loa-goa) *m* catalogue
**catarro** (kah-*tah*-rroa) *m* cold, catarrh
**catástrofe** (kah-*tahss*-troa-fay) *f* disaster, catastrophe, calamity
**catedral** (kah-tay-*dhrahl*) *f* cathedral
**catedrático** (kah-tay-*dhrah*-tee-koa) *m* professor
**categoría** (kah-tay-goa-*ree*-ah) *f* category
**católico** (kah-*toa*-lee-koa) *adj* catholic, Roman Catholic

**catorce** (kah-*toar*-thay) *num* fourteen
**caucho** (*kou*-choa) *m* rubber
**causa** (*kou*-sah) *f* cause, reason; case; lawsuit; **a ~ de** because of, on account of, for, owing to
**causar** (kou-*sahr*) *v* cause
**cautela** (kou-*tay*-lah) *f* caution
**cautivar** (kou-tee-*bhahr*) *v* fascinate
**cava** (*kah*-bah) *m* cava, sparkling wine
**cavar** (kah-*bhahr*) *v* *dig
**caviar** (kah-*bh*ʸ*ahr*) *m* caviar
**cavidad** (kah-bhee-*dhahdh*) *f* cavity
**caza** (*kah*-thah) *f* chase, hunt; game; **apeadero de ~** lodge
**cazador** (kah-thah-*dhoar*) *m*, **-a** *f* hunter
**cazar** (kah-*thahr*) *v* hunt; chase; **~ en vedado** poach
**cazo** (kah-thoa) *m* saucepan
**cazuela** (ka-thoo-ay-lah) *f* pan
**cebada** (thay-*bhah*-dhah) *f* barley
**cebo** (*thay*-bhoa) *m* bait
**cebolla** (thay-*bhoa*-lʸah) *f* onion
**cebollino** (thay-bhoa-*l*ʸ*ee*-noa) *m* chives *pl*
**cebra** (*thay*-bhrah) *f* zebra
**ceder** (thay-*dhayr*) *v* indulge, *give in
***cegar** (thay-*gahr*) *v* blind
**ceja** (*thay*-khah) *f* eyebrow
**celda** (*thayl*-dah) *f* cell
**celebración** (thay-lay-bhrah-*th*ʸ*oan*) *f* celebration
**celebrar** (thay-lay-*bhrahr*) *v* celebrate
**célebre** (*thay*-lay-bhray) *adj* famous
**celebridad** (thay-lay-bhree-*dhahdh*) *f* celebrity
**celeste** (thay-*layss*-tay) *adj* heavenly; celestial
**celibato** (thay-lee-*bhah*-toa) *m* celibacy
**celo** (*thay*-loa) *m* zeal; **celos** jealousy
**celofán** (thay-loa-*fahn*) *m* cellophane
**celoso** (thay-*loa*-soa) *adj* zealous; envious, jealous
**célula** (*thay*-loo-lah) *f* cell
**cementerio** (thay-mayn-*tay*-rʸoa) *m* churchyard, graveyard, cemetery
**cemento** (thay-*mayn*-toa) *m* cement
**cena** (*thay*-nah) *f* dinner, supper
**cenar** (thay-*nahr*) *v* dine, *eat
**cenicero** (thay-nee-*thay*-roa) *m* ashtray
**cenit** (thay-*neet*) *m* zenith
**ceniza** (thay-*nee*-thah) *f* ash
**censura** (thayn-*soo*-rah) *f* censorship
**centelleante** (thayn-tay-lʸay-*ahn*-tay) *adj* sparkling
**centígrado** (thayn-*tee*-grah-dhoa) *adj* centigrade
**centímetro** (thayn-*tee*-may-troa) *m* centimetre, centimeter *Am*
**central** (thayn-*trahl*) *adj* central; **~ eléctrica** power station; **~ telefónica** telephone exchange
**centralizar** (thayn-trah-lee-*thahr*) *v* centralize
**centro** (*thayn*-troa) *m* centre, center *Am*; **~ comercial** shopping centre, mall; **~ de la ciudad** town centre; **~ de recreo** recreation centre
**cepillar** (thay-pee-*l*ʸ*ahr*) *v* brush
**cepillo** (thay-*pee*-lʸoa) *m* brush; **~ de dientes** toothbrush; **~ de la ropa** clothes brush; **~ para el cabello** hairbrush; **~ para las uñas** nailbrush
**cera** (*thay*-rah) *f* wax
**cerámica** (thay-*rah*-mee-kah) *f* ceramics *pl*; crockery, pottery
**cerca** (*thayr*-kah) *f* fence
**cerca de** (*thayr*-kah day) near, by; almost
**cercano** (thayr-*kah*-noa) *adj* close, nearby, near
**cercar** (thayr-*kahr*) *v* encircle, surround
**cerdo** (*thayr*-dhoa) *m* pig
**cereales** (thay-ray-*ah*-layss) *mpl*

cereals, grain
**cerebro** (thay-*ray*-bhroa) *m* brain; **conmoción cerebral** concussion
**ceremonia** (thay-ray-*moa*-nʸah) *f* ceremony
**cereza** (thay-*ray*-thah) *f* cherry
**cerilla** (thay-*ree*-lʸah) *f* match
**cerillo** (thay-*ree*-lʸoa) *mMe* match
**cero** (*thay*-roa) *m* zero, nought
**cerrado** (thay-*rrah*-dhoa) *adj* closed; narrow-minded; introverted; overcast; **curva cerrada** tight curve
**cerradura** (thay-rrah-*dhoo*-rah) *f* lock; **ojo de la ~** keyhole
***cerrar** (thay-*rrahr*) *v* close, *shut; fasten; turn off; **~ con llave** lock
**cerrojo** (thay-*rroa*-khoa) *m* bolt
**certificación** (thayr-tee-fee-kah-*thʸoan*) *f* certificate
**certificado** (thayr-tee-fee-*kah*-dhoa) *m* certificate; **~ de salud** health certificate
**certificar** (thayr-tee-fee-*kahr*) *v* register
**cervecería** (thayr-bhay-thay-*ree*-ah) *f* brewery
**cerveza** (thayr-*bhay*-thah) *f* beer; ale
**cesar** (thay-*sahr*) *v* cease, quit, stop, discontinue
**césped** (*thayss*-paydh) *m* lawn; grass
**cesta** (*thayss*-tah) *f* basket
**cesto** (*thayss*-toa) *m* hamper; **~ para papeles** wastepaper basket
**chabacano** (chah-bhah-*kah*-noa) *mMe* apricot
**chal** (chahl) *m* shawl
**chaleco** (chah-*lay*-koa) *m* waistcoat; vest *Am*; **~ salvavidas** lifebelt
**chalet** (chah-*layt*) *m* chalet
**champán** (chahm-*pahn*) *m* champagne
**champú** (chahm-*poo*) *m* shampoo
**chantaje** (chahn-*tah*-khay) *m* blackmail; ***hacer ~** blackmail
**chapa** (*chah*-pah) *f* plate, sheet
**chaparrón** (chah-pah-*rroan*) *m* cloudburst
**chapucero** (chah-poo-*thay*-roa) *adj* sloppy
**chaqueta** (chah-*kay*-tah) *f* jacket; **~ de lana** cardigan; **~ ligera** blazer
**charanga** (chah-*rahng*-gah) *f* brass band
**charco** (*chahr*-koa) *m* puddle; pool
**charla** (*chahr*-lah) *f* chat
**charlar** (chahr-*lahr*) *v* chat
**chasis** (chah-*seess*) *m* chassis
**checo** (*chay*-koa) *adj* Czech; *m* Czech
**cheque** (*chay*-kay) *m* cheque; check *Am*; **~ de viajero** traveller's cheque
**chicle** (*chee*-klay) *m* chewing gum
**chica** (*chee*-kah) *f* girl
**chico** (*chee*-koa) *m* boy; kid
**chichón** (chee-*choan*) *m* lump
**Chile** (*chee*-lay) *m* Chile
**chileno** (chee-*lay*-noa) *adj* Chilean; *m* Chilean
**chillar** (chee-*lʸahr*) *v* scream, shriek
**chillido** (chee-*lʸee*-dhoa) *m* scream, shriek
**chimenea** (chee-may-*nay*-ah) *f* chimney; fireplace
**China** (*chee*-nah) *f* China
**chinche** (*cheen*-chay) *f* bug; drawing pin; thumbtack *Am*
**chino** (*chee*-noa) *adj* Chinese; *m* Chinese; *adjMe* curly
**chiringuito** (chee-reen-*gee*-toa) *m* beach bar
**chisme** (*cheez*-may) *m* gossip; ***contar chismes** gossip
**chispa** (*cheess*-pah) *f* spark
**chiste** (*chees*-tay) *m* joke
**chistoso** (cheess-*toa*-soa) *adj* witty, humorous
**chocante** (choa-*kahn*-tay) *adj* revolting, shocking
**chocar** (choa-*kahr*) *v* collide, crash,

bump; shock; ~ **contra** knock against
**chocolate** (choa-koa-*lah*-tay) *m* chocolate
**chófer** (*choa*-fayr) *m* chauffeur
**choque** (*choa*-kay) *m* crash; shock
**chorizo** (choa-*ree*-thoa) *m* chorizo; *colloquial* thief; rump steak
**chorro** (*choa*-rroa) *m* spout, jet
**chubasco** (choo-*bahs*-koa) *m* shower
**chuleta** (choo-*lay*-tah) *f* chop, cutlet
**chulo** (*choo*-loa) *colloquial adj* fantastic, great; *adj Me* attractive; cocky; *m* pimp
**chupar** (choo-*pahr*) *v* suck
**churro** (*choo*-rroa) *m* fritter; botched job
**cicatriz** (thee-kah-*treeth*) *f* scar
**ciclista** (thee-*kleess*-tah) *m* cyclist
**ciclo** (*thee*-kloa) *m* cycle
**ciego** (*th$^y$ay*-goa) *adj* blind
**cielo** (*th$^y$ay*-loa) *m* heaven; sky; ~ **raso** ceiling
**ciencia** (*th$^y$ayn*-th$^y$ah) *f* science
**científico** (th$^y$ayn-*tee*-fee-koa) *adj* scientific; *m*, **-a** *f* scientist
**ciento** (*th$^y$ayn*-toa) *num* hundred; **por** ~ percent
**cierre** (*th$^y$ay*-rray) *m* fastener; ~ **relámpago** zipper
**cierto** (*th$^y$ayr*-toa) *adj* certain; **por** ~ indeed
**ciervo** (*th$^y$ayr*-bhoa) *m* deer
**cifra** (*thee*-frah) *f* number, figure
**cigarrillo** (thee-gah-*rree*-l$^y$oa) *m* cigarette
**cigüeña** (thee-*gway*-ñah) *f* stork
**cigüeñal** (thee-gway-*ñahl*) *m* crankshaft
**cilindro** (thee-*leen*-droa) *m* cylinder; **culata del** ~ cylinder head
**cima** (*thee*-mah) *f* top, summit; hilltop
**cinc** (theengk) *m* zinc
**cincel** (theen-*thayl*) *m* chisel
**cinco** (*theeng*-koa) *num* five
**cincuenta** (theeng-*kwayn*-tah) *num* fifty
**cine** (*thee*-nay) *m* pictures
**cinematógrafo** (thee-nay-mah-*toa*-grah-foa) *m* cinema
**cinta** (*theen*-tah) *f* ribbon, tape; ~ **adhesiva** scotch tape, adhesive tape; ~ **de goma** elastic band; ~ **métrica** tape-measure
**cintura** (theen-*too*-rah) *f* waist
**cinturón** (theen-too-*roan*) *m* belt; bypass; ~ **de seguridad** seat belt
**circo** (*theer*-koa) *m* circus
**circulación** (theer-koo-lah-*th$^y$oan*) *f* circulation
**circular** (theer-koo-*lahr*) *v* circulate
**círculo** (*theer*-koo-loa) *m* circle, ring; club
**circundante** (theer-koon-*dahn*-tay) *adj* surrounding
**circundar** (theer-koon-*dahr*) *v* circle
**circunstancia** (theer-koons-*tahn*-th$^y$ah) *f* circumstance, condition
**ciruela** (thee-*rway*-lah) *f* plum; ~ **pasa** prune
**cirujano** (thee-roo-*khah*-noa) *m* surgeon
**cisne** (*theez*-nay) *m* swan
**cistitis** (theess-*tee*-teess) *f* cystitis
**cita** (*thee*-tah) *f* date, appointment; meeting; quotation
**citar** (thee-*tahr*) *v* make an appointment with; quote
**ciudad** (th$^y$oo-*dhahdh*) *f* city, town
**ciudadanía** (th$^y$oo-dhah-dhah-*nee*-ah) *f* citizenship
**ciudadano** (th$^y$oo-dhah-*dhah*-noa) *m*, **-a** *f* citizen
**cívico** (*thee*-bhee-koa) *adj* civic
**civil** (thee-*bheel*) *adj* civilian, civil
**civilización** (thee-bhee-lee-thah-*th$^y$oan*) *f* civilization
**civilizado** (thee-bhee-lee-*thah*-dhoa) *adj* civilized

**claridad** (klah-ree-*dhahdh*) *f* clarity
**clarificar** (klah-ree-fee-*kahr*) *v* clarify
**claro** (*klah*-roa) *adj* clear; plain, distinct; serene, bright; *m* clearing
**clase** (*klah*-say) *f* class; sort; form; classroom; ~ **media** middle class; ~ **turista** tourist class; **de primera** ~ first-rate; **toda** ~ **de** all sorts of
**clásico** (*klah*-see-koa) *adj* classical
**clasificar** (klah-see-fee-*kahr*) *v* classify, assort, sort, arrange
**cláusula** (*klou*-soo-lah) *f* clause
**clavar** (klah-*bhahr*) *v* pin
**clavicémbalo** (klah-bhee-*thaym*-bah-loa) *m* harpsichord
**clavícula** (klah-*bhee*-koo-lah) *f* collarbone
**clavo** (*klah*-bhoa) *m* nail
**clemencia** (klay-*mayn*-th$^y$ah) *f* mercy
**clérigo** (*klay*-ree-goa) *m* clergyman, minister
**cliente** (*kl$^y$ayn*-tay) *m* client, customer
**clima** (*klee*-mah) *m* climate
**climatizado** (klee-mah-tee-*thah*-dhoa) *adj* air-conditioned
**clínica** (*klee*-nee-kah) *f* clinic
**cloro** (*kloa*-roa) *m* chlorine
**club de yates** yacht club
**cobarde** (koa-*bhahr*-dhay) *adj* cowardly; *m* coward
**cobertizo** (koa-bhayr-*tee*-thoa) *m* shed
**cobrador** (koa-bhrah-*dhoar*) *m* conductor
**cobrar** (koa-*bhrahr*) *v* cash
**cobre** (*koa*-bhray) *m* copper, brass; **cobres** *mpl* brassware
**cocaína** (koa-kah-*ee*-nah) *f* cocaine
**cocer** (koa-*thayr*) *v* cook; boil; bake; **cocerse** cook; boil; bake; *colloquial* be roasting
**cocido** (koa-*thee*-doa) *adj* boiled; *m* stew
**cocina** (koa-*thee*-nah) *f* kitchen; cooker, stove; ~ **de gas** gas cooker
**cocinar** (koa-thee-*nahr*) *v* cook
**cocinero** (koa-thee-*nay*-roa) *m* cook
**coco** (*koa*-koa) *m* coconut
**cocodrilo** (koa-koa-*dhree*-l$^y$oa) *m* crocodile
**cóctel** (*koak*-tayl) *m* cocktail
**coche** (*koa*-chay) *m* car; carriage; ~ **cama** sleeping-car; ~ **comedor** dining-car; ~ **de carreras** sports-car; ~ **Pullman** Pullman
**cochecillo** (koa-chay-*thee*-l$^y$oa) *m* pram; baby carriage *Am*
**cochinillo** (koa-chee-*nee*-l$^y$oa) *m* piglet
**codicioso** (koa-dhee-*th$^y$oa*-soa) *adj* greedy
**código** (*koa*-dhee-goa) *m* code; ~ **postal** zip code *Am*
**codo** (*koa*-dhoa) *m* elbow
**codorniz** (koa-dhoar-*neeth*) *f* quail
**coger** (koa-*khayr*) *v* *catch; *take; **llegar a** ~ *catch
**coherencia** (koa-ay-*rayn*-th$^y$ah) *f* coherence
**cohete** (koa-*ay*-tay) *m* rocket
**coincidencia** (koa-een-thee-*dhayn*-th$^y$ah) *f* concurrence
**coincidir** (koa-een-thee-*dheer*) *v* coincide
**cojear** (koa-khay-*ahr*) *v* limp
**cojo** (*koa*-khoa) *adj* lame
**col** (koal) *m* cabbage; ~ **de Bruselas** Brussels sprouts *pl*
**cola** (*koa*-lah) *f* queue, file, line; tail; gum, glue; ***hacer** ~ queue
**colaboración** (koa-lah-bhoa-rah-*th$^y$oan*) *f* cooperation
**colcha** (*koal*-chah) *f* bedspread
**colchón** (koal-*choan*) *m* mattress
**colección** (koa-layk-*th$^y$oan*) *f* collection; ~ **de arte** art collection
**coleccionar** (koa-layk-th$^y$oa-*nahr*) *v* gather

**coleccionista** (koa-layk-th$^{y}$oa-*neess*-tah) *m* collector

**colectivo** (koa-layk-*tee*-bhoa) *adj* collective

**colector** (koa-layk-*toar*) *m* collector

**colega** (koa-*lay*-gah) *m* colleague

**colegio** (koa-*lay*-kh$^{y}$oa) *m* college

**cólera** (*koa*-lay-rah) *f* anger, passion, temper

**colérico** (koa-*lay*-ree-koa) *adj* hot-tempered

***colgar** (koal-*gahr*) *v* *hang

**coliflor** (koa-lee-*floar*) *f* cauliflower

**colina** (koa-*lee*-nah) *f* hill

**colisión** (koa-lee-*s$^{y}$oan*) *f* collision

**colmena** (koal-*may*-nah) *f* beehive

**colmo** (*koal*-moa) *m* height

**colocar** (koa-loa-*kahr*) *v* *lay, place, *put

**Colombia** (koa-*loam*-b$^{y}$ah) *f* Colombia

**colombiano** (koa-loam-*b$^{y}$ah*-noa) *adj* Colombian; *m* Colombian

**colonia** (koa-*loa*-n$^{y}$ah) *f* colony; **~ veraniega** holiday camp

**color** (koa-*loar*) *m* colo(u)r; **~ de aguada** watercolo(u)r; **de ~** colo(u)red

**colorado** (koa-loa-*rah*-dhoa) *adj* colo(u)rful

**colorante** (koa-loa-*rahn*-tay) *m* colo(u)rant

**colorete** (koa-loa-*ray*-tay) *m* blush

**columna** (koa-*loom*-nah) *f* column, pillar; **~ del volante** steering column

**columpiarse** (koa-loom-*p$^{y}$ahr*-say) *v* *swing

**columpio** (koa-*loom*-p$^{y}$oa) *m* swing; seesaw

**collar** (koa-*l$^{y}$ahr*) *m* beads *pl*, necklace; collar

**coma** (*koa*-mah) *f* comma; *m* coma

**comadrona** (koa-mah-*dhroa*-nah) *f* midwife

**comandante** (koa-mahn-*dahn*-tay) *m* commander; captain

**comarca** (koa-*mahr*-kah) *f* district

**comba** (*koam*-bah) *f* bend

**combate** (koam-*bah*-tay) *m* combat, battle, struggle, fight; **~ de boxeo** boxing match

**combatir** (koam-bah-*teer*) *v* combat, battle, *fight

**combinación** (koam-bee-nah-*th$^{y}$oan*) *f* combination; slip

**combinar** (koam-bee-*nahr*) *v* combine

**combustible** (koam-booss-*tee*-bhlay) *m* fuel; **~ líquido** fuel oil

**comedia** (koa-*may*-dh$^{y}$ah) *f* comedy; **~ musical** musical

**comediante** (koa-may-*dh$^{y}$ahn*-tay) *m*, **-a** *f* actor; comedian

**comedor** (koa-may-*dhoar*) *m* dining room

**comentar** (koa-mayn-*tahr*) *v* comment

**comentario** (koa-mayn-*tah*-r$^{y}$oa) *m* comment

***comenzar** (koa-mayn-*thahr*) *v* commence, *begin

**comer** (koa-*mayr*) *v* *eat

**comercial** (koa-mayr-*th$^{y}$ahl*) *adj* commercial

**comerciante** (koa-mayr-*th$^{y}$ahn*-tay) *m/f* merchant; trader, dealer; **~ al por menor** retailer

**comerciar** (koa-mayr-*th$^{y}$ahr*) *v* trade

**comercio** (koa-*mayr*-th$^{y}$oa) *m* commerce, trade, business; **~ al por menor** retail trade

**comestible** (koa-mayss-*tee*-bhlay) *adj* edible

**comestibles** (koa-mayss-*tee*-bhlayss) *mpl* groceries *pl*; **tienda de ~ finos** delicatessen

**cometer** (koa-may-*tayr*) *v* commit

**cómico** (*koa*-mee-koa) *adj* comic,

funny; *m* comedian; entertainer
**comida** (koa-*mee*-dhah) *f* food; meal; **~ principal** dinner
**comidilla** (koa-mee-*dhee*-l$^{y}$ah) *f* hobby-horse
**comienzo** (koa-*m$^{y}$ayn*-thoa) *m* beginning, start
**comillas** (koa-*mee*-l$^{y}$ahss) *fpl* quotation marks
**comisaría** (koa-mee-sah-*ree*-ah) *f* police station
**comisión** (koa-mee-*s$^{y}$oan*) *f* committee, commission
**comité** (koa-mee-*tay*) *m* committee
**comitiva** (koa-mee-*tee*-bhah) *f* group
**como** (*koa*-moa) *adv* as, like, like; **así ~** as well as; **~ máximo** at most; **~ si** as if
**cómo** (*koa*-moa) *adv* how
**cómoda** (*koa*-moa-dhah) *f* chest of drawers; bureau *Am*
**comodidad** (koa-moa-dhee-*dhahdh*) *f* comfort, leisure
**cómodo** (*koa*-moa-dhoa) *adj* convenient, easy
**compacto** (koam-*pahk*-toa) *adj* compact
**compadecerse de** (koam-pah-dhay-*thayr*-say) pity
**compañero** (koam-pah-*ñay*-roa) *m*, **-a** *f* companion; partner; associate; **~ de clase** classmate
**compañía** (koam-pah-*ñee*-ah) *f* company; society
**comparación** (koam-pah-rah-*th$^{y}$oan*) *f* comparison
**comparar** (koam-pah-*rahr*) *v* compare
**compartimento** (koam-pahr-tee-*mayn*-toa) *m* compartment; **~ para fumadores** smoking compartment
**compartir** (koam-pahr-*teer*) *v* share
**compasión** (koam-pah-*s$^{y}$oan*) *f* compassion; sympathy
**compasivo** (koam-pah-*see*-bhoa) *adj* compassionate, sympathetic
**compatriota** (koam-pah-*tr$^{y}$oa*-tah) *m* countryman
**compeler** (koam-pay-*layr*) *v* compel
**compensación** (koam-payn-sah-*th$^{y}$oan*) *f* compensation
**compensar** (koam-payn-*sahr*) *v* compensate; *make good
**competencia** (koam-pay-*tayn*-th$^{y}$ah) *f* competition, rivalry; competence
**competente** (koam-pay-*tayn*-tay) *adj* expert, qualified, competent
**competidor** (koam-pay-tee-*dhoar*) *m*, **-a** *f* competitor, rival
***competir** (koam-pay-*teer*) *v* compete
**compilar** (koam-pee-*lahr*) *v* compile
***complacer** (koam-plah-*thayr*) *v* please; *give satisfaction
**complejo** (koam-*play*-khoa) *adj* complex; *m* complex
**completamente** (koam-play-tah-*mayn*-tay) *adv* completely, quite
**completar** (koam-play-*tahr*) *v* complete; fill in; fill out *Am*
**completo** (koam-*play*-toa) *adj* complete; whole, total, utter; full up
**complicado** (koam-plee-*kah*-dhoa) *adj* complicated
**cómplice** (*koam*-plee-thay) *m* accomplice
**complot** (koam-*ploat*) *m* plot
***componer** (koam-poa-*nayr*) *v* compose
**comportarse** (koam-poar-*tahr*-say) *v* behave, act
**composición** (koam-poa-see-*th$^{y}$oan*) *f* composition; essay
**compositor** (koam-poa-see-*toar*) *m*, **-a** *f* composer
**compra** (*koam*-prah) *f* purchase; ***ir de compras** shop, go shopping; **saco de compras** shopping bag
**comprador** (koam-prah-*dhoar*) *m*, **-a**

*f* purchaser, buyer
**comprar** (koam-*prahr*) *v* purchase, *buy
**comprender** (koam-prayn-*dayr*) *v* *understand; *see, *take; comprise, contain
**comprensión** (koam-prayn-*s$^y$oan*) *m* understanding
**compresa** (koam-*pray*-sah) *f* sanitary towel, sanitary napkin *Am*
**comprimido** (koam-pree-*mee*-doa) *m* pill
**comprobante** (koam-proa-*bhahn*-tay) *m* voucher
***comprobar** (koam-proa-*bhahr*) *v* ascertain, diagnose, establish, note; prove
**comprometerse** (koam-proa-may-*tayr*-say) *v* engage
**compromiso** (koam-proa-*mee*-soa) *m* compromise; engagement
**compuerta** (koam-*pwayr*-tah) *f* sluice
**computadora** (koam-poo-tah-*doa*-rah) *f L.Am* computer; ~ **portatíl** laptop
**común** (koa-*moon*) *adj* common; ordinary; **en ~** joint
**comuna** (koa-*moo*-nah) *f* commune
**comunicación** (koa-moo-nee-kah-*th$^y$oan*) *f* communication
**comunicado** (koa-moo-nee-*kah*-dhoa) *m* communiqué, information
**comunicar** (koa-moo-nee-*kahr*) *v* communicate, inform
**comunidad** (koa-moo-nee-*dhahdh*) *f* congregation
**comunismo** (koa-moo-*neez*-moa) *m* communism
**comunista** (koa-moo-*neess*-tah) *m* communist
**con** (koan) *prep* with; by
***concebir** (koan-thay-*bheer*) *v* conceive
**conceder** (koan-thay-*dhayr*) *v* extend, grant; award
**concentración** (koan-thayn-trah-*th$^y$oan*) *f* concentration
**concentrarse** (koan-thayn-*trahr*-say) *v* concentrate
**concepción** (koan-thayp-*th$^y$oan*) *f* conception
**concepto** (koan-*thayp*-toa) *m* idea
***concernir** (koan-thayr-*neer*) *v* touch, concern; **concerniente a** concerning
**concesión** (koan-thay-*s$^y$oan*) *f* concession
**conciencia** (koan-*th$^y$ayn*-th$^y$ah) *f* conscience; consciousness
**concierto** (koan-*th$^y$ayr*-toa) *m* concert
**conciso** (koan-*thee*-soa) *adj* concise
***concluir** (koang-*klweer*) *v* conclude, finish; infer
**conclusión** (koang-kloo-*s$^y$oan*) *f* conclusion; ending
***concordar** (koang-koar-*dhahr*) *v* agree
**concreto** (koang-*kray*-toa) *adj* concrete
**concurrido** (koang-koo-*rree*-dhoa) *adj* busy
**concurrir** (koang-koo-*rreer*) *v* coincide; concur
**concurso** (koang-*koor*-soa) *m* competition, contest; quiz
**concha** (*koan*-chah) *f* shell; seashell
**condado** (koan-*dah*-dhoa) *m* county
**conde** (*koan*-day) *m* count, earl
**condena** (koan-*day*-nah) *f* conviction
**condenado** (koan-day-*nah*-dhoa) *m* convict
**condenar** (koan-day-*nahr*) *v* sentence; condemn
**condesa** (koan-*day*-sah) *f* countess
**condición** (koan-dee-*th$^y$oan*) *f* condition, term
**condicional** (koan-dee-th$^y$oa-*nahl*) *adj* conditional

**condimentado** (koan-dee-mayn-*tah*-dhoa) *adj* spiced
***conducir** (koan-doo-*theer*) *v* *lead, carry, conduct; *drive
**conducta** (koan-*dook*-tah) *f* behavio(u)r, conduct
**conducto** (koan-*dook*-toa) *m* pipe
**conductor** (koan-dook-*toar*) *m* driver; *mMe* conductor
**conectar** (koa-nayk-*tahr*) *v* connect
**conejo** (koa-*nay*-khoa) *m* rabbit; **conejillo de Indias** guinea pig
**conexión** (koa-nayk-*s*$^{y}$*oan*) *f* connection
**confeccionado** (koan-fayk-th$^{y}$oa-*nah*-dhoa) *adj* ready-made
**confederación** (koan-fay-day-rah-*th*$^{y}$*oan*) *f* union
**conferencia** (koan-fay-*rayn*-th$^{y}$ah) *f* conference; lecture; **~ interurbana** long-distance call
***confesarse** (koan-fay-*sahr*-say) *v* confess
**confesión** (koan-fay-*s*$^{y}$*oan*) *f* confession
**confiable** (koan-*f*$^{y}$*ah*-bhlay) *adj* trustworthy
**confianza** (koan-*f*$^{y}$*ahn*-thah) *f* faith, trust, confidence; **indigno de ~** untrustworthy
**confiar** (koan-*f*$^{y}$*ahr*) *v* commit; **~ en** trust
**confidencial** (koan-fee-dhayn-*th*$^{y}$*ahl*) *adj* confidential
**confirmación** (koan-feer-mah-*th*$^{y}$*oan*) *f* confirmation
**confirmar** (koan-feer-*mahr*) *v* confirm, acknowledge
**confiscar** (koan-feess-*kahr*) *v* confiscate, impound
**confitería** (koan-fee-tay-*ree*-ah) *f* sweetshop; candy store *Am*
**confitero** (koan-fee-*tay*-roa) *m* confectioner
**confitura** (koan-fee-*too*-rah) *f* marmalade
**conflicto** (koan-*fleek*-toa) *m* conflict
**conforme** (koan-*foar*-may) *adj* alike; in agreement; **~ a** according to, in agreement with
**conformidad** (koan-foar-mee-*dhahdh*) *f* agreement
**confort** (koan-*foart*) *m* comfort
**confortable** (koan-foar-*tah*-bhlay) *adj* comfortable; cosy
**confundir** (koan-foon-*deer*) *v* *mistake, confuse
**confusión** (koan-foo-*s*$^{y}$*oan*) *f* confusion; disturbance
**confuso** (koan-*foo*-soa) *adj* confused
**congelado** (koang-khay-*lah*-dhoa) *adj* frozen; **alimento ~** frozen food
**congelador** (koang-khay-lah-*dhoar*) *m* deep-freeze
**congelar** (koang-khay-*lahr*) *v* *freeze
**congestión** (koang-khayss-*t*$^{y}$*oan*) *f* congestion
**congregación** (koang-gray-gah-*th*$^{y}$*oan*) *f* congregation
**congreso** (koang-*gray*-soa) *m* congress
**conjetura** (koang-khay-*too*-rah) *f* guess
**conjuración** (koang-khoo-rah-*th*$^{y}$*oan*) *f* plot, conspiracy
**conmemoración** (koan-may-moa-rah-*th*$^{y}$*oan*) *f* commemoration
**conmovedor** (koan-moa-bhay-*dhoar*) *adj* touching; moving
***conmover** (koan-moa-*bhayr*) *v* move
***conocer** (koa-noa-*thayr*) *v* *know
**conocido** (koa-noa-*thee*-dhoa) *m* acquaintance
**conocimiento** (koa-noa-thee-*m*$^{y}$*ayn*-toa) *m* knowledge
**conquista** (koang-*keess*-tah) *f* conquest, capture
**conquistador** (koang-keess-tah-

*dhoar*) *m* conqueror
**conquistar** (koang-keess-*tahr*) *v* conquer, capture
**consciente** (koan-*th$^{y}$ayn*-tay) *adj* conscious, aware
**consecuencia** (koan-say-*kwayn*-th$^{y}$ah) *f* consequence, result; issue
***conseguir** (koan-say-*geer*) *v* *get; *make, obtain
**consejero** (koan-say-*khay*-roa) *m* counsel(l)or; council(l)or
**consejo** (koan-*say*-khoa) *m* advice, counsel; council, board
**consentimiento** (koan-sayn-tee-*m$^{y}$ayn*-toa) *m* consent; approval
***consentir** (koan-sayn-*teer*) *v* agree, consent
**conserje** (koan-*sayr*-khay) *m* concierge, janitor
**conservación** (koan-sayr-bhah-*th$^{y}$oan*) *f* preservation
**conservador** (koan-sayr-bhah-*dhoar*) *adj* conservative
**conservar** (koan-sayr-*bhahr*) *v* preserve
**conservas** (koan-*sayr*-bhahss) *fpl* tinned food, canned food *Am*
**conservatorio** (koan-sayr-bhah-*toa*-r$^{y}$oa) *m* music academy
**considerable** (koan-see-dhay-*rah*-bhlay) *adj* considerable
**consideración** (koan-see-dhay-rah-*th$^{y}$oan*) *f* consideration
**considerado** (koan-see-dhay-*rah*-dhoa) *adj* considerate
**considerar** (koan-see-dhay-*rahr*) *v* regard, consider; *think over; count, reckon
**consigna** (koan-*seeg*-nah) *f* left luggage office, baggage check *Am*
**consiguiente: por ~** (poar koan-see-*g$^{y}$ayn*-tay) consequently
**consistir en** (koan-seess-*teer*) consist of
***consolar** (koan-soa-*lahr*) *v* comfort
**consorcio** (koan-*soar*-th$^{y}$oa) *m* concern
**conspirar** (koans-pee-*rahr*) *v* conspire
**constante** (koans-*tahn*-tay) *adj* even, constant; steadfast
**constar de** (koans-*tahr*) consist of
**constitución** (koans-tee-too-*th$^{y}$oan*) *f* constitution
***constituir** (koans-tee-*tweer*) *v* constitute; represent
**construcción** (koans-trook-*th$^{y}$oan*) *f* construction
***construir** (koans-*trweer*) *v* construct, *build
**consuelo** (koan-*sway*-loa) *m* comfort
**cónsul** (*koan*-sool) *m* consul
**consulado** (koan-soo-*lah*-dhoa) *m* consulate
**consulta** (koan-*sool*-tah) *f* consultation
**consultar** (koan-sool-*tahr*) *v* consult
**consultorio** (koan-sool-*toa*-r$^{y}$oa) *m* surgery; doctor's office *Am*
**consumidor** (koan-soo-mee-*dhoar*) *m*, **-a** *f* consumer
**consumir** (koan-soo-*meer*) *v* use up; consume; eat; eat away at
**contacto** (koan-*tahk*-toa) *m* contact; touch
**contador** (koan-tah-*dhoar*) *m* meter
**contagioso** (koan-tah-*kh$^{y}$oa*-soa) *adj* infectious, contagious
**contaminación** (koan-tah-mee-nah-*th$^{y}$oan*) *f* pollution
***contar** (koan-*tahr*) *v* count; relate, *tell; **~ con** rely on
**contemplar** (koan-taym-*plahr*) *v* contemplate
**contemporáneo** (koan-taym-poa-*rah*-nay-oa) *adj* contemporary; *m* contemporary
**contenedor** (koan-tay-nay-*dhoar*) *m* container

***contener** (koan-tay-*nayr*) *v* contain; restrain
**contenido** (koan-tay-*nee*-dhoa) *m* contents *pl*
**contentar** (koan-tayn-*tahr*) *v* satisfy
**contento** (koan-*tayn*-toa) *adj* happy, glad, content, joyful; pleased
**contestar** (koan-tayss-*tahr*) *v* answer
**contienda** (koan-*t$^{y}$ayn*-dah) *f* dispute
**contiguo** (koan-*tee*-gwoa) *adj* neighbo(u)ring; adjacent
**continental** (koan-tee-nayn-*tahl*) *adj* continental
**continente** (koan-tee-*nayn*-tay) *m* continent
**continuación** (koan-tee-nwah-*th$^{y}$oan*) *f* sequel; continuation
**continuamente** (koan-tee-nwah-*mayn*-tay) *adv* all the time, continually
**continuar** (koan-tee-*nwahr*) *v* *go on, *go ahead; carry on, continue, *keep on; *keep
**continuo** (koan-*tee*-nwoa) *adj* continuous, continual
**contorno** (koan-*toar*-noa) *m* outline, contour
**contra** (*koan*-trah) *prep* against, versus
**contrabandear** (koan-trah-bhahn-day-*ahr*) *v* smuggle
***contradecir** (koan-trah-dhay-*theer*) *v* contradict
**contradictorio** (koan-trah-dheek-*toa*-r$^{y}$oa) *adj* contradictory
**contrahecho** (koan-trah-*ay*-choa) *adj* deformed
**contralto** (koan-*trahl*-toa) *m* alto
**contrario** (koan-*trah*-r$^{y}$oa) *adj* opposite, contrary; *m* contrary, reverse; **al ~** on the contrary
**contraste** (koan-*trahss*-tay) *m* contrast
**contratiempo** (koan-trah-*t$^{y}$aym*-poa) *m* misfortune
**contratista** (koan-trah-*teess*-tah) *m* contractor
**contrato** (koan-*trah*-toa) *m* agreement, contract
**contribución** (koan-tree-bhoo-*th$^{y}$oan*) *f* contribution
***contribuir** (koan-tree-*bhweer*) *v* contribute
**contrincante** (koan-treeng-*kahn*-tay) *m/f* opponent
**control** (koan-*troal*) *m* inspection, control
**controlar** (koan-troa-*lahr*) *v* check, control
**controvertible** (koan-troa-bhayr-*tee*-bhlay) *adj* controversial
**controvertido** (koan-troa-bhayr-*tee*-dhoa) *adj* controversial
**convencer** (koam-bayn-*thayr*) *v* convince, persuade; convict
**convencimiento** (koam-bayn-thee-*m$^{y}$ayn*-toa) *m* conviction
**conveniente** (koam-bay-*n$^{y}$ayn*-tay) *adj* adequate, proper; convenient
**convenio** (koam-*bay*-n$^{y}$oa) *m* settlement
***convenir** (koam-bay-*neer*) *v* agree; fit, suit
**convento** (koam-*bayn*-toa) *m* cloister, convent
**conversación** (koam-bayr-sah-*th$^{y}$oan*) *f* conversation, talk, discussion
***convertir** (koam-bayr-*teer*) *v* convert; ***convertirse en** turn into
**convicción** (koam-beek-*th$^{y}$oan*) *f* conviction; persuasion
**convidar** (koam-bee-*dhahr*) *v* invite
**convulsión** (koam-bool-*s$^{y}$oan*) *f* convulsion
**cónyuges** (*koan*-$^{y}$oo-khayss) *mpl* married couple
**coñac** (koa-*ñahk*) *m* cognac

**cooperación** (koa-oa-pay-rah-*th$^{y}$oan*) *f* co-operation
**cooperador** (koa-oa-pay-rah-*dhoar*) *adj* cooperative
**cooperativa** (koa-oa-pay-rah-*tee*-bhah) *f* cooperative
**cooperativo** (koa-oa-pay-rah-*tee*-bhoa) *adj* cooperative
**coordinación** (koa-oar-dhee-nah-*th$^{y}$oan*) *f* coordination
**coordinar** (koa-oar-dhee-*nahr*) *v* coordinate
**copa** (*koa*-pah) *f* cup
**copia** (*koa*-p$^{y}$ah) *f* copy, carbon copy
**copiar** (koa-*p$^{y}$ahr*) *v* copy
**coraje** (koa-*rah*-khay) *m* courage, bravery
**coral** (koa-*rahl*) *m* coral
**corazón** (koa-rah-*thoan*) *m* heart; core
**corbata** (koar-*bhah*-tah) *f* tie, necktie; **~ de lazo** bow tie
**corbatín** (koar-bhah-*teen*) *m* bow tie
**corcino** (koar-*thee*-noa) *m* fawn
**corcho** (*koar*-choa) *m* cork
**cordel** (koar-*dhayl*) *m* string
**cordero** (koar-*dhay*-roa) *m* lamb
**cordial** (koar-*dh$^{y}$ahl*) *adj* cordial, hearty, sympathetic
**cordillera** (koar-dhee-*l$^{y}$ay*-rah) *f* mountain range
**cordón** (koar-*dhoan*) *m* cord, line; lace, shoe-lace; **~ de extensión** extension cord; **~ flexible** flex
**cornamenta** (koar-nah-*mayn*-tah) *f* antlers *pl*
**corneja** (koar-*nay*-khah) *f* crow
**coro** (*koa*-roa) *m* choir
**corona** (koa-*roa*-nah) *f* crown
**coronar** (koa-roa-*nahr*) *v* crown
**coronel** (koa-roa-*nayl*) *m* colonel
**corpulento** (koar-poo-*layn*-toa) *adj* corpulent, stout
**corral** (koa-*rrahl*) *m* yard; **aves de ~** poultry
**correa** (koa-*rray*-ah) *f* leash, strap; **~ del ventilador** fan belt; **~ de reloj** watch-strap
**corrección** (koa-rrayk-*th$^{y}$oan*) *f* correction
**correcto** (koa-*rrayk*-toa) *adj* correct; right
**corredor** (koa-rray-*dhoar*) *m*, **-a** *f* runner; agent; **~ de apuestas** bookmaker; **~ de bolsa** stockbroker; **~ de casas** house agent
***corregir** (koa-rray-*kheer*) *v* correct
**correo** (koa-*rray*-oa) *m* post, mail; **~ aéreo** airmail; **enviar por ~** mail; **sello de correos** postage stamp
**correr** (koa-*rrayr*) *v* *run; dash; flow
**correspondencia** (koa-rrayss-poan-*dayn*-th$^{y}$ah) *f* correspondence
**corresponder** (koa-rrayss-poan-*dayr*) *v* correspond; **corresponderse** *v* correspond
**corresponsal** (koa-rrayss-poan-*sahl*) *m/f* correspondent
**corrida de toros** (koa-*rree*-dhah day *toa*-roass) bullfight
**corriente** (koa-*rr$^{y}$ayn*-tay) *adj* current; regular, customary, plain; *f* current; stream; **~ alterna** alternating current; **~ continua** direct current; **~ de aire** draught, draft *Am*
**corromper** (koa-rroam-*payr*) *v* corrupt
**corrupción** (koa-rroop-*th$^{y}$oan*) *f* corruption
**corrupto** (koa-*rroop*-toa) *adj* corrupt
**corsé** (koar-*say*) *m* corset
**cortado** (koar-*tah*-doa) *adj* cut; closed; curdled; shy; **quedarse ~** be embarrassed; *m* coffee with a dash of milk
**cortadura** (koar-tah-*dhoo*-rah) *f* cut
**cortaplumas** (koar-tah-*ploo*-mahss) *m* penknife

**cortar** (koar-*tahr*) *v* *cut; chip, *cut off
**corte** (*koar*-tay) *f* court
**cortés** (koar-*tayss*) *adj* civil, courteous, polite
**corteza** (koar-*tay*-thah) *f* bark; crust
**cortijo** (koar-*tee*-khoa) *m* farmhouse
**cortina** (koar-*tee*-nah) *f* curtain
**corto** (*koar*-toa) *adj* short
**cortocircuito** (koar-toa-theer-*kwee*-toa) *m* short circuit
**cosa** (*koa*-sah) *f* thing; **entre otras cosas** among other things
**cosecha** (koa-*say*-chah) *f* harvest, crop
**coser** (koa-*sayr*) *v* sew
**cosméticos** (koaz-*may*-tee-koass) *mpl* cosmetics *pl*
**cosquillear** (koass-kee-*l$^y$ahr*) *v* tickle
**costa** (*koass*-tah) *f* coast
***costar** (koass-*tahr*) *v* *cost
**coste** (*koass*-tay) *m* cost
**costilla** (koass-*tee*-l$^y$ah) *f* rib
**costoso** (koass-*toa*-soa) *adj* expensive
**costumbre** (koass-*toom*-bray) *f* custom; **costumbres** morals
**costura** (koass-*too*-rah) *f* seam; **sin ~** seamless
**cotidiano** (koa-tee-*dh$^y$ah*-noa) *adj* everyday
**cráneo** (*krah*-nay-oa) *m* skull
**cráter** (*krah*-tayr) *m* crater
**creación** (kray-ah-*th$^y$oan*) *f* creation
**crear** (kray-*ahr*) *v* create
***crecer** (kray-*thayr*) *v* *grow
**crecimiento** (kray-thee-*m$^y$ayn*-toa) *m* growth
**crédito** (*kray*-dhee-toa) *m* credit
**crédulo** (*kray*-dhoo-loa) *adj* credulous
**creencia** (kray-*ayn*-th$^y$ah) *f* belief
***creer** (kray-*ayr*) *v* believe; guess, reckon
**crema** (*kray*-mah) *f* cream; **~ de afeitar** shaving cream; **~ de base** foundation cream; **~ de noche** night cream; **~ facial** face cream; **~ hidratante** moisturizing cream; **~ para la piel** skin cream; **~ para las manos** hand cream
**cremallera** (kray-mah-*l$^y$ay*-rah) *f* zip, zipper *Am*
**cremoso** (kray-*moa*-soa) *adj* creamy
**crepúsculo** (kray-*pooss*-koo-loa) *m* twilight, dusk
**crespo** (*krayss*-poa) *adj* curly
**cresta** (*krayss*-tah) *f* ridge
**creta** (*kray*-tah) *f* chalk
**criada** (*kr$^y$ah*-dhah) *f* (house)maid
**criado** (*kr$^y$ah*-dhoa) *m* servant
**criar** (kr$^y$ahr) *v* rear; raise
**criatura** (kr$^y$ah-*too*-rah) *f* creature; infant
**crimen** (*kree*-mayn) *m* crime
**criminal** (kree-mee-*nahl*) *adj* criminal; *m* criminal
**criminalidad** (kree-mee-nah-lee-*dhahdh*) *f* criminality
**crisis** (*kree*-seess) *f* crisis
**cristal** (kreess-*tahl*) *m* crystal; pane; **de ~** crystal
**cristiano** (kreess-*t$^y$ah*-noa) *adj* Christian; *m* Christian
**Cristo** (*kreess*-toa) Christ
**criterio** (kree-*tay*-r$^y$oa) *m* criterion
**crítica** (*kree*-tee-kah) *f* criticism
**criticar** (kree-tee-*kahr*) *v* criticize
**crítico** (*kree*-tee-koa) *adj* critical; *m*, **-a** *f* critic
**cromo** (*kroa*-moa) *m* chromium
**crónica** (*kroa*-nee-kah) *f* chronicle
**crónico** (*kroa*-nee-koa) *adj* chronic
**cronológico** (kroa-noa-*loa*-khee-koa) *adj* chronological
**cruce** (*kroo*-thay) *m* crossroads; **~ para peatones** pedestrian crossing; crosswalk *Am*
**crucero** (kroo-*thay*-roa) *m* cruise
**crucificar** (kroo-thee-fee-*kahr*) *v*

crucify

**crucifijo** (kroo-thee-*fee*-khoa) *m* crucifix

**crucifixión** (kroo-thee-feek-*s*$^{y}$*oan*) *f* crucifixion

**crudo** (*kroo*-dhoa) *adj* raw

**cruel** (krwayl) *adj* harsh, cruel

**crujido** (kroo-*khee*-dhoa) *m* crack

**crujiente** (kroo-*kh*$^{y}$*ayn*-tay) *adj* crisp

**crujir** (kroo-*kheer*) *v* creak, crack

**cruz** (krooth) *f* cross

**cruzada** (kroo-*thah*-dhah) *f* crusade

**cruzar** (kroo-*thahr*) *v* cross

**cuaderno** (kwah-*dhayr*-noa) *m* notebook; exercise book

**cuadrado** (kwah-*dhrah*-dhoa) *adj* square; *m* square

**cuadriculado** (kwah-dhree-koo-*lah*-dhoa) *adj* chequered

**cuadro** (*kwah*-dhroa) *m* cadre; picture; **a cuadros** chequered; **~ de distribución** switchboard

**cuál** (kwahl) *pron* which

**cualidad** (kwah-lee-*dhahdh*) *f* property

**cualquiera** (kwahl-*k*$^{y}$*ay*-rah) *pron* anyone, anybody; whichever; **cualquier cosa** anything

**cuando** (*kwahn*-doa) *conj* when; **~ quiera que** whenever

**cuándo** (*kwahn*-doa) *adv* when

**cuánto** (*kwahn*-toa) *adv* how much; how many; **cuanto más ... más** the ... the; **en cuanto a** as regards

**cuarenta** (kwah-*rayn*-tah) *num* forty

**cuarentena** (kwah-rayn-*tay*-nah) *f* quarantine

**cuartel** (kwahr-*tayl*) *m* barracks *pl*; **~ general** headquarters *pl*

**cuarto**$^{1}$ (*kwahr*-toa) *num* fourth; *m* quarter; **~ de hora** quarter of an hour

**cuarto**$^{2}$ (*kwahr*-toa) *m* chamber; **~ de aseo** lavatory; washroom *Am*; **~ de baño** bathroom; **~ de niños** nursery; **~ para huéspedes** spare room

**cuatro** (*kwah*-troa) *num* four

**Cuba** (*koo*-bhah) *f* Cuba

**cubano** (koo-*bhah*-noa) *adj* Cuban; *m* Cuban

**cubierta** (koo-*bh*$^{y}$*ayr*-tah) *f* cover; deck

**cubierto** (koo-*bh*$^{y}$*ayr*-toa) *adj* cloudy

**cubiertos** (koo-*bh*$^{y}$*ayr*-toass) *mpl* cutlery

**cubo** (*koo*-bhoa) *m* cube; **~ de la basura** dustbin

**cubrir** (koo-*bhreer*) *v* cover

**cuclillo** (koo-*klee*-l$^{y}$oa) *m* cuckoo

**cuchara** (koo-*chah*-rah) *f* spoon; tablespoon

**cucharada** (koo-chah-*rah*-dhah) *f* spoonful

**cucharadita** (koo-chah-rah-*dhee*-tah) *f* teaspoonful

**cucharilla** (koo-chah-*ree*-l$^{y}$ah) *f* teaspoon

**cuchillo** (koo-*chee*-l$^{y}$oa) *m* knife

**cuello** (*kway*-l$^{y}$oa) *m* neck; collar; **~ de botella** bottleneck

**cuenta** (*kwayn*-tah) *f* account; bill; check *Am*; bead; **~ de banco** bank account; ***darse ~** *see

**cuento** (*kwayn*-toa) *m* story, tale

**cuerda** (*kwayr*-dhah) *f* cord; string; ***dar ~** *wind

**cuerno** (*kwayr*-noa) *m* horn

**cuero** (*kway*-roa) *m* leather; **~ vacuno** cowhide

**cuerpo** (*kwayr*-poa) *m* body

**cuervo** (*kwayr*-bhoa) *m* raven

**cuestión** (kwayss-*t*$^{y}$*oan*) *f* matter, issue, question

**cueva** (*kway*-bhah) *f* cavern, cave; wine cellar

**cuidado** (kwee-*dhah*-dhoa) *m* care; ***tener ~** watch out, look out

**cuidadoso** (kwee-dhah-*dhoa*-soa) *adj* careful; diligent

**cuidar de** (kwee-*dhahr*) attend to, look after, tend, *take care of
**cuidarse** (kwee-*dhahr*-say) look after oneself, take care of oneself; **~ de hacer** take care to do
**culebra** (koo-*lay*-bhrah) *f* snake
**culo** (*koo*-loa) *m vulgar* ass, arse; *colloquial* butt, bum; **ser ~ de mal asiento** *colloquial* be restless
**culpa** (*kool*-pah) *f* guilt, fault, blame
**culpable** (kool-*pah*-bhlay) *adj* guilty
**culpar** (kool-*pahr*) *v* blame, accuse
**cultivar** (kool-tee-*bhahr*) *v* cultivate; *grow, raise
**cultivo** (kool-*tee*-bhoa) *m* cultivation
**culto** (*kool*-toa) *adj* cultured; *m* worship
**cultura** (kool-*too*-rah) *f* culture
**cultural** (kool-too-*rahl*) *adj* cultural
**cumbre** (*koom*-bray) *f* peak
**cumpleaños** (koom-play-*ah*-ñoass) *m* birthday
**cumplimentar** (koom-plee-mayn-*tahr*) *v* compliment
**cumplimiento** (koom-plee-*m*$^{y}$*ayn*-toa) *m* compliment
**cumplir** (koom-*pleer*) *v* comply, carry out
**cuna** (*koo*-nah) *f* cradle; **~ de viaje** carrycot
**cuneta** (koo-*nay*-tah) *f* ditch; gutter
**cuña** (*koo*-ñah) *f* wedge
**cuñada** (koo-*ñah*-dhah) *f* sister-in-law
**cuñado** (koo-*ñah*-dhoa) *m* brother-in-law
**cuota** (*kwoa*-tah) *f* quota
**cupón** (koo-*poan*) *m* coupon
**cúpula** (*koo*-poo-lah) *f* dome
**cura** (*koo*-rah) *m* priest; *f* cure
**curación** (koo-rah-*th*$^{y}$*oan*) *f* cure, recovery
**curandero** (koo-rahn-*day*-roa) *m* quack
**curar** (koo-*rahr*) *v* cure, heal; **curarse** *v* recover
**curato** (koo-*rah*-toa) *m* parsonage
**curiosidad** (koo-r$^{y}$oa-see-*dhahdh*) *f* curiosity; sight; curio
**curioso** (koo-*r*$^{y}$*oa*-soa) *adj* curious; inquisitive; quaint
**cursi** (*koor*-see) *adj colloquial* affected
**cursiva** (koor-*see*-bhah) *f* italics *pl*
**curso** (*koor*-soa) *m* course; lecture; **~ intensivo** intensive course
**curva** (koor-bhah) *f* turn, curve, bend
**curvado** (koor-*bhah*-dhoa) *adj* curved
**curvo** (*koor*-bhoa) *adj* crooked, bent
**custodia** (kooss-*toa*-dh$^{y}$ah) *f* custody
**cuyo** (*koo*-$^{y}$oa) *pron* whose; of which

# D

**dadivoso** (dah-dhee-*bhoa*-soa) *adj* lavish with gifts
**dado**[1] (*dah*-doa) *m* dice
**dado**[2] (*dah*-doa) *adj* given
**daltoniano** (dahl-toa-*n*$^{y}$*ah*-noa) *adj* colo(u)r-blind
**dama** (*dah*-mah) *f* lady
**danés** (dah-*nayss*) *adj* Danish; *m* Dane
**dañar** (dah-*ñahr*) *v* damage; *hurt
**daño** (*dah*-ñoa) *m* mischief; harm; ***hacer ~** *hurt
**dañoso** (dah-*ñoa*-soa) *adj* harmful
***dar** (dahr) *v* *give; **dado que** supposing that
**dátil** (*dah*-teel) *m* date

**dato** (*dah*-toa) *m* data *pl*
**de** (day) *prep* of; out of, from, off; with
**debajo** (day-*bhah*-khoa) *adv* underneath, beneath, below; **~ de** under, beneath, below
**debate** (day-*bhah*-tay) *m* debate, discussion
**debatir** (day-bhah-*teer*) *v* discuss
**deber** (day-*bhayr*) *m* duty; *v* *have to, need to, need; owe; **~ de** *be bound to
**debido** (day-*bhee*-dhoa) *adj* due; proper; **~ a** owing to
**débil** (*day*-bheel) *adj* faint, weak, feeble
**debilidad** (day-bhee-lee-*dhahdh*) *f* weakness
**decencia** (day-*thayn*-th$^y$ah) *f* decency
**decente** (day-*thayn*-tay) *adj* decent
**decepcionar** (day-thayp-th$^y$oa-*nahr*) *v* *let down, disappoint
**decidir** (day-thee-*dheer*) *v* decide; **decidido** resolute
**décimo** (*day*-thee-moa) *num* tenth
**decimoctavo** (day-thee-moak-*tah*-bhoa) *num* eighteenth
**decimonono** (day-thee-moa-*noa*-noa) *num* nineteenth
**decimoséptimo** (day-thee-moa-*sayp*-tee-moa) *num* seventeenth
**decimosexto** (day-thee-moa-*sayks*-toa) *num* sixteenth
***decir** (day-*theer*) *v* *say, *tell; ***querer ~** *mean
**decisión** (day-thee-*s$^y$oan*) *f* decision
**decisivo** (day-thee-*see*-bhoa) *adj* decisive
**declaración** (day-klah-rah-*th$^y$oan*) *f* statement, declaration
**declarar** (day-klah-*rahr*) *v* state, declare
**decoración** (day-koa-rah-*th$^y$oan*) *f* decoration
**decorativo** (day-koa-rah-*tee*-bhoa) *adj* decorative
**decreto** (day-*kray*-toa) *m* decree
**dedal** (day-*dhahl*) *m* thimble
**dédalo** (*day*-dhah-loa) *m* muddle
**dedicar** (day-dhee-*kahr*) *v* devote, dedicate
**dedo** (*day*-dhoa) *m* finger; **~ auricular** little finger; **~ del pie** toe
***deducir** (day-dhoo-*theer*) *v* infer, deduce; deduct
**defecto** (day-*fayk*-toa) *m* fault
**defectuoso** (day-fayk-*twoa*-soa) *adj* defective, faulty
***defender** (day-fayn-*dayr*) *v* defend
**defensa** (day-*fayn*-sah) *f* defence, defense *Am*; plea; *Me* fender
**defensor** (day-fayn-*soar*) *m* defender, proponent; champion
**déficit** (*day*-fee-theet) *m* deficit
**definición** (day-fee-nee-*th$^y$oan*) *f* definition
**definir** (day-fee-*neer*) *v* define; **definido** definite
**definitivo** (day-fee-nee-*tee*-bhoa) *adj* definitive
**deforme** (day-*foar*-may) *adj* deformed
**dejar** (day-*khahr*) *v* *let, *leave; *leave behind, desert; **~ de** stop
**del** (dayl) *contraction of* de el
**delantal** (day-lahn-*tahl*) *m* apron
**delante de** (day-*lahn*-tay day) before, in front of, ahead of
**delegación** (day-lay-gah-*th$^y$oan*) *f* delegation
**delegado** (day-lay-*gah*-dhoa) *m* delegate
**deleite** (day-*lay*-tay) *m* delight
**deleitoso** (day-lay-*toa*-soa) *adj* delightful
**deletrear** (day-lay-tray-*ahr*) *v* *spell
**deletreo** (day-lay-*tray*-oa) *m* spelling
**delgado** (dayl-*gah*-dhoa) *adj* thin
**deliberación** (day-lee-bhay-rah-*th$^y$oan*) *f* deliberation

**deliberar** (day-lee-bhay-*rahr*) *v* deliberate; **deliberado** *adj* deliberate

**delicado** (day-lee-*kah*-dhoa) *adj* delicate, tender

**delicia** (day-*lee*-th$^y$ah) *f* joy, delight

**delicioso** (day-lee-*th$^y$oa*-soa) *adj* wonderful, delightful, delicious, lovely

**delincuente** (day-leeng-*kwayn*-tay) *m* criminal

**delito** (day-*lee*-toa) *m* crime

**demanda** (day-*mahn*-dah) *f* request; application; demand

**demás** (day-*mahss*) *adj* other; remaining; **lo ~** the rest; **los ~** the others

**demasiado** (day-mah-*s$^y$ah*-dhoa) *adv* too

**democracia** (day-moa-*krah*-th$^y$ah) *f* democracy

**democrático** (day-moa-*krah*-tee-koa) *adj* democratic

***demoler** (day-moa-*layr*) *v* demolish

**demolición** (day-moa-lee-*th$^y$oan*) *f* demolition

**demonio** (day-*moa*-n$^y$oa) *m* devil

**demostración** (day-moass-trah-*th$^y$oan*) *f* demonstration

***demostrar** (day-moass-*trahr*) *v* demonstrate, *show, prove

***denegar** (day-nay-*gahr*) *v* deny

**denominación** (day-noa-mee-nah-*th$^y$oan*) *f* denomination

**denso** (*dayn*-soa) *adj* thick, dense

**dentadura postiza** (dayn-tah-*dhoo*-rah poass-*tee*-thah) false teeth, dentures

**dentista** (dayn-*teess*-tah) *m* dentist

**dentro** (*dayn*-troa) *adv* inside; **de ~** within; **~ de** inside, within; into; in

**departamento** (day-pahr-tah-*mayn*-toa) *m* department; section, division

**depender de** (day-payn-*dayr*) depend on

**dependiente** (day-payn-*d$^y$ayn*-tay) *adj* dependant; *m*, **-a** *f* sales clerk *Am*, shop assistant

**deporte** (day-*poar*-tay) *m* sport; **conjunto de ~** sportswear; **chaqueta de ~** sports jacket

**deportista** (day-poar-*teess*-tah) *m* sportsman

**depositar** (day-poa-see-*tahr*) *v* bank

**depósito** (day-*poa*-see-toa) *m* deposit; **~ de gasolina** petrol tank, gas tank *Am*

**depresión** (day-pray-*s$^y$oan*) *f* depression

**deprimente** (day-pree-*mayn*-tay) *adj* depressing

**deprimir** (day-pree-*meer*) *v* depress; **deprimido** blue, depressed, low

**derecha** (day-*ray*-chah) *f* right; **la ~** the right(-hand); **a la ~** on the right; to the right

**derecho** (day-*ray*-choa) *m* right; law, right, justice, straight; *adj* upright; right-hand; **~ administrativo** administrative law; **~ civil** civil law; **~ comercial** commercial law; **~ electoral** franchise, suffrage; **~ penal** criminal law

**derivar de** (day-ree-*bhahr*) *be derived from

**derramar** (day-rrah-*mahr*) *v* *shed

**derribar** (day-rree-*bhahr*) *v* knock down

**derrochador** (day-rroa-chah-*dhoar*) *adj* wasteful

**derrota** (day-*rroa*-tah) *f* defeat

**derrotar** (day-rroa-*tahr*) *v* defeat

**derrumbarse** (day-rroom-*bahr*-say) *v* collapse

**desabotonar** (day-sah-bhoa-toa-*nahr*) *v* unbutton

**desacelerar** (day-sah-thay-lay-*rahr*) *v* slow down

**desacostumbrado** (day-sah-koass-

toom-*brah*-dhoa) *adj* unaccustomed
**desacostumbrar** (day-sah-koass-toom-*brahr*) *v* unlearn
**desafiar** (day-sah-*f$^y$ahr*) *v* dare; challenge
**desafilado** (day-sah-fee-*lah*-dhoa) *adj* blunt
**desafortunado** (day-sah-foar-too-*nah*-dhoa) *adj* unlucky, unfortunate
**desagradable** (day-sah-grah-*dhah*-bhlay) *adj* nasty, disagreeable, unpleasant; unkind
**desagradar** (day-sah-grah-*dhahr*) *v* displease
**desagüe** (day-*sah*-gway) *m* sewer, drain
**desaliñado** (day-sah-lee-*ñah*-doa) *adj* untidy
**desánimo** (day-*sah*-nee-moa) *m* depression, discouragement
***desaparecer** (day-sah-pah-ray-*thayr*) *v* disappear; vanish
**desaparecido** (day-sah-pah-ray-*thee*-dhoa) *adj* lost; *m* missing person
**desapasionado** (day-sah-pah-s$^y$oa-*nah*-dhoa) *adj* matter-of-fact; dispassionate
***desaprobar** (day-sah-proa-*bhahr*) *v* disapprove
**desarrollar** (day-sah-rroa-*l$^y$ahr*) *v* develop; unfold; unwind
**desarrollo** (day-sah-*rroa*-l$^y$oa) *m* development; unfolding
**desasosiego** (day-sah-soa-*s$^y$ay*-goa) *m* unrest
**desastre** (day-*sahss*-tray) *m* disaster, calamity
**desastroso** (day-sahss-*troa*-soa) *adj* disastrous
**desatar** (day-sah-*tahr*) *v* *undo, untie, unfasten
**desautorizado** (day-sou-toa-ree-*thah*-dhoa) *adj* unauthorized
**desayunar** (day-sah-$^y$oo-*nahr*) *v* have breakfast
**desayuno** (day-sah-*$^y$oo*-noa) *m* breakfast
**descafeinado** (dayss-kah-fay-*nah*-dhoa) *adj* decaffeinated
**descansar** (dayss-kahn-*sahr*) *v* rest; relax
**descanso** (dayss-*kahn*-soa) *m* rest; break; half-time
**descarado** (dayss-kah-*rah*-dhoa) *adj* bold, impertinent
**descargar** (dayss-kahr-*gahr*) *v* discharge, unload
**descendencia** (day-thayn-*dayn*-th$^y$ah) *f* origin; descendants
***descender** (day-thayn-*dhayr*) *v* *fall
**descendiente** (day-thayn-*d$^y$ayn*-tay) *m/f* descendant; *adj* descending
**descolorido** (dayss-koa-loa-*ree*-dhoa) *adj* discolo(u)red
**descompostura** (dayss-koam-poass-*too*-rah) *fMe* breakdown
***desconcertar** (dayss-koan-thayr-*tahr*) *v* overwhelm, embarrass
**desconectar** (dayss-koa-nayk-*tahr*) *v* disconnect
**desconfiado** (dayss-koan-*f$^y$ah*-dhoa) *adj* suspicious; distrusting
**desconfianza** (dayss-koan-*f$^y$ahn*-thah) *f* suspicion; distrust
**desconfiar de** (dayss-koan-*f$^y$ahr*) *v* distrust
**descongelarse** (dayss-koang-khay-*lahr*-say) *v* thaw
***desconocer** (dayss-koa-noa-*thayr*) *v* not to *know, fail to recognize
**desconocido** (dayss-koa-noa-*thee*-dhoa) *adj* unknown; unfamiliar
**descontento** (dayss-koan-*tayn*-toa) *adj* discontented
**descorchar** (dayss-koar-*chahr*) *v* uncork
**descortés** (dayss-koar-*tayss*) *adj* impolite

**describir** (dayss-kree-*bheer*) *v* describe
**descripción** (dayss-kreep-*th^y oan*) *f* description
**descubierto** (dayss-koo-*bh^y ayr*-toa) *m* overdraft
**descubrimiento** (dayss-koo-bhree-*m^y ayn*-toa) *m* discovery
**descubrir** (dayss-koo-*bhreer*) *v* discover, detect
**descuento** (dayss-*kwayn*-toa) *m* discount; ~ **bancario** bank rate
**descuidar** (dayss-kwee-*dhahr*) *v* neglect; **descuidado** careless, negligent, slovenly
**descuido** (dayss-*kwee*-dhoa) *m* carelessness, negligence; oversight
**desde** (*dayz*-dhay) *prep* from; since; ~ **entonces** since; ~ **que** since
**desdén** (dayz-*dhayn*) *m* disdain
**desdichado** (dayz-dhee-*chah*-dhoa) *adj* unhappy
**deseable** (day-say-*ah*-bhlay) *adj* desirable
**desear** (day-say-*ahr*) *v* desire; wish, want
**desecar** (day-say-*kahr*) *v* drain
**desechable** (day-say-*chah*-bhlay) *adj* disposable
**desechar** (day-say-*chahr*) *v* discard
**desecho** (day-*say*-choa) *m* refuse
**desembarcar** (day-saym-bahr-*kahr*) *v* disembark; land
**desembocadura** (day-saym-boa-kah-*dhoo*-rah) *f* mouth
**desempaquetar** (day-saym-pah-kay-*tahr*) *v* unpack
**desempeñar** (day-saym-pay-*ñahr*) *v* perform
**desempleo** (day-saym-*play*-oa) *m* unemployment
**desengaño** (day-sayng-*gah*-ñoa) *m* disappointment
**desenvoltura** (day-saym-boal-*too*-rah) *f* ease; eloquence
***desenvolver** (day-saym-boal-*bhayr*) *v* unwrap; expound
**deseo** (day-*say*-oa) *m* wish, desire
**desertar** (day-sayr-*tahr*) *v* desert
**desesperación** (day-sayss-pay-rah-*th^y oan*) *f* despair
**desesperado** (day-sayss-pay-*rah*-dhoa) *adj* hopeless, desperate; ***estar** ~ despair
**desfavorable** (dayss-fah-bhoa-*rah*-bhlay) *adj* unfavo(u)rable
**desfile** (dayss-*fee*-lay) *m* parade
**desgarrar** (dayz-gah-*rrahr*) *v* *tear
**desgracia** (dayz-*grah*-th^yah) *f* misfortune
**desgraciadamente** (dayz-grah-th^yah-dhah-*mayn*-tay) *adv* unfortunately
***deshacer** (day-sah-*thayr*) *v* *undo; **deshacerce de** get rid of
**deshielo** (day-*s^y ay*-loa) *m* thaw
**deshonesto** (day-soa-*nayss*-toa) *adj* dishonest
**deshonor** (day-soa-*noar*) *m* dishonor; disgrace
**deshonra** (day-*soan*-rah) *f* dishonor; shame
**deshuesar** (day-sway-*sahr*) *v* bone
**desierto** (day-*s^y ayr*-toa) *adj* desert; *m* desert
**designar** (day-seeg-*nahr*) *v* designate; appoint
**desigual** (day-see-*gwahl*) *adj* unequal, uneven
**desinclinado** (day-seeng-klee-*nah*-dhoa) *adj* unwilling
**desinfectante** (day-seen-fayk-*tahn*-tay) *m* disinfectant
**desinfectar** (day-seen-fayk-*tahr*) *v* disinfect
**desinteresado** (day-seen-tay-ray-*sah*-dhoa) *adj* unselfish
**desliz** (dayz-*leeth*) *m* slide; slip
**deslizarse** (dayz-lee-*thahr*-say) *v*

*slide; slip
**deslucido** (dayz-loo-*thee*-dhoa) *adj* dim
**desmayarse** (dayz-mah-$^{y}$*ahr*-say) *v* faint
**desnudarse** (dayz-noo-*dhahr*-say) *v* undress
**desnudo** (dayz-*noo*-dhoa) *adj* naked, nude, bare; *m* nude
**desnutrición** (dayz-noo-tree-*th$^{y}$oan*) *f* malnutrition
**desocupado** (day-soa-koo-*pah*-dhoa) *adj* unoccupied; unemployed
**desodorante** (day-soa-dhoa-*rahn*-tay) *m* deodorant
**desolador** (day-soa-lah-*doar*) *adj* bleak
**desorden** (day-*soar*-dayn) *m* disorder; mess
**despachar** (dayss-pah-*chahr*) *v* dispatch, despatch, *send off
**despacho** (dayss-*pah*-choa) *m* study; office
**despedida** (dayss-pay-*dhee*-dhah) *f* parting; departure
***despedir** (dayss-pay-*dheer*) *v* dismiss; fire; ***despedirse** *v* check out
**despegar** (dayss-pay-*gahr*) *v* *take off
**despegue** (dayss-*pay*-gay) *m* take-off
**despensa** (dayss-*payn*-sah) *f* pantry, larder
**desperdicio** (dayss-payr-*dhee*-th$^{y}$oa) *m* litter; waste
**despertador** (dayss-payr-tah-*dhoar*) *m* alarm clock
***despertar** (dayss-payr-*tahr*) *v* *wake, *awake; ***despertarse** *v* wake up
**despierto** (dayss-*p$^{y}$ayr*-toa) *adj* awake; vigilant
***desplegar** (dayss-play-*gahr*) *v* unfold; expand
**desplomarse** (dayss-ploa-*mahr*-say) *v* collapse
**despreciar** (dayss-pray-*th$^{y}$ahr*) *v* scorn, despise
**desprecio** (dayss-*pray*-th$^{y}$oa) *m* scorn, contempt
**despreocupado** (dayss-pray-oa-koo-*pah*-dhoa) *adj* carefree
**después** (dayss-*pwayss*) *adv* afterwards; then; **~ de** after; **~ de que** after
**destacado** (dayss-tah-*kah*-dhoa) *adj* outstanding
**destacarse** (dayss-tah-*kahr*-say) *v* *stand out
**destapar** (dayss-tah-*pahr*) *v* uncover
**destello** (dayss-*tay*-l$^{y}$oa) *m* glare
***desteñirse** (dayss-tay-*ñeer*-say) *v* fade, discolo(u)r; **no destiñe** fast-dyed
**destinar** (dayss-tee-*nahr*) *v* destine; address
**destinatario** (dayss-tee-nah-*tah*-r$^{y}$oa) *m*, **-a** *f* addressee
**destino** (dayss-*tee*-noa) *m* fate, destiny, lot; destination
**destornillador** (dayss-toar-nee-l$^{y}$ah-*dhoar*) *m* screwdriver
**destornillar** (dayss-toar-nee-*l$^{y}$ahr*) *v* unscrew
**destrucción** (dayss-trook-*th$^{y}$oan*) *f* destruction
***destruir** (dayss-*trweer*) *v* destroy; wreck
**desvalorización** (dayz-bhah-loa-ree-thah-*th$^{y}$oan*) *f* devaluation
**desvalorizar** (dayz-bhah-loa-ree-*thahr*) *v* devalue
**desvelado** (dayz-bhay-*lah*-dhoa) *adj* sleepless
**desventaja** (dayz-bhayn-*tah*-khah) *f* disadvantage
**desviar** (dayz-*bh$^{y}$ahr*) *v* avert; **desviarse** *v* deviate
**desvío** (dayz-*bhee*-oa) *m* detour; diversion

**detallado** (day-tah-*l$^{y}$ah*-dhoa) *adj* detailed
**detalle** (day-*tah*-l$^{y}$ay) *m* detail; **vender al ~** sell retail
**detective** (day-tayk-*tee*-bhay) *m/f* detective
**detención** (day-tayn-*th$^{y}$oan*) *f* custody
***detener** (day-tay-*nayr*) *v* detain
**detergente** (day-tayr-*khayn*-tay) *m* detergent
**determinar** (day-tayr-mee-*nahr*) *v* define, determine; **determinado** definite
**detestar** (day-tayss-*tahr*) *v* hate, dislike
**detrás** (day-*trahss*) *adv* behind; **~ de** behind, after
**deuda** (*day$^{oo}$*-dhah) *f* debt
***devolver** (day-bhoal-*bhayr*) *v* *bring back; *send back
**día** (*dee*-ah) *m* day; **¡buenos días!** hello!; **de ~** by day; **~ de trabajo** working day; **~ laborable** weekday; **el otro ~** recently
**diabetes** (d$^{y}$ah-*bhay*-tayss) *f* diabetes
**diabético** (d$^{y}$ah-*bhay*-tee-koa) *m*, **-a** *f* diabetic
**diablo** (*d$^{y}$ah*-bhloa) *m* devil
**diagnosis** (d$^{y}$ahg-*noa*-seess) *m* diagnosis
**diagnosticar** (d$^{y}$ahg-noass-tee-*kahr*) *v* diagnose
**diagonal** (d$^{y}$ah-goa-*nahl*) *adj* diagonal; *f* diagonal
**dialecto** (d$^{y}$ah-*layk*-toa) *m* dialect
**diamante** (d$^{y}$ah-*mahn*-tay) *m* diamond
**diapositiva** (d$^{y}$ah-poa-see-*tee*-bhah) *f* slide
**diario** (*d$^{y}$ah*-r$^{y}$oa) *adj* daily; *m* daily, newspaper; diary; **a ~** per day; **~ matutino** morning paper
**diarrea** (d$^{y}$ah-*rray*-ah) *f* diarrh(o)ea
**dibujar** (dee-bhoo-*khahr*) *v* sketch, *draw
**dibujo** (dee-*bhoo*-khoa) *m* sketch, drawing; **dibujos animados** cartoon
**diccionario** (deek-th$^{y}$oa-*nah*-r$^{y}$oa) *m* dictionary
**diciembre** (dee-*th$^{y}$aym*-bray) December
**dictado** (deek-*tah*-dhoa) *m* dictation
**dictador** (deek-tah-*dhoar*) *m* dictator
**dictadura** (deek-tah-*dhoo*-rah) *f* dictatorship
**dictáfono** (deek-*tah*-foa-noa) *m* dictaphone
**dictar** (deek-*tahr*) *v* dictate
**dichoso** (dee-*choa*-soa) *adj* happy
**diecinueve** (d$^{y}$ay-thee-*nway*-bhay) *num* nineteen
**dieciocho** (d$^{y}$ay-*th$^{y}$oa*-choa) *num* eighteen
**dieciséis** (d$^{y}$ay-thee-*sayss*) *num* sixteen
**diecisiete** (d$^{y}$ay-thee-*s$^{y}$ay*-tay) *num* seventeen
**diente** (*d$^{y}$ayn*-tay) *m* tooth; **~ de león** dandelion
**diesel** (*dee*-sayl) *m* diesel
**diestro** (*d$^{y}$ayss*-troa) *adj* skil(l)ful
**diez** (d$^{y}$ayth) *num* ten
**diferencia** (dee-fay-*rayn*-th$^{y}$ah) *f* difference; contrast, distinction
**diferente** (dee-fay-*rayn*-tay) *adj* different; unlike
***diferir** (dee-fay-*reer*) *v* vary, differ; delay
**difícil** (dee-*fee*-theel) *adj* hard, difficult
**dificultad** (dee-fee-kool-*tahdh*) *f* difficulty
**difteria** (deef-*tay*-r$^{y}$ah) *f* diphtheria
**difunto** (dee-*foon*-toa) *adj* deceased; dead
**difuso** (dee-*foo*-soa) *adj* dim; diffused
**digerible** (dee-khayss-*tee*-bhlay) *adj* digestible

***digerir** (dee-khay-*reer*) *v* digest
**digestión** (dee-khayss-*t$^y$oan*) *f* digestion
**digital** (dee-khee-*tahl*) *adj* digital
**dignidad** (deeg-nee-*dhahdh*) *f* dignity
**digno de** (*dee*-ñoa day) worthy of
**dilación** (dee-lah-*th$^y$oan*) *f* delay, respite
**diligencia** (dee-lee-*khayn*-th$^y$ah) *f* diligence
**diligente** (dee-lee-*khayn*-tay) *adj* diligent
**dimensión** (dee-mayn-*s$^y$oan*) *f* extent, size
**Dinamarca** (dee-nah-*mahr*-kah) *f* Denmark
**dínamo** (*dee*-nah-moa) *f* dynamo
**dinero** (dee-*nay*-roa) *m* money; **~ contante** cash
**dios** (d$^y$oass) *m* god
**diosa** (*d$^y$oa*-sah) *f* goddess
**diploma** (dee-*ploa*-mah) *m* diploma, certificate
**diplomático** (dee-ploa-*mah*-tee-koa) *m* diplomat
**diputado** (dee-poo-*tah*-dhoa) *m* Member of Parliament
**dirección** (dee-rayk-*th$^y$oan*) *f* direction; way; address; leadership, lead; **~ de escena** direction; **~ única** one-way traffic
**directamente** (dee-rayk-tah-*mayn*-tay) *adv* straight; straight away
**directo** (dee-*rayk*-toa) *adj* direct
**director** (dee-rayk-*toar*) *m*, **-a** *f* director, manager; conductor; **~ de escuela** head teacher, headmaster; principal
**dirigir** (dee-ree-*kheer*) *v* head; direct
**disciplina** (dee-thee-*plee*-nah) *f* discipline
**discípulo** (deess-*thee*-poo-loa) *m* disciple; pupil
**disco** (*deess*-koa) *m* disc; record
**disco compacto** (*deess*-koa koam-*pahk*-toa) *m* compact disc; **reproductor de ~s ~s** CD player
**discreto** (deess-*kray*-toa) *adj* discreet; inconspicuous
**disculpa** (deess-*kool*-pah) *f* apology
**disculpar** (deess-kool-*pahr*) *v* excuse; **disculparse** *v* apologize; **¡disculpe!** sorry!
**discurso** (deess-*koor*-soa) *m* speech
**discusión** (deess-koo-*s$^y$oan*) *f* discussion, argument
**discutir** (deess-koo-*teer*) *v* discuss, deliberate, argue
***disentir** (dee-sayn-*teer*) *v* disagree
**diseñar** (dee-say-*ñahr*) *v* design
**diseño** (dee-*say*-ñoa) *m* design; pattern; **cuaderno de ~** sketch-book
**disfraz** (deess-*frahth*) *m* disguise
**disfrazarse** (deess-frah-*thahr*-say) *v* disguise
**disfrutar** (deess-froo-*tahr*) *v* enjoy
**disgustar** (deez-gooss-*tahr*) *v* displease
**disimular** (dee-see-moo-*lahr*) *v* conceal
**dislocar** (deez-loa-*kahr*) *v* dislocate
**disminución** (deez-mee-noo-*th$^y$oan*) *f* decrease
***disminuir** (deez-mee-*nweer*) *v* reduce, lessen, decrease
***disolver** (dee-soal-*bhayr*) *v* dissolve
**disparar** (deess-pah-*rahr*) *v* fire
**disparo** (deess-*pah*-roa) *m* shot
**dispensar** (deess-payn-*sahr*) *v* exempt; **~ de** discharge of; **¡dispense usted!** sorry!
**dispensario** (deess-payn-*sah*-r$^y$oa) *m* health centre (center *Am*)
***disponer** (deess-poa-*nayr*) *v* sort; **~ de** dispose of
**disponible** (deess-poa-*nee*-bhlay) *adj* available; spare
**disposición** (deess-poa-see-*th$^y$oan*) *f*

disposal
**dispuesto** (deess-*pwayss*-toa) *adj* inclined, willing
**disputa** (deess-*poo*-tah) *f* dispute, argument, quarrel
**disputar** (deess-poo-*tahr*) *v* argue, quarrel; dispute
**distancia** (deess-*tahn*-th$^y$ah) *f* distance; space, way
**distinción** (deess-teen-*th$^y$oan*) *f* distinction, difference
**distinguido** (deess-teeng-*gee*-dhoa) *adj* distinguished, dignified
**distinguir** (deess-teeng-*geer*) *v* distinguish; **distinguirse** *v* excel
**distinto** (deess-*teen*-toa) *adj* distinct
**distracción** (deess-trahk-*th$^y$oan*) *f* distraction; amusement
***distraer** (deess-trah-*ayr*) *v* distract
**distribuidor** (deess-tree-bhwee-*dhoar*) *m* distributor
***distribuir** (deess-tree-*bhweer*) *v* distribute; issue
**distrito** (deess-*tree*-toa) *m* district; ~ **electoral** constituency
**disturbio** (deess-*toor*-bh$^y$oa) *m* disturbance
**disuadir** (dee-swah-*dheer*) *v* dissuade from
**diversión** (dee-bhayr-*s$^y$oan*) *f* pleasure, fun; diversion, entertainment
**diverso** (dee-*bhayr*-soa) *adj* diverse
**divertido** (dee-bhayr-*tee*-dhoa) *adj* amusing, entertaining
***divertir** (dee-bhayr-*teer*) *v* amuse, entertain
**dividir** (dee-bhee-*dheer*) *v* divide
**divino** (dee-*bhee*-noa) *adj* divine
**división** (dee-bhee-*s$^y$oan*) *f* division; section
**divorciado** (dee-bhoar-*th$^y$ah*-doa) *adj* divorced; *m*, **-a** (dee-bhoar-*th$^y$ah*-dah) *f* divorcee
**divorciar** (dee-bhoar-*th$^y$ahr*) *v* divorce
**divorcio** (dee-*bhoar*-th$^y$oa) *m* divorce
**doblar** (doa-*bhlahr*) *v* *bend; fold
**doble** (*doa*-bhlay) *adj* double
**doce** (*doa*-thay) *num* twelve
**docena** (doa-*thay*-nah) *f* dozen
**doctor** (doak-*toar*) *m* doctor
**doctrina** (doak-*tree*-nah) *f* doctrine
**documento** (doa-koo-*mayn*-toa) *m* document
***doler** (doa-*layr*) *v* ache
**dolor** (doa-*loar*) *m* ache, pain; grief; **dolores** *mpl* labo(u)r; **sin** ~ painless
**dolorido** (doa-loa-*ree*-dhoa) *adj* painful
**doloroso** (doa-loa-*roa*-soa) *adj* sore
**domesticado** (doa-mayss-tee-*kah*-dhoa) *adj* tame
**domesticar** (doa-mayss-tee-*kahr*) *v* tame
**doméstico** (doa-*mayss*-tee-koa) *adj* domestic; **faenas domésticas** housework
**domicilio** (doa-mee-*thee*-l$^y$oa) *m* domicile
**dominación** (doa-mee-nah-*th$^y$oan*) *f* domination
**dominante** (doa-mee-*nahn*-tay) *adj* leading
**dominar** (doa-mee-*nahr*) *v* dominate; master
**domingo** (doa-*meeng*-goa) *m* Sunday
**dominio** (doa-*mee*-n$^y$oa) *m* dominion, rule
**don** (doan) *m* talent; ability
**donación** (doa-nah-*th$^y$oan*) *f* donation
**donante** (doa-*nahn*-tay) *m* donor
**donar** (doa-*nahr*) *v* donate
**donde** (*doan*-day) *conj* where; **en ~ sea** anywhere
**dónde** (*doan*-day) *adv* where
**dondequiera** (doan-day-*k$^y$ay*-rah) *adv* anywhere; ~ **que** wherever
**dorado** (doa-*rah*-dhoa) *adj* gilt;

golden
**dormido** (doar-*mee*-dhoa) *adj* asleep; **quedarse ~** *oversleep
***dormir** (doar-*meer*) *v* *sleep
**dormitorio** (doar-mee-*toa*-r$^y$oa) *m* bedroom; dormitory
**dos** (doass) *num* two; **~ veces** twice
**dosis** (*doa*-seess) *f* dose
**dotado** (doa-*tah*-dhoa) *adj* talented
**dragón** (drah-*goan*) *m* dragon
**drama** (*drah*-mah) *m* drama
**dramático** (drah-*mah*-tee-koa) *adj* dramatic
**drenar** (dray-*nahr*) *v* drain
**droga** (*droa*-ghah) *f* drug; **~ de diseño** designer drug
**droguería** (droa-gay-*ree*-ah) *f* chemist's, pharmacy; drugstore *Am*
**ducha** (*doo*-chah) *f* shower
**ducharse** (doo-*chahr*-say) *v* have a shower, shower
**duda** (*doo*-dhah) *f* doubt; ***poner en ~** query; **sin ~** undoubtedly, without doubt
**dudar** (doo-*dhahr*) *v* doubt
**dudoso** (doo-*dhoa*-soa) *adj* doubtful
**duelo** (*dway*-loa) *m* duel; grief
**duende** (*dwayn*-dhay) *m* elf
**dueña** (*dway*-ñah) *f* landlady, owner
**dueño** (*dway*-ñoa) *m* landlord, owner
**dulce** (*dool*-thay) *adj* sweet; smooth; *m* sweet; **dulces** cake; sweets; candy *Am*
**duna** (*doo*-nah) *f* dune
**duodécimo** (dwoa-*day*-thee-moa) *num* twelfth
**duque** (*doo*-kay) *m* duke
**duquesa** (doo-*kay*-sah) *f* duchess
**duración** (doo-rah-*th$^y$oan*) *f* duration
**duradero** (doo-rah-*dhay*-roa) *adj* permanent, lasting
**durante** (doo-*rahn*-tay) *prep* for, during
**durar** (doo-*rahr*) *v* last; continue
**duro** (*doo*-roa) *adj* hard; tough

# E

**ébano** (*ay*-bhah-noa) *m* ebony
**eclipse** (ay-*kleep*-say) *m* eclipse
**eco** (*ay*-koa) *m* echo
**economía** (ay-koa-noa-*mee*-ah) *f* economy
**económico** (ay-koa-*noa*-mee-koa) *adj* economic; thrifty, economical; cheap
**economista** (ay-koa-noa-*meess*-tah) *m* economist
**economizar** (ay-koa-noa-mee-*thahr*) *v* economize
**Ecuador** (ay-kwah-*dhoar*) *m* Ecuador
**ecuador** (ay-kwah-*dhoar*) *m* equator
**ecuatoriano** (ay-kwah-toa-*r$^y$ah*-noa) *m* Ecuadorian
**eczema** (ayk-*thay*-mah) *m* eczema
**echar** (ay-*chahr*) *v* toss, throw; **~ abajo** demolish; **~ al correo** post; **~ a perder** *spoil; **~ la culpa** blame; **echarse** lie down
**edad** (ay-*dhahdh*) *f* age; **mayor de ~** of age; **menor de ~** under age
**Edad Media** (ay-*dhahdh may*-dh$^y$ah) Middle Ages
**edición** (ay-dhee-*th$^y$oan*) *f* issue, edition; **~ de mañana** morning edition
**edificar** (ay-dhee-fee-*kahr*) *v* construct
**edificio** (ay-dhee-*fee*-th$^y$oa) *m*

construction, building
**editor** (ay-dhee-*toar*) *m*, **-a** *f* publisher
**edredón** (ay-dhray-*dhoan*) *m* eiderdown
**educación** (ay-dhoo-kah-*th$^y$oan*) *f* education
**educar** (ay-dhoo-*kahr*) *v* educate, *bring up, raise
**efectivamente** (ay-fayk-tee-bhah-*mayn*-tay) *adv* as a matter of fact, in fact
**efectivo** (ay-fayk-*tee*-bhoa) *m* cash; ***hacer ~** cash
**efecto** (ay-*fayk*-toa) *m* effect
**efectuar** (ay-fayk-*twahr*) *v* effect; implement
**eficacia** (ay-fee-*kah*-th$^y$ah) *f* effectiveness; efficacy
**eficaz** (ay-fee-*kahth*) *adj* effective
**eficiente** (ay-fee-*th$^y$ayn*-tay) *adj* efficient
**egipcio** (ay-*kheep*-th$^y$oa) *adj* Egyptian; *m* Egyptian
**Egipto** (ay-*kheep*-toa) *m* Egypt
**egoísmo** (ay-goa-*eez*-moa) *m* ego(t)ism, selfishness
**egoísta** (ay-goa-*eess*-tah) *adj* ego(t)istic, selfish
**eje** (*ay*-khay) *m* axle; axis; main point
**ejecución** (ay-khay-koo-*th$^y$oan*) *f* execution
**ejecutar** (ay-khay-koo-*tahr*) *v* perform, execute
**ejecutivo** (ay-khay-koo-*tee*-bhoa) *adj* executive; *m*, **-a** *f* executive
**ejemplar** (ay-khaym-*plahr*) *m* copy
**ejemplo** (ay-*khaym*-ploa) *m* instance, example; **por ~** for instance, for example
**ejercer** (ay-khayr-*thayr*) *v* exercise; to practice; to manage
**ejercicio** (ay-khayr-*thee*-th$^y$oa) *m* exercise
**ejercitar** (ay-khayr-thee-*tahr*) *v* exercise
**ejército** (ay-*khayr*-thee-toa) *m* army
**el** (ayl) *art* (f la; pl los, las) the *art*
**él** (ayl) *pron* he
**elaborar** (ay-lah-boa-*rahr*) *v* elaborate
**elasticidad** (ay-lahss-tee-thee-*dhahdh*) *f* elasticity
**elástico** (ay-*lahss*-tee-koa) *adj* elastic; *m* rubber band
**elección** (ay-layk-*th$^y$oan*) *f* choice, pick, selection; election
**electricidad** (ay-layk-tree-thee-*dhahdh*) *f* electricity
**electricista** (ay-layk-tree-*theess*-tah) *m/f* electrician
**eléctrico** (ay-*layk*-tree-koa) *adj* electric
**electrónico** (ay-layk-*troa*-nee-koa) *adj* electronic
**elefante** (ay-lay-*fahn*-tay) *m* elephant
**elegancia** (ay-lay-*gahn*-th$^y$ah) *f* elegance
**elegante** (ay-lay-*gahn*-tay) *adj* elegant, stylish
***elegir** (ay-lay-*kheer*) *v* elect, select
**elemental** (ay-lay-mayn-*tahl*) *adj* primary
**elemento** (ay-lay-*mayn*-toa) *m* element
**elevador** (ay-lay-bhah-*dhoar*) *mMe* lift; elevator *Am*
**elevar** (ay-lay-*bhahr*) *v* elevate
**eliminar** (ay-lee-mee-*nahr*) *v* eliminate
**elogio** (ay-*loa*-kh$^y$oa) *m* praise, glory
**ella** (*ay*-l$^y$ah) *pron* she
**ello** (*ay*-l$^y$oa) *pron* it
**ellos** (*ay*-l$^y$oass) *pron* they
**emancipación** (ay-mahn-thee-pah-*th$^y$oan*) *f* emancipation
**embajada** (aym-bah-*khah*-dhah) *f* embassy
**embajador** (aym-bah-khah-*dhoar*) *m* ambassador

**embalaje** (aym-bah-*lah*-khay) *m* packing
**embalar** (aym-bah-*lahr*) *v* pack
**embalse** (aym-*bahl*-say) *m* reservoir
**embarazada** (aym-bah-rah-*thah*-dhah) *adj* pregnant
**embarazoso** (aym-bah-rah-*thoa*-soa) *adj* embarrassing, awkward; puzzling
**embarcación** (aym-bahr-kah-*th$^{y}$oan*) *f* vessel; embarkation
**embarcar** (aym-bahr-*kahr*) *v* embark
**embargar** (aym-bahr-*gahr*) *v* confiscate
**embargo** (aym-*bahr*-goa) *m* embargo; **sin ~** yet, however, though, still
**emblema** (aym-*blay*-mah) *m* emblem
**embotellamiento** (aym-boa-tay-l$^{y}$ah-*m$^{y}$ayn*-toa) *m* traffic jam
**embrague** (aym-*brah*-gay) *m* clutch
**embriagado** (aym-br$^{y}$ah-*gah*-dhoa) *adj* intoxicated
**embrollar** (aym-broa-*l$^{y}$ahr*) *v* muddle
**embrollo** (aym-*broa*-l$^{y}$oa) *m* muddle
**embromar** (aym-broa-*mahr*) *v* tease, kid
**embudo** (aym-*boo*-dhoa) *m* funnel
**emergencia** (ay-mayr-*khayn*-th$^{y}$ah) *f* emergency
**emigración** (ay-mee-*grah-th$^{y}$oan*) *f* emigration
**emigrante** (ay-mee-*grahn*-tay) *m* emigrant
**emigrar** (ay-mee-*grahr*) *v* emigrate
**eminente** (ay-mee-*nayn*-tay) *adj* eminent; outstanding
**emisión** (ay-mee-*s$^{y}$oan*) *f* issue
**emisor** (ay-mee-*soar*) *m* transmitter
**emitir** (ay-mee-*teer*) *v* *broadcast; utter
**emoción** (ay-moa-*th$^{y}$oan*) *f* emotion
**empalme** (aym-*pahl*-may) *m* junction
**empanada** (aym-pah-*nah*-dah) *f* pie
**empapar** (aym-pah-*pahr*) *v* soak
**empaquetar** (aym-pah-kay-*tahr*) *v* pack up
**emparedado** (aym-pah-ray-*dhah*-dhoa) *m* sandwich
**emparentado** (aym-pah-rayn-*tah*-dhoa) *adj* related
**empaste** (aym-*pahss*-tay) *m* filling
**empeñar** (aym-pay-*ñahr*) *v* pawn
**empeño** (aym-*pay*-ñoa) *m* pawn; determination
**emperador** (aym-pay-rah-*dhoar*) *m* emperor
**emperatriz** (aym-pay-rah-*treeth*) *f* empress
***empezar** (aym-pay-*thahr*) *v* *begin, start
**empleado** (aym-play-*ah*-dhoa) *m*, **-a** *f* employee; **~ de oficina** clerk
**emplear** (aym-play-*ahr*) *v* employ; engage
**empleo** (aym-*play*-oa) *m* job, employment
**emprender** (aym-prayn-*dayr*) *v* *undertake
**empresa** (aym-*pray*-sah) *f* undertaking, enterprise; concern, business
**empujar** (aym-poo-*khahr*) *v* push; press
**empujón** (aym-poo-*khoan*) *m* push
**en** (ayn) *prep* at, in; inside, to
**enamorado** (ay-nah-moa-*rah*-dhoa) *adj* in love
**enamorarse** (aynah-moa-*rahr*-say) *v* *fall in love
**encaje** (ayn-kah-khay-) *m* lace
**enano** (ay-*nah*-noa) *m* dwarf
**encantado** (ayng-kahn-*tah*-dhoa) *adj* delighted; pleased
**encantador** (ayng-kahn-tah-*dhoar*) *adj* glamorous; charming, enchanting
**encantar** (ayng-kahn-*tahr*) *v* delight; bewitch
**encanto** (ayng-*kahn*-toa) *m* glamour, charm; spell

**encarcelamiento** (ayng-kahr-thay-lah-*m$^y$ayn*-toa) *m* imprisonment
**encarcelar** (ayng-kahr-thay-*lahr*) *v* imprison
**encargarse de** (ayng-kahr-*gahr*-say) *take over, *take charge of
**encargo** (ayng-*kahr*-goa) *m* assignment
**encariñado con** (ayng-kah-ree-*ñah*-dhoa koan) attached to
**encendedor** (ayn-thayn-day-*dhoar*) *m* cigarette lighter
***encender** (ayn-thayn-*dayr*) *v* *light; turn on, switch on
**encendido** (ayn-thayn-*dee*-dhoa) *m* ignition
***encerrar** (ayn-thay-*rrahr*) *v* *shut in; encircle
**encía** (ayn-*thee*-ah) *f* gum
**enciclopedia** (ayn-thee-kloa-*pay*-dh$^y$ah) *f* encyclop(a)edia
**encima** (ayn-*thee*-mah) *adv* above; over; ~ **de** over, above, on top of
**encinta** (ayn-*theen*-tah) *adj* pregnant
**encogerse** (ayng-koa-*khayr*-say) *v* *shrink; **no encoge** shrinkproof
***encontrar** (ayng-koan-*trahr*) *v* *come across, *find; ***encontrarse con** *meet, encounter, run into
**encorvado** (ayng-koar-*bhah*-dhoa) *adj* curved
**encuentro** (ayng-*kwayn*-troa) *m* meeting, encounter
**encuesta** (ayng-*kwayss*-tah) *f* survey
**encurtidos** (ayng-koor-*tee*-dhoass) *mpl* pickles *pl*
**enchufar** (ayn-choo-*fahr*) *v* plug in
**enchufe** (ayn-*choo*-fay) *m* plug
**endosar** (ayn-doa-*sahr*) *v* endorse
**endulzar** (ayn-dool-*thahr*) *v* sweeten
**enemigo** (ay-nay-*mee*-goa) *m*, **-a** *f* enemy
**energía** (ay-nayr-*khee*-ah) *f* energy; power; zest; ~ **nuclear** nuclear energy
**enérgico** (ay-*nayr*-khee-koa) *adj* energetic
**enero** (ay-*nay*-roa) January
**enfadado** (ayn-fah-*dhah*-dhoa) *adj* angry, cross
**énfasis** (*ayn*-fah-seess) *m* emphasis, stress
**enfatizar** (ayn-fah-tee-*thahr*) *v* emphasize
**enfermedad** (ayn-fayr-may-*dhahdh*) *f* disease; ailment, sickness, illness; ~ **venérea** venereal disease
**enfermera** (ayn-fayr-*may*-rah) *f* nurse
**enfermo** (ayn-*fayr*-moa) *adj* sick, ill
**enfoque** (ayn-*foa*-kay) *m* approach
**enfrentarse con** (ayn-frayn-*tahr*-say) confront; face up to
**enfrente de** (ayn-*frayn*-tay day) facing, opposite
**engañar** (ayng-gah-*ñahr*) *v* cheat, deceive; fool
**engaño** (ayng-*gah*-ñoa) *m* deceit
**engrasar** (ayng-grah-*sahr*) *v* grease
**enhorabuena** (ayn-*oa*-rah-*bway*-nah) *f* congratulations *pl*; **dar la ~** congratulate
**enigma** (ay-*neeg*-mah) *m* mystery, enigma, puzzle
**enjuagar** (ayng-khwah-*gahr*) *v* rinse
**enjugar** (ayng-khoo-*gahr*) *v* wipe
**enlace** (ayn-*lah*-thay) *m* connection, link
**enlazar** (ayn-lah-*thahr*) *v* link
**enojado** (ay-noa-*khah*-doa) *adj* angry, cross
**enojo** (ay-*noa*-khoa) *m* anger
**enorme** (ay-*noar*-may) *adj* huge, enormous, immense
**enrollar** (ayn-roa-*l$^y$ahr*) *v* *wind
**ensaimada** (ayn-say-*mah*-dhah) *f* pastry in the form of a spiral
**ensalada** (ayn-sah-*lah*-dhah) *f* salad
**ensaladilla** (ayn-sah-lah-*dee*-l$^y$ah) *f*:

~ **rusa** Russian salad
**ensamblar** (ayn-sahm-*blahr*) *v* join
**ensayar** (ayn-sah-$^{y}$*ahr*) *v* test; rehearse; **ensayarse** *v* practise
**ensayo** (ayn-*sah*-$^{y}$oa) *m* test; rehearsal; essay
**ensenada** (ayn-say-*nah*-dhah) *f* inlet, creek
**enseñanza** (ayn-say-*ñahn*-thah) *f* tuition; teachings *pl*
**enseñar** (ayn-say-*ñahr*) *v* *teach; *show
**ensueño** (ayn-*sway*-ñoa) *m* day-dream
**entallar** (ayn-tah-*l*$^{y}$*ahr*) *v* carve
***entender** (ayn-tayn-*dayr*) *v* conceive; *take
**entendimiento** (ayn-tayn-dee-*m*$^{y}$*ayn*-toa) *m* insight; conception
**enteramente** (ayn-tay-rah-*mayn*-tay) *adv* completely, entirely, quite
**enterar** (ayn-tay-*rahr*) *v* inform**; ~se de** find out about
**entero** (ayn-*tay*-roa) *adj* whole, entire
***enterrar** (ayn-tay-*rrahr*) *v* bury
**entierro** (ayn-*t*$^{y}$*ay*-*rroa*) *m* burial
**entonces** (ayn-*toan*-thayss) *adv* then; **desde ~** since then
**entrada** (ayn-*trah*-dhah) *f* entry, entrance, way in; admission; appearance; entrance-fee; **prohibida la ~** no admittance
**entrañas** (ayn-*trah*-ñahss) *fpl* insides
**entrar** (ayn-*trahr*) *v* *go in, enter
**entre** (*ayn*-tray) *prep* among, amid; between
**entreacto** (ayn-tray-*ahk*-toa) *m* intermission
**entrega** (ayn-*tray*-gah) *f* delivery
**entregar** (ayn-tray-*gahr*) *v* *give; deliver; commit; extradite
**entremeses** (ayn-tray-*may*-sayss) *mpl* hors-d'œuvre
**entrenador** (ayn-tray-nah-*dhoar*) *m*, **-a** *f* trainer, coach
**entrenamiento** (ayn-tray-nah-*m*$^{y}$*ayn*-toa) *m* training
**entrenar** (ayn-tray-*nahr*) *v* train, drill
**entresuelo** (ayn-tray-*sway*-loa) *m* mezzanine
**entretanto** (ayn-tray-*tahn*-toa) *adv* meanwhile, in the meantime
***entretener** (ayn-tray-tay-*nayr*) *v* amuse, entertain
**entretenido** (ayn-tray-tay-*nee*-dhoa) *adj* entertaining
**entretenimiento** (ayn-tray-tay-nee-*m*$^{y}$*ayn*-toa) *m* amusement, entertainment
**entrevista** (ayn-tray-*bheess*-tah) *f* interview
**entrometido** (ayn-troa-may-*tee*-dhoa) *adj* interfering; nosy
**entusiasmo** (ayn-too-*s*$^{y}$*ahz*-moa) *m* enthusiasm
**entusiasta** (ayn-too-*s*$^{y}$*ahss*-tah) *adj* enthusiastic, keen
**envase** (aym-*bah*-say) *m* container; (empty) bottle; **~ de cartón** carton; **~ no retornable** nonreturnable bottle
**envenenar** (aym-bay-nay-*nahr*) *v* poison
**enviado** (aym-*b*$^{y}$*ah*-dhoa) *m* envoy
**enviar** (aym-*b*$^{y}$*ahr*) *v* dispatch, *send
**envidia** (aym-*bee*-dh$^{y}$ah) *f* envy
**envidiar** (aym-bee-*dh*$^{y}$*ahr*) *v* envy, grudge
**envidioso** (aym-bee-*dh*$^{y}$*oa*-soa) *adj* envious
**envío** (aym-*bee*-oa) *m* expedition, consignment
***envolver** (aym-boal-*bhayr*) *v* wrap; involve
**epidemia** (ay-pee-*dhay*-m$^{y}$ah) *f* epidemic
**epilepsia** (ay-pee-*layp*-s$^{y}$ah) *f* epilepsy
**epílogo** (ay-*pee*-loa-goa) *m* epilogue
**episodio** (ay-pee-*soa*-dheeoa) *m*

episode
**época** (*ay*-poa-kah) *f* period
**equilibrio** (ay-kee-*lee*-bhr$^{y}$oa) *m* balance
**equipaje** (ay-kee-*pah*-khay) *m* baggage, luggage; **~ de mano** hand luggage; hand baggage *Am*; **furgón de equipajes** luggage van
**equipar** (ay-kee-*pahr*) *v* equip
**equipo** (ay-*kee*-poa) *m* outfit, equipment; gang, team; crew; soccer team
**equitación** (ay-kee-tah-*th$^{y}$oan*) *f* riding
**equivalente** (ay-kee-bhah-*layn*-tay) *adj* equivalent
**equivocación** (ay-kee-bhoa-kah-*th$^{y}$oan*) *f* misunderstanding, mistake
**equivocado** (ay-kee-bhoa-*kah*-dhoa) *adj* mistaken
**equivocarse** (ay-kee-bhoa-*kahr*-say) *v* *be mistaken
**equívoco** (ay-*kee*-bhoa-koa) *adj* ambiguous
**era** (*ay*-rah) *f* era
**erguido** (ayr-*gee*-dhoa) *adj* erect
**erigir** (ay-ree-*kheer*) *v* erect
**erizo** (ay-*ree*-thoa) *m* hedgehog; **~ de mar** sea-urchin
***errar** (ay-*rrahr*) *v* err; wander
**erróneo** (ay-*rroa*-nay-oa) *adj* wrong
**error** (ay-*rroar*) *m* mistake, error
**erudito** (ay-roo-*dhee*-toa) *m*, **-a** *f* scholar
**esbelto** (ayz-*bhayl*-toa) *adj* slim, slender
**escala** (ayss-*kah*-lah) *f* scale; **~ de incendios** fire escape; **~ musical** scale
**escalar** (ayss-kah-*lahr*) *v* ascend
**escalera** (ayss-kah-*lay*-rah) *f* stairs *pl*, staircase; **~ de mano** ladder; **~ móvil** escalator
**escalofrío** (ayss-kah-loa-*free*-oa) *m* chill, shiver
**escalope** (ayss-kah-*loa*-pay) *m* escalope
**escama** (ayss-*kah*-mah) *f* scale
**escándalo** (ayss-*kahn*-dah-loa) *m* scandal; offence, offense *Am*
**Escandinavia** (ayss-kahn-dee-*nah*-bh$^{y}$ah) *f* Scandinavia
**escandinavo** (ayss-kahn-dee-*nah*-bhoa) *adj* Scandinavian; *m* Scandinavian
**escapar** (ayss-kah-*pahr*) *v* escape
**escaparate** (ayss-kah-pah-*rah*-tay) *m* shopwindow
**escape** (ayss-*kah*-pay) *m* exhaust; **gases de ~** exhaust gases
**escarabajo** (ayss-kah-rah-*bhah*-khoa) *m* beetle, bug
**escarcha** (ayss-*kahr*-chah) *f* frost
**escarnio** (ayss-*kahr*-n$^{y}$oa) *m* scorn
**escasez** (ayss-kah-*sayth*) *f* scarcity, shortage
**escaso** (ayss-*kah*-soa) *adj* scarce; minor
**escena** (ay-*thay*-nah) *f* scene; setting
**escenario** (ayss-thay-*nah*-r$^{y}$oa) *m* stage
**esclavo** (ayss-*klah*-bhoa) *m* slave
**esclusa** (ayss-*kloo*-sah) *f* lock
**escoba** (ayss-*koa*-bhah) *f* broom
**escobilla** (ayss-koa-*bee*-l$^{y}$ah) *f* small brush; wiper blade
**escocés** (ayss-koa-*thayss*) *adj* Scottish, Scotch; *m* Scot
**Escocia** (ayss-*koa*-th$^{y}$ah) *f* Scotland
**escoger** (ayss-koa-*khayr*) *v* *choose, pick
**escolta** (ayss-*koal*-tah) *f* escort
**escoltar** (ayss-koal-*tahr*) *v* escort
**escombro** (ayss-*koam*-broa) *m* mackerel
**esconder** (ayss-koan-*dayr*) *v* *hide
**escribano** (ayss-kree-*bhah*-noa) *m* clerk

**escribir** (ayss-kree-*bheer*) *v* *write; ~ **a máquina** type; **papel de ~** notepaper; **por escrito** written, in writing
**escrito** (ayss-*kree*-toa) *m* writing
**escritor** (ayss-kree-*toar*) *m* writer
**escritorio** (ayss-kree-*toa*-r$^{y}$oa) *m* desk, bureau
**escritura** (ayss-kree-*too*-rah) *f* handwriting
**escrupuloso** (ayss-kroo-poo-*loa*-soa) *adj* careful
**escuchar** (ayss-koo-*chahr*) *v* listen; ~ **a escondidas** eavesdrop
**escuela** (ayss-*kway*-lah) *f* school; **director de ~** head teacher, headmaster; ~ **secundaria** secondary school
**escultor** (ayss-kool-*toar*) *m*, **-a** *f* sculptor
**escultura** (ayss-kool-*too*-rah) *f* sculpture
**escupir** (ayss-koo-*peer*) *v* *spit
**ese** (*ay*-say) *adj* that; **ése** *pron* that
**esencia** (ay-*sayn*-th$^{y}$ah) *f* essence
**esencial** (ay-sayn-*th$^{y}$ahl*) *adj* essential; vital
**esfera** (ayss-*fay*-rah) *f* sphere; atmosphere
***esforzarse** (ayss-foar-*thahr*-say) *v* try, bother
**esfuerzo** (ayss-*fwayr*-thoa) *m* effort; strain; stress
**eslabón** (ayz-lah-*bhoan*) *m* link
**esmaltar** (ayz-mahl-*tahr*) *v* glaze
**esmalte** (ayz-*mahl*-tay) *m* enamel
**esmeralda** (ayz-may-*rahl*-dah) *f* emerald
**esnórquel** (ayz-*noar*-kayl) *m* snorkel
**eso** (*ay*-soa) *pron* that
**espaciar** (ayss-pah-*th$^{y}$ahr*) *v* space
**espacio** (ayss-*pah*-th$^{y}$oa) *m* room; space
**espacioso** (ayss-pah-*th$^{y}$oa*-soa) *adj* spacious, roomy, large
**espada** (ayss-*pah*-dhah) *f* sword
**espalda** (ayss-*pahl*-dah) *f* back; **dolor de ~** backache
**espantado** (ayss-pahn-*tah*-dhoa) *adj* frightened
**espantar** (ayss-pahn-*tahr*) *v* frighten
**espanto** (ayss-*pahn*-toa) *m* fright; horror
**espantoso** (ayss-pahn-*toa*-soa) *adj* dreadful
**España** (ayss-*pah*-ñah) *f* Spain
**español** (ayss-pah-*ñoal*) *adj* Spanish; *m*, **-a** *f* Spaniard; **los Españoles** the Spanish
**esparadrapo** (ayss-pah-rah-*dhrah*-poa) *m* adhesive tape, plaster
**esparcir** (ayss-pahr-*theer*) *v* scatter, *shed
**espárrago** (ayss-*pah*-rrah-goa) *m* asparagus
**especia** (ayss-*pay*-th$^{y}$ah) *f* spice
**especial** (ayss-pay-*th$^{y}$ahl*) *adj* special; peculiar, particular
**especialidad** (ayss-pay-th$^{y}$ah-lee-*dhahdh*) *f* speciality
**especialista** (ayss-pay-th$^{y}$ah-*leess*-tah) *m/f* specialist
**especializarse** (ayss-pay-th$^{y}$ah-lee-*thahr*-say) *v* specialize; **especializado** skilled
**especialmente** (ayss-pay-th$^{y}$ahl-*mayn*-tay) *adv* especially
**especie** (ayss-*payth$^{y}$ay*) *f* species, breed
**específico** (ayss-pay-*thee*-fee-koa) *adj* specific
**espécimen** (ayss-*pay*-thee-mayn) *m* specimen
**espectáculo** (ayss-payk-*tah*-koo-loa) *m* spectacle, show; ~ **de variedades** floor show
**espectador** (ayss-payk-tah-*dhoar*) *m* spectator

**espectro** (ayss-*payk*-troa) *m* ghost; spectrum
**especular** (ayss-pay-koo-*lahr*) *v* speculate
**espejo** (ayss-*pay*-khoa) *m* mirror, looking-glass
**espera** (ayss-*pay*-rah) *f* waiting, wait
**esperanza** (ayss-pay-*rahn*-thah) *f* hope; expectation
**esperar** (ayss-pay-*rahr*) *v* hope; wait; expect, await
**espesar** (ayss-pay-*sahr*) *v* thicken
**espeso** (ayss-*pay*-soa) *adj* thick
**espesor** (ayss-pay-*soar*) *m* thickness
**espía** (ayss-*pee*-ah) *m* spy
**espiar** (ayss-*p$^y$ahr*) *v* peep
**espina** (ayss-*pee*-nah) *f* thorn; fishbone; **~ dorsal** backbone
**espinacas** (ayss-pee-*nah*-kahss) *fpl* spinach
**espinazo** (ayss-pee-*nah*-thoa) *m* spine
**espirar** (ayss-pee-*rahr*) *v* expire
**espíritu** (ayss-*pee*-ree-too) *m* spirit; ghost
**espiritual** (ayss-pee-ree-*twahl*) *adj* spiritual
**espléndido** (ayss-*playn-dee*-dhoa) *adj* splendid; glorious, enchanting, magnificent
**esplendor** (ayss-playn-*doar*) *m* splendo(u)r
**esponja** (ayss-*poang*-khah) *f* sponge
**esposa** (ayss-*poa*-sah) *f* wife; **esposas** *fpl* handcuffs *pl*
**esposo** (ayss-*poa*-soa) *m* husband
**espuma** (ayss-*poo*-mah) *f* froth, foam, lather
**espumante** (ayss-poo-*mahn*-tay) *adj* sparkling
**espumar** (ayss-poo-*mahr*) *v* foam
**espumoso** (ayss-poo-*moa*-ssoa) *adj* frothy, foamy; sparkling
**esputo** (ayss-*poo*-toa) *m* spit
**esqueleto** (ayss-kay-*lay*-toa) *m* skeleton
**esquema** (ayss-*kay*-mah) *m* diagram; scheme
**esquí** (ayss-*kee*) *m* ski; skiing; **~ acuático** water ski; **salto de ~** ski jump
**esquiador** (ayss-k$^y$ah-*dhoar*) *m* skier
**esquiar** (ayss-*k$^y$ahr*) *v* ski
**esquina** (ayss-*kee*-nah) *f* corner
**esquivo** (ayss-*kee*-bhoa) *adj* shy
**estable** (ayss-*tah*-bhlay) *adj* permanent, stable
***establecer** (ayss-tah-bhlay-*thayr*) *v* establish
**establo** (ayss-*tah*-bhloa) *m* stable
**estación** (ayss-tah-*th$^y$oan*) *f* season; station; depot *Am*; **~ central** central station; **~ de servicio** filling station; **~ terminal** terminal
**estacionamiento** (ayss-tah-th$^y$oa-nah-*m$^y$ayn*-toa) *m* parking lot *Am*; **derechos de ~** parking fee
**estacionar** (ayss-tah-th$^y$oa-*nahr*) *v* park; **prohibido estacionarse** no parking
**estadio** (ayss-*tah*-dh$^y$oa) *m* stadium
**estadística** (ayss-tah-*dheess*-tee-kah) *f* statistics *pl*
**Estado** (ayss-*tah*-doa) *m* state
**estado** (ayss-*tah*-dhoa) *m* state, condition
**Estados Unidos** (ayss-*tah*-dhoass oo-*nee*-dhoass) the States, United States
**estafa** (ayss-*tah*-fah) *f* swindle
**estafador** (ayss-tah-fah-*dhoar*) *m*, **-a** *f* swindler
**estafar** (ayss-tah-*fahr*) *v* cheat, swindle
**estallar** (ayss-tah-*l$^y$ahr*) *v* explode
**estampa** (ayss-*tahm*-pah) *f* engraving
**estampilla** (ayss-tahm-*pee*-l$^y$ah) *fMe* stamp
**estancia** (ayss-*tahn*-th$^y$ah) *f* stay
**estanco** (ayss-*tahng*-koa) *m* cigar

shop, tobacconist's
**estanque** (ayss-*tahng*-kay) *m* pond
**estanquero** (ayss-tahng-*kay*-roa) *m* tobacconist
**estante** (ayss-*tahn*-tay) *m* shelf
**estaño** (ayss-*tah*-ñoa) *m* tin; pewter
***estar** (ayss-*tahr*) *v* *be
**estatua** (ayss-*tah*-twah) *f* statue
**estatura** (ayss-tah-*too*-rah) *f* figure
**este**[1] (*ayss*-tay) *m* east
**este**[2] (*ayss*-tay) *adj* this; **éste** *pron* this
**estera** (ayss-*tay*-rah) *f* mat
**estéril** (ayss-*tay*-reel) *adj* sterile
**esterilizar** (ayss-tay-ree-lee-*thahr*) *v* sterilize
**estético** (ayss-*tay*-tee-koa) *adj* aesthetic
**estiércol** (ayss-tyayr-koal) *m* dung
**estilo** (ayss-*tee*-loa) *m* style
**estilográfica** (ayss-tee-loa-*grah*-fee-kah) *f* fountain pen
**estima** (ayss-*tee*-mah) *f* esteem
**estimación** (ayss-tee-mah-*th*$^y$*oan*) *f* respect; estimate
**estimar** (ayss-tee-*mahr*) *v* esteem; estimate
**estimulante** (ayss-tee-moo-*lahn*-tay) *m* stimulant
**estimular** (ayss-tee-moo-*lahr*) *v* stimulate; urge
**estímulo** (ayss-*tee*-moo-loa) *m* impulse
**estipulación** (ayss-tee-poo-lah-*th*$^y$*oan*) *f* stipulation
**estirar** (ayss-tee-*rahr*) *v* stretch
**estirón** (ayss-tee-*roan*) *m* tug
**esto** (*ayss*-toa) *adj* this
**estola** (ayss-*toa*-lah) *f* stole
**estómago** (ayss-*toa*-mah-goa) *m* stomach; **dolor de ~** stomachache
**estorbar** (ayss-toar-*bhahr*) *v* disturb, embarrass
**estornino** (ayss-toar-*nee*-noa) *m* starling
**estornudar** (ayss-toar-noo-*dhahr*) *v* sneeze
**estrangular** (ayss-trahng-goo-*lahr*) *v* choke, strangle
**estrato** (ayss-*trah*-toa) *m* layer
**estrechar** (ayss-tray-*chahr*) *v* tighten
**estrecho** (ayss-*tray*-choa) *adj* narrow; tight
**estrella** (ayss-*tray*-l$^y$ah) *f* star
**estremecimiento** (ayss-tray-may-thee-*m*$^y$*ayn*-toa) *m* shudder
**estreñido** (ayss-tray-*ñee*-dhoa) *adj* constipated
**estreñimiento** (ayss-tray-ñee-*m*$^y$*ayn*-toa) *m* constipation
**estrés** (ay-*strayss*) *m* stress
**estribor** (ayss-tree-*bhoar*) *m* starboard
**estricto** (ayss-*treek*-toa) *adj* strict
**estrofa** (ayss-*troa*-fah) *f* stanza
**estropeado** (ayss-troa-pay-*ah*-dhoa) *adj* broken; crippled
**estropear** (ayss-troa-pay-*ahr*) *v* mess up
**estructura** (ayss-trook-*too*-rah) *f* structure; fabric
**estuche** (ayss-*too*-chay) *m* case
**estudiante** (ayss-too-*dh*$^y$*ahn*-tay) *m* student
**estudiar** (ayss-too-*dh*$^y$*ahr*) *v* study
**estudio** (ayss-*too*-dh$^y$oa) *m* study
**estufa** (ayss-*too*-fah) *f* stove; **~ de gas** gas stove
**estupendo** (ayss-too-*payn*-doa) *adj* wonderful
**estúpido** (ayss-*too*-pee-dhoa) *adj* stupid; dumb
**etapa** (ay-*tah*-pah) *f* stage
**etcétera** (ayt-*thay*-tay-rah) and so on, etcetera
**eternidad** (ay-tayr-nee-*dhahdh*) *f* eternity
**eterno** (ay-*tayr*-noa) *adj* eternal
**etíope** (ay-*tee*-oa-pay) *adj* Ethiopian;

*m* Ethiopian
**Etiopía** (ay-*t$^{y}$oa*-p$^{y}$ah) *f* Ethiopia
**etiqueta** (ay-tee-*kay*-tah) *f* tag
**Europa** (ay$^{oo}$-*roa*-pah) *f* Europe
**europeo** (ay$^{oo}$-roa-*pay*-oa) *adj* European; *m* European
**evacuar** (ay-bhah-*kwahr*) *v* evacuate
**evaluar** (ay-bhah-*lwahr*) *v* evaluate, estimate
**evaporar** (ay-bhah-poa-*rahr*) *v* evaporate
**evasión** (ay-bhah-*s$^{y}$oan*) *f* escape
**eventual** (ay-bhayn-*twahl*) *adj* eventual; possible
**evidente** (ay-bhee-*dhayn*-tay) *adj* evident; self-evident
**evidentemente** (ay-bhee-dhayn-tay-*mayn*-tay) *adv* apparently
**evitar** (ay-bhee-*tahr*) *v* avoid
**evolución** (ay-bhoa-loo-*th$^{y}$oan*) *f* evolution
**exactamente** (ayk-sahk-tah-*mayn*-tay) *adv* exactly
**exactitud** (ayk-sahk-tee-*toodh*) *f* correctness
**exacto** (ayk-*sahk*-toa) *adj* precise, exact, accurate
**exagerar** (ayk-sah-khay-*rahr*) *v* exaggerate
**examen** (ayk-*sah*-mayn) *m* examination
**examinar** (ayk-sah-mee-*nahr*) *v* examine
**excavación** (ayks-kah-bhah-*th$^{y}$oan*) *f* excavation
**exceder** (ayk-thay-*dhayr*) *v* exceed
**excelencia** (ayk-thay-*layn*-th$^{y}$ah) *f* excellence
**excelente** (ayk-thay-*layn*-tay) *adj* excellent, fine
**excéntrico** (ayk-*thayn*-tree-koa) *adj* eccentric
**excepción** (ayk-thayp-*th$^{y}$oan*) *f* exception
**excepcional** (ayk-thayp-th$^{y}$oa-*nahl*) *adj* exceptional
**excepto** (ayk-*thayp*-toa) *prep* except
**excesivo** (ayk-thay-*see*-bhoa) *adj* excessive
**exceso** (ayk-*thay*-soa) *m* excess; **~ de velocidad** speeding
**excitación** (ayk-thee-tah-*th$^{y}$oan*) *f* excitement
**excitante** (ayk-thee-*tahn*-tay) *adj* exciting
**excitar** (ayk-thee-*tahr*) *v* excite
**exclamación** (ayks-klah-mah-*th$^{y}$oan*) *f* exclamation
**exclamar** (ayks-klah-*mahr*) *v* exclaim
***excluir** (ayks-*klweer*) *v* exclude
**exclusivamente** (ayks-kloo-see-bhah-*mayn*-tay) *adv* exclusively, solely
**exclusivo** (ayks-kloo-*see*-bhoa) *adj* exclusive
**excursión** (ayks-koor-*s$^{y}$oan*) *f* trip, excursion
**excusa** (ayks-*koo*-sah) *f* apology, excuse
**excusar** (ayks-koo-*sahr*) *v* excuse
**exento** (ayk-*sayn*-toa) *adj* exempt; **~ de impuestos** duty-free
**exhausto** (ayk-*souss*-toa) *adj* exhausted
**exhibir** (ayk-see-*bheer*) *v* exhibit, display
**exigencia** (ayk-see-*khayn*-th$^{y}$ah) *f* demand; requirement
**exigente** (ayk-see-*khayn*-tay) *adj* demanding; particular
**exigir** (ayk-see-*kheer*) *v* demand
**exiliado** (ayk-see-*l$^{y}$ah*-dhoa) *m* exile
**exilio** (ayk-*see*-l$^{y}$oa) *m* exile
**eximir** (ayk-see-*meer*) *v* exempt
**existencia** (ayk-seess-*tayn*-th$^{y}$ah) *f* existence; **existencias** *fpl* supply, stock; ***tener en ~** stock
**existir** (ayk-seess-*teer*) *v* exist

**éxito** (*ayk*-see-toa) *m* success, luck; hit; **de ~** successful; ***tener ~** manage, succeed
**exorbitante** (ayk-soar-bhee-*tahn*-tay) *adj* prohibitive
**exótico** (ayk-*soa*-tee-koa) *adj* exotic
**expansión** (ayks-pahn-*s*$^y$*oan*) *f* expansion
**expedición** (ayks-pay-dhee-*th*$^y$*oan*) *f* expedition; shipment
**expediente** (ayks-pay-*dh*$^y$*ayn*-tay) *m* file; means; record
**expedir** (ayks-pay-*deer*) *v* issue; send, dispatch
**experiencia** (ayks-pay-*r*$^y$*ayn*-th$^y$ah) *f* experience
**experimentar** (ayks-pay-ree-mayn-*tahr*) *v* experiment; experience
**experimentado** experienced
**experimento** (ayks-pay-ree-*mayn*-toa) *m* experiment
**experto** (ayks-*payr*-toa) *m* expert
**expirar** (ayks-pee-*rahr*) *v* expire
**explicable** (ayks-plee-*kah*-bhlay) *adj* explainable
**explicación** (ayks-plee-kah-*th*$^y$*oan*) *f* explanation
**explicar** (ayks-plee-*kahr*) *v* explain; account for
**explícito** (ayks-*plee*-thee-toa) *adj* express, explicit
**explorador** (ayks-ploa-rah-*dhoar*) *m* explorer; scout; boy scout
**exploradora** (ayks-ploa-rah-*dhoa*-rah) *f* girl guide; scout *Am*
**explorar** (ayks-ploa-*rahr*) *v* explore
**explosión** (ayks-ploa-*s*$^y$*oan*) *f* explosion, blast; outbreak
**explosivo** (ayks-ploa-*see*-bhoa) *adj* explosive; *m* explosive
**explotar** (ayks-ploa-*tahr*) *v* exploit
***exponer** (ayks-poa-*nayr*) *v* exhibit
**exportación** (ayks-poar-tah-*th*$^y$*oan*) *f* exportation, export
**exportar** (ayks-poar-*tahr*) *v* export
**exposición** (ayks-poa-see-*th*$^y$*oan*) *f* exposition, exhibition, display, show; exposure; **~ de arte** art exhibition
**exposímetro** (ayks-poa-*see*-may-troa) *m* exposure meter
**expresar** (ayks-pray-*sahr*) *v* express
**expresión** (ayks-pray-*s*$^y$*oan*) *f* expression
**expresivo** (ayks-pray-*see*-bhoa) *adj* expressive
**expreso** (ayks-*pray*-soa) *adj* explicit; express; **por ~** special delivery
**expulsar** (ayks-pool-*sahr*) *v* expel; eject
**exquisito** (ayks-kee-*see*-toa) *adj* exquisite; delicious
**éxtasis** (*ayks*-tah-seess) *m* ecstasy
***extender** (ayks-tayn-*dayr*) *v* *spread, expand
**extenso** (ayks-*tayn*-soa) *adj* comprehensive, extensive
**extenuar** (ayks-tay-*nwahr*) *v* exhaust; weaken
**exterior** (ayks-tay-*r*$^y$*oar*) *adj* external, exterior; *m* exterior, outside
**externo** (ayks-*tayr*-noa) *adj* outward
**extinguir** (ayks-teeng-*geer*) *v* extinguish
**extintor** (ayks-teen-*toar*) *m* fire-extinguisher
**extorsión** (ayks-toar-*s*$^y$*oan*) *f* extortion
**extorsionar** (ayks-toar-s$^y$oa-*nahr*) *v* extort
**extra** (*ayks*-trah) *adj* extra
**extracto** (ayks-*trahk*-toa) *m* excerpt
***extraer** (ayks-trah-*ayr*) *v* extract
**extranjero** (ayks-trahng-*khay*-roa) *adj* alien, foreign; *m*, **-a** *f* alien, foreigner; stranger; **en el ~** abroad
**extrañar** (ayks-trah-*ñahr*) *v* amaze, surprise; banish
**extraño** (ayks-*trah*-ñoa) *adj* strange; peculiar, queer, funny, foreign

**extraoficial** (ayks-trah-oa-fee-*th$^y$ahl*) *adj* unofficial
**extraordinario** (ayks-trah-oar-dhee-*nah*-r$^y$oa) *adj* extraordinary, exceptional
**extravagante** (ayks-trah-bhah-*gahn*-tay) *adj* extravagant
**extraviar** (ayks-trah-*bh$^y$ahr*) *v* *mislay
**extremo** (ayks-*tray*-moa) *adj* extreme; very, utmost; *m* extreme; end
**exuberante** (ayk-soo-bhay-*rahn*-tay) *adj* exuberant

# F

**fábrica** (*fah*-bhree-kah) *f* factory; works *pl*, mill; **~ de gas** gasworks
**fabricante** (fah-bhree-*kahn*-tay) *m* manufacturer
**fabricar** (fah-bhree-*kahr*) *v* manufacture
**fábula** (*fah*-bhoo-lah) *f* fable
**fácil** (*fah*-theel) *adj* easy
**facilidad** (fah-thee-lee-*dhahdh*) *f* ease; facility
**facilitar** (fah-thee-lee-*tahr*) *v* facilitate
**factor** (fahk-*toar*) *m* factor
**factura** (fahk-*too*-rah) *f* invoice
**facturar** (fahk-too-*rahr*) *v* invoice; bill
**facultad** (fah-kool-*tahdh*) *f* faculty
**fachada** (fah-*chah*-dhah) *f* façade
**faisán** (figh-*sahn*) *m* pheasant
**falda** (*fahl*-dah) *f* skirt
**fallo** (*fah*-l$^y$oa) *m* mistake; fault; judg(e)ment; **~ cardiaco** heart failure
**falsificación** (fahl-see-fee-kah-*th$^y$oan*) *f* fake
**falsificar** (fahl-see-fee-*kahr*) *v* forge, counterfeit
**falso** (*fahl*-soa) *adj* false; untrue
**falta** (*fahl*-tah) *f* error; want, lack; offence; **sin ~** without fail
**faltar** (fahl-*tahr*) *v* fail
**fallar** (fah-*l$^y$ahr*) *v* fail
***fallecer** (fah-l$^y$ay-*thayr*) *v* die, pass away
**fama** (*fah*-mah) *f* fame; **de ~ mundial** world-famous; **de mala ~** notorious
**familia** (fah-*mee*-l$^y$ah) *f* family
**familiar** (fah-mee-*l$^y$ahr*) *adj* familiar
**famoso** (fah-*moa*-soa) *adj* famous
**fanático** (fah-*nah*-tee-koa) *adj* fanatical
**fantasía** (fahn-tah-*see*-ah) *f* fantasy
**fantasma** (fahn-*tahz*-mah) *m* spook, phantom, ghost
**fantástico** (fahn-*tahss*-tee-koa) *adj* fantastic
**farallón** (fah-rah-*l$^y$oan*) *m* cliff, bluff
**farmacéutico** (fahr-mah-*thay$^{oo}$*-tee-koa) *m* chemist, pharmacist *Am*
**farmacia** (fahr-*mah*-th$^y$ah) *f* chemist's, pharmacy; drugstore *Am*
**faro** (*fah*-roa) *m* headlight; lighthouse
**farol trasero** (fah-*roal* trah-*say*-roa) taillight
**farsa** (*fahr*-sah) *f* farce
**fascismo** (fah-*theez*-moa) *m* fascism
**fascista** (fah-*theess*-tah) *adj* fascist; *m* fascist
**fase** (*fah*-say) *f* stage, phase
**fastidiar** (fahss-tee-*dh$^y$ahr*) *v* annoy, bother
**fastidioso** (fahss-tee-*dh$^y$oa*-soa) *adj* annoying, bothersome
**fatal** (fah-*tahl*) *adj* fatal; mortal
**fatigar** (fah-tee-*gahr*) *v* tire; **fatigarse** get tired
**favor** (fah-*bhoar*) *m* favo(u)r; **a ~ de**

on behalf of; **por ~** please
**favorable** (fah-bhoa-*rah*-bhlay) *adj* favo(u)rable
***favorecer** (fah-bhoa-ray-*thayr*) *v* favo(u)r
**favorecido** (fah-bhoa-ray-*thee*-dhoa) *m*, **-a** *f* payee
**favorito** (fah-bhoa-*ree*-toa) *adj* pet; *m*, **-a** *f* favo(u)rite
**fax** (fahks) *m* fax; **enviar un ~** send a fax
**fe** (fay) *f* faith
**febrero** (fay-*bhray*-roa) February
**febril** (fay-*bhreel*) *adj* feverish, hectic
**fecundo** (fay-*koon*-doa) *adj* fertile
**fecha** (*fay*-chah) *f* date
**federación** (fay-dhay-rah-*th*$^{y}$*oan*) *f* federation
**federal** (fay-dhay-*rahl*) *adj* federal
**felicidad** (fay-lee-thee-*dhahdh*) *f* happiness
**felicitación** (fay-lee-thee-tah-*th*$^{y}$*oan*) *f* congratulation
**felicitar** (fay-lee-thee-*tahr*) *v* congratulate
**feliz** (fay-*leeth*) *adj* happy
**femenino** (fay-may-*nee*-noa) *adj* feminine; female
**fenómeno** (fay-*noa*-may-noa) *m* phenomenon
**feo** (*fay*-oa) *adj* ugly
**feria** (*fay*-r$^{y}$ah) *f* fair
**fermentar** (fayr-mayn-*tahr*) *v* ferment
**feroz** (fay-*roath*) *adj* wild
**ferretería** (fay-rray-tay-*ree*-ah) *f* hardware store
**ferrocarril** (fay-rroa-kah-*rreel*) *m* railway; railroad *Am*
**fértil** (*fayr*-teel) *adj* fertile
**fertilidad** (fayr-tee-lee-*dhahdh*) *f* fertility
**festival** (fayss-tee-*bhahl*) *m* festival
**festivo** (fayss-*tee*-bhoa) *adj* festive
**feudal** (fay$^{oo}$-*dhahl*) *adj* feudal

**fiable** (*f*$^{y}$*ah*-bhlay) *adj* reliable
**fianza** (*f*$^{y}$*ahn*-thah) *f* security; bail; deposit
**fiasco** (*f*$^{y}$*ahss*-koa) *m* failure
**fibra** (*fee*-bhrah) *f* fibre
**ficción** (feek-*th*$^{y}$*oan*) *f* fiction
**ficha** (*fee*-chah) *f* chip, token
**fiebre** (*f*$^{y}$*ay*-bhray) *f* fever; **~ del heno** hay fever
**fiel** (f$^{y}$ayl) *adj* faithful, true
**fieltro** (*f*$^{y}$*ayl*-troa) *m* felt
**fiero** (*f*$^{y}$*ay*-roa) *adj* fierce
**fiesta** (*f*$^{y}$*ayss*-tah) *f* feast; party; holiday
**figura** (fee-*goo*-rah) *f* figure
**figurarse** (fee-goo-*rahr*-say) *v* imagine
**fijador** (fee-khah-*dhoar*) *m* setting lotion, hair gel, hair spray
**fijar** (fee-*khahr*) *v* attach; **fijarse en** mind
**fijo** (*fee*-khoa) *adj* fixed; permanent
**fila** (*fee*-lah) *f* row, rank
**Filipinas** (fee-lee-*pee*-nahss) *fpl* Philippines *pl*
**filipino** (fee-lee-*pee*-noa) *adj* Philippine; *m* Filipino
**filmar** (feel-*mahr*) *v* film
**filme** (*feel*-may) *m* film
**filosofía** (fee-loa-soa-*fee*-ah) *f* philosophy
**filósofo** (fee-*loa*-soa-foa) *m*, **-a** *f* philosopher
**filtrar** (feel-*trahr*) *v* strain
**filtro** (*feel*-troa) *m* filter; **~ de aire** air-filter; **~ del aceite** oil filter
**fin** (feen) *m* end; aim, purpose; **a ~ de** so that; **al ~** at last
**final** (fee-*nahl*) *adj* eventual, final; *m* end; **al ~** at last
**financiar** (fee-nahn-*th*$^{y}$*ahr*) *v* finance
**financiero** (fee-nahn-*th*$^{y}$*ay*-roa) *adj* financial
**finanzas** (fee-*nahn*-thahss) *fpl* finances *pl*

**finca** (*feeng*-kah) *f* country estate; property
**fingir** (feeng-*kheer*) *v* pretend
**finlandés** (feen-lahn-*dayss*) *adj* Finnish; *m* Finn
**Finlandia** (feen-*lahn*-d$^{y}$ah) *f* Finland
**fino** (*fee*-noa) *adj* delicate, fine; sheer
**firma** (*feer*-mah) *f* signature; firm
**firmar** (feer-*mahr*) *v* sign
**firme** (*feer*-may) *adj* steady, firm; secure
**física** (*fee*-see-kah) *f* physics
**físico** (*fee*-see-koa) *adj* physical; *m* physicist
**flaco** (*flah*-koa) *adj* thin
**flamenco** (flah-*mayng*-koa) *m* flamingo
**flan** (flahn) *m* crème caramel
**flauta** (*flou*-tah) *f* flute
**flecha** (*flay*-chah) *f* arrow
**flexible** (flayk-*see*-bhlay) *adj* flexible; supple, elastic
**flojo** (*floa*-khoa) *adj* weak
**flor** (floar) *f* flower
**florista** (floa-*reess*-tah) *m/f* florist
**floristería** (floa-reess-tay-*ree*-ah) *f* flower-shop
**flota** (*floa*-tah) *f* fleet
**flotador** (floa-tah-*dhoar*) *m* float
**flotar** (floa-*tahr*) *v* float
**fluido** (*floo*-ee-dhoa) *adj* fluid; *m* fluid
***fluir** (flweer) *v* flow, stream
**foca** (*foa*-kah) *f* seal
**foco** (*foa*-koa) *m* focus; spotlight; *mMe* light bulb
**folklore** (foal-*kloa*-ray) *m* folklore
**folleto** (foa-*l$^{y}$ay*-toa) *m* brochure
**fondo** (*foan*-doa) *m* background; ground, bottom; *mMe* slip; **fondos** *mpl* fund
**fontanero** (foan-tah-*nay*-roa) *m* plumber
**footing** (*foo*-teengh) *m* jogging; **hacer ~** go jogging, jog
**forastero** (foa-rahss-*tay*-roa) *m*, **-a** *f* foreigner; stranger
**forma** (*foar*-mah) *f* form, shape
**formación** (foar-mah-*th$^{y}$oan*) *f* formation
**formal** (foar-*mahl*) *adj* formal
**formalidad** (foar-mah-lee-*dhahdh*) *f* formality
**formar** (foar-*mahr*) *v* form, shape; educate
**formato** (foar-*mah*-toa) *m* size
**formidable** (foar-mee-*dhah*-bhlay) *adj* huge
**fórmula** (*foar*-moo-lah) *f* formula
**formulario** (foar-moo-*lah*-r$^{y}$oa) *m* form; **~ de matriculación** registration form
**forro** (*foa*-rroa) *m* lining
**fortaleza** (foar-tah-*lay*-thah) *f* fortress, fort
**fortuna** (foar-*too*-nah) *f* fortune; good luck
**forúnculo** (foa-*roong*-koo-loa) *m* boil
***forzar** (foar-*thahr*) *v* force; strain
**forzosamente** (foar-thoa-sah-*mayn*-tay) *adv* by force
**foso** (*foa*-soa) *m* moat
**foto** (*foa*-toa) *f* photo
**fotocopia** (foa-toa-*koa*-p$^{y}$ah) *f* photocopy
**fotocopiar** (foa-toa-koa-*p$^{y}$ahr*) *v* photocopy
**fotografía** (foa-toa-grah-*fee*-ah) *f* photograph; photography; **~ de pasaporte** passport photograph
**fotografiar** (foa-toa-grah-*f$^{y}$ahr*) *v* photograph
**fotógrafo** (foa-*toa*-grah-foa) *m* photographer
**fracasado** (frah-kah-*sah*-dhoa) *adj* unsuccessful
**fracaso** (frah-*kah*-soa) *m* failure
**fracción** (frahk-*th$^{y}$oan*) *f* fraction
**fractura** (frahk-*too*-rah) *f* fracture,

break
**fracturar** (frahk-too-*rahr*) *v* fracture
**frágil** (*frah*-kheel) *adj* fragile
**fragmento** (frahg-*mayn*-toa) *m* fragment, piece; extract
**frambuesa** (frahm-*bway*-sah) *f* raspberry
**francés** (frahn-*thayss*) *adj* French; *m* Frenchman
**Francia** (*frahn*-th$^y$ah) *f* France
**franco** (*frahng*-koa) *adj* postage paid, post-paid
**francotirador** (frahng-koa-tee-rah-*dhoar*) *m* sniper
**franela** (frah-*nay*-lah) *f* flannel
**franja** (*frahng*-khah) *f* fringe; trimming
**franqueo** (frahng-*kay*-oa) *m* postage
**frasco** (*frahss*-koa) *m* flask
**frase** (*frah*-say) *f* sentence; phrase
**fraternidad** (frah-tayr-nee-*dhahdh*) *f* fraternity
**fraude** (*frou*-dhay) *m* fraud
**frecuencia** (fray-*kwayn*-th$^y$ah) *f* frequency
**frecuentar** (fray-kwayn-*tahr*) *v* associate with
**frecuente** (fray-*kwayn*-tay) *adj* frequent
**frecuentemente** (fray-kwayn-tay-*mayn*-tay) *adv* frequently, often
***fregar** (fray-*gahr*) *v* wash up; scrub
***freír** (fray-*eer*) *v* fry
**frenar** (fray-*nahr*) *v* slow down
**freno** (*fray*-noa) *m* brake; ~ **de mano** handbrake; ~ **de pie** foot brake
**frente** (*frayn*-tay) *f* forehead; *m* front
**fresa** (*fray*-sah) *f* strawberry
**fresco** (*frayss*-koa) *adj* fresh; chilly, cool
**fricción** (freek-*th$^y$oan*) *f* friction
**frigorífico** (free-goa-*ree*-fee-koa) *m* refrigerator
**frío** (*free*-oa) *adj* cold; *m* cold
**frito** (*free*-toa) (p freír); *adj* fried; **fritos** fried food
**frontera** (froan-*tay*-rah) *f* frontier, border; boundary
**frotar** (froa-*tahr*) *v* rub
**fruta** (*froo*-tah) *f* fruit
**fruto** (*froo*-toa) *m* fruit, result, consequence
**fuego** (*fway*-goa) *m* fire
**fuente** (*fwayn*-tay) *f* source, fountain; dish
**fuera** (*fway*-rah) *adv* out; off, away; ~ **de** outside, out of; ~ **de lugar** misplaced; ~ **de temporada** off season
**fuerte** (*fwayr*-tay) *adj* powerful, strong; mighty; loud
**fuerza** (*fwayr*-thah) *f* force; power, might, energy; strength; ~ **de voluntad** will-power; ~ **motriz** driving force; **fuerzas armadas** military force, armed forces
**fugarse** (foo-*gahr*-say) *v* run away; escape
**fugitivo** (foo-khee-*tee*-bhoa) *m* runaway
**fumador** (foo-mah-*dhoar*) *m* smoker; **compartimento para fumadores** smoker
**fumar** (foo-*mahr*) *v* smoke; **prohibido** ~ no smoking
**función** (foon-*th$^y$oan*) *f* function
**funcionamiento** (foon-th$^y$oa-nah-*m$^y$ayn*-toa) *m* working, operation
**funcionar** (foon-th$^y$oa-*nahr*) *v* work, operate
**funcionario** (foon-th$^y$oa-*nah*-r$^y$oa) *m* civil servant
**funda** (*foon*-dah) *f* case, cover; ~ **de almohada** pillowcase
**fundación** (foon-dah-*th$^y$oan*) *f* foundation
**fundamentado** (foon-dah-mayn-*tah*-dhoa) *adj* well-founded

**fundamental** (foon-dah-mayn-*tahl*) *adj* fundamental, basic
**fundamento** (foon-dah-*mayn*-toa) *m* basis, base
**fundar** (foon-*dahr*) *v* found
**fundir** (foon-*deer*) *v* melt
**funerales** (foo-nay-*rah*-layss) *mpl* funeral
**furgoneta** (foor-goa-*nay*-tah) *f* delivery van
**furioso** (foo-*r*ʸ*oa*-soa) *adj* furious
**furor** (foo-*roar*) *m* anger, rage
**fusible** (foo-*see*-bhlay) *m* fuse
**fusil** (foo-*seel*) *m* gun
**fusión** (foo-*s*ʸ*oan*) *f* merger
**fútbol** (*foot*-bhoal) *m* soccer; football
**futuro** (foo-*too*-roa) *adj* future

# G

**gabinete** (gah-bhee-*nay*-tay) *m* cabinet
**gafas** (*gah*-fahss) *fpl* glasses, spectacles *pl*; **~ de sol** sunglasses *pl*; **~ submarinas** goggles *pl*
**gaitero** (gigh-*tay*-roa) *adj* gaudy
**galería** (gah-lay-*ree*-ah) *f* gallery; **~ de arte** art gallery
**galgo** (*gahl*-goa) *m* greyhound
**galope** (gah-*loa*-pay) *m* gallop
**galleta** (gah-*l*ʸ*ay*-tah) *f* biscuit, cookie *Am*
**gallina** (gah-*l*ʸ*ee*-nah) *f* hen
**gallo** (*gah*-lʸoa) *m* cock; **~ de bosque** grouse
**gamba** (*gahm*-bah) *f* prawn
**gamuza** (gah-*moo*-thah) *f* suede
**gana** (*gah*-nah) *f* desire; appetite
**ganador** (gah-nah-*dhoar*) *adj* winning
**ganancia** (gah-*nahn*-thʸah) *f* gain, profit
**ganar** (gah-*nahr*) *v* gain; *make, earn
**ganas** (*gah*-nahss) *fpl* desire; **tener ~ de** want to
**gancho** (*gahn*-choa) *m* hook
**ganga** (*gahng*-gah) *f* bargain
**garaje** (gah-*rah*-khay) *m* garage; **dejar en ~** garage
**garante** (gah-*rahn*-tay) *m* guarantor
**garantía** (gah-rahn-*tee*-ah) *f* guarantee
**garantizar** (gah-rahn-tee-*thahr*) *v* guarantee
**garganta** (gahr-*gahn*-tah) *f* throat; **dolor de ~** sore throat
**garra** (*gah*-rrah) *f* claw
**garrafa** (gah-*rrah*-fah) *f* carafe
**garrote** (gah-*rroa*-tay) *m* club, cudgel
**garza** (*gahr*-thah) *f* heron
**gas** (gahss) *m* gas; **cocina de ~** gas cooker
**gasa** (*gah*-sah) *f* gauze
**gasolina** (gah-soa-*lee*-nah) *f* petrol; gasoline *Am*, gas *Am*; **~ sin plomo** unleaded petrol; **puesto de ~** petrol station, gas station *Am*
**gasolinera** (gah-soa-*lee*-*nayh*-rah) *f* gas station *Am*, petrol station
**gastado** (gahss-*tah*-dhoa) *adj* worn-out, worn, threadbare
**gastar** (gahss-*tahr*) *v* *spend; wear out
**gasto** (*gahss*-toa) *m* expense, expenditure; **gastos de viaje** fare, travel(l)ing expenses
**gástrico** (*gahss*-tree-koa) *adj* gastric
**gastrónomo** (gahss-*troa*-noa-moa) *m*, **-a** *f* gourmet
**gatear** (gah-tay-*ahr*) *v* *creep, crawl
**gato** (*gah*-toa) *m* cat; jack

**gaviota** (gah-*bh*$^{y}$*oa*-tah) *f* gull, seagull
**gemelos** (khay-*may*-loass) *mpl* twins *pl*; binoculars *pl*; cuff links *pl*; **~ de campaña** field glasses
***gemir** (khay-*meer*) *v* groan, moan
**generación** (khay-nay-rah-*th*$^{y}$*oan*) *f* generation
**generador** (khay-nay-rah-*dhoar*) *m* generator
**general** (khay-nay-*rahl*) *adj* general; universal, public, broad; *m* general; **en ~** in general
**generalmente** (khay-nay-rahl-*mayn*-tay) *adv* mostly, as a rule
**generar** (khay-nay-*rahr*) *v* generate
**género** (*khay*-nay-roa) *m* gender; kind
**generosidad** (khay-nay-roa-see-*dhahdh*) *f* generosity
**generoso** (khay-nay-*roa*-soa) *adj* generous, liberal
**genial** (khay-*n*$^{y}$*ahl*) *adj* genial
**genio** (*khay*-n$^{y}$oa) *m* genius
**genital** (khay-nee-*tahl*) *adj* genital
**gente** (*khayn*-tay) *f* folk; people; nation *pl*
**gentil** (khayn-*teel*) *adj* polite, genteel, charming
**genuino** (khay-*nwee*-noa) *adj* genuine
**geografía** (khay-oa-grah-*fee*-ah) *f* geography
**geográfico** (khay-oa-*grah*-fee-koa) *adj* geographical
**geología** (khay-oa-loa-*khee*-ah) *f* geology
**geometría** (khay-oa-may-*tree*-ah) *f* geometry
**gerencial** (khay-rayn-*th*$^{y}$*ahl*) *adj* administrative
**germen** (*khayr*-mayn) *m* germ; source
**gesticular** (khayss-tee-koo-*lahr*) *v* gesticulate
**gestión** (khayss-*t*$^{y}$*oan*) *f* administration, management
**gesto** (*khayss*-toa) *m* sign; gesture; grimace
**gigante** (khee-*gahn*-tay) *m* giant
**gigantesco** (khee-gahn-*tayss*-koa) *adj* enormous, gigantic
**gimnasia** (kheem-*nah*-s$^{y}$ah) *f* gymnastics *pl*
**gimnasio** (kheem-*nah*-s$^{y}$oa) *m* gymnasium
**gimnasta** (kheem-*nahss*-tah) *m* gymnast
**ginecólogo** (khee-nay-*koa*-loa-goa) *m*, **-a** *f* gyn(a)ecologist
**girar** (khee-*rahr*) *v* turn, twist, swivel
**giro** (*khee*-roa) *m* draft; **~ postal** postal order
**glaciar** (glah-*th*$^{y}$*ahr*) *m* glacier
**glándula** (*glahn*-doo-lah) *f* gland
**globo** (*gloa*-bhoa) *m* globe; balloon
**gloria** (*gloa*-r$^{y}$ah) *f* glory
**glorieta** (gloa-*r*$^{y}$*ay*-tah) *f* roundabout, traffic circle
**glosario** (gloa-*sah*-r$^{y}$oa) *m* vocabulary
**gobernador** (goa-bhayr-nah-*dhoar*) *m* governor
**gobernante** (goa-bhayr-*nahn*-tay) *m* ruler
***gobernar** (goa-bhayr-*nahr*) *v* reign, rule
**gobierno** (goa-*bh*$^{y}$*ayr*-noa) *m* government, rule; **~ de la casa** housekeeping
**goce** (*goa*-thay) *m* enjoyment
**gol** (goal) *m* goal
**golf** (goalf) *m* golf; **campo de ~** golf links, golf course *Am*
**golfo** (*goal*-foa) *m* gulf
**golondrina** (goa-loan-*dree*-nah) *f* swallow
**golosina** (goa-loa-*see*-nah) *f* delicacy; **golosinas** sweets; candy *Am*
**golpe** (*goal*-pay) *m* blow; knock, bump; ***dar golpes** bump
**golpear** (goal-pay-*ahr*) *v* *beat,

knock, *strike; thump, tap
**golpecito** (goal-pay-*thee*-toa) *m* tap
**gollerías** (goa-l$^y$ay-*ree*-ahss) *fpl* delicacies
**goma** (*goa*-mah) *f* gum; **~ de borrar** eraser, rubber; **~ de mascar** chewing gum; **~ espumada** foam rubber
**góndola** (*goan*-doa-lah) *f* gondola
**gordo** (*goar*-dhoa) *adj* big; fat, stout
**gorra** (*goa*-rrah) *f* cap
**gorrión** (goa-*rr$^y$oan*) *m* sparrow
**gorro** (*goa*-rroa) *m* cap; **~ de baño** bathing cap
**gota** (*goa*-tah) *f* drop; gout
**gotear** (goa-tay-*ahr*) *v* leak
**goteo** (goa-*tay*-oa) *m* leak
**gótico** (*goa*-tee-koa) *adj* Gothic
**gozar** (goa-*thahr*) *v* enjoy
**grabación** (grah-bhah-*th$^y$oan*) *f* recording
**grabado** (grah-*bhah*-dhoa) *m* engraving; picture, print
**grabador** (grah-bhah-*dhoar*) *m* engraver
**grabar** (grah-*bhahr*) *v* engrave
**gracia** (*grah-th$^y$ah*) *f* grace; **de ~** free, gratis
**gracias** (*grah*-th$^y$ahss) thank you
**gracioso** (grah-*th$^y$oa*-soa) *adj* funny, humorous; graceful
**grado** (*grah*-dhoa) *m* degree; grade; **a tal ~** so
**gradual** (grah-*dhwahl*) *adj* gradual
**graduar** (grah-*dhwahr*) *v* grade; classify; **graduarse** *v* graduate
**gráfico** (*grah*-fee-koa) *adj* graphic; *m* graph, chart, diagram
**gramática** (grah-*mah*-tee-kah) *f* grammar
**gramatical** (grah-mah-tee-*kahl*) *adj* grammatical
**gramo** (*grah*-moa) *m* gram
**Gran Bretaña** (grahn bray-*tah*-ñah) Great Britain
**grande** (*grahn*-day) *adj* big; great, large, major
**grandeza** (grahn-*day*-thah) *f* greatness; grandness
**grandioso** (grahn-*d$^y$oa*-soa) *adj* superb, magnificent
**granero** (grah-*nay*-roa) *m* barn
**granito** (grah-*nee*-toa) *m* granite
**granizo** (grah-*nee*-thoa) *m* hail
**granja** (*grahng*-khah) *f* farm
**granjera** (grahng-*khay*-rah) *f* farmer's wife
**granjero** (grahng-*khay*-roa) *m* farmer
**grano** (*grah*-noa) *m* grain; corn; pimple
**grapa** (*grah*-pah) *f* clamp; staple
**grasa** (*grah*-sah) *f* fat, grease; *fMe* shoe polish
**grasiento** (grah-*s$^y$ayn*-toa) *adj* fatty, greasy
**graso** (*grah*-soa) *adj* fat
**grasoso** (grah-*soa*-soa) *adj* greasy
**gratis** (*grah*-teess) *adv* free of charge
**gratitud** (grah-tee-*toodh*) *f* gratitude
**grato** (*grah*-toa) *adj* enjoyable
**gratuito** (grah-*twee*-toa) *adj* gratis, free of charge, free
**grava** (*grah*-bhah) *f* gravel
**grave** (*grah*-bhay) *adj* grave; bad
**gravedad** (grah-bhay-*dhahdh*) *f* gravity
**Grecia** (*gray*-th$^y$ah) *f* Greece
**griego** (*gr$^y$ay*-goa) *adj* Greek; *m* Greek
**grieta** (*gr$^y$ay*-tah) *f* cleft, chasm; cave
**grifo** (*gree*-foa) *m* tap; faucet *Am*
**grillo** (*gree*-l$^y$oa) *m* cricket
**gripe** (*gree*-pay) *f* influenza, flu
**gris** (greess) *adj* grey
**gritar** (gree-*tahr*) *v* cry; yell, scream, shout
**grito** (*gree*-toa) *m* cry; yell, scream, shout
**grosella** (groa-*say*-l$^y$ah) *f* currant; **~**

**espinosa** gooseberry; ~ **negra** blackcurrant
**grosero** (groa-*say*-roa) *adj* gross; coarse, rude, impertinent
**grotesco** (groa-*tayss*-koa) *adj* ludicrous
**grúa** (*groo*-ah) *f* crane
**gruesa** (*grway*-sah) *f* gross
**grueso** (*grway*-soa) *adj* corpulent
**grumo** (*groo*-moa) *m* lump
***gruñir** (groo-*ñeer*) *v* growl
**grupo** (*groo*-poa) *m* group; party, set, bunch
**gruta** (*groo*-tah) *f* grotto
**guante** (*gwahn*-tay) *m* glove
**guapo** (*gwah*-poa) *adj* handsome
**guarda** (gwahr-dhah) *m* custodian
**guardabarros** (gwahr-dhah-*bhah*-rroass) *m* mudguard
**guardabosques** (gwahr-dhah-*bhoass*-kayss) *m* forester
**guardar** (gwahr-*dhahr*) *v* *keep, *put away; guard; ~ **con llave** lock up; **guardarse** *v* beware
**guardarropa** (gwahr-dhah-*rroa*-pah) *m* wardrobe; cloakroom; checkroom *Am*
**guardería** (gwahr-dhay-*ree*-ah) *f* nursery
**guardia** (*gwahr*-dh$^y$ah) *f* guard; *m* policeman; ~ **personal** bodyguard
**guardián** (gwahr-*dh$^y$ahn*) *m* attendant, warden; caretaker
**guateque** (gwah-*tay*-kay) *m* party
**guerra** (*gay*-rrah) *f* war; ~ **mundial** world war
**guía** (*gee*-ah) *m* guide; *f* guidebook; ~ **telefónica** telephone directory; telephone book *Am*
**guiar** (g$^y$ahr) *v* guide
**guión** (g$^y$oan) *m* dash; hyphen
**guisante** (gee-*sahn*-tay) *m* pea
**guisar** (gee-*sahr*) *v* cook
**guiso** (*gee*-soa) *m* stew, casserole
**guitarra** (gee-*tah*-rrah) *f* guitar
**gusano** (goo-*sah*-noa) *m* worm
**gustar** (gooss-*tahr*) *v* care for, like; fancy
**gusto** (*gooss*-toa) *m* taste; **con mucho** ~ with pleasure
**gustosamente** (gooss-toa-sah-*mayn*-tay) *adv* willingly, gladly

# H

***haber** (ah-*bhayr*) *v* *have
**hábil** (*ah*-bheel) *adj* able, skilful, skilled
**habilidad** (ah-bhee-lee-*dhahdh*) *f* ability; skill, art
**habitable** (ah-bhee-*tah*-bhlay) *adj* inhabitable, habitable
**habitación** (ah-bhee-tah-*th$^y$oan*) *f* room; ~ **para huéspedes** guest room
**habitante** (ah-bhee-*tahn*-tay) *m* inhabitant
**habitar** (ah-bhee-*tahr*) *v* inhabit
**hábito** (*ah*-bhee-toa) *m* habit
**habitual** (ah-bhee-*twahl*) *adj* habitual
**habitualmente** (ah-bhee-twahl-*mayn*-tay) *adv* usually
**habla** (*ah*-bhlah) *f* speech; language
**hablar** (ah-*bhlahr*) *v* *speak, talk
***hacer** (ah-*thayr*) *v* act; *do; *have, cause to, *make; **hace** ago; ***hacerse** *v* *become; *grow, *go, *get
**hacia** (*ah*-th$^y$ah) *prep* at, towards, to; about; ~ **abajo** down; ~ **adelante** forward; ~ **arriba** upwards, up; ~

**atrás** backwards
**hacienda** (ah-*th*$^{y}$*ayn*-dah) *f* estate
**hacha** (*ah*-chah) *f* axe
**hada** (*ah*-dhah) *f* fairy; **cuento de hadas** fairytale
**halcón** (ahl-*koan*) *m* hawk
**halibut** (ah-lee-*bhoot*) *m* halibut
**hallar** (ah-*l*$^{y}$*ahr*) *v* *come across
**hallazgo** (ah-*l*$^{y}$*ahdh*-goa) *m* finding
**hamaca** (ah-*mah*-kah) *f* hammock
**hambre** (*ahm*-bray) *f* hunger
**hambriento** (ahm-*br*$^{y}$*ayn*-toa) *adj* hungry
**harina** (ah-*ree*-nah) *f* flour
**harto de** (*ahr*-toa day) fed up with, tired of
**hasta** (*ahss*-tah) *prep* to, till, until; ~ **ahora** so far; ~ **que** till
**hay** (ah$^{y}$) there is; there are; ~ **que** it is necessary
**haya** (*ah*-$^{y}$ah) *f* beech
**hebilla** (ay-*bhee*-l$^{y}$ah) *f* buckle
**hebreo** (ay-*bhray*-oa) *m* Hebrew
**hechizar** (ay-chee-*thahr*) *v* bewitch
**hecho** (*ay*-choa) *m* fact
***heder** (ay-*dhayr*) *v* *smell
**hediondo** (ay-*dh*$^{y}$*oan*-doa) *adj* smelly
**helado** (ay-*lah*-dhoa) *adj* freezing; *m* ice-cream
***helar** (ay-*lahr*) *v* *freeze
**hélice** (*ay*-lee-thay) *f* propeller
**hemorragia** (ay-moa-*rrah*-kh$^{y}$ah) *f* h(a)emorrhage; ~ **nasal** nosebleed
**hemorroides** (ay-moa-*rroi*-dhayss) *fpl* h(a)emorrhoids *pl*, piles *pl*
**hendidura** (ayn-dee-*dhoo*-rah) *f* chink, crack
**heno** (*ay*-noa) *m* hay
**heredar** (ay-ray-*dhahr*) *v* inherit
**hereditario** (ay-ray-dhee-*tah*-r$^{y}$oa) *adj* hereditary
**herencia** (ay-rayn-*th*$^{y}$*ah*) *f* inheritance, legacy
**herida** (ay-*ree*-dhah) *f* injury, wound
**herido** (ay-*ree*-doa) *adj* wounded; injured; *m* wounded man; injured man
***herir** (ay-*reer*) *v* injure, wound
**hermana** (ayr-*mah*-nah) *f* sister
**hermano** (ayr-*mah*-noa) *m* brother
**hermético** (ayr-*may*-tee-koa) *adj* airtight
**hermoso** (ayr-*moa*-soa) *adj* beautiful
**hernia** (*ayr*-n$^{y}$ah) *f* hernia; ~ **intervertebral** slipped disc
**héroe** (*ay*-roa-ay) *m* hero
**heroico** (ay-*roi*-koa) *adj* heroic
**heroísmo** (ay-roa-*eez*-moa) *m* heroism
**herradura** (ay-rrah-*dhoo*-rah) *f* horseshoe
**herramienta** (ay-rrah-*m*$^{y}$*ayn*-tah) *f* tool, utensil, implement; **bolsa de herramientas** tool kit
**herrería** (ay-rray-*ree*-ah) *f* ironworks
**herrero** (ay-*rray*-roa) *m* smith, blacksmith
**herrumbre** (ay-*rroom*-bray) *f* rust
***hervir** (ayr-*bheer*) *v* boil
**heterosexual** (ay-tay-roa-sayk-*swahl*) *adj* heterosexual
**hidalgo** (ee-*dhahl*-goa) *m* nobleman
**hidrógeno** (ee-*dhroa*-khay-noa) *m* hydrogen
**hiedra** ($^{y}$*ay*-dhrah) *f* ivy
**hielo** ($^{y}$*ay*-loa) *m* ice
**hierba** ($^{y}$*ayr*-bhah) *f* herb; **brizna de ~** blade of grass; **mala ~** weed
**hierro** ($^{y}$*ay*-rroa) *m* iron; **de ~** iron; **~ fundido** cast iron
**hígado** (*ee*-gah-dhoa) *m* liver
**higiene** (ee-*kh*$^{y}$*ay*-nay) *f* hygiene
**higiénico** (ee-*kh*$^{y}$*ay*-nee-koa) *adj* hygienic; **papel ~** toilet paper
**higo** (*ee*-goa) *m* fig
**hija** (*ee*-khah) *f* daughter
**hijastra** (*ee-khahss*-trah) *f* stepdaughter

**hijastro** (ee-*khahss*-troa) *m* stepchild
**hijo** (*ee*-khoa) *m* son
**hilar** (ee-*lahr*) *v* *spin
**hilo** (*ee*-loa) *m* yarn, thread; ~ **de zurcir** darning wool
**himno** (*eem*-noa) *m* hymn; ~ **nacional** national anthem
**hinchar** (een-*chahr*) *v* inflate; **hincharse** *v* *swell
**hinchazón** (een-chah-*thoan*) *f* swelling
**hipo** (*ee*-poa) *m* hiccup
**hipocresía** (ee-poa-kray-*see*-ah) *f* hypocrisy
**hipócrita** (ee-*poa*-kree-tah) *adj* hypocritical; *m* hypocrite
**hipódromo** (ee-*poa*-dhroa-moa) *m* race-course
**hipoteca** (ee-poa-*tay*-kah) *f* mortgage
**hispanoamericano** (eess-pah-noa-ah-may-ree-*kah*-noa) *adj* Spanish-American
**histérico** (eess-*tay*-ree-koa) *adj* hysterical
**historia** (eess-*toa*-r$^y$ah) *f* history; ~ **de amor** love story; ~ **del arte** art history
**histórico** (eess-*toa*-ree-koa) *adj* historical, historic
**hocico** (oa-*thee*-koa) *m* mouth, snout
**hogar** (oa-*gahr*) *m* hearth
**hoja** (*oa*-khah) *f* leaf; sheet; blade; ~ **de afeitar** razor blade; ~ **de pedido** order form; **hojas de oro** gold leaf
**¡hola!** (*oa*-lah) hello!
**Holanda** (oa-*lahn*-dah) *f* Holland
**holandés** (oa-lahn-*dayss*) *adj* Dutch; *m* Dutchman
**hombre** (*oam*-bray) *m* man
**hombro** (*oam*-broa) *m* shoulder
**homenaje** (oa-may-*nah*-khay) *m* tribute, homage
**homosexual** (oa-moa-sayk-*swahl*) *adj* homosexual
**hondo** (*oan*-doa) *adj* deep
**honesto** (oa-*nayss*-toa) *adj* honest; honourable, straight
**hongo** (*oang*-goa) *m* mushroom; toadstool
**honor** (oa-*noar*) *m* hono(u)r; glory
**honorarios** (oa-noa-*rah*-r$^y$oass) *mpl* fee
**honra** (*oan*-rrah) *f* honour
**honradez** (oan-rah-*dhayth*) *f* honesty
**honrado** (oan-*rrah*-dhoa) *adj* honest
**honrar** (oan-*rahr*) *v* honour
**hora** (*oa*-rah) *f* hour; ~ **de llegada** time of arrival; ~ **de salida** time of departure; ~ **punta** rush hour; **horas extraordinarias** overtime; **horas de consulta** consultation hours; **horas de oficina** office hours, business hours; **horas de visita** visiting hours; **horas hábiles** business hours
**horario** (oa-*rah*-r$^y$oa) *m* schedule; timetable; ~ **comercial** business hours *pl*; ~ **de verano** summer time
**horca** (*oar*-kah) *f* gallows *pl*
**horizontal** (oa-ree-thoan-*tahl*) *adj* horizontal
**horizonte** (oa-ree-*thoan*-tay) *m* horizon
**hormiga** (oar-*mee*-gah) *f* ant
**hormigón** (oar-mee-*goan*) *m* concrete
**hornear** (oar-nay-*ahr*) *v* bake
**horno** (*oar*-noa) *m* oven; furnace; ~ **de microonda** microwave oven
**horquilla** (oar-*kee*-l$^y$ah) *f* hairpin, hair-grip; bobby pin *Am*
**horrible** (oa-*rree*-bhlay) *adj* horrible; hideous
**horror** (oa-*rroar*) *m* horror
**horticultura** (oar-tee-kool-*too*-rah) *f* horticulture
**hospedar** (oass-pay-*dhahr*) *v* entertain; **hospedarse** *v* stay
**hospedería** (oass-pay-dhay-*ree*-ah) *f* hostel
**hospicio** (oass-*pee*-th$^y$oa) *m* home

**hospital** (oass-pee-*tahl*) *m* hospital
**hospitalario** (oass-pee-tah-*lah*-r$^y$oa) *adj* hospitable
**hospitalidad** (oass-pee-tah-lee-*dhahdh*) *f* hospitality
**hostal** (oass-*tahl*) *m* hostel
**hostil** (oass-*teel*) *adj* hostile
**hotel** (oa-*tayl*) *m* hotel
**hoy** (oi) *adv* today; **~ en día** nowadays
**hoyo** (*oa*-$^y$oa) *m* pit
**hueco** (*way*-koa) *adj* hollow; *m* gap
**huelga** (*wayl*-gah) *f* strike; ***estar en ~** *strike
**huella** (*way*-l$^y$ah) *f* trace
**huérfano** (*wayr*-fah-noa) *m* orphan
**huerto** (*wayr*-toa) *m* kitchen garden
**hueso** (*way*-soa) *m* bone; stone
**huésped** (*wayss*-paydh) *m* guest; lodger, boarder
**hueva** (*way*-bhah) *f* roe
**huevera** (way-*bhay*-rah) *f* egg-cup
**huevo** (*way*-bhoa) *m* egg; **yema de ~** egg yolk
***huir** (weer) *v* escape
**hule** (*oo*-lay) *mMe* rubber
**humanidad** (oo-mah-nee-*dhahdh*) *f* humanity, mankind
**humano** (oo-*mah*-noa) *adj* human
**humedad** (oo-may-*dhahdh*) *f* moisture, humidity, damp
***humedecer** (oo-may-dhay-*thayr*) *v* moisten, damp
**húmedo** (*oo*-may-dhoa) *adj* moist, humid, damp; wet
**humilde** (oo-*meel*-day) *adj* humble, meek
**humo** (*oo*-moa) *m* smoke, steam, vapo(u)r
**humor** (oo-*moar*) *m* spirit, mood; humo(u)r; **de buen ~** good-tempered, good-humo(u)red
**humorístico** (oo-moa-*reess*-tee-koa) *adj* humorous
**hundirse** (oon-*deer*-say) *v* *sink; collapse
**húngaro** (*oong*-gah-roa) *adj* Hungarian; *m* Hungarian
**Hungría** (oong-*gree*-ah) *m* Hungary
**huracán** (oo-rah-*kahn*) *m* hurricane
**hurtar** (oor-*tahr*) *v* *steal
**hurto** (*oor*-toa) *m* theft

# I

**ibérico** (ee-*bhay*-ree-koa) *adj* Iberian
**icono** (ee-*koa*-noa) *m* icon
**ictericia** (eek-tay-*ree*-th$^y$ah) *f* jaundice
**ida** (*ee*-dah) *f* outward journey; (**billete de**) **~ y vuelta** round trip (ticket), return (ticket)
**idea** (ee-*dhay*-ah) *f* idea
**ideal** (ee-dhay-*ahl*) *adj* ideal; *m* ideal
**idéntico** (ee-*dhayn*-tee-koa) *adj* identical
**identidad** (ee-dhayn-tee-*dhahdh*) *f* identity; **carnet de ~** identity card
**identificación** (ee-dhayn-tee-fee-kah-*th$^y$oan*) *f* identification
**identificar** (ee-dhayn-tee-fee-*kahr*) *v* identify
**idioma** (ee-*dh$^y$oa*-mah) *m* language
**idiomático** (ee-dh$^y$oa-*mah*-tee-koa) *adj* idiomatic
**idiota** (ee-*dh$^y$oa*-tah) *adj* idiotic; *m* idiot, fool
**ídolo** (*ee*-dhoa-loa) *m* idol
**iglesia** (ee-*glay*-s$^y$ah) *f* church
**ignorancia** (eeg-noa-*rahn*-th$^y$ah) *f*

ignorance
**ignorante** (eeg-noa-*rahn*-tay) *adj* ignorant
**ignorar** (eeg-noa-*rahr*) *v* ignore
**igual** (ee-*gwahl*) *adj* equal, alike; level, even; **sin ~** unsurpassed
**igualar** (ee-gwah-*lahr*) *v* level, equalize; equal
**igualdad** (ee-gwahl-*dahdh*) *f* equality
**igualmente** (ee-gwahl-*mayn*-tay) *adv* alike; equally
**ilegal** (ee-lay-*gahl*) *adj* illegal, unlawful
**ilegible** (ee-lay-*khee*-bhlay) *adj* illegible
**ileso** (ee-*lay*-soa) *adj* unhurt
**ilimitado** (ee-lee-mee-*tah*-dhoa) *adj* unlimited
**iluminación** (ee-loo-mee-nah-*th$^y$oan*) *f* illumination
**iluminar** (ee-loo-mee-*nahr*) *v* illuminate
**ilusión** (ee-loo-*s$^y$oan*) *f* illusion
**ilustración** (ee-looss-trah-*th$^y$oan*) *f* illustration; picture
**ilustrar** (ee-looss-*trahr*) *v* illustrate
**ilustre** (ee-*looss*-tray) *adj* illustrious
**imagen** (ee-*mah*-khayn) *f* image, picture; **~ reflejada** reflection
**imaginación** (ee-mah-khee-nah-*th$^y$oan*) *f* imagination
**imaginar** (ee-mah-khee-*nahr*) *v* imagine; conceive; **imaginarse** *v* fancy, imagine
**imaginario** (ee-mah-khee-*nah*-r$^y$oa) *adj* imaginary
**imbécil** (eem-*bay*-theel) *adj* stupid; *m/f* idiot, imbecile
**imitación** (ee-mee-tah-*th$^y$oan*) *f* imitation
**imitar** (ee-mee-*tahr*) *v* imitate, copy
**impaciente** (eem-pah-*th$^y$ayn*-tay) *adj* eager, impatient
**impar** (eem-*pahr*) *adj* odd
**imparcial** (eem-pahr-*th$^y$ahl*) *adj* impartial
**impecable** (eem-pay-*kah*-bhlay) *adj* faultless
**impedimento** (eem-pay-dhee-*mayn*-toa) *m* impediment
***impedir** (eem-pay-*dheer*) *v* hinder, impede; restrain, prevent
**impeler** (eem-pay-*layr*) *v* propel
**imperdible** (eem-payr-*dhee*-bhlay) *m* safety pin
**imperfección** (eem-payr-fayk-*th$^y$oan*) *f* fault
**imperfecto** (eem-payr-*fayk*-toa) *adj* imperfect
**imperial** (eem-pay-*r$^y$ahl*) *adj* imperial
**imperio** (eem-*pay*-r$^y$oa) *m* empire
**impermeable** (eem-payr-may-*ah*-bhlay) *adj* waterproof, rainproof; *m* raincoat, mackintosh
**impersonal** (eem-payr-soa-*nahl*) *adj* impersonal
**impertinencia** (eem-payr-tee-*nayn*-th$^y$ah) *f* impertinence
**impertinente** (eem-payr-tee-*nayn*-tay) *adj* bold, impertinent
**impetuoso** (eem-pay-*twoa*-soa) *adj* impetuous; violent; hasty
**implicar** (eem-plee-*kahr*) *v* implicate, imply
**imponente** (eem-poa-*nayn*-tay) *adj* grand, imposing
**importación** (eem-poar-tah-*th$^y$oan*) *f* import
**importador** (eem-poar-tah-*dhoar*) *m* importer
**importancia** (eem-poar-*tahn*-th$^y$ah) *f* importance; ***tener ~** matter
**importante** (eem-poar-*tahn*-tay) *adj* important; considerable, capital, big
**importar** (eem-poar-*tahr*) *v* import
**importuno** (eem-poar-*too*-noa) *adj* annoying
**imposible** (eem-poa-*see*-bhlay) *adj*

impossible
**impotencia** (eem-poa-*tayn*-th$^y$ah) *f* impotence
**impotente** (eem-poa-*tayn*-tay) *adj* powerless; impotent
**impresora** (eem-pray-*soah-rah*.) *f* printer
**impresión** (eem-pray-*s$^y$oan*) *f* impression; ~ **digital** fingerprint
**impresionante** (eem-pray-s$^y$oa-*nahn*-tay) *adj* impressive; striking
**impresionar** (eem-pray-s$^y$oa-*nahr*) *v* *strike, impress
**impreso** (eem-*pray*-soa) *m* printed matter
**imprevisto** (eem-pray-*bheess*-toa) *adj* unexpected, incidental
***imprimir** (eem-pree-*meer*) *v* print
**improbable** (eem-proa-*bhah*-bhlay) *adj* unlikely, improbable
**impropio** (eem-*proa*-p$^y$oa) *adj* improper; wrong
**improvisar** (eem-proa-bhee-*sahr*) *v* improvise
**imprudente** (eem-proo-*dhayn*-tay) *adj* imprudent; unwise, indiscreet
**impudente** (eem-poo-*dhayn*-tay) *adj* impudent; shameless
**impuesto** (eem-*pwayss*-toa) *m* taxation, tax; Customs duty; ~ **de aduana** Customs duty; **impuestos de importación** import duty; **libre de impuestos** tax-free
**impulsivo** (eem-pool-*see*-bhoa) *adj* impulsive
**impulso** (eem-*pool*-soa) *m* urge, impulse
**inaccesible** (ee-nahk-thay-*see*-bhlay) *adj* inaccessible
**inaceptable** (ee-nah-thayp-*tah*-bhlay) *adj* unacceptable
**inadecuado** (ee-nah-dhay-*kwah*-dhoa) *adj* inadequate; unfit, unsuitable
**inapreciable** (ee-nah-pray-*th$^y$ah*-bhlay) *adj* priceless; imperceptible
**incapaz** (eeng-kah-*pahth*) *adj* unable, incapable
**incendio** (een-*thayn*-d$^y$oa) *m* fire
**incidente** (een-thee-*dhayn*-tay) *m* incident
**incienso** (een-*th$^y$ayn*-soa) *m* incense
**incierto** (een-*th$^y$ayr*-toa) *adj* uncertain
**incineración** (een-thee-nay-rah-*th$^y$oan*) *f* cremation
**incinerar** (een-thee-nay-*rahr*) *v* cremate
**incisión** (een-thee-*s$^y$oan*) *f* cut
**incitar** (een-thee-*tahr*) *v* incite
**inclinación** (eeng-klee-nah-*th$^y$oan*) *f* tendency, inclination; incline
**inclinar** (eeng-klee-*nahr*) *v* bow; **inclinado** inclined; sloping, slanting; **inclinarse** *v* *be inclined to; slope, slant
***incluir** (eeng-*klweer*) *v* include; enclose; count; **todo incluido** all in
**incluso** (eeng-*kloo*-soa) *adj* inclusive, included
**incombustible** (eeng-koam-booss-*tee*-bhlay) *adj* fireproof
**incomodidad** (eeng-koa-moa-dhee-*dhahdh*) *f* inconvenience
**incómodo** (eeng-*koa*-moa-dhoa) *adj* uncomfortable
**incompetente** (eeng-koam-pay-*tayn*-tay) *adj* incompetent; unqualified
**incompleto** (eeng-koam-*play*-toa) *adj* incomplete
**inconcebible** (eeng-koan-thay-*bhee*-bhlay) *adj* inconceivable
**incondicional** (eeng-koan-dee-th$^y$oa-*nahl*) *adj* unconditional
**inconsciente** (eeng-koan-*th$^y$ayn*-tay) *adj* unaware; unconscious
**inconveniencia** (eeng-koam-bay-*n$^y$ayn*-th$^y$ah) *f* inconvenience
**incorrecto** (eeng-koa-*rrayk*-toa) *adj*

incorrect
**increíble** (eeng-kray-*ee*-bhlay) *adj* incredible
**incrementar** (eeng-kray-mayn-*tahr*) *v* increase
**inculto** (eeng-*kool*-toa) *adj* uncultivated; uneducated
**incurable** (eeng-koo-*rah*-bhlay) *adj* incurable
**indagación** (een-dah-gah-*th$^{y}$oan*) *f* inquiry
**indecente** (een-day-*thayn*-tay) *adj* indecent
**indefenso** (een-day-*fayn*-soa) *adj* unprotected
**indefinido** (een-day-fee-*nee*-dhoa) *adj* indefinite
**indemnización** (een-daym-nee-thah-*th$^{y}$oan*) *f* compensation, indemnity
**independencia** (een-day-payn-*dayn*-th$^{y}$ah) *f* independence
**independiente** (een-day-payn-*d$^{y}$ayn*-tay) *adj* independent; self-employed,
**indeseable** (een-day-say-*ah*-bhlay) *adj* undesirable
**India** (*een*-d$^{y}$ah) *f* India
**indicación** (een-dee-kah-*th$^{y}$oan*) *f* indication
**indicador** (een-dee-kah-*dhoar*) *m* trafficator, indicator, blinker *Am*
**indicar** (een-dee-*kahr*) *v* indicate; declare
**indicativo** (een-dee-kah-*tee*-bhoa) *m* indicative
**índice** (*een*-dee-thay) *m* index, table of contents; index finger
**indiferencia** (een-dee-fay-*rayn*-th$^{y}$ah) *f* indifference
**indiferente** (een-dee-fay-*rayn*-tay) *adj* indifferent; careless
**indígena** (een-*dee*-khay-nah) *m* native
**indigestión** (een-dee-khayss-*t$^{y}$oan*) *f* indigestion
**indignación** (een-deeg-nah-*th$^{y}$oan*) *f* indignation
**indio** (*een*-d$^{y}$oa) *adj* Indian; *m* Indian
**indirecto** (een-dee-*rayk*-toa) *adj* indirect
**indispensable** (een-deess-payn-*sah*-bhlay) *adj* essential
**indispuesto** (een-deess-*pwayss*-toa) *adj* unwell
**individual** (een-dee-bhee-*dhwahl*) *adj* individual
**individuo** (een-dee-*bhee*-dhwoa) *m* individual
**Indonesia** (een-doa-*nay*-s$^{y}$ah) *f* Indonesia
**indonesio** (een-doa-*nay*-s$^{y}$oa) *adj* Indonesian; *m* Indonesian
**indudable** (een-doo-*dhah*-bhlay) *adj* undoubtable; unquestionable
**indulto** (een-*dool*-toa) *m* pardon
**industria** (een-*dooss*-tr$^{y}$ah) *f* industry; ingenuity
**ineficiente** (ee-nay-fee-*th$^{y}$ayn*-tay) *adj* inefficient
**inesperado** (ee-nayss-pay-*rah*-dhoa) *adj* unexpected
**inestable** (ee-nayss-*tah*-bhlay) *adj* unsteady, unstable
**inevitable** (ee-nay-bhee-*tah*-bhlay) *adj* unavoidable, inevitable
**inexacto** (ee-nayk-*sahk*-toa) *adj* incorrect, inaccurate; false
**inexperto** (ee-nayks-*payr*-toa) *adj* inexperienced
**inexplicable** (ee-nayks-plee-*kah*-bhlay) *adj* unaccountable
**infancia** (een-*fahn*-th$^{y}$ah) *f* infancy
**infantil** (een-fahn-*teel*) *adj* childlike
**infección** (een-fayk-*th$^{y}$oan*) *f* infection
**infectar** (een-fayk-*tahr*) *v* infect; **infectarse** *v* *become infected
**inferior** (een-fay-*r$^{y}$oar*) *adj* inferior; bottom
**infiel** (een-*f$^{y}$ayl*) *adj* unfaithful
**infierno** (een-*f$^{y}$ayr*-noa) *m* hell

**infinidad** (een-fee-nee-*dhahdh*) *f* infinity
**infinitivo** (een-fee-nee-*tee*-bhoa) *m* infinitive
**infinito** (een-fee-*nee*-toa) *adj* endless, infinite
**inflable** (een-*flah*-bhlay) *adj* inflatable
**inflación** (een-flah-*th$^y$oan*) *f* inflation
**inflamable** (een-flah-*mah*-bhlay) *adj* inflammable
**inflamación** (een-flah-mah-*th$^y$oan*) *f* inflammation
**influencia** (een-*flwayn*-th$^y$ah) *f* influence
***influir** (een-*flweer*) *v* influence
**influjo** (een-*floo*-khoa) *m* influence
**influyente** (een-floo-*$^y$ayn*-tay) *adj* influential
**información** (een-foar-mah-*th$^y$oan*) *f* enquiry, information; **oficina de informaciones** inquiry office
**informal** (een-foar-*mahl*) *adj* informal; casual
**informar** (een-foar-*mahr*) *v* report, inform; **informarse** *v* inquire
**informe** (een-*foar*-may) *m* report; **informes** *mpl* information; ***pedir informes** inquire
**infrarrojo** (een-frah-*rroa*-khoa) *adj* infra-red
**ingeniero** (eeng-khay-*n$^y$ay*-roa) *m* engineer
**ingenio** (eeng-khay-nyoa) *n* wit
**ingenioso** (eeng-khay-*n$^y$oa*-soa) *adj* ingenious; witty
**ingenuo** (eeng-*khay*-nwoa) *adj* naïve; simple
**Inglaterra** (eeng-glah-*tay*-rrah) *f* England; Britain
**ingle** (*eeng*-glay) *f* groin
**inglés** (eeng-*glayss*) *adj* English; *m* Englishman; Briton
**ingrato** (eeng-*grah*-toa) *adj* ungrateful
**ingrediente** (eeng-gray-*dh$^y$ayn*-tay) *m* ingredient
**ingresar** (eeng-gray-*sahr*) *v* deposit
**ingreso** (eenggray-soa) *m* entry
**ingresos** (eeng-*gray*-soass) *mpl* revenue, earnings *pl*, income; **impuesto sobre los ~** income tax
**inhabitable** (ee-nah-bhee-*tah*-bhlay) *adj* uninhabitable
**inhabitado** (ee-nah-bhee-*tah*-dhoa) *adj* uninhabited
**inhalar** (ee-nah-*lahr*) *v* inhale
**inicial** (ee-nee-*th$^y$ahl*) *adj* initial; *f* initial
**iniciar** (ee-nee-*th$^y$ahr*) *v* initiate
**iniciativa** (ee-nee-th$^y$ah-*tee*-bhah) *f* initiative
**ininterrumpido** (ee-neen-tay-rroom-*pee*-dhoa) *adj* continuous
**injusticia** (eeng-khooss-*tee*-th$^y$ah) *f* injustice
**injusto** (eeng-*khooss*-toa) *adj* unfair, unjust
**inmaculado** (een-mah-koo-*lah*-dhoa) *adj* immaculate; stainless, spotless
**inmediatamente** (een-may-dh$^y$ah-tah-*mayn*-tay) *adv* instantly, immediately
**inmediato** (een-may-*dh$^y$ah*-toa) *adj* immediate, prompt; **de ~** immediately
**inmenso** (een-*mayn*-soa) *adj* immense
**inmigración** (een-mee-grah-*th$^y$oan*) *f* immigration
**inmigrante** (een-mee-*grahn*-tay) *m* immigrant
**inmigrar** (een-mee-*grahr*) *v* immigrate
**inmodesto** (een-moa-*dhayss*-toa) *adj* immodest
**inmueble** (een-*mway*-bhlay) *m* building
**inmunidad** (een-moo-nee-*dhahdh*) *f* immunity

**inmunizar** (een-moo-nee-*thahr*) *v* immunize
**innato** (een-*nah*-toa) *adj* innate; natural
**innecesario** (een-nay-thay-*sah*-r$^{y}$oa) *adj* unnecessary
**innumerable** (een-noo-may-*rah*-bhlay) *adj* innumerable
**inocencia** (ee-noa-*thayn*-th$^{y}$ah) *f* innocence
**inocente** (ee-noa-*thayn*-tay) *adj* innocent
**inoculación** (ee-noa-koo-lah-*th$^{y}$oan*) *f* inoculation
**inocuo** (ee-*noa*-kwoa) *adj* harmless
**inoportuno** (ee-noa-poar-*too*-noa) *adj* inconvenient; misplaced
**inquietarse** (eeng-k$^{y}$ay-*tahr*-say) *v* worry
**inquieto** (een-*k$^{y}$ay*-toa) *adj* restless; uneasy, worried
**inquietud** (eeng-k$^{y}$ay-*toodh*) *f* unrest; worry
**inquilino** (eeng-kee-*lee*-noa) *m* tenant
**insalubre** (een-sah-*loo*-bhray) *adj* unhealthy
**insatisfecho** (een-sah-teess-*fay*-choa) *adj* dissatisfied
**inscribir** (eens-kree-*bheer*) *v* enter, book, list; **inscribirse** *v* register, check in; enro(l)l
**inscripción** (eens-kreep-*th$^{y}$oan*) *f* inscription; registration
**insecticida** (een-sayk-tee-*thee*-dhah) *m* insecticide
**insecto** (een-*sayk*-toa) *m* insect; bug *Am*
**inseguro** (een-say-*goo*-roa) *adj* unsafe; doubtful
**insensato** (een-sayn-*sah*-toa) *adj* senseless
**insensible** (een-sayn-*see*-bhlay) *adj* insensitive; heartless
**insertar** (een-sayr-*tahr*) *v* insert
**insignificante** (een-seeg-nee-fee-*kahn*-tay) *adj* unimportant, petty, insignificant
**insípido** (een-*see*-pee-dhoa) *adj* insipid; tasteless
**insistir** (een-seess-*teer*) *v* insist
**insolación** (een-soa-lah-*th$^{y}$oan*) *f* sunstroke
**insolencia** (een-soa-*layn*-th$^{y}$ah) *f* insolence
**insolente** (een-soa-*layn*-tay) *adj* insolent
**insólito** (een-*soa*-lee-toa) *adj* uncommon, unusual
**insomnio** (een-*soam*-n$^{y}$oa) *m* insomnia
**insonorizado** (een-soa-noa-ree-*thah*-dhoa) *adj* soundproof
**insoportable** (een-soa-poar-*tah*-bhlay) *adj* intolerable
**inspección** (eens-payk-*th$^{y}$oan*) *f* inspection; **~ de pasaportes** passport control
**inspeccionar** (eens-payk-th$^{y}$oa-*nahr*) *v* inspect
**inspector** (eens-payk-*toar*) *m*, **-a** *f* inspector
**inspirar** (een-spee-*rahr*) *v* inspire
**instalación** (eens-tah-lah-*th$^{y}$oan*) *f* installation; plant
**instalar** (eens-tah-*lahr*) *v* install; furnish
**instantánea** (eens-tahn-*tah*-nay-ah) *f* snapshot
**instantáneamente** (eens-tahn-tah-nay-ah-*mayn*-tay) *adv* instantly
**instante** (eens-*tahn*-tay) *m* instant; second; **al ~** instantly
**instinto** (een-*steen*-toa) *m* instinct
**institución** (eens-tee-too-*th$^{y}$oan*) *f* institution, institute
***instituir** (eens-tee-*tweer*) *v* institute
**instituto** (eens-tee-*too*-toa) *m* institution, institute

**instrucción** (eens-trook-*th$^{y}$oan*) *f* instruction; direction
**instructivo** (eens-trook-*tee*-bhoa) *adj* instructive
**instructor** (eens-trook-*toar*) *m*, **-a** *f* instructor
***instruir** (eens-*trweer*) *v* instruct
**instrumento** (eens-troo-*mayn*-toa) *m* instrument; **~ músico** musical instrument
**insuficiente** (een-soo-fee-*th$^{y}$ayn*-tay) *adj* insufficient
**insufrible** (een-soo-*free*-bhlay) *adj* unbearable
**insultante** (een-sool-*tahn*-tay) *adj* offensive, insulting
**insultar** (een-sool-*tahr*) *v* insult
**insulto** (een-*sool*-toa) *m* insult
**intacto** (een-*tahk*-toa) *adj* intact; unbroken, whole
**integral** (een-tay-*grahl*) *adj* integral
**integrar** (een-tay-*grahr*) *v* integrate
**intelecto** (een-tay-*layk*-toa) *m* intellect
**intelectual** (een-tay-layk-*twahl*) *adj* intellectual
**inteligencia** (een-tay-lee-*khayn*-th$^{y}$ah) *f* intelligence, brain
**inteligente** (een-tay-lee-*khayn*-tay) *adj* intelligent; clever, smart
**intención** (een-tayn-*th$^{y}$oan*) *f* intention, purpose; ***tener la ~ de** intend to
**intencionado** (een-tayn-th$^{y}$oa-*nah*-dhoa) *adj* on purpose
**intencional** (een-tayn-th$^{y}$oa-*nahl*) *adj* intentional
**intensidad** (een-tayn-see-*dhahdh*) *f* intensity
**intenso** (een-*tayn*-soa) *adj* intense
**intentar** (een-tayn-*tahr*) *v* attempt, try; intend
**intercambiar** (een-tayr-kahm-*b$^{y}$ahr*) *v* exchange
**interés** (een-tay-*rayss*) *m* interest
**interesado** (een-tay-ray-*sah*-dhoa) *adj* interested; concerned; *m* candidate
**interesante** (een-tay-ray-*sahn*-tay) *adj* interesting
**interesar** (een-tay-ray-*sahr*) *v* interest
**interferencia** (een-tayr-fay-*rayn*-th$^{y}$ah) *f* interference
**interferir** (een-tayr-fay-*reer*) *v* interfere
**ínterin** (*een*-tay-reen) *m* interim
**interior** (een-tay-*r$^{y}$oar*) *adj* inside, inner; domestic; *m* interior, inside
**intermediario** (een-tayr-may-*dh$^{y}$ah*-r$^{y}$oa) *m* intermediary
**intermedio** (een-tayr-*may*-dh$^{y}$oa) *m* interlude
**intermitente** (een-tayr-mee-*tayn*-tay) *adj* intermittent; *m* turn signal, indicator
**internacional** (een-tayr-nah-th$^{y}$oa-*nahl*) *adj* international
**internado** (een-tayr-*nah*-dhoa) *m* boarding school
**interno** (een-*tayr*-noa) *adj* internal
**interpretar** (een-tayr-pray-*tahr*) *v* interpret
**intérprete** (een-*tayr*-pray-tay) *m* interpreter
**interrogar** (een-tay-rroa-*gahr*) *v* interrogate
**interrogativo** (een-tay-rroa-gah-*tee*-bhoa) *adj* interrogative
**interrogatorio** (een-tay-rroa-gah-*toa*-r$^{y}$oa) *m* interrogation, examination
**interrumpir** (een-tay-rroom-*peer*) *v* interrupt
**interrupción** (een-tay-rroop-*th$^{y}$oan*) *f* interruption
**interruptor** (een-tay-rroop-*toar*) *m* switch
**intersección** (een-tayr-sayk-*th$^{y}$oan*) *f* intersection
**intervalo** (een-tayr-*bhah*-loa) *m*

interval
**intervención** (een-tayr-bhayn-*th$^y$oan*) *f* intervention
***intervenir** (een-tayr-bhay-*neer*) *v* intervene
**intestino** (een-tayss-*tee*-noa) *m* intestine, gut; **~ recto** rectum; **intestinos** intestines *pl*, bowels *pl*
**intimidad** (een-tee-mee-*dhahdh*) *f* privacy; intimacy
**íntimo** (*een*-tee-moa) *adj* intimate
**intoxicación alimentaria** (een-toak-see-kah-*th$^y$oan* ah-lee-mayn-*tah*-r$^y$ah) food poisoning
**intransitable** (een-trahn-see-*tah*-bhlay) *adj* impassable
**intriga** (een-*tree*-gah) *f* intrigue
**introducción** (een-troa-dhook-*th$^y$oan*) *f* introduction
***introducir** (een-troa-dhoo-*theer*) *v* introduce; *bring up
**intruso** (een-*troo*-soa) *m* intruder; trespasser
**inundación** (ee-noon-dah-*th$^y$oan*) *f* flood
**inusitado** (ee-noo-see-*tah*-dhoa) *adj* unusual
**inútil** (ee-*noo*-teel) *adj* useless
**inútilmente** (ee-noo-teel-*mayn*-tay) *adv* in vain
**invadir** (eem-bah-*dheer*) *v* invade
**inválido** (eem-*bah*-lee-dhoa) *adj* invalid, disabled; *m* invalid
**invasión** (eem-bah-*s$^y$oan*) *f* invasion
**invención** (eem-bayn-*th$^y$oan*) *f* invention
**inventar** (eem-bayn-*tahr*) *v* invent
**inventario** (eem-bayn-*tah*-r$^y$oa) *m* inventory
**inventivo** (eem-bayn-*tee*-bhoa) *adj* inventive
**inventor** (eem-bayn-*toar*) *m* inventor
**invernadero** (eem-bayr-nah-*dhay*-roa) *m* greenhouse
**inversión** (eem-bayr-*s$^y$oan*) *f* investment
**inversionista** (eem-bayr-s$^y$oa-*neess*-tah) *m* investor
**inverso** (eem-*bayr*-soa) *adj* reverse
***invertir** (eem-bayr-*teer*) *v* invert; invest
**investigación** (eem-bayss-tee-gah-*th$^y$oan*) *f* research; investigation, enquiry
**investigador** (eem-bhayss-tee-gah-*dhoar*) *m* research worker
**investigar** (eem-bayss-tee-*gahr*) *v* investigate, enquire
**invierno** (eem-*b$^y$ayr*-noa) *m* winter; **deportes de ~** winter sports
**invisible** (eem-bee-*see*-bhlay) *adj* invisible
**invitación** (eem-bee-tah-*th$^y$oan*) *f* invitation
**invitado** (eem-bee-*tah*-dhoa) *m* guest
**invitar** (eem-bee-*tahr*) *v* invite; ask
**inyección** (een-$^y$ayk-*th$^y$oan*) *f* shot, injection
**inyectar** (een-$^y$ayk-*tahr*) *v* inject
***ir** (eer) *v* *go; **~ por** fetch; ***irse** *v* *go away
**Irak** (ee-*rahk*) *m* Iraq
**Irán** (ee-*rahn*) *m* Iran
**iraní** (ee-rah-*nee*) *adj* Iranian; *m* Iranian
**iraquí** (ee-rah-*kee*) *adj* Iraqi; *m* Iraqi
**irascible** (ee-rahss-*thee*-bhlay) *adj* irascible, quick-tempered
**Irlanda** (eer-*lahn*-dah) *f* Ireland
**irlandés** (eer-lahn-*dayss*) *adj* Irish; *m* Irishman
**ironía** (ee-roa-*nee*-ah) *f* irony
**irónico** (ee-*roa*-nee-koa) *adj* ironical
**irrazonable** (ee-rrah-thoa-*nah*-bhlay) *adj* unreasonable
**irreal** (ee-rray-*ahl*) *adj* unreal
**irreflexivo** (ee-rray-flayk-*see*-bhoa) *adj* rash, impetuous

**irregular** (ee-rray-goo-*lahr*) *adj* irregular; uneven
**irrelevante** (ee-rray-lay-*bhahn*-tay) *adj* insignificant
**irreparable** (ee-rray-pah-*rah*-bhlay) *adj* irreparable
**irrevocable** (ee-rray-bhoa-*kah*-bhlay) *adj* irrevocable
**irritable** (ee-rree-*tah*-bhlay) *adj* irritable
**irritante** (ee-rree-*tahn*-tay) *adj* irritating, annoying
**irritar** (ee-rree-*tahr*) *v* annoy, irritate
**irrompible** (ee-rroam-*pee*-bhlay) *adj* unbreakable
**irrupción** (ee-rroop-*th$^y$oan*) *f* invasion, raid
**isla** (*eez*-lah) *f* island
**islandés** (eez-lahn-*dayss*) *adj* Icelandic; *m* Icelander
**Islandia** (eez-*lahn*-d$^y$ah) *f* Iceland
**Israel** (eess-rah-*ayl*) *m* Israel
**israelí** (eess-rah-ay-*lee*) *adj* Israeli; *m* Israeli
**istmo** (*eest*-moa) *m* isthmus
**Italia** (ee-*tah*-l$^y$ah) *f* Italy
**italiano** (ee-tah-*l$^y$ah*-noa) *adj* Italian; *m* Italian
**itinerario** (ee-tee-nay-*rah*-r$^y$oa) *m* itinerary
**IVA** (*ee*-bah) (= *impuesto sobre el valor añadido*) *sales tax*, VAT (= value-added tax)
**izar** (ee-*thahr*) *v* hoist
**izquierda** (eeth-*k$^y$ayr*-dah) *f* left; **por la ~** on the left
**izquierdo** (eeth-*k$^y$ayr*-dhoa) *adj* left; left-hand

# J

**jabón** (khah-*bhoan*) *m* soap; **~ de afeitar** shaving soap; **~ en polvo** soap powder, washing powder
**jade** (*khah*-dhay) *m* jade
**jadear** (khah-dhay-*ahr*) *v* pant
**jalar** (khah-*lahr*) *vMe* *draw
**jalea** (khah-*lay*-ah) *f* jelly
**jamás** (khah-*mahss*) *adv* ever
**jamón** (khah-*moan*) *m* ham
**Japón** (khah-*poan*) *m* Japan
**japonés** (khah-poa-*nayss*) *adj* Japanese; *m* Japanese
**¡jaque!** (*khah*-kay) check!
**jarabe** (khah-*rah*-bhay) *m* syrup
**jardín** (khahr-*dheen*) *m* garden; **~ de infancia** kindergarten; **~ público** public garden; **~ zoológico** zoological gardens, zoo
**jardinero** (khahr-dhee-*nay*-roa) *m*, **-a** *f* gardener
**jarra** (*khah*-rrah) *f* jar
**jaula** (*khou*-lah) *f* cage
**jefe** (*khay*-fay) *m* chief, manager, boss; leader; chieftain; **~ de cocina** chef; **~ de Estado** head of state; **~ de gobierno** premier
**jengibre** (khayng-*khee*-bhray) *m* ginger
**jerarquía** (khay-rahr-*kee*-ah) *f* hierarchy
**jerez** (khay-*rayth*) *m* sherry
**jeringa** (khay-*reeng*-gah) *f* syringe
**jersey** (khayr-*say*) *m* jersey, sweater; jumper
**jinete** (khee-*nay*-tay) *m* horseman, rider
**jitomate** (khee-toa-*mah*-tay) *mMe* tomato

**Jordania** (khoar-*dhah*-n$^y$ah) *f* Jordan
**jordano** (khoar-*dhah*-noa) *adj* Jordanian; *m* Jordanian
**jornada** (khoar-*nah*-dhah) *f* day trip; working day
**joven** (*khoa*-bhayn) *adj* young; *m* lad
**jovial** (khoa-*bh$^y$ahl*) *adj* jovial; jolly
**joya** (*khoa*-$^y$ah) *f* jewel, gem
**joyería** (khoa-$^y$ay-*ree*-ah) *f* jewel(le)ry
**joyero** (khoa-$^y$*ay*-roa) *m*, **-a** *f* jewel(l)er
**jubilado** (khoo-bhee-*lah*-dhoa) *adj* retired
**judía** (khoo-*dhee*-ah) *f* bean
**judío** (khoo-*dhee*-oa) *adj* Jewish; *m*, **-a** *f* Jew
**juego** (*khway*-goa) *m* game, play; set; ***hacer ~ con** match; **~ de bolos** bowling; **~ de damas** draughts, checkers *Am*; **~ de té** tea set; **~ electrónico** electronic game
**juerga** (*khwayr*-gah) *f colloquial* partying; **irse de ~** *colloquial* go out on the town, go out partying
**jueves** (*khway*-bhayss) *m* Thursday
**juez** (khwayth) *m/f* judge
**jugada** (khoo-*gah*-dhah) *f* move
**jugador** (khoo-gah-*dhoar*) *m* player
***jugar** (khoo-*gahr*) *v* play
**juguete** (khoo-*gay*-tay) *m* toy
**juguetería** (khoo-gay-tay-*ree*-ah) *f* toy store
**juicio** (*khwee*-th$^y$oa) *m* sense; judgment
**julio** (*khoo*-l$^y$oa) July
**junco** (*khoong*-koa) *m* rush, reed
**jungla** (*khoong*-glah) *f* jungle
**junio** (*khoo*-n$^y$oa) June
**junta** (*khoon*-tah) *f* meeting, council
**juntamente** (khoon-tah-*mayn*-tay) *adv* jointly
**juntar** (khoon-*tahr*) *v* attach; collect; join; **juntarse** *v* gather
**junto a** (*khoon*-toa ah) beside; next to
**juntos** (*khoon*-toass) *adv* together
**jurado** (khoo-*rah*-dhoa) *m* jury
**juramento** (khoo-rah-*mayn*-toa) *m* vow, oath; **prestar ~** vow
**jurar** (khoo-*rahr*) *v* *swear
**jurídico** (khoo-*ree*-dhee-koa) *adj* legal
**jurista** (khoo-*reess*-tah) *m* lawyer
**justamente** (khooss-tah-*mayn*-tay) *adv* rightly; just
**justicia** (khooss-*tee*-th$^y$ah) *f* justice
**justificar** (khooss-tee-fee-*kahr*) *v* justify
**justo** (*khooss*-toa) *adj* fair, just, righteous, right; correct, appropriate, proper
**juvenil** (khoo-bhay-*neel*) *adj* juvenile
**juventud** (khoo-bhayn-*toodh*) *f* youth
**juzgar** (khoodh-*gahr*) *v* judge

# K

**Kenya** (*kay*-n$^y$ah) *m* Kenya
**kilogramo** (kee-loa-*grah*-moa) *m* kilogram
**kilometraje** (kee-loa-may-*trah*-khay) *m* distance in kilometres, kilometers *Am*
**kilómetro** (kee-*loa*-may-troa) *m* kilometre, kilometer *Am*

# L

**la** (lah) *pron* her
**laberinto** (lah-bhay-*reen*-toa) *m* maze, labyrinth
**labio** (*lah*-bh$^{y}$oa) *m* lip
**labor** (lah-*bhoar*) *f* labo(u)r
**laboratorio** (lah-bhoa-rah-*toa*-r$^{y}$oa) *m* laboratory; **~ de lenguas** language laboratory
**laca** (*lah*-kah) *f* lacquer; **~ para el cabello** hair-spray
**ladera** (lah-*dhay*-rah) *f* hillside
**lado** (*lah*-dhoa) *m* side; way; **al ~** next-door; **al otro ~** across; **al otro ~ de** across
**ladrar** (lah-*dhrahr*) *v* bark
**ladrillo** (lah-*dhree*-l$^{y}$oa) *m* brick
**ladrón** (lah-*dhroan*) *m*, **ladrona** *f* thief, robber; burglar
**lago** (*lah*-goa) *m* lake
**lágrima** (*lah*-gree-mah) *f* tear
**laguna** (lah-*goo*-nah) *f* lagoon
**lamentable** (lah-mayn-*tah*-bhlay) *adj* lamentable
**lamentar** (lah-mayn-*tahr*) *v* lament; grieve
**lamer** (lah-*mayr*) *v* lick
**lámpara** (*lahm*-pah-rah) *f* lamp; **~ para lectura** reading lamp; **~ sorda** hurricane lamp
**lana** (*lah*-nah) *f* wool; **de ~** wool(l)en
**landa** (*lahn*-dhah) *f* heath, moorland
**langosta** (lahng-*goass*-tah) *f* lobster
**lanza** (*lahn*-thah) *f* spear
**lanzamiento** (lahn-thah-*m$^{y}$ayn*-toa) *m* throw
**lanzar** (lahn-*thahr*) *v* *cast; launch
**lápiz** (*lah*-peeth) *m* pencil; **~ labial** lipstick; **~ para las cejas** eyebrow pencil
**largo** (*lahr*-goa) *adj* long; **a lo ~ de** along, past; **pasar de ~** pass by; *m* length
**laringitis** (lah-reeng-*khee*-teess) *f* laryngitis
**lástima: ¡qué lástima!** (kay *lahss*-tee-mah) what a pity!
**lata** (*lah*-tah) *f* tin, canister, can
**lateralmente** (lah-tay-rahl-*mayn*-tay) *adv* sideways
**latín** (lah-*teen*) *m* Latin
**latinoamericano** (lah-tee-noa-ah-may-ree-*kah*-noa) *adj* Latin American
**latitud** (lah-tee-*toodh*) *f* latitude
**latón** (lah-*toan*) *m* brass
**lavable** (lah-*bhah*-bhlay) *adj* washable
**lavabos** (lah-*bhah*-bhoass) *mpl* bathroom; **~ para caballeros** men's room; **~ para señoras** ladies' room
**lavado** (lah-*bhah*-dhoa) *m* washing
**lavadora** (lah-bhah-*dhoa*-rah) *f* washing machine
**lavandería** (lah-bhahn-day-*ree*-ah) *f* laundry; **~ de autoservicio** launderette
**lavar** (lah-*bhahr*) *v* wash
**laxante** (lahk-*sahn*-tay) *m* laxative
**le** (lay) *pron* him; her
**leal** (lay-*ahl*) *adj* true, loyal
**lección** (layk-*th$^{y}$oan*) *f* lesson
**lector** (layk-toar) *m*, **-a** *f* reader
**lectura** (layk-*too*-rah) *f* reading
**leche** (*lay*-chay) *f* milk; **batido de ~** milk-shake
**lechería** (lay-chay-*ree*-ah) *f* dairy
**lechero** (lay-*chay*-roa) *m* milkman
**lechoso** (lay-*choa*-soa) *adj* milky
**lechuga** (lay-*choo*-gah) *f* lettuce
***leer** (lay-*ayr*) *v* *read
**legación** (lay-gah-*th$^{y}$oan*) *f* legation
**legal** (lay-*gahl*) *adj* legal
**legalización** (lay-gah-lee-thah-*th$^{y}$oan*) *f* legalization
**legible** (lay-*khee*-bhlay) *adj* legible

**legítimo** (lay-*khee*-tee-moa) *adj* legitimate, legal
**legumbre** (lay-*goom*-bray) *f* vegetable
**lejano** (lay-*khah*-noa) *adj* remote, far, distant
**lejos** (*lay*-khoass) *adv* far
**lema** (*lay*-mah) *f* motto, slogan
**lengua** (*layng*-gwah) *f* tongue; language; **~ materna** native language, mother tongue
**lenguado** (layng-*gwah*-dhoa) *m* sole
**lenguaje** (layng-*gwah*-khay) *m* speech
**lente** (*layn*-tay) *m/f* lens; **~ de aumento** magnifying glass; **lentillas** *fpl* contact lenses
**lento** (*layn*-toa) *adj* slow; slack
**león** (lay-*oan*) *m* lion
**lepra** (*lay*-prah) *f* leprosy
**lerdo** (*layr*-dhoa) *adj* slow; clumsy; dull
**les** (layss) *pron* them
**lesión** (lay-*s$^{y}$oan*) *f* injury
**letra** (*lay*-trah) *f* letter
**levadura** (lay-bhah-*dhoo*-rah) *f* yeast
**levantamiento** (lay-bhahn-tah-*m$^{y}$ayn*-toa) *m* rise; rising
**levantar** (lay-bhahn-*tahr*) *v* lift; *bring up; **levantarse** *v* *rise, *get up
**levante** (lay-*bhan*-tay) *m* east
**leve** (*lay*-bhay) *adj* slight
**ley** (lay) *f* law
**leyenda** (lay-*$^{y}$ayn*-dah) *f* legend
**liar** (l$^{y}$ahr) *v* bundle; tie, tie up
**libanés** (lee-bhah-*nayss*) *adj* Lebanese; *m* Lebanese
**Líbano** (*lee*-bhah-noa) *m* Lebanon
**liberación** (lee-bhay-rah-*th$^{y}$oan*) *f* liberation; delivery
**liberal** (lee-bhay-*rahl*) *adj* liberal
**liberalismo** (lee-bhay-rah-*leez*-moa) *m* liberalism
**Liberia** (lee-*bhay*-r$^{y}$ah) *f* Liberia
**liberiano** (lee-bhay-*r$^{y}$ah*-noa) *adj* Liberian; *m* Liberian
**libertad** (lee-bhayr-*tahdh*) *f* liberty, freedom
**libra** (*lee*-bhrah) *f* pound
**libranza** (lee-*bhrahn*-thah) *f* money order
**librar** (lee-*bhrahr*) *v* deliver; rescue
**libre** (*lee*-bhray) *adj* free
**librería** (lee-bhray-*ree*-ah) *f* bookstore
**librero** (lee-*bhray*-roa) *m*, **-a** *f* bookseller
**libro** (*lee*-bhroa) *m* book; **~ de bolsillo** paperback; **~ de cocina** cook(ery)-book; **~ de reclamaciones** complaints book; **~ de texto** textbook
**licencia** (lee-*thayn*-th$^{y}$ah) *f* permission, licence, license *Am*; leave
**lícito** (*lee*-thee-toa) *adj* lawful
**licor** (lee-*koar*) *m* liquor; liqueur
**líder** (*lee*-dhayr) *m* leader
**liebre** (*l$^{y}$ay*-bhray) *f* hare
**liga** (*lee*-gah) *f* union, league
**ligar** (lee-*gahr*) *v* bind; tie; **~ con** *colloquial* pick up
**ligero** (lee-*khay*-roa) *adj* light; slight
**lima** (*lee*-mah) *f* file; lime; **~ para las uñas** nail file
**limitar** (lee-mee-*tahr*) *v* limit
**límite** (*lee*-mee-tay) *m* boundary, limit; **~ de velocidad** speed limit
**limón** (lee-*moan*) *m* lemon
**limonada** (lee-moa-*nah*-dhah) *f* lemonade
**limpiaparabrisas** (leem-p$^{y}$ah-pah-rah-*bhree*-sahss) *m* windscreen wiper, windshield wiper *Am*
**limpiar** (leem-*p$^{y}$ahr*) *v* clean; **~ en seco** dry-clean
**limpieza** (leem-*p$^{y}$ay*-thah) *f* cleaning
**limpio** (*leem*-p$^{y}$oa) *adj* clean
**lindo** (*leen*-doa) *adj* pretty, lovely, nice
**línea** (*lee*-nay-ah) *f* line; **~ de navegación** shipping line; **~ de**

**pesca** fishing line; ~ **principal** main line
**lino** (*lee*-noa) *m* linen
**linterna** (leen-*tayr*-nah) *f* lantern; torch, flashlight
**liquidación** (lee-kee-dhah-*th*$^{y}$*oan*) *f* clearance sale
**líquido** (*lee*-kee-dhoa) *adj* liquid
**liso** (*lee*-soa) *adj* smooth, plain, flat
**lista** (*leess*-tah) *f* list; ~ **de correos** poste restante; ~ **de espera** waiting list; ~ **de precios** price list
**listín telefónico** (leess-*teen* tay-lay-*foa*-nee-koa) telephone directory; telephone book *Am*
**listo** (*leess*-toa) *adj* bright; clever, smart; ready
**litera** (lee-*tay*-rah) *f* berth
**literario** (lee-tay-*rah*-r$^{y}$oa) *adj* literary
**literatura** (lee-tay-rah-*too*-rah) *f* literature
**litoral** (lee-toa-*rahl*) *m* seacoast
**litro** (*lee*-troa) *m* litre, liter *Am*
**llaga** (*l*$^{y}$*ah*-gah) *f* sore; wound
**llama** (*l*$^{y}$*ah*-mah) *f* flame
**llamada** (l$^{y}$ah-*mah*-dhah) *f* call; ~ **local** local call; ~ **telefónica** telephone call
**llamar** (l$^{y}$ah-*mahr*) *v* cry, call; **así llamado** so-called; ~ **por teléfono** phone; **llamarse** *v* *be called
**llano** (*l*$^{y}$*ah*-noa) *adj* flat; level, even, smooth; *m* plain
**llanta** (*l*$^{y}$*ahn*-tah) *f* rim; *fMe* tire
**llave** (*l*$^{y}$*ah*-bhay) *f* key; **ama de llaves** housekeeper; **guardar con** ~ lock up; ~ **de la casa** latchkey; ~ **inglesa** spanner, wrench *Am*
**llegada** (l$^{y}$ay-*gah*-dhah) *f* arrival; coming
**llegar** (l$^{y}$ay-*gahr*) *v* arrive; ~ **a** attain
**llenar** (l$^{y}$ay-*nahr*) *v* fill; fill in; fill out *Am*; fill up
**lleno** (*l*$^{y}$*ay*-noa) *adj* full
**llevar** (l$^{y}$ay-*bhahr*) *v* *take; *bear, carry; *wear; **llevarse** *v* *take away
**llorar** (l$^{y}$oa-*rahr*) *v* cry, *weep
***llover** (l$^{y}$oa-*bhayr*) *v* rain
**llovizna** (l$^{y}$oa-*bheeth*-nah) *f* drizzle
**lluvia** (*l*$^{y}$*oo*-bh$^{y}$ah) *f* rain
**lluvioso** (l$^{y}$oo-*bh*$^{y}$*oa*-soa) *adj* rainy
**lo** (loa) *pron* it; ~ **que** what
**lobo** (*loa*-bhoa) *m* wolf
**local** (loa-*kahl*) *adj* local
**localidad** (loa-kah-lee-*dhahdh*) *f* locality; seat
**localizar** (loa-kah-lee-*thahr*) *v* locate
**loción** (loa-*th*$^{y}$*oan*) *f* lotion
**loco** (*loa*-koa) *adj* crazy; mad
**locomotora** (loa-koa-moa-*toa*-rah) *f* engine, locomotive
**locuaz** (loa-*kwahth*) *adj* talkative
**locura** (loa-*koo*-rah) *f* madness, lunacy
**lodo** (*loa*-dhoa) *m* mud
**lodoso** (loa-*dhoa*-soa) *adj* muddy
**lógica** (*loa*-khee-kah) *f* logic
**lógico** (*loa*-khee-koa) *adj* logical
**lograr** (loa-*grahr*) *v* achieve; secure
**lomo** (*loa*-moa) *m* back; loin; **a lomos de burro** on a donkey
**lona** (*loa*-nah) *f* canvas
**longitud** (loang-khee-*toodh*) *f* length; longitude; ~ **de onda** wavelength
**lonja** (*loan*-khah) *f* fish market; slice
**loro** (*loa*-roa) *m* parrot
**lotería** (loa-tay-*ree*-ah) *f* lottery
**loza** (*loa*-thah) *f* earthenware; pottery, faience, crockery
**lubricación** (loo-bhree-kah-*th*$^{y}$*oan*) *f* lubrication
**lubricar** (loo-bhree-*kahr*) *v* lubricate
**lucio** (*loo*-th$^{y}$oa) *m* pike
***lucir** (loo-*theer*) *v* *shine
**lucha** (*loo*-chah) *f* combat, fight; contest; struggle
**luchar** (loo-*chahr*) *v* struggle, *fight
**luego** (*lway*-goa) *adv* later; **¡hasta**

**luego!** so long!
**lugar** (loo-*gahr*) *m* place; spot; **en ~ de** instead of; **~ de camping** camping site; **~ de descanso** holiday resort; **~ de nacimiento** place of birth; **~ de reunión** meeting place; ***tener ~** *take place
**lujo** (*loo*-khoa) *m* luxury
**lujoso** (loo-*khoa*-soa) *adj* luxurious
**lumbago** (loom-*bah*-goa) *m* lumbago
**luminoso** (loo-mee-*noa*-soa) *adj* luminous
**luna** (*loo*-nah) *f* moon; **~ de miel** honeymoon
**lunático** (loo-*nah*-tee-koa) *adj* insane, lunatic
**lunes** (*loo*-nayss) *m* Monday
**lúpulo** (*loo*-poo-loa) *m* hop
**lustroso** (looss-*troa*-soa) *adj* glossy
**luto** (*loo*-toa) *m* mourning
**luz** (looth) *f* light; **luces de freno** brake lights; **~ de estacionamiento** parking light; **~ de la luna** moonlight; **~ del día** daylight; **~ del sol** sunlight; **~ lateral** sidelight; **~ trasera** rear light

# M

**macizo** (mah-*thee*-thoa) *adj* solid, massive
**machacar** (mah-chah-*kahr*) *v* mash
**macho** (*mah*-choa) *adj* male; masculine
**madera** (mah-*dhay*-rah) *f* wood; **de ~** wooden; **~ de construcción** timber
**madero** (mah-*dhay*-roa) *m* log
**madrastra** (mah-*dhrahss*-trah) *f* stepmother
**madre** (*mah*-dhray) *f* mother
**madriguera** (mah-dhree-*gay*-rah) *f* den
**madrugada** (mah-dhroo-*gah*-dhah) *f* daybreak
**madrugar** (mah-dhroo-*gahr*) *v* *rise early
**madurez** (mah-dhoo-*rayth*) *f* maturity
**maduro** (mah-*dhoo*-roa) *adj* mature, ripe
**maestro** (mah-*ayss*-troa) *m*, **-a** *f* master; schoolteacher, schoolmaster, teacher; **~ particular** tutor
**magia** (*mah*-kh$^{y}$ah) *f* magic
**mágico** (*mah*-khee-koa) *adj* magic
**magistrado** (mah-kheess-*trah*-dhoa) *m* magistrate
**magnético** (mahg-*nay*-tee-koa) *adj* magnetic
**magneto** (mahg-*nay*-toa) *m* magneto
**magnetófono** (mahg-nay-*toa*-foa-noa) *m* tape recorder
**magnífico** (mahg-*nee*-fee-koa) *adj* splendid, gorgeous, magnificent, swell
**magro** (*mah*-groa) *adj* lean
**magulladura** (mah-goo-l$^{y}$ah-*dhoo*-rah) *f* bruise
**magullar** (mah-goo-*l$^{y}$ahr*) *v* bruise
**majo** (*mah*-khoa) *adj colloquial* nice; pretty
**maíz** (mah-*eeth*) *m* maize, corn *Am*; **~ en la mazorca** corn on the cob
**majestad** (mah-khayss-*tahdh*) *f* majesty
**mal** (mahl) *m* harm, evil; wrong; mischief
**malaria** (mah-*lah*-r$^{y}$ah) *f* malaria
**Malasia** (mah-*lah*-s$^{y}$ah) *f* Malaysia
**malayo** (mah-*lah*-$^{y}$oa) *adj* Malaysian;

*m* Malay
***maldecir** (mahl-day-*theer*) *v* curse
**maldición** (mahl-dee-*th$^{y}$oan*) *f* curse
**malentendido** (mahl-ayn-tan-*dee*-doah) *m* misunderstanding
**maleta** (mah-*lay*-tah) *f* suitcase, bag
**maletín** (mah-lay-*teen*) *m* briefcase
**malévolo** (mah-*lay*-bhoa-loa) *adj* spiteful
**malicia** (mah-*lee*-th$^{y}$ah) *f* mischief
**malicioso** (mah-lee-*th$^{y}$oa*-soa) *adj* malicious
**maligno** (mah-*leeg*-noa) *adj* malignant; ill
**malo** (*mah*-loa) *adj* bad; evil, ill
**malva** (*mahl*-bhah) *adj* mauve
**malvado** (mahl-*bhah*-dhoa) *adj* wicked, evil
**malla** (*mah*-l$^{y}$ah) *f* mesh
**mamífero** (mah-*mee*-fay-roa) *m* mammal
**mamut** (mah-*moot*) *m* mammoth
**manada** (mah-*nah*-dhah) *f* herd
**manantial** (mah-nahn-*t$^{y}$ahl*) *m* spring
**mancuernillas** (mahn-kwayr-*nee*-l$^{y}$ahss) *fplMe* cuff links *pl*
**mancha** (*mahn*-chah) *f* stain, spot, speck; blot
**manchado** (mahn-*chah*-dhoa) *adj* soiled
**manchar** (mahn-*chahr*) *v* stain
**mandar** (mahn-*dahr*) *v* command; *send; **~ a buscar** *send for
**mandarina** (mahn-dah-*ree*-nah) *f* mandarin, tangerine
**mandato** (mahn-*dah*-toa) *m* mandate; order
**mandíbula** (mahn-*dee*-bhoo-lah) *f* jaw
**mando** (*mahn*-doa) *m* command
**manejable** (mah-nay-*khah*-bhlay) *adj* handy; manageable
**manejar** (mah-nay-*khahr*) *v* handle
**manejo** (mah-*nay*-khoa) *m* management
**manera** (mah-*nay*-rah) *f* way, manner; **de otra ~** otherwise
**manga** (*mahng*-gah) *f* sleeve
**mango** (*mahng*-goa) *m* handle
**manía** (mah-*nee*-ah) *f* craze; mania
**manicura** (mah-nee-*koo*-rah) *f* manicure; ***hacer la ~** manicure
**manifestación** (mah-nee-fayss-tah-*th$^{y}$oan*) *f* demonstration; ***hacer una ~** demonstrate
***manifestar** (mah-nee-fayss-*tahr*) *v* reveal, manifest, express
**maniquí** (mah-nee-*kee*) *m* model, mannequin
**mano** (*mah*-noa) *f* hand; **de segunda ~** second-hand; **hecho a ~** hand-made
**mansión** (mahn-*s$^{y}$oan*) *f* mansion
**manso** (*mahn*-soa) *adj* tame
**manta** (*mahn*-tah) *f* blanket
**mantel** (mahn-*tayl*) *m* tablecloth
***mantener** (mahn-tay-*nayr*) *v* maintain; support; service
**mantenimiento** (mahn-tay-nee-*m$^{y}$ayn*-toa) *m* maintenance; servicing
**mantequilla** (mahn-tay-*kee*-l$^{y}$ah) *f* butter
**manual** (mah-*nwahl*) *adj* manual; *m* handbook; **~ de conversación** phrase book
**manuscrito** (mah-nooss-*kree*-toa) *m* manuscript
**manutención** (mah-noo-tayn-*th$^{y}$oan*) *f* upkeep; maintenance; support
**manzana** (mahn-*thah*-nah) *f* apple; **~ de casas** block *Am*
**manzanilla** (mahn-tha-*nee*-l$^{y}$ah) *f* camomile tea
**mañana** (mah-*ñah*-nah) *f* morning; *adv* tomorrow; **esta ~** this morning
**mapa** (*mah*-pah) *m* map; **~ de carreteras** road map
**maquillaje** (mah-kee-*l$^{y}$ah*-khay) *m*

make-up
**máquina** (*mah*-kee-nah) *f* engine, machine; ~ **de billetes** ticket machine; ~ **de coser** sewing-machine; ~ **de escribir** typewriter; ~ **de lavar** washing machine; ~ **tragamonedas** slot machine
**mar** (mahr) *m* sea; **orilla del** ~ seaside, seashore
**maravilla** (mah-rah-*bhee*-l$^y$ah) *f* marvel
**maravillarse** (mah-rah-bhee-*l$^y$ahr*-say) *v* marvel
**maravilloso** (mah-rah-bhee-*l$^y$oa*-soa) *adj* wonderful, marvel(l)ous, fine
**marca** (*mahr*-kah) *f* brand; mark; ~ **de fábrica** trademark
**marcar** (mahr-*kahr*) *v* mark; score
**marco** (*mahr*-koa) *m* frame
**marcha** (*mahr*-chah) *f* march; ***dar** ~ **atrás** reverse; ~ **atrás** reverse
**marchar** (mahr-*chahr*) *v* march
**marea** (mah-*ray*-ah) *f* tide ; ~ **alta** high tide; ~ **baja** low tide
**mareado** (mah-ray-*ah*-dhoa) *adj* dizzy, giddy; seasick
**mareo** (mah-*ray*-oa) *m* dizziness; giddiness; seasickness
**marfil** (mahr-*feel*) *m* ivory
**margarina** (mahr-gah-*ree*-nah) *f* margarine
**margen** (*mahr*-khayn) *m* margin
**marido** (mah-*ree*-dhoa) *m* husband
**marina** (mah-*ree*-nah) *f* navy; seascape
**marinero** (mah-ree-*nay*-roa) *m* sailor
**marino** (mah-*ree*-noa) *m* seaman; *adj* marine
**mariposa** (mah-ree-*poa*-sah) *f* butterfly
**marisco** (mah-*reess*-koa) *m*, **mariscos** *pl* seafood
**marisma** (mah-*reez*-mah) *f* swamp
**marítimo** (mah-*ree*-tee-moa) *adj* maritime
**mármol** (*mahr*-moal) *m* marble
**marqués** (mahr-*kayss*) *m* marquis
**marrón** (mah-rroan) *adj* brown
**marroquí** (mah-rroa-*kee*) *adj* Moroccan; *m* Moroccan
**Marruecos** (mah-*rway*-koass) *m* Morocco
**martes** (*mahr*-tayss) *m* Tuesday
**martillo** (mahr-*tee*-l$^y$oa) *m* hammer
**mártir** (*mahr*-teer) *m* martyr
**marzo** (*mahr*-thoa) March
**mas** (mahss) *conj* but
**más** (mahss) *adv* more; plus; **algo** ~ some more; **el** ~ most; ~ **de** over
**masa** (*mah*-sah) *f* mass; crowd, lot; dough, batter
**masaje** (mah-*sah*-khay) *m* massage; ***dar** ~ massage; ~ **facial** face massage
**masajista** (mah-sah-*kheess*-tah) *m* masseur
**máscara** (*mahss*-kah-rah) *f* mask; ~ **facial** face pack
**masculino** (mahss-koo-*lee*-noa) *adj* masculine
**masticar** (mahss-tee-*kahr*) *v* chew
**mástil** (*mahss*-teel) *m* mast
**matar** (mah-*tahr*) *v* kill
**mate** (*mah*-tay) *adj* matt, dim, dull
**matemáticas** (mah-tay-*mah*-tee-kahss) *fpl* mathematics
**matemático** (mah-tay-*mah*-tee-koa) *adj* mathematical
**materia** (mah-*tay*-r$^y$ah) *f* matter; ~ **prima** raw material
**material** (mah-tay-*r$^y$ahl*) *adj* material, substantial; *m* material
**matiz** (mah-*teeth*) *m* nuance
**matorral** (mah-toa-*rrahl*) *m* scrub, bush
**matrícula** (mah-*tree*-koo-lah) *f* registration number
**matrimonial** (mah-tree-moa-*n$^y$ahl*) *adj* matrimonial
**matrimonio** (mah-tree-*moa*-n$^y$oa) *m*

wedding, marriage; matrimony
**matriz** (mah-*treeth*) *f* uterus
**máximo** (*mahk*-see-moa) *m* maximum
**mayo** (*mah*-$^y$oa) May
**mayor** (mah-$^y$*oar*) *adj* superior, major; bigger; main, eldest; *m* major; **mayores** *mpl* ancestors; elders
**mayoría** (mah-$^y$oa-*ree*-ah) *f* majority; bulk
**mayorista** (mah-$^y$oa-*reess*-tah) *m* wholesale dealer
**mayúscula** (mah-$^y$*ooss*-koo-lah) *f* capital letter
**mazo** (*mah*-thoa) *m* mallet
**me** (may) *pron* me; myself
**mecánico** (may-*kah*-nee-koa) *adj* mechanical; *m* mechanic
**mecanismo** (may-kah-*neez*-moa) *m* mechanism, machinery
**mecer** (may-*thayr*) *v* rock; swing
**mecha** (*may*-chah) *f* fuse; wick
**mechero** (may-*chay*-roa) *m* cigarette lighter
**medalla** (may-*dhah*-l$^y$ah) *f* medal
**media** (*may*-dh$^y$ah) *f* stocking; **medias elásticas** support hose
**mediador** (may-dh$^y$ah-*dhoar*) *m* mediator
**medianamente** (may-dh$^y$ah-nah-*mayn*-tay) *adv* fairly
**mediano** (may-*dh$^y$ah*-noa) *adj* medium
**medianoche** (may-dh$^y$ah-*noa*-chay) *f* midnight
**mediante** (may-*dh$^y$ahn*-tay) *adv* by means of
**mediar** (may-*dh$^y$ahr*) *v* mediate
**medicamento** (may-dhee-kah-*mayn*-toa) *m* medicine, drug
**medicina** (may-dhee-*thee*-nah) *f* medicine
**médico** (*may*-dhee-koa) *adj* medical; *m*, **-a** *f* doctor, physician; **~ de cabecera** general practitioner
**medida** (may-*dhee*-dhah) *f* measure; **hecho a la ~** made to order, tailor-made
**medidor** (may-dhee-*dhoar*) *m* gauge
**medieval** (may-dh$^y$ay-*bhahl*) *adj* medi(a)eval
**medio** (*may*-dh$^y$oa) *adj* half; medium; middle; *m* midst, middle; means; **en ~ de** amid; **~ ambiente** milieu, environment
**mediocre** (may-*dh$^y$oa*-kray) *adj* mediocre; below average
**mediodía** (may-dh$^y$oa-*dhee*-ah) *m* midday, noon
***medir** (may-*dheer*) *v* measure
**meditación** (may-dhee-tah-*th$^y$oan*) *f* meditation
**meditar** (may-dhee-*tahr*) *v* meditate
**Mediterráneo** (may-dhee-tay-*rrah*-nay-oa) Mediterranean
**médula** (*may*-dhoo-lah) *f* marrow
**medusa** (may-*dhoo*-sah) *f* jellyfish
**mejicano** (may-khee-*kah*-noa) *adj* Mexican; *m* Mexican
**Méjico** (*may*-khee-koa) *m* Mexico
**mejilla** (may-*khee*-l$^y$ah) *f* cheek
**mejillón** (may-khee-*l$^y$oan*) *m* mussel
**mejor** (may-*khoar*) *adj* better; superior
**mejora** (may-*khoa*-rah) *f* improvement
**mejorar** (may-khoa-*rahr*) *v* improve
**melancolía** (may-lahng-koa-*lee*-ah) *f* melancholy
**melancólico** (may-lahng-*koa*-lee-koa) *adj* sad
**melocotón** (may-loa-koa-*toan*) *m* peach
**melodía** (may-loa-*dhee*-ah) *f* melody
**melodioso** (may-loa-*dh$^y$oa*-soa) *adj* melodious
**melodrama** (may-loa-*dhrah*-mah) *m* melodrama

**melón** (may-*loan*) *m* melon
**memorable** (may-moa-*rah*-bhlay) *adj* memorable
**memoria** (may-*moa*-r$^{y}$ah) *f* memory; **de ~** by heart
**menaje** (may-*nah*-khay) *m* household
**mención** (mayn-*th$^{y}$oan*) *f* mention
**mencionar** (mayn-th$^{y}$oa-*nahr*) *v* mention
**mendigar** (mayn-dee-*gahr*) *v* beg
**mendigo** (mayn-*dee*-goa) *m*, **-a** *f* beggar
**menor** (may-*noar*) *adj* minor; junior
**menos** (*may*-noass) *adv* less; minus; but; **a ~ que** unless; **por lo ~** at least
**menosprecio** (may-noass-*pray*-th$^{y}$oa) *m* contempt; disdain
**mensaje** (mayn-*sah*-khay) *m* message
**mensajero** (mayn-sah-*khay*-roa) *m* messenger
**menstruación** (mayns-trwah-*th$^{y}$oan*) *f* menstruation
**mensual** (mayn-*swahl*) *adj* monthly
**menta** (*mayn*-tah) *f* mint; peppermint
**mental** (mayn-*tahl*) *adj* mental
**mente** (*mayn*-tay) *f* mind
***mentir** (mayn-*teer*) *v* lie
**mentira** (mayn-*tee*-rah) *f* lie
**menú** (may-*noo*) *m* menu
**menudo** (may-*noo*-dhoa) *adj* minute, small, tiny; **a ~** often
**mercado** (mayr-*kah*-dhoa) *m* market; **~ negro** black market
**mercancía** (mayr-kahn-*thee*-ah) *f* merchandise
**mercería** (mayr-thay-*ree*-ah) *f* haberdashery; notions store *Am*
**mercurio** (mayr-*koo*-r$^{y}$oa) *m* mercury
***merecer** (may-ray-*thayr*) *v* merit, deserve
**meridional** (may-ree-dh$^{y}$oa-*nahl*) *adj* southern, southerly
**merienda** (may-*r$^{y}$ayn*-dah) *f* snack; lunch
**mérito** (*may*-ree-toa) *m* merit
**merluza** (mayr-*loo*-thah) *f* whiting
**mermelada** (mayr-may-*lah*-dhah) *f* jam
**mes** (mayss) *m* month
**mesa** (*may*-sah) *f* table
**mesera** (may-*say*-rah) *fMe* waitress
**mesero** (may-*say*-roa) *mMe* waiter
**meseta** (may-*say*-tah) *f* plateau
**meta** (*may*-tah) *f* goal; finish
**metal** (may-*tahl*) *m* metal
**metálico** (may-*tah*-lee-koa) *adj* metal
**meter** (may-*tayr*) *v* *put
**meticuloso** (may-tee-koo-*loa*-soa) *adj* meticulous; precise
**metódico** (may-*toa*-dhee-koa) *adj* methodical
**método** (*may*-toa-dhoa) *m* method
**metro** (*may*-troa) *m* metre; underground; subway *Am*
**mezcla** (*mayth*-klah) *f* mixture
**mezclar** (mayth-*klahr*) *v* mix; **mezclarse en** interfere with
**mezquino** (mayth-*kee*-noa) *adj* narrow-minded, stingy; mean
**mezquita** (mayth-*kee*-tah) *f* mosque
**mi** (mee) *adj* my
**micrófono** (mee-*kroa*-foa-noa) *m* microphone
**microscopio** (mee-kroass-*koa*-p$^{y}$oa) *m* microscope
**miedo** (*m$^{y}$ay*-dhoa) *m* fear, fright; ***tener ~** *be afraid
**miel** (m$^{y}$ayl) *f* honey
**miembro** (*m$^{y}$aym*-broa) *m* limb; member
**mientras** (*m$^{y}$ayn*-trahss) *conj* whilst, while
**miércoles** (*m$^{y}$ayr*-koa-layss) *m* Wednesday
**migaja** (mee-*gah*-khah) *f* crumb
**migraña** (mee-*grah*-ñah) *f* migraine
**mil** (meel) *num* thousand
**milagro** (mee-*lah*-*groa*) *m* miracle;

wonder
**milagroso** (mee-lah-*groa*-soa) *adj* miraculous
**militar** (mee-lee-*tahr*) *adj* military; *m* soldier
**milla** (*mee*-l$^y$ah) *f* mile
**millaje** (mee-*l$^y$ah*-khay) *m* mileage
**millón** (mee-*l$^y$oan*) *m* million
**millonario** (mee-l$^y$oa-*nah*-r$^y$oa) *m*, **-a** *f* millionaire
**mimar** (mee-*mahr*) *v* *spoil
**mina** (*mee*-nah) *f* mine; pit; **~ de oro** goldmine
**mineral** (mee-nay-*rahl*) *m* mineral; ore
**minería** (mee-nay-*ree*-ah) *f* mining
**minero** (mee-*nay*-roa) *m* miner
**miniatura** (mee-n$^y$ah-*too*-rah) *f* miniature
**mínimo** (*mee*-nee-moa) *adj* least
**mínimum** (*mee*-nee-moom) *m* minimum
**ministerio** (mee-neess-*tay*-r$^y$oa) *m* ministry
**ministro** (mee-*neess*-troa) *m* minister
**minoría** (mee-noa-*ree*-ah) *f* minority
**minorista** (mee-noa-*reess*-tah) *m/f* retailer
**minucioso** (mee-noo-*th$^y$oa*-soa) *adj* thorough
**minusválido** (mee-nooz-*bhah*-lee-*dhoa*) *adj* disabled, handicapped
**minuto** (mee-*noo*-toa) *m* minute
**mío** (*mee*-oa) *pron* mine
**miope** (*m$^y$oa*-pay) *adj* short-sighted
**mirada** (mee-*rah*-dhah) *f* look; gaze
**mirador** (mee-rah-*dhoar*) *m* viewpoint
**mirar** (mee-*rahr*) *v* look; watch, view, look at; stare, gaze
**mirlo** (*meer*-loa) *m* blackbird
**misa** (*mee*-sah) *f* Mass
**misceláneo** (mee-thay-*lah*-nay-oa) *adj* miscellaneous
**miserable** (mee-say-*rah*-bhlay) *adj* unfortunate, stingy, vile
**miseria** (mee-*say*-r$^y$ah) *f* poverty; misery
**misericordia** (mee-say-ree-*koar*-d$^y$ah) *f* mercy
**misericordioso** (mee-say-ree-koar-*d$^y$oa*-soa) *adj* merciful
**misión** (mee-*s$^y$oan*) *f* mission
**mismo** (*meez*-moa) *adj* same
**misterio** (meess-*tay*-r$^y$oa) *m* mystery
**misterioso** (meess-tay-*r$^y$oa*-soa) *adj* mysterious; obscure
**mitad** (mee-*tahdh*) *f* half; **partir por la ~** halve
**mito** (*mee*-toa) *m* myth
**mixto** (*meeks*-toa) *adj* mixed; joint
**moción** (moa-*th$^y$oan*) *f* motion
**mochila** (moa-*chee*-lah) *f* rucksack, knapsack; backpack
**moda** (*moa*-dhah) *f* fashion; **a la ~** fashionable
**modales** (moa-*dhah*-layss) *mpl* manners *pl*
**modelar** (moa-dhay-*lahr*) *v* model
**modelo** (moa-*dhay*-loa) *m* model
**moderado** (moa-dhay-*rah*-dhoa) *adj* moderate
**moderno** (moa-*dhayr*-noa) *adj* modern
**modestia** (moa-dhayss-*t$^y$ah*) *f* modesty
**modesto** (moa-*dhayss*-toa) *adj* modest
**modificación** (moa-dhee-fee-kah-*th$^y$oan*) *f* change
**modificar** (moa-dhee-fee-*kahr*) *v* change, modify
**modismo** (moa-*dheez*-moa) *m* idiom
**modista** (moa-*dheess*-tah) *f* dressmaker
**modo** (*moa*-dhoa) *m* fashion, manner; **de cualquier ~** anyhow; **de ningún ~** by no means; **de todos modos** any

way; at any rate; **en ~ alguno** at all; **~ de empleo** directions for use
**moho** (*moa*-oa) *m* mildew
**mojado** (moa-*khah*-dhoa) *adj* wet; moist, damp
**mojigato** (moa-khee-*gah*-toa) *adj* hypocritical
**mojón** (moa-*khoan*) *m* landmark
*__moler__ (moa-*layr*) *v* *grind
**molestar** (moa-layss-*tahr*) *v* disturb, trouble, bother
**molestia** (moa-*layss*-t$^{y}$ah) *f* trouble, nuisance, bother
**molesto** (moa-*layss*-toa) *adj* troublesome, inconvenient
**molinero** (moa-lee-*nay*-roa) *m* miller
**molino** (moa-*lee*-noa) *m* mill; **~ de viento** windmill
**momentáneo** (moa-mayn-*tah*-nay-oa) *adj* momentary
**momento** (moa-*mayn*-toa) *m* moment
**monarca** (moa-*nahr*-kah) *m* monarch, ruler
**monarquía** (moa-nahr-*kee*-ah) *f* monarchy
**monasterio** (moa-nahss-*tay*-r$^{y}$oa) *m* monastery
**moneda** (moa-*nay*-dhah) *f* currency; coin; change; **~ extranjera** foreign currency
**monedero** (moa-nay-*dhay*-roa) *m* purse, wallet *Am*
**monetario** (moa-nay-*tah*-r$^{y}$oa) *adj* monetary; **unidad monetaria** monetary unit
**monja** (*moang*-khah) *f* nun
**monje** (*moang*-khay) *m* monk
**mono** (*moa*-noa) *m* monkey; overalls *pl*
**monólogo** (moa-*noa*-loa-goa) *m* monologue
**monopolio** (moa-noa-*poa*-l$^{y}$oa) *m* monopoly
**monótono** (moa-*noa*-toa-noa) *adj* monotonous
**monstruo** (*moans*-trwoa) *m* monster
**montaña** (moan-*tah*-ñah) *f* mountain
**montañismo** (moan-tah-*ñeez*-moa) *m* mountaineering
**montañoso** (moan-tah-*ñoa*-soa) *adj* mountainous
**montar** (moan-*tahr*) *v* mount, *get on; assemble; *ride
**monte** (*moan*-tay) *m* mount
**montículo** (moan-*tee*-koo-loa) *m* mound
**montón** (moan-*toan*) *m* heap, stack, pile
**montuoso** (moan-*twoa*-soa) *adj* hilly
**monumento** (moa-noo-*mayn*-toa) *m* monument; memorial
**mora** (*moa*-rah) *f* mulberry; blackberry
**morado** (moa-*rah*-dhoa) *adj* violet
**moral** (moa-*rahl*) *adj* moral; *f* moral; spirits
**moralidad** (moa-rah-lee-*dhahdh*) *f* morality
**mordaza** (moar-*dhah*-thah) *f* clamp
**mordedura** (moar-dhay-*dhoo*-rah) *f* bite
*__morder__ (moar-*dhayr*) *v* *bite
**morena** (moa-*ray*-nah) *f* brunette
**moreno** (moa-*ray*-noa) *adj* dark brown
**moretón** (moa-ray-*toan*) *m* bruise
**morfina** (moar-*fee*-nah) *f* morphine, morphia
*__morir__ (moa-*reer*) *v* die
**moro** (*moa*-roa) *m* Moor
**mortal** (moar-*tahl*) *adj* mortal; fatal
**mosaico** (moa-*sigh*-koa) *m* mosaic
**mosca** (*moass*-kah) *f* fly
**mosquitero** (moass-kee-*tay*-roa) *m* mosquito-net
**mosquito** (moass-*kee*-toa) *m* mosquito

**mostaza** (moass-*tah*-thah) *f* mustard
**mostrador** (moass-trah-*dhoar*) *m* counter
***mostrar** (moass-*trahr*) *v* display, *show
**mote** (*moa*-tay) *m* nickname
**moteado** (moa-tay-*ah*-dhoa) *adj* spotted
**motel** (moa-*tayl*) *m* motel
**motín** (moa-*teen*) *m* riot
**motivo** (moa-*tee*-bhoa) *m* motive; cause, occasion
**motocicleta** (moa-toa-thee-*klay*-tah) *f* motorcycle; motorbike *Am*
**motoneta** (moa-toa-*nay*-tah) *f* scooter
**motor** (moa-*toar*) *m* motor, engine; **~ de arranque** starter motor
***mover** (moa-*bhayr*) *v* move; stir
**movible** (moa-*bhee*-bhlay) *adj* movable
**móvil** (*moa*-bheel) *adj* mobile
**movimiento** (moa-bhee-*m*$^{y}$*ayn*-toa) *m* movement, motion
**mozo** (*moa*-thoa) *m* youth; porter
**muchacha** (moo-*chah*-chah) *f* girl; maid
**muchacho** (moo-*chah*-choa) *m* boy
**muchedumbre** (moo-chay-*dhoom*-bray) *f* crowd
**mucho** (*moo*-choa) *adv* much; far, very; *adj* much; **con ~** by far; **muchos** *adj* many
**mudanza** (moo-*dhahn*-thah) *f* move
**mudarse** (moo-*dhahr*-say) *v* move; change
**mudo** (*moo-dhoa*) *adj* mute, dumb
**muebles** (*mway*-bhlayss) *mpl* furniture
**muela** (*mway*-lah) *f* molar; **dolor de muelas** toothache
**muelle** (*mway*-l$^{y}$ay) *m* dock, wharf, quay; pier, jetty; spring
**muerte** (*mwayr*-tay) *f* death
**muerto** (*mwayr*-toa) *adj* dead
**muestra** (*mwayss*-trah) *f* sample
**mugir** (moo-*kheer*) *v* roar
**mujer** (moo-*khayr*) *f* woman; wife
**mújol** (*moo*-khoal) *m* mullet
**muleta** (moo-*lay*-tah) *f* crutch
**mulo** (*moo*-loa) *m* mule
**multa** (*mool*-tah) *f* fine; ticket
**multiplicación** (mool-tee-plee-kah-*th*$^{y}$*oan*) *f* multiplication
**multiplicar** (mool-tee-plee-*kahr*) *v* multiply
**multitud** (mool-tee-*toodh*) *f* crowd
**mundial** (moon-*d*$^{y}$*ahl*) *adj* world-wide, global
**mundo** (*moon*-doa) *m* world; **todo el ~** everyone
**municipal** (moo-nee-thee-*pahl*) *adj* municipal
**municipalidad** (moo-nee-thee-pah-lee-*dhahdh*) *f* municipality
**muñeca** (moo-*ñay*-kah) *f* doll; wrist
**muralla** (moo-*rah*-l$^{y}$ah) *f* wall
**muro** (*moo*-roa) *m* wall
**músculo** (*mooss*-koo-loa) *m* muscle
**musculoso** (mooss-koo-*loa*-soa) *adj* muscular
**museo** (moo-*say*-oa) *m* museum; **~ de figuras de cera** waxworks *pl*
**musgo** (*mooz*-goa) *m* moss
**música** (*moo*-see-kah) *f* music
**musical** (moo-see-*kahl*) *adj* musical; **comedia ~** musical comedy
**músico** (*moo*-see-koa) *m*, **-a** *f* musician
**muslo** (*mooz*-loa) *m* thigh
**musulmán** (moo-sool-*mahn*) *m* Muslim
**mutuo** (*moo*-twoa) *adj* mutual
**muy** (moo$^{ee}$) *adv* very, quite

# N

**nácar** (*nah*-kahr) *m* mother-of-pearl
***nacer** (nah-*thayr*) *v* *be born
**nacido** (nah-*thee*-dhoa) *adj* born
**nacimiento** (nah-thee-*m$^y$ayn*-toa) *m* birth; source; origin
**nación** (nah-*th$^y$oan*) *f* nation
**nacional** (nah-th$^y$oa-*nahl*) *adj* national
**nacionalidad** (nah-th$^y$oa-nah-lee-*dhahdh*) *f* nationality
**nacionalizar** (nah-th$^y$oa-nah-lee-*thahr*) *v* nationalize
**nada** (*nah*-dhah) nothing; nil; **de ~** you're welcome
**nadador** (nah-dhah-*dhoar*) *m*, **-a** *f* swimmer
**nadar** (nah-*dhahr*) *v* *swim
**nadie** (*nah*-dh$^y$ay) *pron* nobody, no one
**naipe** (*nigh*-pay) *m* playing card
**nalga** (*nahl*-gah) *m* buttock
**naranja** (nah-*rahng*-khah) *f* orange
**narciso** (nahr-*thee*-soa) *m* daffodil
**narcosis** (nahr-*koa*-seess) *f* narcosis
**narcótico** (nahr-*koa*-tee-koa) *m* narcotic
**nariz** (nah-*reeth*) *f* nose
**narración** (nah-rrah-*th$^y$oan*) *f* narration
**nata** (*nah*-tah) *f* cream
**natación** (nah-tah-*th$^y$oan*) *f* swimming
**nativo** (nah-*tee*-bhoa) *adj* native
**natural** (nah-too-*rahl*) *adj* natural; *m* nature
**naturaleza** (nah-too-rah-*lay*-thah) *f* nature
**naturalmente** (nah-too-rahl-*mayn*-tay) *adv* naturally
**náusea** (*nou*-say-ah) *f* nausea, sickness
**navaja** (nah-*bhah*-khah) *f* jack-knife; razor
**naval** (nah-*bhahl*) *adj* naval
**nave** (*nah*-bay) *f* ship; nave; **~ espacial** spacecraft
**navegable** (nah-bhay-*gah*-bhlay) *adj* navigable
**navegación** (nah-bhay-gah-*th$^y$oan*) *f* navigation
**navegar** (nah-bhay-*gahr*) *v* sail; navigate
**Navidad** (nah-bhee-*dhahdh*) *f* Christmas
**nebuloso** (nay-bhoo-*loa*-soa) *adj* cloudy; misty
**necesario** (nay-thay-*sah*-r$^y$oa) *adj* necessary; requisite
**neceser** (nay-thay-*sayr*) *m* toilet case
**necesidad** (nay-thay-see-*dhahdh*) *f* need, necessity; want; misery
**necesitar** (nay-thay-see-*tahr*) *v* need
**necio** (*nay*-th$^y$oa) *adj* foolish, silly
***negar** (nay-*gahr*) *v* deny
**negativa** (nay-gah-*tee*-bhah) *f* refusal
**negativo** (nay-gah-*tee*-bhoa) *adj* negative; *m* negative
**negligencia** (nay-glee-*khayn*-th$^y$ah) *f* negligence; neglect
**negligente** (nay-glee-*khayn*-tay) *adj* negligent, careless
**negociación** (nay-goa-th$^y$ah-*th$^y$oan*) *f* negotiation
**negociante** (nay-goa-*th$^y$ahn*-tay) *m/f* dealer
**negociar** (nay-goa-*th$^y$ahr*) *v* negotiate
**negocio** (nay-*goa*-th$^y$oa) *m* business; ***hacer negocios con** *deal with; **hombre de negocios** businessman; **~ fotográfico** camera shop; **viaje de negocios** business trip
**neón** (nay-*oan*) *m* neon
**nervio** (*nayr*-bh$^y$oa) *m* nerve
**nervioso** (nayr-*bh$^y$oa*-soa) *adj*

nervous
**neto** (*nay*-toa) *adj* net
**neumático** (nay$^{oo}$-*mah*-tee-koa) *adj* pneumatic; *m* tyre, tire *Am*; **~ de repuesto** spare tyre; **~ desinflado** flat tyre
**neumonía** (nay$^{oo}$-moa-*nee*-ah) *f* pneumonia
**neuralgia** (nay$^{oo}$-*rahl*-kh$^{y}$ah) *f* neuralgia
**neurosis** (nay$^{oo}$-*roa*-seess) *f* neurosis
**neutral** (nay$^{oo}$-*trahl*) *adj* neutral
**neutro** (*nay$^{oo}$*-troa) *adj* neuter
***nevar** (nay-*bhahr*) *v* snow
**nevasca** (nay-*bhahss*-kah) *f* snowstorm
**nevoso** (nay-*bhoa*-soa) *adj* snowy
**ni … ni** (nee) neither … nor
**nicotina** (nee-koa-*tee*-nah) *f* nicotine
**nido** (*nee*-dhoa) *m* nest
**niebla** (*n$^{y}$ay*-bhlah) *f* mist, fog; haze; **faro de ~** foglamp; **~ tóxica** smog
**nieta** (*n$^{y}$ay*-tah) *f* granddaughter
**nieto** (*n$^{y}$ay*-toa) *m* grandson
**nieve** (*n$^{y}$ay*-bhay) *f* snow
**Nigeria** (nee-*khay*-r$^{y}$ah) *f* Nigeria
**nigeriano** (nee-khay-*r$^{y}$ah*-noa) *adj* Nigerian; *m* Nigerian
**ninguno** (neeng-*goo*-noa) *adj* no; *pron* none; **~ de los dos** neither
**niñera** (nee-*ñay*-rah) *f* nanny
**niño** (*nee*-ñoa) *m* child; boy
**níquel** (*nee*-kayl) *m* nickel
**nitrógeno** (nee-*troa*-khay-noa) *m* nitrogen
**nivel** (nee-*bhayl*) *m* level; **~ de vida** standard of living; **paso a ~** level crossing
**nivelar** (nee-bhay-*lahr*) *v* level
**no** (noa) not; no; **si ~** otherwise, else
**noble** (*noa*-bhlay) *adj* noble
**nobleza** (noa-*bhlay*-thah) *f* nobility
**noción** (noa-*th$^{y}$oan*) *f* notion; idea
**nocturno** (noak-*toor*-noa) *adj* nightly
**noche** (*noa*-chay) *f* night; **de ~** overnight, by night; **esta ~** tonight
**Nochebuena** (noa-chay-*bway*-nah) *f* Christmas Eve
**Nochevieja** (noa-chay-*b$^{y}$ay*-khah) *f* New Year's Eve
**nogal** (noa-*gahl*) *m* walnut
**nombramiento** (noam-brah-*m$^{y}$ayn*-toa) *m* appointment, nomination
**nombrar** (noam-*brahr*) *v* name, mention; appoint, nominate
**nombre** (*noam*-bray) *m* noun; name; denomination; **en ~ de** on behalf of, in the name of; **~ de pila** Christian name, first name
**nominación** (noa-mee-nah-*th$^{y}$oan*) *f* nomination
**nominal** (noa-mee-*nahl*) *adj* nominal
**nordeste** (noar-*dhayss*-tay) *m* north-east
**norma** (*noar*-mah) *f* standard
**normal** (noar-*mahl*) *adj* normal; regular, standard
**noroeste** (noa-roa-*ayss*-tay) *m* north-west
**norte** (*noar*-tay) *m* north; **del ~** northerly; **polo ~** North Pole
**norteño** (noar-*tay*-ñoa) *adj* northern
**Noruega** (noa-*rway*-gah) *f* Norway
**noruego** (noa-*rway*-goa) *adj* Norwegian; *m* Norwegian
**nos** (noass) *pron* ourselves
**nosotros** (noa-*soa*-troass) *pron* we; us
**nostalgia** (noass-*tahl*-kh$^{y}$ah) *f* homesickness
**nota** (*noa*-tah) *f* ticket; note; mark
**notable** (noa-*tah*-bhlay) *adj* considerable; remarkable, striking, noticeable
**notar** (noa-*tahr*) *v* notice; note
**notario** (noa-*tah*-r$^{y}$oa) *m* notary
**noticia** (noa-*tee*-th$^{y}$ah) *f* news, notice; **noticias** *fpl* news
**noticiario** (noa-tee-*th$^{y}$ah*-r$^{y}$oa) *m*

news; newscast
**notificar** (noa-tee-fee-*kahr*) *v* notify
**notorio** (noa-*toa*-r$^y$oa) *adj* well-known
**novedad** (noa-bhay-*dhahdh*) *f* novelty
**novela** (noa-*bhay*-lah) *f* novel; ~ **policíaca** detective story; ~ **por entregas** serial
**novelista** (noa-bhay-*leess*-tah) *m/f* novelist
**noveno** (noa-*bhay*-noa) *num* ninth
**noventa** (noa-*bhayn*-tah) *num* ninety
**novia** (*noa*-bh$^y$ah) *f* fiancée; bride
**noviazgo** (noa-*bh$^y$ahth*-goa) *m* engagement
**noviembre** (noa-*bh$^y$aym*-bray) November
**novillos: *hacer ~** (ah-*thayr* noa-*bhee*-l$^y$oass) play truant
**novio** (*noa*-bh$^y$oa) *m* fiancé; bridegroom
**nube** (*noo*-bhay) *f* cloud
**nublado** (noo-*bhlah*-dhoa) *adj* cloudy, overcast
**nuca** (*noo*-kah) *f* nape of the neck
**nuclear** (noo-klay-*ahr*) *adj* nuclear
**núcleo** (*noo*-klay-oa) *m* nucleus; heart, essence, core
**nudillo** (noo-*dhee*-l$^y$oa) *m* knuckle
**nudo** (*noo*-dhoa) *m* knot; lump; ~ **corredizo** loop
**nuestro** (*nwayss*-troa) *adj* our
**Nueva Zelanda** (*nway*-bhah thay-*lahn*-dah) New Zealand
**nueve** (*nway*-bhay) *num* nine
**nuevo** (*nway*-bhoa) *adj* new; **de ~** again
**nuez** (nwayth) *f* nut; ~ **moscada** nutmeg
**nulo** (*noo*-loa) *adj* invalid, void
**numeral** (noo-may-*rahl*) *m* numeral
**número** (*noo*-may-roa) *m* number; digit; quantity; size; act
**numeroso** (noo-may-*roa*-soa) *adj* numerous
**nunca** (*noong*-kah) *adv* never
**nutritivo** (noo-tree-*tee*-bhoa) *adj* nutritious, nourishing
**nylon** (*nigh*-loan) *m* nylon

# O

**o** (oa) *conj* or; **o … o** either … or
**oasis** (oa-*ah*-seess) *f* oasis
***obedecer** (oa-bhay-dhay-*thayr*) *v* obey
**obediencia** (oa-bhay-*dh$^y$ayn*-th$^y$ah) *f* obedience
**obediente** (oa-bhay-*dh$^y$ayn*-tay) *adj* obedient
**obertura** (oa-bhayr-*too*-rah) *f* overture
**obesidad** (oa-bhay-see-*dhahdh*) *f* obesity
**obeso** (oa-*bhay*-soa) *adj* obese, corpulent
**obispo** (oa-*bheess*-poa) *m* bishop
**objeción** (oabh-khay-*th$^y$oan*) *f* objection; ***hacer ~ a** mind
**objetar** (oabh-khay-*tahr*) *v* object
**objetivo** (oabh-khay-*tee*-bhoa) *adj* objective; *m* design, objective, target
**objeto** (oabh-*khay*-toa) *m* object; **objetos de valor** valuables *pl*; **objetos perdidos** lost and found
**oblea** (oa-*bhlay*-ah) *f* wafer
**oblicuo** (oa-*bhlee*-kwoa) *adj* slanting
**obligar** (oa-bhlee-*gahr*) *v* oblige; force
**obligatorio** (oa-bhlee-gah-*toa*-r$^y$oa) *adj* compulsory, obligatory
**oblongo** (oa-*bhloang*-goa) *adj* oblong

**obra** (*oa*-bhrah) *f* work; ~ **de arte** work of art; ~ **de teatro** play; ~ **hecha a mano** handwork; ~ **maestra** masterpiece
**obrar** (oa-*bhrahr*) *v* work; perform
**obrero** (oa-*bhray*-roa) *m*, **-a** *f* worker; ~ **portuario** docker
**obsceno** (oabh-*thay*-noa) *adj* obscene
**obscuridad** (oabhs-koo-ree-*dhahdh*) *f* gloom; obscurity
**obscuro** (oabhs-*koo*-roa) *adj* dark, gloomy; obscure
**observación** (oabh-sayr-bhah-*th$^{y}$oan*) *f* observation; remark; ***hacer una ~** remark
**observar** (oabh-sayr-*bhahr*) *v* watch, observe, notice, note
**observatorio** (oabh-sayr-bhah-*toa*-r$^{y}$oa) *m* observatory
**obsesión** (oabh-say-*s$^{y}$oan*) *f* obsession
**obstáculo** (oabhs-*tah*-koo-loa) *m* obstacle
**obstante: no ~** (noa oabhs-*tahn*-tay) nevertheless
**obstinado** (oabhs-tee-*nah*-dhoa) *adj* dogged, obstinate
***obstruir** (oabhs-*trweer*) *v* block
***obtener** (oabh-tay-*nayr*) *v* obtain
**obtenible** (oabh-tay-*nee*-bhlay) *adj* available
**obtuso** (oabh-*too*-soa) *adj* blunt
**obvio** (*oabh*-bh$^{y}$oa) *adj* apparent, obvious
**oca** (*oa*-kah) *f* goose
**ocasión** (oa-kah-*s$^{y}$oan*) *f* occasion; chance
**ocasionalmente** (oa-kah-s$^{y}$oa-nahl-*mayn*-tay) *adv* occasionally
**ocaso** (oa-*kah*-soa) *m* sunset
**occidental** (oak-thee-dhayn-*tahl*) *adj* westerly; western
**occidente** (oak-thee-*dhayn*-tay) *m* west
**océano** (oa-*thay*-ah-noa) *m* ocean; **Océano Pacífico** Pacific Ocean
**ocio** (*oa*-th$^{y}$oa) *m* leisure
**ocioso** (oa-*th$^{y}$oa*-soa) *adj* idle
**octavo** (oak-*tah*-bhoa) *num* eighth
**octubre** (oak-*too*-bhray) October
**oculista** (oa-koo-*leess*-tah) *m/f* oculist
**ocultar** (oa-kool-*tahr*) *v* *hide
**ocupación** (oa-koo-pah-*th$^{y}$oan*) *f* occupation; business
**ocupante** (oa-koo-*pahn*-tay) *m* occupant
**ocupar** (oa-koo-*pahr*) *v* occupy; *take up; **ocupado** *adj* engaged, busy; occupied; **ocuparse de** look after
**ocurrencia** (oa-koo-*rrayn*-th$^{y}$ah) *f* idea
**ocurrir** (oa-koo-*rreer*) *v* occur
**ochenta** (oa-*chayn*-tah) *num* eighty
**ocho** (*oa*-choa) *num* eight
**odiar** (oa-*dh$^{y}$ahr*) *v* hate
**odio** (*oa*-dh$^{y}$oa) *m* hatred, hate
**oeste** (oa-*ayss*-tay) *m* west
**ofender** (oa-fayn-*dayr*) *v* offend; wound, *hurt
**ofensa** (oa-*fayn*-sah) *f* offence, offense *Am*
**ofensivo** (oa-fayn-*see*-bhoa) *adj* offensive; *m* offensive
**oferta** (oa-*fayr*-tah) *f* offer, supply
**oficial** (oa-fee-*th$^{y}$ahl*) *adj* official; *m* officer; ~ **de aduanas** Customs officer
**oficina** (oa-fee-*thee*-nah) *f* office; ~ **de cambio** exchange office; ~ **de colocación** employment exchange; ~ **de informaciones** information bureau; ~ **de objetos perdidos** lost property office
**oficinista** (oa-fee-thee-*neess*-tah) *m/f* clerk, office worker
**oficio** (oa-*fee*-th$^{y}$oa) *m* trade
***ofrecer** (oa-fray-*thayr*) *v* offer
**oído** (oa-*ee*-dhoa) *m* hearing; **dolor de**

**oídos** earache
***oír** (oa-*eer*) *v* *hear
**ojal** (oa-*khahl*) *m* buttonhole
**ojeada** (oa-khay-*ah*-dhah) *f* glimpse, glance; look
**ojear** (oa-khay-*ahr*) *v* glance
**ojo** (*oa*-khoa) *m* eye
**ola** (*oa*-lah) *f* wave
***oler** (oa-*layr*) *v* *smell
**olmo** (*oal*-moa) *m* elm
**olor** (oa-*loar*) *m* smell, odo(u)r
**olvidadizo** (oal-bhee-dhah-*dhee*-thoa) *adj* forgetful
**olvidar** (oal-bhee-*dhahr*) *v* *forget
**olla** (*oa*-l$^y$ah) *f* pot; kettle; **~ a presión** pressure cooker
**ombligo** (oam-*blee*-goa) *m* navel
**omitir** (oa-mee-*teer*) *v* *leave out, omit; fail
**omnipotente** (oam-nee-poa-*tayn*-tay) *adj* omnipotent
**once** (*oan*-thay) *num* eleven
**onceno** (oan-*thay*-noa) *num* eleventh
**onda** (*oan*-dah) *f* wave
**ondulación** (oan-doo-lah-*th$^y$oan*) *f* wave; **~ permanente** permanent wave
**ondulado** (oan-doo-*lah*-dhoa) *adj* wavy
**ópalo** (*oa*-pah-loa) *m* opal
**opcional** (oap-th$^y$oa-*nahl*) *adj* optional
**ópera** (*oa*-pay-rah) *f* opera
**operación** (oa-pay-rah-*th$^y$oan*) *f* operation, surgery
**operar** (oa-pay-*rahr*) *v* operate
**opinar** (oa-pee-*nahr*) *v* consider
**opinión** (oa-pee-*n$^y$oan*) *f* view, opinion
***oponerse** (oa-poa-*nayr*-say) *v* oppose; **~ a** object to
**oportunidad** (oa-poar-too-nee-*dhahdh*) *f* chance, opportunity
**oportuno** (oa-poar-*too*-noa) *adj* convenient; appropriate
**oposición** (oa-poa-see-*th$^y$oan*) *f* opposition
**oprimir** (oa-pree-*meer*) *v* oppress
**óptico** (*oap*-tee-koa) *m*, **-a** *f* optician
**optimismo** (oap-tee-*meez*-moa) *m* optimism
**optimista** (oap-tee-*meess*-tah) *adj* optimistic; *m/f* optimist
**óptimo** (*oap*-tee-moa) *adj* best; optimal
**opuesto** (oa-*pwayss*-toa) *adj* opposite; averse
**oración** (oa-rah-*th$^y$oan*) *f* prayer
**oral** (oa-*rahl*) *adj* oral
**orar** (oa-*rahr*) *v* pray
**orden** (*oar*-dhayn) *f* command; order; *m* method; **de primer ~** first-rate; **~ del día** agenda
**ordenador** (oar-dhay-nah-*dhoar*) *m* computer; **~ personal** personal computer, PC; **~ portatíl** laptop
**ordenar** (oar-dhay-*nahr*) *v* arrange; order
**ordinario** (oar-dhee-*nah*-r$^y$oa) *adj* simple, ordinary; common, vulgar
**oreja** (oa-*ray*-khah) *f* ear
**orfebre** (oar-*fay*-bhray) *m* goldsmith
**orgánico** (oar-*gah*-nee-koa) *adj* organic
**organismo** (oar-gah-*neez*-moa) *m* organism
**organización** (oar-gah-nee-thah-*th$^y$oan*) *f* organization
**organizar** (oar-gah-nee-*thahr*) *v* organize; arrange
**órgano** (*oar*-gah-noa) *m* organ
**orgullo** (oar-*goo*-l$^y$oa) *m* pride
**orgulloso** (oar-goo-*l$^y$oa*-soa) *adj* proud
**orientación** (oa-r$^y$ayn-tah-*th$^y$oan*) *f* orientation
**oriental** (oa-r$^y$ayn-*tahl*) *adj* eastern; oriental

**orientarse** (oa-r$^y$ayn-*tahr*-say) *v* orient
**oriente** (oa-*r$^y$ayn*-tay) *m* Orient
**origen** (oa-*ree*-khayn) *m* origin
**original** (oa-ree-khee-*nahl*) *adj* original
**originalmente** (oa-ree-khee-nahl-*mayn*-tay) *adv* originally
**originar** (oa-ree-khee-*nahr*) *v* originate
**orilla** (oa-*ree*-l$^y$ah) *f* bank; shore
**orina** (oa-*ree*-nah) *f* urine
**ornamental** (oar-nah-mayn-*tahl*) *adj* ornamental
**oro** (*oa*-roa) *m* gold
**orquesta** (oar-*kayss*-tah) *f* orchestra; band
**ortodoxo** (oar-toa-*dhoak*-soa) *adj* orthodox
**os** (oass) *pron* you
**osar** (oa-*sahr*) *v* dare
**oscilar** (oa-thee-*lahr*) *v* *swing
**oscuridad** (oass-koo-ree-*dhahdh*) *f* dark
**oscuro** (oass-*koo*-roa) *adj* dark, dim, obscure
**oso** (*oa*-soa) *m* bear
**ostra** (*oass*-trah) *f* oyster
**otoño** (oa-*toa*-ñoa) *m* autumn; fall *Am*
**otro** (*oa*-troa) *adj* other, different; another; ~ **más** another
**ovalado** (oa-bhah-*lah*-dhoa) *adj* oval
**oveja** (oa-*bhay*-khah) *f* sheep
**overol** (oa-bhay-*roal*) *mMe* overalls *pl*
**oxidado** (oak-see-*dhah*-dhoa) *adj* rusty
**oxígeno** (oak-*see*-khay-noa) *m* oxygen
**oyente** (oa-*$^y$ayn*-tay) *m* auditor, listener
**ozono** (oa-*thoa*-noa) *m* ozone

# P

**pabellón** (pah-bhay-*l$^y$oan*) *m* pavilion
***pacer** (pah-*thayr*) *v* graze
**paciencia** (pah-*th$^y$ayn*-th$^y$ah) *f* patience
**paciente** (pah-*th$^y$ayn*-tay) *adj* patient; *m/f* patient
**pacifismo** (pah-thee-*feez*-moa) *m* pacifism
**pacifista** (pah-thee-*feess*-tah) *adj* pacifist; *m* pacifist
***padecer** (pah-dhay-*thayr*) *v* suffer
**padrastro** (pah-*dhrahss*-troa) *m* stepfather
**padre** (*pah*-dhray) *m* father
**padres** (*pah*-dhrayss) *mpl* parents *pl*; ~ **adoptivos** foster-parents *pl*; ~ **políticos** parents-in-law *pl*
**padrino** (pah-*dhree*-noa) *m* godfather
**paella** (pah-*ay*-l$^y$ah) *f* paella
**paga** (*pah*-gah) *f* wages *pl*
**pagano** (pah-*gah*-noa) *adj* heathen, pagan; *m* heathen, pagan
**pagar** (pah-*gahr*) *v* *pay; **pagado por adelantado** prepaid; ~ **a plazos** *pay on account
**página** (*pah*-khee-nah) *f* page
**pago** (*pah*-goa) *m* payment; **primer** ~ down payment
**painel** (pigh-*nayl*) *m* panel
**país** (pah-*eess*) *m* country, land; region; area; ~ **natal** native country
**paisaje** (pigh-*sah*-khay) *m* scenery, landscape
**paisano** (pigh-*sah*-noa) *m* civilian
**Países Bajos** (pah-*ee*-sayss-*bah*-khoass) *mpl* the Netherlands

**paja** (*pah*-khah) *f* straw

**pájaro** (*pah*-khah-roa) *m* bird

**paje** (*pah*-khay) *m* pageboy

**pala** (*pah*-lah) *f* spade, shovel

**palabra** (pah-*lah*-bhrah) *f* word

**palacio** (pah-*lah*-th$^{y}$oa) *m* palace

**palanca** (pah-*lahng*-kah) *f* lever; **~ de cambios** gear lever

**palangana** (pah-lahng-*gah*-nah) *f* basin; washbasin

**pálido** (*pah*-lee-dhoa) *adj* pale; dull; light

**palillo** (pah-*lee*-l$^{y}$oa) *m* toothpick

**palma** (*pahl*-mah) *f* palm

**palmera** (pahl-*may*-rah) *f* palm tree; heart-shaped pastry

**palo** (*pah*-loa) *m* stick; **~ de golf** golf club

**paloma** (pah-*loa*-mah) *f* pigeon

**palpable** (pahl-*pah*-bhlay) *adj* palpable

**palpar** (pahl-*pahr*) *v* *feel; touch

**palpitación** (pahl-pee-tah-*th$^{y}$oan*) *f* palpitation

**pan** (pahn) *m* bread, loaf; **~ integral** wholemeal bread; **~ tostado** toast

**pana** (*pah*-nah) *f* corduroy, velveteen

**panadería** (pah-nah-dhay-*ree*-ah) *f* bakery

**panadero** (pah-nah-*dhay*-roa) *m* baker

**panecillo** (pah-nay-*thee*-l$^{y}$oa) *m* roll

**pánico** (*pah*-nee-koa) *m* panic

**pantalones** (pahn-tah-*loa*-nayss) *mpl* trousers *pl*; slacks *pl*; pants *plAm*; **~ cortos** shorts *pl*; **~ de esquí** ski pants; **~ de gimnasia** trunks, shorts

**pantalla** (pahn-*tah*-l$^{y}$ah) *f* lampshade; screen

**pantano** (pahn-*tah*-noa) *m* marsh, bog

**pantanoso** (pahn-tah-*noa*-soa) *adj* marshy

**pantorrilla** (pahn-toa-*rree*-l$^{y}$ah) *f* calf

**panty media** (*pahn*-tee *may*-dh$^{y}$ah) *f* panty hose

**pañal** (pah-*ñahl*) *m* nappy; diaper *Am*

**pañería** (pah-ñay-*ree*-ah) *f* drapery

**pañero** (pah-*ñay*-roa) *m* draper

**paño** (*pah*-ñoa) *m* cloth

**pañuelo** (pah-*ñway*-loa) *m* handkerchief; **~ de papel** tissue, Kleenex®

**Papa** (*pah*-pah) *m* pope

**papa** (*pah*-pah) *fMe* potato

**papá** (pah-*pah*) *m* dad

**papel** (pah-*payl*) *m* paper; role; **de ~** paper; **~ de aluminio** foil; **~ de envolver** wrapping paper; **~ de escribir** writing-paper; **~ de estaño** tinfoil; **~ de lija** sandpaper; **~ higiénico** toilet paper; **~ para cartas** notepaper; **~ pintado** wallpaper; **~ (de) regalo** giftwrap

**papelera** (pah-pay-*lay*-rah) *f* wastepaper basket

**papelería** (pah-pay-lay-*ree*-ah) *f* stationery; stationer's

**paperas** (pah-*pay*-rahss) *fpl* mumps

**paquete** (pah-*kay*-tay) *m* packet, package, parcel; bundle

**Paquistán** (pah-keess-*tahn*) *m* Pakistan

**paquistaní** (pah-keess-tah-*nee*) *adj* Pakistani; *m* Pakistani

**par** (pahr) *adj* even (number); like; *m* pair

**para** (*pah*-rah) *prep* to, for; to, in order to; **~ con** towards; **~ qué?** what for?

**parabrisas** (pah-rah-*bhree*-sahss) *m* windscreen; windshield *Am*

**parachoques** (pah-rah-*choa*-kayss) *m* fender, bumper

**parada** (pah-*rah*-dhah) *f* parade; stop; **~ de taxis** taxi rank; taxi stand *Am*

**parado** (pah-*rah*-dhoa) *adjMe* erect; standing; **los ~s** the unemployed

**parador** (pah-rah-*dhoar*) *m* inn; hotel

**parafina** (pah-rah-*fee*-nah) *f* paraffin
**paraguas** (pah-*rah*-gwahss) *m* umbrella
**paraíso** (pah-rah-*ee*-soa) *m* paradise
**paralelo** (pah-rah-*lay*-loa) *adj* parallel; *m* parallel
**paralítico** (pah-rah-*lee*-tee-koa) *adj* lame
**paralizar** (pah-rah-lee-*thahr*) *v* paralise
**pararse** (pah-*rahr*-say) *v* stop; pull up; *Me* stand up
**parcela** (pahr-*thay*-lah) *f* plot
**parcial** (pahr-*th$^{y}$ahl*) *adj* partial
**parecer** (pah-ray-*thayr*) *m* view, opinion
***parecer** (pah-ray-*thayr*) *v* appear, seem, look
**parecido** (pah-ray-*thee*-dhoa) *adj* alike; **bien ~** good-looking
**pared** (pah-*raydh*) *f* wall
**pareja** (pah-*ray*-khah) *f* couple; partner
**pariente** (pah-*r$^{y}$ayn*-tay) *m* relative, relation
**parking** (*pahr*-keengh) *m* parking lot, car park
**parlamentario** (pahr-lah-mayn-*tah*-r$^{y}$oa) *adj* parliamentary
**parlamento** (pahr-lah-*mayn*-toa) *m* parliament
**paro** (*pah*-roa) *m* unemployment; **estar en ~** be unemployed; **~ cardíaco** cardiac arrest
**párpado** (*pahr*-pah-dhoa) *m* eyelid
**parque** (*pahr*-kay) *m* park; **~ de estacionamiento** car park; **~ de reserva zoológica** game reserve; **~ nacional** national park
**parquímetro** (pahr-*kee*-may-troa) *m* parking meter
**párrafo** (*pah*-rrah-foa) *m* paragraph
**parrilla** (pah-*ree*-l$^{y}$ah) *f* grill; grill-room; **asar en ~** grill
**parroquia** (pah-*rroa*-k$^{y}$ah) *f* parish
**parsimonioso** (pahr-see-moa-*n$^{y}$oa*-soa) *adj* economical
**parte** (*pahr*-tay) *f* part; share; **en alguna ~** somewhere; **en ninguna ~** nowhere; **en ~** partly; **otra ~** elsewhere; **~ posterior** rear; **~ superior** top, top side; **por otra ~** besides; **por todas partes** everywhere, throughout
**participante** (pahr-tee-thee-*pahn*-tay) *m/f* participant
**participar** (pahr-tee-thee-*pahr*) *v* participate
**particular** (pahr-tee-koo-*lahr*) *adj* private; particular; **en ~** specially, in particular
**particularidad** (pahr-tee-koo-lah-ree-*dhahdh*) *f* detail; peculiarity
**partida** (pahr-*tee*-dhah) *f* departure; certificate
**partido** (pahr-*tee*-dhoa) *m* side, party; match; **~ de fútbol** football match
**partir** (pahr-*teer*) *v* *leave, depart, pull out, *set out; **a ~ de** as from; from
**parto** (*pahr*-toa) *m* childbirth, delivery
**pasa** (*pah*-sah) *f* raisin; **~ de Corinto** currant
**pasado** (pah-*sah*-dhoa) *adj* past; *m* past
**pasaje** (pah-*sah*-khay) *m* passage
**pasajero** (pah-sah-*khay*-roa) *m* , **-a** *f* passenger
**pasaporte** (pah-sah-*poar*-tay) *m* passport
**pasar** (pah-*sahr*) *v* happen; *go through; pass; *spend; **~ por alto** overlook; **pasarse sin** spare
**pasarela** (pah-sah-*ray*-lah) *f* gangway; catwalk
**pasatiempo** (pah-sah-*t$^{y}$aym*-poa) *m* pastime
**Pascua** (*pahss*-kwah) Easter
**paseante** (pah-say-*ahn*-tay) *m* walker;

stroller
**pasear** (pah-say-*ahr*) *v* walk, stroll
**paseo** (pah-*say*-oa) *m* stroll; ride; promenade
**pasillo** (pah-*see*-l$^y$oa) *m* corridor; aisle
**pasión** (pah-*s$^y$oan*) *f* passion
**pasivo** (pah-*see*-bhoa) *adj* passive
**paso** (*pah*-soa) *m* step, pace; move, gait; crossing; mountain pass; **de ~** casual; **~ a nivel** crossing; **prioridad de ~** right of way; **prohibido el ~** no entry
**pasta** (*pahss*-tah) *f* paste; **~ dentífrica** toothpaste
**pastel** (pahss-*tayl*) *m* cake
**pastelería** (pahss-tay-lay-*ree*-ah) *f* pastry, cake; pastry shop
**pastilla** (pahss-*tee*-l$^y$ah) *f* tablet
**pastor** (pahss-*toar*) *m* shepherd; clergyman, parson, rector
**pata** (*pah*-tah) *f* paw; leg
**patada** (pah-*tah*-dhah) *f* kick
**patata** (pah-*tah*-tah) *f* potato; **patatas fritas** chips, French fries *Am*
**patear** (pah-tay-*ahr*) *v* kick; stamp
**patente** (pah-*tayn*-tay) *f* patent
**patillas** (pah-*tee*-l$^y$ahss) *fpl* whiskers *pl*, sideburns *pl*
**patín** (pah-*teen*) *m* skate; scooter
**patinaje** (pah-tee-*nah*-khay) *m* skating
**patinar** (pah-tee-*nahr*) *v* skate; skid
**pato** (*pah*-toa) *m* duck
**patria** (*pah*-tr$^y$ah) *f* native country, homeland
**patriota** (pah-*tr$^y$oa*-tah) *m/f* patriot
**patrón** (pah-*troan*) *m* boss, master; employer; landlord
**patrona** (pah-*troa*-nah) *f* employer, landlady
**patrulla** (pah-*troo*-l$^y$ah) *f* patrol
**pausa** (*pou*-sah) *f* pause; ***hacer una ~** pause
**pavimentar** (pah-bhee-mayn-*tahr*) *v* pave
**pavimento** (pah-bhee-*mayn*-toa) *m* pavement
**pavo** (*pah*-bhoa) *m* peacock; turkey
**payaso** (pah-*$^y$ah*-soa) *m* clown
**paz** (pahth) *f* peace; quiet
**peaje** (pay-*ah*-khay) *m* toll
**peatón** (pay-ah-*toan*) *m* pedestrian; **prohibido para los peatones** no pedestrians
**pecado** (pay-*kah*-dhoa) *m* sin
**peculiar** (pay-koo-*l$^y$ahr*) *adj* peculiar
**pecho** (*pay*-choa) *m* chest; bosom
**pechuga** (pay-*choo*-gah) *f* breast; L.Am. *colloquial* nerve
**pedal** (pay-*dhahl*) *m* pedal
**pedazo** (pay-*dhah*-thoa) *m* piece; scrap
**pedernal** (pay-dhayr-*nahl*) *m* flint
**pedicuro** (pay-dhee-*koo*-roa) *m* chiropodist, pedicure
**pedido** (pay-*dhee*-dhoa) *m* order
***pedir** (pay-*dheer*) *v* beg; order; charge
**pegajoso** (pay-gah-*khoa*-soa) *adj* sticky
**pegar** (pay-*gahr*) *v* smack, slap, *hit; *stick, paste; **pegarse** *v* *burn
**peinado** (pay-*nah*-dhoa) *m* hairdo
**peinar** (pay-*nahr*) *v* comb
**peine** (*pay*-nay) *m* comb
**pelar** (pay-*lahr*) *v* peel
**peldaño** (payl-*dah*-ñoa) *m* step
**pelea** (pay-*lay*-ah) *f* battle
**peletero** (pay-lay-*tay*-roa) *m* furrier
**pelícano** (pay-*lee*-kah-noa) *m* pelican
**película** (pay-*lee*-koo-lah) *f* film; **~ en colores** colo(u)r film
**peligro** (pay-*lee*-groa) *m* danger; peril, risk; distress
**peligroso** (pay-lee-*groa*-soa) *adj* dangerous; perilous
**pelo** (*pay*-loa) *m* hair; fur; **a ~** unprepared; **montar a ~** ride bareback

**pelota** (pay-*loa*-tah) *f* ball

**peluca** (pay-*loo*-kah) *f* wig

**peluquero** (pay-loo-*kay*-roa) *m*, **-a** *f* hairdresser

**pelvis** (*payl*-bheess) *m* pelvis

**pellizcar** (pay-l$^{y}$eeth-*kahr*) *v* pinch

**pena** (*pay*-nah) *f* sorrow; pains; penalty; ~ **de muerte** death penalty

**pendiente** (payn-*d$^{y}$ayn*-tay) *adj* slanting; *m* earring, pendant; *f* gradient, slope

**penetrar** (pay-nay-*trahr*) *v* penetrate

**penicilina** (pay-nee-thee-*lee*-nah) *f* penicillin

**península** (pay-*neen*-soo-lah) *f* peninsula

**pensamiento** (payn-sah-*m$^{y}$ayn*-toa) *m* idea, thought

***pensar** (payn-*sahr*) *v* *think; ~ **en** *think of

**pensativo** (payn-sah-*tee*-bhoa) *adj* thoughtful

**pensión** (payn-*s$^{y}$oan*) *f* guesthouse, pension, boardinghouse; board; ~ **alimenticia** alimony; ~ **completa** full board, board and lodging

**Pentecostés** (payn-tay-koass-*tayss*) *m* Whitsun, Pentecost *Am*

**peña** (*pay*-ñah) *f* boulder

**peón** (pay-*oan*) *m* pawn; unskilled worker

**peor** (pay-*oar*) *adj* worse; *adv* worse

**pepino** (pay-*pee*-noa) *m* cucumber

**pepita** (pay-*pee*-tah) *f* pip

**pequeño** (pay-*kay*-ñoa) *adj* small, little; petty, minor

**pera** (*pay*-rah) *f* pear

**perca** (*payr*-kah) *f* perch, bass

**percepción** (payr-thayp-*th$^{y}$oan*) *f* perception

**perceptible** (payr-thayp-*tee*-bhlay) *adj* perceptible, noticeable

**percibir** (payr-thee-*bheer*) *v* perceive

**percha** (*payr*-chah) *f* hanger, coat-hanger, peg; hat rack

***perder** (payr-*dhayr*) *v* *lose; miss; waste

**pérdida** (*payr*-dhee-dhah) *f* loss

**perdiz** (payr-*dheeth*) *f* partridge

**perdón** (payr-*dhoan*) *m* pardon; grace; **¡perdón!** sorry!

**perdonar** (payr-dhoa-*nahr*) *v* *forgive

**perecedero** (pay-ray-thay-*dhay*-roa) *adj* perishable

***perecer** (pay-ray-*thayr*) *v* perish

**peregrinación** (pay-ray-gree-nah-*th$^{y}$oan*) *f* pilgrimage

**peregrino** (pay-ray-*gree*-noa) *m* pilgrim

**perejil** (pay-ray-*kheel*) *m* parsley

**perezoso** (pay-ray-*thoa*-soa) *adj* lazy

**perfección** (payr-fayk-*th$^{y}$oan*) *f* perfection

**perfecto** (payr-*fayk*-toa) *adj* perfect; faultless

**perfil** (payr-*feel*) *m* profile

**perfume** (payr-*foo*-may) *m* perfume; scent

**perico** (pay-*ree*-koa) *m* parakeet

**periódico** (pay-*r$^{y}$oa*-dhee-koa) *adj* periodical; *m* periodical, paper; **vendedor de periódicos** newsagent

**periodismo** (pay-r$^{y}$oa-*deez*-moa) *m* journalism

**periodista** (pay-r$^{y}$oa-*dheess*-tah) *m/f* journalist

**período** (pay-*ree*-oa-dhoa) *m* period, term

**perito** (pay-*ree*-toa) *m* expert, connoisseur

**perjudicar** (payr-khoo-dhee-*kahr*) *v* harm

**perjudicial** (payr-khoo-dhee-*th$^{y}$ahl*) *adj* harmful, hurtful

**perjuicio** (payr-*khwee*-th$^{y}$oa) *m* harm, damage

**perjurio** (payr-*khoo*-r$^{y}$oa) *m* perjury

**perla** (*payr*-lah) *f* pearl

***permanecer** (payr-mah-nay-*thayr*) *v* remain
**permanente** (payr-mah-*nayn*-tay) *adj* permanent; **planchado ~** permanent press
**permiso** (payr-*mee*-soa) *m* permission, authorization; permit, licence, license *Am*; **~ de conducir** driving licence; **~ de pesca** fishing licence; **~ de residencia** residence permit; **~ de trabajo** work permit; labor permit *Am*
**permitir** (payr-mee-*teer*) *v* permit, allow; enable; **permitirse** *v* afford
**pero** (*pay*-roa) *conj* yet, only, but
**perpendicular** (payr-payn-dee-koo-*lahr*) *adj* perpendicular
**perpetuo** (payr-*pay*-twoa) *adj* perpetual
**perra** (*pay*-rrah) *f* bitch
**perrera** (pay-*rray*-rah) *f* kennel
**perro** (*pay*-rroa) *m* dog; **~ lazarillo** guide dog
**persa** (*payr*-sah) *adj* Persian; *m* Persian
***perseguir** (payr-say-*geer*) *v* pursue
**perseverar** (payr-say-bhay-*rahr*) *v* *keep up
**Persia** (*payr*-s$^y$ah) *f* Persia
**persiana** (payr-*s$^y$ah*-nah) *f* shutter, blind
**persistir** (payr-seess-*teer*) *v* insist
**persona** (payr-*soa*-nah) *f* person; **por ~** per person
**personal** (payr-soa-*nahl*) *adj* personal, private; *m* personnel, staff
**personalidad** (payr-soa-nah-lee-*dhahdh*) *f* personality
**perspectiva** (payrs-payk-*tee*-bhah) *f* perspective; prospect
**persuadir** (payr-swah-dheer) *v* persuade
***pertenecer** (payr-tay-nay-*thayr*) *v* belong
**pertenencias** (payr-tay-*nayn*-th$^y$ahss) *fpl* belongings *pl*
**pertinaz** (payr-tee-*nahth*) *adj* persistent
**pesado** (pay-*sah*-dhoa) *adj* heavy; tedious
**pesadumbre** (pay-sah-*dhoom*-bray) *f* grief
**pesar** (pay-*sahr*) *v* weigh; **a ~ de** despite, in spite of
**pesca** (*payss*-kah) *f* fishing; fishing industry
**pescadería** (payss-kah-dhay-*ree*-ah) *f* fish shop
**pescado** (payss-*kah-dhoa*) *m* fish
**pescador** (payss-kah-*dhoar*) *m* fisherman
**pescar** (payss-*kahr*) *v* fish; **~ con caña** angle
**pesebre** (pay-*say*-bhray) *m* manger
**pesimismo** (pay-see-*meez*-moa) *m* pessimism
**pesimista** (pay-see-*meess*-tah) *adj* pessimistic; *m/f* pessimist
**pésimo** (*pay*-see-moa) *adj* worst; terrible
**peso** (*pay*-soa) *m* weight; burden
**pestaña** (payss-*tah*-ñah) *f* eyelash
**petaca** (pay-*tah*-kah) *f* pouch; tobacco pouch
**pétalo** (*pay*-tah-loa) *m* petal
**petición** (pay-tee-*th$^y$oan*) *f* petition
**petirrojo** (pay-tee-*rroa*-khoa) *m* robin
**petróleo** (pay-*troa*-lay-oa) *m* petroleum, oil; **~ lampante** kerosene; **pozo de ~** oil well; **refinería de ~** oil refinery
**pez** (payth) *m* fish
**piadoso** (p$^y$ah-*dhoa*-soa) *adj* pious
**pianista** (p$^y$ah-*neess*-tah) *m* pianist
**piano** (*p$^y$ah*-noa) *m* piano; **~ de cola** grand piano
**picadero** (pee-kah-*dhay*-roa) *m* riding school

**picadura** (pee-kah-*dhoo*-rah) *f* sting, bite; cigarette tobacco
**picante** (pee-*kahn*-tay) *adj* spicy, savo(u)ry
**picar** (pee-*kahr*) *v* itch; mince; *sting; nibble
**pícaro** (*pee*-kah-roa) *m* rascal
**picazón** (pee-kah-*thoan*) *f* itch
**pico** (*pee*-koa) *m* beak; peak; pick-axe
**pie** (p$^{y}$ay) *m* foot; **a ~** on foot; walking; **de ~** upright; ***estar de ~** *stand; **~ de cabra** crowbar
**piedad** (p$^{y}$ay-*dhahdh*) *f* pity; ***tener ~ de** pity
**piedra** (*p*$^{y}$*ay*-dhrah) *f* stone; **de ~** stone; **~ miliar** milestone; **~ pómez** pumice stone; **~ preciosa** stone
**piel** (p$^{y}$ayl) *f* skin; fur, hide; peel; **de ~** leather; **~ de cerdo** pigskin
**pierna** (*p*$^{y}$*ayr*-nah) *f* leg
**pieza** (*p*$^{y}$*ay*-thah) *f* part; **de dos piezas** two-piece; **~ de repuesto** spare part; **~ en un acto** one-act play
**pijama** (pee-*khah*-mah) *m* pyjamas *pl*
**pilar** (pee-*lahr*) *m* pillar
**píldora** (*peel*-doa-rah) *f* pill
**pileta** (pee-*lay*-tah) *f* sink
**piloto** (pee-*loa*-toa) *m* pilot
**pillo** (*pee*-l$^{y}$oa) *m* rascal
**pimienta** (pee-*m*$^{y}$*ayn*-tah) *f* pepper
**pimiento** (pee-*m*$^{y}$*ayn*-toa) *m* pepper
**pincel** (peen-*thayl*) *m* paint-brush
**pinchado** (peen-*chah*-dhoa) *adj* punctured
**pinchar** (peen-*chahr*) *v* puncture
**pinchazo** (peen-*chah*-thoa) *m* puncture
**pingüino** (peeng-*gwee*-noa) *m* penguin
**pintar** (peen-*tahr*) *v* paint
**pintor** (peen-*toar*) *m*, **-a** *f* painter
**pintoresco** (peen-toa-*rayss*-koa) *adj* picturesque, scenic
**pintura** (peen-*too*-rah) *f* paint; painting; **~ al óleo** oil painting
**pinzas** (*peen*-thahss) *fpl* tweezers *pl*
**pinzón** (peen-*thoan*) *m* finch
**piña** (*pee*-ñah) *f* pineapple
**pío** (*pee*-oa) *adj* pious
**piojo** (*p*$^{y}$*oa*-khoa) *m* louse
**pionero** (p$^{y}$oa-*nay*-roa) *m* pioneer
**pipa** (*pee*-pah) *f* pipe
**pirata** (pee-*rah*-tah) *m* pirate
**pisar** (pee-*sahr*) *v* step on; walk on
**piscina** (pee-*thee*-nah) *f* swimming pool
**piso** (*pee*-soa) *m* stor(e)y, floor; flat; apartment *Am*; **~ bajo** ground floor
**pista** (*peess*-tah) *f* ring; track; lane; **~ de aterrizaje** runway; **~ de patinaje** skating rink; **~ para carreras** racecourse
**pistola** (peess-*toa*-lah) *f* pistol
**pistón** (peess-*toan*) *m* piston
**pitar** (*pee*-tahr) *v* whistle; beep, hoot; L.Am. smoke
**pitillera** (pee-tee-*l*$^{y}$*ay*-rah) *f* cigarette case
**pizarra** (pee-*thah*-rrah) *f* slate; blackboard
**placa** (*plah*-kah) *f* registration plate
**placer** (plah-*thayr*) *m* pleasure
***placer** (plah-*thayr*) *v* please
**plaga** (*plah*-gah) *f* plague
**plan** (plahn) *m* plan, project
**plancha** (*plahn*-chah) *f* iron; **no precisa ~** wash and wear, drip-dry
**planchar** (plahn-*chahr*) *v* iron; press
**planeador** (plah-nay-ah-*dhoar*) *m* glider
**planear** (plah-nay-*ahr*) *v* plan
**planeta** (plah-*nay*-tah) *m* planet
**planetario** (plah-nay-*tah*-r$^{y}$oa) *m* planetarium
**plano** (*plah*-noa) *adj* level, even, plane; *m* plan, map; **primer ~** foreground
**planta** (*plahn*-tah) *f* plant

**plantación** (plahn-tah-*th$^{y}$oan*) *f* plantation
**plantar** (plahn-*tahr*) *v* plant
**plantear** (plahn-tay-*ahr*) *v* *put
**plástico** (*plahss*-tee-koa) *m* plastic; **de ~** plastic
**plata** (*plah*-tah) *f* silver; **de ~** silver; **~ labrada** silverware
**plátano** (*plah*-tah-noa) *m* banana
**platero** (plah-*tay*-roa) *m* silversmith
**platija** (plah-*tee*-khah) *f* plaice
**platillo** (plah-*tee*-l$^{y}$oa) *m* saucer
**platino** (plah-*tee*-noa) *m* platinum
**plato** (*plah*-toa) *m* dish, plate; course
**playa** (*plah*-$^{y}$ah) *f* beach; **~ de veraneo** seaside resort; **~ para nudistas** nudist beach
**plaza** (*plah*-thah) *f* square; **~ de mercado** market-place; **~ de toros** bullring; **~ fuerte** stronghold
**plazo** (*plah*-thoa) *m* term; instal(l)ment; **compra a plazos** instal(l)ment plan
**pleamar** (play-ah-*mahr*) *f* high tide
**plegable** (play-*gah*-blay) *adj* collapsible, folding
***plegar** (play-*gahr*) *v* crease
**pliegue** (*pl$^{y}$ay*-gay) *m* crease, fold
**plomero** (ploa-*may*-roa) *m* plumber
**plomo** (*ploa*-moa) *m* lead
**pluma** (*ploo*-mah) *f* feather; pen
**plural** (ploo-*rahl*) *m* plural
**población** (poa-bhlah-*th$^{y}$oan*) *f* population
**pobre** (*poa*-bhray) *adj* poor
**pobreza** (poa-*bhray*-thah) *f* poverty
**poco** (*poa*-koa) *adj* little; *m* bit; **dentro de ~** presently; **un ~** some; **pocos** *adj* few
**poder** (poa-*dhayr*) *m* power; authority
***poder** (poa-*dhayr*) *v* *be able to, *can; *might, *may
**poderoso** (poa-dhay-*roa*-soa) *adj* powerful
**podrido** (poa-*dhree*-dhoa) *adj* rotten
**poema** (poa-*ay*-mah) *m* poem; **~ épico** epic
**poesía** (poa-ay-*see*-ah) *f* poetry
**poeta** (poa-*ay*-tah) *m* poet
**poético** (poa-*ay*-tee-koa) *adj* poetic
**polaco** (poa-*lah*-koa) *adj* Polish; *m* Pole
**polea** (poa-*lay*-ah) *f* pulley
**policía** (poa-lee-*thee*-ah) *f* police *pl*
**polilla** (poa-*lee*-l$^{y}$ah) *f* moth
**polio** (*poa*-l$^{y}$oa) *f* polio
**poliomielitis** (poa-l$^{y}$oa-m$^{y}$ay-*lee*-teess) *f* polio
**política** (poa-*lee*-tee-kah) *f* policy; politics
**político** (poa-*lee*-tee-koa) *adj* political; *m* politician
**póliza** (*poa*-lee-thah) *f* policy
**Polonia** (poa-*loa*-n$^{y}$ah) *f* Poland
**polución** (poa-loo-*th$^{y}$oan*) *f* pollution
**polvera** (poal-*bhay*-rah) *f* powder compact
**polvo** (*poal*-bhoa) *m* dust; powder; grit; **~ facial** face powder; **~ para los dientes** toothpowder; **~ para los pies** foot powder
**pólvora** (*poal*-bhoa-rah) *f* gunpowder
**polvoriento** (poal-bhoa-*r$^{y}$ayn*-toa) *adj* dusty
**pollero** (poa-*l$^{y}$ay*-roa) *m* poulterer
**pollo** (*poa*-l$^{y}$oa) *m* chicken
**pomelo** (poa-*may*-loa) *m* grapefruit
**pómulo** (*poa*-moo-loa) *m* cheekbone
**ponderado** (poan-day-*rah*-dhoa) *adj* cautious; steady
***poner** (poa-*nayr*) *v* place, *lay, *put, *set; ***ponerse** *v* *put on
**pony** (*poa*-nee) *m* pony
**popular** (poa-poo-*lahr*) *adj* popular; vulgar; **canción ~** folk song; **danza ~** folk dance
**populoso** (poa-poo-*loa*-soa) *adj* populous

**por** (poar) *prep* by; for; via; times
**porcelana** (poar-thay-*lah*-nah) *f* china, porcelain
**porcentaje** (poar-thayn-*tah*-khay) *m* percentage
**porción** (poar-*th$^{y}$oan*) *f* portion, helping
**porque** (*poar*-kay) *conj* because, for, as; **por qué?** why?
**porra** (*poa*-rrah) *f* club
**portabagajes** (poar-tah-bah-*khah*-gayss) *m* luggage rack
**portador** (poar-tah-*dhoar*) *m* carrier
**portaequipajes** (poar-tah-ay-kee-*pah*-khayss) *m* boot; trunk *Am*
**portafolio** (poar-tah-*foa*-l$^{y}$oa) *m* attaché case, briefcase
**portátil** (poar-*tah*-teel) *adj* portable
**portero** (poar-*tay*-roa) *m* doorman, door-keeper, porter; goalkeeper
**portilla** (poar-*tee*-l$^{y}$ah) *f* porthole
**portón** (poar-*toan*) *m* gate
**Portugal** (poar-too-*gahl*) *m* Portugal
**portugués** (poar-too-*gayss*) *adj* Portuguese; *m* Portuguese
**porvenir** (poar-bhay-*neer*) *m* future
**posada** (poa-*sah*-dhah) *f* inn
**posadero** (poa-sah-*dhay*-roa) *m* innkeeper
***poseer** (poa-say-*ayr*) *v* own, possess
**posesión** (poa-say-*s$^{y}$oan*) *f* possession
**posibilidad** (poa-see-bhee-lee-*dhahdh*) *f* possibility
**posible** (poa-*see*-bhlay) *adj* possible
**posición** (poa-see-*th$^{y}$oan*) *f* position
**positiva** (poa-see-*tee*-bhah) *f* positive, print
**positivo** (poa-see-*tee*-bhoa) *adj* positive
**postal ilustrada** (poass-*tahl* ee-looss-*trah*-dhah) picture postcard
**poste** (*poass*-tay) *m* post, pole; **~ de farol** lamppost; **~ de indicador** signpost
**posterior** (poass-tay-*r$^{y}$oar*) *adj* subsequent
**postizo** (poass-*tee*-thoa) *adj* false, artificial; *m* hairpiece
**postre** (*poass*-tray) *m* dessert
**potable** (poa-*tah*-bhlay) *adj* drinkable
**potencia** (poa-*tayn*-th$^{y}$ah) *f* capacity; power
**pozo** (*poa*-thoa) *m* well; **~ de petróleo** oil well
**práctica** (*prahk*-tee-kah) *f* practice
**practicar** (prahk-tee-*kahr*) *v* practise
**práctico** (*prahk*-tee-koa) *adj* practical; skilled; *m* pilot
**prado** (*prah*-dhoa) *m* meadow, pasture
**precario** (pray-*kah*-r$^{y}$oa) *adj* critical, precarious
**precaución** (pray-kou-*th$^{y}$oan*) *f* precaution
**precedente** (pray-thay-*dhayn*-tay) *adj* previous, preceding, last
**preceder** (pray-thay-*dhayr*) *v* precede
**precio** (*pray*-th$^{y}$oa) *m* price; charge, cost, rate; **~ de compra** purchase price; **~ del billete** fare
**precioso** (pray-*th$^{y}$oa*-soa) *adj* precious; lovely
**precipicio** (pray-thee-*pee*-th$^{y}$oa) *m* precipice
**precipitación** (pray-thee-pee-tah-*th$^{y}$oan*) *f* precipitation
**precipitarse** (pray-thee-pee-*tahr*-say) *v* rush; crash; **precipitado** *adj* rash
**preciso** (pray-*thee*-soa) *adj* precise; very
**predecesor** (pray-dhay-thay-*soar*) *m* predecessor
***predecir** (pray-dhay-*theer*) *v* predict
**predicar** (pray-dhee-*kahr*) *v* preach
**preferencia** (pray-fay-*rayn*-th$^{y}$ah) *f* preference
**preferible** (pray-fay-*ree*-bhlay) *adj* preferable

***preferir** (pray-fay-*reer*) *v* prefer; **preferido** *adj* favo(u)rite
**prefijo** (pray-*fee*-khoa) *m* prefix
**pregunta** (pray-*goon*-tah) *f* question; query, inquiry
**preguntar** (pray-goon-*tahr*) *v* ask; enquire; **preguntarse** *v* wonder
**prejuicio** (pray-*khwee*-th$^y$oa) *m* prejudice
**preliminar** (pray-lee-mee-*nahr*) *adj* preliminary
**prematuro** (pray-mah-*too*-roa) *adj* premature
**premio** (*pray*-m$^y$oa) *m* award, prize; ~ **de consolación** consolation prize
**prender** (prayn-*dayr*) *v* attach
**prensa** (*prayn*-sah) *f* press; **conferencia de** ~ press conference
**preocupación** (pray-oa-koo-pah-*th$^y$oan*) *f* concern, anxiety, worry; trouble
**preocupado** (pray-oa-koo-*pah*-dhoa) *adj* concerned, anxious
**preocuparse de** (pray-oa-koo-*pahr*-say) care about; see to
**preparación** (pray-pah-rah-*th$^y$oan*) *f* preparation
**preparado** (pray-pah-*rah*-dhoa) *adj* prepared, ready
**preparar** (pray-pah-*rahr*) *v* prepare; cook
**preposición** (pray-poa-see-*th$^y$oan*) *f* preposition
**presa** (*pray*-sah) *f* dam
**prescindir** (pray-theen-*deer*) *v* omit; disregard; **prescindiendo de** apart from
**prescribir** (prayss-kree-*bheer*) *v* prescribe
**prescripción** (prayss-kreep-*th$^y$oan*) *f* prescription
**presencia** (pray-*sayn*-th$^y$ah) *f* presence
**presenciar** (pray-sayn-*th$^y$ahr*) *v* witness
**presentación** (pray-sayn-tah-*th$^y$oan*) *f* introduction
**presentar** (pray-sayn-*tahr*) *v* introduce, present; offer; **presentarse** *v* report
**presente** (pray-*sayn*-tay) *adj* present; *m* present
**preservativo** (pray-sayr-bhah-*tee*-bhoa) *m* condom
**preservar** (pray-sayr-*bhahr*) *v* preserve
**presidente** (pray-see-*dhayn*-tay) *m* president, chairman
**presidir** (pray-see-*dheer*) *v* preside at
**presión** (pray-*s$^y$oan*) *f* pressure; ~ **atmosférica** atmospheric pressure; ~ **del aceite** oil pressure; ~ **del neumático** tyre pressure, tire pressure *Am*
**preso** (*pray*-soa) *m* prisoner; **coger** ~ capture
**préstamo** (*prayss*-tah-moa) *m* loan
**prestar** (prayss-*tahr*) *v* *lend; ~ **atención a** attend to, *pay attention to; **tomar prestado** borrow
**prestigio** (prayss-*tee*-kh$^y$oa) *m* prestige
**presumible** (pray-soo-*mee*-bhlay) *adj* presumable
**presumido** (pray-soo-*mee*-dhoa) *adj* presumptuous
**presumir** (pray-soo-*meer*) *v* assume; boast
**presuntuoso** (pray-soon-*twoa*-soa) *adj* conceited; presumptuous
**presupuesto** (pray-soo-*pwayss*-toa) *m* budget
**pretender** (pray-tayn-*dayr*) *v* claim
**pretensión** (pray-tayn-*s$^y$oan*) *f* claim
**pretexto** (pray-*tayks*-toa) *m* pretext, pretence, pretense *Am*
***prevenir** (pray-bhay-*neer*) *v* anticipate, prevent

**preventivo** (pray-bhayn-*tee*-bhoa) *adj* preventive
***prever** (pray-*bhayr*) *v* anticipate
**previo** (*pray*-bh$^{y}$oa) *adj* previous
**previsión** (pray-bhee-*s$^{y}$oan*) *f* outlook, forecast
**prima** (*pree*-mah) *f* cousin; premium
**primario** (pree-*mah*-r$^{y}$oa) *adj* primary
**primavera** (pree-mah-*bhay*-rah) *f* springtime, spring
**primero** (pree-*may*-roa) *num* first; *adj* foremost; primary
**primitivo** (pree-mee-*tee*-bhoa) *adj* primitive
**primo** (*pree*-moa) *m* cousin
**primordial** (pree-moar-*dh$^{y}$ahl*) *adj* primary
**princesa** (preen-*thay*-sah) *f* princess
**principal** (preen-thee-*pahl*) *adj* principal; chief, main, cardinal; *m* principal
**principalmente** (preen-thee-pahl-*mayn*-tay) *adv* mainly
**príncipe** (*preen*-thee-pay) *m* prince
**principiante** (preen-thee-*p$^{y}$ahn*-tay) *m* beginner, novice
**principio** (preen-*thee*-p$^{y}$oa) *m* principle; **al ~** at first
**prioridad** (pr$^{y}$oa-ree-*dhahdh*) *f* priority
**prisa** (*pree*-sah) *f* haste, speed, hurry; ***dar ~** *speed; ***darse ~** hurry; **de ~** in a hurry
**prisión** (pree-*s$^{y}$oan*) *f* prison
**prisionero** (pree-s$^{y}$oa-*nay*-roa) *m* prisoner; **~ de guerra** prisoner of war
**prismáticos** (preez-*mah*-tee-koass) *mpl* binoculars *pl*
**privado** (pree-*bhah*-dhoa) *adj* private
**privar de** (pree-*bhahr*) deprive of
**privilegio** (pree-bhee-*lay*-kh$^{y}$oa) *m* privilege
**probable** (proa-*bhah*-bhlay) *adj* probable; likely
**probablemente** (proa-bhah-bhlay-*mayn*-tay) *adv* probably
**probador** (proa-bhah-*dhoar*) *m* fitting room
***probar** (proa-*bhahr*) *v* attempt; test; taste; ***probarse** *v* try on
**problema** (proa-*bhlay*-mah) *m* problem, question
**procedencia** (proa-thay-*dhayn*-th$^{y}$ah) *f* origin
**proceder** (proa-thay-*dhayr*) *v* proceed
**procedimiento** (proa-thay-dhee-*m$^{y}$ayn*-toa) *m* procedure; process
**procesión** (proa-thay-*s$^{y}$oan*) *f* procession
**proceso** (proa-*thay*-soa) *m* process, trial, lawsuit
**proclamar** (proa-klah-*mahr*) *v* proclaim
**procurador** (proa-koo-rah-*dhoar*) *m* solicitor
**procurar** (proa-koo-*rahr*) *v* furnish
**pródigo** (*proa*-dhee-goa) *adj* lavish
**producción** (proa-dhook-*th$^{y}$oan*) *f* production, output; **~ en serie** mass production
***producir** (proa-dhoo-*theer*) *v* produce
**producto** (proa-*dhook*-toa) *m* product, produce
**productor** (proa-dhook-*toar*) *m* producer
**profano** (proa-*fah*-noa) *m* layman
**profesar** (proa-fay-*sahr*) *v* confess
**profesión** (proa-fay-*s$^{y}$oan*) *f* profession
**profesional** (proa-fay-s$^{y}$oa-*nahl*) *adj* professional
**profesor** (proa-fay-*soar*) *m*, **-a** *f* teacher; professor
**profesora** (proa-fay-*soa*-rah) *f* teacher
**profeta** (proa-*fay*-tah) *m* prophet
**profundidad** (proa-foon-dee-*dhahdh*) *f* depth

**profundo** (proa-*foon*-doa) *adj* low; profound

**programa** (proa-*grah*-mah) *m* programme

**progresista** (proa-gray-*seess*-tah) *adj* progressive

**progresivo** (proa-gray-*see*-bhoa) *adj* progressive

**progreso** (proa-*gray*-soa) *m* progress

**prohibición** (proa-ee-bhee-*th$^{y}$oan*) *f* prohibition

**prohibido** (proa-ee-*bhee*-dhoa) *adj* prohibited

**prohibir** (proa-ee-*bheer*) *v* prohibit, *forbid

**prolongación** (proa-loang-gah-*th$^{y}$oan*) *f* prolongation

**prolongar** (proa-loang-*gahr*) *v* extend

**promedio** (proa-*may*-dh$^{y}$oa) *adj* average; *m* average, mean; **en ~** on the average

**promesa** (proa-*may*-sah) *f* promise

**prometer** (proa-may-*tayr*) *v* promise

**prometido** (proa-may-*tee*-dhoa) *adj* engaged

**promoción** (proa-moa-*th$^{y}$oan*) *f* promotion

***promover** (proa-moa-*bhayr*) *v* promote; advance

**pronombre** (proa-*noam*-bray) *m* pronoun

**pronosticar** (proa-noass-tee-*kahr*) *v* forecast

**pronto** (*proan*-toa) *adj* prompt; *adv* soon, shortly; **tan ~ como** as soon as

**pronunciación** (proa-noon-th$^{y}$ah-*th$^{y}$oan*) *f* pronunciation

**pronunciar** (proa-noon-*th$^{y}$ahr*) *v* pronounce

**propaganda** (proa-pah-*gahn*-dah) *f* propaganda

**propicio** (proa-*pee*-th$^{y}$oa) *adj* favo(u)rable; well-disposed

**propiedad** (proa-p$^{y}$ay-*dhahdh*) *f* property; estate

**propietario** (proa-p$^{y}$ay-*tah*-r$^{y}$oa) *m*, **-a** *f* owner, proprietor; landlord

**propina** (proa-*pee*-nah) *f* gratuity, tip

**propio** (*proa*-p$^{y}$oa) *adj* own

***proponer** (proa-poa-*nayr*) *v* propose

**proporción** (proa-poar-*th$^{y}$oan*) *f* proportion

**proporcional** (proa-poar-th$^{y}$oa-*nahl*) *adj* proportional

**proporcionar** (proa-poar-th$^{y}$oa-*nahr*) *v* adjust; procure

**propósito** (proa-*poa*-see-toa) *m* purpose; **a ~** by the way

**propuesta** (proa-*pwayss*-tah) *f* proposition, proposal

**prórroga** (*proa*-rroa-gah) *f* extension

**prosa** (*proa*-sah) *f* prose

***proseguir** (proa-say-*geer*) *v* proceed, continue, carry on

**prospecto** (proass-*payk*-toa) *m* prospectus

**prosperidad** (proass-pay-ree-*dhahdh*) *f* prosperity

**próspero** (*proass*-pay-roa) *adj* prosperous

**prostituta** (proass-tee-*too*-tah) *f* prostitute

**protección** (proa-tayk-*th$^{y}$oan*) *f* protection

**proteger** (proa-tay-*khayr*) *v* protect

**proteína** (proa-tay-*ee*-nah) *f* protein

**protesta** (proa-*tayss*-tah) *f* protest

**protestante** (proa-tayss-*tahn*-tay) *adj* Protestant

**protestar** (proa-tayss-*tahr*) *v* protest

**provechoso** (proa-bhay-*choa*-soa) *adj* profitable

***proveer** (proa-bhay-*ayr*) *v* provide; **~ de** furnish with

**proverbio** (proa-*bhayr*-bh$^{y}$oa) *m* proverb

**provincia** (proa-*bheen*-th$^{y}$ah) *f* province

**provincial** (proa-bheen-*th$^y$ahl*) *adj* provincial
**provisional** (proa-bhee-s$^y$oa-*nahl*) *adj* provisional, temporary
**provisiones** (proa-bhee-*s$^y$oa*-nayss) *fpl* provisions *pl*
**provocar** (proa-bhoa-*kahr*) *v* cause
**próximamente** (*proak*-see-mah-mayn-tay) *adv* shortly
**próximo** (*proak*-see-moa) *adj* next
**proyectar** (proa-$^y$ayk-*tahr*) *v* project
**proyecto** (proa-*$^y$ayk*-toa) *m* project, scheme
**proyector** (proa-$^y$ayk-*toar*) *m* spotlight
**prudente** (proo-*dhayn*-tay) *adj* cautious, wary; sensible; wise
**prueba** (*prway*-bhah) *f* experiment, trial, test; proof, token, evidence; **a ~** on approval
**psicoanalista** (see-koa-ah-nah-*leess*-tah) *m* analyst, psychoanalyst
**psicología** (see-koa-loa-*khee*-ah) *f* psychology
**psicológico** (see-koa-*loa*-khee-koa) *adj* psychological
**psicólogo** (see-*koa*-loa-goa) *m* psychologist
**psiquiatra** (see-*k$^y$ah*-trah) *m* psychiatrist
**psíquico** (*see*-kee-koa) *adj* psychic
**publicación** (poo-bhlee-kah-*th$^y$oan*) *f* publication
**publicar** (poo-bhlee-*kahr*) *v* publish
**publicidad** (poo-bhlee-thee-*dhahdh*) *f* advertising, publicity
**público** (*poo*-bhlee-koa) *adj* public; *m* public
**pueblo** (*pway*-bhloa) *m* nation, people; village
**puente** (*pwayn*-tay) *m* bridge; **~ colgante** suspension bridge; **~ levadizo** drawbridge; **~ superior** main deck
**puerta** (*pwayr*-tah) *f* door; **~ corrediza** sliding door; **~ giratoria** revolving door
**puerto** (*pwayr*-toa) *m* harbo(u)r, port; **~ de mar** seaport
**pues** (pwayss) *conj* since; *adv* well then
**puesta** (*pwayss*-tah) *f* bet
**puesto** (loo-*gahr*) *m* spot; job, post, position; stand, stall, booth; **~ de gasolina** service station; gas station *Am*; **~ de libros** bookstand
**puesto que** (*pwayss*-toa kay) because, since
**pulcro** (*pool*-kroa) *adj* neat, tidy; clean
**pulgar** (pool-*gahr*) *m* thumb
**pulir** (poo-*leer*) *v* polish
**pulmón** (pool-*moan*) *m* lung
**pulóver** (poo-*loa*-bhayr) *m* pullover
**púlpito** (*pool*-pee-toa) *m* pulpit
**pulpo** (*pool*-poa) *m* octopus
**pulsera** (pool-*say*-rah) *f* bracelet, bangle
**pulso** (*pool*-soa) *m* pulse
**pulverizador** (pool-bhay-ree-thah-*dhoar*) *m* atomizer
**punta** (*poon*-tah) *f* tip, point
**puntiagudo** (poon-t$^y$ah-*goo*-dhoa) *adj* pointed
**puntilla** (poon-*tee*-l$^y$ah) *f* lace edging; nib
**punto** (*poon*-toa) *m* point; item, issue; period, full stop; stitch; **géneros de ~** hosiery; ***hacer ~** *knit; **~ de congelación** freezing-point; **~ de partida** starting-point; **~ de vista** point of view; **~ y coma** semi-colon
**puntual** (poon-*twahl*) *adj* punctual
**punzada** (poon-*thah*-dhah) *f* stitch
**punzar** (poon-*thahr*) *v* pierce, prick
**puñado** (poo-*ñah*-dhoa) *m* handful
**puñetazo** (poo-ñay-*tah*-thoa) *m* punch; ***dar puñetazos** punch

**puño** (*poo*-ñoa) *m* fist; cuff

**pupitre** (poo-*pee*-tray) *m* school desk

**puro** (*poo*-roa) *adj* pure; clean, neat, sheer; *m* cigar

**purpúreo** (poor-*poo*-ray-oa) *adj* purple

**pus** (pooss) *f* pus

**puta** (*poo*-tah) *f vulgar* whore

# Q

**que** (kay) *pron* who, which, that; *conj* that; as, than

**qué** (kay) *pron* what; *adv* how

**quebradizo** (kay-bhrah-*dhee*-thoa) *adj* crumbly; brittle, frail

**quebrantar** (kay-bhrahn-*tahr*) *v* *break

***quebrar** (kay-*bhrahr*) *v* crack, *break, *burst

**quedar** (kay-*dhahr*) *v* remain, stay; **~ con uno** make a date with; **quedarse** *v* remain, stay; **~ con** hold on to

**queja** (*kay*-khah) *f* complaint

**quejarse** (kay-*khahr*-say) *v* complain

**quemadura** (kay-mah-*dhoo*-rah) *f* burn; **~ del sol** sunburn

**quemar** (kay-*mahr*) *v* *burn

***querer** (kay-*rayr*) *v* *will, want; like, *be fond of

**querida** (kay-*ree*-dhah) *f* sweetheart; mistress

**querido** (kay-*ree*-dhoa) *adj* beloved, dear; precious; *m* darling

**queso** (*kay*-soa) *m* cheese

**quien** (k$^{y}$ayn) *pron* who; **a ~** whom

**quienquiera** (k$^{y}$ayng-*k$^{y}$ay*-rah) *pron* whoever

**quieto** (*k$^{y}$ay*-toa) *adj* still, quiet; ***estarse ~** *keep quiet

**quilate** (kee-*lah*-tay) *m* carat

**quilla** (*kee*-l$^{y}$ah) *f* keel

**química** (*kee*-mee-kah) *f* chemistry

**químico** (*kee*-mee-koa) *adj* chemical

**quincalla** (keeng-*kah*-l$^{y}$ah) *f* small hardware

**quince** (*keen*-thay) *num* fifteen

**quincena** (keen-*thay*-nah) *f* fortnight

**quinceno** (keen-*thay*-noa) *num* fifteenth

**quinta** (*keen*-tah) *f* country house

**quinto**[1] (*keen*-toa) *num* fifth

**quinto**[2] (*keen*-toa) *m* conscript

**quiosco** (*k$^{y}$oass*-koa) *m* kiosk; **~ de periódicos** newsstand

**quitamanchas** (kee-tah-*mahn*-chahss) *m* cleaning fluid, stain remover

**quitar** (kee-*tahr*) *v* *take away

**quitasol** (kee-tah-*soal*) *m* sunshade

**quizás** (kee-*thahss*) *adv* maybe, perhaps

# R

**rábano** (*rah*-bhah-noa) *m* radish; **~ picante** horseradish

**rabia** (*rah*-bh$^{y}$ah) *f* rage; rabies

**rabiar** (rah-*bh$^{y}$ahr*) *v* rage

**rabioso** (rah-*bh$^y$oa*-soa) *adj* mad
**racial** (rah-*th$^y$ahl*) *adj* racial
**ración** (rah-*th$^y$oan*) *f* ration
**radiador** (rah-dh$^y$ah-*dhoar*) *m* radiator
**radical** (rah-dhee-*kahl*) *adj* radical
**radio** (*rah*-dh$^y$oa) *m* radius; spoke; *f* radio
**radiografía** (rah-dh$^y$oa-grah-*fee*-ah) *f* X-ray
**radiografiar** (rah-dh$^y$oa-grah-*f$^y$ahr*) *v* X-ray
**raedura** (rah-ay-*dhoo*-rah) *f* scratch; ***hacer raeduras** scratch
**ráfaga** (*rah*-fah-gah) *f* gust, blow
**raíz** (rah-*eeth*) *f* root
**rallar** (rah-*l$^y$ahr*) *v* grate
**rama** (*rah*-mah) *f* branch, bough
**ramita** (rah-*mee*-tah) *f* twig
**ramo** (*rah*-moa) *m* bouquet
**rampa** (*rahm*-pah) *f* ramp
**rana** (*rah*-nah) *f* frog
**rancio** (*rahn*-th$^y$oa) *adj* rancid
**rancho** (*rahn*-choa) *mMe* farmhouse
**rango** (*rahng*-goa) *m* rank
**ranura** (rah-*noo*-rah) *f* slot
**rápidamente** (*rah*-pee-dah-mayn-tay) *adv* soon
**rapidez** (*rah*-pee-dhayth) *f* speed
**rápido** (*rah*-pee-dhoa) *adj* fast, rapid, quick; **rápidos de río** rapids *pl*
**raptar** (rahp-*tahr*) *v* kidnap
**raqueta** (rah-*kay*-tah) *f* rackuet
**raro** (*rah*-roa) *adj* uncommon, rare; strange, odd; **raras veces** rarely
**rascacielos** (rahss-kah-*th$^y$ay*-loass) *m* skyscraper
**rascar** (rahss-*kahr*) *v* scratch
**rasgar** (rahz-*gahr*) *v* rip; tear up
**rasgo** (*rahz*-goa) *m* trait; feature; **~ característico** characteristic
**rasgón** (rahz-*goan*) *m* tear
**rasguño** (rahz-*goo*-ñoa) *m* scratch
**raso** (*rah*-soa) *adj* bare; *m* satin
**raspar** (rahss-*pahr*) *v* scrape
**rastrear** (rahss-tray-*ahr*) *v* trace
**rastrillo** (rahss-*tree*-l$^y$oa) *m* rake
**rastro** (*rahss*-troa) *m* trail
**rasurarse** (rah-soo-*rahr*-say) *v* shave
**rata** (*rah*-tah) *f* rat
**rato** (*rah*-toa) *m* while
**ratón** (rah-*toan*) *m* mouse
**raya** (*rah*-$^y$ah) *f* line, stripe; crease; parting
**rayado** (rah-*$^y$ah*-dhoa) *adj* striped
**rayador** (rah-$^y$ah-*dhoar*) *m* grater
**rayo** (*rah*-$^y$oa) *m* beam, ray
**rayón** (rah-*$^y$oan*) *m* rayon
**raza** (*rah*-thah) *f* race; breed
**razón** (rah-*thoan*) *f* wits *pl*, sense, reason; **no *tener ~** *be wrong; ***tener ~** *be right
**razonable** (rah-thoa-*nah*-bhlay) *adj* reasonable
**razonar** (rah-thoa-*nahr*) *v* reason
**reacción** (ray-ahk-*th$^y$oan*) *f* reaction
**reaccionar** (ray-ahk-th$^y$oa-*nahr*) *v* react
**real** (ray-*ahl*) *adj* factual, true, substantial; royal
**realidad** (ray-ah-lee-*dhahdh*) *f* reality; **en ~** actually, as a matter of fact
**realizable** (ray-ah-lee-*thah*-bhlay) *adj* feasible, realizable
**realización** (ray-ah-lee-thah-*th$^y$oan*) *f* achievement
**realizar** (ray-ah-lee-*thahr*) *v* realize; attain; carry out
**rebaja** (ray-*bhah*-khah) *f* reduction, rebate; **rebajas** *fpl* sales
**rebajar** (ray-bhah-*khahr*) *v* lower, reduce
**rebaño** (ray-*bhah*-ñoa) *m* flock
**rebelde** (ray-*bhayl*-day) *m* rebel
**rebelión** (ray-bhay-*l$^y$oan*) *f* revolt, rebellion
**recado** (ray-*kah*-dhoa) *m* errand
**recambio** (ray-*kahm*-b$^y$oa) *m* spare

part; refill

**recepción** (ray-thayp-*th*$^y$*oan*) *f* reception

**recepcionista** (ray-thayp-th$^y$oa-*neess*-tah) *m/f* receptionist

**receptáculo** (ray-thayp-*tah*-koo-loa) *m* container

**receptor** (ray-thayp-*toar*) *m* receiver

**receta** (ray-*thay*-tah) *f* recipe

**recibir** (ray-thee-*bheer*) *v* receive

**recibo** (ray-*thee*-bhoa) *m* voucher, receipt; **oficina de ~** reception office

**reciclable** (ray-thee-*clah*-bhlay) *adj* recyclable

**reciclar** (ray-thee-*clahr*) *v* recycle

**recién** (ray-*th*$^y$*ayn*) *adv* recently

**reciente** (ray-*th*$^y$*ayn*-tay) *adj* recent

**recientemente** (ray-th$^y$ayn-tay-*mayn*-tay) *adv* lately, recently

**recíproco** (ray-*thee*-proa-koa) *adj* mutual

**recital** (ray-thee-*tahl*) *m* recital

**reclamar** (ray-klah-*mahr*) *v* claim

**recluta** (ray-*kloo*-tah) *m* recruit

**recoger** (ray-koa-*khayr*) *v* pick up, pick; collect, gather; *overtake

**recogida** (ray-koa-*khee*-dhah) *f* collection

**recomendación** (ray-koa-mayn-dah-*th*$^y$*oan*) *f* recommendation

***recomendar** (ray-koa-mayn-*dahr*) *v* recommend

***recomenzar** (ray-koa-mayn-*thahr*) *v* recommence

**recompensa** (ray-koam-*payn*-sah) *f* prize, reward

**recompensar** (ray-koam-payn-*sahr*) *v* reward

**reconciliación** (ray-koan-thee-l$^y$ah-*th*$^y$*oan*) *f* reconciliation

***reconocer** (ray-koa-noa-*thayr*) *v* recognize; admit, confess, acknowledge; realize

**reconocimiento** (ray-koa-noa-thee-*m*$^y$*ayn*-toa) *m* recognition; medical check-up

**récord** (*ray*-koardh) *m* record

***recordar** (ray-koar-*dhahr*) *v* remind; *think of

**recorrer** (ray-koa-*rrayr*) *v* cross; go through

**recorrido** (ray-koa-*rree*h-doa) *m* route; round

**recortar** (ray-koar-*tahr*) *v* trim

**recreación** (ray-kray-ah-*th*$^y$*oan*) *f* recreation

**recreo** (ray-*kray*-oa) *m* recreation; **patio de ~** playground

**recriar** (ray-*kr*$^y$*ahr*) *v* *breed

**rectangular** (rayk-tahng-goo-*lahr*) *adj* rectangular

**rectángulo** (rayk-*tahng*-goo-loa) *m* oblong, rectangle

**rectificación** (rayk-tee-fee-kah-*th*$^y$*oan*) *f* correction

**recto** (*rayk*-toa) *adj* straight; direct; upright

**rector** (rayk-*toar*) *m* rector

**rectoría** (rayk-toa-*ree*-ah) *f* rectory

**recuerdo** (ray-*kwayr*-dhoa) *m* remembrance, memory; souvenir; **~s** regards

**recuperación** (ray-koo-pay-rah-*th*$^y$*oan*) *f* recovery

**recuperar** (ray-koo-pay-*rahr*) *v* recover

**rechazar** (ray-chah-*thahr*) *v* reject, turn down

**red** (raydh) *f* net; network; **~ de carreteras** road system; **~ de pescar** fishing net

**redacción** (ray-dhahk-*th*$^y$*oan*) *f* wording; editorial staff

**redactar** (ray-dhahk-*tahr*) *v* *write up; *draw up; edit

**redactor** (ray-dhahk-*toar*) *m* editor

**redecilla** (ray-dhay-*thee*-l$^y$ah) *f* hair net

**redimir** (ray-dhee-*meer*) *v* redeem

**rédito** (*ray*-dhee-toa) *m* revenue, income, interest

**redondeado** (ray-dhoan-day-*ah*-dhoa) *adj* rounded

**redondo** (ray-*dhoan*-doa) *adj* round

**reducción** (ray-dhook-*th$^{y}$oan*) *f* reduction, rebate

***reducir** (ray-dhoo-*theer*) *v* *cut, decrease, reduce

**reembolsar** (ray-aym-boal-*sahr*) *v* reimburse

**reemplazar** (ray-aym-plah-*thahr*) *v* replace

**reemprender** (ray-aym-prayn-*dayr*) *v* resume

**reexpedir** (ray-ayks-pay-*dheer*) *v* forward

**referencia** (ray-fay-*rayn*-th$^{y}$ah) *f* reference; **punto de ~** landmark

***referir** (ray-fay-*reer*) *v* refer; narrate

**refinería** (ray-fee-nay-*ree*-ah) *f* refinery

**reflector** (ray-flayk-*toar*) *m* reflector; searchlight

**reflejar** (ray-flay-*khahr*) *v* reflect

**reflejo** (ray-*flay*-khoa) *m* reflection

**reflexionar** (ray-flayk-s$^{y}$oa-*nahr*) *v* *think

**Reforma** (ray-*foar*-mah) *f* reformation

**refractario** (ray-frahk-*tah*-r$^{y}$oa) *adj* fireproof

**refrenar** (ray-fray-*nahr*) *v* curb

**refrescar** (ray-frayss-*kahr*) *v* refresh

**refresco** (ray-*frayss*-koa) *m* refreshment

**refrigerador** (ray-free-khay-rah-*dhoar*) *m* fridge, refrigerator

**refugio** (ray-*foo*-kh$^{y}$oa) *m* cover, shelter

**refugiado** (ray-*foo-kh$^{y}$ah*-doa) *m*, **-a** *f* refugee

**refunfuñar** (ray-foon-foo-*ñahr*) *v* grumble

**regalar** (ray-gah-*lahr*) *v* present

**regaliz** (ray-gah-*leeth*) *m* liquorice

**regalo** (ray-*gah*-loa) *m* present, gift

**regata** (ray-*gah*-tah) *f* regatta

**regatear** (ray-gah-tay-*ahr*) *v* bargain

**régimen** (*ray*-khee-mayn) *m* (pl regímenes) régime; government, rule; diet

**regimiento** (ray-khee-*m$^{y}$ayn*-toa) *m* regiment

**región** (ray-*kh$^{y}$oan*) *f* region; zone, country, area

**regional** (ray-kh$^{y}$oa-*nahl*) *adj* regional

***regir** (ray-*kheer*) *v* govern, rule

**registrar** (ray-kheess-*trahr*) *v* book, record

**registro** (ray-*kheess*-troa) *m* record

**regla** (*ray*-glah) *f* rule; regulation; ruler; **en ~** in order; **por ~ general** as a rule

**reglamento** (ray-glah-*mayn*-toa) *m* regulation

**regocijo** (ray-goa-*thee*-khoa) *m* joy; rejoicing

**regordete** (ray-goar-*dhay*-tay) *adj* plump

**regresar** (ray-gray-*sahr*) *v* *go back, *get back

**regreso** (ray-*gray*-soa) *m* return; **viaje de ~** return journey; **vuelo de ~** return flight

**regulación** (ray-goo-lah-*th$^{y}$oan*) *f* regulation

**regular** (ray-goo-*lahr*) *v* regulate; *adj* regular

**rehabilitación** (ray-ah-bhee-lee-tah-*th$^{y}$oan*) *f* rehabilitation

**rehén** (ray-*ayn*) *m* hostage

**rehusar** (ray$^{oo}$-*sahr*) *v* refuse; reject

**reina** (*ray*-nah) *f* queen

**reinado** (ray-*nah*-dhoa) *m* reign

**reino** (*ray*-noa) *m* kingdom

**reintegrar** (rayn-tay-*grahr*) *v* *repay, refund

**reintegro** (rayn-*tay*-groa) *m* repayment, refund
***reír** (ray-*eer*) *v* laugh
**reivindicación** (ray-bheen-dee-kah-*th$^y$oan*) *f* claim
**reivindicar** (ray-bheen-dee-*kahr*) *v* claim
**reja** (*ray*-khah) *f* grate; fence, gate
**rejilla** (ray-*khee*-l$^y$ah) *f* luggage rack
**relación** (ray-lah-*th$^y$oan*) *f* connection, relation(ship); reference; report
**relacionar** (ray-lah-th$^y$oa-*nahr*) *v* relate
**relajación** (ray-lah-khah-*th$^y$oan*) *f* relaxation
**relajado** (ray-lah-*khah*-dhoa) *adj* relaxed; easygoing
**relámpago** (ray-*lahm*-pah-goa) *m* lightning; flash
**relatar** (ray-lah-*tahr*) *v* report
**relativo** (ray-lah-*tee*-bhoa) *adj* comparative, relative; ~ **a** regarding
**relato** (ray-*lah*-toa) *m* report; narrative
**relevar** (ray-lay-*bhahr*) *v* relieve
**relieve** (ray-*l$^y$ay*-bhay) *m* relief
**religión** (ray-lee-*kh$^y$oan*) *f* religion
**religioso** (ray-lee-*kh$^y$oa*-soa) *adj* religious
**reliquia** (ray-lee-kyah) *f* relic
**reloj** (ray-*loakh*) *m* clock; watch; ~ **de pulsera** wristwatch
**relojero** (ray-loa-*khay*-roa) *m*, **-a** *f* watchmaker
**reluciente** (ray-loo-*th$^y$ayn*-tay) *adj* bright
***relucir** (ray-loo-*theer*) *v* *shine
**rellenado** (ray-l$^y$ay-*nah*-doa) *adj* stuffed
**relleno** (ray-*l$^y$ay*-noa) *m* stuffing; filling
**remanente** (ray-mah-*nayn*-tay) *m* remnant
**remar** (ray-*mahr*) *v* row
**remedio** (ray-*may*-dh$^y$oa) *m* remedy
***remendar** (ray-mayn-*dahr*) *v* mend; patch
**remesa** (ray-*may*-sah) *f* remittance
**remitente** (ray-mee-*tayn-tay*) *m/f* sender
**remitir** (ray-mee-*teer*) *v* remit; ~ **a** refer to
**remo** (*ray*-moa) *m* paddle, oar
**remoción** (ray-moa-*th$^y$oan*) *f* removal
**remojar** (ray-moa-*khahr*) *v* soak
**remolacha** (ray-moa-*lah*-chah) *f* beetroot, beet
**remolcador** (ray-moal-kah-*dhoar*) *m* tug
**remolcar** (ray-moal-*kahr*) *v* tug, tow
**remolque** (ray-*moal*-kay) *m* trailer
**remoto** (ray-*moa*-toa) *adj* remote, far-away, far-off
***remover** (ray-moa-*bhayr*) *v* remove
**remuneración** (ray-moo-nay-rah-*th$^y$oan*) *f* remuneration
**remunerar** (ray-moo-nay-*rahr*) *v* remunerate
**Renacimiento** (ray-nah-thee-*m$^y$ayn*-toa) *m* Renaissance
**rendición** (rayn-dee-*th$^y$oan*) *f* surrender
***rendir** (rayn-*deer*) *v* *pay; ~ **homenaje** hono(u)r; ***rendirse** *v* surrender
**renglón** (rayng-*gloan*) *m* line
**reno** (*ray*-noa) *m* reindeer
**renombre** (ray-*noam*-bray) *m* reputation
***renovar** (ray-noa-*bhahr*) *v* renew
**renta** (*rayn*-tah) *f* revenue
**rentable** (rayn-*tah*-bhlay) *adj* paying
**renunciar** (ray-noon-*th$^y$ahr*) *v* *give up
***reñir** (ray-*ñeer*) *v* dispute, quarrel
**reparación** (ray-pah-rah-*th$^y$oan*) *f* reparation; repair
**reparar** (ray-pah-*rahr*) *v* repair, mend

**repartir** (ray-pahr-*teer*) *v* divide, *deal, share out
**reparto** (ray-*pahr*-toa) *m* delivery; **camioneta de ~** pick-up van
**repelente** (ray-pay-*layn*-tay) *adj* repellent, revolting
**repentinamente** (ray-payn-tee-nah-*mayn*-tay) *adv* suddenly
**repertorio** (ray-payr-*toa*-r$^{y}$oa) *m* repertory
**repetición** (ray-pay-tee-*th$^{y}$oan*) *f* repetition
**repetidamente** (ray-pay-tee-dhah-*mayn*-tay) *adv* again and again
***repetir** (ray-pay-*teer*) *v* repeat
**repleto** (ray-*play*-toa) *adj* crowded
**reportero** (ray-poar-*tay*-roa) *m*, **-a** *f* reporter
**reposado** (ray-poa-*sah*-dhoa) *adj* restful
**reposo** (ray-*poa*-soa) *m* rest
**reprender** (ray-prayn-*dayr*) *v* reprimand, scold
**representación** (ray-pray-sayn-tah-*th$^{y}$oan*) *f* representation; show, performance
**representante** (ray-pray-sayn-*tahn*-tay) *m* agent
**representar** (ray-pray-sayn-*tahr*) *v* represent
**representativo** (ray-pray-sayn-tah-*tee*-bhoa) *adj* representative
**reprimir** (ray-pree-*meer*) *v* suppress
***reprobar** (ray-proa-*bhahr*) *v* reject
**reprochar** (ray-proa-*chahr*) *v* reproach
**reproche** (ray-*proa*-chay) *m* reproach, blame
**reproducción** (ray-proa-dhook-*th$^{y}$oan*) *f* reproduction
***reproducir** (ray-proa-dhoo-*theer*) *v* reproduce
**reptil** (rayp-*teel*) *m* reptile
**república** (ray-*poo*-bhlee-kah) *f* republic
**republicano** (ray-poo-bhlee-*kah*-noa) *adj* republican
**repuesto** (ray-*pwayss*-toa) *m* store; refill
**repugnancia** (ray-poog-*nahn*-th$^{y}$ah) *f* dislike
**repugnante** (ray-poog-*nahn*-tay) *adj* repellent, disgusting, revolting
**repulsivo** (ray-pool-*see*-bhoa) *adj* repulsive
**reputación** (ray-poo-tah-*th$^{y}$oan*) *f* reputation, fame
**requerimiento** (ray-kay-ree-*m$^{y}$ayn*-toa) *m* requirement
***requerir** (ray-kay-*reer*) *v* require, demand
**resaca** (ray-*sah*-kah) *f* undercurrent; hangover
**resbaladizo** (rayz-bhah-lah-*dhee*-thoa) *adj* slippery
**resbalar** (rayz-bhah-*lahr*) *v* slip, glide
**rescatar** (rayss-kah-*tahr*) *v* rescue
**rescate** (rayss-*kah*-tay) *m* rescue; ransom
***resentirse por** (ray-sayn-*teer*-say) resent
**reseña** (ray-*say*-ñah) *f* review
**reserva** (ray-*sayr*-bhah) *f* qualification; reserve; booking; **de ~** spare
**reservación** (ray-sayr-bhah-*th$^{y}$oan*) *f* reservation, booking
**reservar** (ray-sayr-*bhahr*) *v* engage; reserve, book
**resfriado** (rayss-*fr$^{y}$ah*-dhoa) *m* cold
**resfriarse** (rayss-*fr$^{y}$ahr*-say) *v* catch a cold
**residencia** (ray-see-*dhayn*-th$^{y}$ah) *f* residence
**residente** (ray-see-*dhayn*-tay) *adj* resident; *m*/*f* resident
**residir** (ray-see-*dheer*) *v* reside
**residuo** (ray-*see*-dhwoa) *m* remnant

**resignación** (ray-seeg-nah-*th^y^oan*) *f* resignation
**resignar** (ray-seeg-*nahr*) *v* resign
**resina** (ray-*see*-nah) *f* resin
**resistencia** (ray-seess-*tayn*-th^y^ah) *f* resistance
**resistir** (ray-seess-*teer*) *v* resist
**resolución** (ray-soa-loo-*th^y^oan*) *f* resolution
***resolver** (ray-soal-*bhayr*) *v* solve
***resonar** (ray-soa-*nahr*) *v* sound
**respectivo** (rayss-payk-*tee*-bhoa) *adj* respective
**respecto a** (rayss-*payk*-toa ah) about, regarding
**respetable** (rayss-pay-*tah*-bhlay) *adj* respectable
**respetar** (rayss-pay-*tahr*) *v* respect
**respeto** (rayss-*pay-toa*) *m* respect, esteem, regard
**respetuoso** (rayss-pay-*twoa*-soa) *adj* respectful
**respiración** (rayss-pee-rah-*th^y^oan*) *f* respiration, breathing
**respirar** (rayss-pee-*rahr*) *v* breathe
***resplandecer** (rayss-plahn-day-*thayr*) *v* *shine
**resplandor** (rayss-plahn-*doar*) *m* glare
**responder** (rayss-poan-*dayr*) *v* reply, answer
**responsabilidad** (rayss-poan-sah-bhee-lee-*dhahdh*) *f* responsibility; liability
**responsable** (rayss-poan-*sah*-bhlay) *adj* responsible; liable
**respuesta** (rayss-*pwayss*-tah) *f* reply, answer
***restablecerse** (rayss-tah-bhlay-*thayr*-say) *v* recover
**restablecimiento** (rayss-tah-bhlay-thee-*m^y^ayn*-toa) *m* recovery
**restante** (rayss-*tahn*-tay) *adj* remaining
**restar** (rayss-*tahr*) *v* subtract
**restaurante** (rayss-tou-*rahn*-tay) *m* restaurant; **~ de autoservicio** self-service restaurant
**resto** (*rayss*-toa) *m* rest; remnant, remainder
**restricción** (rayss-treek-*th^y^oan*) *f* restriction; qualification
**resuelto** (ray-*swayl*-toa) *adj* resolute, determined
**resultado** (ray-sool-*tah*-dhoa) *m* result; issue, outcome, effect
**resultar** (ray-sool-*tahr*) *v* result; prove
**resumen** (ray-*soo*-mayn) *m* résumé, survey, summary
**retardar** (ray-tahr-*dhahr*) *v* delay
***retener** (ray-tay-*nayr*) *v* *hold
**retina** (ray-*tee*-nah) *f* retina
**retirar** (ray-tee-*rahr*) *v* *withdraw
**reto** (*ray*-toa) *m* challenge
**retrasado** (ray-trah-*sah*-dhoa) *adj* late
**retraso** (ray-*trah*-soa) *m* delay
**retrato** (ray-*trah*-toa) *m* portrait
**retrete** (ray-*tray*-tay) *m* toilet
**retroceso** (ray-troa-*thay*-soa) *m* recession; retreat
**retumbo** (ray-*toom*-boa) *m* boom; reverberation; rumble
**reumatismo** (ray^oo^-mah-*teez*-moa) *m* rheumatism
**reunión** (ray^oo^-*n^y^oan*) *f* meeting, assembly, rally
**reunir** (ray^oo^-*neer*) *v* join, assemble; reunite
**revelación** (ray-bhay-lah-*th^y^oan*) *f* revelation
**revelar** (ray-bhay-*lahr*) *v* reveal; *give away; develop
**revendedor** (ray-bhayn-day-*dhoar*) *m*, **-a** *f* retailer
***reventar** (ray-bhayn-*tahr*) *v* crack, *burst
**reventón** (ray-bhayn-*toan*) *m* blow-out

**reverencia** (ray-bhay-*rayn*-th$^{y}$ah) *f* respect
**reverso** (ray-*bhayr*-soa) *m* reverse
**revés** (ray-*bhayss*) *m* reverse; **al ~** the other way round; upside-down; inside out
**revisar** (ray-bhee-*sahr*) *v* revise, overhaul
**revisión** (ray-bhee-*s$^{y}$oan*) *f* revision
**revisor** (ray-bhee-*soar*) *m* ticket collector
**revista** (ray-*bheess*-tah) *f* journal; review, magazine; revue; **~ mensual** monthly magazine
**revocar** (ray-bhoa-*kahr*) *v* revoke; recall
**revolución** (ray-bhoa-loo-*th$^{y}$oan*) *f* revolution
**revolucionar** (ray-bhoa-loo-th$^{y}$oa-*nahr*) *v* rebel
**revolucionario** (ray-bhoa-loo-th$^{y}$oa-*nah*-r$^{y}$oa) *adj* revolutionary
***revolver** (ray-bhoal-*bhayr*) *v* stir
**revólver** (ray-*bhoal*-bhayr) *m* revolver, gun
**revuelta** (ray-*bhwayl*-tah) *f* revolt
**rey** (ray) *m* king
**rezar** (ray-*thahr*) *v* pray
**ribera** (ree-*bhay*-rah) *f* riverside, river bank, shore
**rico** (*ree*-koa) *adj* rich; wealthy; nice, enjoyable, tasty
**ridiculizar** (ree-dhee-koo-lee-*thahr*) *v* ridicule
**ridículo** (ree-*dhee*-koo-loa) *adj* ridiculous, ludicrous
**riesgo** (*r$^{y}$ayz*-goa) *m* hazard, chance, risk
**rima** (*ree*-mah) *f* rhyme
**rímel** (*ree*-mayl) *m* mascara
**rincón** (reeng-*koan*) *m* angle
**rinoceronte** (ree-noa-thay-*roan*-tay) *m* rhinoceros
**riña** (*ree*-ñah) *f* dispute
**riñón** (ree-*ñoan*) *m* kidney
**río** (*ree*-oa) *m* river; **~ abajo** downstream; **~ arriba** upstream
**riqueza** (ree-*kay*-thah) *f* riches *pl*, wealth
**risa** (*ree*-sah) *f* laughter, laugh
**ritmo** (*reet*-moa) *m* rhythm; pace
**rival** (ree-*bhahl*) *m/f* rival
**rivalidad** (ree-bhah-lee-*dhahdh*) *f* rivalry
**rivalizar** (ree-bhah-lee-*thahr*) *v* rival
**rizadores** (ree-thah-*dhoa*-rayss) *mpl* hair rollers
**rizar** (ree-*thahr*) *v* curl
**rizo** (*ree*-thoa) *m* curl
**robar** (roa-*bhahr*) *v* rob; burgle
**roble** (*roa*-bhlay) *m* oak
**robo** (*roa*-bhoa) *m* robbery, theft
**robusto** (roa-*bhooss*-toa) *adj* solid, robust
**roca** (*roa*-kah) *f* rock
**rocío** (roa-*thee*-oa) *m* dew
**rocoso** (roa-*koa*-soa) *adj* rocky
**rodaballo** (roa-dhah-*bhah*-l$^{y}$oa) *m* brill
***rodar** (roa-*dhahr*) *v* roll
**rodear** (roa-dhay-*ahr*) *v* circle, surround; by-pass
**rodilla** (roa-*dhee*-l$^{y}$ah) *f* knee
***rogar** (roa-*gahr*) *v* ask
**rojo** (*roa*-khoa) *adj* red
**rollo** (*roa*-l$^{y}$oa) *m* roll
**romano** (roa-*mah*-noa) *adj* Roman
**romántico** (roa-*mahn*-tee-koa) *adj* romantic
**rompecabezas** (roam-pay-kah-*bhay*-thahss) *m* puzzle; jigsaw puzzle
**romper** (roam-*payr*) *v* *break
**roncar** (roang-*kahr*) *v* snore
**ronco** (*roang*-koa) *adj* hoarse
**ropa** (*roa*-pah) *f* clothes *pl*; **~ blanca** linen; **~ de cama** bedding; **~ interior** underwear; **~ interior de mujer** lingerie; **~ sucia** washing, laundry

**rosa** (*roa*-sah) *f* rose; *adj* rose
**rosado** (roa-*sah*-dhoa) *adj* pink
**rosario** (roa-*sah*-r$^y$oa) *m* beads *pl*, rosary
**rostro** (*roas*-troa) *m* face
**rota** (*roa*-tah) *f* rattan
**roto** (*roa*-toa) *adj* broken
**rótula** (*roa*-too-lah) *f* kneecap
**rotular** (roa-too-*lahr*) *v* label
**rótulo** (*roa*-too-loa) *m* label
**rozadura** (roa-thah-*dhoo*-rah) *f* graze
**rubí** (roo-*bhee*) *m* ruby
**rubia** (*roo*-bh$^y$ah) *f* blonde
**rubio** (*roo*-bh$^y$oa) *adj* fair, blond
**ruborizarse** (roo-bhoa-ree-*thahr*-say) blush
**rueda** (*rway*-dhah) *f* wheel; ring; **patinaje de ruedas** roller-skating; ~ **de repuesto** spare wheel
**ruego** (*rway*-goa) *m* request
**rugido** (roo-*khee*-dhoa) *m* roar
**rugir** (roo-*kheer*) *v* roar
**ruibarbo** (rwee-*bhahr*-bhoa) *m* rhubarb
**ruido** (*rwee*-dhoa) *m* noise
**ruidoso** (rwee-*dhoa*-soa) *adj* noisy
**ruina** (*rwee*-nah) *f* ruins; ruin, destruction
**ruinoso** (rwee-*noa*-soa) *adj* dilapidated
**ruiseñor** (rwee-say-*ñoar*) *m* nightingale
**ruleta** (roo-*lay*-tah) *f* roulette
**rulo** (*roo*-loa) *m* curler
**Rumania** (roo-*mah*-n$^y$ah) *f* Rumania
**rumano** (roo-*mah*-noa) *adj* Rumanian; *m* Rumanian
**rumbo** (*room*-boa) *m* course
**rumor** (roo-*moar*) *m* rumo(u)r
**rural** (roo-*rahl*) *adj* rural
**Rusia** (*roo*-s$^y$ah) *f* Russia
**ruso** (*roo*-soa) *adj* Russian; *m* Russian
**rústico** (*rooss*-tee-koa) *adj* rustic
**ruta** (*roo*-tah) *f* route; ~ **principal** thoroughfare
**rutina** (roo-*tee*-nah) *f* routine

# S

**sábado** (*sah*-bhah-dhoa) *m* Saturday
**sábana** (*sah*-bhah-nah) *f* sheet
***saber** (sah-*bhayr*) *v* *know; *be able to; **a** ~ namely; ~ **a** taste
**sabiduría** (sah-bhee-dhoo-*ree*-ah) *f* wisdom
**sabio** (*sah*-bh$^y$oa) *adj* wise
**sabor** (sah-*bhoar*) *m* flavo(u)r
**sabroso** (sah-*bhroa*-soa) *adj* savo(u)ry, tasty
**sacacorchos** (sah-kah-*koar*-choass) *mpl* corkscrew
**sacapuntas** (sah-kah-*poon*-tahss) *m* pencil sharpener
**sacar** (sah-*kahr*) *v* *take out; *draw; ~ **brillo** brush
**sacerdote** (sah-thayr-*dhoa*-tay) *m* priest
**saco** (*sah*-koa) *m* sack; *mMe* jacket; ~ **de compras** shopping bag; ~ **de dormir** sleeping bag
**sacrificar** (sah-kree-fee-*kahr*) *v* sacrifice
**sacrificio** (sah-kree-*fee*-th$^y$oa) *m* sacrifice
**sacrilegio** (sah-kree-*lay*-kh$^y$oa) *m* sacrilege
**sacudir** (sah-koo-*dheer*) *v* *shake
**sagrado** (sah-*grah*-dhoa) *adj* sacred
**sal** (sahl) *f* salt; **sales de baño** bath

salts

**sala** (*sah*-lah) *f* hall; lounge; **~ de conciertos** concert hall; **~ de espera** waiting room; **~ de estar** sitting room, living room; **~ de lectura** reading room; **~ para fumar** smoking room

**salado** (sah-*lah*-dhoa) *adj* salty

**salario** (sah-*lah*-r$^y$oa) *m* pay

**salchicha** (sahl-*chee*-chah) *f* sausage

**saldo** (*sahl*-doa) *m* balance

**salero** (sah-*lay*-roa) *m* salt cellar, salt shaker *Am*

**salida** (sah-*lee*-dhah) *f* issue, exit, way out; **~ de emergencia** emergency exit

***salir** (sah-*leer*) *v* *go out; appear

**saliva** (sah-*lee*-bhah) *f* spit

**salmón** (sahl-*moan*) *m* salmon

**salón** (sah-*loan*) *m* salon, lounge, drawing-room; **~ de baile** ballroom; **~ de belleza** beauty parlo(u)r; **~ de demostraciones** showroom; **~ de té** tea-shop

**salpicar** (sahl-pee-*kahr*) *v* splash; splatter; sprinkle

**salsa** (*sahl*-sah) *f* sauce; gravy

**saltamontes** (sahl-tah-*moan*-tayss) *m* grasshopper

**saltar** (sahl-*tahr*) *v* jump, *leap; skip, hop

**salto** (*sahl*-toa) *m* jump, leap, hop

**salud** (sah-*loodh*) *f* health

**saludable** (sah-loo-*dhah*-bhlay) *adj* wholesome

**saludar** (sah-loo-*dhahr*) *v* greet; salute

**saludo** (sah-*loo*-dhoa) *m* greeting

**salvador** (sahl-bhah-*dhoar*) *m* savio(u)r

**salvaje** (sahl-*bhah*-khay) *adj* wild, savage; fierce, desert

**salvar** (sahl-*bhahr*) *v* save

**sanatorio** (sah-nah-*toa*-r$^y$oa) *m* sanatorium

**sandalia** (sahn-*dah*-l$^y$ah) *f* sandal

**sandía** (sahn-*dee*-ah) *f* watermelon

**sangrar** (sahng-*grahr*) *v* *bleed

**sangre** (*sahng*-gray) *f* blood

**sangriento** (sahng-*gr$^y$ayn*-toa) *adj* bloody

**sanitario** (sah-nee-*tah*-r$^y$oa) *adj* sanitary

**sano** (*sah*-noa) *adj* healthy, well

**santo** (*sahn*-toa) *adj* holy; *m* saint; **~ y seña** password

**santuario** (sahn-*twah*-r$^y$oa) *m* shrine

**sapo** (*sah*-poa) *m* toad

**sarampión** (sah-rahm-*p$^y$oan*) *m* measles

**sardina** (sahr-*dhee*-nah) *f* sardine

**sartén** (sahr-*tayn*) *f* frying pan

**sastre** (*sahss*-tray) *m* tailor

**satélite** (sah-*tay*-lee-tay) *m* satellite

**satisfacción** (sah-teess-fahk-*th$^y$oan*) *f* satisfaction

***satisfacer** (sah-teess-fah-*thayr*) *v* satisfy; **satisfecho** satisfied

**saudí** (sou-*dhee*) *adj* Saudi Arabian

**sauna** (*sou*-nah) *f* sauna

**sazonar** (sah-thoa-*nahr*) *v* season, flavo(u)r

**se** (say) *pron* himself; herself; yourselves; themselves

**secadora** (say-kah-*dhoa*-rah) *f* dryer

**secar** (say-*kahr*) *v* dry

**sección** (sayk-*th$^y$oan*) *f* section; agency

**seco** (*say*-koa) *adj* dry

**secretario** (say-kray-*tah*-r$^y$oa) *m*, **-a** *f* secretary

**secreto** (say-*kray*-toa) *adj* secret; *m* secret

**sector** (sayk-*toar*) *m* sector

**secuencia** (say-*kwayn*-th$^y$ah) *f* shot

**secuestrador** (say-kwayss-trah-*dhoar*) *m* hijacker

**secundario** (say-koon-*dah*-r$^y$oa) *adj* secondary; minor

**sed** (saydh) *f* thirst
**seda** (*say*-dhah) *f* silk
**sede** (*say*-dhay) *f* seat; headquarters
**sediento** (say-*dh$^y$ayn*-toa) *adj* thirsty
***seducir** (say-dhoo-*theer*) *v* seduce
**en seguida** (ayn say-*gee*-dhah) straight away, at once, presently
***seguir** (say-*geer*) *v* follow; **~ el paso** *keep up with; **todo seguido** straight on, straight ahead
**según** (say-*goon*) *prep* according to
**segundo** (say-*goon*-doa) *num* second; *m* second
**seguramente** (say-goo-rah-*mayn*-tay) *adv* surely
**seguridad** (say-goo-ree-*dhahdh*) *f* security, safety; **cinturón de ~** safety belt
**seguro** (say-*goo*-roa) *adj* safe; sure; *m* insurance; **póliza de ~** insurance policy; **~ de viaje** travel insurance; **~ de vida** life insurance
**seis** (sayss) *num* six
**selección** (say-layk-*th$^y$oan*) *f* selection; choice
**seleccionado** (say-layk-th$^y$oa-*nah*-dhoa) *adj* select
**seleccionar** (say-layk-th$^y$oa-*nahr*) *v* select
**selecto** (say-*layk*-toa) *adj* select
**selva** (*sayl*-bhah) *f* jungle, forest
**selvoso** (sayl-*bhoa*-soa) *adj* wooded
**sellar** (say-*l$^y$ahr*) *v* stamp; seal
**sello** (*say*-l$^y$oa) *m* stamp; seal
**semáforo** (say-*mah*-foa-roa) *m* traffic light
**semana** (say-*mah*-nah) *f* week; **fin de ~** weekend
**semanal** (say-mah-*nahl*) *adj* weekly
***sembrar** (saym-*brahr*) *v* *sow
**semejante** (say-may-*khahn*-tay) *adj* like
**semejanza** (say-may-*khahn*-thah) *f* resemblance, similarity
**semi-** (*say*-mee) semi-
**semicírculo** (say-mee-*theer*-koo-loa) *m* semicircle
**semilla** (say-*mee*-l$^y$ah) *f* seed
**senado** (say-*nah*-dhoa) *m* senate
**senador** (say-nah-*dhoar*) *m* senator
**sencillo** (sayn-*thee*-l$^y$oa) *adj* plain
**senda** (*sayn*-dah) *f* footpath
**sendero** (sayn-*day*-roa) *m* trail
**senil** (say-*neel*) *adj* senile
**seno** (*say*-noa) *m* bosom; breast
**sensación** (sayn-sah-*th$^y$oan*) *f* sensation; feeling
**sensacional** (sayn-sah-th$^y$oa-*nahl*) *adj* sensational
**sensato** (sayn-*sah*-toa) *adj* sensible; down-to-earth
**sensibilidad** (sayn-see-bhee-lee-*dhahdh*) *f* sensibility
**sensible** (sayn-*see*-bhlay) *adj* sensitive; noticeable; sentient
**sensitivo** (sayn-see-*tee*-bhoa) *adj* sensitive
***sentarse** (sayn-*tahr*-say) *v* *sit down; ***estar sentado** *sit; ***sentar bien** *become
**sentencia** (sayn-*tayn*-th$^y$ah) *f* sentence, verdict
**sentenciar** (sayn-tayn-*th$^y$ahr*) *v* sentence
**sentido** (sayn-*tee*-dhoa) *m* sense; reason; **~ del honor** sense of hono(u)r; **sin ~** meaningless
**sentimental** (sayn-tee-mayn-*tahl*) *adj* sentimental
**sentimiento** (sayn-tee-*m$^y$ayn*-toa) *m* sentiment
***sentir** (sayn-*teer*) *v* *feel, sense; regret
**seña** (*say*-ñah) *f* sign; **señas personales** description
**señal** (say-*ñahl*) *f* signal, sign, indication; *m* token, tick; ***hacer señales** signal; wave; **~ de alarma** distress signal

**señalar** (say-ñah-*lahr*) *v* tick off, indicate
**señor** (say-*ñoar*) *m* mister; sir
**señora** (say-*ñoa*-rah) *f* lady; madam
**señorita** (say-ñoa-*ree*-tah) *f* young lady; miss
**separación** (say-pah-rah-*th$^{y}$oan*) *f* division
**separadamente** (say-pah-rah-dhah-*mayn*-tay) *adv* apart
**separado** (say-pah-*rah*-dhoa) *adj* separate; **por ~** apart, separately
**separar** (say-pah-*rahr*) *v* separate, part; divide; detach
**sepia** (*say*-p$^{y}$ah) *f* cuttlefish
**septentrional** (sayp-tayn-tr$^{y}$oa-*nahl*) *adj* north
**septicemia** (sayp-tee-*thay*-m$^{y}$ah) *f* blood-poisoning
**séptico** (*sayp*-tee-koa) *adj* septic
**septiembre** (sayp-*t$^{y}$aym*-bray) September
**séptimo** (*sayp*-tee-moa) *num* seventh
**sepulcro** (say-*pool*-kroa) *m* sepulchre, sepulcher *Am*
**sepultura** (say-pool-*too*-rah) *f* grave
**sequía** (say-*kee*-ah) *f* drought
**ser** (sayr) *m* being, creature; **~ humano** human being
***ser** (sayr) *v* *be
**sereno** (say-*ray*-noa) *adj* serene
**serie** (*say*-r$^{y}$ay) *f* series; sequence
**seriedad** (say-r$^{y}$ay-*dhahdh*) *f* seriousness, gravity
**serio** (*say*-r$^{y}$oa) *adj* serious
**sermón** (sayr-*moan*) *m* sermon
**serpiente** (sayr- *p$^{y}$ayn*-tay) *f* snake; **~ de cascabel** rattlesnake
**serrín** (say-*rreen*) *m* sawdust
**servicial** (sayr-bhee-*th$^{y}$ahl*) *adj* helpful
**servicio** (sayr-*bhee*-th$^{y}$oa) *m* service; service charge; **~ de habitación** room service; **~ de mesa** dinner service; **~ postal** postal service
**servilleta** (sayr-bhee-*l$^{y}$ay*-tah) *f* napkin, serviette; **~ de papel** paper napkin
***servir** (sayr-*bheer*) *v* serve; attend on, wait on; *be of use
**sesenta** (say-*sayn*-tah) *num* sixty
**sesión** (say-*s$^{y}$oan*) *f* session
**seta** (*say*-tah) *f* mushroom
**setenta** (say-*tayn*-tah) *num* seventy
**seto** (*say*-toa) *m* hedge
**severo** (say-*bhay*-roa) *adj* harsh, strict, severe
**sexo** (*sayk*-soa) *m* sex
**sexto** (*sayks*-toa) *num* sixth
**sexual** (sayk-*swahl*) *adj* sexual
**sexualidad** (sayk-swah-lee-*dhahdh*) *f* sexuality; sex
**si** (see) *conj* if; in case; whether; **si … o** whether … or; **~ bien** though
**sí** (see) yes
**siamés** (s$^{y}$ah-*mayss*) *adj* Siamese; *m* Siamese
**SIDA** (*see*-dhah) *m* AIDS
**siempre** (*s$^{y}$aym*-pray) *adv* ever, always
**sien** (s$^{y}$ayn) *f* temple
**sierra** (*s$^{y}$ay*-rrah) *f* saw
**siesta** (*s$^{y}$ayss*-tah) *f* nap
**siete** (*s$^{y}$ay*-tay) *num* seven
**siglo** (*see*-gloa) *m* century
**significado** (seeg-nee-fee-*kah*-dhoa) *m* meaning
**significar** (seeg-nee-fee-*kahr*) *v* *mean
**significativo** (seeg-nee-fee-kah-*tee*-bhoa) *adj* significant
**signo** (*seeg*-noa) *m* sign; **~ de interrogación** question mark
**siguiente** (see-*g$^{y}$ayn*-tay) *adj* following
**sílaba** (*see*-lah-bhah) *f* syllable
**silbar** (seel-*bhahr*) *v* whistle
**silbato** (seel-*bhah*-toa) *m* whistle
**silenciador** (see-layn-th$^{y}$ah-*dhoar*) *m*

silencer
**silencio** (see-*layn*-th$^y$oa) *m* quiet, silence
**silencioso** (see-layn-*th$^y$oa*-soa) *adj* silent
**silla** (*see*-l$^y$ah) *f* chair; ~ **de montar** saddle; **de ruedas** wheelchair
**sillón** (see-*l$^y$oan*) *m* armchair
**simbólico** (seem-*boa*-lee-koa) *adj* symbolic
**símbolo** (*seem*-boa-loa) *m* symbol
**similar** (see-mee-*lahr*) *adj* similar
**simpatía** (seem-pah-*tee*-ah) *f* sympathy
**simpático** (seem-*pah*-tee-koa) *adj* nice, pleasant; obliging
**simple** (*seem*-play) *adj* simple
**simular** (see-moo-*lahr*) *v* simulate
**simultáneo** (see-mool-*tah*-nay-oa) *adj* simultaneous
**sin** (seen) *prep* without
**sinagoga** (see-nah-*goa*-gah) *f* synagogue
**sincero** (seen-*thay*-roa) *adj* sincere; open, honest
**sindicato** (seen-dee-*kah*-toa) *m* trade-union
**sinfonía** (seen-foa-*nee*-ah) *f* symphony
**singular** (seeng-goo-*lahr*) *adj* singular, queer; *m* singular
**siniestro** (see-*n$^y$ayss*-troa) *adj* ominous, sinister
**sino** (*see*-noa) *conj* but
**sinónimo** (see-*noa*-nee-moa) *m* synonym
**sintético** (seen-*tay*-tee-koa) *adj* synthetic
**síntoma** (*seen*-toa-mah) *m* symptom
**sintonizar** (seen-toa-nee-*thahr*) *v* tune in
**siquiera** (see-*k$^y$ay*-rah) *adv* at least; *conj* even though
**sirena** (see-*ray*-nah) *f* siren; mermaid
**Siria** (*see*-r$^y$ah) *f* Syria
**sirio** (*see*-r$^y$oa) *adj* Syrian; *m* Syrian
**sirviente** (seer-*bh$^y$ayn*-tay) *m* domestic
**sistema** (seess-*tay*-mah) *m* system; ~ **decimal** decimal system; ~ **de lubricación** lubrication system; ~ **de refrigeración** cooling system
**sistemático** (seess-tay-*mah*-tee-koa) *adj* systematic
**sitio** (*see*-t$^y$oa) *m* site; seat, room; siege
**situación** (see-twah-*th$^y$oan*) *f* situation
**situado** (see-*twah*-dhoa) *adj* situated
**situar** (see-*twahr*) *v* locate
**slogan** (*sloa*-gahn) *m* slogan
**smoking** (*smoa*-keeng) *m* dinner jacket; tuxedo *Am*
**soberano** (soa-bhay-*rah*-noa) *m* sovereign
**soberbio** (soa-*bhayr*-bh$^y$oa) *adj* superb
**sobornar** (soa-bhoar-*nahr*) *v* bribe
**soborno** (soa-*bhoar*-noa) *m* bribery
**sobra** (*soa*-bhrah) *f* surplus
**sobrar** (soa-*bhrahr*) *v* *be left over; *be in plenty
**sobre** (*soa*-bhray) *prep* on, upon; *m* envelope
**sobrecubierta** (soa-bhray-koo-*bh$^y$ayr*-tah) *f* jacket (of book)
**sobreexcitado** (soa-bhray-ayk-thee-*tah*-dhoa) *adj* overexcited
**sobrepeso** (soa-bhray-*pay*-soa) *m* overweight
**sobretasa** (soa-bhray-*tah*-sah) *f* surcharge
**sobrevivir** (soa-bhray-bhee-*bheer*) *v* survive
**sobrina** (soa-*bhree*-nah) *f* niece
**sobrino** (soa-*bhree*-noa) *m* nephew
**sobrio** (*soa*-bhr$^y$oa) *adj* sober
**social** (soa-*th$^y$ahl*) *adj* social
**socialismo** (soa-th$^y$ah-*leez*-moa) *m*

socialism
**socialista** (soa-th$^y$ah-*leess*-tah) *adj* socialist; *m* socialist
**sociedad** (soa-th$^y$ay-*dhahdh*) *f* community, society; company
**socio** (*soa*-th$^y$oa) *m*, **-a** *f* associate; partner
**socorro** (soa-*koa*-rroa) *m* aid; **puesto de ~** first aid post
**soda** (*soa*-dhah) *f* soda water
**sofá** (soa-*fah*) *m* sofa
**sofocante** (soa-foa-*kahn*-tay) *adj* stuffy
**sofocarse** (soa-foa-*kahr*-say) *v* choke
**soga** (*soa*-gah) *f* rope
**sol** (soal) *m* sun; **tomar el ~** sunbathe
**solamente** (soa-lah-*mayn*-tay) *adv* merely, only
**solapa** (soa-*lah*-pah) *f* lapel
**soldado** (soal-*dah*-dhoa) *m* soldier
**soldadura** (soal-dah-*dhoo*-rah) *f* joint
**soleado** (soa-lay-*ah*-dhoa) *adj* sunny
**soledad** (soa-lay-*dhahdh*) *f* solitude
**solemne** (soa-*laym*-nay) *adj* solemn
***soler** (soa-*layr*) *v* would
**solicitar** (soa-lee-thee-*tahr*) *v* request; **~ un puesto** apply
**solicitud** (soa-lee-thee-*toodh*) *f* application
**sólido** (*soa*-lee-dhoa) *adj* solid, firm; *m* solid
**solitario** (soa-lee-*tah*-r$^y$oa) *adj* lonely
**solo** (*soa*-loa) *adj* alone, lonely, single
**sólo** (*soa*-loa) *adv* only; solely; just
**solomillo** (soa-loa-*mee*-l$^y$oa) *m* sirloin
***soltar** (soal-*tahr*) *v* loosen
**soltero** (soal-*tay*-roa) *adj* single, unmarried
**solterón** (soal-tay-*roan*) *m* confirmed bachelor
**solterona** (soal-tay-*roa*-nah) *f* spinster
**soluble** (soa-*loo*-bhlay) *adj* soluble
**solución** (soa-loo-*th$^y$oan*) *f* solution
**sombra** (*soam*-brah) *f* shade; shadow; **~ para los ojos** eye shadow
**sombreado** (soam-bray-*ah*-dhoa) *adj* shady
**sombrerera** (soam-bray-*ray*-rah) *f* milliner
**sombrero** (soam-*bray*-roa) *m* hat
**sombrío** (soam-*bree*-oa) *adj* sombre, somber *Am*; gloomy
**someter** (soa-may-*tayr*) *v* subject; **someterse** *v* submit
**somnífero** (soam-*nee*-fay-roa) *m* sleeping pill
***sonar** (soa-*nahr*) *v* sound; *ring
**sonido** (soa-*nee*-dhoa) *m* sound
**sonreír** (soan-ray-*eer*) *v* smile
**sonrisa** (soan-*ree*-sah) *f* smile
***soñar** (soa-*ñahr*) *v* *dream
**soñoliento** (soa-ñoa-*l$^y$ayn*-toa) *adj* sleepy
**sopa** (*soa*-pah) *f* soup
**soplar** (soa-*plahr*) *v* *blow
**soportar** (soa-poar-*tahr*) *v* *bear, endure, sustain; support
**sóquet** (*soa*-kayt) *mMe* socket
**sorbo** (*soar*-bhoa) *m* sip
**sórdido** (*soar*-dhee-dhoa) *adj* filthy
**sordo** (*soar*-dhoa) *adj* deaf
**sorprender** (soar-prayn-*dayr*) *v* surprise; *catch
**sorpresa** (soar-*pray*-sah) *f* surprise; astonishment
**sorteo** (soar-*tay*-oa) *m* draw
**soso** (*soa*-soa) *adj* dull, boring; tasteless
**sospecha** (soass-*pay*-chah) *f* suspicion
**sospechar** (soass-pay-*chahr*) *v* suspect
**sospechoso** (soass-pay-*choa*-soa) *adj* suspicious; **persona sospechosa** suspect
**sostén** (soass-*tayn*) *m* brassière, bra; support

***sostener** (soass-tay-*nayr*) *v* support, *hold up
**sota** (*soa*-tah) *f* knave
**sótano** (*soa*-tah-noa) *m* basement; cellar
**soto** (*soa*-toa) *m* grove
**stárter** (*stahr*-tayr) *m* choke
**su** (soo) *adj* his; her; their
**suahili** (swah-*ee*-lee) *m* Swahili
**suave** (*swah*-bhay) *adj* mild, mellow; gentle
**subacuático** (soo-bhah-*kwah*-tee-koa) *adj* underwater
**subalterno** (soo-bhahl-*tayr*-noa) *adj* subordinate
**subasta** (soo-*bhahss*-tah) *f* auction
**súbdito** (*soobh*-dhee-toa) *m* subject
**subestimar** (soo-bhayss-tee-*mahr*) *v* underestimate
**subida** (soo-*bhee*-dhah) *f* climb, rise, ascent
**subir** (soo-*bheer*) *v* *rise, ascend; *get on
**súbito** (*soo*-bhee-toa) *adj* sudden
**sublevación** (soo-bhlay-bhah-*th$^y$oan*) *f* rebellion
**sublevarse** (soo-bhlay-*bhahr*-say) *v* revolt
**subordinado** (soo-bhoar-dhee-*nah*-dhoa) *adj* subordinate
**subrayar** (soobh-rah-*$^y$ahr*) *v* underline
**subsidio** (soobh-*see*-dh$^y$oa) *m* subsidy
**substancia** (soobhs-*tahn*-th$^y$ah) *f* substance
**substantivo** (soobh-stahn-*tee*-bhoa) *m* noun
***substituir** (soobhs-tee-*tweer*) *v* replace
**subterráneo** (soobh-tay-*rrah*-nay-oa) *adj* underground
**subtítulo** (soobh-*tee*-too-loa) *m* subtitle
**suburbano** (soo-bhoor-*bhah*-noa) *adj* suburban; *m* commuter
**suburbio** (soo-*bhoor*-bh$^y$oa) *m* suburb
**subvención** (soobh-bhayn-*th$^y$oan*) *f* grant
**suceder** (soo-thay-*dhayr*) *v* happen, occur; succeed
**sucesión** (soo-thay-*s$^y$oan*) *f* sequence
**suceso** (soo-*thay*-soa) *m* event
**suciedad** (soo-th$^y$ay-*dhahdh*) *f* dirt; filth
**sucio** (*soo*-th$^y$oa) *adj* dirty; unclean, foul
**sucursal** (soo-koor-*sahl*) *f* branch
**sudar** (soo-*dhahr*) *v* perspire, sweat
**sudeste** (soo-*dhayss*-tay) *m* south-east
**sudoeste** (soo-dhoa-*ayss*-tay) *m* south-west
**sudor** (soo-*dhoar*) *m* perspiration, sweat
**Suecia** (*sway*-th$^y$ah) *f* Sweden
**sueco** (*sway*-koa) *adj* Swedish; *m* Swede
**suegra** (*sway*-grah) *f* mother-in-law
**suegro** (*sway*-groa) *m* father-in-law
**suela** (*sway*-lah) *f* sole
**sueldo** (*swayl*-doa) *m* salary, pay; **aumento de ~** rise; raise *Am*
**suelo** (*sway*-loa) *m* soil, earth; floor
**suelto** (*swayl*-toa) *adj* loose; free; detached
**sueño** (*sway*-ñoa) *m* sleep; dream
**suero** (*sway*-roa) *m* serum
**suerte** (*swayr*-tay) *f* luck; fortune, lot; chance; **mala ~** bad luck
**suéter** (*sway*-tayr) *m* sweater
**suficiente** (soo-fee-*th$^y$ayn*-tay) *adj* enough, sufficient; ***ser ~** *do
**sufragio** (soo-*frah*-kh$^y$oa) *m* suffrage
**sufrimiento** (soo-free-*m$^y$ayn*-toa) *m* affliction, sorrow, suffering
**sufrir** (soo-*freer*) *v* suffer
***sugerir** (soo-khay-*reer*) *v* suggest

**sugestión** (soo-khayss-*t$^y$oan*) *f* suggestion
**suicidio** (swee-*thee*-dh$^y$oa) *m* suicide
**Suiza** (*swee*-thah) *f* Switzerland
**suizo** (*swee*-thoa) *adj* Swiss; *m* Swiss
**sujetador** (soo-khay-tah-*dhoar*) *m* fastener; clip; bra
**sujeto** (soo-*khay*-toa) *m* subject; theme
**sujeto a** (soo-*khay*-toa ah) liable to, subject to
**suma** (*soo*-mah) *f* amount, sum
**sumar** (soo-*mahr*) *v* add; amount to
**sumario** (soo-*mah*-r$^y$oa) *m* summary
**suministrar** (soo-mee-neess-*trahr*) *v* furnish, supply
**suministro** (soo-mee-*neess*-troa) *m* supply
**sumo** (*soo*-moa) *adj* supreme; **a lo ~** at most
**superar** (soo-pay-*rahr*) *v* exceed, *outdo
**superficial** (soo-payr-fee-*th$^y$ahl*) *adj* superficial
**superficie** (soo-payr-*fee*-th$^y$ay) *f* surface; area
**superfluo** (soo-*payr*-flwoa) *adj* superfluous, redundant
**superior** (soo-pay-*r$^y$oar*) *adj* superior, upper; top
**superlativo** (soo-payr-lah-*tee*-bhoa) *adj* superlative; *m* superlative
**supermercado** (soo-payr-mayr-*kah*-dhoa) *m* supermarket
**superstición** (soo-payrs-tee-*th$^y$oan*) *f* superstition
**supervisar** (soo-payr-bhee-*sahr*) *v* supervise
**supervisión** (soo-payr-bhee-*s$^y$oan*) *f* supervision
**supervisor** (soo-payr-bhee-*soar*) *m*, **-a** *f* supervisor
**supervivencia** (soo-payr-bhee-*bhayn*-th$^y$ah) *f* survival
**suplemento** (soo-play-*mayn*-toa) *m* supplement
**suplicar** (soo-plee-*kahr*) *v* beg
***suponer** (soo-poa-*nayr*) *v* assume, suppose
**supositorio** (soo-poa-see-*toa*-r$^y$oa) *m* suppository
**supremo** (soo-*pray*-moa) *adj* supreme
**suprimir** (soo-pree-*meer*) *v* discontinue
**por supuesto** (poar soo-*pwayss*-toa) naturally, of course
**sur** (soor) *m* south; **polo ~** South Pole
**surco** (*soor*-koa) *m* groove
**surgir** (soor-*kheer*) *v* *arise
**surtido** (soor-*tee*-dhoa) *m* assortment
**suscribir** (sooss-kree-*bheer*) *v* sign
**suscripción** (sooss-kreep-*th$^y$oan*) *f* subscription
**suspender** (sooss-payn-*dayr*) *v* suspend; ***ser suspendido** fail
**suspensión** (sooss-payn-*s$^y$oan*) *f* suspension
**suspicacia** (sooss-pee-*kah*-th$^y$ah) *f* suspicion
**suspicaz** (sooss-pee-*kahth*) *adj* suspicious
**sustancia** (sooss-*tahn*-th$^y$ah) *f* substance
**sustancial** (sooss-tahn-*th$^y$ahl*) *adj* substantial
**sustento** (sooss-*tayn*-toa) *m* livelihood
***sustituir** (sooss-tee-*tweer*) *v* substitute
**sustituto** (sooss-tee-*too*-toa) *m*, **-a** *f* deputy, substitute
**susto** (*sooss*-toa) *m* scare
**susurrar** (soo-soo-*rrahr*) *v* whisper
**susurro** (soo-*soo*-rroa) *m* whisper
**sutil** (soo-*teel*) *adj* subtle; fine; delicate
**sutura** (soo-*too*-rah) *f* stitch; ***hacer una ~** sew up
**suyo** (*soo*-$^y$oa) *pron* his

# T

**tabaco** (tah-*bhah*-koa) *m* tobacco; **~ de pipa** pipe tobacco
**taberna** (tah-*bhayr*-nah) *f* public house, pub; tavern; **moza de ~** barmaid
**tabla** (*tah*-bhlah) *f* board; chart, table; **~ de conversión** conversion chart; **~ para surf** surfboard
**tablero** (tah-*bhlay*-roa) *m* board; **~ de ajedrez** chessboard; **~ de damas** draughtboard, checkerboard *AmAm*; **~ de instrumentos** dashboard
**tablón** (tah-*bhloan*) *m* plank
**tabú** (tah-*bhoo*) *m* taboo
**taburete** (tah-bhoo-*ray*-tay) *m* stool
**tacón** (tah-*koan*) *m* heel
**táctica** (*tahk*-tee-kah) *f* tactics *pl*
**tacto** (*tahk*-toa) *m* touch; tact
**tailandés** (tigh-lahn-*dayss*) *adj* Thai; *m* Thai
**Tailandia** (tigh-*lahn*-d$^{y}$ah) *f* Thailand
**tajada** (tah-*khah*-dhah) *f* slice
**tajar** (tah-*khahr*) *v* chop
**tal** (tahl) *adj* such; **con ~ que** provided that; **~ como** such as
**taladrar** (tah-lah-*dhrahr*) drill, bore
**taladro** (tah-*lah*-dhroa) *m* drill
**talco** (*tahl*-koa) *m* talc powder
**talento** (tah-*layn*-toa) *m* gift, talent
**talentoso** (tah-layn-*toa*-soa) *adj* gifted, talented
**talismán** (tah-leez-*mahn*) *m* lucky charm
**talón** (tah-*loan*) *m* heel; counterfoil, stub
**talonario** (tah-loa-*nah*-r$^{y}$oa) *m* chequebook; checkbook *Am*
**talla** (*tah*-l$^{y}$ah) *f* carving
**tallar** (tah-*l$^{y}$ahr*) *v* carve
**taller** (tah-*l$^{y}$ayr*) *m* workshop
**tallo** (*tah*-l$^{y}$oa) *m* stem
**tamaño** (tah-*mah*-ñoa) *m* size; **~ extraordinario** outsize
**también** (tahm-*b$^{y}$ayn*) *adv* too, also, as well; **así ~** likewise
**tambor** (tahm-*boar*) *m* drum; **~ del freno** brake drum
**tamiz** (tah-*meeth*) *m* sieve
**tamizar** (tah-mee-*thahr*) *v* sift, sieve
**tampoco** (tahm-*poa*-koa) *adv* not … either
**tampón** (tahm-*poan*) *m* tampon
**tan** (tahn) *adv* so, such
**tangible** (tahng-*khee*-bhlay) *adj* tangible
**tanque** (*tahng*-kay) *m* tank
**tanteo** (tahn-*tay*-oa) *m* score
**tanto** (*tahn*-toa) *adv* as much; as; **por lo ~** therefore; **por ~** so; **tanto … como** both … and
**tapa** (*tah*-pah) *f* lid, top, cover; appetizer
**tapizar** (tah-pee-*thahr*) *v* upholster
**tapón** (tah-*poan*) *m* stopper, cork
**taquigrafía** (tah-kee-grah-*fee*-ah) *f* shorthand
**taquilla** (tah-*kee*-l$^{y}$ah) *f* box office
**tararear** (tah-rah-ray-*ahr*) *v* hum
**tardanza** (tahr-*dhahn*-thah) *f* delay
**tardar** (tahr-*dahr*) *v* take a long time; **a más ~** at the latest; **¡no tardes!** don't be late; **¿cuánto se tarda …?** how long does it take to …?
**tarde** (*tahr*-dhay) *f* afternoon; evening
**tardío** (tahr-*dhee*-oa) *adj* late
**tarea** (tah-*ray*-ah) *f* duty, task; job
**tarifa** (tah-*ree*-fah) *f* rate; **~ nocturna** night rate
**tarjeta** (tahr-*khay*-tah) *f* card; **~ de crédito** credit card; charge plate *Am*; **~ de temporada** season ticket; **~ de visita** visiting-card; **~ postal** postcard, card; **~ postal ilustrada**

picture postcard; ~ **telefónica** phone card; ~ **verde** green card
**tarta** (*tahr*-tah) *f* cake
**taxi** (*tahk*-see) *m* cab, taxi
**taxímetro** (tahk-*see*-may-troa) *m* taximeter
**taxista** (tahk-*seess*-tah) *m/f* cab driver, taxi driver
**taza** (*tah*-thah) *f* cup; mug; ~ **de café** cup of coffee; ~ **de té** cup of tea
**tazón** (tah-*thoan*) *m* bowl, basin
**te** (tay) *pron* yourself
**té** (tay) *m* tea
**teatro** (tay-*ah*-troa) *m* drama; theatre; ~ **de la ópera** opera house; ~ **de variedades** music hall, variety theatre (theater *Am*); ~ **guiñol** puppet show
**tebeo** (tay-*bhay*-oa) *m* comics *pl*
**técnica** (*tayk*-nee-kah) *f* technique
**técnico** (*tayk*-nee-koa) *adj* technical; *m* technician
**tecnología** (tayk-noa-loa-*khee*-ah) *f* technology
**techo** (*tay*-choa) *m* roof; ~ **de paja** thatched roof
**tecla** (*tay*-klah) *f* key
**teja** (*tay*-khah) *f* tile
**tejado** (tay-*khah*-doa) *m* roof
**tejedor** (tay-khay-*dhoar*) *m*, **-a** *f* weaver
**tejer** (tay-*khayr*) *v* *weave
**tejido** (tay-*khee*-dhoa) *m* fabric, tissue, material
**tele** (*tay*-lay) *f* TV
**tela** (*tay*-lah) *f* cloth; ~ **para toallas** towel(l)ing
**telaraña** (tay-lah-*rah*-ñah) *f* spider's web
**telefax** (tay-lay-*fahks*) *m* fax; **mandar un** ~ send a fax
**telefonear** (tay-lay-foa-nay-*ahr*) *v* phone; call up *Am*
**telefonista** (tay-lay-foa-*neess*-tah) *f* telephonist, telephone operator
**teléfono** (tay-*lay*-foa-noa) *m* phone, telephone; **llamar por** ~ ring up
**telegrafiar** (tay-lay-grah-*f*ʸ*ahr*) *v* telegraph
**teleobjetivo** (tay-lay-oabh-khay-*tee*-bhoa) *m* telephoto lens
**telepatía** (tay-lay-pah-*tee*-ah) *f* telepathy
**telesilla** (tay-lay-*see*-lʸah) *m* ski lift
**televisión** (tay-lay-bhee-*s*ʸ*oan*) *f* television; ~ **por cable** cable television; ~ **por satélite** satellite television
**televisor** (tay-lay-bhee-*soar*) *m* television set
**télex** (*tay*-layks) *m* telex
**telón** (tay-*loan*) *m* stage curtain
**tema** (*tay*-mah) *m* theme
***temblar** (taym-*bhlahr*) *v* tremble, shiver
**temer** (tay-*mayr*) *v* fear, dread
**temor** (tay-*moar*) *m* fear, dread
**temperamento** (taym-pay-rah-*mayn*-toa) *m* temperament
**temperatura** (taym-pay-rah-*too*-rah) *f* temperature; ~ **ambiente** room temperature
**tempestad** (taym-payss-*tahdh*) *f* tempest
**tempestuoso** (taym-payss-*twoa*-soa) *adj* stormy
**templo** (*taym*-ploa) *m* temple
**temporada** (taym-poa-*rah*-dhah) *f* season; **alta** ~ high season; ~ **baja** low season
**temporal** (taym-poa-*rahl*) *adj* temporary
**temprano** (taym-*prah*-noa) *adj* early
**tenazas** (tay-*nah*-thahss) *f* tongs *pl*, pincers *pl*
**tendencia** (tayn-*dayn*-thʸah) *f* tendency
***tender** (tayn-*dayr*): ~ **a** tend;

***tenderse** *v* *lie down
**tendero** (tayn-*day*-roa) *m*, **-a** *f* shopkeeper; tradesman
**tendón** (tayn-*doan*) *m* sinew, tendon
**tenedor** (tay-nay-*dhoar*) *m* fork
***tener** (tay-*nayr*) *v* *have; *keep, *hold; **~ que** *must; *ought to, *should, *shall; *be obliged to; **tenga usted** here you are
**teniente** (tay-*n$^y$ayn*-tay) *m* lieutenant
**tenis** (*tay*-neess) *m* tennis; **~ de mesa** ping-pong, table tennis
**tensión** (tayn-*s$^y$oan*) *f* strain, pressure, tension; **~ arterial** blood pressure
**tenso** (*tayn*-soa) *adj* tense
**tentación** (tayn-tah-*th$^y$oan*) *f* temptation
***tentar** (tayn-*tahr*) *v* tempt
**tentativa** (tayn-tah-*tee*-bhah) *f* attempt, try
**tentempié** (tayn-taym-*p$^y$ay*) *m* snack
***teñir** (tay-*ñeer*) *v* dye
**teología** (tay-oa-loa-*khee*-ah) *f* theology
**teoría** (tay-oa-*ree*-ah) *f* theory
**teórico** (tay-*oa*-ree-koa) *adj* theoretical
**terapia** (tay-*rah*-p$^y$ah) *f* therapy
**tercero** (tayr-*thay*-roa) *num* third
**terciopelo** (tayr-th$^y$oa-*pay*-loa) *m* velvet
**terminación** (tayr-mee-nah-*th$^y$oan*) *f* finish
**terminar** (tayr-mee-*nahr*) *v* end, finish; accomplish; **terminarse** *v* expire, end
**término** (*tayr*-mee-noa) *m* term; issue
**termo** (*tayr*-moa) *m* vacuum flask, thermos flask
**termómetro** (tayr-*moa*-may-troa) *m* thermometer
**termostato** (tayr-moass-*tah*-toa) *m* thermostat
**ternero** (tayr-*nay*-roa) *m* calf
**ternura** (tayr-*noo*-rah) *f* tenderness
**terraplén** (tay-rrah-*playn*) *m* embankment
**terraza** (tay-*rrah*-thah) *f* terrace
**terremoto** (tay-rray-*moa*-toa) *m* earthquake
**terreno** (tay-*rray*-noa) *m* terrain; field, grounds
**terrible** (tay-*rree*-bhlay) *adj* frightful; awful, horrible, terrible, dreadful
**territorio** (tay-rree-*toa*-r$^y$oa) *m* territory
**terrón** (tay-*rroan*) *m* lump
**terror** (tay-*rroar*) *m* terror; terrorism
**terrorismo** (tay-rroa-*reez*-moa) *m* terrorism
**terrorista** (tay-rroa-*reess*-tah) *m/f* terrorist
**tesis** (*tay*-seess) *f* thesis
**Tesorería** (tay-soa-ray-*ree*-ah) *f* treasury
**tesorero** (tay-soa-*ray*-roa) *m* treasurer
**tesoro** (tay-*soa*-roa) *m* treasure
**testamento** (tayss-tah-*mayn*-toa) *m* will
**testarudo** (tayss-tah-*roo*-dhoa) *adj* pig-headed, stubborn
**testigo** (tayss-*tee*-goa) *m* witness; **~ de vista** eyewitness
**testimoniar** (tayss-tee-moa-*n$^y$ahr*) *v* testify
**testimonio** (tayss-tee-*moa*-n$^y$oa) *m* testimony
**tetera** (tay-*tay*-rah) *f* teapot
**textil** (tayks-*teel*) *m* textile
**texto** (*tayks*-toa) *m* text
**textura** (tayks-*too*-rah) *f* texture
**tez** (tayth) *f* complexion
**ti** (tee) *pron* you
**tía** (*tee*-ah) *f* aunt
**tibio** (*tee*-bh$^y$oa) *adj* tepid, lukewarm
**tiburón** (tee-bhoo-*roan*) *m* shark
**tiempo** (*t$^y$aym*-poa) *m* time; weather; period; tense; tempo; **a ~** in time; **~**

**libre** spare time
**tienda** (*t*$^y$*ayn*-dah) *f* shop; tent
**tierno** (*t*$^y$*ayr*-noa) *adj* gentle, tender
**tierra** (*t*$^y$*ay*-rrah) *f* earth; ground, soil; land; **en ~** ashore; **~ baja** lowlands *pl*; **~ firme** mainland
**tieso** (*t*$^y$*ay*-soa) *adj* stiff
**tifus** (*tee*-fooss) *m* typhoid
**tigre** (*tee*-gray) *m* tiger
**tijeras** (tee-*khay*-rahss) *fpl* scissors *pl*; **~ para las uñas** nail scissors *pl*
**tilo** (*tee*-loa) *m* limetree, lime
**timbre** (*teem*-bray) *m* tone; bell; doorbell; *mMe* postage stamp
**timidez** (tee-mee-*dhayth*) *f* timidity, shyness
**tímido** (*tee*-mee-dhoa) *adj* timid, embarrassed, shy
**timón** (tee-*moan*) *m* helm, rudder
**timonel** (tee-moa-*nayl*) *m* steersman
**timonero** (tee-moa-*nay*-roa) *m* helmsman
**tímpano** (*teem*-pah-noa) *m* ear-drum
**tinta** (*teen*-tah) *f* ink
**tinto** (*teen*-toa) *adj*: vino **~** red wine
**tintorería** (teen-toa-ray-*ree*-ah) *f* dry-cleaner's
**tintura** (teen-*too*-rah) *f* dye
**tío** (*tee*-oa) *m* uncle
**tiovivo** (tee-oa-*bee*-boa) *m* carousel, merry-go-round
**típico** (*tee*-pee-koa) *adj* typical, characteristic
**tipo** (*tee*-poa) *m* type; fellow, guy
**tirada** (tee-*rah*-dhah) *f* issue
**tirano** (tee-*rah*-noa) *m*, **-a** *f* tyrant
**tirantes** (tee-*rahn*-tayss) *mpl* braces *pl*; suspenders *plAm*
**tirar** (tee-*rahr*) *v* pull; *throw; *shoot
**tirita** (tee-*ree*-tah) *f* Bandaid®, plaster
**tiritar** (tee-ree-*tahr*) *v* shiver
**tiro** (*tee*-roa) *m* shot; throw
**tirón** (tee-*roan*) *m* jerk, tug; pull
**titular** (tee-too-*lahr*) *m* headline
**título** (*tee*-too-loa) *m* heading, title; degree
**toalla** (toa-*ah*-l$^y$ah) *f* towel; **~ de baño** bath towel
**tobera** (toa-*bhay*-rah) *f* nozzle
**tobillo** (toa-*bhee*-l$^y$oa) *m* ankle
**tobogán** (toa-bhoa-*gahn*) *m* slide
**tocadiscos** (toa-kah-*deess*-koass) *m* record player
**tocador** (toa-kah-*dhoar*) *m* dressing table; powder room; **artículos de ~** toiletries
**tocante a** (toa-*kahn*-tay ah) regarding
**tocar** (toa-*kahr*) *v* touch, *hit; play; **no ~** *keep off
**tocino** (toa-*thee*-noa) *m* bacon
**todavía** (toa-dhah-*bhee*-ah) *adv* still, however
**todo** (*toa*-dhoa) *adj* all; entire; *pron* everything; **sobre ~** most of all, essentially, especially; **todos** *pron* everybody
**toldo** (*toal*-doa) *m* awning
**tolerable** (toa-lay-*rah*-bhlay) *adj* tolerable
**tomar** (toa-*mahr*) *v* *catch; *take; **~ el pelo** tease
**tomate** (toa-*mah*-tay) *m* tomato
**tomillo** (toa-*mee*-l$^y$oa) *m* thyme
**tomo** (*toa*-moa) *m* volume
**tonada** (toa-*nah*-dhah) *f* tune
**tonel** (toa-*nayl*) *m* barrel, cask
**tonelada** (toa-nay-*lah*-dhah) *f* ton
**tónico** (*toa*-nee-koa) *m* tonic; **~ para el cabello** hair tonic
**tono** (*toa*-noa) *m* tone; note; shade
**tontería** (toan-tay-*ree*-ah) *f* nonsense, rubbish; ***decir tonterías** talk rubbish
**tonto** (*toan*-toa) *adj* foolish; *m* fool
**topetar** (toa-pay-*tahr*) *v* bump
**topetón** (toa-pay-*toan*) *m* bump
**toque** (*toa*-kay) *m* touch
**torcedura** (toar-thay-*dhoo*-rah) *f*

sprain
***torcer** (toar-*thayr*) *v* twist; ***torcerse** *v* sprain
**tordo** (*toar*-dhoa) *m* thrush
**torero** (toa-*ray*-roa) *m* bullfighter
**tormenta** (toar-*mayn*-tah) *f* storm
**tormento** (toar-*mayn*-toa) *m* torment
**tormentoso** (toar-mayn-*toa*-soa) *adj* stormy
**tornar** (toar-*nahr*) *v* give back; transform
**torneo** (toar-*nay*-oa) *m* tournament
**tornillo** (toar-*nee*-l$^y$oa) *m* screw
**torno** (*toar*-noa): **en ~** about, around; **en ~ de** round, around
**toro** (*toa*-roa) *m* bull
**toronja** (toa-*roan*-khah) *f Me* grapefruit
**torpe** (*toar*-pay) *adj* clumsy, awkward
**torre** (*toa*-rray) *f* tower
**torsión** (toar-*s$^y$oan*) *f* twist
**tortilla** (toar-*tee*-l$^y$ah) *f* omelette; *Me* corn flatcake
**tortuga** (toar-*too*-gah) *f* turtle
**tortuoso** (toar-*twoa*-soa) *adj* winding
**tortura** (toar-*too*-rah) *f* torture
**torturar** (toar-too-*rahr*) *v* torture
**tos** (toass) *f* cough
**toser** (toa-*sayr*) *v* cough
**tostado** (toass-*tah*-dhoa) *adj* toasted; tanned
**tostar** (toas-*tahr*) *v* toast; roast; tan; **tostarse** (toas-*tahr*-say) tan, get brown
**total** (toa-*tahl*) *adj* total; overall, utter; *m* total; whole; **en ~** altogether
**totalitario** (toa-tah-lee-*tah*-r$^y$oa) *adj* totalitarian
**totalmente** (toa-tahl-*mayn*-tay) *adv* completely, altogether, wholly
**tóxico** (*toak*-see-koa) *adj* toxic
**trabajar** (trah-bhah-*khahr*) *v* work; work at; work on
**trabajo** (trah-*bhah*-khoa) *m* work, labo(u)r; difficulty; **~ manual** handicraft
**tractor** (trahk-*toar*) *m* tractor
**tradición** (trah-dhee-*th$^y$oan*) *f* tradition
**tradicional** (trah-dhee-th$^y$oa-*nahl*) *adj* traditional
**traducción** (trah-dhook-*th$^y$oan*) *f* translation
***traducir** (trah-dhoo-*theer*) *v* translate
**traductor** (trah-dhook-*toar*) *m*, **-a** *f* translator
***traer** (trah-*ayr*) *v* *bring
**tragar** (trah-*gahr*) *v* swallow
**tragedia** (trah-*khay*-dh$^y$ah) *f* drama, tragedy
**trágico** (*trah*-khee-koa) *adj* tragic
**trago** (*trah*-goa) *m* mouthful; *colloquial* drink; **de un ~** in one gulp; **pasar un mal ~** have a hard time
**traición** (trigh-*th$^y$oan*) *f* treason
**traicionar** (trigh-th$^y$oa-*nahr*) *v* betray
**traidor** (trigh-*dhoar*) *m* traitor
**traje** (*trah*-khay) *m* suit; gown; robe; **~ de baño** bathing suit; **~ de etiqueta** evening dress; **~ del país** national dress; **~ de malla** tights *pl*; **~ pantalón** pant suit
**trama** (*trah*-mah) *f* plot
**trampa** (*trahm*-pah) *f* trap; hatch
**tranquilidad** (trahng-kee-lee-*dhahdh*) *f* calmness; tranquillity
**tranquilizar** (trahng-kee-lee-*thahr*) *v* reassure; calm
**tranquilo** (trahng-*kee*-loa) *adj* tranquil, quiet, calm; peaceful
**transacción** (trahn-sahk-*th$^y$oan*) *f* transaction, deal; **volumen de transacciones** turnover
**transatlántico** (trahn-saht-*lahn*-tee-koa) *adj* transatlantic
**transbordador** (trahnz-bhoar-dhah-*dhoar*) *m* ferry-boat; **~ de trenes** train ferry

**transcurrir** (trahns-koo-*rreer*) *v* pass

**transeúnte** (trahn-say-*oon*-tay) *m* passer-by

***transferir** (trahns-fay-*reer*) *v* transfer

**transformador** (trahns-foar-mah-*dhoar*) *m* transformer

**transformar** (trahns-foar-*mahr*) *v* transform

**transgredir** (trahnz-gray-*deer*) *v* transgress

**transición** (trahn-see-*th$^y$oan*) *f* transition

**tránsito** (*trahn*-see-toa) *m* traffic

**transmisión** (trahnz-mee-*s$^y$oan*) *f* transmission, broadcast

**transmitir** (trahnz-mee-*teer*) *v* transmit

**transparente** (trahns-pah-*rayn*-tay) *adj* transparent

**transpiración** (trahns-pee-rah-*th$^y$oan*) *f* perspiration

**transpirar** (trahns-pee-*rahr*) *v* perspire

**transportar** (trahns-poar-*tahr*) *v* transport; ship

**transporte** (trahns-*poar*-tay) *m* transportation, transport

**tranvía** (trahm-*bee*-ah) *m* tram; streetcar *Am*

**trapo** (*trah*-poa) *m* rag; ~ **de cocina** tea cloth, kitchen towel *Am*

**tras** (trahss) *prep* behind

**trasbordo: *hacer ~** (ah-*thayr* trahz-*bhoar*-dhoa) change, transfer

**trasero** (trah-*say*-roa) *m* bottom, buttocks, rump; *adj* back, rear

**trasladar** (trahz-lah-*dhahr*) *v* move

**traslúcido** (trahz-*loo*-thee-dhoa) *adj* sheer

**trastornado** (trahss-toar-*nah*-dhoa) *adj* upset

**trastornar** (trahss-toar-*nahr*) *v* upset

**trastos** (*trahss*-toass) *mpl* junk

**tratado** (trah-*tah*-dhoa) *m* essay; treaty

**tratamiento** (trah-tah-*m$^y$ayn*-toa) *m* treatment; ~ **de belleza** beauty treatment

**tratar** (trah-*tahr*) *v* handle, treat; ~ **con** *deal with

**trato** (*trah*-toa) *m* relationship; treatment; manner ~**s** dealings

**través: a ~ de** (ah trah-*bhayss day*) across, through

**travesía** (trah-bhay-*see*-ah) *f* crossing, passage

**travieso** (trah-*bh$^y$ay*-soa) *adj* naughty, bad; mischievous

**trazar** (trah-*thahr*) *v* sketch

**trébol** (*tray*-bhoal) *m* clover, shamrock

**trece** (*tray*-thay) *num* thirteen

**treceno** (tray-*thay*-noa) *num* thirteenth

**trecho** (*tray*-choa) *m* stretch

**treinta** (*trayn*-tah) *num* thirty

**treintavo** (trayn-*tah*-bhoa) *num* thirtieth

**tremendo** (tray-*mayn*-doa) *adj* awful, terrible; tremendous, terrific

**trementina** (tray-mayn-*tee*-nah) *f* turpentine

**tren** (trayn) *m* train; ~ **de cercanías** local train; ~ **de mercancías** goods train; ~ **de pasajeros** passenger train; ~ **directo** through train; ~ **expreso** express train; ~ **nocturno** night train

**trenza** (*trayn*-thah) *f* braid

**trepar** (tray-*pahr*) *v* climb

**tres** (trayss) *num* three

**triangular** (tr$^y$ahng-goo-*lahr*) *adj* triangular

**triángulo** (*tr$^y$ahng*-goo-loa) *m* triangle

**tribu** (*tree*-bhoo) *m* tribe

**tribuna** (tree-*bhoo*-nah) *f* stand

**tribunal** (tree-bhoo-*nahl*) *m* court, law

court
**trigal** (tree-*gahl*) *m* cornfield
**trigo** (*tree*-goa) *m* grain, corn; wheat
**trimestral** (tree-mayss-*trahl*) *adj* quarterly
**trimestre** (tree-*mayss*-tray) *m* quarter
**trinchar** (treen-*chahr*) *v* carve
**trineo** (tree-*nay*-oa) *m* sleigh, sledge, sled *Am*
**triste** (*treess*-tay) *adj* sad
**tristeza** (treess-*tay*-thah) *f* sorrow, sadness
**triturar** (tree-too-*rahr*) *v* *grind
**triunfante** (tr$^{y}$oon-*fahn*-tay) *adj* triumphant
**triunfar** (tr$^{y}$oon-*fahr*) *v* triumph
**triunfo** (*tr$^{y}$oon*-foa) *m* triumph
***trocar** (troa-*kahr*) *v* swap
**trompeta** (troam-*pay*-tah) *f* trumpet
**tronada** (troa-*nah*-dhah) *f* thunderstorm
***tronar** (troa-*nahr*) *v* thunder
**tronco** (*troang*-koa) *m* trunk
**trono** (*troanoa*) *m* throne
**tropas** (*troa*-pahss) *fpl* troops *pl*
***tropezarse** (troa-pay-*thahr*-say) *v* stumble
**tropical** (troa-pee-*kahl*) *adj* tropical
**trópicos** (*troa*-pee-koass) *mpl* tropics *pl*
**trozo** (*troa*-thoa) *m* chunk, morsel, bit; fragment, passage
**truco** (*troo*-koa) *m* trick
**trucha** (*troo*-chah) *f* trout
**trueno** (*trway*-noa) *m* thunder
**tu** (too) *adj* your
**tú** (too) *pron* you
**tuberculosis** (too-bhayr-koo-*loa*-seess) *f* tuberculosis
**tubo** (*too*-bhoa) *m* tube
**tuerca** (*twayr*-kah) *f* nut
**tulipán** (too-lee-*pahn*) *m* tulip
**tumba** (*toom*-bah) *f* tomb
**tumbona** (toom-*boa*-nah *f* (sun) lounger
**tumor** (too-*moar*) *m* growth, tumo(u)r
**tunecino** (too-nay-*thee*-noa) *adj* Tunisian; *m* Tunisian
**túnel** (*too*-nayl) *m* tunnel
**Túnez** (*too*-nayth) *m* Tunisia
**túnica** (*too*-nee-kah) *f* tunic, robe
**turbar** (toor-*bhahr*) *v* disturb; upset
**turbina** (toor-*bhee*-nah) *f* turbine
**turco** (*toor*-koa) *adj* Turkish; *m* Turk
**turismo** (too-*reez*-moa) *m* tourism
**turista** (too-*reess*-tah) *m/f* tourist; **oficina para turistas** tourist office
**turno** (*toor*-noa) *m* turn; shift
**Turquía** (toor-*kee*-ah) *f* Turkey
**turrón** (too-*rroan*) *m* nougat
**tutela** (too-*tay*-lah) *f* custody
**tutor** (too-*toar*) *m* tutor; guardian
**tuyos** (*too*-$^{y}$oass) *adj* your

# U

**ubicación** (oo-bhee-kah-*th$^{y}$oan*) *f* situation, location
**UE** (oo-ay) *f* EU
**úlcera** (*ool*-thay-rah) *f* ulcer, sore; **~ gástrica** gastric ulcer
**ulterior** (ool-tay-*r$^{y}$oar*) *adj* further; subsequent
**últimamente** (*ool*-tee-mah-mayn-tay) *adv* lately; finally
**último** (*ool*-tee-moa) *adj* ultimate; last; latest
**ultramar** (ool-trah-*mahr*) *adv* overseas

**ultravioleta** (ool-trah-bh$^y$oa-*lay*-tah) *adj* ultraviolet
**umbral** (oom-*brahl*) *m* threshold
**un** (oon) *art* a
**unánime** (oo-*nah*-nee-may) *adj* unanimous
**ungüento** (oong-*gwayn*-toa) *m* ointment, salve
**únicamente** (*oo*-nee-kah-mayn-tay) *adv* exclusively
**único** (*oo*-nee-koa) *adj* unique, sole
**unidad** (oo-nee-*dhahdh*) *f* unity; unit
**unido** (oo-*nee*-dhoa) *adj* joint
**uniforme** (oo-nee-*foar*-may) *adj* uniform; *m* uniform
**unilateral** (oo-nee-lah-tay-*rahl*) *adj* one-sided
**unión** (oo-*n$^y$oan*) *f* union
**Unión Europea** (oo-*n$^y$oan* ay$^{oo}$-roa-*pay*-ah) European Union
**unir** (oo-*neer*) *v* unite; combine; **unirse a** join
**universal** (oo-nee-bhayr-*sahl*) *adj* universal
**universidad** (oo-nee-bhayr-see-*dhahdh*) *f* university
**universo** (oo-nee-*bhayr*-soa) *m* universe
**uno** (*oo*-noa) *num* one; *pron* one; **unos** *adj* some; *pron* some
**untar** (oon-*tahr*) *v* rub, spread
**uña** (*oo*-ñah) *f* nail
**urbano** (oor-*bhah*-noa) *adj* urban
**urgencia** (oor-*khayn*-th$^y$ah) *f* urgency; emergency; **botiquín de ~** first-aid kit
**urgente** (oor-*khayn*-tay) *adj* pressing, urgent
**urraca** (oo-*rrah*-kah) *f* magpie
**Uruguay** (oo-roo-*gwigh*) *m* Uruguay
**uruguayo** (oo-roo-*gwah*-$^y$oa) *adj* Uruguayan; *m* Uruguayan
**usar** (oo-*sahr*) *v* use
**uso** (*oo*-soa) *m* use, usage
**usted** (ooss-*taydh*) *pron* you; **a ~** you; **de ~** your
**usual** (oo-*swahl*) *adj* common, customary, usual
**usuario** (oo-*swah*-r$^y$oa) *m* user
**utensilio** (oo-tayn-*see*-l$^y$oa) *m* utensil
**útil** (*oo*-teel) *adj* useful
**utilidad** (oo-tee-lee-*dhahdh*) *f* utility, use
**utilizable** (oo-tee-lee-*thah*-bhlay) *adj* usable
**utilizar** (oo-tee-lee-*thahr*) *v* utilize
**uva** (*oo*-bhah) *f* grape; **uvas** *fpl* grapes *pl*

# V

**vaca** (*bah*-kah) *f* cow
**vacaciones** (bah-kah-*th$^y$oa*-nayss) *fpl* holiday, vacation; **de ~** on holiday
**vacante** (bah-*kahn*-tay) *adj* vacant; *f* vacancy
**vaciar** (bah-*th$^y$ahr*) *v* empty; vacate
**vacilante** (bah-thee-lahn-tay) *adj* unsteady, shaky
**vacilar** (bah-thee-*lahr*) *v* hesitate; falter
**vacío** (bah-*thee*-oa) *adj* empty; *m* vacuum
**vacunación** (bah-koo-nah-*th$^y$oan*) *f* vaccination
**vacunar** (bah-koo-*nahr*) *v* vaccinate, inoculate
**vadear** (bah-dhay-*ahr*) *v* wade
**vado** (*bah*-dhoa) *m* ford

**vagabundear** (bah-gah-bhoon-day-*ahr*) *v* tramp, roam
**vagabundo** (bah-gah-*bhoon*-doa) *m* tramp
**vagar** (bah-*gahr*) *v* wander
**vago** (*bah*-goa) *adj* vague; faint, dim; idle
**vagón** (bah-*goan*) *m* wag(g)on, carriage; coach
**vainilla** (bigh-*nee*-l$^y$ah) *f* vanilla
**vale** (*bah*-lay) *m* voucher; coupon; receipt
***valer** (bah-*layr*) *v* *be worth; **~ la pena** *be worthwhile
**valiente** (bah-*l$^y$ayn*-tay) *adj* courageous, brave; bold
**valija** (bah-*lee*-khah) *f* case; valise
**valioso** (bah-*l$^y$oa*-soa) *adj* valuable
**valor** (bah-*loar*) *m* worth, value; courage; **bolsa de valores** stock exchange; **sin ~** worthless
**vals** (bahls) *m* waltz
**valuar** (bah-*lwahr*) *v* value; appreciate
**válvula** (*bahl*-bhoo-lah) *f* valve
**valle** (*bah*-l$^y$ay) *m* valley
**vanidoso** (bah-nee-*dhoa*-soa) *adj* vain
**vano** (*bah*-noa) *adj* idle, vain; **en ~** in vain
**vapor** (bah-*poar*) *m* steam, vapo(u)r; steamer; **~ de línea** liner
**vaporizador** (bah-poa-ree-thah-*dhoar*) *m* atomizer
**vaqueros** (bah-*kay*-roass) *mpl* jeans *pl*
**variable** (bah-*r$^y$ah*-bhlay) *adj* variable
**variación** (bah-r$^y$ah-*th$^y$oan*) *f* variation
**variado** (bah-*r$^y$ah*-dhoa) *adj* varied
**variar** (bah-*r$^y$ahr*) *v* vary
**varice** (*bah*-ree-thay) *f* varicose vein
**varicela** (bah-ree-*thay*-lah) *f* chickenpox
**variedad** (bah-r$^y$ay-*dhahdh*) *f* variety; **espectáculo de variedades** variety show
**varios** (*bah*-r$^y$oass) *adj* various, several
**vaselina** (bah-say-*lee*-nah) *f* vaseline
**vasija** (bah-*see*-khah) *f* receptacle
**vaso** (*bah*-soa) *m* glass; mug, tumbler; vase; **~ sanguíneo** blood vessel
**vasto** (*bahss*-toa) *adj* wide, vast; extensive
**vatio** (*bah*-t$^y$oa) *m* watt
**Vd.** *pron* (usted)
**vecindad** (bay-theen-*dahdh*) *f* neighbo(u)rhood, vicinity
**vecindario** (bay-theen-*dah*-r$^y$oa) *m* community
**vecino** (bay-*thee*-noa) *adj* neighbo(u)ring; *m*, **-a** *f* neighbo(u)r
**vegetación** (bay-khay-tah-*th$^y$oan*) *f* vegetation
**vegetariano** (bay-khay-tah-*r$^y$ah*-noa) *m*, **-a** *f* vegetarian
**vehículo** (bay-*ee*-koo-loa) *m* vehicle
**veinte** (*bayn*-tay) *num* twenty
**vejez** (bay-*khayth*) *f* old age
**vejiga** (bay-*khee*-gah) *f* bladder
**vela** (*bay*-lah) *f* sail; **deporte de ~** yachting
**velo** (*bay*-loa) *m* veil
**velocidad** (bay-loa-thee-*dhahdh*) *f* speed; rate; gear; **límite de ~** speed limit; **~ de cruce** cruising speed
**velocímetro** (bay-loa-*thee*-may-troa) *m* speedometer
**veloz** (bay-*loath*) *adj* swift
**vena** (*bay*-nah) *f* vein
**vencedor** (bayn-thay-*dhoar*) *m* winner
**vencer** (bayn-*thayr*) *v* *overcome, conquer; *win
**vencimiento** (bayn-thee-*m$^y$ayn*-toa) *m* expiry
**vendaje** (bayn-*dah*-khay) *m* bandage
**vendar** (bayn-*dahr*) *v* bandage

**vendedor** (bayn-day-*dhoar*) *m* salesman
**vendedora** (bayn-day-*dhoa*-rah) *f* salesgirl
**vender** (bayn-*dayr*) *v* *sell; **~ al detalle** retail
**vendible** (bayn-*dee*-bhlay) *adj* saleable
**vendimia** (bayn-*dee*-m$^{y}$ah) *f* vintage
**veneno** (bay-*nay*-noa) *m* poison
**venenoso** (bay-nay-*noa*-soa) *adj* poisonous
**venerable** (bay-nay-*rah*-bhlay) *adj* venerable
**venerar** (bay-nay-*rahr*) *v* worship
**venezolano** (bay-nay-thoa-*lah*-noa) *adj* Venezuelan; *m* Venezuelan
**Venezuela** (bay-nay-*thway*-lah) *f* Venezuela
**venganza** (bayng-*gahn*-thah) *f* revenge
**venidero** (bay-nee-*dhay*-roa) *adj* upcoming; future
***venir** (bay-*neer*) *v* *come
**venta** (*bayn*-tah) *f* sale; **de ~** for sale; **~ al por mayor** wholesale
**ventaja** (bayn-*tah*-khah) *f* benefit, advantage; profit; lead
**ventajoso** (bayn-tah-*khoa*-soa) *adj* advantageous; profitable
**ventana** (bayn-*tah*-nah) *f* window; **~ de la nariz** nostril
**ventanilla** (bayn-*tah-nee*-l$^{y}$ah) *f* window; porthole
**ventarrón** (bayn-tah-*rroan*) *m* gale
**ventilación** (bayn-tee-lah-*th$^{y}$oan*) *f* ventilation
**ventilador** (bayn-tee-lah-*dhoar*) *m* fan, ventilator
**ventilar** (bayn-tee-*lahr*) *v* ventilate
**ventisca** (bhayn-*teess*-kah) *f* blizzard
**ventoso** (bayn-*toa*-soa) *adj* windy
***ver** (bayr) *v* *see, notice
**veranda** (bay-*rahn*-dah) *f* veranda
**verano** (bay-*rah*-noa) *m* summer; **pleno ~** midsummer
**verbal** (bayr-*bhahl*) *adj* verbal
**verbena** (bayr-*bay*-nah) *f* party
**verbo** (*bayr*-bhoa) *m* verb
**verdad** (bayr-*dhahdh*) *f* truth
**verdaderamente** (bayr-dhah-dhay-rah-*mayn*-tay) *adv* really
**verdadero** (bayr-dhah-*dhay*-roa) *adj* true; real, very; actual
**verde** (*bayr*-dhay) *adj* green
**verdulero** (bayr-dhoo-*lay*-roa) *m* greengrocer
**veredicto** (bay-ray-*dheek*-toa) *m* verdict
**vergel** (*bayr*-gayl) *m* orchard
**vergüenza** (bayr-*gwayn*-thah) *f* shame; **¡qué vergüenza!** shame!
**verídico** (bay-*ree*-dhee-koa) *adj* truthful
**verificar** (bay-ree-fee-*kahr*) *v* check, verify
**verosímil** (bay-roa-*see*-meel) *adj* credible
**versión** (bayr-*s$^{y}$oan*) *f* version
**verso** (*bayr*-soa) *m* verse
***verter** (bayr-*tayr*) *v* pour; *spill
**vertical** (bayr-tee-*kahl*) *adj* vertical
**vestíbulo** (bayss-*tee*-bhoo-loa) *m* hall, lobby; foyer
**vestido** (bayss-*tee*-dhoa) *m* dress; garment; **vestidos** *mpl* clothes *pl*
***vestir** (bayss-*teer*) *v* dress; ***vestirse** *v* dress
**vestuario** (bayss-*twah*-r$^{y}$oa) *m* wardrobe; dressing room
**veterinario** (bay-tay-ree-*nah*-r$^{y}$oa) *m*, **-a** *f* veterinary surgeon
**vez** (bayth) *f* time; **alguna ~** some time; **a veces** sometimes; **de ~ en cuando** occasionally, now and then; **otra ~** again, once more; **pocas veces** seldom; **una ~** once
**vía** (*bee*-ah) *f* way; track; **~ del tren**

railroad *Am*; ~ **navegable** waterway
**viaducto** (b$^{y}$ah-*dhook*-toa) *m* viaduct
**viajar** (b$^{y}$ah-*khahr*) *v* travel
**viaje** (*b$^{y}$ah*-khay) *m* journey; trip, voyage
**viajero** (b$^{y}$ah-*khay*-roa) *m*, **-a** *f* travel(l)er
**vibración** (bee-bhrah-*th$^{y}$oan*) *f* vibration
**vibrar** (bee-*bhrahr*) *v* tremble, vibrate
**vicario** (bee-*kah*-r$^{y}$oa) *m* vicar
**vicepresidente** (bee-thay-pray-see-*dhayn*-tay) *m* vice-president
**vicio** (*bee*-th$^{y}$oa) *m* vice; **pasarlo de** ~ *colloquial* have a great time
**vicioso** (bee-*th$^{y}$oa*-soa) *adj* vicious
**víctima** (*beek*-tee-mah) *f* casualty, victim
**victoria** (beek-*toa*-r$^{y}$ah) *f* victory
**vida** (*bee*-dhah) *f* life; lifetime; **en** ~ alive; ~ **privada** privacy
**videocámara** (bee-dhay-oa-*kah*-mah-rah) *f* video camera
**videocasete** (bee-dhay-oa-kah-*say*-tay) *m* video cassette
**videograbadora** (bee-dhay-oa-grah-bhah-*dhoa*-rah) *f* video recorder
**vidrio** (*bee*-dhr$^{y}$oa) *m* glass; **de** ~ glass; ~ **de color** stained glass
**viejo** (*b$^{y}$ay*-khoa) *adj* old; ancient, aged; stale
**viento** (*b$^{y}$ayn*-toa) *m* wind
**vientre** (*b$^{y}$ayn*-tray) *m* belly
**viernes** (*b$^{y}$ayr*-nayss) *m* Friday
**vigente** (bee-*khayn*-tay) *adj* in force
**vigésimo** (bee-*khay*-see-moa) *num* twentieth
**vigilar** (bee-khee-*lahr*) *v* watch, patrol
**villa** (*bee*-l$^{y}$ah) *f* villa
**villano** (bee-*l$^{y}$ah*-noa) *adj* villainous, base
**vinagre** (bee-*nah*-gray) *m* vinegar
**vino** (*bee*-noa) *m* wine
**viña** (*bee*-ñah) *f* vineyard
**violación** (b$^{y}$oa-lah-*th$^{y}$oan*) *f* violation
**violar** (b$^{y}$oa-*lahr*) *v* violate; rape; force
**violencia** (b$^{y}$oa-*layn*-th$^{y}$ah) *f* violence
**violento** (b$^{y}$oa-*layn*-toa) *adj* violent; fierce, severe
**violeta** (b$^{y}$oa-*lay*-tah) *f* violet
**violín** (b$^{y}$oa-*leen*) *m* violin
**virgen** (*beer*-khayn) *f* virgin
**virtud** (beer-*toodh*) *f* virtue
**visado** (bee-*sah*-dhoa) *m* visa
**visar** (bee-*sahr*) *v* endorse
**visibilidad** (bee-see-bhee-lee-*dhahdh*) *f* visibility
**visible** (bee-*see*-bhlay) *adj* visible
**visión** (bee-*s$^{y}$oan*) *f* vision
**visita** (bee-*see*-tah) *f* visit, call
**visitante** (bee-see-*tahn*-tay) *m*/*f* visitor
**visitar** (bee-see-*tahr*) *v* visit, call on
**vislumbrar** (beez-loom-*brahr*) *v* glimpse
**vislumbre** (beez-*loom*-bray) *m* glimpse
**visón** (bee-*soan*) *m* mink
**visor** (bee-*soar*) *m* viewfinder
**vista** (*beess*-tah) *f* sight; view; **punto de** ~ point of view
**vistoso** (beess-*toa*-soa) *adj* colo(u)rful; showy
**vital** (bee-*tahl*) *adj* vital
**vitamina** (bee-tah-*mee*-nah) *f* vitamin
**vitrina** (bee-*tree*-nah) *f* showcase
**viuda** (*b$^{y}$oo*-dhah) *f* widow
**viudo** (*b$^{y}$oo*-dhoa) *m* widower
**vivaz** (bee-*bhahth*) *adj* lively
**vivero** (bee-*bhay*-roa) *m* tree nursery; hatchery
**vivienda** (bee-*bh$^{y}$ayn*-dah) *f* accommodation; dwelling
**vivir** (bee-*bheer*) *v* live; experience
**vivo** (*bee*-bhoa) *adj* alive, live; brisk, vivid, lively
**vocabulario** (boa-kah-bhoo-*lah*-r$^{y}$oa) *m* vocabulary

**vocación** (boa-kah-*th$^y$oan*) *f* vocation
**vocal** (boa-*kahl*) *f* vowel; *adj* vocal
**vocalista** (boa-kah-*leess*-tah) *m* vocalist
**volante** (boa-*lahn*-tay) *m* steering-wheel
***volar** (boa-*lahr*) *v* *fly
**volatería** (boa-lah-tay-*ree*-ah) *f* fowls
**volcán** (boal-*kahn*) *m* volcano
**voleibol** (boa-lay-*boal*) *m* volleyball
**voltaje** (boal-*tah*-khay) *m* voltage
**voltio** (*boal*-t$^y$oa) *m* volt
**volumen** (boa-*loo*-mayn) *m* volume
**voluminoso** (boa-loo-mee-*noa*-soa) *adj* bulky; big
**voluntad** (boa-loon-*tahdh*) *f* will; **buena ~** goodwill
**voluntario** (boa-loon-*tah*-r$^y$oa) *adj* voluntary; *m* volunteer
***volver** (boal-*bhayr*) *v* return, turn back; turn over, turn, turn round; **~ a casa** *go home; ***volverse** *v* turn round
**vomitar** (boa-mee-*tahr*) *v* vomit
**vosotros** (boa-*soa*-troass) *pron* you
**votación** (boa-tah-*th$^y$oan*) *f* vote
**votar** (boa-*tahr*) *v* vote
**voto** (*boa*-toa) *m* vote; vow
**voz** (boath) *f* voice; cry; **en ~ alta** aloud
**vuelo** (*bway*-loa) *m* flight; **~ charter** charter flight; **~ nocturno** night flight
**vuelta** (*bwayl*-tah) *f* return journey, way back; tour; turning, turn; round; reverse; **ida y ~** round trip *Am*
**vuestro** (*bwayss*-troa) *adj* your
**vulgar** (bool-*gahr*) *adj* vulgar
**vulnerable** (bool-nay-*rah*-bhlay) *adj* vulnerable

# Y

**y** (ee) *conj* and
**ya** ($^y$ah) *adv* already; **~ no** no longer; **~ que** as
***yacer** ($^y$ah-*thayr*) *v* *lie
**yacimiento** ($^y$ah-thee-*m$^y$ayn*-toa) *m* deposit
**yate** ($^y$*ah*-tay) *m* yacht
**yegua** ($^y$*ay*-gwah) *f* mare
**yema** ($^y$*ay*-mah) *f* yolk
**yerno** ($^y$*ayr*-noa) *m* son-in-law
**yeso** ($^y$*ay*-soa) *m* plaster
**yo** ($^y$oa) *pron* I
**yodo** ($^y$*oa*-dhoa) *m* iodine
**yugo** ($^y$*oo*-goa) *m* yoke
**yogur** ($^y$oa-*goor*) *m* yog(h)urt

# Z

**zafiro** (thah-*fee*-roa) *m* sapphire
**zanahoria** (thah-nah-*oa*-r$^y$ah) *f* carrot
**zanja** (*thahng*-khah) *f* ditch
**zapatería** (thah-pah-tay-*ree*-ah) *f* shoe shop
**zapatero** (thah-pah-*tay*-roa) *m* shoemaker
**zapatilla** (thah-pah-*tee*-l$^y$ah) *f* slipper

**zapato** (thah-*pah*-toa) *m* shoe; **zapatos de gimnasia** *pl* plimsolls; sneakers *Am*; **zapatos de tenis** tennis shoes
**zodíaco** (thoa-*dhee*-ah-koa) *m* zodiac
**zona** (*thoa*-nah) *f* zone; area; **~ industrial** industrial area
**zoología** (thoa-oa-loa-*khee*-ah) *f* zoology
**zorro** (*thoa*-rroa) *m* fox
**zueco** (*thway*-koa) *m* wooden shoe
**zumo** (*thoo*-moa) *m* juice; squash
**zurcir** (thoor-*theer*) *v* darn
**zurdo** (*thoor*-dhoa) *adj* left-handed
**zurra** (*thoo*-rrah) *f* spanking

# Menu Reader

## Food

**a caballo** steak topped with two eggs
**acedera** sorrel
**aceite** oil
**aceituna** olive
**achicoria** endive (US chicory)
**(al) adobo** marinated
**aguacate** avocado (pear)
**ahumado** smoked
**ajiaceite** garlic mayonnaise
**ajiaco bogotano** chicken soup with potatoes
**(al) ajillo** cooked in garlic and oil
**ajo** garlic
**al, a la** in the style of, with
**albahaca** basil
**albaricoque** apricot
**albóndiga** spiced meat- or fishball
**alcachofa** artichoke
**alcaparra** caper
**aliñado** seasoned
**alioli** garlic mayonnaise
**almeja** clam, cockle
**almejas a la marinera** cooked in hot, pimento sauce
**almendra** almond
~ **garrapiñada** sugared almond
**almíbar** syrup
**almuerzo** lunch
**alubia** bean
**anchoa** anchovy
**anguila** eel
**angula** baby eel
**anticucho** beef heart grilled on a skewer with green peppers
**apio** celery
**a punto** medium (done)
**arenque** herring
~ **en escabeche** marinated, pickled herring
**arepa** flapjack made of maize (corn)
**arroz** rice
~ **blanco** boiled, steamed
~ **escarlata** with tomatoes and prawns
~ **a la española** with chicken liver, pork, tomatoes, fish stock
~ **con leche** rice pudding
~ **con pollo** chicken and rice
~**primavera** with spring vegetables
~ **a la valenciana** with vegetables, chicken, shellfish (and sometimes eel)
**asado** roast
~ **antiguo a la venezolana mechado** roast beef stuffed with capers
**asturias** a strong, fermented cheese with a sharp flavour
**atún** tunny (US tuna)
**avellana** hazelnut
**azafrán** saffron
**azúcar** sugar
**bacalao** cod
~ **a la vizcaína** with green peppers, potatoes, tomato sauce
**barbo** barbel (fish)
**batata** sweet potato, yam
**becada** woodcock
**berberecho** cockle
**berenjena** aubergine (US eggplant)
**berraza** parsnip
**berro** cress
**berza** cabbage
**besugo** sea bream
**bien hecho** well-done
**biftec, bistec** beef steak
**bizcocho** sponge cake, sponge finger (US ladyfinger)
~ **borracho** cake steeped in rum (or wine) and syrup

**bizcotela** glazed biscuit (US cookie)
**blando** soft
**bocadillo** 1) sandwich 2) sweet (Colombia)
**bollito, bollo** roll, bun
**bonito** a kind of tunny (US tuna)
**boquerón** 1) anchovy 2) whitebait
**(en) brocheta** (on a) skewer
**budín** blancmange, custard
**buey** ox
**buñuelo** 1) doughnut 2) fritter with ham, mussels and prawns (sometimes flavoured with brandy)
**burgos** a popular soft, creamy cheese named after the Spanish province of its origin
**burrito** Mexican tortilla wrap with cheese or meat filling
**butifarra** spiced sausage
**caballa** fish of the mackerel family
**cabeza de ternera** calf's head
**cabra** goat
**cabrales** blue-veined goat's-milk cheese
**cabrito** kid
**cacahuete** peanut
**cachelos** diced potatoes boiled with cabbage, paprika, garlic, bacon, chorizo sausage
**calabacín** vegetable marrow, courgette (US zucchini)
**calabaza** pumpkin
**calamar** squid
**calamares a la romana** squids fried in batter
**caldereta de cabrito** kid stew (often cooked in red wine)
**caldillo de congrio** conger-eel soup with tomatoes and potatoes
**caldo** consommé
~ **gallego** meat and vegetable broth
**callos** tripe (often served in pimento sauce)
~ **a la madrileña** in piquant sauce with chorizo sausage and tomatoes
**camarón** shrimp
**canela** cinnamon
**cangrejo de mar** crab
**cangrejo de río** crayfish
**cantarela** chanterelle mushroom
**caracol** snail
**carbonada criolla** baked pumpkin stuffed with diced beef
**carne** meat
~ **asada al horno** roast meat
~ **molida** minced beef
~ **a la parrilla** charcoal-grilled steak
~ **picada** minced beef
**carnero** mutton
**carpa** carp
**casero** home made
**castaña** chestnut
**castañola** sea perch
**(a la) catalana** with onions, parsley, tomatoes and herbs
**caza** game
**(a la) cazadora** with mushrooms, spring onions, herbs in wine
**cazuela de cordero** lamb stew with vegetables
**cebolla** onion
**cebolleta** chive
**cebrero** blue-veined cheese of creamy texture with a pale, yellow rind; sharp taste
**cena** dinner, supper
**centolla** spider-crab, served cold
**cerdo** pork
**cereza** cherry
**ceviche** fish marinated in lemon and lime juice
**cigala** Dublin Bay prawn
**cincho** a hard cheese made from sheep's milk
**ciruela** plum
~ **pasa** prune
**cocido** 1) cooked, boiled 2) stew of beef with ham, fowl, chick peas,

potatoes and vegetables (the broth is eaten first)
**cochifrito de cordero** highly seasoned stew of lamb or kid
**cochinillo** roasted suckling pig
**codorniz** quail
**col** cabbage
~ **de Bruselas** brussels sprout
**coliflor** cauliflower
**comida** meal
**compota** stewed fruit
**conejo** rabbit
**confitura** jam
**congrio** conger eel
**consomé al jerez** chicken broth with sherry
**copa nuria** egg-yolk and egg-white, whipped and served with jam
**corazón de alcachofa** artichoke heart
**corazonada** heart stewed in sauce
**cordero** lamb
~ **recental** spring lamb
**cortadillo** small pancake with lemon
**corzo** deer
**costilla** chop
**crema** 1) cream or mousse
~ **batida** whipped cream
~ **española** dessert of milk, eggs, fruit jelly
~ **nieve** frothy egg-yolk, sugar, rum (or wine)
**crema** 2) soup
**criadillas (de toro)** glands (of bull)
**(a la) criolla** with green peppers, spices and tomatoes
**croqueta** croquette, fish or meat dumpling
**crudo** raw
**cubierto** cover charge
**cuenta** bill (US check)
**curanto** dish consisting of seafood, vegetables and suck(l)ing pig, all cooked in an earthen well, lined with charcoal
**chabacano** apricot
**chalote** shallot
**champiñón** mushroom
**chancho adobado** pork braised with sweet potatoes, orange and lemon juice
**chanfaina** goat's liver and kidney stew, served in a thick sauce
**chanquete** whitebait
**chile** chili pepper
**chiles en nogada** green peppers stuffed with whipped cream and nut sauce
**chimichurri** hot parsley sauce
**chipirón** small squid
**chopa** a kind of sea bream
**chorizo** pork sausage, highly seasoned with garlic and paprika
**chuleta** cutlet
**chupe de mariscos** scallops served with a creamy sauce and gratinéed with cheese
**churro** sugared tubular fritter
**damasco** variety of apricot
**dátil** date
**desayuno** breakfast
**dorada** gilt-head
**dulce** sweet
~ **de naranja** marmalade
**durazno** peach
**embuchado** stuffed with meat
**embutido** spicy sausage
**empanada** pie or tart with meat or fish filling
~ **de horno** dough filled with minced meat, similar to ravioli
**empanadilla** small patty stuffed with seasoned meat or fish
**empanado** breaded
**emperador** swordfish
**encurtido** pickle
**enchilada** a maizeflour (US cornmeal) pancake (tortilla) stuffed

and usually served with vegetable garnish and sauce
~ **roja** sausage-filled maizeflour pancake dipped into a red sweet-pepper sauce
~ **verde** maizeflour pancake stuffed with meat or fowl and braised in a green-tomato sauce
**endibia** chicory (US endive)
**eneldo** dill
**ensalada** salad
~ **común** green
~ **de frutas** fruit salad
~ **(a la) primavera** spring
~ **valenciana** with green peppers, lettuce and oranges
**ensaladilla rusa** diced cold vegetables with mayonnaise
**entremés** appetizer, hors-d'oeuvre
**erizo de mar** sea urchin
**(en) escabeche** marinated, pickled
~ **de gallina** chicken marinated in vinegar
**escarcho** red gurnard (fish)
**escarola** endive (US chicory)
**espalda** shoulder
**(a la) española** with tomatoes
**espárrago** asparagus
**especia** spice
**especialidad de la casa** chef's speciality
**espinaca** spinach
**esqueixada** mixed fish salad
**(al) estilo de** in the style of
**estofado** stew(ed)
**estragón** tarragon
**fabada (asturiana)** stew of pork, beans, bacon and sausage
**faisán** pheasant
**fajitas** spiced pork slices served with condiments, guacamole and tortillas
**fiambres** cold meat (US cold cuts)
**fideo** thin noodle
**filete** steak
~ **de lomo** fillet steak (US tenderloin)
~ **de res** beef steak
~ **de lenguado empanado** breaded fillet of sole
**(a la) flamenca** with onions, peas, green peppers, tomatoes and spiced sausage
**flan** caramel mould, custard
**frambuesa** raspberry
**(a la) francesa** sautéed in butter
**fresa** strawberry
~ **de bosque** wild
**fresco** fresh, chilled
**fresón** large strawberry
**fricandó** veal bird, thin slice of meat rolled in bacon and braised
**frijol** bean
**frijoles refritos** fried mashed beans
**frío** cold
**frito** 1) fried 2) fry
~ **de patata** deep-fried potato croquette
**fritura** fry
~ **mixta** meat, fish or vegetables deep-fried in batter
**fruta** fruit
~ **escarchada** crystallized (US candied) fruit
**galleta** salted or sweet biscuit (US cracker or cookie)
~ **de nata** cream biscuit (US sandwich cookie)
**gallina** hen
~ **de Guinea** guinea fowl
**gallo** cockerel
**gamba** shrimp
~ **grande** prawn
**gambas** shrimp
~ **al ajillo** shrimp in garlic sauce
~ **con mayonesa** shrimp cocktail
**ganso** goose
**garbanzo** chick pea
**gazpacho** seasoned broth made of

raw onions, garlic, tomatoes, cucumber and green pepper; served chilled
(a la) **gitanilla** with garlic
**gordo** fatty, rich (of food)
**granada** pomegranate
**grande** large
(al) **gratín** gratinéed
**gratinado** gratinéed
**grelo** turnip greens
**grosella** currant
~ **espinosa** gooseberry
~ **negra** blackcurrant
~ **roja** redcurrant
**guacamole** a purée of avocado and spices used as a dip, in a salad, for a tortilla filling or as a garnish
**guarnición** garnish, trimming
**guayaba** guava (fruit)
**guinda** sour cherry
**guindilla** chili pepper
**guisado** stew(ed)
**guisante** green pea
**haba** broad bean
**habichuela verde** French bean (US green bean)
**hamburguesa** hamburger
**hayaca central** maizeflour (US cornmeal) pancake, usually with a minced-meat filling
**helado** ice-cream, ice
**hervido** 1) boiled 2) stew of beef and vegetables (Latin America)
**hielo** ice
**hierba** herb
**hierbas finas** finely chopped mixture of herbs
**hígado** liver
**higo** fig
**hinojo** fennel
**hongo** mushroom
(al) **horno** baked
**hortaliza** greens
**hueso** bone
**huevo** egg
~ **cocido** boiled
~ **duro** hard-boiled
~ **escalfado** poached
~ **a la española** stuffed with tomatoes and served with cheese sauce
~ **a la flamenca** baked with asparagus, peas, peppers, onions, tomatoes and sausage
~ **frito** fried
~ **al nido** egg-yolk placed into small, soft roll, fried, then covered with egg-white
~ **pasado por agua** soft-boiled
~ **revuelto** scrambled
~ **con tocino** bacon and egg
**humita** boiled maize (US corn) with tomatoes, green peppers, onions and cheese
(a la) **inglesa** 1) underdone (of meat) 2) boiled 3) served with boiled vegetables
**jabalí** wild boar
**jalea** jelly
**jamón** ham
~ **cocido** boiled (often referred to as jamón de York)
~ **en dulce** boiled and served cold
~ **gallego** smoked and cut thinly
~ **serrano** cured and cut thinly
(a la) **jardinera** with carrots, peas and other vegetables
**jengibre** ginger
(al) **jerez** braised in sherry
**judía** bean
~ **verde** French bean (US green bean)
**jugo** gravy, meat juice
**en su** ~ in its own juice
**juliana** with shredded vegetables
**jurel** variety of mackerel
**lacón** shoulder of pork
~ **curado** salted pork

**lamprea** lamprey
**langosta** spiny lobster
**langostino** Norway lobster, Dublin Bay prawn
**laurel** bay leaf
**leche frita** sweet fried custard squares
**lechón** suck(l)ing pig
**lechuga** lettuce
**legumbre** vegetable
**lengua** tongue
**lenguado** sole, flounder
~ **frito** fried fillet of sole on bed of vegetables
**lenteja** lentil
**liebre** hare
~ **estofada** jugged hare
**lima** 1) lime 2) sweet lime (Latin America)
**limón** lemon
**lista de platos** menu
**lista de vinos** wine list
**lobarro** a variety of bass
**lombarda** red cabbage
**lomo** loin
**longaniza** long, highly seasoned sausage
**lonja** slice of meat
**lubina** bass
**macarrones** macaroni
(**a la**) **madrileña** with chorizo sausage, tomatoes and paprika
**magras al estilo de Aragón** cured ham in tomato sauce
**maíz** maize (US corn)
(**a la**) **mallorquina** usually refers to highly seasoned fish and shellfish
**manchego** hard cheese from La Mancha, made from sheep's milk, white or golden-yellow in colour
**maní** peanut
**mantecado** 1) small butter cake 2) custard ice-cream
**mantequilla** butter
**manzana** apple
~ **en dulce** in honey
(**a la**) **marinera** usually with mussels, onions, tomatoes, herbs and wine
**marisco** seafood
**matambre** rolled beef stuffed with vegetables
**mayonesa** mayonnaise
**mazapán** marzipan, almond paste
**mejillón** mussel
**mejorana** marjoram
**melaza** treacle, molasses
**melocotón** peach
**membrillo** quince
**menestra** boiled green vegetable soup
~ **de pollo** chicken and vegetable soup
**menta** mint
**menú** menu
~ **del día** set menu
~ **turístico** tourist menu
**menudillos** giblets
**merengue** meringue
**merienda** snack
**merluza** hake
**mermelada** jam
**mezclado** mixed
**miel** honey
(**a la**) **milanesa** with cheese, generally baked
**minuta** menu
**mixto** mixed
**mole poblano** chicken served with a sauce of chili peppers, spices and chocolate
**molusco** mollusc (snail, mussel, clam)
**molleja** sweetbread
**mora** mulberry
**morcilla** black pudding (US blood sausage)
**morilla** morel mushroom
**moros y cristianos** rice and black beans with diced ham, garlic, green peppers and herbs
**mostaza** mustard

**mújol** mullet
**nabo** turnip
**naranja** orange
**nata** cream
~ **batida** whipped cream
**natillas** custard
~ **al limón** lemon cream
**níspola** medlar (fruit)
**nopalito** young cactus leaf served with salad dressing
**nuez** nut
~ **moscada** nutmeg
**olla** stew
~ **gitana** vegetable stew
~ **podrida** stew made of vegetables, meat, fowl and ham
**ostra** oyster
**oveja** ewe
**pabellón criollo** beef in tomato sauce garnished with beans, rice and bananas
**paella** consists basically of saffron rice with assorted seafood and sometimes meat
~ **alicantina** with green peppers, onions, tomatoes, artichokes and fish
~ **catalana** with sausages, pork, squid, tomatoes, red sweet peppers and peas
~ **marinera** with fish, shellfish and meat
~ (**a la**) **valenciana** with chicken, shrimps, peas, tomatoes, mussels and garlic
**palmito** palm heart
**palta** avocado (pear)
**pan** bread
**panecillo** roll
**papa** potato
**papas a la huancaína** with cheese and green peppers
(**a la**) **parrilla** grilled
**parrillada mixta** mixed grill
**pasado** done, cooked
**bien** ~ well-done
**poco** ~ underdone (US rare)
**pastas** noodles, macaroni, spaghetti
**pastel** cake, pie
~ **de choclo** maize with minced beef, chicken, raisins and olives
**pastelillo** small tart
**pata** trotter (US foot)
**patatas** potatoes
~ **bravas** in a spicy tomato sauce
~ **fritas** fried; usually chips (US french fries)
~ (**a la**) **leonesa** with onions
~ **nuevas** new
**pato** duck, duckling
**pavo** turkey
**pechuga** breast (of fowl)
**pepinillo** gherkin (US pickle)
**pepino** cucumber
(**en**) **pepitoria** stewed with onions, green peppers and tomatoes
**pera** pear
**perca** perch
**percebe** barnacle (shellfish)
**perdiz** partridge
~ **en escabeche** cooked in oil with vinegar, onions, parsley, carrots and green pepper; served cold
~ **estofada** stewed and served with a white-wine sauce
**perejil** parsley
**perifollo** chervil
**perilla** a firm, bland cheese
**pescadilla** whiting
**pescado** fish
**pez espada** swordfish
**picadillo** minced meat, hash
**picado** minced
**picante** sharp, spicy, highly seasoned
**picatoste** deep-fried slice of bread
**pichoncillo** young pigeon (US squab)
**pierna** leg
**pimentón** chili pepper
**pimienta** pepper

**pimiento** sweet pepper
~ **morrón** red (sweet) pepper
**pincho moruno** grilled meat (often kidneys) on a skewer, sometimes served with spicy sauces
**pintada** guinea fowl
**piña** pineapple
**pisto** diced and sautéed vegetables: mainly aubergines, green peppers and tomatoes; served cold
(**a la**) **plancha** grilled on a girdle
**plátano** banana
**plato** plate, dish, portion
~ **típico de la región** regional speciality
**pollito** spring chicken
**pollo** chicken
~ **pibil** simmered in fruit juice and spices
**polvorón** hazelnut biscuit (US cookie)
**pomelo** grapefruit
**porción** portion
**porotos granados** shelled beans served with pumpkin and maize (US corn)
**postre** dessert, sweet
**potaje** vegetable soup
**puchero** stew
**puerro** leek
**pulpo** octopus
**punta de espárrago** asparagus tip
**punto de nieve** dessert of whipped cream with beaten egg-whites
**puré de patatas** mashed potatoes
**queso** cheese
**quisquilla** shrimp
**rábano** radish
~ **picante** horse-radish
**raja** slice or portion
**rallado** grated
**rape** angler fish
**ravioles** ravioli
**raya** skate, ray
**rebanada** slice
**rebozado** breaded or fried in batter
**recargo** extra charge
**rehogada** sautéed
**relleno** stuffed
**remolacha** beetroot
**repollo** cabbage
**requesón** a fresh-curd cheese
**riñón** kidney
**róbalo** haddock
**rodaballo** turbot, flounder
(**a la**) **romana** dipped in batter and fried
**romero** rosemary
**roncal** cheese made from sheep's milk; close grained and hard in texture with a few small holes; piquant flavour
**ropa vieja** cooked, left-over meat and vegetables, covered with tomatoes and green peppers
**rosbif** roast beef
**rosquilla** doughnut
**rubio** red mullet
**ruibarbo** rhubarb
**sal** salt
**salado** salted, salty
**salchicha** small pork sausage for frying
**salchichón** salami
**salmón** salmon
**salmonete** red mullet
**salsa** sauce
~ **blanca** white
~ **española** brown sauce with herbs, spices and wine
~ **mayordoma** butter and parsley
~ **picante** hot pepper
~ **romana** bacon or ham, egg, cream (sometimes flavoured with nutmeg)
~ **tártara** tartar
~ **verde** parsley
**salsifí** salsify
**salteado** sauté(ed)

**salvia** sage
**san simón** a firm, bland cheese resembling perilla; shiny yellow rind
**sandía** watermelon
**sardina** sardine, pilchard
**sémola** semolina
**sencillo** plain
**sepia** cuttlefish
**servicio** service
~ **(no) incluido** (not) included
**sesos** brains
**seta** mushroom
**sobrasada** pork sausage from Mallorca
**solomillo** fillet steak (US tenderloin)
**sopa** soup
~ **(de) cola de buey** oxtail
~ **sevillana** a highly spiced fish soup
**suave** soft
**suflé** soufflé
**suizo** bun
**surtido** assorted
**taco** wheat or maizeflour (US cornmeal) shell usually with a meat filling and garnished with chile sauce
**tajada** slice
**tallarín** noodle
**tamal** a pastry dough of coarsely ground maizeflour with meat or fruit filling, steamed in maizehusks (US corn husks)
**tapa** appetizer, snack
**tarta** cake, tart
~ **helada** ice-cream tart
**ternera** veal
**tocino** bacon
~ **de cielo** 1) caramel mould 2) custard-filled cake
**tomate** tomato
**tomillo** thyme
**tordo** thrush
**toronja** variety of grapefruit
**torrijas** bread dipped in a milk-egg mixture and fried
**tortilla** 1) potato omelet 2) a type of pancake made with maizeflour (US cornmeal)
~ **de chorizo** with pieces of a spicy sausage
~ **a la española** with onions, potatoes and seasoning
~ **a la francesa** plain
~ **gallega** potatoes with ham, red sweet peppers and peas
~ **a la jardinera** with mixed, diced vegetables
~ **al ron** rum
**tortita** waffle
**tortuga** turtle
**tostada** toast
**tripas** tripe
**trucha** trout
~ **frita a la asturiana** floured and fried in butter, garnished with lemon
**trufa** truffle
**turrón** nougat
**ulloa** a soft cheese from Galicia, rather like a mature camembert
**uva** grape
~ **pasa** raisin
**vaca salada** corned beef
**vainilla** vanilla
**(a la) valenciana** with rice, tomatoes and garlic
**variado** varied, assorted
**varios** sundries
**venado** venison
**venera** scallop, coquille St. Jacques
**verdura** greens
**vieira** scallop
**villalón** a cheese from sheep's milk
**vinagre** vinegar
**vinagreta** a piquant vinegar dressing (vinaigrette) to accompany salads
**(a la)** ~ marinated in oil and vinegar or lemon juice with mixed herbs
**(a la) vizcaína** with green peppers, tomatoes, garlic and paprika

**yema** egg-yolk
**yemas** a dessert of whipped egg-yolks and sugar
**zanahoria** carrot
**zarzamora** blackberry
**zarzuela** savoury stew of assorted fish and shellfish
~ **de mariscos** seafood stew
~ **de pescado** selection of fish served with a highly seasoned sauce
~ **de verduras** vegetable stew

## Drinks

**abocado** sherry made from a blend of sweet and dry wines
**agua** water
**aguardiente** spirits
**Alicante** this region to the south of Valencia produces a large quantity of red table wine and some good rosé, particularly from Yecla
**Amontillado** medium-dry sherry, light amber in colour, with a nutty flavour
**Andalucía** a drink of dry sherry and orange juice
**Angélica** a Basque herb liqueur similar to yellow Chartreuse
**anís** aniseed liqueur
**Anís del Mono** a Calatonian aniseed liqueur
**anís seco** aniseed brandy
**anisado** an aniseed-based soft drink which may be slightly alcoholic
**batido** milk shake
**bebida** drink
**Bobadilla Gran Reserva** a wine-distilled brandy
**botella** bottle
**media** ~ half bottle
**café** coffee
~ **cortado** small cup of espresso coffee with a dash of milk or cream
~ **descafeinado** coffeine-free
~ **exprés** espresso
~ **granizado** iced (white)
~ **con leche** white (US with milk)
~ **negro/solo** black
**Calisay** a quinine-flavoured liqueur
**Carlos I** a wine-distilled brandy
**Cataluña** Catalonia; this region southwest of Barcelona is known for its xampañ, bearing little resemblance to the famed French sparkling wine
**Cazalla** an aniseed liqueur
**cerveza** beer
~ **de barril** draught (US draft)
~ **dorada** light
~ **negra** dark
**cola de mono** a blend of coffee, milk, rum and pisco
**coñac** 1) French Cognac 2) term applied to any Spanish wine-distilled brandy
**Cordoníu** a brand-name of Catalonian sparkling wine locally referred to as xampañ (champagne)
**cosecha** harvest; indicates the vintage of wine
**crema de cacao** cocoa liqueur, crème de cacao
**Cuarenta y Tres** an egg liqueur
**Cuba libre** rum and Coke
**champán, champaña** 1) French Champagne 2) term applied to any Spanish sparkling wine
**chicha de manzana** apple brandy

**Chinchón** an aniseed liqueur
**chocolate** chocolate drink
~ **con leche** hot chocolate with milk
**Dulce** dessert wine
**Fino** dry sherry wine, very pale and straw-coloured
**Fundador** a wine-distilled brandy
**Galicia** this Atlantic coastal region has good table wines
**gaseosa** fizzy (US carbonated) water
**ginebra** gin
**gran vino** term found on Chilean wine labels to indicate a wine of exceptional quality
**granadina** pomegranate syrup mixed with wine or brandy
**horchata de almendra** (or **de chufa**) drink made from ground almonds (or Jerusalem artichoke)
**Jerez** 1) sherry 2) the Spanish region near the Portuguese border, internationally renowned for its Jerez
**jugo** fruit juice
**leche** milk
**limonada** lemonade, lemon squash
**Málaga** 1) dessert wine 2) the region in the south of Spain, is particularly noted for its dessert wine
**Manzanilla** dry sherry, very pale and straw-coloured
**margarita** tequila with lime juice
**Montilla** a dessert wine from near Cordoba, often drunk as an aperitif
**Moscatel** fruity dessert wine
**naranjada** orangeade
**Oloroso** sweet, dark sherry, drunk as dessert wine, resembles brown cream sherry
**Oporto** port (wine)
**pisco** grape brandy
**ponche crema** eggnog liquor
**Priorato** the region south of Barcelona produces good quality red and white wine but also a dessert wine, usually called Priorato but renamed Tarragona when it is exported
**refresco** a soft drink
**reservado** term found on Chilean wine labels to indicate a wine of exceptional quality
**Rioja** the northern region near the French border is considered to produce Spain's best wines-especially red; some of the finest Rioja wines resemble good Bordeaux wines
**ron** rum
**sangría** a mixture of red wine, ice, orange, lemon, brandy and sugar
**sangrita** tequila with tomato, orange and lime juices
**sidra** cider
**sol y sombra** a blend of wine-distilled brandy and aniseed liqueur
**sorbete** (iced) fruit drink
**té** tea
**tequila** brandy made from agave (US aloe)
**tinto** 1) red wine 2) black coffee with sugar (Colombia)
**Tío Pepe** a brand-name sherry
**Triple Seco** an orange liqueur
**Valdepeñas** the region south of Madrid is an important wine-producing area
**vermú** vermouth
**Veterano Osborne** a wine-distilled brandy
**vino** wine
~ **blanco** white
~ **clarete** rosé
~ **común** table wine
~ **dulce** dessert
~ **espumoso** sparkling
~ **de mesa** table wine
~ **del país** local wine

~ **rosado** rosé
~ **seco** dry
~ **suave** sweet
~ **tinto** red

**xampañ** Catalonian sparkling wine
**Yerba mate** South American holly tea
**zumo** juice

# Mini-Grammar

## Articles

Nouns in Spanish are either masculine or feminine. Articles agree in gender and number with the noun.

1. Definite article (the):

| | singular | | plural |
|---|---|---|---|
| masc. | **el tren** | the train | **los trenes** |
| fem. | **la casa** | the house | **las casas** |

2. Indefinite article (a/an):

| | | | |
|---|---|---|---|
| masc. | **un lápiz** | a pencil | **unos lápices** |
| fem. | **una carta** | a letter | **unas cartas** |

## Nouns

1. Most nouns which end in **o** are masculine. Those ending in **a** are generally feminine.
2. Normally, nouns which end in a vowel add **s** to form the plural; nouns ending in a consonant add **es.**
3. To show possession, use the preposition **de** (of).

| | |
|---|---|
| **el fin de la fiesta** | the end of the party |
| **el principio del* mes** | the beginning of the month |
| **las maletas de los viajeros** | the travellers' suitcases |
| **los ojos de las niñas** | the girls' eyes |
| **la habitación de Roberto** | Robert's room |

## Adjectives

1. Adjectives agree with the noun in gender and number. If the masculine form ends in **o** the feminine ends in **a.** As a rule, the adjective comes after the noun.

| | |
|---|---|
| **el niño pequeño** | the small boy |
| **la niña pequeña** | the small girl |

If the masculine form ends in **e** or with a consonant, the feminine keeps in general the same form.

| | |
|---|---|
| **el muro/la casa grande** | the big wall/house |
| **el mar/la flor azul** | the blue sea/flower |

2. Most adjectives form their plurals in the same way as nouns.

---

* (**del** is the contraction of **de** + **el**)

| | |
|---|---|
| **un coche inglés** | an English car |
| **dos coches ingleses** | two English cars |

3. Possessive adjectives: They agree with the thing possessed, not with the possessor.

| | sing. | plur. |
|---|---|---|
| my | **mi** | **mis** |
| your (fam.) | **tu** | **tus** |
| your (polite form) | **su** | **sus** |
| his/her/its | **su** | **sus** |
| our | **nuestro(a)** | **nuestros(as)** |
| your | **vuestro(a)** | **vuestros(as)** |
| their | **su** | **sus** |

| | |
|---|---|
| **su hijo** | *his* or *her* son |
| **su habitación** | *his* or *her* or *their* room |
| **sus maletas** | *his* or *her* or *their* suitcases |

4. Comparative and superlative: These are formed by adding **más** (more) or **menos** (less) and **lo más** or **lo menos,** respectively, before the adjective.

| | | | |
|---|---|---|---|
| **alto** | high | **más alto** | lo más alto |

## Adverbs

These are generally formed by adding **-mente** to the feminine form of the adjective (if it differs from the masculine); otherwise to the masculine.

| | | | |
|---|---|---|---|
| **cierto(a)** | sure | **fácil** | easy |
| **ciertamente** | surely | **fácilmente** | easily |

## Possessive pronouns

| | sing. | plur. |
|---|---|---|
| mine | **mío(a)** | **míos(as)** |
| yours (fam. sing.) | **tuyo(a)** | **tuyos(as)** |
| yours (polite form) | **suyo(a)** | **suyos(as)** |
| his/hers/its | **suyo(a)** | **suyos(as)** |
| ours | **nuestro(a)** | **nuestros(as)** |
| yours (fam. pl.) | **vuestro(a)** | **vuestros(as)** |
| theirs | **suyo(a)** | **suyos(as)** |

## Demonstrative pronouns

| | masc. | fem. | neut. |
|---|---|---|---|
| this | **éste** | **ésta** | **esto** |
| these | **éstos** | **éstas** | **estos** |
| that | **ése/aquél** | **ésa/aquélla** | **eso/aquello** |
| those | **ésos/aquéllos** | **ésas/aquéllas** | **esos/aquellos** |

The above masculine and feminine forms are also used as demonstrative adjectives, but accents are dropped. The two forms for "that" designate difference in place; **ése** means "that one", **aquél** "that one over there".

| | |
|---|---|
| **Esos libros no me gustan.** | I don't like those books. |
| **Eso no me gusta.** | I don't like that. |

## Personal pronouns

| | subject | direct object | indirect object |
|---|---|---|---|
| I | **yo** | **me** | **me** |
| you | **tú** | **te** | **te** |
| you | **usted** | **lo** | **le** |
| he | **él** | **lo** | **le** |
| she | **ella** | **la** | **le** |
| it | **él/ella** | **lo/la** | **le** |
| we | **nosotros(as)** | **nos** | **nos** |
| you | **vosotros(as)** | **os** | **os** |
| | **ustedes** | **los** | **les** |
| they | **ellos(as)** | **los** | **les** |

Subject pronouns are generally omitted, except in the polite form (**usted, ustedes**) which corresponds to "you". **Tú** (sing.) and **vosotros** (plur.) are used when talking to relatives, close friends and children and between young people; **usted** and the plural **ustedes** (often abbreviated to **Vd./Vds.**) are used in all other cases.

## Negatives

Negatives are formed by placing **no** before the verb.

| | | | |
|---|---|---|---|
| **Es nuevo.** | It's new. | **No es nuevo.** | It's not new. |

## Questions

In Spanish, questions are often formed by changing the intonation of your voice. Very often, the personal pronoun is left out, both in affirmative sentences and in questions.

| | |
|---|---|
| **Hablo español.** | I speak Spanish. |
| **¿Habla español?** | Do you speak Spanish? |

Note the double question mark used in Spanish.
The same is true of exclamation marks.

| | |
|---|---|
| **¡Qué tarde se hace!** | How late it's getting! |

# Verbs

Below are some examples of Spanish verbs in the three regular conjugations, grouped by families according to their infinitive endings, *-ar*, *-er* and *-ir*. Verbs which do not follow the conjugations below are considered irregular (see irregular verb list). Note that there are some verbs which follow the regular conjugation of the category they belong to, but present some minor changes in spelling. Examples: *tocar*, *toque*; *cargar*, *cargue*. The personal pronoun is not generally expressed, since the verb endings clearly indicate the person.

| | | 1st conj. | 2nd conj. | 3rd conj. |
|---|---|---|---|---|
| | | **am ar** | **tem er** | **viv ir** |
| Infinitive | | (*to love*) | (*to fear*) | (*to live*) |
| Present | (yo) | am **o** | tem **o** | viv **o** |
| | (tú) | am **as** | tem **es** | viv **es** |
| | (él) | am **a** | tem **e** | viv **e** |
| | (nosotros) | am **amos** | tem **emos** | viv **imos** |
| | (vosotros) | am **áis** | tem **éis** | viv **ís** |
| | (ellos) | am **an** | tem **en** | viv **en** |
| Imperfect | (yo) | am **aba** | tem **ía** | viv **ía** |
| | (tú) | am **abas** | tem **ías** | viv **ías** |
| | (él) | am **aba** | tem **ía** | viv **ía** |
| | (nosotros) | am **ábamos** | tem **íamos** | viv **íamos** |
| | (vosotros) | am **abais** | tem **íais** | viv **íais** |
| | (ellos) | am **aban** | tem **ían** | viv **ían** |
| Past. def. | (yo) | am **é** | tem **í** | viv **í** |
| | (tú) | am **aste** | tem **iste** | viv **iste** |
| | (él) | am **ó** | tem **ió** | viv **ió** |
| | (nosotros) | am **amos** | tem **imos** | viv **imos** |
| | (vosotros) | am **asteis** | tem **isteis** | viv **isteis** |
| | (ellos) | am **aron** | tem **ieron** | viv **ieron** |
| Future | (yo) | am **aré** | tem **eré** | viv **iré** |
| | (tú) | am **arás** | tem **erás** | viv **irás** |
| | (él) | am **ará** | tem **erá** | viv **irá** |
| | (nosotros) | am **aremos** | tem **eremos** | viv **iremos** |
| | (vosotros) | am **aréis** | tem **eréis** | viv **iréis** |
| | (ellos) | am **arán** | tem **erán** | viv **irán** |
| Conditional | (yo) | am **aría** | tem **ería** | viv **iría** |
| | (tú) | am **arías** | tem **erías** | viv **irías** |
| | (él) | am **aría** | tem **ería** | viv **iría** |
| | (nosotros) | am **aríamos** | tem **eríamos** | viv **iríamos** |
| | (vosotros) | am **aríais** | tem **eríais** | viv **iríais** |
| | (ellos) | am **arían** | tem **erían** | viv **irían** |

| | | | | |
|---|---|---|---|---|
| Subj. Pres. | (yo) | am **e** | tem **a** | viv **a** |
| | (tú) | am **es** | tem **as** | viv **as** |
| | (él) | am **e** | tem **a** | viv **a** |
| | (nosotros) | am **emos** | tem **amos** | viv **amos** |
| | (vosotros) | am **éis** | tem **áis** | viv **áis** |
| | (ellos) | am **en** | tem **an** | viv **an** |
| Pres. Part./Gerund | | am **ando** | tem **iendo** | viv **iendo** |
| Past. Part. | | am **ado** | tem **ido** | viv **ido** |

## Auxiliary verbs

The verb **to have** is translated either by *haber* or by *tener. Haber* is the auxiliary (e.g. he has gone) and *tener* (see list of irregular verbs) is a transitive verb, which conveys the idea of possession (e.g. she has a house).

The verb **to be** is translated either by *ser* or *estar. Ser* is used as an auxiliary verb to form the passive (e.g. they are understood) and to express an intrinsic quality of a fundamental characteristic (e.g. man is mortal). *Estar* (see list of irregular verbs) expresses a state or an attitude, whether lasting or not, of a thing or a person (e.g. she is hungry).

| | **haber** (*to have*) | | **ser** (*to be*) | |
|---|---|---|---|---|
| | *Present* | *Imperfect* | *Present* | *Imperfect* |
| (yo) | he | había | soy | era |
| (tú) | has | habías | eres | eras |
| (él) | ha | había | es | era |
| (nosotros) | hemos | habíamos | somos | éramos |
| (vosotros) | habéis | habíais | sois | erais |
| (ellos) | han | habían | son | eran |
| | *Future* | *Conditional* | *Future* | *Conditional* |
| (yo) | habré | habría | seré | sería |
| (tú) | habrás | habrías | serás | serías |
| (él) | habrá | habría | será | sería |
| (nosotros) | habremos | habríamos | seremos | seríamos |
| (vosotros) | habréis | habríais | seréis | seríais |
| (ellos) | habrán | habrían | serán | serían |
| | *Present subjunctive* | *Present perfect* | *Present subjunctive* | *Present perfect* |
| (yo) | haya | he habido | sea | he sido |
| (tú) | hayas | has habido | seas | has sido |
| (él) | haya | ha habido | sea | ha sido |
| (nosotros) | hayamos | hemos habido | seamos | hemos sido |
| (vosotros) | hayáis | habéis habido | seáis | habéis sido |
| (ellos) | hayan | han habido | sean | han sido |

| Present participle | Past participle | Present participle | Past participle |
|---|---|---|---|
| habiendo | habido | siendo | sido |

## Irregular verbs

Below is a list of the verbs and tenses commonly used in spoken Spanish. In the listing, a) stands for the present tense, b) for the imperfect, c) for the past def., d) for the future, e) for the present participle and f) for the past participle. The only forms given below are the irregular ones commonly used. There can be other irregular forms, but they are considered rare. In tenses other than present, all persons can be regularly formed from the first person. Unless otherwise indicated, verbs with prefixes (*ad-*, *ante-*, *com-*, *con-*, *de-*, *des-*, *dis-*, *en-*, *ex-*, *im-*, *pos-*, *pre-*, *pro-*, *re-*, *sobre-*, *sub-*, *tras-*, etc.) are conjugated like the stem verb.

**abstenerse** *refrain* →tener

**acertar** *guess* →cerrar

**acontecer** *happen* →agradecer

**acordar** *agree; decide* →contar

**acostarse** *lie down* →contar

**acrecentar** *increase; advance* →cerrar

**adormecer** *put to sleep* →agradecer

**adquirir** *acquire* a) adquiero, adquieres, adquiere, adquirimos, adquirís, adquieren; b) adquiría; c) adquirí; d) adquiriré; e) adquiriendo; f) adquirido

**advertir** *notice* →sentir

**agradecer** *thank* a) agradezco, agradeces, agradece, agradecemos, agradecéis, agradecen; b) agradecía; c) agradecí; d) agradeceré; e) agradeciendo; f) agradecido

**alentar** *encourage* →cerrar

**almorzar** *have lunch* →contar

**amanecer** *dawn* →agradecer

**andar** *walk* a) ando, andas, anda, andamos, andáis, andan; b) andaba; c) anduve; d) andaré; e) andando; f) andado
**anochecer** *begin to get dark* →agradecer
**apetecer** *want* →agradecer
**apostar** *bet* →contar
**apretar** *tighten, squeeze* →cerrar
**arrendar** *let, lease, rent* →cerrar
**arrepentirse** *repent, regret* →sentir
**ascender** *climb, reach* →perder
**atenerse** *obey; rely on* →tener
**atravesar** *cross, pierce* →cerrar
**atribuir** *attribute* →instruir
**aventar** *fan, air* →cerrar
**avergonzar** *put to shame, embarrass* →contar
**bendecir** *bless* →decir
**caber** *contain; fit* a) quepo, cabes, cabe, cabemos, cabéis, caben; b) cabía; c) cupe; d) cabré; e) cabiendo; f) cabido
**caer** *fall* a) caigo, caes, cae, caemos, caéis, caen; b) caía; c) caí; d) caeré; e) cayendo; f) caído
**calentar** *heat* →cerrar
**carecer** *lack* →agradecer
**cegar** *blind* →cerrar
**cerrar** *close* a) cierro, cierras, cierra, cerramos, cerráis, cierran; b) cerraba; c) cerré; d) cerraré; e) cerrando; f) cerrado
**cocer** *boil* a) cuezo, cueces, cuece, cocemos, cocéis, cuecen; b) cocía; c) cocí; d) coceré; e) cociendo; f) cocido

**colar** →contar
*strain; filter*

**colgar** →contar
*hang*

**comenzar** →cerrar
*begin*

**competir** →pedir
*compete*

**concebir** →pedir
*conceive*

**concernir** →sentir
*concern*

**concluir** →instruir
*conclude, finish*

**concordar** →contar
*agree, reconcile*

**conducir** →traducir
*drive*

**conferir** →sentir
*confer*

**confesar** →cerrar
*confess*

**conocer** a) conozco, conoces, conoce, conocemos, conocéis, conocen; b) conocía; c) conocí; d) conoceré; e) conociendo; f) conocido
*know*

**consolar** →contar
*console, comfort*

**constituir** →instruir
*constitute, be*

**construir** →instruir
*build, erect*

**contar** a) cuento, cuentas, cuenta, contamos, contáis, cuentan; b) contaba; c) conté; d) contaré; e) contando; f) contado
*count, bear in mind*

**contribuir** →instruir
*contribute*

**convertir** →sentir
*convert*

**corregir** →pedir
*correct*

**costar** →contar
*cost*

**crecer** →agradecer
*grow, rise*

**dar** a) doy, das, da, damos, dais, dan; b) daba; c) di; d) daré; e) dando; f) dado
*give*

**decir** a) digo, dices, dice, decimos, decís, dicen; b) decía; c) dije; d) diré e) diciendo; f) dicho
*say*

**deducir** →traducir
*deduce*

**defender** →perder
*defend*

**derretir** →pedir
*melt*

**descender** →perder
*descend, let down*

**descollar** →contar
*be outstanding*

**desconcertar** →cerrar
*damage; upset*

**despertar** →cerrar
*awaken, revive*

**desterrar** →cerrar
*banish*

**destituir** →instruir
*deprive, dismiss*

**destruir** →instruir
*destroy*

**desvanecer** →agradecer
*make disappear, take out*

**diferir** →sentir
*defer*

**digerir** →sentir
*digest*

**diluir** →instruir
*dilute*

**discernir** →sentir
*discern*

**disminuir** →instruir
*diminish*

**disolver** →morder
*dissolve*

**distribuir** →instruir
*distribute*

**divertir** →sentir
*entertain, distract*

**doler** →morder
*hurt*

**dormir** a) duermo, duermes, duerme, dormimos, dormís duermen; b) dormía; c) dormí; d) dormiré; e) durmiendo; f) dormido
*sleep*

**elegir** →pedir
*elect, choose*

**embestir** →pedir
*assault*

**empezar** →cerrar
*begin, start*

**enaltecer** →agradecer
*exalt, praise*

**enardecer** →agradecer
*excite; inflame*

**encender** →perder
*light, ignite*

**encomendar** →cerrar
*entrust*

**encontrar** →contar
*find*

**engrandecer** →agradecer
*enlarge, exaggerate*

**enloquecer** →agradecer
*madden*

**enmendar** →cerrar
*emend, correct*

**enmudecer** →agradecer
*silence*

**enorgullecer** →agradecer
*fill with pride*

**enriquecer** →agradecer
*enrich*

**ensangrentar** →cerrar
*stain with blood*

**ensoberbecer** →agradecer
*make proud*

**ensordecer** →agradecer
*deafen*

**enternecer** →agradecer
*soften; affect*

**enterrar** →cerrar
*bury*
**entristecer** →agradecer
*sadden*
**envejecer** →agradecer
*age*
**errar** →cerrar
*miss; wander*
**escarmentar** →cerrar
*chastise, punish*
**escarnecer** →agradecer
*scoff*
**establecer** →agradecer
*establish*
**estar** a) estoy, estás, está, estamos, estáis, están; b) estaba; c) estuve;
*be* d) estaré; e) estando; f) estado
**estremecer** →agradecer
*shake*
**excluir** →instruir
*exclude*
**fallecer** →agradecer
*die*
**favorecer** →agradecer
*favour*
**florecer** →agradecer
*blossom*
**fluir** →instruir
*flow*
**fortalecer** →agradecer
*strengthen*
**forzar** →contar
*compel, force*
**fregar** →cerrar
*wash up; scrub*
**freír** →reír
*fry*
**gemir** →pedir
*groan*
**gobernar** →cerrar
*govern*
**gruñir** a) gruño, gruñes, gruñe, gruñimos, gruñís, gruñen; b) gruñía;
*grunt* c) gruñí; d) gruñiré; e) gruñiendo; f) gruñido
**haber** a) he, has, ha, hemos, habéis, han; b) había; c) hube; d) habré;
*have* e) habiendo; f) habido

| | |
|---|---|
| **hacer** *make* | a) hago, haces, hace, hacemos, hacéis, hacen; b) hacía; c) hice; d) haré; e) haciendo; f) hecho |
| **heder** *stink* | →perder |
| **helar** *freeze* | →cerrar |
| **hender** *crack* | →perder |
| **herir** *injure* | →sentir |
| **hervir** *boil* | →sentir |
| **huir** *escape* | →instruir |
| **humedecer** *humidify* | →agradecer |
| **incluir** *include* | →instruir |
| **inducir** *induce* | →traducir |
| **ingerir** *swallow; consume* | →sentir |
| **instituir** *institute* | →instruir |
| **instruir** *instruct* | a) instruyo, instruyes, instruye, instruimos, instruís, instruyen; b) instruía; c) instruí; d) instruiré; e) instruyendo; f) instruido |
| **introducir** *introduce* | →traducir |
| **invertir** *invest* | →sentir |
| **ir** *go* | a) voy, vas, va, vamos, vais, van; b) iba; c) fui; d) iré; e) yendo; f) ido |
| **jugar** *play* | a) juego, juegas, juega, jugamos, jugáis, juegan; b) jugaba; c) jugué; d) jugaré; e) jugando; f) jugado |
| **lucir** *shine* | a) luzco, luces, luce, lucimos, lucís, lucen; b) lucía; c) lucí; d) luciré; e) luciendo; f) lucido |
| **llover** *rain* | a) llueve; b) llovía; c) llovió; d) lloverá; e) lloviendo; f) llovido |
| **manifestar** *manifest* | →cerrar |
| **mantener** *maintain* | →tener |

| | |
|---|---|
| **medir**<br>*measure* | →pedir |
| **mentir**<br>*tell a lie* | →sentir |
| **merecer**<br>*deserve* | →agradecer |
| **merendar**<br>*have tea, snack* | →cerrar |
| **moler**<br>*grind* | →morder |
| **morder**<br>*bite* | a) muerdo, muerdes, muerde, mordemos, mordéis, muerden; b) mordía; c) mordí; d) morderé; e) mordiendo; f) mordido |
| **morir**<br>*die* | →dormir |
| **mostrar**<br>*show* | →contar |
| **mover**<br>*move* | →morder |
| **nacer**<br>*be born* | a) nazco, naces, nace, nacemos, nacéis, nacen; b) nacía; c) nací; d) naceré; e) naciendo; f) nacido |
| **negar**<br>*deny* | →cerrar |
| **nevar**<br>*snow* | a) nieva; b) nevaba; c) nevó; d) nevará; e) nevando; f) nevado |
| **obedecer**<br>*obey* | →agradecer |
| **obscurecer**<br>*darken* | →agradecer |
| **obstruir**<br>*obstruct* | →instruir |
| **obtener**<br>*obtain* | →tener |
| **ofrecer**<br>*offer* | →agradecer |
| **oír**<br>*hear, listen* | a) oigo, oyes, oye, oímos, oís, oyen; b) oía; c) oí; d) oiré; e) oyendo; f) oído |
| **oler**<br>*smell* | →morder |
| **pacer**<br>*graze* | →nacer |
| **padecer**<br>*suffer* | →agradecer |
| **parecer**<br>*seem* | →agradecer |

**pedir** a) pido, pides, pide, pedimos, pedís, piden; b) pedía; c) pedí; d)
*ask for, request* pediré; e) pidiendo; f) pedido

**pensar** →cerrar
*think*

**perder** a) pierdo, pierdes, pierde, perdemos, perdéis, pierden; b)
*lose* perdía; c) perdí; d) perderé; e) perdiendo; f) perdido

**perecer** →agradecer
*perish*

**permanecer** →agradecer
*stay*

**pertenecer** →agradecer
*belong to*

**pervertir** →sentir
*pervert*

**placer** a) plazco, places, place, placemos, placéis, placen; b) placía; c)
*please* plací; d) placeré; e) placiendo; f) placido

**plegar** →cerrar
*fold*

**poblar** →contar
*populate*

**poder** a) puedo, puedes, puede, podemos, podéis, pueden; b) podía;
*can, be able* c) pude; d) podré; e) pudiendo; f) podido

**poner** a) pongo, pones, pone, ponemos, ponéis, ponen; b) ponía; c)
*put* puse; d) pondré; e) poniendo; f) puesto

**preferir** →sentir
*prefer*

**probar** →contar
*try*

**producir** →traducir
*produce*

**proferir** →sentir
*utter*

**quebrar** →cerrar
*break*

**querer** a) quiero, quieres, quiere, queremos, queréis, quieren; b)
*want, wish* quería; c) quise; d) querré; e) queriendo; f) querido

**recomendar** →cerrar
*recommend*

**recordar** →contar
*remember*

**reducir** →traducir
*reduce*

**referir** →sentir
*refer, relate*

**regar** →cerrar
*water*

**regir** →pedir
*govern*

**reír** a) río, ríes, ríe, reímos, reís, ríen; b) reía; c) reí; d) reiré; e) riendo; f) reído
*laugh*

**remendar** →cerrar
*mend*

**rendir** →pedir
*produce; overcome*

**renovar** →contar
*renew*

**reñir** →teñir
*scold; quarrel*

**repetir** →pedir
*repeat*

**requerir** →sentir
*request*

**resolver** →morder
*resolve*

**resplandecer** →agradecer
*shine*

**restituir** →instruir
*restore, return*

**retribuir** →instruir
*pay; reward*

**reventar** →cerrar
*burst*

**robustecer** →agradecer
*strengthen*

**rodar** →contar
*drive; roll*

**rogar** →contar
*beg, plead*

**saber** a) sé, sabes, sabe, sabemos, sabéis, saben; b) sabía; c) supe; d) sabré; e) sabiendo; f) sabido
*know*

**salir** a) salgo, sales, sale, salimos, salís, salen; b) salía; c) salí; d) saldré; e) saliendo; f) salido
*go out*

**satisfacer** →hacer
*satisfy*

**seducir** →traducir
*seduce*

**seguir** →pedir
*follow*

**sembrar** →cerrar
*sow*

**sentar** →cerrar
*sit, seat*

**sentir** a) siento, sientes, siente, sentimos, sentís, sienten; b) sentía; c) sentí; d) sentiré; e) sintiendo; f) sentido
*feel*

**ser** a) soy, eres, es, somos, sois, son; b) era c) fui; d) seré; e) siendo; f) sido
*be*

**servir** →pedir
*serve*

**soldar** →contar
*solder; join*

**soler** a) suelo, sueles, suele, solemos, soléis, suelen; b) solía; c) solí; e) soliendo; f) solido
*be used to*

**soltar** →contar
*release; loosen*

**sonar** →contar
*ring, sound*

**soñar** →contar
*dream*

**sugerir** →sentir
*suggest*

**sustituir** →instruir
*substitute*

**temblar** →cerrar
*tremble*

**tender** →perder
*stretch, extend*

**tener** a) tengo, tienes, tiene, tenemos, tenéis, tienen; b) tenía; c) tuve; d) tendré; e) teniendo; f) tenido
*have (got)*

**tentar** →cerrar
*touch; try*

**teñir** a) tiño, tiñes, tiñe, teñimos, teñís, tiñen; b) teñía; c) teñí; d) teñiré; e) tiñiendo; f) teñido
*dye*

**torcer** →cocer
*twist*

**tostar** →contar
*roast*

**traducir** a) traduzco, traduces, traduce, traducimos, traducís, traducen; b) traducía; c) traduje; d) traduciré; e) traduciendo; f) traducido
*translate*

| | |
|---|---|
| **traer**<br>*bring* | a) traigo, traes, trae, traemos, traéis, traen; b) traía; c) traje; d) traeré; e) trayendo; f) traído |
| **transferir**<br>*transfer* | →sentir |
| **trocar**<br>*(ex)change* | →contar |
| **tronar**<br>*thunder* | a) trueno, truenas, truena, tronamos, tronáis, truenan; b) tronaba; c) troné; d) tronaré; e) tronando; f) tronado |
| **tropezar**<br>*stumble* | →cerrar |
| **valer**<br>*protect; be worth* | a) valgo, vales, vale, valemos, valéis, valen; b) valía; c) valí; d) valdré; e) valiendo; f) valido |
| **venir**<br>*come* | a) vengo, vienes, viene, venimos, venís, vienen; b) venía; c) vine; d) vendré; e) viniendo; f) venido |
| **ver**<br>*see* | a) veo, ves, ve, vemos, veis, ven; b) veía; c) vi; d) veré; e) viendo; f) visto |
| **verter**<br>*pour; spill* | →perder |
| **vestir**<br>*dress* | →pedir |
| **volar**<br>*fly* | →contar |
| **volcar**<br>*tip over* | →contar |
| **volver**<br>*(re)turn* | →morder |
| **yacer**<br>*lie, rest* | →nacer |
| **zambullir**<br>*plunge* | a) zambullo, zambulles, zambulle, zambullimos, zambullís, zambullen; b) zambullía; c) zambullí; d) zambulliré; e) zambullendo; f) zambullido |

## Spanish Abbreviations

| | | |
|---|---|---|
| **a.C.** | *antes de Cristo* | B.C. |
| **A.C.** | *año de Cristo* | A.D. |
| **admón.** | *administración* | administration |
| **A.L.A.L.C.** | *Asociación Latino-Americana de Libre Comercio* | Latin American Free Trade Association |
| **apdo.** | *apartado de correos* | P.O. Box |
| **Av./Avda.** | *Avenida* | avenue |
| **Barna.** | *Barcelona* | Barcelona |
| **C/** | *Calle* | street, road |
| **c/c.** | *cuenta corriente* | current account |
| **Cía.** | *Compañía* | company |
| **cta.** | *cuenta* | account; bill |
| **cte.** | *corriente* | inst., of this month |
| **CV.** | *caballos de vapor* | horsepower |
| **D.** | *Don* | courtesy title for gentlemen only used together with the Christian name |
| **D.ª** | *Doña* | courtesy title for ladies, only used together with the Christian name |
| **dcha.** | *derecha* | right (direction) |
| **D.N.I.** | *Documento Nacional de Identidad* | identity card |
| **d. v.** | *días de visita* | open days |
| **EE.UU.** | *Estados Unidos* | USA |
| **Exc.ª** | *Excelencia* | Your Excellency |
| **f.c.** | *ferrocarril* | railway |
| **G.C.** | *Guardia Civil* | Spanish police force |
| **gral.** | *general* | general |
| **h.** | *hora* | hour |
| **hab.** | *habitantes* | inhabitants, population |
| **hnos.** | *hermanos* | brothers (in firms) |
| **íd.** | *ídem* | ditto |
| **igla.** | *iglesia* | church |
| **izq./izqda.** | *izquierda* | left (direction) |
| **lic.** | *licenciado* | licentiate; lawyer |
| **M.I.T.** | *Ministerio de Información y Turismo* | Spanish Ministry of Information and Tourism |
| **Mons.** | *Monseñor* | Roman Catholic title (approx. Your Grace) |
| **N.ª S.ª** | *Nuestra Señora* | Our Lady, Virgin Mary |

| | | |
|---|---|---|
| **n.º/núm.** | *número* | number |
| **O.E.A.** | *Organización de Estados Americanos* | Organization of American States |
| **P.** | *Padre* | Father (ecclesiastical title) |
| **pág.** | *página* | page |
| **P.D.** | *posdata* | P.S. |
| **p. ej.** | *por ejemplo* | e.g. |
| **P.P.** | *porte pagado* | postage paid |
| **P.V.P.** | *precio de venta al público* | retail price |
| **R.A.C.E.** | *Real Automóvil Club de España* | Royal Automobile Association of Spain |
| **R.A.E.** | *Real Academia Española* | Royal Academy of the Spanish Language |
| **R.C.** | *Real Club…* | Royal… Association |
| **RENFE** | *Red Nacional de los Ferrocarriles Españoles* | Spanish National Railways |
| **R.M.** | *Reverenda Madre* | Mother Superior, abbess |
| **R.P.** | *Reverendo Padre* | Reverend Father (title for Catholic priests and abbots) |
| **Rte.** | *Remite, Remitente* | sender (of a letter) |
| **RTVE** | *Radio Televisión Española* | Spanish Radio and Television Corporation |
| **S./Sto./Sta.** | *San/Santo/Santa* | saint |
| **S.A.** | *Sociedad Anónima* | Ltd., Inc. |
| **S.A.R.** | *Su Alteza Real* | His/Her Royal Highness |
| **s.a.s.s.** | *su atento y seguro servidor* | approx. Yours faithfully |
| **S.E.** | *Su Excelencia* | His Excellency |
| **sgte.** | *siguiente* | following |
| **S.M.** | *Su Majestad* | His/Her Majesty |
| **Sr.** | *Señor* | Mr. |
| **Sra.** | *Señora* | Mrs. |
| **S.R.C.** | *se ruega contestación* | please reply |
| **Sres./Srs.** | *Señores* | Sirs, Gentlemen |
| **Srta.** | *Señorita* | Miss |
| **S.S.** | *Su Santidad* | His Holiness |
| **Ud./Vd.** | *Usted* | you (singular) |
| **Uds./Vds.** | *Ustedes* | you (plural) |
| **Vda.** | *viuda* | widow |
| **v.g./v.gr.** | *verbigracia* | e.g. |

# Numerals

## Cardinal numbers

| | |
|---|---|
| 0 | cero |
| 1 | uno |
| 2 | dos |
| 3 | tres |
| 4 | cuatro |
| 5 | cinco |
| 6 | seis |
| 7 | siete |
| 8 | ocho |
| 9 | nueve |
| 10 | diez |
| 11 | once |
| 12 | doce |
| 13 | trece |
| 14 | catorce |
| 15 | quince |
| 16 | dieciséis |
| 17 | diecisiete |
| 18 | dieciocho |
| 19 | diecinueve |
| 20 | veinte |
| 21 | veintiuno |
| 30 | treinta |
| 31 | treinta y uno |
| 40 | cuarenta |
| 50 | cincuenta |
| 60 | sesenta |
| 70 | setenta |
| 80 | ochenta |
| 90 | noventa |
| 100 | ciento (cien) |
| 101 | ciento uno |
| 230 | doscientos treinta |
| 500 | quinientos |
| 700 | setecientos |
| 900 | novecientos |
| 1.000 | mil |
| 100.000 | cien mil |
| 1.000.000 | un millón |

## Ordinal numbers

| | |
|---|---|
| 1.º | primero |
| 2.º | segundo |
| 3.º | tercero |
| 4.º | cuarto |
| 5.º | quinto |
| 6.º | sexto |
| 7.º | séptimo |
| 8.º | octavo |
| 9.º | noveno (nono) |
| 10.º | décimo |
| 11.º | undécimo |
| 12.º | duodécimo |
| 13.º | decimotercero |
| 14.º | decimocuarto |
| 15.º | decimoquinto |
| 16.º | decimosexto |
| 17.º | decimoséptimo |
| 18.º | decimoctavo |
| 19.º | decimonoveno |
| 20.º | vigésimo |
| 21.º | vigésimo primero |
| 22.º | vigésimo segundo |
| 30.º | trigésimo |
| 40.º | cuadragésimo |
| 50.º | quincuagésimo |
| 60.º | sexagésimo |
| 70.º | septuagésimo |
| 80.º | octogésimo |
| 90.º | nonagésimo |
| 100.º | centésimo |
| 230.º | ducentésimo trigésimo |
| 300.º | tricentésimo |
| 400.º | cuadringentésimo |
| 500.º | quingentésimo |
| 600.º | sexcentésimo |
| 700.º | septingentésimo |
| 800.º | octingentésimo |
| 900.º | noningentésimo |
| 1.000.º | milésimo |

## Time

Although official time in Spain is based on the 24-hour clock, the 12-hour system is used in conversation.

In some Latin American countries you can specify *a.m.* or *p.m.* as in English, but it is far more common to add *de la mañana*, *de la tarde* or *de la noche* as in Spain.

Thus:

| | |
|---|---|
| *las ocho de la mañana* | 8 a.m. |
| *la una de la tarde* | 1 p.m. |
| *las ocho de la noche* | 8 p.m. |

## Days of the Week

| | |
|---|---|
| *domingo* | Sunday |
| *lunes* | Monday |
| *martes* | Tuesday |
| *miércoles* | Wednesday |
| *jueves* | Thursday |
| *viernes* | Friday |
| *sábado* | Saturday |

## Some Basic Phrases / Algunas expresiones útiles

| | |
|---|---|
| Please. | Por favor. |
| Thank you very much. | Muchas gracias. |
| Don't mention it. | No hay de qué. |
| Good morning. | Buenos días. |
| Good afternoon. | Buenas tardes. |
| Good evening. | Buenas noches. |
| Good night. | Buenas noches (despedida). |
| Good-bye. | Adiós. |
| See you later. | Hasta luego. |
| Where is/Where are…? | ¿Dónde está/Dónde están…? |
| What do you call this? | ¿Cómo se llama esto? |
| What does that mean? | ¿Qué quiere decir eso? |
| Do you speak English? | ¿Habla usted inglés? |
| Do you speak German? | ¿Habla usted alemán? |
| Do you speak French? | ¿Habla usted francés? |
| Do you speak Spanish? | ¿Habla usted español? |
| Do you speak Italian? | ¿Habla usted italiano? |
| Could you speak more slowly, please? | ¿Puede usted hablar más despacio, por favor? |
| I don't understand. | No comprendo. |
| Can I have…? | ¿Puede darme…? |
| Can you show me…? | ¿Puede usted enseñarme…? |
| Can you tell me…? | ¿Puede usted decirme…? |
| Can you help me, please? | ¿Puede usted ayudarme, por favor? |
| I'd like… | Quisiera… |
| We'd like… | Quisiéramos… |
| Please give me… | Por favor, déme… |
| Please bring me… | Por favor, tráigame… |
| I'm hungry. | Tengo hambre. |
| I'm thirsty. | Tengo sed. |
| I'm lost. | Me he perdido. |
| Hurry up! | ¡Dése prisa! |
| There is/There are… | Hay… |
| There isn't/There aren't… | No hay… |

### Arrival / Llegada

| | |
|---|---|
| Your passport, please. | Su pasaporte, por favor. |
| Have you anything to declare? | ¿Tiene usted algo que declarar? |
| No, nothing at all. | No, nada en absoluto. |
| Can you help me with my luggage, please? | ¿Puede usted ayudarme con mi equipaje, por favor? |

| | |
|---|---|
| Where's the bus to the centre of town, please? | ¿Dónde está el autobús que va al centro, por favor? |
| This way, please. | Por aquí, por favor. |
| Where can I get a taxi? | ¿Dónde puedo tomar un taxi? |
| What's the fare to...? | ¿Cuánto es la tarifa a...? |
| Take me to this address, please. | Lléveme a esta dirección, por favor. |
| I'm in a hurry. | Tengo mucha prisa. |
| **Hotel** | **Hotel** |
| My name is... | Me llamo... |
| Have you a reservation? | ¿Ha hecho usted una reserva? |
| I'd like a room with a bath. | Quisiera una habitación con baño. |
| What's the price per night? | ¿Cuánto cuesta por noche? |
| May I see the room? | ¿Puedo ver la habitación? |
| What's my room number, please? | ¿Cuál es el número de mi habitación, por favor? |
| There's no hot water. | No hay agua caliente. |
| May I see the manager, please? | ¿Puedo ver al director, por favor? |
| Did anyone telephone me? | ¿Me ha llamado alguien? |
| Is there any mail for me? | ¿Hay correo para mí? |
| May I have my bill (check), please? | ¿Puede darme la cuenta, por favor? |
| **Eating out** | **Restaurante** |
| Do you have a fixed-price menu? | ¿Tiene usted un menú de precio fijo? |
| May I see the menu? | ¿Puedo ver la carta? |
| May we have an ashtray, please? | ¿Nos puede traer un cenicero, por favor? |
| Where's the toilet, please? | ¿Dónde están los servicios, por favor? |
| I'd like an hors d'œuvre (starter). | Quisiera entremeses. |
| Have you any soup? | ¿Tiene usted sopa? |
| I'd like some fish. | Quisiera pescado. |
| What kind of fish do you have? | ¿Qué clases de pescado tiene usted? |
| I'd like a steak. | Quisiera un bistec. |
| What vegetables have you got? | ¿Qué verduras tiene usted? |
| Nothing more, thanks. | Nada más, gracias. |
| What would you like to drink? | ¿Qué le gustaría beber? |
| I'll have a beer, please. | Tomaré una cerveza, por favor. |
| I'd like a bottle of wine. | Quisiera una botella de vino. |
| May I have the bill (check), please? | ¿Podría darme la cuenta, por favor? |
| Is service included? | ¿Está incluido el servicio? |
| Thank you, that was a very good meal. | Gracias. Ha sido una comida muy buena. |

| **Travelling** | **Viajes** |
|---|---|
| Where's the railway station, please? | ¿Dónde está la estación de ferrocarril, por favor? |
| Where's the ticket office, please? | ¿Dónde está la taquilla, por favor? |
| I'd like a ticket to… | Quisiera un billete para… |
| First or second class? | ¿Primera o segunda clase? |
| First class, please. | Primera clase, por favor. |
| Single or return (one way or roundtrip)? | ¿Ida, o ida y vuelta? |
| Do I have to change trains? | ¿Tengo que transbordar? |
| What platform does the train for … leave from? | ¿De qué andén sale el tren para…? |
| Where's the nearest underground (subway) station? | ¿Dónde está la próxima estación de Metro? |
| Where's the bus station, please? | ¿Dónde está la estación de autobuses, pot favor? |
| When's the first bus to…? | ¿Cuándo sale el primer autobús para…? |
| Please let me off at the next stop. | Por favor, deténgase en la próxima parada. |

| **Relaxing** | **Diversiones** |
|---|---|
| What's on at the cinema (movies)? | ¿Qué dan en el cine? |
| What time does the film begin? | ¿A qué hora empieza la película? |
| Are there any tickets for tonight? | ¿Quedan entradas para esta noche? |
| Where can we go dancing? | ¿Dónde se puede ir a bailar? |

| **Meeting people** | **Presentaciones — Citas** |
|---|---|
| How do you do. | Buenos días Señora/Señorita/Señor. |
| How are you? | ¿Cómo está usted? |
| Very well, thank you. And you? | Muy bien, gracias. ¿Y usted? |
| May I introduce…? | ¿Me permite presentarle a…? |
| My name is… | Me llamo… |
| I'm very pleased to meet you. | Tanto gusto (en conocerle). |
| How long have you been here? | ¿Cuánto tiempo lleva usted aquí? |
| It was nice meeting you. | Ha sido un placer conocerle. |
| Do you mind if I smoke? | ¿Le molesta si fumo? |
| Do you have a light, please? | ¿Tiene usted fuego, por favor? |
| May I get you a drink? | ¿Me permite invitarle a una bebida (una copa)? |
| May I invite you for dinner tonight? | ¿Me permite invitarle a cenar esta noche? |
| Where shall we meet? | ¿Dónde quedamos citados? |

| **Shops, stores and services** | **Comercios y servicios** |
|---|---|
| Where's the nearest bank, please? | Dónde está el banco más cercano, por favor? |
| Where can I cash some travellers' cheques? | ¿Dónde puedo cambiar unos cheques de viaje? |
| Can you give me some small change, please? | ¿Puede usted darme algún dinero suelto, por favor? |
| Where's the nearest chemist's (pharmacy)? | ¿Dónde está la farmacia más cercana? |
| How do I get there? | ¿Cómo podría ir hasta allí? |
| Is it within walking distance? | ¿Se puede ir andando? |
| Can you help me, please? | ¿Puede usted atenderme, por favor? |
| How much is this? And that? | ¿Cuánto cuesta éste? ¿Y ése? |
| It's not quite what I want. | No es exactamente lo que quiero. |
| I like it. | Me gusta. |
| Can you recommend something for sunburn? | ¿Podría recomendarme algo para las quemaduras del sol? |
| I'd like a haircut, please. | Quisiera cortarme el pelo, por favor. |
| I'd like a manicure, please. | Quisiera una manicura, por favor. |

| **Street directions** | **Direcciones** |
|---|---|
| Can you show me on the map where I am? | ¿Puede enseñarme en el mapa dónde estoy? |
| You are on the wrong road. | Está usted equivocado de camino. |
| Go/Walk straight ahead. | Siga todo derecho. |
| It's on the left/on the right. | Está a la izquierda/a la derecha. |

| **Emergencies** | **Urgencias** |
|---|---|
| Call a doctor quickly. | Llame a un médico rápidamente. |
| Call an ambulance. | Llame a una ambulancia. |
| Please call the police. | Llame a la policía, por favor. |

# Inglés-Español

# English-Spanish

# Introducción

Este diccionario ha sido concebido para resolver de la mejor manera posible sus problemas prácticos de lenguaje. Se han suprimido las informaciones lingüísticas innecesarias. Los vocablos se suceden en un estricto orden alfabético, sin tener en cuenta si la palabra es simple o compuesta, o si se trata de una expresión formada por dos o más términos separados. Como única excepción, algunas expresiones idiomáticas están colocadas en orden alfabético, considerando para ello la palabra más característica. Cuando un término principal va seguido de otras palabras, expresiones o locuciones, éstas se hallan anotadas también en orden alfabético.

Cada palabra va seguida de una transcripción fonética (véase la guía de pronunciación). Después de la transcripción fonética se encuentra una indicación de la parte de la oración a la que pertenece el vocablo. Cuando una palabra puede desempeñar distintos oficios en la oración, las diferentes traducciones se dan una a continuación de la otra, precedidas de la indicación correspondiente.

Se indica el plural de los nombres cuando son irregulares y en algunos otros casos dudosos.

Cuando haya que repetir una palabra para formar el plural irregular o en las series de palabras se usa la tilde (~) para representar el vocablo principal.

En los plurales irregulares de las palabras compuestas sólo se escribe la parte que cambia, mientras que la parte invariable se representa por un guión (-).

Un asterisco (*) colocado antes de un verbo indica que dicho verbo es irregular. Para más detalles puede consultar la lista de los verbos irregulares.

Las palabras de este diccionario están escritas en su forma inglesa. La forma y significado americanos están señalados como tales (véase la lista de abreviaturas empleadas en el texto).

## Abreviaturas

| | |
|---|---|
| *adj* | adjetivo |
| *adv* | adverbio |
| *Am* | inglés americano |
| *art* | artículo |
| *conj* | conjunción |
| *f* | femenino |
| *fMe* | femenino (mexicano) |
| *fpl* | femenino plural |
| *fplMe* | femenino plural (mexicano) |
| *L.Am.* | América Latina |
| *m* | masculino |
| *Me* | mexicano |
| *mMe* | masculino (mexicano) |
| *mpl* | masculino plural |
| *mplMe* | masculino plural (mexicano) |

| | |
|---|---|
| *n* | nombre (sustantivo) |
| *nAm* | nombre (inglés americano) |
| *num* | numeral |
| *p* | tiempo pasado |
| *pl* | plural |
| *plAm* | plural (inglés americano) |
| *pp* | participio pasado |
| *pr* | tiempo presente |
| *pref* | prefijo |
| *prep* | preposición |
| *pron* | pronombre |
| *v* | verbo |
| *vAm* | verbo (inglés americano) |
| *vMe* | verbo (mexicano) |

# Guía de pronunciación

Cada vocablo principal de esta parte del diccionario va acompañado de una transcripción fonética destinada a indicar la pronunciación. Esta representación fonética debe leerse como si se tratara del idioma español hablado en Castilla. A continuación figuran tan solo las letras y los símbolos ambiguos o particularmente difíciles de comprender.
Cada sílaba está separada por un guión y la que lleva el acento está impresa en letra *bastardilla*.
Por supuesto, los sonidos de dos lenguas rara vez coinciden exactamente, pero siguiendo con atención nuestras explicaciones, el lector de habla española llegará a pronunciar las palabras extranjeras de manera que pueda ser comprendido. A fin de facilitar su tarea, algunas veces nuestras transcripciones simplifican ligeramente el sistema fonético del idioma, sin dejar por ello de reflejar las diferencias de sonido esenciales.

## Consonantes

| | |
|---|---|
| b | como en **b**ueno |
| dd | como en **d**ía |
| ð | como **d** en rui**d**o |
| ʤ | como la **ll** argentina, precedida por una **d** |
| gh | como **g** en **g**ato |
| h | sonido que es una espiración suave |
| ng | como **n** en bla**n**co |
| r | ponga la lengua en la misma posición que para pronunciar ʒ (véase más abajo), luego abra ligeramente la boca y baje la lengua |
| s | sonido siempre suave y sonoro como en mi**s**mo |
| ʃ | como **ch** en mu**ch**o, pero sin la **t** inicial que compone el sonido |
| v | más o menos como en la**v**a; sonido que se obtiene colocando los dientes incisivos superiores sobre el labio inferior y expulsando suavemente el aire |
| ʒ | como la **ll** argentina |

## Vocales y diptongos

**æ** sonido que combina el de la **a** en c**a**so con el de la **e** en sab**e**r
**ê** como **e** en sab**e**r
**o** como **o** en p**o**r
**ö** vocal neutral; sonido parecido al de la **a** española, pero con los labios extendidos

1) Las vocales largas están impresas a doble.
2) Las letras situadas más arriba que las otras (por ej.: **$^{u}$i, u$^{ö}$**) deben pronunciarse con menor intensidad y rápidamente.
3) Algunas palabras inglesas toman del francés las vocales nasales, que están indicadas con un símbolo de vocal mas **~~ng~~** (por ej.: **a~~ng~~**). Este signo **~~ng~~** *no* se debe pronunciar y sólo sirve para indicar la nasalidad de la vocal precedente. Las vocales nasales se pronuncian con la boca y la nariz simultáneamente.

## Pronunciación americana

Nuestra transcripción representa la pronunciación de Gran Bretaña. Aunque existen notables variaciones regionales en la lengua americana, ésta presenta en general algunas diferencias importantes respecto al inglés de Gran Bretaña.

He aquí algunos ejemplos:
1) La **r,** delante de una consonante o al final de una palabra, siempre se pronuncia, lo cual es contrario a la costumbre inglesa.
2) En muchas palabras (por ej.: *ask*, *castle*, *laugh*, etc.) la **aa** se transforma en **ææ.**
3) El sonido inglés **o** se pronuncia **a** o también **oo.**
4) En palabras como *duty*, *tune*, *new*, etc., el sonido **y** se omite a menudo antes de **uu.**
5) Por último, el acento tónico de algunas palabras puede variar considerablemente.

# A

**a** (ei, ö) *art* (an) un *art*

**abbey** (æ-bi) *n* abadía *f*

**abbreviation** (ö-brii-vi-*ei*-ʃön) *n* abreviatura *f*

**ability** (ö-*bi*-lö-ti) *n* habilidad *f*

**able** (*ei*-böl) *adj* capaz; hábil; ***be ~ to** *ser capaz de; *saber, *poder

**aboard** (ö-*bood*) *adv* a bordo

**abolish** (ö-*bo*-liʃ) *v* abolir

**abortion** (ö-*boo*-ʃön) *n* aborto *m*

**about** (ö-*baut*) *prep* acerca de; respecto a; alrededor de; *adv* hacia, aproximadamente; en torno

**above** (ö-*bav*) *prep* encima de; *adv* encima

**abroad** (ö-*brood*) *adv* en el extranjero

**abscess** (*æb*-ssêss) *n* absceso *m*

**absence** (*æb*-ssönss) *n* ausencia *f*

**absent** (*æb*-ssönt) *adj* ausente

**absolutely** (*æb*-ssö-luut-li) *adv* absolutamente

**abstain from** (öb-*sstein*) *abstenerse de

**abstract** (*æb*-sstrækt) *adj* abstracto

**absurd** (öb-*ssööd*) *adj* absurdo

**abundance** (ö-*ban*-dönss) *n* abundancia *f*

**abundant** (ö-*ban*-dönt) *adj* abundante

**abuse** (ö-*byuuss*) *n* abuso *m*

**abyss** (ö-*biss*) *n* abismo *m*

**academy** (ö-*kæ*-dö-mi) *n* academia *f*

**accelerate** (ök-*ssê*-lö-reit) *v* acelerar

**accelerator** (ök-*ssê*-lö-rei-tö) *n* acelerador *m*

**accent** (*æk*-ssönt) *n* acento *m*

**accept** (ök-*ssêpt*) *v* aceptar

**access** (*æk*-ssêss) *n* acceso *m*

**accessible** (ök-*ssê*-ssö-böl) *adj* accesible

**accessories** (ök-*ssê*-ssö-ris) *pl* accesorios *mpl*

**accident** (*æk*-ssi-dönt) *n* accidente *m*

**accidental** (æk-ssi-*dên*-töl) *adj* accidental

**accommodate** (ö-*ko*-mö-deit) *v* acomodar

**accommodation** (ö-ko-mö-*dei*-ʃön) *n* acomodación *f*, alojamiento *m*

**accompany** (ö-*kam*-pö-ni) *v* acompañar

**accomplish** (ö-*kam*-pliʃ) *v* terminar; cumplir

**accordance: in ~ with** (in ö-*koo*-dönss $^{u}$i) con arreglo a; conforme a

**according to** (ö-*koo*-ding tuu) según

**account** (ö-*kaunt*) *n* cuenta *f*; factura *f*; relato *m*; **~ for** explicar; **on ~ of** a causa de

**accountable** (ö-*kaun*-tö-böl) *adj* explicable; responsable

**accurate** (æ-kyu-röt) *adj* exacto; preciso; acertado

**accuse** (ö-*kyuus*) *v* acusar

**accused** (ö-*kyuusd*) *n* acusado *m*, -a *f*

**accustom** (ö-*ka*-sstöm) *v* acostumbrar; **accustomed** acostumbrado

**ache** (eik) *v* *doler; *n* dolor *m*

**achieve** (ö-*chiiv*) *v* alcanzar; lograr

**achievement** (ö-*chiiv*-mönt) *n* realización *f*

**acid** (æ-ssid) *n* ácido *m*

**acknowledge** (ök-*no*-lidʒ) *v* *reconocer; admitir; confirmar

**acne** (*æk*-ni) *n* acné *m*

**acorn** (*ei*-koon) *n* bellota *f*

**acquaintance** (ö-*k$^{u}$ein*-tönss) *n* conocido *m*

**acquire** (ö-*k$^{u}$ai$^{ö}$*) *v* *adquirir

**acquisition** (æ-k$^{u}$i-*si*-ʃön) *n* adquisición *f*

**acquittal** (ö-*k$^{u}$i*-töl) *n* absolución *f*

**across** (ö-*kross*) *prep* a través de; al otro lado de; *adv* al otro lado

**act** (ækt) *n* acto *m*; hecho *m*; *v* actuar, *hacer; comportarse
**action** (*æk*-ʃön) *n* acción *f*
**active** (*æk*-tiv) *adj* activo; vivaz
**activity** (æk-*ti*-vö-ti) *n* actividad *f*
**actor** (*æk*-tö) *n* actor *m*
**actress** (*æk*-triss) *n* actriz *f*
**actual** (*æk*-chu-öl) *adj* verdadero
**actually** (*æk*-chu-ö-li) *adv* en realidad
**acute** (ö-*kyuut*) *adj* agudo
**adapt** (ö-*dæpt*) *v* adaptar
**adaptor** (ö-*dæpt*-tö) *n* adaptador *m*
**add** (æd) *v* sumar, adicionar; añadir
**addition** (ö-*di*-ʃön) *n* adición *f*
**additional** (ö-*di*-ʃö-nöl) *adj* adicional; accesorio
**address** (ö-*drêss*) *n* dirección *f*; senas *fpl*; *v* destinar; dirigirse a
**addressee** (æ-drê-*ssii*) *n* destinatario *m*, -a *f*
**adequate** (*æ*-di-k$^{u}$öt) *adj* adecuado; conveniente
**adjective** (*æ*-dʒik-tiv) *n* adjetivo *m*
**adjourn** (ö-*dʒöön*) *v* aplazar
**adjust** (ö-*dʒasst*) *v* ajustar
**administer** (öd-*mi*-ni-sstö) *v* administrar
**administration** (öd-mi-ni-*sstrei*-ʃön) *n* administración *f*; gestión *f*
**administrative** (öd-*mi*-ni-sströ-tiv) *adj* gerencial; administrativo; **~ law** derecho administrativo
**admiration** (æd-mö-*rei*-ʃön) *n* admiración *f*
**admire** (öd-*mai*$^{ö}$) *v* admirar
**admission** (öd-*mi*-ʃön) *n* entrada *f*; admisión *f*
**admit** (öd-*mit*) *v* admitir; *reconocer
**admittance** (öd-*mi*-tönss) *n* admisión *f*; **no ~** prohibida la entrada
**adopt** (ö-*dopt*) *v* adoptar
**adorable** (ö-*doo*-rö-böl) *adj* adorable
**adult** (*æ*-dalt) *n* adulto *m*; *adj* adulto
**advance** (öd-*vaanss*) *n* adelanto *m*; anticipo *m*; *v* avanzar; anticipar; **in ~** por adelantado
**advanced** (öd-*vaansst*) *adj* avanzado
**advantage** (öd-*vaan*-tidʒ) *n* ventaja *f*
**advantageous** (æd-vön-*tei*-dʒöss) *adj* ventajoso
**adventure** (öd-*vên*-chö) *n* aventura *f*
**adverb** (*æd*-vööb) *n* adverbio *m*
**advertise** (*æd*-vöö-tais) *v* anunciar; anunciarse, poner un anuncio
**advertisement** (öd-*vöö*-tiss-mönt) *n* anuncio *m*
**advertising** (*æd*-vö-tai-sing) *n* publicidad *f*
**advice** (öd-*vaiss*) *n* consejo *m*
**advise** (öd-*vais*) *v* aconsejar
**advocate** (*æd*-vö-köt) *n* abogado *m*
**aerial** (*ê*$^{ö}$-ri-öl) *n* antena *f*
**aeroplane** (*ê*$^{ö}$-rö-plein) *n* avión *m*
**affair** (ö-*fê*$^{ö}$) *n* asunto *m*; amorío *m*
**affect** (ö-*fêkt*) *v* afectar
**affected** (ö-*fêk*-tid) *adj* afectado
**affection** (ö-*fêk*-ʃön) *n* afección *f*; cariño *m*
**affectionate** (ö-*fêk*-ʃö-nit) *adj* cariñoso
**affiliated** (ö-*fi*-li-ei-tid) *adj* afiliado
**affirmative** (ö-*föö*-mö-tiv) *adj* afirmativo
**afford** (ö-*food*) *v* permitirse
**afraid** (ö-*freid*) *adj* angustioso, asustado; ***be ~** *tener miedo
**Africa** (*æ*-fri-kö) África *f*
**African** (*æ*-fri-kön) *adj* africano
**after** (*aaf*-tö) *prep* después de; detrás de; tras; *conj* después de que
**afternoon** (aaf-tö-*nuun*) *n* tarde *f*
**afterwards** (*aaf*-tö-$^{u}$öds) *adv* después, más tarde
**again** (ö-*ghên*) *adv* otra vez; de nuevo; **~ and again** repetidamente
**against** (ö-*ghênsst*) *prep* contra
**age** (eidʒ) *n* edad *f*; vejez *f*; época *f*; **of ~** mayor de edad; **under ~** menor de

edad
**aged** (*ei*-dʒid) *adj* viejo; anciano
**agency** (*ei*-dʒön-ssi) *n* agencia *f*; sección *f*
**agenda** (ö-*dʒên*-dö) *n* orden del día
**agent** (*ei*-dʒönt) *n* agente *m*, representante *m*
**aggressive** (ö-*ghrê*-ssiv) *adj* agresivo
**ago** (ö-*ghou*) *adv* hace; **long ~** hace mucho tiempo
**agree** (ö-*ghrii*) *v* *convenir, *concordar; *consentir; *acordar
**agreeable** (ö-*ghrii*-ö-böl) *adj* agradable
**agreement** (ö-*ghrii*-mönt) *n* contrato *m*; acuerdo *m*; conformidad *f*
**agriculture** (*æ*-ghri-kal-chö) *n* agricultura *f*
**ahead** (ö-*hêd*) *adv* adelante; **~ of** delante de; ***go ~** continuar; **straight ~** todo seguido
**aid** (eid) *n* socorro *m*; *v* asistir, ayudar
**AIDS** (eids) *n* SIDA *m*
**aim** (eim) *n* fin *m*; **~ at** apuntar; aspirar a
**air** (êᶷ) *n* aire *m*; *v* airear
**air conditioning** (*êᶷ*-kön-di-ʃö-ning) *n* aire acondicionado; **air conditioned** *adj* climatizado
**aircraft** (*êᶷ*-kraaft) *n* (pl **~**) avión *m*
**airfield** (*êᶷ*-fiild) *n* campo de aviación
**airline** (*êᶷ*-lain) *n* aerolínea *f*
**airmail** (*êᶷ*-meil) *n* correo aéreo
**airplane** (*êᶷ*-plein) *nAm* avión *m*
**airport** (*êᶷ*-poot) *n* aeropuerto *m*
**airsickness** (*êᶷ*-ssik-nöss) *n* mal de las alturas; mareo *m*
**airtight** (*êᶷ*-tait) *adj* hermético
**airy** (*êᶷ*-ri) *adj* espacioso; ventilado; ligero
**aisle** (ail) *n* nave lateral; pasillo *m*
**alarm** (ö-*laam*) *n* alarma *f*; *v* alarmar; **~ clock** despertador *m*
**album** (*æl*-böm) *n* álbum *m*
**alcohol** (*æl*-kö-hol) *n* alcohol *m*
**alcoholic** (æl-kö-*ho*-lik) *adj* alcohólico
**ale** (eil) *n* cerveza *f*
**algebra** (*æl*-dʒi-brö) *n* álgebra *f*
**Algeria** (æl-*dʒiᶷ*-ri-ö) Argelia *f*
**Algerian** (æl-*dʒiᶷ*-ri-ön) *adj* argelino
**alien** (*ei*-li-ön) *n* extranjero *m*, -a *f*; *adj* extranjero
**alike** (ö-*laik*) *adj* igual, parecido; *adv* igualmente
**alive** (ö-*laiv*) *adj* en vida, vivo
**all** (ool) *adj* todo; *adv* del todo; **~ day** todo el día; **~ in ~** con todo; **~ right!** ¡está bien!; **at ~** en modo alguno; siquiera
**allergy** (*æ*-lö-dʒi) *n* alergia *f*
**alley** (*æ*-li) *n* callejón *m*
**alliance** (ö-*lai*-önss) *n* alianza *f*
**allow** (ö-*lau*) *v* permitir, autorizar; **~ to** autorizar a; ***be allowed** *estar autorizado
**allowance** (ö-*lau*-önss) *n* asignación *f*
**all-round** (ool-*raund*) *adj* polifacético
**almond** (*aa*-mönd) *n* almendra *f*
**almost** (*ool*-mousst) *adv* casi; cerca de
**alone** (ö-*loun*) *adv* sólo
**along** (ö-*long*) *prep* a lo largo de
**aloud** (ö-*laud*) *adv* en voz alta
**alphabet** (*æl*-fö-bêt) *n* abecedario *m*
**already** (ool-*rê*-di) *adv* ya
**also** (*ool*-ssou) *adv* también; asimismo
**altar** (*ool*-tö) *n* altar *m*
**alter** (*ool*-tö) *v* cambiar, alterar
**alteration** (ool-tö-*rei*-ʃön) *n* cambio *m*, alteración *f*
**alternate** (ool-*töö*-nöt) *adj* alternativo
**alternative** (ool-*töö*-nö-tiv) *n* alternativa *f*
**although** (ool-*ðou*) *conj* aunque
**altitude** (*æl*-ti-tyuud) *n* altitud *f*
**alto** (*æl*-tou) *n* (pl **~**s) contralto *m*
**altogether** (ool-tö-*ghê*-ðö) *adv* en total

**always** (*ool*-ᵘeis) *adv* siempre
**am** (æm) *v* (pr be)
**amaze** (ö-*meis*) *v* extrañar, asombrar
**amazement** (ö-*meis*-mönt) *n* asombro *m*
**amazing** (ö-*mei*-sing) *adj* asombroso; alucinante
**ambassador** (æm-*bæ*-ssö-dö) *n* embajador *m*
**amber** (*æm*-bö) *n* ámbar *m*
**ambiguous** (æm-*bi*-ghyu-öss) *adj* ambiguo; equívoco
**ambition** (*æm*-bi-ʃön) *n* ambición *f*
**ambitious** (æm-*bi*-ʃöss) *adj* ambicioso
**ambulance** (*æm*-byu-lönss) *n* ambulancia *f*
**ambush** (*æm*-buʃ) *n* emboscada *f*
**America** (ö-*mê*-ri-kö) América *f*
**American** (ö-*mê*-ri-kön) *adj* americano
**amethyst** (*æ*-mi-zisst) *n* amatista *f*
**amid** (ö-*mid*) *prep* entre; en medio de
**ammonia** (ö-*mou*-ni-ö) *n* amoníaco *m*
**amnesty** (*æm*-ni-ssti) *n* amnistía *f*
**among** (ö-*mang*) *prep* entre; ~ **other things** entre otras cosas
**amount** (ö-*maunt*) *n* cantidad *f*; suma *f*; ~ **to** sumar
**amuse** (ö-*myuus*) *v* *divertir, *entretener
**amusement** (ö-*myuus*-mönt) *n* distracción *f*, entretenimiento *m*
**amusing** (ö-*myuu*-sing) *adj* divertido
**an(a)emia** (ö-*nii*-mi-ö) *n* anemia *f*
**an(a)esthesia** (æ-niss-*zii*-si-ö) *n* anestesia *f*
**analyse** (*æ*-nö-lais) *v* analizar
**analysis** (ö-*næ*-lö-ssiss) *n* (pl -ses) análisis *f*
**analyst** (*æ*-nö-lisst) *n* analista *m*; psicoanalista *m*
**anarchy** (*æ*-nö-ki) *n* anarquía *f*
**anatomy** (ö-*næ*-tö-mi) *n* anatomía *f*
**ancestor** (*æn*-ssê-sstö) *n* antepasado *m*, -a *f*
**anchor** (*æng*-kö) *n* ancla *f*
**anchovy** (*æn*-chö-vi) *n* anchoa *f*
**ancient** (*ein*-ʃönt) *adj* viejo, antiguo; anticuado
**and** (ænd, önd) *conj* y
**angel** (*ein*-dʒöl) *n* ángel *m*
**anger** (*æng*-ghö) *n* cólera *f*, enojo *m*; furia *f*; *v* enojar
**angle** (*æng*-ghöl) *v* pescar con caña; *n* ángulo *m*
**angry** (*æng*-ghri) *adj* enfadado, enojado
**animal** (*æ*-ni-möl) *n* animal *m*
**ankle** (*æng*-köl) *n* tobillo *m*
**annex**¹ (*æ*-nêkss) *n* anexo *m*
**annex**² (ö-*nêkss*) *v* anexar
**anniversary** (æ-ni-*vöö*-ssö-ri) *n* aniversario *m*
**announce** (ö-*naunss*) *v* anunciar; informar; proclamar
**announcement** (ö-*naunss*-mönt) *n* anuncio *m*; informe *m*; proclama *f*
**annoy** (ö-*noi*) *v* irritar, fastidiar; molestar
**annoyance** (ö-*noi*-önss) *n* molestia *f*; fastidio *m*
**annoying** (ö-*noi*-ing) *adj* molesto; fastidioso
**annual** (*æ*-nyu-öl) *adj* anual; *n* anuario *m*
**annum: per ~** (pör *æ*-nöm) al año
**anonymous** (ö-*no*-ni-möss) *adj* anónimo
**another** (ö-*na*-ðö) *adj* otro más; otro
**answer** (*aan*-ssö) *v* responder a; *n* respuesta *f*
**ant** (ænt) *n* hormiga *f*
**antibiotic** (æn-ti-bai-*o*-tik) *n* antibiótico *m*
**anticipate** (æn-*ti*-ssi-peit) *v* *prever; *prevenir
**antifreeze** (*æn*-ti-friis) *n* anticongelante *m*

**antipathy** (æn-*ti*-pö-zi) *n* antipatía *f*
**antique** (æn-*tiik*) *adj* antiguo; *n* antigüedad *f*; ~ **dealer** anticuario *m*
**antiquity** (æn-*ti*-k$^{u}$ö-ti) *n* Antigüedad *f*; **antiquities** *pl* antigüedades *fpl*
**anxiety** (æng-*sai*-ö-ti) *n* ansiedad *f*; preocupación *f*
**anxious** (*ængk*-ʃöss) *adj* ansioso; preocupado
**any** (*ê*-ni) *adj* alguno, alguna
**anybody** (*ê*-ni-bo-di) *pron* cualquiera
**anyhow** (*ê*-ni-hau) *adv* de cualquier modo
**anyone** (*ê*-ni-$^{u}$an) *pron* cualquiera
**anything** (*ê*-ni-zing) *pron* cualquier cosa
**anyway** (*ê*-ni-$^{u}$ei) *adv* en todo caso
**anywhere** (*ê*-ni-$^{u}$ê$^{ö}$) *adv* en donde sea; dondequiera
**apart** (ö-*paat*) *adv* por separado, separadamente; ~ **from** aparte de
**apartment** (ö-*paat*-mönt) *nAm* apartamento *m*; piso *m*; ~ **house** *Am* casa de pisos
**aperitif** (ö-*pê*-rö-tiv) *n* aperitivo *m*
**apologize** (ö-*po*-lö-dʒais) *v* disculparse
**apology** (ö-*po*-lö-dʒi) *n* excusa *f*, disculpa *f*
**apparatus** (æ-pö-*rei*-töss) *n* aparato *m*
**apparent** (ö-*pæ*-rönt) *adj* aparente; obvio
**apparently** (ö-*pæ*-rönt-li) *adv* por lo visto; evidentemente
**appeal** (ö-*piil*) *n* apelación *f*
**appear** (ö-*pi*$^{ö}$) *v* *parecer; *salir; *aparecer
**appearance** (ö-*pi*$^{ö}$-rönss) *n* apariencia *f*; aspecto *m*; entrada *f*
**appendicitis** (ö-pên-di-*ssai*-tiss) *n* apendicitis *f*
**appendix** (ö-*pên*-dikss) *n* (pl -dices, -dixes) apéndice *m*
**appetite** (*æ*-pö-tait) *n* apetito *m*
**appetizer** (*æ*-pö-tai-sö) *n* tapa *f*; aperitivo *m*
**appetizing** (*æ*-pö-tai-sing) *adj* apetitoso
**applaud** (ö-*plood*) *v* aplaudir
**applause** (ö-*ploos*) *n* aplauso *m*
**apple** (*æ*-pöl) *n* manzana *f*
**appliance** (ö-*plai*-önss) *n* aparato *m*
**application** (æ-pli-*kei*-ʃön) *n* aplicación *f*; demanda *f*; solicitud *f*
**apply** (ö-*plai*) *v* aplicar; solicitar un puesto; aplicarse a
**appoint** (ö-*point*) *v* designar, nombrar
**appointment** (ö-*point*-mönt) *n* cita *f*; nombramiento *m*
**appreciate** (ö-*prii*-ʃi-eit) *v* valuar; apreciar
**appreciation** (ö-prii-ʃi-*ei*-ʃön) *n* aprecio *m*
**apprentice** (ö-*prên*-tis) aprendiz *m*, -a *f*
**approach** (ö-*prouch*) *v* acercarse; *n* enfoque *m*; acceso *m*
**appropriate** (ö-*prou*-pri-öt) *adj* justo, apropiado, adecuado
**approval** (ö-*pruu*-völ) *n* aprobación *f*; consentimiento *m*, acuerdo *m*; **on** ~ a prueba
**approve** (ö-*pruuv*) *v* *aprobar; ~ **of** *estar de acuerdo con
**approximate** (ö-*prok*-ssi-möt) *adj* aproximado
**approximately** (ö-*prok*-ssi-möt-li) *adv* aproximadamente
**apricot** (*ei*-pri-kot) *n* albaricoque *m*; chabacano *mMe*
**April** (*ei*-pröl) abril
**apron** (*ei*-prön) *n* delantal *m*
**Arab** (*æ*-röb) *adj* árabe
**arbitrary** (*aa*-bi-trö-ri) *adj* arbitrario
**arcade** (aa-*keid*) *n* pórtico *m*, arcada *f*
**arch** (aach) *n* arco *m*; bóveda *f*
**arch(a)eologist** (aa-ki-*o*-lö-dʒisst) *n* arqueólogo *m*, -a *f*

**arch(a)eology** (aa-ki-*o*-lö-dʒi) *n* arqueología *f*
**archbishop** (aach-*bi*-ʃöp) *n* arzobispo *m*
**arched** (aacht) *adj* arqueado
**architect** (*aa*-ki-têkt) *n* arquitecto *m*
**architecture** (*aa*-ki-têk-chö) *n* arquitectura *f*
**archives** (*aa*-kaivs) *pl* archivo *m*
**are** (aa) *v* (pr be)
**area** (*ê*ö-ri-ö) *n* región *f*; zona *f*; superficie *f*; ~ **code** indicativo *m*
**Argentina** (aa-dʒön-*tii*-nö) Argentina *f*
**Argentinian** (aa-dʒön-*ti*-ni-ön) *adj* argentino
**argue** (*aa*-ghyuu) *v* argumentar, discutir; disputar; razonar
**argument** (*aa*-ghyu-mönt) *n* argumento *m*; discusión *f*; disputa *f*
***arise** (ö-*rais*) *v* surgir
**arm** (aam) *n* brazo *m*; arma *f*; *v* armar
**armchair** (*aam*-chêö) *n* butaca *f*, sillón *m*
**armed** (aamd) *adj* armado; ~ **forces** fuerzas armadas
**armour** (*aa*-mö) *n* armadura *f*
**army** (*aa*-mi) *n* ejército *m*
**aroma** (ö-*rou*-mö) *n* aroma *m*
**around** (ö-*raund*) *prep* alrededor de, en torno de; *adv* en torno; **all** ~ por todas partes
**arrange** (ö-*reind*ʒ) *v* clasificar, ordenar; organizar
**arrangement** (ö-*reind*ʒ-mönt) *n* arreglo *m*; orden *m*; acuerdo *m*
**arrest** (ö-*rêsst*) *v* arrestar; *n* arresto *m*
**arrival** (ö-*rai*-völ) *n* llegada *f*
**arrive** (ö-*raiv*) *v* llegar
**arrow** (*æ*-rou) *n* flecha *f*
**art** (aat) *n* arte *m/f*; habilidad *f*; ~ **collection** colección de arte; ~ **exhibition** exposición de arte; ~ **gallery** galería de arte; ~ **history** historia del arte; **arts and crafts** artes industriales; ~ **school** academia de bellas artes
**artery** (*aa*-tö-ri) *n* arteria *f*
**artichoke** (*aa*-ti-chouk) *n* alcachofa *f*
**article** (*aa*-ti-köl) *n* artículo *m*
**artificial** (aa-ti-*fi*-ʃöl) *adj* artificial
**artist** (*aa*-tisst) *n* artista *m/f*
**artistic** (aa-*ti*-sstik) *adj* artístico
**as** (æs) *conj* como; tanto; que; ya que, porque; ~ **from** a partir de; ~ **if** como si
**asbestos** (æs-*bê*-sstoss) *n* asbesto *m*
**ascend** (ö-*ssênd*) *v* subir; escalar
**ascent** (ö-*ssênt*) *n* subida *f*
**ascertain** (æ-ssö-*tein*) *v* *comprobar; asegurarse de
**ash** (æʃ) *n* ceniza *f*
**ashamed** (ö-*ʃeimd*) *adj* avergonzado; ***be** ~ *avergonzarse
**ashore** (ö-*ʃoo*) *adv* en tierra
**ashtray** (*æ*ʃ-trei) *n* cenicero *m*
**Asia** (*ei*-ʃö) Asia *f*
**Asian** (*ei*-ʃön) *adj* asiático
**aside** (ö-*ssaid*) *adv* aparte
**ask** (aassk) *v* preguntar; *rogar; invitar
**asleep** (ö-*ssliip*) *adj* dormido
**asparagus** (ö-*sspæ*-rö-ghöss) *n* espárrago *m*
**aspect** (*æ*-sspêkt) *n* aspecto *m*
**asphalt** (*æss*-fælt) *n* asfalto *m*
**aspire** (ö-*sspai*ö) *v* aspirar
**aspirin** (*æ*-sspö-rin) *n* aspirina *f*
**assassination** (ö-ssæ-ssi-*nei*-ʃön) *n* asesinato *m*
**assault** (ö-*ssoolt*) *v* atacar; violar
**assemble** (ö-*ssêm*-böl) *v* reunir; montar
**assembly** (ö-*ssêm*-bli) *n* reunión *f*, asamblea *f*
**assignment** (ö-*ssain*-mönt) *n* encargo *m*
**assign to** (ö-*ssain*) asignar a; *atribuir a

**assist** (ö-*ssisst*) *v* asistir
**assistance** (ö-*ssi*-sstönss) *n* auxilio *m*; apoyo *m*, asistencia *f*
**assistant** (ö-*ssi*-sstönt) *n* asistente *m*
**associate**[1] (ö-*ssou*-ʃi-öt) *n* compañero *m*, -a *f*; colega *m/f*; aliado *m*, -a *f*; socio *m*, -a *f*
**associate**[2] (ö-*ssou*-ʃi-eit) *v* asociar; ~ **with** frecuentar
**association** (ö-ssou-ssi-*ei*-ʃön) *n* asociación *f*
**assort** (ö-*ssoot*) *v* clasificar
**assortment** (ö-*ssoot*-mönt) *n* surtido *m*
**assume** (ö-*ssyuum*) *v* *suponer, presumir
**assure** (ö-*ʃuö*) *v* asegurar
**asthma** (*æss*-mö) *n* asma *f*
**astonish** (ö-*ssto*-niʃ) *v* asombrar
**astonishing** (ö-*ssto*-ni-ʃing) *adj* asombroso
**astonishment** (ö-*ssto*-niʃ-mönt) *n* asombro *m*; sorpresa *f*
**astronaut** (*æss*-tro-noot) astronauta *m/f*
**astronomy** (ö-*sstro*-nö-mi) *n* astronomía *f*
**asylum** (ö-*ssai*-löm) *n* asilo *m*
**at** (æt) *prep* en, a; hacia
**ate** (êt) *v* (p eat)
**atheist** (*ei*-zi-isst) *n* ateo *m*
**athlete** (*æz*-liit) *n* atleta *m*
**athletics** (æz-*lê*-tikss) *pl* atletismo *m*
**Atlantic** (öt-*læn*-tik) Atlántico *m*
**atmosphere** (*æt*-möss-fiö) *n* atmósfera *f*; esfera *f*, ambiente *m*
**atom** (*æ*-töm) *n* átomo *m*
**atomic** (ö-*to*-mik) *adj* atómico
**atomizer** (*æ*-tö-mai-sö) *n* vaporizador *m*; aerosol *m*, pulverizador *m*
**attach** (ö-*tæch*) *v* prender; fijar; juntar; **attached to** encariñado con
**attack** (ö-*tæk*) *v* atacar; *n* ataque *m*
**attain** (ö-*tein*) *v* llegar a
**attainable** (ö-*tei*-nö-böl) *adj* alcanzable
**attempt** (ö-*têmpt*) *v* intentar; *probar; *n* tentativa *f*
**attend** (ö-*tênd*) *v* asistir a; ~ **on** *servir; ~ **to** cuidar de, *atender a; prestar atención a
**attendance** (ö-*tên*-dönss) *n* asistencia *f*; presencia *f*
**attendant** (ö-*tên*-dönt) *n* asistente *m*; acompañante *m*
**attention** (ö-*tên*-ʃön) *n* atención *f*; ***pay** ~ prestar atención
**attentive** (ö-*tên*-tiv) *adj* atento
**attic** (*æ*-tik) *n* buhardilla *f*
**attitude** (*æ*-ti-tyuud) *n* actitud *f*
**attorney** (ö-*töö*-ni) *n* abogado *m*
**attract** (ö-*trækt*) *v* *atraer
**attraction** (ö-*træk*-ʃön) *n* atracción *f*
**attractive** (ö-*træk*-tiv) *adj* atractivo
**auction** (*ook*-ʃön) *n* subasta *f*
**audible** (*oo*-di-böl) *adj* audible
**audience** (*oo*-di-önss) *n* auditorio *m*
**auditor** (*oo*-di-tö) *n* auditor *m*, -a *f*
**auditorium** (oo-di-*too*-ri-öm) *n* aula *f*
**August** (*oo*-ghösst) agosto
**aunt** (aant) *n* tía *f*
**Australia** (o-*sstrei*-li-ö) Australia *f*
**Australian** (o-*sstrei*-li-ön) *adj* australiano
**Austria** (*o*-sstri-ö) Austria *f*
**Austrian** (*o*-sstri-ön) *adj* austríaco
**authentic** (oo-*zên*-tik) *adj* auténtico
**author** (*oo*-zö) *n* autor *m*
**authoritarian** (oo-zo-ri-*têö*-ri-ön) *adj* autoritario
**authority** (oo-*zo*-rö-ti) *n* autoridad *f*; poder *m*
**authorization** (oo-zö-rai-*sei*-ʃön) *n* autorización *f*; permiso *m*
**authorize** (*oo*-zö-rais) *v* autorizar; **be authorized to** estar autorizado para
**automatic** (oo-tö-*mæ*-tik) *adj* automático; ~ **teller** cajero

automático

**automobile** (*oo*-tö-mö-biil) *n* automóvil *m*; ~ **club** automóvil club

**autonomous** (oo-*to*-nö-möss) *adj* autónomo

**autopsy** (*oo*-to-pssi) *n* autopsia *f*

**autumn** (*oo*-töm) *n* otoño *m*

**available** (ö-*vei*-lö-böl) *adj* adquirible, obtenible, disponible

**avalanche** (æ-vö-laanʃ) *n* avalancha *f*

**avenue** (æ-vö-nyuu) *n* avenida *f*

**average** (æ-vö-ridʒ) *adj* medio; mediano; *n* promedio *m*; **on the** ~ por término medio

**averse** (ö-*vööss*) *adj* opuesto, contrario

**aversion** (ö-*vöö*-ʃön) *n* aversión *f*

**avert** (ö-*vööt*) *v* desviar

**avoid** (ö-*void*) *v* evitar

**await** (ö-$^{u}$*eit*) *v* esperar

**awake** (ö-$^{u}$*eik*) *adj* despierto

***awake** (ö-$^{u}$*eik*) *v* *despertar

**award** (ö-$^{u}$*ood*) *n* premio *m*; *v* conceder

**aware** (ö-$^{u}$*ê*$^{ö}$) *adj* consciente

**away** (ö-$^{u}$*ei*) *adv* fuera; ***go** ~ *irse

**awful** (*oo*-föl) *adj* terrible, tremendo

**awkward** (*oo*-k$^{u}$öd) *adj* embarazoso; torpe

**awning** (*oo*-ning) *n* toldo *m*

**axe** (ækss) *n* hacha *f*

**axle** (*æk*-ssöl) *n* eje *m*

# B

**baby** (*bei*-bi) *n* bebé *m*; ~ **carriage** *Am* cochecillo *m*

**babysitter** (*bei*-bi-ssi-tö) *n* babysitter *m*

**bachelor** (*bæ*-chö-lö) *n* soltero *m*

**back** (bæk) *n* espalda *f*; *adv* atrás; ***go** ~ regresar

**backache** (*bæ*-keik) *n* dolor de espalda

**backbone** (*bæk*-boun) *n* espina dorsal

**background** (*bæk*-ghraund) *n* fondo *m*; antecedentes *mpl*

**backwards** (*bæk*-$^{u}$öds) *adv* hacia atrás

**bacon** (*bei*-kön) *n* tocino *m*

**bacterium** (bæk-*tii*-ri-öm) *n* (pl -ria) bacteria *f*

**bad** (bæd) *adj* malo; grave; travieso

**bag** (bægh) *n* bolsa *f*; bolso *m*, cartera *f*; maleta *f*

**baggage** (*bæ*-ghidʒ) *n* equipaje *m*; ~ **check** *nAm* consigna *f*; **hand** ~ *Am* equipaje de mano

**bail** (beil) *n* fianza *f*

**bait** (beit) *n* cebo *m*

**bake** (beik) *v* cocer al horno

**baker** (*bei*-kö) *n* panadero *m*

**bakery** (*bei*-kö-ri) *n* panadería *f*

**balance** (*bæ*-lönss) *n* equilibrio *m*; balance *m*; saldo *m*

**balcony** (*bæl*-kö-ni) *n* balcón *m*

**bald** (boold) *adj* calvo

**ball** (bool) *n* pelota *f*; baile *m*

**ballet** (*bæ*-lei) *n* ballet *m*

**balloon** (bö-*luun*) *n* globo *m*

**ballpoint pen** (*bool*-point-pên) *n* bolígrafo *m*

**ballroom** (*bool*-ruum) *n* salón de baile

**bamboo** (bæm-*buu*) *n* (pl ~s) bambú *m*

**banana** (bö-*naa*-nö) *n* plátano *m*

**band** (bænd) *n* orquesta *f*; banda *f*

**bandage** (*bæn*-didʒ) *n* vendaje *m*

**bandit** (*bæn*-dit) *n* bandido *m*

**bangle** (*bæng*-ghöl) *n* pulsera *f*

**bank** (bængk) *n* orilla *f*; banco *m*; *v* depositar; ~ **account** cuenta bancaria; ~ **rate** descuento bancario
**banknote** (*bængk*-nout) *n* billete de banco
**bankrupt** (*bængk*-rapt) *adj* en quiebra
**banner** (*bæ*-nö) *n* bandera *f*; estandarte *m*
**banquet** (*bæng*-k$^u$it) *n* banquete *m*
**baptism** (*bæp*-ti-söm) *n* bautismo *m*, bautizo *m*
**baptize** (bæp-*tais*) *v* bautizar
**bar** (baa) *n* bar *m*; barra *f*; barrote *m*
**barbecue** (*baa*-bi-kyuu) *n* barbacoa *f*; *v* cocinar en la barbacoa
**barbed wire** (baarbd- $^u$*ai*$^ö$) alambre *f* de espino
**barber** (*baa*-bö) *n* barbero *m*; peluquero *m*
**bare** (bê$^ö$) *adj* desnudo; raso
**barely** (*bê*$^ö$-li) *adv* apenas
**bargain** (*baa*-ghin) *n* ganga *f*; *v* regatear
**baritone** (*bæ*-ri-toun) *n* barítono *m*
**bark** (baak) *n* corteza *f*; *v* ladrar
**barley** (*baa*-li) *n* cebada *f*
**barman** (*baa*-mön) *n* (pl -men) barman *m*
**barn** (baan) *n* granero *m*
**barometer** (bö-*ro*-mi-tö) *n* barómetro *m*
**baroque** (bö-*rok*) *adj* barroco
**barracks** (*bæ*-rökss) *pl* cuartel *m*
**barrel** (*bæ*-röl) *n* tonel *m*, barril *m*
**barrier** (*bæ*-ri-ö) *n* barrera *f*
**barrister** (*bæ*-ri-sstö) *n* abogado *m*
**bartender** (*baa*-tên-dö) *n* barman *m*
**base** (beiss) *n* base *f*; fundamento *m*; *v* basar
**baseball** (*beiss*-bool) *n* béisbol *m*
**basement** (*beiss*-mönt) *n* sótano *m*
**basic** (*bei*-ssik) *adj* fundamental; **the basics** *npl* lo básico, los fundamentos; **get down to basics** centrarse en lo esencial
**basilica** (bö-*si*-li-kö) *n* basílica *f*
**basin** (*bei*-ssön) *n* tazón *m*, palangana *f*
**basis** (*bei*-ssiss) *n* (pl bases) fundamento *m*, base *f*
**basket** (*baa*-sskit) *n* cesta *f*
**bass**[1] (beiss) *n* bajo *m*
**bass**[2] (bæss) *n* (pl ~) perca *f*
**bastard** (*baa*-sstöd) *n* bastardo *m*
**batch** (bæch) *n* carga *f*
**bath** (baaz) *n* baño *m*; ~ **salts** sales de baño; ~ **towel** toalla de baño
**bathe** (beið) *v* bañarse
**bathing cap** (*bei*-ðing-kæp) *n* gorro de baño
**bathing suit** (*bei*-ðing-ssuut) *n* traje de baño
**bathing trunks** (*bei*-ðing-trangkss) *n* bañador *m*
**bathrobe** (*baaz*-roub) *n* bata de baño
**bathroom** (*baaz*-ruum) *n* cuarto de baño; lavabos *mpl*; baño *mMe*
**batter** (*bæ*-tö) *n* masa *f*
**battery** (*bæ*-tö-ri) *n* batería *f*; acumulador *m*
**battle** (*bæ*-töl) *n* batalla *f*; pelea *f*, combate *m*; *v* combatir
**bay** (bei) *n* bahía *f*; *v* aullar
***be** (bii) *v* *estar, *ser
**beach** (biich) *n* playa *f*; **nudist** ~ playa para nudistas
**bead** (biid) *n* cuenta *f*; **beads** *pl* collar *m*; rosario *m*
**beak** (biik) *n* pico *m*
**beam** (biim) *n* rayo *m*; viga *f*
**bean** (biin) *n* judía *f*; ejote *mMe*
**bear** (bê$^ö$) *n* oso *m*
***bear** (bê$^ö$) *v* llevar; aguantar; soportar
**beard** (bi$^ö$d) *n* barba *f*
**bearer** (*bê*$^ö$-rö) *n* portador *m*
**beast** (biisst) *n* animal *m*; ~ **of prey** animal de presa
***beat** (biit) *v* batir, golpear

**beautiful** (*byuu*-ti-föl) *adj* hermoso
**beauty** (*byuu*-ti) *n* belleza *f*; ~ **parlo(u)r** salón de belleza; ~ **salon** salón de belleza; ~ **treatment** tratamiento de belleza
**beaver** (*bii*-vö) *n* castor *m*
**because** (bi-*kos*) *conj* porque; puesto que; ~ **of** a causa de
***become** (bi-*kam*) *v* *hacerse; *sentar bien
**bed** (bêd) *n* cama *f*; ~ **and board** pensión completa; ~ **and breakfast** cama y desayuno
**bedding** (*bê*-ding) *n* ropa de cama
**bedroom** (*bêd*-ruum) *n* dormitorio *m*
**bee** (bii) *n* abeja *f*
**beech** (bii-ch) *n* haya *f*
**beef** (biif) *n* carne de vaca; **beefburger** hamburguesa *f*
**beehive** (*bii*-haiv) *n* colmena *f*
**been** (biin) *v* (pp be)
**beer** (bi$^{ö}$) *n* cerveza *f*
**beet** (biit) *n* remolacha *f*
**beetle** (*bii*-töl) *n* escarabajo *m*
**beetroot** (*biit*-ruut) *n* remolacha *f*
**before** (bi-*foo*) *prep* antes de; delante de; *conj* antes de que; *adv* antes
**beg** (bêgh) *v* mendigar; suplicar; *pedir
**beggar** (*bê*-ghö) *n* mendigo *m*, -a *f*
***begin** (bi-*ghin*) *v* *empezar; *comenzar
**beginner** (bi-*ghi*-nö) *n* principiante *m*
**beginning** (bi-*ghi*-ning) *n* comienzo *m*
**behalf** (bi-*haaf*): **on ~ of** en nombre de; a favor de; **on my/his ~** en nombre mío/suyo
**behave** (bi-*heiv*) *v* comportarse
**behavio(u)r** (bi-*hei*-vyö) *n* conducta *f*
**behind** (bi-*haind*) *prep* detrás de; *adv* detrás
**beige** (beiʒ) *adj* beige
**being** (*bii*-ing) *n* ser *m*
**Belgian** (*bêl*-dʒön) *adj* belga
**Belgium** (*bêl*-dʒöm) Bélgica *f*
**belief** (bi-*liif*) *n* creencia *f*
**believe** (bi-*liiv*) *v* *creer
**bell** (bêl) *n* campana *f*; timbre *m*
**bellboy** (*bêl*-boi) *n* botones *mpl*
**belly** (*bê*-li) *n* vientre *m*; panza *f*
**belong** (bi-*long*) *v* *pertenecer
**belongings** (bi-*long*-ings) *pl* pertenencias *fpl*
**beloved** (bi-*lavd*) *adj* querido
**below** (bi-*lou*) *prep* debajo de; bajo; *adv* debajo
**belt** (bêlt) *n* cinturón *m*
**bench** (bênch) *n* banco *m*
**bend** (bênd) *n* comba *f*, curva *f*
***bend** (bênd) *v* doblar; ~ **down** bajarse
**beneath** (bi-*niiz*) *prep* debajo de; *adv* debajo
**benefit** (*bê*-ni-fit) *n* beneficio *m*; ventaja *f*; *v* aprovechar
**bent** (bênt) *adj* (pp bend) doblado; torcido
**beret** (*bê*-rei) *n* boina *f*
**berry** (*bê*-ri) *n* baya *f*
**beside** (bi-*ssaid*) *prep* junto a
**besides** (bi-*ssaids*) *adv* además; por otra parte; *prep* además de
**best** (bêsst) *adj* óptimo
**bet** (bêt) *n* apuesta *f*
***bet** (bêt) *v* *apostar
**betray** (bi-*trei*) *v* traicionar
**better** (*bê*-tö) *adj* mejor
**between** (bi-*t*$^{u}$*iin*) *prep* entre
**beverage** (*bê*-vö-ridʒ) *n* bebida *f*
**beware** (bi-$^{u}$*ê*$^{ö}$) *v* precaverse, guardarse
**bewitch** (bi-$^{u}$*ich*) *v* hechizar, encantar
**beyond** (bi-*yond*) *prep* más allá de; además de; *adv* más allá
**bible** (*bai*-böl) *n* biblia *f*
**bicycle** (*bai*-ssi-köl) *n* bicicleta *f*; biciclo *m*

**bid** (bid) *n* puja *f*; intento *m*
***bid** (bid) *v* pujar
**big** (bigh) *adj* grande; voluminoso; gordo; importante
**bike** (baik) *n colloquial* bici *f*; moto *f*; *v* ir en bici
**bile** (bail) *n* bilis *f*
**bilingual** (bai-*ling*-ghuöl) *adj* bilingüe
**bill** (bil) *n* cuenta *f*; factura *f*; billete *mAm*; *v* facturar
**billiards** (*bil*-yöds) *pl* billar *m*
**billion** (*bil*-yön) mil millones *mpl*, millardo *m*
***bind** (baind) *v* atar
**binding** (*bain*-ding) *n* atadura *f*
**binoculars** (bi-*no*-kyö-lös) *pl* prismáticos *mpl*; gemelos *mpl*
**biology** (bai-*o*-lö-dʒi) *n* biología *f*
**birch** (bööch) *n* abedul *m*
**bird** (bööd) *n* pájaro *m*
**Biro** (*bai*-rou) *n* bolígrafo *m*
**birth** (bööz) *n* nacimiento *m*
**birthday** (*bööz*-dei) *n* cumpleaños *m*
**biscuit** (*biss*-kit) *n* galleta *f*; bollo *mAm*
**bishop** (*bi*-ʃöp) *n* obispo *m*
**bit** (bit) *n* trozo *m*; poco *m*
**bitch** (bich) *n* perra *f*
**bite** (bait) *n* bocado *m*; mordedura *f*; picadura *f*
***bite** (bait) *v* *morder
**bitter** (*bi*-tö) *adj* amargo
**black** (blæk) *adj* negro; **~ market** mercado negro
**blackberry** (*blæk*-bö-ri) *n* mora *f*
**blackbird** (*blæk*-bööd) *n* mirlo *m*
**blackboard** (*blæk*-bood) *n* pizarra *f*
**blackcurrant** (blæk-*ka*-rönt) *n* grosella negra
**blackmail** (*blæk*-meil) *n* chantaje *m*; *v* *hacer chantaje
**blacksmith** (*blæk*-ssmiz) *n* herrero *m*
**bladder** (*blæ*-dö) *n* vejiga *f*
**blade** (bleid) *n* hoja *f*; **~ of grass** brizna de hierba
**blame** (bleim) *n* culpa *f*; reproche *m*; *v* echar la culpa, culpar
**blank** (blængk) *adj* blanco
**blanket** (*blæng*-kit) *n* manta *f*
**blast** (blaasst) *n* explosión *f*
**blazer** (*blei*-sö) *n* chaqueta de sport, chaqueta ligera
**bleach** (bliich) *v* blanquear
**bleak** (bliik) *adj* desolador
***bleed** (bliid) *v* sangrar
**bless** (blêss) *v* *bendecir
**blessing** (*blê*-ssing) *n* bendición *f*
**blind** (blaind) *n* persiana *f*; *adj* ciego; *v* *cegar
**blinker** (*bling*-kö) *nAm* indicador *m*
**blister** (*bli*-sstö) *n* ampolla *f*
**blizzard** (*bli*-söd) *n* ventisca *f*
**block** (blok) *v* *obstruir, bloquear; *n* bloque *m*; **~ of flats** casa de pisos
**blond** (blond) *adj* rubio
**blonde** (blond) *n* rubia *f*
**blood** (blad) *n* sangre *f*; **~ poisoning** septicemia *f*; **~ pressure** tensión arterial; **~ vessel** vaso sanguíneo
**bloody** (*bla*-di) *adj* ensangrentado; sangriento; *colloquial* maldito, puñetero; **bloody ~!** ¡ostras!
**blossom** (*bla*-söm) *n* flores *fpl*; *v* florecer
**blot** (blot) *n* borrón *m*; mancha *f*; **blotting paper** papel secante
**blouse** (blaus) *n* blusa *f*
**blow** (blou) *n* golpe *m*; ráfaga *f*
***blow** (blou) *v* soplar; **~ up** volar; hinchar; ampliar; explotar
**blowout** (*blou*-aut) *n* reventón *m*
**blue** (bluu) *adj* azul; deprimido
**blunt** (blant) *adj* desafilado; directo, abrupto
**blush** (blaʃ) *v* ruborizarse; *n* rubor *m*, sonrojo *m*
**board** (bood) *n* tabla *f*; tablero *m*; pensión *f*; consejo *m*; **~ and lodging**

pensión completa
**boarder** (*boo*-dö) *n* huésped *m*
**boardinghouse** (*boo*-ding-hauss) *n* pensión *f*
**boarding school** (*boo*-ding-sskuul) *n* internado *m*
**boast** (bousst) *v* presumir
**boat** (bout) *n* barco *m*, barca *f*
**body** (*bo*-di) *n* cuerpo *m*
**bodyguard** (*bo*-di-ghaad) *n* guardaespaldas *m*/*f*
**bog** (bogh) *n* pantano *m*
**boil** (boil) *v* *hervir; *n* forúnculo *m*
**bold** (bould) *adj* audaz; impertinente, atrevido
**Bolivia** (bö-*li*-vi-ö) Bolivia *f*
**Bolivian** (bö-*li*-vi-ön) *adj* boliviano
**bolt** (boult) *n* cerrojo *m*; perno *m*
**bomb** (bom) *n* bomba *f*; *v* bombardear
**bond** (bond) *n* vínculo *m*; obligación *f*
**bone** (boun) *n* hueso *m*; espina *f*; *v* deshuesar
**bonnet** (*bo*-nit) *n* capó *m*
**book** (buk) *n* libro *m*; *v* reservar; inscribir, registrar
**booking** (*bu*-king) *n* reservación *f*, reserva *f*
**bookmaker** (*buk*-mei-kö) *n* corredor *m* de apuestas
**bookseller** (*buk*-ssê-lö) *n* librero *m*, -a *f*
**bookstand** (*buk*-sstænd) *n* puesto de libros
**bookstore** (*buk*-sstoo) *n* librería *f*
**boot** (buut) *n* bota *f*; portaequipajes *m*
**booth** (buuð) *n* puesto *m*; cabina *f*
**booze** (buus) *n* *colloquial* bebida *f*, priva *f*
**border** (*boo*-dö) *n* frontera *f*; borde *m*
**bore**[1] (boo) *v* aburrir; taladrar; *n* pelmazo *m*
**bore**[2] (boo) *v* (p bear)
**boring** (*boo*-ring) *adj* aburrido
**born** (boon) *adj* nacido
**borrow** (*bo*-rou) *v* tomar prestado
**bosom** (*bu*-söm) *n* pecho *m*; seno *m*
**boss** (boss) *n* jefe *m*, patrón *m*
**botany** (*bo*-tö-ni) *n* botánica *f*
**both** (bouz) *adj* ambos; **both … and** tanto … como
**bother** (*bo*-ðö) *v* fastidiar, molestar; *esforzarse; *n* molestia *f*
**bottle** (*bo*-töl) *n* botella *f*; **~ opener** destapador de botellas; **hot-water ~** calorífero *m*
**bottleneck** (*bo*-töl-nêk) *n* atasco de tráfico; atascadero *m*
**bottom** (*bo*-töm) *n* fondo *m*; trasero *m*; *adj* inferior
**bought** (boot) *v* (p, pp buy)
**boulder** (*boul*-dö) *n* pedrón *m*
**bound** (baund) *n* límite *m*; ***be ~ to** deber de; **~ for** camino de
**boundary** (*baun*-dö-ri) *n* límite *m*; frontera *f*
**bouquet** (bu-*kei*) *n* ramo *m*
**bourgeois** (*bu*$^{ö}$-ʒ$^{u}$aa) *adj* burgués
**boutique** (bu-*tiik*) *n* boutique *f*
**bow**[1] (bau) *v* inclinar
**bow**[2] (bou) *n* arco *m*; **~ tie** corbata de lazo, corbatín *m*
**bowels** (bau$^{ö}$ls) *pl* intestinos *mpl*
**bowl** (boul) *n* tazón *m*
**bowling** (*bou*-ling) *n* bowling *m*, juego de bolos; **~ alley** bolera *f*
**box**[1] (bokss) *v* boxear; **boxing match** partido de boxeo
**box**[2] (bokss) *n* caja *f*
**box office** (*bokss*-o-fiss) *n* taquilla *f*
**boy** (boi) *n* muchacho *m*; chico *m*, mozo *m*; sirviente *m*; **~ scout** explorador *m*
**boyfriend** (*boi*-frênd) novio *m*
**bra** (braa) *n* sujetador *m*, sostén *m*
**bracelet** (*breiss*-lit) *n* pulsera *f*
**braces** (*brei*-ssis) *pl* tirantes *mpl*
**brain** (brein) *n* cerebro *m*; **~s** inteligencia *f*

**brainwave** (*brein-*ᵘeiv) *n* inspiración *f*
**brake** (breik) *n* freno *m*; ~ **drum** tambor del freno; ~ **lights** luces de freno
**branch** (braanch) *n* rama *f*; sucursal *f*
**brand** (brænd) *n* marca *f*
**brand-new** (brænd-*nyuu*) *adj* novísimo
**brass** (braass) *n* latón *m*; cobre *m*, cobre amarillo; ~ **band** *n* charanga *f*
**brave** (breiv) *adj* valiente
**Brazil** (brö-*sil*) Brasil *m*
**Brazilian** (brö-*sil*-yön) *adj* brasileño
**breach** (briich) *n* brecha *f*
**bread** (brêd) *n* pan *m*; **wholemeal** ~ pan integral
**breadth** (brêdz) *n* ancho *m*
**break** (breik) *n* fractura *f*; descanso *m*
***break** (breik) *v* *quebrar, quebrantar; ~ **down** averiarse; romperse; detallar, desglosar
**breakdown** (*breik*-daun) *n* avería *f*; colapso *m*; descompostura *fMe*
**breakfast** (*brêk*-fösst) *n* desayuno *m*
**breast** (brêsst) *n* seno *m*
**breaststroke** (*brêsst*-sstrouk) *n* braza *f*
**breath** (brêz) *n* aliento *m*; respiración *f*
**breathe** (briið) *v* respirar
**breathing** (*brii*-ðing) *n* respiración *f*
**breed** (briid) *n* raza *f*; especie *f*
***breed** (briid) *v* recriar
**breeze** (briis) *n* brisa *f*
**brew** (bruu) *v* fabricar cerveza
**brewery** (*bruu*-ö-ri) *n* cervecería *f*
**bribe** (braib) *v* sobornar
**bribery** (*brai*-bö-ri) *n* soborno *m*
**brick** (brik) *n* ladrillo *m*
**bricklayer** (*brik*-leiᵒ) *n* albañil *m*
**bride** (braid) *n* novia *f*
**bridegroom** (*braid*-ghruum) *n* novio *m*
**bridge** (bridʒ) *n* puente *m*; bridge *m*
**brief** (briif) *adj* breve
**briefcase** (*briif*-keiss) *n* portafolio *m*; maletín *m*
**briefs** (briifss) *pl* bragas *f*, calzoncillos *mpl*
**bright** (brait) *adj* claro; reluciente; listo
**brill** (bril) *n* rodaballo *m*
**brilliant** (*bril*-yönt) *adj* brillante
**brim** (brim) *n* borde *m*
***bring** (bring) *v* *traer; ~ **back** *devolver; ~ **up** educar; *introducir, levantar
**brisk** (brissk) *adj* enérgico, rápido
**Britain** (*bri*-tön) Inglaterra *f*
**British** (*bri*-tiʃ) *adj* británico
**Briton** (*bri*-tön) *n* británico *m*; inglés *m*
**broad** (brood) *adj* ancho; amplio; general
**broadcast** (*brood*-kaasst) *n* transmisión *f*
***broadcast** (*brood*-kaasst) *v* emitir
**brochure** (*brou*-ʃuᵒ) *n* folleto *m*
**broke**[1] (brouk) *v* (p break)
**broke**[2] (brouk) *adj* arruinado
**broken** (*brou*-kön) *adj* (pp break) estropeado, roto
**broker** (*brou*-kö) *n* corredor *m*, bolsista *m*
**bronchitis** (brong-*kai*-tiss) *n* bronquitis *f*
**bronze** (brons) *n* bronce *m*; *adj* de bronce
**brooch** (brouch) *n* broche *m*
**brook** (bruk) *n* arroyo *m*
**broom** (bruum) *n* escoba *f*
**brothel** (*bro*-zöl) *n* burdel *m*
**brother** (*bra*-ðö) *n* hermano *m*
**brother-in-law** (*bra*-ðö-rin-loo) *n* (pl brothers-) cuñado *m*
**brought** (broot) *v* (p, pp bring)
**brown** (braun) *adj* marrón
**bruise** (bruus) *n* moretón *m*,

magulladura *f*; *v* magullar
**brunette** (bruu-*nêt*) *n* morena *f*
**brush** (braʃ) *n* cepillo *m*; brocha *f*; *v* sacar brillo, cepillar
**brutal** (*bruu*-töl) *adj* brutal
**bubble** (*ba*-böl) *n* burbuja *f*
**buck** (bak) *n colloquial* dólar *m*
**bucket** (*ba*-kit) *n* balde *m*
**buckle** (*ba*-köl) *n* hebilla *f*
**bud** (bad) *n* capullo *m*
**buddy** (*ba*-di) *colloquial* amigo *m*, -a *f*, colega *m/f*, *L.Am.* compadre *m/f*
**budget** (*ba*-dʒit) *n* presupuesto *m*
**buffet** (*bu*-fei) *n* buffet *m*
**bug** (bagh) *n* chinche *f*; escarabajo *m*; *nAm* insecto *m*
***build** (bild) *v* *construir
**building** (*bil*-ding) *n* edificio *m*
**bulb** (balb) *n* bulbo *m*; **light ~** bombilla *f*; foco *mMe*
**Bulgaria** (bal-*ghê*ö-ri-ö) Bulgaria *f*
**Bulgarian** (bal-*ghê*ö-ri-ön) *adj* búlgaro
**bulk** (balk) *n* bulto *m*; mayoría *f*
**bulky** (*bal*-ki) *adj* voluminoso
**bull** (bul) *n* toro *m*
**bullet** (*bu*-lit) *n* bala *f*
**bulletin** (*bu*-li-tin) boletín *m*
**bullfight** (*bul*-fait) *n* corrida de toros
**bullring** (*bul*-ring) *n* plaza de toros
**bump** (bamp) *v* topetar; chocar; darse contra; *dar golpes; *n* golpe *m*, topetón *m*
**bumper** (*bam*-pö) *n* parachoques *m*
**bumpy** (*bam*-pi) *adj* lleno de baches
**bun** (ban) *n* bollo *m*
**bunch** (banch) *n* ramo *m*; grupo *m*
**bundle** (*ban*-döl) *n* paquete *m*; *v* atar, liar
**bunk** (bangk) *n* camastro *m*
**buoy** (boi) *n* boya *f*
**burden** (*böö*-dön) *n* peso *m*; carga *f*
**bureau** (*byu*ö-rou) *n* (pl ~x, ~s) escritorio *m*; *nAm* cómoda *f*
**bureaucracy** (byuö-*ro*-krö-ssi) *n* burocracia *f*
**burglar** (*böö*-ghlö) *n* ladrón *m*, ladrona *f*
**burgle** (*böö*-ghöl) *v* robar
**burial** (*bê*-ri-öl) *n* entierro *m*
**burn** (böön) *n* quemadura *f*
***burn** (böön) *v* quemar; pegarse
***burst** (böösst) *v* *reventar; *quebrar
**bury** (*bê*-ri) *v* *enterrar
**bus** (bass) *n* autobús *m*
**bush** (buʃ) *n* matorral *m*
**business** (*bis*-nöss) *n* negocios *mpl*, comercio *m*; empresa *f*, negocio *m*; ocupación *f*; asunto *m*; **~ hours** horas hábiles, horas de oficina; **~ trip** viaje de negocios; **on ~** por asuntos de negocio
**business-like** (*bis*-niss-laik) *adj* práctico; serio
**businessman** (*bis*-nöss-mön) *n* (pl -men) hombre de negocios
**bust** (basst) *n* busto *m*
**bustle** (*ba*-ssöl) *n* bullicio *m*
**busy** (*bi*-si) *adj* ocupado; concurrido, atareado
**but** (bat) *conj* mas; pero; *prep* menos
**butcher** (*bu*-chö) *n* carnicero *m*
**butter** (*ba*-tö) *n* mantequilla *f*
**butterfly** (*ba*-tö-flai) *n* mariposa *f*; **~ stroke** braza de mariposa
**buttock** (*ba*-tök) *n* nalga *m*
**button** (*ba*-tön) *n* botón *m*; *v* abrochar
**buttonhole** (ba-tön-houl) *n* ojal *m*
**buzz** (bas) *n* zumbido *m*; *v* zumbar; llamar por el interfono
***buy** (bai) *v* comprar; *adquirir
**buyer** (*bai*-ö) *n* comprador *m*, -a *f*
**by** (bai) *prep* por; con; cerca de
**by-pass** (*bai*-paass) *n* desviación *f*; *v* evitar; pasar por alto

# C

**cab** (kæb) *n* taxi *m*; ~ **driver** taxista *m/f*
**cabaret** (*kæ*-bö-rei) *n* cabaret *m*
**cabbage** (*kæ*-bidʒ) *n* col *m*
**cabin** (*kæ*-bin) *n* cabina *f*; cabaña *f*
**cabinet** (*kæ*-bi-nöt) *n* gabinete *m*
**cable** (*kei*-böl) *n* cable *m*
**café** (*kæ*-fei) *n* cafetería *f*, café *m*
**cafeteria** (kæ-fö-*ti*ö-ri-ö) *n* cafetería *f*
**caffeine** (*kæ*-fiin) *n* cafeína *f*
**cage** (keidʒ) *n* jaula *f*
**cake** (keik) *n* pastel *m*; pastelería *f*, tarta *f*, dulces; **sponge** ~ bizcocho *m*
**calamity** (kö-*læ*-mö-ti) *n* calamidad *f*; desastre *m*, catástrofe *f*
**calcium** (*kæl*-ssi-öm) *n* calcio *m*
**calculate** (*kæl*-kyu-leit) *v* calcular
**calculation** (kæl-kyu-*lei*-ʃön) *n* cálculo *m*
**calculator** (*kæl*-kyu-lei-tö) *n* calculadora *f*
**calendar** (*kæ*-lön-dö) *n* calendario *m*
**calf** (kaaf) *n* (pl calves) ternero *m*; pantorrilla *f*; ~ **skin** becerro *m*
**call** (kool) *v* llamar; *n* llamada *f*; visita *f*; ***be called** llamarse; ~ **names** insultar; ~ **off** cancelar; ~ **on** visitar; ~ **up** *Am* telefonear; ; **long-distance** ~ conferencia interurbana
**calm** (kaam) *adj* tranquilo; ~ **down** calmar
**calorie** (*kæ*-lö-ri) *n* caloría *f*
**Calvinism** (*kæl*-vi-ni-söm) *n* calvinismo *m*
**came** (keim) *v* (p come)
**camel** (*kæ*-möl) *n* camello *m*
**cameo** (*kæ*-mi-ou) *n* (pl ~s) camafeo *m*
**camera** (*kæ*-mö-rö) *n* cámara fotográfica; cámara *f*; ~ **shop** negocio fotográfico
**camp** (kæmp) *n* campamento *m*; *v* acampar; ~ **bed** catre de campaña, cama de tijera
**campaign** (kæm-*pein*) *n* campaña *f*
**camper** (*kæm*-pö) *n* acampador *m*
**camping** (*kæm*-ping) *n* camping *m*; ~ **site** camping *m*, lugar de camping
**can** (kæn) *n* lata *f*; bote *m*; ~ **opener** abrelatas *m*
***can** (kæn) *v* *poder
**Canada** (*kæ*-nö-dö) Canadá *m*
**Canadian** (kö-*nei*-di-ön) *adj* canadiense
**canal** (kö-*næl*) *n* canal *m*
**canary** (kö-*nê*ö-ri) *n* canario *m*
**cancel** (*kæn*-ssöl) *v* cancelar; anular
**cancellation** (kæn-ssö-*lei*-ʃön) *n* cancelación *f*
**cancer** (*kæn*-ssö) *n* cáncer *m*
**candidate** (*kæn*-di-döt) *n* candidato *m*, interesado *m*
**candle** (*kæn*-döl) *n* vela *f*; candela *f*
**candy** (*kæn*-di) *nAm* bombón *m*; dulces, golosinas
**cane** (kein) *n* caña *f*; bastón *m*
**canister** (*kæ*-ni-sstö) *n* caja metálica, lata *f*
**canoe** (kö-*nuu*) *n* canoa *f*
**canteen** (kæn-*tiin*) *n* cantina *f*
**canvas** (*kæn*-vöss) *n* lona *f*
**cap** (kæp) *n* gorra *f*, gorro *m*
**capable** (*kei*-pö-böl) *adj* capaz
**capacity** (kö-*pæ*-ssö-ti) *n* capacidad *f*; potencia *f*; competencia *f*
**cape** (keip) *n* capa *f*; cabo *m*
**capital** (*kæ*-pi-töl) *n* capital *f*; capital *m*; *adj* importante, capital; ~ **letter** mayúscula *f*
**capitalism** (*kæ*-pi-tö-li-söm) *n* capitalismo *m*
**capitulation** (kö-pi-tyu-*lei*-ʃön) *n* capitulación *f*
**capsule** (*kæp*-ssyuul) *n* cápsula *f*
**captain** (*kæp*-tin) *n* capitán *m*;

comandante *m*
**capture** (*kæp*-chö) *v* coger preso, capturar; conquistar; *n* captura *f*; conquista *f*
**car** (kaa) *n* coche *m*; carro *m**Me*; **~ hire** alquiler de coches; **~ park** parque de estacionamiento; aparcamiento *m*
**caramel** (*kæ*-rö-möl) *n* caramelo *m*
**carat** (*kæ*-röt) *n* quilate *m*
**caravan** (*kæ*-rö-væn) *n* caravana *f*; remolque *m*
**carburet(t)or** (kaa-byu-*rê*-tö) *n* carburador *m*
**card** (kaad) *n* tarjeta *f*; tarjeta postal
**cardboard** (*kaad*-bood) *n* cartón *m*; *adj* de cartón
**cardigan** (*kaa*-di-ghön) *n* chaqueta *f* de punto
**cardinal** (*kaa*-di-nöl) *n* cardenal *m*; *adj* cardinal, principal
**care** (kê$^{ö}$) *n* cuidado *m*; **~ about** preocuparse de; **~ for** gustar; ***take ~ of** cuidar de
**career** (kö-*ri*$^{ö}$) *n* carrera *f*
**carefree** (*kê*$^{ö}$-frii) *adj* despreocupado
**careful** (*kê*$^{ö}$-föl) *adj* cuidadoso; escrupuloso
**careless** (*kê*$^{ö}$-löss) *adj* descuidado; indiferente; negligente
**caretaker** (*kê*$^{ö}$-tei-kö) *n* guardián *m*
**cargo** (*kaa*-ghou) *n* (pl ~es) carga *f*
**carnival** (*kaa*-ni-völ) *n* carnaval *m*
**carp** (kaap) *n* (pl ~) carpa *f*
**carpenter** (*kaa*-pin-tö) *n* carpintero *m*
**carpet** (*kaa*-pit) *n* alfombra *f*
**carriage** (*kæ*-ridʒ) *n* vagón *m*; coche *m*, carruaje *m*; **baby ~** *Am* cochecillo de niño
**carriageway** (*kæ*-ridʒ-$^{u}$ei) *n* calzada *f*
**carrot** (*kæ*-röt) *n* zanahoria *f*
**carry** (*kæ*-ri) *v* llevar; *conducir; **~ on** continuar; *proseguir; **~ out** realizar
**carrycot** (*kæ*-ri-kot) *n* cuna de viaje
**cart** (kaat) *n* carro *m*
**carton** (*kaa*-tön) *n* caja de cartón; cartón *m*
**cartoon** (kaa-*tuun*) *n* dibujos animados
**cartridge** (*kaa*-tridʒ) *n* cartucho *m*
**carve** (kaav) *v* trinchar; entallar, tallar
**carving** (*kaa*-ving) *n* talla *f*
**case** (keiss) *n* caso *m*; causa *f*; valija *f*; estuche *m*; funda *f*; **attaché ~** portafolio *m*; **in ~ of** en caso de; **just in ~** por si acaso
**cash** (kæʃ) *n* dinero contante, efectivo *m*; *v* cobrar, *hacer efectivo; **~ dispenser** cajero automático
**cashier** (kæ-*ʃi*$^{ö}$) *n* cajero *m*; cajera *f*
**cashmere** (*kæʃ*-mi$^{ö}$) *n* cachemira *f*
**casino** (kö-*ssii*-nou) *n* casino *m*
**cask** (kaassk) *n* barril *m*, tonel *m*
**cassette** (kö-*sset*) cinta *f*, casete *f*
**cast** (kaasst) *n* echada *f*; molde *m*; reparto *m*
***cast** (kaasst) *v* lanzar; **cast iron** hierro fundido
**castle** (*kaa*-ssöl) *n* castillo *m*
**casual** (*kæ*-ʒu-öl) *adj* informal; de paso, por casualidad
**casualty** (*kæ*-ʒu-öl-ti) *n* víctima *f*
**cat** (kæt) *n* gato *m*
**catacomb** (*kæ*-tö-koum) *n* catacumba *f*
**catalogue** (*kæ*-tö-logh) *n* catálogo *m*
**catarrh** (kö-*taa*) *n* catarro *m*
**catastrophe** (kö-*tæ*-sströ-fi) *n* catástrofe *f*
***catch** (kæch) *v* coger; sorprender
**category** (*kæ*-ti-ghö-ri) *n* categoría *f*
**cathedral** (kö-*zii*-dröl) *n* catedral *f*
**catholic** (*kæ*-zö-lik) *adj* católico
**cattle** (*kæ*-töl) *pl* ganado *m*
**caught** (koot) *v* (p, pp catch)
**cauliflower** (*ko*-li-flau$^{ö}$) *n* coliflor *f*
**cause** (koos) *v* causar; provocar; *n* causa *f*; motivo *m*; **~ to** *hacer
**causeway** (*koos*-$^{u}$ei) *n* calzada *f*

**caution** (*koo*-ʃön) *n* cautela *f*; *v* *advertir
**cautious** (*koo*-ʃöss) *adj* cauteloso, cauto
**cave** (keiv) *n* cueva *f*; grieta *f*
**cavern** (*kæ*-vön) *n* caverna *f*
**caviar** (*kæ*-vi-aa) *n* caviar *m*
**cavity** (*kæ*-vö-ti) *n* cavidad *f*
**cease** (ssiiss) *v* cesar
**cease-fire** *n* (*ssiiss*- fai$^{ö}$) alto *m* el fuego
**ceiling** (*ssii*-ling) *n* techo *m*, cielo raso *m*
**celebrate** (*ssê*-li-breit) *v* celebrar
**celebration** (ssê-li-*brei*-ʃön) *n* celebración *f*
**celebrity** (ssi-*lê*-brö-ti) *n* celebridad *f*
**celery** (*ssê*-lö-ri) *n* apio *m*
**cell** (ssêl) *n* celda *f*; célula *f*
**cellar** (*ssê*-lö) *n* sótano *m*
**cement** (ssi-*mênt*) *n* cemento *m*
**cemetery** (*ssê*-mi-tri) *n* cementerio *m*
**censorship** (*ssên*-ssö-ʃip) *n* censura *f*
**center** (*ssên*-tö) *n* centro *m*
**centigrade** (*ssên*-ti-ghreid) *adj* centígrado
**centimetre** (*ssên*-ti-mii-tö) *n* centímetro *m*
**central** (*ssên*-tröl) *adj* central; ~ **heating** calefacción central; ~ **station** estación central
**centralize** (*ssên*-trö-lais) *v* centralizar
**centre** (*ssên*-tö) *n* centro *m*
**century** (*ssên*-chö-ri) *n* siglo *m*
**ceramics** (ssi-*ræ*-mikss) *pl* cerámica *f*
**ceremony** (*ssê*-rö-mö-ni) *n* ceremonia *f*
**certain** (*ssöö*-tön) *adj* cierto; **certainly** *adv* ciertamiente, por cierto; **certainly not!** ¡por supuesto que no!
**certificate** (ssö-*ti*-fi-köt) *n* certificado *m*; certificación *f*, acta *f*, diploma *m*
**chain** (chein) *n* cadena *f*
**chair** (chê$^{ö}$) *n* silla *f*
**chairman** (*chê*$^{ö}$-mön) *n* (pl -men) presidente *m*
**chalet** (*ʃæ*-lei) *n* chalet *m*
**chalk** (chook) *n* creta *f*
**challenge** (*chæ*-lönd3) *v* desafiar; *n* reto *m*, desafío *m*
**chamber** (*cheim*-bö) *n* cámara *f*; recámara *f*
**champagne** (ʃæm-*pein*) *n* champán *m*
**champion** (*chæm*-pyön) *n* campeón *m*, campeona *f*; abanderado *m*, -a *f*
**chance** (chaanss) *n* azar *m*; casualidad *f*, ocasión *f*; riesgo *m*; suerte *f*; oportunidad *f*; **by ~** por casualidad
**change** (cheind3) *v* modificar, cambiar; mudarse; *hacer trasbordo; *n* modificación *f*, cambio *m*; moneda *f*
**channel** (*chæ*-nöl) *n* canal *m*; **English Channel** Canal de la Mancha
**chaos** (*kei*-oss) *n* caos *m*
**chaotic** (kei-*o*-tik) *adj* caótico
**chap** (chæp) *n* tipo *m*, chico *m*, tío *m*
**chapel** (*chæ*-pöl) *n* capilla *f*
**chaplain** (*chæ*-plin) *n* capellán *m*
**character** (*kæ*-rök-tö) *n* carácter *m*
**characteristic** (kæ-rök-tö-*ri*-sstik) *adj* típico, característico; *n* característica *f*, rasgo característico
**characterize** (*kæ*-rök-tö-rais) *v* caracterizar
**charcoal** (*chaa*-koul) *n* carbón de leña
**charge** (chaad3) *v* *pedir; cargar; acusar; *n* precio *m*; carga *f*; acusación *f*; **free of ~** gratuito; **in ~ of** encargado de; ***take ~ of** encargarse de
**charity** (*chæ*-rö-ti) *n* caridad *f*
**charm** (chaam) *n* encanto *m*; amuleto *m*
**charming** (*chaa*-ming) *adj* encantador
**chart** (chaat) *n* tabla *f*; gráfico *m*; carta marina; **conversion ~** tabla de conversión

**chase** (cheiss) *v* cazar; expulsar, ahuyentar; perseguir; *n* caza *f*
**chasm** (*kæ*-söm) *n* grieta *f*
**chassis** (*ʃæ*-ssi) *n* (pl ~) chasis *m*
**chaste** (cheisst) *adj* casto
**chat** (chæt) *v* charlar; *n* charla *f*
**chatterbox** (*chæ*-tö-bokss) *n* charlador(a) *m/f*; parlanchín(ina) *m/f*
**chauffeur** (*ʃou*-fö) *n* chófer *m*
**cheap** (chiip) *adj* barato; económico
**cheat** (chiit) *v* engañar; estafar
**check** (chêk) *v* controlar, verificar; *n* escaque *m*; *nAm* cuenta *f*; cheque *m*; **check!** ¡jaque!; ~ **in** inscribirse; ~ **out** *despedirse
**checkbook** (*chêk*-buk) *nAm* talonario *m*
**checkerboard** (*chê*-kö-bood) *nAm* tablero de damas
**checkroom** (*chêk*-ruum) *nAm* guardarropa *m*
**checkup** (*chê*-kap) *n* reconocimiento *m*
**cheek** (chiik) *n* mejilla *f*
**cheekbone** (*chiik*-boun) *n* pómulo *m*
**cheer** (chi^ö^) *v* aclamar; alentar; ~ **up** alegrar
**cheerful** (*chi^ö^*-föl) *adj* alegre
**cheese** (chiis) *n* queso *m*
**chef** (ʃêf) *n* jefe de cocina
**chemical** (*kê*-mi-köl) *adj* químico
**chemist** (*kê*-misst) *n* farmacéutico *m*; **chemist's** farmacia *f*; droguería *f*
**chemistry** (*kê*-mi-sstri) *n* química *f*
**cheque** (chêk) *n* cheque *m*
**chequebook** (*chêk*-buk) *n* talonario *m*
**chequered** (*chê*-köd) *adj* a cuadros, cuadriculado
**cherry** (*chê*-ri) *n* cereza *f*
**chess** (chêss) *n* ajedrez *m*
**chest** (chêsst) *n* pecho *m*; arca *f*; cofre *m*; ~ **of drawers** cómoda *f*
**chestnut** (*chêss*-nat) *n* castaña *f*
**chew** (chuu) *v* masticar
**chewing gum** (*chuu*-ing-gham) *n* goma de mascar, chicle *m*
**chic** (ʃik) *adj* elegante
**chicken** (*chi*-kin) *n* pollo *m*
**chickenpox** (*chi*-kin-pokss) *n* varicela *f*
**chief** (chiif) *n* jefe *m*; *adj* principal
**chiefly** (*chiif*-li) *adv* sobre todo
**chieftain** (*chiif*-tön) *n* cacique *m*
**child** (chaild) *n* (pl children) niño *m*, niña *f*
**childbirth** (*chaild*-bööz) *n* parto *m*
**childhood** (*chaild*-hud) *n* infancia *f*
**Chile** (*chi*-li) Chile *m*
**Chilean** (*chi*-li-ön) *adj* chileno
**chill** (chil) *n* escalofrío *m*
**chilly** (*chi*-li) *adj* fresco
**chimes** (chaims) *pl* carillón *m*
**chimney** (*chim*-ni) *n* chimenea *f*
**chin** (chin) *n* barbilla *f*
**China** (*chai*-nö) China *f*
**china** (*chai*-nö) *n* porcelana *f*
**Chinese** (chai-*niis*) *adj* chino
**chip** (chip) *n* astilla *f*; ficha *f*; *v* cortar, astillar; **chips** patatas fritas
**chisel** (*chi*-söl) *n* cincel *m*
**chives** (chaivs) *pl* cebollino *m*
**chlorine** (*kloo*-riin) *n* cloro *m*
**chocolate** (*cho*-klöt) *n* chocolate *m*
**choice** (choiss) *n* elección *f*; selección *f*
**choir** (k^u^ai^ö^) *n* coro *m*
**choke** (chouk) *v* sofocarse; estrangular; *n* starter *m*
***choose** (chuus) *v* escoger
**chop** (chop) *n* chuleta *f*; *v* tajar
**Christ** (kraisst) Cristo
**christen** (*kri*-ssön) *v* bautizar
**christening** (*kri*-ssö-ning) *n* bautizo *m*
**Christian** (*kriss*-chön) *adj* cristiano; ~ **name** nombre de pila
**Christmas** (*kriss*-möss) Navidad *f*

**chromium** (*krou*-mi-öm) *n* cromo *m*
**chronic** (*kro*-nik) *adj* crónico
**chronological** (kro-nö-*lo*-dʒi-köl) *adj* cronológico
**chuckle** (*cha*-köl) *v* *reírse entre dientes
**chunk** (changk) *n* trozo *m*; pedazo *m*
**church** (chööch) *n* iglesia *f*
**churchyard** (*chööch*-yaad) *n* cementerio *m*
**cigar** (ssi-*ghaa*) *n* puro *m*; cigarro *m*; ~ **shop** estanco *m*
**cigarette** (ssi-ghö-*rêt*) *n* cigarrillo *m*; ~ **lighter** encendedor *m*; ~ **tobacco** picadura *f*
**cinema** (*ssi*-nö-mö) *n* cinematógrafo *m*
**cinnamon** (*ssi*-nö-mön) *n* canela *f*
**circle** (*ssöö*-köl) *n* círculo *m*; balcón *m*; *v* rodear, circundar
**circulation** (ssöö-kyu-*lei*-ʃön) *n* circulación *f*; circulación de la sangre
**circumstance** (*ssöö*-köm-sstænss) *n* circunstancia *f*
**circus** (*ssöö*-köss) *n* circo *m*
**citizen** (*ssi*-ti-sön) *n* ciudadano *m*, -a *f*
**citizenship** (*ssi*-ti-sön-ʃip) *n* ciudadanía *f*
**city** (*ssi*-ti) *n* ciudad *f*
**civic** (*ssi*-vik) *adj* cívico
**civil** (*ssi*-völ) *adj* civil; cortés; ~ **law** derecho civil; ~ **servant** funcionario *m*
**civilian** (ssi-*vil*-yön) *adj* civil; *n* paisano *m*
**civilization** (ssi-vö-lai-*sei*-ʃön) *n* civilización *f*
**civilized** (*ssi*-vö-laisd) *adj* civilizado
**claim** (kleim) *v* reivindicar, reclamar; afirmar; *n* reivindicación *f*, pretensión *f*
**clamp** (klæmp) *n* mordaza *f*; grapa *f*
**clap** (klæp) *v* aplaudir
**clarify** (*klæ*-ri-fai) *v* aclarar, clarificar
**class** (klaass) *n* clase *f*
**classical** (*klæ*-ssi-köl) *adj* clásico
**classify** (*klæ*-ssi-fai) *v* clasificar
**classmate** (*klaass*-meit) *n* compañero *m*, -a *f* de clase
**classroom** (*klaass*-ruum) *n* clase *f*
**clause** (kloos) *n* cláusula *f*
**claw** (kloo) *n* garra *f*
**clay** (klei) *n* arcilla *f*
**clean** (kliin) *adj* puro, limpio; *v* limpiar
**cleaning** (*klii*-ning) *n* limpieza *f*; ~ **fluid** quitamanchas *m*
**clear** (kliö) *adj* claro; *v* limpiar
**clearing** (*kliö*-ring) *n* claro *m*
**cleft** (klêft) *n* grieta *f*
**clergyman** (*klöö*-dʒi-mön) *n* (pl -men) pastor *m*; clérigo *m*
**clerk** (klaak) *n* oficinista *m/f*; dependiente *m*, -a *f*
**clever** (*klê*-vö) *adj* inteligente; astuto, listo
**click** (klik) *n* clic *m*; *v* hacer clic
**client** (*klai*-önt) *n* cliente *m*
**cliff** (klif) *n* acantilado *m*, farallón *m*
**climate** (*klai*-mit) *n* clima *m*
**climb** (klaim) *v* trepar; *n* subida *f*
***cling** (kling) *v* adherirse; pegarse al cuerpo
**clinic** (*kli*-nik) *n* clínica *f*
**cloak** (klouk) *n* capa *f*; manto *m*
**cloakroom** (*klouk*-ruum) *n* guardarropa *m*
**clock** (klok) *n* reloj *m*; **at … o'clock** a las …
**cloister** (*kloi*-sstö) *n* claustro *m*
**close**[1] (klous) *v* *cerrar
**close**[2] (klouss) *adj* cercano
**closet** (*klo*-sit) *n* armario *m*; ropero *m*
**cloth** (kloz) *n* tela *f*; paño *m*
**clothes** (klouðs) *pl* ropa *f*, vestidos *mpl*
**clothing** (*klou*-ðing) *n* ropa *f*
**cloud** (klaud) *n* nube *f*
**cloudy** (*klau*-di) *adj* cubierto, nublado

**clover** (*klou*-vö) *n* trébol *m*
**clown** (klaun) *n* payaso *m*
**club** (klab) *n* club *m*; círculo *m*, asociación *f*; porra *f*, garrote *m*
**clumsy** (*klam*-si) *adj* torpe
**clutch** (klach) *n* embrague *m*; apretón *m*
**coach** (kouch) *n* autobús *m*; vagón *m*; carroza *f*; entrenador *m*, -a *f*
**coal** (koul) *n* carbón *m*
**coarse** (kooss) *adj* burdo; grosero
**coast** (kousst) *n* costa *f*
**coat** (kout) *n* sobretodo *m*, abrigo *m*
**coathanger** (*kout*-hæng-ö) *n* percha *f*
**cocaine** (kou-*kein*) *n* cocaína *f*
**cock** (kok) *n* gallo *m*
**cocktail** (*kok*-teil) *n* cóctel *m*
**coconut** (*kou*-kö-nat) *n* coco *m*
**cod** (kod) *n* (pl ~) bacalao *m*
**code** (koud) *n* código *m*
**coffee** (*ko*-fi) *n* café *m*; ~ **shop** *n* café *m*
**cognac** (*ko*-nyæk) *n* coñac *m*
**coherence** (kou-*hi*ö-rönss) *n* coherencia *f*
**coin** (koin) *n* moneda *f*
**coincide** (kou-in-*ssaid*) *v* coincidir
**cold** (kould) *adj* frío; *n* frío *m*; resfriado *m*; **catch a** ~ resfriarse
**collaborate** (kö-*læ*-bö-reit) *v* colaborar
**collapse** (kö-*læpss*) *v* desplomarse, derrumbarse
**collar** (*ko*-lö) *n* collar *m*; cuello *m*; ~ **stud** botón del cuello
**collarbone** (*ko*-lö-boun) *n* clavícula *f*
**colleague** (*ko*-liigh) *n* colega *m/f*
**collect** (kö-*lêkt*) *v* juntar; recoger; coleccionar; *hacer una colecta
**collection** (kö-*lêk*-ʃön) *n* colección *f*; recogida *f*
**collective** (kö-*lêk*-tiv) *adj* colectivo
**collector** (kö-*lêk*-tö) *n* coleccionista *m*; colector *m*
**college** (*ko*-lidʒ) *n* colegio *m*; universidad *f*
**collide** (kö-*laid*) *v* chocar
**collision** (kö-*li*-ʒön) *n* colisión *f*
**Colombia** (kö-*lom*-bi-ö) Colombia *f*
**Colombian** (kö-*lom*-bi-ön) *adj* colombiano
**colonel** (*köö*-nöl) *n* coronel *m*
**colony** (*ko*-lö-ni) *n* colonia *f*
**colo(u)r** (*ka*-lö) *n* color *m*; *v* colorear; ~ **film** película en colores
**colo(u)r-blind** (*ka*-lö-blaind) *adj* daltoniano
**colo(u)red** (*ka*-löd) *adj* de color
**colo(u)rful** (*ka*-lö-föl) *adj* colorado, lleno de color
**column** (*ko*-löm) *n* columna *f*
**coma** (*kou*-mö) *n* coma *m*
**comb** (koum) *v* peinar; *n* peine *m*
**combat** (*kom*-bæt) *n* lucha *f*, combate *m*; *v* combatir
**combination** (kom-bi-*nei*-ʃön) *n* combinación *f*
**combine** (köm-*bain*) *v* combinar; unir
***come** (kam) *v* *venir; ~ **across** *encontrar; hallar
**comedian** (kö-*mii*-di-ön) *n* humorista *m/f*; cómico *m*, -a *f*
**comedy** (*ko*-mö-di) *n* comedia *f*; **musical** ~ comedia musical
**comfort** (*kam*-föt) *n* comodidad *f*, confort *m*; consuelo *m*; *v* *consolar
**comfortable** (*kam*-fö-tö-böl) *adj* confortable
**comic** (*ko*-mik) *adj* cómico
**comics** (*ko*-mikss) *pl* tebeo *m*
**coming** (*ka*-ming) *n* llegada *f*
**comma** (*ko*-mö) *n* coma *f*
**command** (kö-*maand*) *v* mandar; *n* orden *f*
**commander** (kö-*maan*-dö) *n* comandante *m*
**commemoration** (kö-mê-mö-*rei*-ʃön) *n* conmemoración *f*

**commence** (kö-*mênss*) *v* *comenzar
**comment** (*ko*-mênt) *n* comentario *m*; *v* comentar
**commerce** (*ko*-mööss) *n* comercio *m*
**commercial** (kö-*möö*-ʃöl) *adj* comercial; *n* anuncio publicitario; ~ **law** derecho comercial
**commission** (kö-*mi*-ʃön) *n* comisión *f*
**commit** (kö-*mit*) *v* confiar, entregar; cometer
**committee** (kö-*mi*-ti) *n* comisión *f*, comité *m*
**common** (*ko*-mön) *adj* común; usual; ordinario
**commune** (*ko*-myuun) *n* comuna *f*
**communicate** (kö-*myuu*-ni-keit) *v* comunicar
**communication** (kö-myuu-ni-*kei*-ʃön) *n* comunicación *f*
**communiqué** (kö-*myuu*-ni-kei) *n* comunicado *m*
**communism** (*ko*-myu-ni-söm) *n* comunismo *m*
**community** (kö-*myuu*-nö-ti) *n* sociedad *f*, vecindario *m*
**commuter** (kö-*myuu*-tö) *n* viajero *m*, -a *f* (al trabajo)
**compact** (*kom*-pækt) *adj* compacto
**compact disc** (*kom*-pækt dissk) *n* disco compacto *m*; ~ **player** reproductor de discos compactos
**companion** (köm-*pæ*-nyön) *n* compañero *m*, -a *f*
**company** (*kam*-pö-ni) *n* compañía *f*; sociedad *f*
**comparative** (köm-*pæ*-rö-tiv) *adj* relativo
**compare** (köm-*pê*ö) *v* comparar
**comparison** (köm-*pæ*-ri-ssön) *n* comparación *f*
**compartment** (köm-*paat*-mönt) *n* compartimento *m*
**compass** (*kam*-pöss) *n* brújula *f*
**compel** (köm-*pêl*) *v* compeler
**compensate** (*kom*-pön-sseit) *v* compensar
**compensation** (kom-pön-*ssei*-ʃön) *n* compensación *f*; indemnización *f*
**compete** (köm-*piit*) *v* *competir
**competition** (kom-pö-*ti*-ʃön) *n* concurso *m*; competencia *f*
**competitor** (köm-*pê*-ti-tör) *n* competidor *m*
**compile** (köm-*pail*) *v* compilar
**complain** (köm-*plein*) *v* quejarse
**complaint** (köm-*pleint*) *n* queja *f*
**complete** (köm-*pliit*) *adj* completo; *v* completar
**completely** (köm-*pliit*-li) *adv* enteramente, totalmente, completamente
**complex** (*kom*-plêkss) *n* complejo *m*; *adj* complejo
**complexion** (köm-*plêk*-ʃön) *n* tez *f*
**complicated** (*kom*-pli-kei-tid) *adj* complicado
**compliment** (*kom*-pli-mönt) *n* cumplido *m*; piropo *m*; *v* cumplimentar
**compose** (köm-*pous*) *v* *componer
**composer** (köm-*pou*-sö) *n* compositor *m*, -a *f*
**composition** (kom-pö-*si*-ʃön) *n* composición *f*
**comprehensive** (kom-pri-*hên*-ssiv) *adj* extenso
**comprise** (köm-*prais*) *v* comprender
**compromise** (*kom*-prö-mais) *n* compromiso *m*
**compulsory** (köm-*pal*-ssö-ri) *adj* obligatorio
**computer** (köm-*pyu*-tö) *n* ordenador *m*
**comrade** (*kom*-reid) *n* camarada *m*
**conceal** (kön-*ssiil*) *v* disimular; ocultar
**conceited** (kön-*ssii*-tid) *adj* presuntuoso

**conceive** (kön-*ssiiv*) *v* *concebir, *entender; imaginar
**concentrate** (*kon*-ssön-treit) *v* concentrarse
**concentration** (kon-ssön-*trei*-ʃön) *n* concentración *f*
**concern** (kön-*ssöön*) *v* *concernir, atañer; *n* preocupación *f*; asunto *m*; empresa *f*, consorcio *m*
**concerned** (kön-*ssöönd*) *adj* preocupado; interesado
**concerning** (kön-*ssöö*-ning) *prep* en lo que se refiere a: acerca de
**concert** (*kon*-ssöt) *n* concierto *m*; ~ **hall** sala de conciertos
**concession** (kön-*ssê*-ʃön) *n* concesión *f*
**concierge** (koñg-ssi-*ê*ö ʒ) *n* conserje *m*
**concise** (kön-*ssaiss*) *adj* conciso
**conclusion** (köng-*kluu*-ʒön) *n* conclusión *f*
**concrete** (*kong*-kriit) *adj* concreto; *n* hormigón *m*
**concurrence** (köng-*ka*-rönss) *n* conformidad *f*
**concussion** (köng-*ka*-ʃön) *n* conmoción cerebral
**condemn** (kön-*dêm*) *v* condenar
**condition** (kön-*di*-ʃön) *n* condición *f*; estado *m*; circunstancia *f*
**conditional** (kön-*di*-ʃö-nöl) *adj* condicional
**conditioner** (kön-*di*-ʃö-nö) *n* suavizante de cabello *m*
**condom** (*kon*-dom) *n* preservativo *m*
**conduct** (*kon*-dakt) *n* conducta *f*
**conductor** (kön-*dak*-tö) *n* director *m*, -a *f* de orquestra; revisor *m*, -a *f*; conductor *m*
**conference** (*kon*-fö-rönss) *n* conferencia *f*
**confess** (kön-*fêss*) *v* *reconocer; *confesarse; profesar
**confession** (kön-*fê*-ʃön) *n* confesión *f*
**confidence** (*kon*-fi-dönss) *n* confianza *f*
**confident** (*kon*-fi-dönt) *adj* lleno de confianza; seguro
**confidential** (kon-fi-*dên*-ʃöl) *adj* confidencial
**confirm** (kön-*fööm*) *v* confirmar
**confirmation** (kon-fö-*mei*-ʃön) *n* confirmación *f*
**confiscate** (*kon*-fi-sskeit) *v* embargar, confiscar
**conflict** (*kon*-flikt) *n* conflicto *m*
**confuse** (kön-*fyuus*) *v* confundir; **confused** *adj* confuso
**confusion** (kön-*fyuu*-ʒön) *n* confusión *f*
**congratulate** (köng-*ghræ*-chu-leit) *v* felicitar
**congratulation** (köng-ghræ-chu-*lei*-ʃön) *n* felicitación *f*
**congregation** (kong-ghri-*ghei*-ʃön) *n* comunidad *f*, congregación *f*
**congress** (*kong*-ghrêss) *n* congreso *m*
**connect** (kö-*nêkt*) *v* conectar
**connection** (kö-*nêk*-ʃön) *n* relación *f*; conexión *f*; enlace *m*
**connoisseur** (ko-nö-*ssöö*) *n* perito *m*
**connotation** (ko-nö-*tei*-ʃön) *n* connotación *f*
**conquer** (*kong*-kö) *v* conquistar; vencer
**conqueror** (*kong*-kö-rö) *n* conquistador *m*
**conquest** (*kong*-kuêsst) *n* conquista *f*
**conscience** (*kon*-ʃönss) *n* conciencia *f*
**conscious** (*kon*-ʃöss) *adj* consciente
**consciousness** (*kon*-ʃöss-nöss) *n* conciencia *f*
**conscript** (*kon*-sskript) *n* quinto *m*
**consent** (kön-*ssênt*) *v* *consentir; *n* consentimiento *m*
**consequence** (*kon*-ssi-kuönss) *n* consecuencia *f*

**consequently** (*kon*-ssi-k$^{u}$önt-li) *adv* por consiguiente
**conservative** (kön-*ssöö*-vö-tiv) *adj* conservador
**consider** (kön-*ssi*-dö) *v* considerar; opinar
**considerable** (kön-*ssi*-dö-rö-böl) *adj* considerable; importante, notable
**considerate** (kön-*ssi*-dö-röt) *adj* considerado; respetuoso
**consideration** (kön-ssi-dö-*rei*-ʃön) *n* consideración *f*; atención *f*
**considering** (kön-*ssi*-dö-ring) *prep* considerando
**consignment** (kön-*ssain*-mönt) *n* envío *m*
**consist of** (kön-*ssisst*) constar de
**conspire** (kön-*sspai*$^{ö}$) *v* conspirar
**constant** (*kon*-sstönt) *adj* constante
**constipation** (kon-ssti-*pei*-ʃön) *n* estreñimiento *m*
**constituency** (kön-*ssti*-chu-ön-ssi) *n* distrito electoral
**constitution** (kon-ssti-*tyuu*-ʃön) *n* constitución *f*
**construct** (kön-*sstrakt*) *v* *construir; edificar
**construction** (kön-*sstrak*-ʃön) *n* construcción *f*; edificio *m*
**consul** (*kon*-ssöl) *n* cónsul *m*
**consulate** (*kon*-ssyu-löt) *n* consulado *m*
**consult** (kön-*ssalt*) *v* consultar
**consultation** (kon-ssöl-*tei*-ʃön) *n* consulta *f*; ~ **hours** *n* horas de consulta
**consume** (kön-*ssyuum*) *v* consumir
**consumer** (kön-*ssyuu*-mö) *n* consumidor *m*, -a *f*
**contact** (*kon*-tækt) *n* contacto *m*; *v* *ponerse en contacto con; ~ **lenses** lentillas *fpl*
**contagious** (kön-*tei*-dʒöss) *adj* contagioso
**contain** (kön-*tein*) *v* *contener; comprender
**container** (kön-*tei*-nö) *n* recipiente *m*; contenedor *m*
**contemporary** (kön-*têm*-pö-rö-ri) *adj* contemporáneo; de entonces; *n* contemporáneo *m*
**contempt** (kön-*têmpt*) *n* desprecio *m*, menosprecio *m*
**content** (kön-*tênt*) *adj* contento
**contents** (*kon*-têntss) *pl* contenido *m*
**contest** (*kon*-têsst) *n* lucha *f*; concurso *m*
**continent** (*kon*-ti-nönt) *n* continente *m*
**continental** (kon-ti-*nên*-töl) *adj* continental
**continual** (kön-*ti*-nyu-öl) *adj* continuo
**continue** (kön-*ti*-nyuu) *v* continuar; *proseguir, durar
**continuous** (kön-*ti*-nyu-öss) *adj* continuo, ininterrumpido
**contour** (*kon*-tu$^{ö}$) *n* contorno *m*
**contraceptive** (kon-trö-*ssêp*-tiv) *n* anticonceptivo *m*
**contract**[1] (*kon*-trækt) *n* contrato *m*
**contract**[2] (kön-*trækt*) *v* atrapar
**contractor** (kön-*træk*-tö) *n* contratista *m/f*; **building** ~ constructora *f*
**contradict** (kon-trö-*dikt*) *v* *contradecir
**contradictory** (kon-trö-*dik*-tö-ri) *adj* contradictorio
**contrary** (*kon*-trö-ri) *n* contrario *m*; *adj* contrario; **on the** ~ al contrario
**contrast** (*kon*-traasst) *n* contraste *m*; diferencia *f*
**contribution** (kon-tri-*byuu*-ʃön) *n* contribución *f*
**control** (kön-*troul*) *n* control *m*; *v* controlar
**controversial** (kon-trö-*vöö*-ʃöl) *adj* controvertido, controvertible
**convenience** (kön-*vii*-nyönss) *n*

comodidad *f*
**convenient** (kön-*vii*-nyönt) *adj* cómodo; adecuado, conveniente
**convent** (*kon*-vönt) *n* convento *m*
**conversation** (kon-vö-*ssei*-ʃön) *n* conversación *f*
**convert** (kön-*vööt*) *v* *convertir
**convict**[1] (kön-*vikt*) *v* condenar
**convict**[2] (*kon*-vikt) *n* condenado *m*
**conviction** (kön-*vik*-ʃön) *n* convencimiento *m*; condena *f*
**convince** (kön-*vinss*) *v* convencer
**convulsion** (kön-*val*-ʃön) *n* convulsión *f*
**cook** (kuk) *n* cocinero *m*; *v* cocinar; guisar, preparar comidas
**cooker** (*ku*-kö) *n* cocina *f*; **gas ~** cocina de gas
**cook(ery) book** (*ku*-kö-ri-buk) *n* libro de cocina
**cookie** (*ku*-ki) *nAm* galleta *f*
**cool** (kuul) *adj* fresco
**cooperation** (kou-o-pö-*rei*-ʃön) *n* cooperación *f*; colaboración *f*
**cooperative** (kou-*o*-pö-rö-tiv) *adj* cooperativo; cooperador; *n* cooperativa *f*
**coordinate** (kou-*oo*-di-neit) *v* coordinar
**coordination** (kou-oo-di-*nei*-ʃön) *n* coordinación *f*
**cope** (koup) *v* arreglárselas; **~ with** poder con
**copper** (*ko*-pö) *n* cobre *m*
**copy** (*ko*-pi) *n* copia *f*; ejemplar *m*; *v* copiar; imitar; **carbon ~** copia *f*
**coral** (*ko*-röl) *n* coral *m*
**cord** (kood) *n* cuerda *f*; cordón *m*
**cordial** (*koo*-di-öl) *adj* cordial
**corduroy** (*koo*-dö-roi) *n* pana *f*
**core** (koo) *n* núcleo *m*; corazón *m*
**cork** (kook) *n* corcho *m*; tapón *m*
**corkscrew** (*kook*-sskruu) *n* sacacorchos *mpl*
**corn** (koon) *n* grano *m*; cereales *mpl*, trigo *m*; maíz *m*; callo *m*; **~ on the cob** maíz en la mazorca
**corner** (*koo*-nö) *n* esquina *f*
**cornfield** (*koon*-fiild) *n* trigal *m*
**corpse** (koopss) *n* cadáver *m*
**corpulent** (*koo*-pyu-lönt) *adj* corpulento; grueso
**correct** (kö-*rêkt*) *adj* correcto, justo; *v* *corregir
**correction** (kö-*rêk*-ʃön) *n* corrección *f*; rectificación *f*
**correctness** (kö-*rêkt*-nöss) *n* exactitud *f*
**correspond** (ko-ri-*sspond*) *v* corresponderse; corresponder
**correspondence** (ko-ri-*sspon*-dönss) *n* correspondencia *f*
**correspondent** (ko-ri-*sspon*-dönt) *n* corresponsal *m/f*
**corridor** (*ko*-ri-doo) *n* pasillo *m*
**corrupt** (kö-*rapt*) *adj* corrupto; *v* corromper
**corruption** (kö-*rap*-ʃön) *n* corrupción *f*
**corset** (*koo*-ssit) *n* corsé *m*
**cosmetics** (kos-*mê*-tikss) *pl* productos cosméticos, cosméticos *mpl*
**cost** (kosst) *n* coste *m*; precio *m*
***cost** (kosst) *v* *costar
**cosy** (*kou*-si) *adj* acogedor; confortable
**cot** (kot) *nAm* catre *m*
**cottage** (*ko*-tidʒ) *n* casita de campo
**cotton** (*ko*-tön) *n* algodón *m*; de algodón
**cotton wool** (*ko*-tön-ᵘul) *n* algodón *m*
**couch** (kauch) *n* diván *m*
**cough** (kof) *n* tos *f*; *v* toser
**could** (kud) *v* (p can)
**council** (*kaun*-ssöl) *n* consejo *m*
**councillor** (*kaun*-ssö-lö) *n* consejal *m*, -a *f*

**counsel** (*kaun*-ssöl) *n* consejo *m*
**counsellor** (*kaun*-ssö-lö) *n* consejero *m*
**count** (kaunt) *v* *contar; adicionar; *incluir; considerar; *n* conde *m*
**counter** (*kaun*-tö) *n* mostrador *m*; barra *f*
**counterfeit** (*kaun*-tö-fiit) *v* falsificar
**counterfoil** (*kaun*-tö-foil) *n* talón *m*
**countess** (*kaun*-tiss) *n* condesa *f*
**country** (*kan*-tri) *n* país *m*; campo *m*; región *f*; ~ **estate** finca *f*; ~ **house** quinta *f*
**countryman** (*kan*-tri-mön) *n* (pl -men) compatriota *m*
**countryside** (*kan*-tri-ssaid) *n* campo *m*
**county** (*kaun*-ti) *n* condado *m*
**couple** (*ka*-pöl) *n* pareja *f*; par *m*
**coupon** (*kuu*-pon) *n* cupón *m*
**courage** (*ka*-ridʒ) *n* valor *m*
**courageous** (kö-*rei*-dʒöss) *adj* valiente
**course** (kooss) *n* rumbo *m*; plato *m*; curso *m*; **intensive** ~ curso intensivo; **of** ~ por supuesto
**court** (koot) *n* tribunal *m*; corte *f*
**courteous** (*köö*-ti-öss) *adj* cortés
**cousin** (*ka*-sön) *n* prima *f*, primo *m*
**cover** (*ka*-vö) *v* cubrir; *n* refugio *m*; tapa *f*; cubierta *f*; ~ **charge** precio del cubierto
**cow** (kau) *n* vaca *f*
**coward** (*kau*-öd) *n* cobarde *m*
**cowardly** (*kau*-öd-li) *adj* cobarde
**cozy** (*kou*-si) *adj* acogedor; confortable
**crab** (kræb) *n* cangrejo *m*
**crack** (kræk) *n* crujido *m*; hendidura *f*; *v* crujir; *quebrar, *reventar
**cradle** (*krei*-döl) *n* cuna *f*
**cramp** (kræmp) *n* calambre *m*
**crane** (krein) *n* grúa *f*
**crash** (kræʃ) *n* choque *m*; *v* chocar; precipitarse; ~ **barrier** barrera de protección
**crate** (kreit) *n* caja *f*
**crater** (*krei*-tö) *n* cráter *m*
**crawl** (krool) *v* arrastrarse; *n* crawl *m*
**craze** (kreis) *n* manía *f*
**crazy** (*krei*-si) *adj* loco
**creak** (kriik) *v* crujir
**cream** (kriim) *n* crema *f*; nata *f*; *adj* de color crema
**creamy** (*krii*-mi) *adj* cremoso
**crease** (kriiss) *v* *plegar; *n* raya *f*; pliegue *m*
**create** (kri-*eit*) *v* crear
**creative** (kri-*ei*-tiv) *adj* creativo
**creature** (*krii*-chö) *n* criatura *f*; ser *m*
**credible** (*krê*-di-böl) *adj* creíble; verosímil
**credit** (*krê*-dit) *n* crédito *m*; *v* acreditar; ~ **card** tarjeta de crédito
**creditor** (*krê*-di-tö) *n* acreedor *m*
**credulous** (*krê*-dyu-löss) *adj* crédulo
**creek** (kriik) *n* ensenada *f*
***creep** (kriip) *v* gatear; arrastrarse
**creepy** (*krii*-pi) *adj* lúgubre, espeluznante
**cremate** (kri-*meit*) *v* incinerar
**cremation** (kri-*mei*-ʃön) *n* incineración *f*
**crew** (kruu) *n* equipo *m*; tripulación *f*
**cricket** (*kri*-kit) *n* grillo *m*
**crime** (kraim) *n* crimen *m*
**criminal** (*kri*-mi-nöl) *n* delincuente *m*, criminal *m*; *adj* criminal; ~ **law** derecho penal
**criminality** (kri-mi-*næ*-lö-ti) *n* criminalidad *f*
**crimson** (*krim*-sön) *adj* carmesí
**crippled** (*kri*-pöld) *adj* lisiado; incapacitado; minusválido
**crisis** (*krai*-ssiss) *n* (pl crises) crisis *f*
**crisp** (krissp) *adj* crujiente, quebradizo
**critic** (*kri*-tik) *n* crítico *m*, -a *f*

**critical** (*kri*-ti-köl) *adj* crítico; precario
**criticism** (*kri*-ti-ssi-söm) *n* crítica *f*
**criticize** (*kri*-ti-ssais) *v* criticar
**crochet** (*krou*-ʃei) *v* *hacer ganchillo
**crockery** (*kro*-kö-ri) *n* cerámica *f*, loza *f*
**crocodile** (*kro*-kö-dail) *n* cocodrilo *m*
**crooked** (*kru*-kid) *adj* torcido, curvo; deshonesto
**crop** (krop) *n* cosecha *f*
**cross** (kross) *v* *atravesar; *adj* enojado, enfadado; *n* cruz *f*
**cross-eyed** (*kross*-aid) *adj* bizco
**crossing** (*kro*-ssing) *n* travesía *f*; encrucijada *f*; paso *m*; paso a nivel
**crossroads** (*kross*-rouds) *n* encrucijada *f*
**crosswalk** (*kross*-$^{u}$ook) *nAm* cruce para peatones
**crow** (krou) *n* corneja *f*
**crowbar** (*krou*-baa) *n* pie de cabra
**crowd** (kraud) *n* masa *f*, muchedumbre *f*
**crowded** (*krau*-did) *adj* animado; repleto; concurrido
**crown** (kraun) *n* corona *f*; *v* coronar
**crucifix** (*kruu*-ssi-fikss) *n* crucifijo *m*
**crucifixion** (kruu-ssi-*fik*-ʃön) *n* crucifixión *f*
**crucify** (*kruu*-ssi-fai) *v* crucificar
**cruel** (kru$^{ö}$l) *adj* cruel
**cruise** (kruus) *n* crucero *m*
**crumb** (kram) *n* migaja *f*
**crusade** (kruu-*sseid*) *n* cruzada *f*
**crust** (krasst) *n* corteza *f*
**crutch** (krach) *n* muleta *f*
**cry** (krai) *v* llorar; gritar; llamar; *n* grito *m*
**crystal** (*kri*-sstöl) *n* cristal *m*; *adj* de cristal
**Cuba** (*kyuu*-bö) Cuba *f*
**Cuban** (*kyuu*-bön) *adj* cubano
**cube** (kyuub) *n* cubo *m*
**cuckoo** (*ku*-kuu) *n* cuclillo *m*
**cucumber** (*kyuu*-köm-bö) *n* pepino *m*
**cuddle** (*ka*-döl) *v* acariciar
**cuff links** (*kaf*-lingkss) *pl* gemelos *mpl*; mancuernillas *fplMe*
**cul-de-sac** (*kal*-dö-ssæk) *n* callejon sin salida
**cultivate** (*kal*-ti-veit) *v* cultivar
**culture** (*kal*-chö) *n* cultura *f*
**cultured** (*kal*-chöd) *adj* culto
**cunning** (*ka*-ning) *adj* astuto
**cup** (kap) *n* taza *f*; copa *f*
**cupboard** (*ka*-böd) *n* armario *m*
**curb** (kööb) *n* bordillo *m*; *v* refrenar
**cure** (kyu$^{ö}$) *v* curar; *n* cura *f*; curación *f*
**curiosity** (kyu$^{ö}$-ri-*o*-ssö-ti) *n* curiosidad *f*
**curious** (*kyu$^{ö}$*-ri-öss) *adj* curioso
**curl** (kööl) *v* rizar; *n* rizo *m*
**curler** (*köö*-lö) *n* rulo *m*
**curly** (*köö*-li) *adj* crespo; chino *adjMe*
**currant** (*ka*-rönt) *n* pasa de Corinto; grosella *f*
**currency** (*ka*-rön-ssi) *n* moneda *f*; **foreign ~** moneda extranjera
**current** (*ka*-rönt) *n* corriente *f*; *adj* corriente; **alternating ~** corriente alterna; **direct ~** corriente continua
**curry** (*ka*-ri) *n* curry *m*
**curse** (kööss) *v* *maldecir; *n* maldición *f*
**curtain** (*köö*-tön) *n* cortina *f*; telón *m*
**curve** (kööv) *n* curva *f*
**curved** (köövd) *adj* curvado, encorvado
**cushion** (*ku*-ʃön) *n* almohadón *m*; cojín *m*
**custody** (*ka*-sstö-di) *n* detención *f*; custodia *f*; tutela *f*
**custom** (*ka*-sstöm) *n* costumbre *f*
**customary** (*ka*-sstö-mö-ri) *adj* usual, corriente, acostumbrado
**customer** (*ka*-sstö-mö) *n* cliente *m*
**Customs** (*ka*-sstöms) *pl* aduana *f*; **~ duty** impuesto *m*; **~ officer** oficial de

aduanas
**cut** (kat) *n* incisión *f*; cortadura *f*
***cut** (kat) *v* cortar; *reducir; **~ off** cortar
**cutlery** (*kat*-lö-ri) *n* cubiertos *mpl*
**cutlet** (*kat*-löt) *n* chuleta *f*
**cycle** (*ssai*-köl) *n* biciclo *m*; bicicleta *f*; ciclo *m*
**cyclist** (*ssai*-klisst) *n* ciclista *m*
**cylinder** (*ssi*-lin-dö) *n* cilindro *m*; **~ head** culata del cilindro
**Cyprus** (*ssai*-prös) Chipre *f*
**cystitis** (ssi-*sstai*-tiss) *n* cistitis *f*
**Czech** (chêk) *adj* checo

# D

**dad** (dæd) *n* papá *m*
**daffodil** (*dæ*-fö-dil) *n* narciso *m*
**daily** (*dei*-li) *adj* diario; *n* diario *m*
**dairy** (*dê*ö-ri) *n* lechería *f*
**dam** (dæm) *n* presa *f*; dique *m*
**damage** (*dæ*-midʒ) *n* perjuicio *m*; *v* dañar
**damn** (dæm) *colloquial adj* maldito; **damn!** ¡mecachis!; *v* condenar; **damn it!** ¡maldita sea!
**damp** (dæmp) *adj* húmedo; mojado; *n* humedad *f*; *v* *humedecer
**dance** (daanss) *v* bailar; *n* baile *m*
**dandelion** (*dæn*-di-lai-ön) *n* diente de león
**dandruff** (*dæn*-dröf) *n* caspa *f*
**Dane** (dein) *n* danés *m*
**danger** (*dein*-dʒö) *n* peligro *m*
**dangerous** (*dein*-dʒö-röss) *adj* peligroso
**Danish** (*dei*-niʃ) *adj* danés
**dare** (dêö) *v* atreverse, osar; desafiar
**daring** (*dê*ö-ring) *adj* atrevido
**dark** (daak) *adj* oscuro, obscuro; *n* oscuridad *f*
**darling** (*daa*-ling) *n* amor *m*, querido *m*, -a *f*
**darn** (daan) *v* zurcir
**dash** (dæʃ) *v* correr; *n* guión *m*
**dashboard** (*dæʃ*-bood) *n* tablero de instrumentos
**data** (*dei*-tö) *pl* datos *m*
**date**[1] (deit) *n* fecha *f*; cita *f*; *v* datar; **out of ~** anticuado
**date**[2] (deit) *n* dátil *m*
**daughter** (*doo*-tö) *n* hija *f*; **daughter-in-law** (pl daughters-in-law) nuera *f*
**dawn** (doon) *n* alba *f*; aurora *f*
**day** (dei) *n* día *m*; **by ~** de día; **~ trip** jornada *f*; **per ~** a diario; **the ~ before yesterday** anteayer
**daybreak** (*dei*-breik) *n* amanecer *m*
**daylight** (*dei*-lait) *n* luz del día
**dead** (dêd) *adj* muerto; difunto
**deaf** (dêf) *adj* sordo
**deal** (diil) *n* transacción *f*
***deal** (diil) *v* repartir; **~ with** *v* tratar con; *hacer negocios con
**dealer** (*dii*-lö) *n* negociante *m/f*, comerciante *m/f*; traficante *m/f*
**dear** (diö) *adj* querido; caro; amado
**death** (dêz) *n* muerte *f*; **~ penalty** pena de muerte
**debate** (di-*beit*) *n* debate *m*
**debit** (*dê*-bit) *n* debe *m*
**debt** (dêt) *n* deuda *f*
**decaffeinated** (dii-*kæ*-fi-nei-tid) *adj* descafeinado
**deceit** (di-*ssiit*) *n* engaño *m*
**deceive** (di-*ssiiv*) *v* engañar
**December** (di-*ssêm*-bö) diciembre
**decency** (*dii*-ssön-ssi) *n* decencia *f*

**decent** (*dii*-ssönt) *adj* decente
**decide** (di-*ssaid*) *v* decidir
**decision** (di-*ssi*-ʒön) *n* decisión *f*
**deck** (dêk) *n* cubierta *f*; **~ cabin** camarote en cubierta; **~ chair** silla de tijera
**declaration** (dê-klö-*rei*-ʃön) *n* declaración *f*
**declare** (di-*klê*$^{ö}$) *v* declarar; indicar
**decorate** (*dê*-kö-reit) *v* pintar; empapelar; decorar; condecorar
**decoration** (dê-kö-*rei*-ʃön) *n* decoración *f*
**decrease** (dii-*kriiss*) *v* *reducir; *disminuir; *n* disminución *f*
**dedicate** (*dê*-di-keit) *v* dedicar
**deduce** (di-*dyuuss*) *v* *deducir
**deduct** (di-*dakt*) *v* *deducir
**deed** (diid) *n* acción *f*, acto *m*
**deep** (diip) *adj* hondo
**deep-freeze** (diip-*friis*) *n* congelador *m*
**deer** (di$^{ö}$) *n* (pl ~) ciervo *m*
**defeat** (di-*fiit*) *v* derrotar; *n* derrota *f*
**defective** (di-*fêk*-tiv) *adj* defectuoso
**defence** (di-*fênss*) *n* defensa *f*
**defend** (di-*fênd*) *v* *defender
**deficiency** (di-*fi*-ʃön-ssi) *n* deficiencia *f*
**deficit** (*dê*-fi-ssit) *n* déficit *m*
**define** (di-*fain*) *v* definir, determinar
**definite** (*dê*-fi-nit) *adj* determinado; definido
**definition** (dê-fi-*ni*-ʃön) *n* definición *f*
**deformed** (di-*foomd*) *adj* deforme
**degree** (di-*ghrii*) *n* grado *m*; título *m*
**delay** (di-*lei*) *v* retardar; *diferir; *n* retraso *m*, tardanza *f*; dilación *f*
**delegate** (*dê*-li-ghöt) *n* delegado *m*
**delegation** (dê-li-*ghei*-ʃön) *n* delegación *f*
**deliberate**[1] (di-*li*-bö-reit) *v* discutir, deliberar
**deliberate**[2] (di-*li*-bö-röt) *adj* deliberado
**deliberation** (di-li-bö-*rei*-ʃön) *n* deliberación *f*
**delicacy** (*dê*-li-kö-ssi) *n* golosina *f*; delicadeza *f*; **delicacies** *n* gollerías *fpl*
**delicate** (*dê*-li-köt) *adj* delicado; fino
**delicatessen** (dê-li-kö-*tê*-ssön) tienda de comestibles finos; tienda de ultramarinos
**delicious** (di-*li*-ʃöss) *adj* exquisito, delicioso
**delight** (di-*lait*) *n* delicia *f*, deleite *m*; *v* encantar
**delighted** (di-*lai*-töd) *adj* encantado; **I'd be ~ to come** me encantaría venir
**delightful** (di-*lait*-föl) *adj* delicioso, deleitoso
**deliver** (di-*li*-vö) *v* entregar; librar
**delivery** (di-*li*-vö-ri) *n* entrega *f*, reparto *m*; parto *m*; liberación *f*; **~ van** furgoneta *f*
**demand** (di-*maand*) *v* *requerir, exigir; *n* exigencia *f*; demanda *f*
**democracy** (di-*mo*-krö-ssi) *n* democracia *f*
**democratic** (dê-mö-*kræ*-tik) *adj* democrático
**demolish** (di-*mo*-liʃ) *v* *demoler
**demolition** (dê-mö-*li*-ʃön) *n* demolición *f*
**demonstrate** (*dê*-mön-sstreit) *v* *demostrar; *hacer una manifestación
**demonstration** (dê-mön-*sstrei*-ʃön) *n* manifestación *f*; demostración *f*
**den** (dên) *n* madriguera *f*
**Denmark** (*dên*-maak) Dinamarca *f*
**denomination** (di-no-mi-*nei*-ʃön) *n* denominación *f*
**dense** (dênss) *adj* denso
**dent** (dênt) *n* abolladura *f*
**dentist** (*dên*-tisst) *n* dentista *m*
**denture** (*dên*-chö) *n* dentadura

postiza
**deny** (di-*nai*) *v* *negar; *denegar
**deodorant** (dii-*ou*-dö-rönt) *n* desodorante *m*
**depart** (di-*paat*) *v* partir; irse; marcharse; *fallecer
**department** (di-*paat*-mönt) *n* departamento *m*; ~ **store** grandes almacenes
**departure** (di-*paa*-chö) *n* despedida *f*, partida *f*
**dependant** (di-*pên*-dönt) *adj* dependiente
**depend on** (di-*pênd*) depender de; **that depends** depende
**deposit** (di-*po*-sit) *n* depósito *m*; fianza *f*; capa *f*, yacimiento *m*; *v* ingresar
**depository** (di-*po*-si-tö-ri) *n* almacén *m*
**depot** (*dê*-pou) *n* deposito *m*; *nAm* estación *f*
**depress** (di-*prêss*) *v* deprimir
**depression** (di-*prê*-ʃön) *n* desánimo *m*; depresión *f*
**deprive of** (di-*praiv*) privar de
**depth** (dêpz) *n* profundidad *f*
**deputy** (*dê*-pyu-ti) *n* segundo *m*, -a *f*; sustituto *m*, -a *f*
**descend** (di-*ssênd*) *v* *descender
**descendant** (di-*ssên*-dönt) *n* descendiente *m/f*
**descent** (di-*ssênt*) *n* bajada *f*
**describe** (di-*sskraib*) *v* describir
**description** (di-*sskrip*-ʃön) *n* descripción *f*
**desert**[1] (*dê*-söt) *n* desierto *m*; *adj* yermo, desierto
**desert**[2] (di-*sööt*) *v* desertar; dejar
**deserve** (di-*sööv*) *v* *merecer
**design** (di-*sain*) *v* diseñar; *n* diseño *m*; objetivo *m*
**designate** (*dê*-sigh-neit) *v* designar
**desirable** (di-*saiö*-rö-böl) *adj* deseable
**desire** (di-*saiö*) *n* deseo *m*; ganas *fpl*; *v* anhelar, desear
**desk** (dêssk) *n* escritorio *m*; pupitre *m*
**despair** (di-*sspêö*) *n* desesperación *f*; *v* *estar desesperado
**despatch** (di-*sspæch*) *v* despachar
**desperate** (*dê*-sspö-röt) *adj* desesperado
**despise** (di-*sspais*) *v* despreciar
**despite** (di-*sspait*) *prep* a pesar de
**dessert** (di-*sööt*) *n* postre *m*
**destination** (dê-ssti-*nei*-ʃön) *n* destino *m*
**destine** (*dê*-sstin) *v* destinar
**destiny** (*dê*-ssti-ni) *n* destino *m*
**destroy** (di-*sstroi*) *v* *destruir
**destruction** (di-*sstrak*-ʃön) *n* destrucción *f*; ruina *f*
**detach** (di-*tæch*) *v* separar
**detail** (*dii*-teil) *n* particularidad *f*, detalle *m*
**detailed** (*dii*-teild) *adj* detallado
**detect** (di-*têkt*) *v* descubrir
**detective** (di-*têk*-tiv) *n* detective *m/f*; ~ **story** novela policíaca
**detergent** (di-*töö*-dʒönt) *n* detergente *m*
**determine** (di-*töö*-min) *v* determinar
**determined** (di-*töö*-mind) *adj* resuelto
**detest** (di-*têsst*) *v* detestar
**detour** (*dii*-tuö) *n* desvío *m*
**devaluation** (dii-væl-yu-*ei*-ʃön) *n* desvalorización *f*
**devalue** (dii-*væl*-yuu) *v* desvalorizar
**develop** (di-*vê*-löp) *v* desarrollar; revelar
**development** (di-*vê*-löp-mönt) *n* desarrollo *m*
**deviate** (*dii*-vi-eit) *v* desviarse
**devil** (*dê*-völ) *n* diablo *m*
**devise** (di-*vais*) *v* idear; proyectar
**devote** (di-*vout*) *v* dedicar
**dew** (dyuu) *n* rocío *m*

**diabetes** (dai-ö-*bii*-tiis) *n* diabetes *f*
**diabetic** (dai-ö-*bê*-tik) *n* diabético *m*, -a *f*
**diagnose** (dai-ögh-*nous*) *v* diagnosticar; *comprobar
**diagnosis** (dai-ögh-*nou*-ssiss) *n* (pl -ses) diagnosis *m*
**diagonal** (dai-*æ*-ghö-nöl) *n* diagonal *f*; *adj* diagonal
**diagram** (*dai*-ö-ghræm) *n* esquema *m*; gráfico *m*
**dial** (*dai*-öl) *n* esfera *f*; cuadrante *m*; disco *m*; *v* marcar
**dialect** (*dai*-ö-lêkt) *n* dialecto *m*
**diamond** (*dai*-ö-mönd) *n* diamante *m*
**diaper** (*dai*-ö-pö) *nAm* pañal *m*
**diaphragm** (*dai*-ö-fræm) *n* membrana *f*
**diarrh(o)ea** (dai-ö-*ri*-ö) *n* diarrea *f*
**diary** (*dai*-ö-ri) *n* agenda *f*; diario *m*
**dictaphone** (*dik*-tö-foun) *n* dictáfono *m*
**dictate** (dik-*teit*) *v* dictar
**dictation** (dik-*tei*-ʃön) *n* dictado *m*
**dictator** (dik-*tei*-tö) *n* dictador *m*
**dictionary** (*dik*-ʃö-nö-ri) *n* diccionario *m*
**did** (did) *v* (p do)
**die** (dai) *v* *morir
**diesel** (*dii*-söl) *n* diesel *m*
**diet** (*dai*-öt) *n* régimen *m*
**differ** (*di*-fö) *v* *diferir
**difference** (*di*-fö-rönss) *n* diferencia *f*; distinción *f*
**different** (*di*-fö-rönt) *adj* diferente; otro
**difficult** (*di*-fi-költ) *adj* difícil; fastidioso
**difficulty** (*di*-fi-köl-ti) *n* dificultad *f*; trabajo *m*
***dig** (digh) *v* cavar
**digest** (di-*dʒêsst*) *v* *digerir
**digestible** (di-*dʒê*-sstö-böl) *adj* digerible
**digestion** (di-*dʒêss*-chön) *n* digestión *f*
**digit** (*di*-dʒit) *n* número *m*
**digital** (*di*-dʒi-töl) *adj* digital
**dignified** (*digh*-ni-faid) *adj* distinguido
**dignity** (*digh*-ni-ti) dignidad *f*
**dilapidated** (di-*læ*-pi-dei-tid) *adj* ruinoso
**diligence** (*di*-li-dʒönss) *n* diligencia *f*
**diligent** (*di*-li-dʒönt) *adj* diligente
**dilute** (dai-*lyuut*) *v* *diluir
**dim** (dim) *adj* deslucido, mate; oscuro, vago, difuso
**dine** (dain) *v* cenar
**dinghy** (*ding*-ghi) *n* chinchorro *m*
**dining car** (*dai*-ning-kaa) *n* coche comedor
**dining room** (*dai*-ning-ruum) *n* comedor *m*
**dinner** (*di*-nö) *n* comida principal; cena *f*
**dinner jacket** (*di*-nö-dʒæ-kit) *n* smoking *m*
**dinner service** (*di*-nö-ssöö-viss) *n* servicio de mesa
**diphtheria** (dif-*ziö*-ri-ö) *n* difteria *f*
**diploma** (di-*plou*-mö) *n* diploma *m*
**diplomat** (*di*-plö-mæt) *n* diplomático *m*
**direct** (di-*rêkt*) *adj* directo; *v* dirigir; administrar
**direction** (di-*rêk*-ʃön) *n* dirección *f*; instrucción *f*; dirección de escena; administración *f*; **directions for use** modo de empleo
**directive** (di-*rêk*-tiv) *n* directriz *f*
**director** (di-*rêk*-tö) *n* director *m*, -a *f*; director de escena
**directory** (di-*rêk*-tö-ri) directorio *m*; guía *f* telefónica
**dirt** (dööt) *n* suciedad *f*
**dirty** (*döö*-ti) *adj* sucio
**disabled** (di-*ssei*-böld) *adj*

minusválido, inválido
**disadvantage** (di-ssöd-*vaan*-tidʒ) *n* desventaja *f*
**disagree** (di-ssö-*ghrii*) *v* no *estar de acuerdo, *disentir
**disagreeable** (di-ssö-*ghrii*-ö-böl) *adj* desagradable
**disappear** (di-ssö-*piö*) *v* *desaparecer
**disappoint** (di-ssö-*point*) *v* decepcionar
**disappointment** (di-ssö-*point*-mönt) *n* desengaño *m*
**disapprove** (di-ssö-*pruuv*) *v* *desaprobar
**disaster** (di-*saa*-sstö) *n* desastre *m*; catástrofe *f*, calamidad *f*
**disastrous** (di-*saa*-sströss) *adj* desastroso
**disc** (dissk) *n* disco *m*; **slipped ~** hernia intervertebral
**discard** (di-*sskaad*) *v* desechar
**discharge** (diss-*chaadʒ*) *v* descargar; **~ of** dispensar de
**discipline** (*di*-ssi-plin) *n* disciplina *f*
**discolo(u)r** (di-*sska*-lö) *v* *desteñirse; **discolo(u)red** descolorido
**disconnect** (di-sskö-*nêkt*) *v* desconectar
**discontented** (di-sskön-*tên*-tid) *adj* descontento
**discontinue** (di-sskön-*ti*-nyuu) *v* suprimir, cesar
**discount** (*di*-sskaunt) *n* descuento *m*
**discourage** (diss-*ka*-ridʒ) *v* disuadir (**from** de); desanimar, desalentar
**discover** (di-*sska*-vö) *v* descubrir
**discovery** (di-*sska*-vö-ri) *n* descubrimiento *m*
**discuss** (di-*sskass*) *v* discutir; debatir
**discussion** (di-*sska*-ʃön) *n* discusión *f*; conversación *f*, debate *m*
**disease** (di-*siis*) *n* enfermedad *f*
**disembark** (di-ssim-*baak*) *v* desembarcar
**disgrace** (diss-*ghreiss*) *n* deshonor *m*
**disguise** (diss-*ghais*) *v* disfrazarse; *n* disfraz *m*
**disgust** (diss-*ghasst*) *n* asco *m*, repugnancia *f*; *v* dar asco, repugnar
**disgusting** (diss-*gha*-ssting) *adj* repugnante, asqueroso
**dish** (diʃ) *n* plato *m*; fuente *f*; guiso *m*
**dishonest** (di-*sso*-nisst) *adj* tramposo; fraudulento
**dishwasher** (*di*ʃ-ᵘo-ʃö) lavaplatos *m*/*f*; lavavajillas *m*, lavaplatos *m*
**disinfect** (di-ssin-*fêkt*) *v* desinfectar
**disinfectant** (di-ssin-*fêk*-tönt) *n* desinfectante *m*
**dislike** (di-*sslaik*) *v* detestar, no gustar; *n* repugnancia *f*, aversión *f*, antipatía *f*
**dislocated** (*di*-sslö-kei-tid) *adj* dislocado
**dismiss** (diss-*miss*) *v* *despedir
**disorder** (di-*ssoo*-dö) *n* desorden *m*
**dispatch** (di-*sspæch*) *v* enviar, despachar
**display** (di-*ssplei*) *v* exhibir; *mostrar; *n* exposición *f*
**displease** (di-*sspliis*) *v* disgustar, desagradar
**disposable** (di-*sspou*-sö-böl) *adj* desechable
**disposal** (di-*sspou*-söl) *n* disposición *f*
**dispose of** (di-*sspous*) *disponer de
**dispute** (di-*sspyuut*) *n* disputa *f*; riña *f*, contienda *f*; *v* *reñir, disputar
**dissatisfied** (di-*ssæ*-tiss-faid) *adj* insatisfecho
**dissolve** (di-*solv*) *v* *disolver
**dissuade from** (di-*ssᵘeid*) disuadir
**distance** (*di*-sstönss) *n* distancia *f*; **~ in kilometres** (**kilometers** *Am*) kilometraje *m*
**distant** (*di*-sstönt) *adj* lejano
**distinct** (di-*sstingkt*) *adj* claro; distinto
**distinction** (di-*sstingk*-ʃön) *n*

distinción *f*, diferencia *f*
**distinguish** (di-*ssting*-gh$^u$iʃ) *v* distinguir
**distinguished** (di-*ssting*-gh$^u$iʃt) *adj* distinguido
**distress** (di-*sstrêss*) *n* peligro *m*; ~ **signal** señal de alarma
**distribute** (di-*sstri*-byuut) *v* *distribuir
**distributor** (di-*sstri*-byu-tö) *n* distribuidor *m*
**district** (*di*-sstrikt) *n* distrito *m*; comarca *f*; barrio *m*
**disturb** (di-*sstööb*) *v* estorbar, molestar
**disturbance** (di-*sstöö*-bönss) *n* disturbio *m*; confusión *f*
**ditch** (dich) *n* zanja *f*, cuneta *f*
**dive** (daiv) *v* bucear
**diversion** (dai-*vöö*-ʃön) *n* desvío *m*; diversión *f*
**divide** (di-*vaid*) *v* dividir; repartir; separar
**divine** (di-*vain*) *adj* divino
**division** (di-*vi*-ʒön) *n* división *f*; separación *f*; departamento *m*
**divorce** (di-*vooss*) *n* divorcio *m*; *v* divorciar
**dizziness** (*di*-si-nöss) *n* vértigo *m*
**dizzy** (*di*-si) *adj* mareado
***do** (duu) *v* *hacer; *ser suficiente
**dock** (dok) *n* dock *m*; muelle *m*; *v* atracar
**docker** (*do*-kö) *n* obrero portuario
**doctor** (*dok*-tö) *n* médico *m*; doctor *m*
**document** (*do*-kyu-mönt) *n* documento *m*
**dog** (dogh) *n* perro *m*
**dogged** (*do*-ghid) *adj* obstinado; tenaz
**doll** (dol) *n* muñeca *f*
**dollar** (*do*-lö) dólar *m*
**dome** (doum) *n* cúpula *f*
**domestic** (dö-*mê*-sstik) *adj* doméstico; interior; *n* sirviente *m*
**domicile** (*do*-mi-ssail) *n* domicilio *m*
**domination** (do-mi-*nei*-ʃön) *n* dominación *f*
**dominion** (dö-*mi*-nyön) *n* dominio *m*
**donate** (dou-*neit*) *v* donar
**donation** (dou-*nei*-ʃön) *n* donación *f*
**done** (dan) *v* (pp do)
**donkey** (*dong*-ki) *n* burro *m*
**donor** (*dou*-nö) *n* donante *m*
**door** (doo) *n* puerta *f*; **revolving** ~ puerta giratoria; **sliding** ~ puerta corrediza
**doorbell** (*doo*-bêl) *n* timbre *m*
**doorman** (*doo*-mön) *n* (pl -men) portero *m*
**dormitory** (*doo*-mi-tri) *n* dormitorio *m* (colectivo)
**dose** (douss) *n* dosis *f*
**dot** (dot) *n* punto *m*
**double** (*da*-böl) *adj* doble
**doubt** (daut) *v* dudar; *n* duda *f*; **without** ~ sin duda
**doubtful** (*daut*-föl) *adj* dudoso; inseguro
**dough** (dou) *n* masa *f*
**down**[1] (daun) *adv* abajo; hacia abajo; *adj* abatido; *prep* a lo largo de, debajo de; ~ **payment** primer pago
**down**[2] (daun) *n* flojel *m*
**downpour** (*daun*-poo) *n* aguacero *m*
**downstairs** (daun-*sstê$^ö$s*) *adv* abajo
**downstream** (daun-*sstriim*) *adv* río abajo
**down-to-earth** (daun-tu-*ööz*) *adj* sensato
**downwards** (*daun*-$^u$öds) *adv* hacia abajo
**dozen** (*da*-sön) *n* (pl ~, ~s) docena *f*
**draft** (draaft) *n* giro *m*; *Am* corriente de aire
**drag** (drægh) *v* arrastrar
**dragon** (*dræ*-ghön) *n* dragón *m*
**drain** (drein) *v* desecar; drenar; *n* desagüe *m*

**drama** (*draa*-mö) *n* drama *m*; tragedia *f*; teatro *m*
**dramatic** (drö-*mæ*-tik) *adj* dramático
**drank** (dræŋgk) *v* (p drink)
**drapery** (*drei*-pö-ri) *n* pañería *f*
**draught** (draaft) *n* corriente de aire; **draughts** juego de damas
**draw** (droo) *n* sorteo *m*
***draw** (droo) *v* dibujar; arrastrar; sacar; jalar *vMe*; **~ up** redactar
**drawbridge** (*droo*-bridʒ) *n* puente levadizo
**drawer** (*droo*-ö) *n* cajón *m*; **drawers** calzoncillos *mpl*
**drawing** (*droo*-ing) *n* dibujo *m*; **~ pin** (*droo*-ing-pin) *n* chinche *f*
**dread** (drêd) *v* temer; *n* temor *m*
**dreadful** (*drêd*-föl) *adj* terrible, espantoso
**dream** (driim) *n* sueño *m*
***dream** (driim) *v* *soñar
**dress** (drêss) *v* *vestir; *vestirse; vendar; *n* vestido *m*
**dressing gown** (*drê*-ssing-ghaun) *n* bata *f*
**dressing room** (*drê*-ssing-ruum) *n* vestuario *m*
**dressing table** (*drê*-ssing-tei-böl) *n* tocador *m*
**dressmaker** (*drêss*-mei-kö) *n* modista *f*
**drill** (dril) *v* taladrar; entrenar; *n* taladro *m*
**drink** (dringk) *n* aperitivo *m*, bebida *f*
***drink** (dringk) *v* beber
**drinking water** (*dring*-king-ᵘoo-tö) *n* agua potable
**drip-dry** (drip-*drai*) *adj* no precisa plancha
**drive** (draiv) *n* calzada *f*; paseo en coche
***drive** (draiv) *v* *conducir
**driver** (*drai*-vö) *n* conductor *m*; **driver's license** *Am*, **driving licence** carné *m* de conducir
**drizzle** (*dri*-söl) *n* llovizna *f*
**drop** (drop) *v* dejar caer; *n* gota *f*
**drought** (draut) *n* sequía *f*
**drown** (draun) *v* ahogar; ***be drowned** ahogarse
**drug** (dragh) *n* droga *f*; estupefaciente *m*; medicamento *m*
**drugstore** (*dragh*-sstoo) *nAm* droguería *f*, farmacia *f*; almacén *m*
**drum** (dram) *n* tambor *m*
**drunk** (drangk) *adj* (pp drink) borracho
**dry** (drai) *adj* seco; *v* secar
**dry-clean** (drai-*kliin*) *v* limpiar en seco
**dry cleaner's** (drai-*klii*-nös) *n* tintorería *f*
**dryer** (*drai*-ö) *n* secadora *f*
**duchess** (da-chiss) *n* duquesa *f*
**duck** (dak) *n* pato *m*
**due** (dyuu) *adj* adeudado; debido
**dues** (dyuus) *pl* derechos *mpl*
**dug** (dagh) *v* (p, pp dig)
**duke** (dyuuk) *n* duque *m*
**dull** (dal) *adj* aburrido; pálido, mate; embotado
**dumb** (dam) *adj* tomto; atontado, estúpido; mudo
**dune** (dyuun) *n* duna *f*
**dung** (dang) *n* estiércol *m*
**dunghill** (*dang*-hil) *n* estercolero *m*
**duration** (dyu-*rei*-ʃön) *n* duración *f*
**during** (*dyu*ᵒ-ring) *prep* durante
**dusk** (dassk) *n* crepúsculo *m*
**dust** (dasst) *n* polvo *m*
**dustbin** (*dasst*-bin) *n* cubo de la basura
**dusty** (*da*-ssti) *adj* polvoriento
**Dutch** (dach) *adj* holandés
**Dutchman** (*dach*-mön) *n* (pl -men) holandés *m*
**duty** (*dyuu*-ti) *n* deber *m*; tarea *f*; arancel *m*; **Customs ~** impuesto de aduana

**duty-free** (dyuu-ti-*frii*) *adj* exento de impuestos
**dwarf** (d[u]oof) *n* enano *m*
**dye** (dai) *v* *teñir; *n* tintura *f*
**dynamo** (*dai*-nö-mou) *n* (pl ~s) dínamo *f*

# E

**each** (iich) *adj* cada; ~ **other** el uno al otro
**eager** (*ii*-ghö) *adj* ansioso, impaciente
**eagle** (*ii*-ghöl) *n* águila *m*
**ear** (i[ö]) *n* oreja *f*
**earache** (*i*[ö]-reik) *n* dolor de oídos
**eardrum** (*i*[ö]-dram) *n* tímpano *m*
**earl** (ööl) *n* conde *m*
**early** (*öö*-li) *adj* temprano
**earn** (öön) *v* ganar
**earnest** (*öö*-nisst) *adj* serio, formal
**earnings** (*öö*-nings) *pl* ingresos *mpl*, ganancias *fpl*
**earring** (*i*[ö]-ring) *n* pendiente *m*
**earth** (ööz) *n* tierra *f*; suelo *m*
**earthquake** (*ööz*-k[u]eik) *n* terremoto *m*
**ease** (iis) *n* desenvoltura *f*, facilidad *f*; bienestar *m*
**east** (iisst) *n* este *m*
**Easter** (*ii*-sstö) Pascua
**easterly** (*ii*-sstö-li) *adj* oriental
**eastern** (*ii*-sstön) *adj* oriental
**easy** (*ii*-si) *adj* fácil; cómodo; ~ **chair** butaca *f*
**easy-going** (*ii*-si-ghou-ing) *adj* relajado; despreocupado
***eat** (iit) *v* comer; cenar
**eavesdrop** (*iivs*-drop) *v* escuchar a escondidas
**ebony** (*ê*-bö-ni) *n* ébano *m*
**eccentric** (ik-*ssên*-trik) *adj* excéntrico
**echo** (*ê*-kou) *n* (pl ~es) eco *m*
**eclipse** (i-*klipss*) *n* eclipse *m*
**economic** (ii-kö-*no*-mik) *adj* económico
**economical** (ii-kö-*no*-mi-köl) *adj* rentable; económico
**economist** (i-*ko*-nö-misst) *n* economista *m*
**economize** (i-*ko*-nö-mais) *v* economizar
**economy** (i-*ko*-nö-mi) *n* economía *f*
**ecstasy** (*êk*-sstö-si) *n* éxtasis *m*
**Ecuador** (*ê*-k[u]ö-doo) Ecuador *m*
**Ecuadorian** (ê-k[u]ö-*doo*-ri-ön) *n* ecuatoriano *m*
**eczema** (*êk*-ssi-mö) *n* eczema *m*
**edge** (êdʒ) *n* borde *m*; filo *m*
**edible** (*ê*-di-böl) *adj* comestible
**edit** (*ê*-dit) *v* corregir; editar; dirigir; montar
**edition** (i-*di*-ʃön) *n* edición *f*; **morning** ~ edición de mañana
**editor** (*ê*-di-tö) *n* redactor *m*
**educate** (*ê*-dʒu-keit) *v* formar, educar
**education** (ê-dʒu-*kei*-ʃön) *n* educación *f*
**eel** (iil) *n* anguila *f*
**effect** (i-*fêkt*) *n* resultado *m*, efecto *m*; *v* efectuar; **in** ~ en realidad
**effective** (i-*fêk*-tiv) *adj* eficaz
**efficient** (i-*fi*-ʃönt) *adj* eficiente
**effort** (*ê*-föt) *n* esfuerzo *m*
**egg** (êgh) *n* huevo *m*; ~ **yolk** yema de huevo
**eggcup** (*êgh*-kap) *n* huevera *f*
**eggplant** (*êgh*-plaant) *n* berenjena *f*
**egoistic** (ê-ghou-*i*-sstik) *adj* egoísta
**Egypt** (*ii*-dʒipt) Egipto *m*

**Egyptian** (i-*dʒip*-ʃön) *adj* egipcio
**eiderdown** (*ai*-dö-daun) *n* edredón *m*
**eight** (eit) *num* ocho
**eighteen** (ei-*tiin*) *num* dieciocho
**eighteenth** (ei-*tiinz*) *num* decimoctavo
**eighth** (eitz) *num* octavo
**eighty** (*ei*-ti) *num* ochenta
**either** (*ai*-ðö) *pron* cualquiera de los dos; **either ... or** o ... o, bien ... bien
**elaborate** (i-*læ*-bö-reit) *v* elaborar
**elastic** (i-*læ*-sstik) *adj* elástico; flexible; **~ band** cinta de goma
**elasticity** (ê-læ-*ssti*-ssö-ti) *n* elasticidad *f*
**elbow** (*êl*-bou) *n* codo *m*
**elder** (*êl*-dö) *adj* mayor
**elderly** (*êl*-dö-li) *adj* anciano
**eldest** (*êl*-disst) *adj* mayor
**elect** (i-*lêkt*) *v* *elegir
**election** (i-*lêk*-ʃön) *n* elección *f*
**electric** (i-*lêk*-trik) *adj* eléctrico; **~ razor** afeitadora eléctrica
**electrician** (i-lêk-*tri*-ʃön) *n* electricista *m/f*
**electricity** (i-lêk-*tri*-ssö-ti) *n* electricidad *f*
**electronic** (i-lêk-*tro*-nik) *adj* electrónico; **~ game** juego electrónico
**elegance** (*ê*-li-ghönss) *n* elegancia *f*
**elegant** (*ê*-li-ghönt) *adj* elegante
**element** (*ê*-li-mönt) *n* elemento *m*
**elephant** (*ê*-li-fönt) *n* elefante *m*
**elevator** (*ê*-li-vei-tö) *nAm* ascensor *m*; elevador *mMe*
**eleven** (i-*lê*-vön) *num* once
**eleventh** (i-*lê*-vönz) *num* onceno
**elf** (êlf) *n* (pl elves) duende *m*
**eliminate** (i-*li*-mi-neit) *v* eliminar
**elm** (êlm) *n* olmo *m*
**else** (êlss) *adv* más; otro; diferente
**elsewhere** (êl-*ss*ᵘ*ê*ᵒ̈) *adv* otra parte
**elucidate** (i-*luu*-ssi-deit) *v* elucidar
**e-mail** (*ii*-meil) *n* correo *m* electrónico; *v* mandar un correo electrónico a
**emancipation** (i-mæn-ssi-*pei*-ʃön) *n* emancipación *f*
**embankment** (im-*bængk*-mönt) *n* terraplén *m*
**embargo** (êm-*baa*-ghou) *n* (pl ~es) embargo *m*
**embark** (im-*baak*) *v* embarcar
**embarkation** (êm-baa-*kei*-ʃön) *n* embarcación *f*
**embarrass** (im-*bæ*-röss) *v* turbar; *desconcertar; estorbar; **embarrassed** tímido; **embarrassment** embarazo *m*, apuro *m*
**embassy** (*êm*-bö-ssi) *n* embajada *f*
**emblem** (*êm*-blöm) *n* emblema *m*
**embrace** (im-*breiss*) *v* abrazar; *n* abrazo *m*
**embroider** (im-*broi*-dö) *v* bordar
**embroidery** (im-*broi*-dö-ri) *n* bordado *m*
**emerald** (*ê*-mö-röld) *n* esmeralda *f*
**emergency** (i-*möö*-dʒön-ssi) *n* caso de urgencia, urgencia *f*; emergencia *f*; **~ exit** salida de emergencia
**emigrant** (*ê*-mi-ghrönt) *n* emigrante *m*
**emigrate** (*ê*-mi-ghreit) *v* emigrar
**emigration** (ê-mi-*ghrei*-ʃön) *n* emigración *f*
**emotion** (i-*mou*-ʃön) *n* emoción *f*
**emotional** (i-*mou*-ʃö-nöl) *adj* sentimental; emotivo
**emperor** (*êm*-pö-rö) *n* emperador *m*
**emphasize** (*êm*-fö-ssais) *v* enfatizar, acentuar
**empire** (*êm*-paiᵒ̈) *n* imperio *m*
**employ** (im-*ploi*) *v* emplear
**employee** (êm-ploi-*ii*) *n* empleado *m*, -a *f*
**employer** (im-*ploi*-ö) *n* jefe *m*; patrón *m*; empresario *m*, -a *f*

**employment** (im-*ploi*-mönt) *n* empleo *m*; **~ exchange** oficina de colocación
**empress** (*êm*-priss) *n* emperatriz *f*
**empty** (*êmp*-ti) *adj* vacío; *v* vaciar
**enable** (i-*nei*-böl) *v* permitir
**enamel** (i-*næ*-möl) *n* esmalte *m*
**enamelled** (i-*næ*-möld) *adj* esmaltado
**enchanting** (in-*chaan*-ting) *adj* espléndido, encantador
**encircle** (in-*ssöö*-köl) *v* *circuir, cercar; *encerrar
**enclose** (ing-*klous*) *v* *incluir
**enclosure** (ing-*klou*-ʒö) *n* anexo *m*
**encounter** (ing-*kaun*-tö) *v* *encontrarse con; *n* encuentro *m*
**encourage** (ing-*ka*-ridʒ) *v* *alentar
**encyclop(a)edia** (ên-ssai-klö-*pii*-di-ö) *n* enciclopedia *f*
**end** (ênd) *n* fin *m*, extremo *m*; final *m*; *v* terminar, acabar; terminarse
**ending** (*ên*-ding) *n* conclusión *f*
**endless** (*ênd*-löss) *adj* infinito
**endorse** (in-*dooss*) *v* visar, endosar
**endure** (in-*dyu*$^{ö}$) *v* soportar
**enemy** (*ê*-nö-mi) *n* enemigo *m*, -a *f*
**energetic** (ê-nö-*dʒê*-tik) *adj* enérgico
**energy** (*ê*-nö-dʒi) *n* energía *f*; fuerza *f*
**engage** (ing-*gheidʒ*) *v* emplear; reservar; comprometerse; **engaged** prometido; ocupado
**engagement** (ing-*gheidʒ*-mönt) *n* noviazgo *m*; compromiso *m*; **~ ring** anillo de esponsales, anillo de compromiso
**engine** (*ên*-dʒin) *n* máquina *f*, motor *m*; locomotora *f*
**engineer** (ên-dʒi-*ni*$^{ö}$) *n* ingeniero *m*
**England** (*ing*-ghlönd) Inglaterra *f*
**English** (*ing*-ghliʃ) *adj* inglés
**Englishman** (*ing*-ghliʃ-mön) *n* (pl -men) inglés *m*
**Englishwoman** (*ing*-ghliʃ-$^{u}$u-mön) (pl -women) inglesa *f*
**engrave** (ing-*ghreiv*) *v* grabar
**engraver** (ing-*ghrei*-vö) *n* grabador *m*
**engraving** (ing-*ghrei*-ving) *n* estampa *f*; grabado *m*
**enigma** (i-*nigh*-mö) *n* enigma *m*
**enjoy** (in-*dʒoi*) *v* disfrutar, gozar
**enjoyable** (in-*dʒoi*-ö-böl) *adj* agradable, grato, deleitable
**enjoyment** (in-*dʒoi*-mönt) *n* disfrute *m*; goce *m*
**enlarge** (in-*laadʒ*) *v* ampliar; aumentar; extender
**enlargement** (in-*laadʒ*-mönt) *n* ampliación *f*
**enormous** (i-*noo*-möss) *adj* gigantesco, enorme
**enough** (i-*naf*) *adv* bastante; *adj* suficiente
**enquire** (ing-*k*$^{u}$*ai*$^{ö}$) *v* preguntar; investigar
**enquiry** (ing-*k*$^{u}$*ai*$^{ö}$-ri) *n* información *f*; investigación *f*; encuesta *f*
**enter** (*ên*-tö) *v* entrar; ingresar
**enterprise** (*ên*-tö-prais) *n* empresa *f*
**entertain** (ên-tö-*tein*) *v* *divertir, *entretener; hospedar
**entertainer** (ên-tö-*tei*-nö) *n* artista *m*
**entertaining** (ên-tö-*tei*-ning) *adj* divertido, entretenido
**entertainment** (ên-tö-*tein*-mönt) *n* diversión *f*, entretenimiento *m*
**enthusiasm** (in-*zyuu*-si-æ-söm) *n* entusiasmo *m*
**enthusiastic** (in-zyuu-si-*æ*-sstik) *adj* entusiasta
**entire** (in-*tai*$^{ö}$) *adj* todo, entero
**entirely** (in-*tai*$^{ö}$-li) *adv* enteramente
**entrance** (*ên*-trönss) *n* entrada *f*; acceso *m*; **~ fee** entrada *f*
**entry** (*ên*-tri) *n* entrada *f*, ingreso *m*; anotación *f*; **no ~** prohibido el paso
**envelop** (in-*vö*-loup) *v* cubrir
**envelope** (*ên*-vö-loup) *n* sobre *m*
**envious** (*ên*-vi-öss) *adj* envidioso, celoso

**environment** (in-*vai*ö-rön-mönt) *n* medio ambiente; alrededores *mpl*
**envoy** (*ên*-voi) *n* enviado *m*
**envy** (*ên*-vi) *n* envidia *f*; *v* envidiar
**epic** (*ê*-pik) *n* poema épico; *adj* épico
**epidemic** (ê-pi-*dê*-mik) *n* epidemia *f*
**epilepsy** (*ê*-pi-lêp-ssi) *n* epilepsia *f*
**epilogue** (*ê*-pi-logh) *n* epílogo *m*
**episode** (*ê*-pi-ssoud) *n* episodio *m*
**equal** (*ii*-kuöl) *adj* igual; *v* igualar
**equality** (i-*ku**o*-lö-ti) *n* igualdad *f*
**equalize** (*ii*-kuö-lais) *v* igualar
**equally** (*ii*-kuö-li) *adv* igualmente
**equator** (i-*ku**ei*-tö) *n* ecuador *m*
**equip** (i-*ku**ip*) *v* equipar
**equipment** (i-*ku**ip*-mönt) *n* equipo *m*
**equivalent** (i-*ku**i*-vö-lönt) *adj* equivalente
**eraser** (i-*rei*-sö) *n* goma de borrar
**erect** (i-*rêkt*) *v* erigir; *adj* erguido, recto; parado *adjMe*
**err** (öö) *v* *errar
**errand** (*ê*-rönd) *n* recado *m*
**error** (*ê*-rö) *n* falta *f*, error *m*
**escalator** (*ê*-sskö-lei-tö) *n* escalera móvil
**escape** (i-*sskeip*) *v* escaparse; *huir, escapar; *n* evasión *f*
**escort**[1] (*ê*-sskoot) *n* escolta *f*
**escort**[2] (i-*sskoot*) *v* escoltar
**especially** (i-*sspê*-ʃö-li) *adv* sobre todo, especialmente
**essay** (*ê*-ssei) *n* ensayo *m*; tratado *m*, composición *f*
**essence** (*ê*-ssönss) *n* esencia *f*; núcleo *m*
**essential** (i-*ssên*-ʃöl) *adj* indispensable; esencial
**essentially** (i-*ssên*-ʃö-li) *adv* sobre todo
**establish** (i-*sstæ*-bliʃ) *v* *establecer; *comprobar
**estate** (i-*ssteit*) *n* propiedad *f*; finca *f*; bienes *mpl*
**esteem** (i-*sstiim*) *n* respeto *m*, estima *f*; *v* estimar
**estimate**[1] (*ê*-ssti-meit) *v* evaluar, estimar
**estimate**[2] (*ê*-ssti-möt) *n* estimación *f*
**estuary** (*êss*-chu-ö-ri) *n* estuario *m*
**etcetera** (êt-*ssê*-tö-rö) etcétera
**etching** (*ê*-ching) *n* aguafuerte *f*
**eternal** (i-*töö*-nöl) *adj* eterno
**eternity** (i-*töö*-nö-ti) *n* eternidad *f*
**ether** (*ii*-zö) *n* éter *m*
**Ethiopia** (i-zi-*ou*-pi-ö) Etiopía *f*
**Ethiopian** (i-zi-*ou*-pi-ön) *adj* etíope
**EU** (ii-*yu*) (= **European Union**) UE *f* (=Unión Europea)
**Europe** (*yu*ö-röp) Europa *f*
**European** (yuö-rö-*pii*-ön) *adj* europeo
**European Union** (yuö-rö-*pii*-ön *yuu*-nyön) Unión Europea
**evacuate** (i-*væ*-kyu-eit) *v* evacuar
**evade** (i-*veid*) *v* evadir
**evaluate** (i-*væl*-yu-eit) *v* evaluar
**evaporate** (i-*væ*-pö-reit) *v* evaporar
**even** (*ii*-vön) *adj* llano, plano, igual; constante; par; *adv* aun
**evening** (*iiv*-ning) *n* tarde *f*; **~ dress** traje de etiqueta
**event** (i-*vênt*) *n* acontecimiento *m*; caso *m*
**eventual** (i-*vên*-chu-öl) *adj* eventual; final; **eventually** *adv* finalmente
**ever** (*ê*-vö) *adv* jamás; siempre; alguna vez
**every** (*êv*-ri) *adj* cada; todo; todos los
**everybody** (*êv*-ri-bo-di) *pron* todos
**everyday** (*êv*-ri-dei) *adj* cotidiano
**everyone** (*êv*-ri-uan) *pron* cada uno, todo el mundo
**everything** (*êv*-ri-zing) *pron* todo
**everywhere** (*êv*-ri-uêö) *adv* por todas partes
**evidence** (*ê*-vi-dönss) *n* prueba *f*
**evident** (*ê*-vi-dönt) *adj* evidente
**evil** (*ii*-völ) *n* mal *m*; *adj* malo,

malvado
**evolution** (ii-vö-*luu*-ʃön) *n* evolución *f*
**exact** (igh-*sækt*) *adj* exacto
**exactly** (igh-*sækt*-li) *adv* exactamente
**exaggerate** (igh-*sæ*-dʒö-reit) *v* exagerar
**exam** (igh-*sæm*) examen *m*; **take an ~** hacer un examen; **pass/fail an ~** aprobar/ suspender un examen
**examination** (igh-sæ-mi-*nei*-ʃön) *n* examen *m*; interrogatorio *m*
**examine** (igh-*sæ*-min) *v* examinar
**example** (igh-*saam*-pöl) *n* ejemplo *m*; **for ~** por ejemplo
**excavation** (êkss-kö-*vei*-ʃön) *n* excavación *f*
**exceed** (ik-*ssiid*) *v* exceder; superar
**excel** (ik-*ssêl*) *v* distinguirse
**excellent** (*êk*-ssö-lönt) *adj* excelente
**except** (ik-*ssêpt*) *prep* excepto
**exception** (ik-*ssêp*-ʃön) *n* excepción *f*
**exceptional** (ik-*ssêp*-ʃö-nöl) *adj* extraordinario, excepcional
**excerpt** (*êk*-ssööpt) *n* extracto *m*
**excess** (ik-*ssêss*) *n* exceso *m*
**excessive** (ik-*ssê*-ssiv) *adj* excesivo
**exchange** (ikss-*cheindʒ*) *v* intercambiar, cambiar; *n* cambio *m*; bolsa *f*; **~ office** oficina de cambio; **~ rate** cambio *m*
**excite** (ik-*ssait*) *v* excitar; **excited** *adj* emocionado, excitado; **get excited about** emocionarse con, excitarse con
**excitement** (ik-*ssait*-mönt) *n* agitación *f*, excitación *f*
**exciting** (ik-*ssai*-ting) *adj* excitante
**exclaim** (ik-*sskleim*) *v* exclamar
**exclamation** (êk-ssklö-*mei*-ʃön) *n* exclamación *f*
**exclude** (ik-*sskluud*) *v* *excluir
**exclusive** (ik-*sskluu*-ssiv) *adj* exclusivo
**exclusively** (ik-*sskluu*-ssiv-li) *adv* exclusivamente, únicamente
**excursion** (ik-*ssköö*-ʃön) *n* excursión *f*
**excuse**[1] (ik-*sskyuuss*) *n* excusa *f*
**excuse**[2] (ik-*sskyuus*) *v* excusar, disculpar
**execute** (*êk*-ssi-kyuut) *v* ejecutar
**execution** (êk-ssi-*kyuu*-ʃön) *n* ejecución *f*
**executioner** (êk-ssi-*kyuu*-ʃö-nö) *n* verdugo *m*
**executive** (igh-*sê*-kyu-tiv) *adj* ejecutivo; *n* poder ejecutivo; ejecutivo *m*, -a *f*
**exempt** (igh-*ʒêmpt*) *v* dispensar, eximir; *adj* exento
**exemption** (igh-*sêmp*-ʃön) *n* exención *f*
**exercise** (*êk*-ssö-ssais) *n* ejercicio *m*; *v* ejercitar; ejercer
**exhale** (êkss-*heil*) *v* exhalar
**exhaust** (igh-*soosst*) *n* tubo de escape, escape *m*; *v* extenuar; **~ gases** gases de escape
**exhibit** (igh-*si*-bit) *v* *exponer; exhibir
**exhibition** (êk-ssi-*bi*-ʃön) *n* exposición *f*
**exile** (*êk*-ssail) *n* exilio *m*; exiliado *m*
**exist** (igh-*sisst*) *v* existir
**existence** (igh-*si*-sstönss) *n* existencia *f*
**exit** (*êk*-ssit) *n* salida *f*
**exotic** (igh-*so*-tik) *adj* exótico
**expand** (ik-*sspænd*) *v* *extender; *desplegar
**expansion** (ik-*sspæn*-ʃön) expansión *f*; dilatación *f*
**expect** (ik-*sspêkt*) *v* aguardar, esperar
**expectation** (êk-sspêk-*tei*-ʃön) *n* esperanza *f*; expectativa *f*
**expedition** (êk-sspö-*di*-ʃön) *n* expedición *f*
**expel** (ik-*sspêl*) *v* expulsar
**expenditure** (ik-*sspên*-di-chö) *n* gasto *m*

**expense** (ik-*sspênss*) *n* gasto *m*
**expensive** (ik-*sspên*-ssiv) *adj* caro; costoso
**experience** (ik-*sspi*$^{\ddot{o}}$-ri-önss) *n* experiencia *f*; *v* experimentar, vivir; **experienced** experimentado
**experiment** (ik-*sspê*-ri-mönt) *n* prueba *f*, experimento *m*; *v* experimentar
**expert** (*êk*-sspööt) *n* perito *m*, experto *m*; *adj* competente
**expire** (ik-*sspai*$^{\ddot{o}}$) *v* expirar, terminarse; espirar; **expired** caducado
**explain** (ik-*ssplein*) *v* explicar
**explanation** (êk-ssplö-*nei*-ʃön) *n* aclaración *f*, explicación *f*
**explicit** (ik-*sspli*-ssit) *adj* expreso, explícito
**explode** (ik-*ssploud*) *v* estallar
**exploit** (ik-*ssploit*) *v* abusar de, explotar
**explore** (ik-*ssploo*) *v* explorar
**explosion** (ik-*ssplou*-ʒön) *n* explosión *f*
**explosive** (ik-*ssplou*-ssiv) *adj* explosivo; *n* explosivo *m*
**export**[1] (ik-*sspoot*) *v* exportar
**export**[2] (*êk*-sspoot) *n* exportación *f*
**exportation** (êk-sspoo-*tei*-ʃön) *n* exportación *f*
**exports** (*êk*-sspootss) *pl* exportación *f*
**expose** (ik-*sspous*) *v* exponer
**exposition** (êk-sspö-*si*-ʃön) *n* exposición *f*
**exposure** (ik-*sspou*-ʒö) *n* exposición *f*; ~ **meter** exposímetro *m*
**express** (ik-*sssprêss*) *v* expresar; *adj* expreso; explícito; ~ **train** tren expreso
**expression** (ik-*ssprê*-ʃön) *n* expresión *f*
**exquisite** (ik-*ssk*$^{u}$*i*-sit) *adj* exquisito
**extend** (ik-*sstênd*) *v* prolongar; ampliar; conceder
**extension** (ik-*sstên*-ʃön) *n* prórroga *f*; ampliación *f*; extensión *f*; ~ **cord** cordón de extensión
**extensive** (ik-*sstên*-ssiv) *adj* extenso; amplio
**extent** (ik-*sstênt*) *n* alcance *m*; dimensión *f*
**exterior** (êk-*ssti*$^{\ddot{o}}$-ri-ö) *adj* exterior; *n* exterior *m*
**external** (êk-*sstöö*-nöl) *adj* exterior
**extinguish** (ik-*ssting*-gh$^{u}$iʃ) *v* extinguir, apagar
**extort** (ik-*sstoot*) *v* extorsionar
**extortion** (ik-*sstoo*-ʃön) *n* extorsión *f*
**extra** (*êk*-sströ) *adj* extra
**extract**[1] (ik-*sstrækt*) *v* *extraer
**extract**[2] (*êk*-sstrækt) *n* fragmento *m*
**extradite** (*êk*-sströ-dait) *v* entregar
**extraordinary** (ik-*sstroo*-dön-ri) *adj* extraordinario
**extravagant** (ik-*sstræ*-vö-ghönt) *adj* exagerado, extravagante
**extreme** (ik-*sstriim*) *adj* extremo; *n* extremo *m*
**exuberant** (igh-*syuu*-bö-rönt) *adj* exuberante
**eye** (ai) *n* ojo *m*; ~ **shadow** sombra para los ojos
**eyebrow** (*ai*-brau) *n* ceja *f*; ~ **pencil** lápiz para las cejas
**eyelash** (*ai*-læʃ) *n* pestaña *f*
**eyelid** (*ai*-lid) *n* párpado *m*
**eyewitness** (*ai*-$^{u}$it-nöss) *n* testigo de vista

# F

**fable** (*fei*-böl) *n* fábula *f*
**fabric** (*fæ*-brik) *n* tejido *m*; estructura *f*
**façade** (fö-*ssaad*) *n* fachada *f*
**face** (feiss) *n* cara *f*; rostro *m*; *v* enfrentarse con; ~ **cream** crema facial; ~ **down** boca abajo; ~ **massage** masaje facial; ~ **pack** máscara facial; ~ **powder** polvo facial
**facing** (*fei*-ssing) enfrente de; frente a
**facilities** (fö-*ssi*-lö-tiis) *npl* instalaciones *fpl*
**fact** (fækt) *n* hecho *m*; **in** ~ efectivamente; en realidad
**factor** (*fæk*-tö) *n* factor *m*
**factory** (*fæk*-tö-ri) *n* fábrica *f*
**factual** (*fæk*-chu-öl) *adj* real
**faculty** (*fæ*-köl-ti) *n* facultad *f*; don *m*, aptitud *f*
**fade** (feid) *v* *desteñirse; descolorarse
**fail** (feil) *v* fallar; faltar; omitir; *ser suspendido; **without** ~ sin falta
**failure** (*feil*-yö) *n* fracaso *m*; fiasco *m*
**faint** (feint) *v* desmayarse; *adj* débil, vago
**fair** (fê^ö^) *n* feria *f*; *adj* justo; rubio; claro
**fairly** (*fê^ö^*-li) *adv* bastante
**fairy** (*fê^ö^*-ri) *n* hada *f*
**fairytale** (*fê^ö^*-ri-teil) *n* cuento de hadas
**faith** (feiz) *n* fe *f*; confianza *f*
**faithful** (*feiz*-ful) *adj* fiel; leal
**fake** (feik) *n* falsificación *f*
**fall** (fool) *n* caída *f*; *nAm* otoño *m*
***fall** (fool) *v* *caer
**false** (foolss) *adj* falso; inexacto; ~ **teeth** dentadura postiza
**falter** (*fool*-tö) *v* vacilar; balbucear
**fame** (feim) *n* fama *f*; reputación *f*
**familiar** (fö-*mil*-yö) *adj* familiar
**family** (*fæ*-mö-li) *n* familia *f*; ~ **name** apellido *m*
**famous** (*fei*-möss) *adj* famoso
**fan** (fæn) *n* ventilador *m*; abanico *m*; admirador *m*, -a *f*, seguidor *m*, -a *f*; ~ **belt** correa del ventilador
**fanatical** (fö-*næ*-ti-köl) *adj* fanático
**fancy** (*fæn*-ssi) *v* gustar, antojarse; imaginarse; *n* capricho *m*; gusto *m*
**fantastic** (fæn-*tæ*-sstik) *adj* fantástico
**fantasy** (*fæn*-tö-si) *n* fantasía *f*
**far** (faa) *adj* lejano; *adv* lejos; **by** ~ con mucho; **so** ~ hasta ahora
**far-away** (*faa*-rö-^u^ei) *adj* remoto
**fare** (fê^ö^) *n* gastos de viaje, precio del billete; comida *f*
**farm** (faam) *n* granja *f*; cortijo *m*;
**farmer** (*faa*-mö) *n* granjero *m*, -a *f*, agricultor *m*, -a *f*
**farmhouse** (*faam*-hauss) *n* cortijo *m*; rancho *mMe*
**far-off** (*faa*-rof) *adj* a lo lejos
**farther** (*faa*- ðö) *adv* más lejos; ~ **away** más allá, más lejos
**fascinate** (*fæ*-ssi-neit) *v* fascinar
**fascism** (*fæ*-ʃi-söm) *n* fascismo *m*
**fascist** (*fæ*-ʃisst) *adj* fascista
**fashion** (*fæ*-ʃön) *n* moda *f*; modo *m*; uso *m*
**fashionable** (*fæ*-ʃö-nö-böl) *adj* de moda
**fast** (faasst) *adj* rápido; firme; *n* ayuno *m*
**fasten** (*faa*-ssön) *v* atar; *cerrar
**fastener** (*faa*-ssö-nö) *n* cierre *m*
**fat** (fæt) *adj* graso, gordo; *n* grasa *f*
**fatal** (*fei*-töl) *adj* fatal, mortal
**fate** (feit) *n* destino *m*
**father** (*faa*-ðö) *n* padre *m*
**father-in-law** (*faa*-ðö-rin-loo) *n* (pl fathers-) suegro *m*
**fatty** (*fæ*-ti) *adj* grasiento
**faucet** (*foo*-ssit) *nAm* grifo *m*
**fault** (foolt) *n* culpa *f*; imperfección *f*,

defecto *m*
**faultless** (*foolt*-löss) *adj* impecable; perfecto
**faulty** (*fool*-ti) *adj* defectuoso
**favo(u)r** (*fei*-vö) *n* favor *m*; *v* *favorecer
**favo(u)rable** (*fei*-vö-rö-böl) *adj* favorable
**favo(u)rite** (*fei*-vö-rit) *n* favorito *m*, -a *f*; *adj* preferido
**fax** (fakss) *n* telefax *m*; **send a ~** mandar un telefax
**fear** (fi$^{ö}$) *n* temor *m*, miedo *m*; *v* temer
**feasible** (*fii*-sö-böl) *adj* realizable
**feast** (fiisst) *n* fiesta *f*
**feat** (fiit) *n* hazaña *f*
**feather** (*fê*-ðö) *n* pluma *f*
**feature** (*fii*-chö) *n* característica *f*; rasgo *m*
**February** (*fê*-bru-ö-ri) febrero
**federal** (*fê*-dö-röl) *adj* federal
**federation** (fê-dö-*rei*-ʃön) *n* federación *f*
**fee** (fii) *n* honorarios *mpl*
**feeble** (*fii*-böl) *adj* débil; enfermizo
***feed** (fiid) *v* alimentar; **fed up with** harto de
***feel** (fiil) *v* *sentir; palpar; **~ like** antojarse; tener ganas de
**feeling** (*fii*-ling) *n* sensación *f*; sentimiento *m*; tacto *m*
**feet** (fiit) *n* (pl foot)
**fell** (fêl) *v* (p fall)
**fellow** (*fê*-lou) *n* tipo *m*; **~ countryman** compatriota *m*/*f*
**felt**[1] (fêlt) *n* fieltro *m*
**felt**[2] (fêlt) *v* (p, pp feel)
**female** (*fii*-meil) *adj* femenino
**feminine** (*fê*-mi-nin) *adj* femenino
**fence** (fênss) *n* cerca *f*; reja *f*; *v* esgrimir
**ferment** (föö-*mênt*) *v* fermentar
**ferry-boat** (*fê*-ri-bout) *n* transbordador *m*
**fertile** (*föö*-tail) *adj* fértil
**festival** (*fê*-ssti-völ) *n* festival *m*
**festive** (*fê*-sstiv) *adj* festivo
**fetch** (fêch) *v* *ir por; *ir a buscar
**feudal** (*fyuu*-döl) *adj* feudal
**fever** (*fii*-vö) *n* fiebre *f*
**feverish** (*fii*-vö-riʃ) *adj* febril
**few** (fyuu) *adj* pocos
**fiancé** (fi-*an̅g̅*-ssei) *n* novio *m*
**fiancée** (fi-*an̅g̅*-ssei) *n* novia *f*
**fibre**(*fai*-bö) *n* fibra *f*
**fiction** (*fik*-ʃön) *n* ficción *f*
**field** (fiild) *n* campo *m*; terreno *m*; **~ glasses** gemelos de campaña
**fierce** (fi$^{ö}$ss) *adj* fiero; salvaje, violento
**fifteen** (fif-*tiin*) *num* quince
**fifteenth** (fif-*tiinz*) *num* quinceno
**fifth** (fifz) *num* quinto
**fifty** (*fif*-ti) *num* cincuenta
**fig** (figh) *n* higo *m*
**fight** (fait) *n* combate *m*, lucha *f*
***fight** (fait) *v* combatir, luchar
**figure** (*fi*-ghö) *n* estatura *f*, figura *f*; cifra *f*
**file** (fail) *n* lima *f*; expediente *m*; cola *f*
**fill** (fil) *v* llenar; **~ in** completar, llenar; **filling station** estación de servicio; **~ out** *Am* completar, llenar; **~ up** llenar
**filling** (*fi*-ling) *n* empaste *m*; relleno *m*
**film** (film) *n* película *f*; *v* filmar
**filter** (*fil*-tö) *n* filtro *m*
**filthy** (*fil*-zi) *adj* sucio; sórdido, inmundo
**final** (*fai*-nöl) *adj* final; **finally** *adv* finalmente, por último; por fin
**finance** (fai-*nænss*) *v* financiar
**finances** (fai-*næn*-ssis) *pl* finanzas *fpl*
**financial** (fai-*næn*-ʃöl) *adj* financiero
**finch** (finch) *n* pinzón *m*
***find** (faind) *v* *encontrar
**fine** (fain) *n* multa *f*; *adj* fino; bello; excelente, maravilloso; **~ arts** bellas artes
**finger** (*fing*-ghö) *n* dedo *m*; **little ~**

dedo meñique
**fingerprint** (*fing*-ghö-print) *n* impresión digital
**finish** (*fi*-niʃ) *v* terminar; *n* terminación *f*; meta *f*; **finished** acabado
**Finland** (*fin*-lönd) Finlandia *f*
**Finn** (fin) *n* finlandés *m*
**Finnish** (*fi*-niʃ) *adj* finlandés
**fire** (faiö) *n* fuego *m*; incendio *m*; *v* disparar; *despedir; ~ **alarm** alarma de incendio; ~ **brigade,** *Am* ~ **department** bomberos *mpl*; ~ **escape** escala de incendios; ~ **extinguisher** extintor *m*
**fireplace** (*faiö*-pleiss) *n* chimenea *f*
**fireproof** (*faiö*-pruuf) *adj* incombustible; refractario
**firm** (fööm) *adj* firme; sólido; *n* firma *f*
**first** (fööst) *num* primero; **at** ~ antes; al principio; ~ **name** nombre de pila
**first aid** (fööst-*eid*) *n* primeros auxilios; ~ **kit** botiquín de urgencia; ~ **post** puesto de socorro
**first-class** (fööst-*klaass*) *adj* de primera calidad
**first-rate** (fööst-*reit*) *adj* de primer orden, de primera clase
**fir tree** (*föö*-trii) *n* abeto *m*
**fish**[1] (fiʃ) *n* (pl ~, ~es) pez *m*; ~ **shop** pescadería *f*
**fish**[2] (fiʃ) *v* pescar; **fishing gear** avíos de pesca; **fishing fly** mosca artificial; **fishing hook** anzuelo *m*; **fishing licence** permiso de pesca; **fishing line** línea de pesca; **fishing net** red de pescar; **fishing rod** caña de pescar; **fishing tackle** aparejo de pesca
**fishbone** (*fiʃ*-boun) *n* espina *f*
**fisherman** (*fi*-ʃö-mön) *n* (pl -men) pescador *m*
**fist** (fisst) *n* puño *m*
**fit** (fit) *adj* apropiado; *n* ataque *m*; *v* *convenir; **fitting room** probador *m*
**five** (faiv) *num* cinco
**fix** (fikss) *v* arreglar
**fixed** (fiksst) *adj* fijo
**fizz** (fis) *n* efervescencia *f*
**flag** (flægh) *n* bandera *f*
**flame** (fleim) *n* llama *f*
**flamingo** (flö-*ming*-ghou) *n* (pl ~s, ~es) flamenco *m*
**flannel** (*flæ*-nöl) *n* franela *f*
**flash** (flæʃ) *n* relámpago *m*
**flash bulb** (*flæʃ*-balb) *n* bombilla de flash
**flashlight** (*flæʃ*-lait) *n* linterna *f*
**flask** (flaassk) *n* frasco *m*; **thermos** ~ termo *m*
**flat** (flæt) *adj* llano; liso; *n* piso *m*; ~ **tire** *Am*, ~ **tyre** neumático desinflado
**flavo(u)r** (*flei*-vö) *n* sabor *m*; gusto m; *v* sazonar
***flee** (flii) *v* escapar, huir
**fleet** (fliit) *n* flota *f*
**flesh** (flêʃ) *n* carne *f*
**flew** (fluu) *v* (p fly)
**flex** (flêkss) *n* cordón flexible; *v* doblar, flexionar
**flexible** (*flêk*-ssi-böl) *adj* flexible
**flight** (flait) *n* vuelo *m*; **charter** ~ vuelo charter
**flint** (flint) *n* pedernal *m*
**float** (flout) *v* flotar; *n* flotador *m*
**flock** (flok) *n* rebaño *m*
**flood** (flad) *n* inundación *f*; riada *f*
**floor** (floo) *n* suelo *m*; piso *m*; ~ **show** espectáculo de variedades
**florist** (*flo*-risst) *n* florista *m/f*
**flour** (flauö) *n* harina *f*
**flow** (flou) *v* correr, *fluir
**flower** (flauö) *n* flor *f*; ~ **shop** floristería *f*
**flowerbed** (*flauö*-bêd) *n* arriate *m*
**flown** (floun) *v* (pp fly)
**flu** (fluu) *n* gripe *f*
**fluent** (*fluu*-önt) *adj* corriente;

elocuente
**fluid** (*fluu*-id) *adj* fluido; *n* fluido *m*
**flute** (fluut) *n* flauta *f*
**fly** (flai) *n* mosca *f*; bragueta *f*
***fly** (flai) *v* *volar
**foam** (foum) *n* espuma *f*; *v* espumar; ~ **rubber** goma espumada
**focus** (*fou*-köss) *n* foco *m*
**fog** (fogh) *n* niebla *f*
**foggy** (*fo*-ghi) *adj* brumoso
**foglamp** (*fogh*-læmp) *n* faro de niebla
**fold** (fould) *v* doblar; *n* pliegue *m*
**folk** (fouk) *n* gente *f*; ~ **dance** danza popular; ~ **song** canción popular
**folklore** (*fouk*-loo) *n* folklore *m*
**follow** (*fo*-lou) *v* *seguir; **following** *adj* siguiente
**fond: *be ~ of** (bii fond ov) *querer
**food** (fuud) *n* comida *f*; alimento *m*; ~ **poisoning** intoxicación alimentaria
**foodstuffs** (*fuud*-sstafss) *pl* comestibles
**fool** (fuul) *n* idiota *m*, tonto *m*; *v* engañar
**foolish** (*fuu*-liʃ) *adj* necio, tonto; absurdo
**foot** (fut) *n* (pl feet) pie *m*; **on ~** a pie; ~ **brake** freno de pie
**football** (*fut*-bool) *n* fútbol *m*; ~ **match** partido de fútbol
**footbridge** (*fut*-bridʒ) *n* puente *m* peatonal
**footpath** (*fut*-paaz) *n* senda *f*
**footwear** (*fut*-ᵘêᵒ) *n* calzado *m*
**for** (foo, fö) *prep* para; durante; a causa de, por; *conj* porque
***forbid** (fö-*bid*) *v* prohibir
**force** (fooss) *v* obligar, *forzar; *n* fuerza *f*; **by ~** forzosamente; **driving ~** fuerza motriz
**forecast** (*foo*-kaasst) *n* pronóstico *m*; previsión *f*; *v* pronosticar; predecir
**foreground** (*foo*-ghraund) *n* primer plano
**forehead** (*fo*-rêd) *n* frente *f*
**foreign** (*fo*-rin) *adj* extranjero; extraño
**foreigner** (*fo*-ri-nö) *n* extranjero *m*; forastero *m*
**foreman** (*foo*-mön) *n* (pl -men) capataz *m*
**foremost** (*foo*-mousst) *adj* primero; principal
**forest** (*fo*-risst) *n* selva *f*, bosque *m*
**forester** (*fo*-ri-sstö) *n* guardabosques *m*
**forever** (fö-*rê*-vö) *adv* siempre; constantemente
**forge** (foodʒ) *v* falsificar
***forget** (fö-*ghêt*) *v* olvidar
**forgetful** (fö-*ghêt*-föl) *adj* olvidadizo
***forgive** (fö-*ghiv*) *v* perdonar
**fork** (fook) *n* tenedor *m*; bifurcación *f*; *v* bifurcarse
**form** (foom) *n* forma *f*; formulario *m*; clase *f*; *v* formar
**formal** (*foo*-möl) *adj* formal
**formality** (foo-*mæ*-lö-ti) *n* formalidad *f*
**former** (*foo*-mö) *adj* antiguo; anterior; **formerly** antes
**formula** (*foo*-myu-lö) *n* (pl ~e, ~s) fórmula *f*
**fortnight** (*foot*-nait) *n* quincena *f*
**fortress** (*foo*-triss) *n* fortaleza *f*
**fortunate** (*foo*-chö-nöt) *adj* afortunado; **fortunately** *adv* afortunadamente
**fortune** (*foo*-chuun) *n* fortuna *f*; suerte *f*
**forty** (*foo*-ti) *num* cuarenta
**forward** (*foo*-ᵘöd) *adv* hacia adelante, adelante; *v* reexpedir
**foster parents** (*fo*-sstö-pêᵒ-röntss) *pl* padres adoptivos
**fought** (foot) *v* (p, pp fight)
**foul** (faul) *adj* sucio; vil; obsceno; *n* falta *f*
**found**[1] (faund) *v* (p, pp find)

**found²** (faund) *v* fundar
**foundation** (faun-*dei*-ʃön) *n* fundación *f*; ~ **cream** crema de base
**fountain** (*faun*-tin) *n* fuente *f*
**fountain pen** (*faun*-tin-pên) *n* estilográfica *f*
**four** (foo) *num* cuatro
**fourteen** (foo-*tiin*) *num* catorce
**fourteenth** (foo-*tiinz*) *num* catorceno
**fourth** (fooz) *num* cuarto
**fowl** (faul) *n* (pl ~s, ~) ave *f* de corral
**fox** (fokss) *n* zorro *m*
**foyer** (*foi*-ei) *n* vestíbulo *m*
**fraction** (*fræk*-ʃön) *n* fracción *f*
**fracture** (*fræk*-chö) *v* fracturar; *n* fractura *f*
**fragile** (*fræ*-dʒail) *adj* frágil
**fragment** (*frægh*-mönt) *n* fragmento *m*; trozo *m*
**frame** (freim) *n* marco *m*; armadura *f*
**France** (fraanss) Francia *f*
**franchise** (*fræn*-chais) *n* derecho electoral
**fraternity** (frö-*töö*-nö-ti) *n* fraternidad *f*
**fraud** (frood) *n* fraude *m*
**fray** (frei) *v* deshilacharse
**free** (frii) *adj* libre; gratuito; ~ **of charge** gratis; ~ **ticket** billete gratuito
**freedom** (*frii*-döm) *n* libertad *f*
***freeze** (friis) *v* *helar; congelar
**freezer** (*frii*-sör) congelador *m*
**freezing** (*frii*-sing) *adj* helado
**freezing point** (*frii*-sing-point) *n* punto de congelación
**freight** (freit) *n* carga *f*, cargo *m*
**French** (frênch) *adj* francés
**Frenchman** (*frênch*-mön) *n* (pl -men) francés *m*
**Frenchwoman** (*frênch*-ᵘu-mön) *n* (pl -women) francesa *f*
**frequency** (*frii*-kᵘön-ssi) *n* frecuencia *f*
**frequent** (*frii*-kᵘönt) *adj* frecuente
**fresh** (frêʃ) *adj* fresco; ~**water** *adj* de agua dulce
**friction** (*frik*-ʃön) *n* fricción *f*
**Friday** (*frai*-di) viernes *m*
**fridge** (fridʒ) *n* frigorífico *m*, refrigerador *m*
**friend** (frênd) *n* amigo *m*; amiga *f*
**friendly** (*frênd*-li) *adj* amable; amistoso
**friendship** (*frênd*-ʃip) *n* amistad *f*
**fright** (frait) *n* miedo *m*, espanto *m*
**frighten** (*frai*-tön) *v* espantar
**frightened** (*frai*-tönd) *adj* espantado; ***be** ~ asustarse
**frightful** (*frait*-föl) *adj* terrible; espantoso
**fringe** (frindʒ) *n* fleco *m*; franja *f*
**frock** (frok) *n* vestido *m*
**frog** (frogh) *n* rana *f*
**from** (from) *prep* desde; de; a partir de
**front** (frant) *n* frente *m*; **in ~ of** delante de
**frontier** (*fran*-tiᵒ) *n* frontera *f*
**frost** (frosst) *n* escarcha *f*
**froth** (froz) *n* espuma *f*
**frozen** (*frou*-sön) *adj* congelado; ~ **food** alimento congelado
**fruit** (fruut) *n* fruta *f*; fruto *m*
**fry** (frai) *v* *freír
**frying pan** (*frai*-ing-pæn) *n* sartén *f*
**fuck** (fak) *v* *vulgar* follar con; *L.Am.* coger; **fuck!** ¡joder!
**fuel** (*fyuu*-öl) *n* combustible *m*; ~ **pump** *Am* bomba de gasolina
**full** (ful) *adj* lleno; ~ **board** pensión completa; ~ **stop** punto *m*; ~ **up** completo
**fun** (fan) *n* diversión *f*
**function** (*fangk*-ʃön) *n* función *f*
**fund** (fand) *n* fondos *mpl*
**fundamental** (fan-dö-*mên*-töl) *adj* fundamental
**funeral** (*fyuu*-nö-röl) *n* funerales *mpl*

**funnel** (*fa*-nöl) *n* embudo *m*
**funny** (*fa*-ni) *adj* gracioso, cómico; extraño
**fur** (föö) *n* piel *f*; ~ **coat** abrigo de pieles
**furious** (*fyu*$^{ö}$-ri-öss) *adj* furioso
**furnace** (*föö*-niss) *n* horno *m*
**furnish** (*föö*-niʃ) *v* suministrar, procurar; instalar, amueblar; ~ **with** *proveer de
**furniture** (*föö*-ni-chö) *n* muebles *mpl*
**furrier** (*fa*-ri-ö) *n* peletero *m*
**further** (*föö*-ðö) *adj* más lejos; adicional
**furthermore** (*föö*-ðö-moo) *adv* además
**furthest** (*föö*-ðisst) *adj* el más alejado
**fuse** (fyuus) *n* fusible *m*; mecha *f*
**fuss** (fass) *n* agitación *f*; lío *m*; ostentación *f*, bulla *f*; **make a** ~ armar un lío
**future** (*fyuu*-chö) *n* porvenir *m*; futuro *m*; *adj* futuro

# G

**gable** (*ghei*-böl) *n* faldón *m*
**gadget** (*ghæ*-dʒit) *n* aparato *m*
**gain** (ghein) *v* ganar; *n* ganancia *f*
**gale** (gheil) *n* ventarrón *m*
**gall** (ghool) *n* bilis *f*; ~ **bladder** vesícula biliar
**gallery** (*ghæ*-lö-ri) *n* galería *f*
**gallon** (*ghæ*-lön) galón *m* (en EE.UU. 3,785 litros, en GB 4,546)
**gallop** (*ghæ*-löp) *n* galope *m*
**gallows** (*ghæ*-lous) *pl* horca *f*
**gallstone** (*ghool*-sstoun) *n* cálculo biliar
**game** (gheim) *n* juego *m*; caza *f*; ~ **reserve** parque de reserva zoológica
**gang** (ghæng) *n* banda *f*; pandilla *f*
**gangway** (*ghæng*-$^{u}$ei) *n* pasarela *f*; pasillo *m*
**gap** (ghæp) *n* hueco *m*
**garage** (*ghæ*-raaʒ) *n* garaje *m*; *v* dejar en garaje
**garbage** (*ghaa*-bidʒ) *n* basura *f*
**garden** (*ghaa*-dön) *n* jardín *m*; **public** ~ jardín público; **zoological gardens** jardín zoológico
**gardener** (*ghaa*-dö-nö) *n* jardinero *m*, -a *f*
**gargle** (*ghaa*-ghöl) *v* *hacer gárgaras
**garlic** (*ghaa*-lik) *n* ajo *m*
**gas** (ghæss) *n* gas *m*; *nAm* gasolina *f*; ~ **cooker** cocina de gas; ~ **station** *Am* puesto de gasolina; ~ **stove** estufa de gas; ~ **tank** *Am* déposito de gasolina
**gasoline** (*ghæ*-ssö-liin) *nAm* gasolina *f*
**gastric** (*ghæ*-sstrik) *adj* gástrico; ~ **ulcer** úlcera gástrica
**gasworks** (*ghæss*-$^{u}$öökss) *n* fábrica de gas
**gate** (gheit) *n* portón *m*; verja *f*; puerta *f*
**gather** (*ghæ*-ðö) *v* coleccionar; juntarse; recoger
**gauge** (gheidʒ) *n* medida *f*; calibre *m*; *v* medir; calibrar
**gave** (gheiv) *v* (p give)
**gay** (ghei) *adj* alegre; gaitero; homosexual
**gaze** (gheis) *v* mirar
**gazetteer** (ghæ-sö-*ti*$^{ö}$) *n* diccionario geográfico
**gear** (ghi$^{ö}$) *n* prendas *fpl*; aparejo *m*;

engranaje *m*; **change ~** cambiar de marcha; **~ lever, ~ shift** palanca de cambios
**gearbox** (*ghi*$^{ö}$-bokss) *n* caja de velocidades
**geese** (giis) *n* (pl goose)
**gem** (dʒêm) *n* joya *f*, gema *f*; alhaja *f*
**gender** (*dʒên*-dö) *n* género *m*
**general** (*dʒê*-nö-röl) *adj* general; *n* general *m*; **~ practitioner** médico de cabecera; **in ~** en general
**generate** (*dʒê*-nö-reit) *v* generar
**generation** (dʒê-nö-*rei*-ʃön) *n* generación *f*
**generator** (*dʒê*-nö-rei-tör) *n* generador *m*
**generosity** (dʒê-nö-*ro*-ssö-ti) *n* generosidad *f*
**generous** (*dʒê*-nö-röss) *adj* generoso
**genital** (*dʒê*-ni-töl) *adj* genital
**genius** (*dʒii*-ni-öss) *n* genio *m*
**gentle** (*dʒên*-töl) *adj* gentil; tierno, suave; prudente
**gentleman** (*dʒên*-töl-mön) *n* (pl -men) caballero *m*
**genuine** (*dʒê*-nyu-in) *adj* genuino
**geography** (dʒi-*o*-ghrö-fi) *n* geografía *f*
**geology** (dʒi-*o*-lö-dʒi) *n* geología *f*
**geometry** (dʒi-*o*-mö-tri) *n* geometría *f*
**germ** (dʒööm) *n* germen *m*
**German** (*dʒöö*-mön) *adj* alemán
**Germany** (*dʒöö*-mö-ni) Alemania *f*
**gesticulate** (dʒi-*ssti*-kyu-leit) *v* gesticular
***get** (ghêt) *v* *conseguir; *ir a buscar; *hacerse; **~ back** regresar; **~ off** apearse; **~ on** subir, montar; adelantar; **~ up** levantarse
**ghost** (ghousst) *n* fantasma *m*; espíritu *m*
**giant** (*dʒai*-önt) *n* gigante *m*
**giddiness** (*ghi*-di-nöss) *n* mareo *m*
**giddy** (*ghi*-di) *adj* mareado
**gift** (ghift) *n* regalo *m*; talento *m*
**gifted** (*ghif*-tid) *adj* talentoso
**gigantic** (dʒai-*ghæn*-tik) *adj* gigantesco
**giggle** (*ghi*-ghöl) *v* *soltar risitas
**gill** (ghil) *n* branquia *f*
**gilt** (ghilt) *adj* dorado
**ginger** (*dʒin*-dʒö) *n* jengibre *m*
**girdle** (*ghöö*-döl) *n* faja *f*
**girl** (ghööl) *n* muchacha *f*; **~ guide** exploradora *f*
**girlfriend** (*ghööl*-frênd) novia *f*; amiga *f*
***give** (ghiv) *v* *dar; entregar; **~ away** revelar; **~ in** ceder; **~ up** renunciar
**glacier** (*ghlæ*-ssi-ö) *n* glaciar *m*
**glad** (ghlæd) *adj* alegre, contento; **gladly** con mucho gusto, gustosamente
**gladness** (*ghlæd*-nöss) *n* alegría *f*
**glamorous** (*ghlæ*-mö-röss) *adj* encantador
**glamour** (*ghlæ*-mö) *n* encanto *m*
**glance** (ghlaanss) *n* ojeada *f*; *v* ojear
**gland** (ghlænd) *n* glándula *f*
**glare** (ghlê$^{ö}$) *n* relumbrón *m*; mirada *f* feroz
**glaring** (*ghlê*$^{ö}$-ring) *adj* deslumbrador
**glass** (ghlaass) *n* vaso *m*; vidrio *m*; de vidrio; **glasses** anteojos *mpl*, gafas *fpl*; **magnifying ~** lente de aumento
**glaze** (ghleis) *v* esmaltar
**glide** (ghlaid) *v* resbalar
**glider** (*ghlai*-dö) *n* planeador *m*
**glimpse** (ghlimpss) *n* vislumbre *m*; ojeada *f*; *v* vislumbrar
**global** (*ghlou*-böl) *adj* mundial; global
**globe** (ghloub) *n* globo *m*
**gloom** (ghluum) *n* oscuridad *f*; lobreguez *f*
**gloomy** (*ghluu*-mi) *adj* sombrío; tenebroso
**glorious** (*ghloo*-ri-öss) *adj* glorioso
**glory** (*ghloo*-ri) *n* gloria *f*; honor *m*,

elogio *m*
**gloss** (ghloss) *n* brillo *m*
**glossy** (*ghlo*-ssi) *adj* lustroso; satinado
**glove** (ghlav) *n* guante *m*
**glow** (ghlou) *v* brillar; *n* brillo *m*
**glue** (ghluu) *n* cola *f*; goma *f*
***go** (ghou) *v* *ir; caminar; *hacerse; ~ **ahead** continuar; ~ **away** *irse; ~ **back** regresar; ~ **home** *volver a casa; ~ **in** entrar; ~ **on** continuar; ~ **out** *salir; ~ **through** pasar
**goal** (ghoul) *n* meta *f*; gol *m*
**goalkeeper** (*ghoul*-kii-pö) *n* portero *m*
**goat** (ghout) *n* cabrón *m*, cabra *f*
**god** (ghod) *n* dios *m*
**goddess** (*gho*-diss) *n* diosa *f*
**godfather** (*ghod*-faa-ðö) *n* padrino *m*
**goggles** (*gho*-ghöls) *pl* gafas *fpl* submarinas
**gold** (ghould) *n* oro *m*; ~ **leaf** hojas de oro
**golden** (*ghoul*-dön) *adj* dorado
**goldmine** (*ghould*-main) *n* mina de oro
**goldsmith** (*ghould*-ssmiz) *n* orfebre *m*
**golf** (gholf) *n* golf *m*; ~ **course**, ~ **links** campo de golf
**golfclub** (*gholf*-klab) *n* palo de golf
**gondola** (*ghon*-dö-lö) *n* góndola *f*
**gone** (ghon) *adv* (pp go) ido
**good** (ghud) *adj* bueno
**goodbye!** (ghud-*bai*) ¡adiós!
**good-humo(u)red** (ghud-*hyuu*-möd) *adj* de buen humor
**good-looking** (ghud-*lu*-king) *adj* bien parecido; guapo
**good-natured** (ghud-*nei*-chöd) *adj* bondadoso
**goods** (ghuds) *pl* mercancías *fpl*, bienes *mpl*; ~ **train** tren de mercancías
**good-tempered** (ghud-*têm*-pöd) *adj* de buen humor
**goodwill** (ghud-$^{u}$*il*) *n* buena voluntad
**goose** (ghuuss) *n* (pl geese) oca *f*; ~ **bumps** *Am*, ~ **flesh** carne de gallina
**gooseberry** (*ghus*-bö-ri) *n* grosella espinosa
**gorge** (ghoodʒ) *n* cañón *m*
**gorgeous** (*ghoo*-dʒöss) *adj* magnífico
**gospel** (*gho*-sspöl) *n* evangelio *m*
**gossip** (*gho*-ssip) *n* chisme *m*; *v* *contar chismes
**got** (ghot) *v* (p, pp get)
**Gothic** (*gho*-zik) *adj* gótico
**gourmet** (*ghu*$^{ö}$-mei) *n* gastrónomo *m*, -a *f*
**gout** (ghaut) *n* gota *f*
**govern** (*gha*-vön) *v* *regir
**governess** (*gha*-vö-niss) *n* aya *f*
**government** (*gha*-vön-mönt) *n* régimen *m*, gobierno *m*
**governor** (*gha*-vö-nö) *n* gobernador *m*
**gown** (ghaun) *n* traje largo (de mujer) *m*
**grace** (ghreiss) *n* gracia *f*; perdón *m*
**graceful** (*ghreiss*-föl) *adj* gracioso
**grade** (ghreid) *n* grado *m*; *v* graduar
**gradient** (*ghrei*-di-önt) *n* pendiente *f*
**gradual** (*ghræ*-dʒu-öl) *adj* gradual; **gradually** *adv* paulatinamente
**graduate** (*ghræ*-dʒu-eit) *v* graduarse
**grain** (ghrein) *n* grano *m*, trigo *m*
**gram** (ghræm) *n* gramo *m*
**grammar** (*ghræ*-mö) *n* gramática *f*
**grammatical** (ghrö-*mæ*-ti-köl) *adj* gramatical
**grand** (ghrænd) *adj* imponente
**grandchild** nieto *m*, -a *f*
**granddad** (*ghræn*-dæd) *n* abuelito *m*
**granddaughter** (*ghræn*-doo-tö) *n* nieta *f*
**grandfather** (*ghræn*-faa-ðö) *n* abuelo *m*
**grandmother** (*ghræn*-ma-ðö) *n*

abuela *f*
**grandparents** (*ghræn*-pê$^{ö}$-röntss) *pl* abuelos *mpl*
**grandson** (*ghræn*-ssan) *n* nieto *m*
**granite** (*ghræ*-nit) *n* granito *m*
**grant** (ghraant) *v* conceder; *n* subvención *f*, beca *f*
**grape** (ghreip) uva *f*
**grapefruit** (*ghreip*-fruut) *n* pomelo *m*; toronja *fMe*
**grapes** (ghreipss) *pl* uvas *fpl*
**graph** (ghræf) *n* gráfico *m*
**graphic** (*ghræ*-fik) *adj* gráfico
**grasp** (ghraassp) *v* agarrar; *n* agarre *m*
**grass** (ghraass) *n* césped *m*
**grasshopper** (*ghraass*-ho-pö) *n* saltamontes *m*
**grate** (ghreit) *n* reja *f*; *v* rallar
**grateful** (*ghreit*-föl) *adj* agradecido
**grater** (*ghrei*-tö) *n* rayador *m*
**gratis** (*ghræ*-tiss) *adj* gratuito
**gratitude** (*ghræ*-ti-tyuud) *n* gratitud *f*
**gratuity** (ghrö-*tyuu*-ö-ti) *n* propina *f*
**grave** (ghreiv) *n* sepultura *f*; *adj* grave
**gravel** (*ghræ*-völ) *n* grava *f*
**gravestone** (*ghreiv*-sstoun) *n* lápida *f*
**graveyard** (*ghreiv*-yaad) *n* cementerio *m*
**gravity** (*ghræ*-vö-ti) *n* gravedad *f*; seriedad *f*
**gravy** (*ghrei*-vi) *n* salsa *f*
**graze** (ghreis) *v* *pacer; *n* rozadura *f*
**grease** (ghriiss) *n* grasa *f*; *v* engrasar
**greasy** (*ghrii*-ssi) *adj* grasiento, grasoso
**great** (ghreit) *adj* grande; **Great Britain** Gran Bretaña
**Greece** (ghriiss) Grecia *f*
**greed** (ghriid) *n* codicia *f*
**greedy** (*ghrii*-di) *adj* codicioso; glotón
**Greek** (ghriik) *adj* griego
**green** (ghriin) *adj* verde; **~ card** tarjeta verde
**greengrocer** (*ghriin*-ghrou-ssö) *n* verdulero *m*
**greenhouse** (*ghriin*-hauss) *n* invernadero *m*, invernáculo *m*
**greens** (ghriins) *pl* legumbres *fpl*
**greet** (ghriit) *v* saludar
**greeting** (*ghrii*-ting) *n* saludo *m*
**grey** (ghrei) *adj* gris
**greyhound** (*ghrei*-haund) *n* galgo *m*
**grief** (ghriif) *n* pesadumbre *f*; aflicción *f*, dolor *m*
**grieve** (ghriiv) *v* *estar afligido
**grill** (ghril) *n* parrilla *f*; *v* asar en parrilla
**grillroom** (*ghril*-ruum) *n* parrilla *f*
**grim** (ghrim) *adj* severo; desolador; lúgubre
**grin** (ghrin) *v* *sonreír; *n* sonrisa sardónica
***grind** (ghraind) *v* *moler; triturar
**grip** (ghrip) *v* *asir; *n* agarradero *m*, agarre *m*; *nAm* maletín *m*
**grit** (ghrit) *n* arena *f*; cascajo *m*; valor *m*
**groan** (ghroun) *v* *gemir
**grocer** (*ghrou*-ssö) *n* abacero *m*; abarrotero *mMe*; **grocer's** abacería *f*; abarrotería *fMe*
**groceries** (*ghrou*-ssö-ris) *pl* comestibles *mpl*
**groin** (ghroin) *n* ingle *f*
**groom** (ghruum) *n* novio *m*; mozo *m* de cuadra; *v* almohazar; preparar; **well groomed** bien arreglado
**groove** (ghruuv) *n* surco *m*
**gross**[1] (ghrouss) *n* (pl ~) gruesa *f*
**gross**[2] (ghrouss) *adj* grosero; bruto
**grotto** (*ghro*-tou) *n* (pl ~es, ~s) gruta *f*
**ground**[1] (ghraund) *n* fondo *m*, tierra *f*; **~ floor** piso bajo; **grounds** terreno *m*
**ground**[2] (ghraund) *v* (p, pp grind)
**group** (ghruup) *n* grupo *m*
**grouse** (ghrauss) *n* (pl ~) gallo de bosque
**grove** (ghrouv) *n* soto *m*

***grow** (ghrou) *v* *crecer; cultivar; *hacerse
**growl** (ghraul) *v* *gruñir
**grown-up** (*ghroun*-ap) *adj* adulto; *n* adulto *m*, -a *f*
**growth** (ghrouz) *n* crecimiento *m*; desarrollo *m*; tumor *m*
**grudge** (ghradʒ) *n* rencor *m*
**grumble** (*ghram*-böl) *v* refunfuñar
**guarantee** (ghæ-rön-*tii*) *n* garantía *f*; *v* garantizar
**guard** (ghaad) *n* guardia *f*; *v* guardar
**guardian** (*ghaa*-di-ön) *n* tutor *m/f*; guardián *m*
**guess** (ghêss) *v* adivinar; *creer, conjeturar; *n* conjetura *f*
**guest** (ghêsst) *n* huésped *m*, invitado *m*; ~ **room** habitación para huéspedes
**guesthouse** (*ghêsst*-hauss) *n* pensión *f*
**guide** (ghaid) *n* guía *m*; *v* guiar
**guidebook** (*ghaid*-buk) *n* guía *f*
**guide dog** (*ghaid*-dogh) *n* perro lazarillo
**guilt** (ghilt) *n* culpa *f*
**guilty** (*ghil*-ti) *adj* culpable
**guinea pig** (*ghi*-ni-pigh) *n* conejillo de Indias
**guitar** (ghi-*taa*) *n* guitarra *f*
**gulf** (ghalf) *n* golfo *m*
**gull** (ghal) *n* gaviota *f*
**gum** (gham) *n* encía *f*; goma *f*; cola *f*
**gun** (ghan) *n* fusil *m*, revólver *m*; cañón *m*
**gunpowder** (*ghan*-pau-dö) *n* pólvora *f*
**gust** (ghasst) *n* ráfaga *f*
**gusty** (*gha*-ssti) *adj* borrascoso
**gut** (ghat) *n* intestino *m*; **guts** coraje *m*
**gutter** (*gha*-tö) *n* cuneta *f*
**guy** (ghai) *n* tipo *m*
**gym** (dʒim) gimnasio *m*
**gymnasium** (dʒim-*nei*-si-öm) *n* (pl ~s, -sia) gimnasio *m*
**gymnast** (*dʒim*-næsst) *n* gimnasta *m*
**gymnastics** (dʒim-*næ*-sstikss) *pl* gimnasia *f*
**gyn(a)ecologist** (ghai-nö-*ko*-lö-dʒisst) *n* ginecólogo *m*, -a *f*

# H

**habit** (*hæ*-bit) *n* hábito *m*
**habitable** (*hæ*-bi-tö-böl) *adj* habitable
**habitual** (hö-*bi*-chu-öl) *adj* habitual
**had** (hæd) *v* (p, pp have)
**haddock** (*hæ*-dök) *n* (pl ~) bacalao *m*
**h(a)emorrhage** (*hê*-mö-ridʒ) *n* hemorragia *f*
**h(a)emorrhoids** (*hê*-mö-roids) *pl* hemorroides *fpl*
**hail** (heil) *n* granizo *m*
**hair** (hêö) *n* cabello *m*; ~ **cream** brillantina *f*; ~ **gel** gel fijador de cabello; ~ **piece** postizo *m*; ~ **rollers** rizadores *mpl*; ~ **tonic** tónico para el cabello
**hairbrush** (*hêö*-braʃ) *n* cepillo para el cabello
**haircut** (*hêö*-kat) *n* corte de pelo
**hairdo** (*hêö*-duu) *n* peinado *m*
**hairdresser** (*hêö*-drê-ssö) *n* peluquero *m*, -a *f*
**hairdrier, hairdryer** (*hêö*-drai-ö) *n* secador para el pelo
**hairgrip** (*hêö*-ghrip) *n* horquilla *f*
**hair net** (*hêö*-nêt) *n* redecilla *f*
**hairpin** (*hêö*-pin) *n* horquilla *f*

**hair spray** (*hê*^ö-ssprei) *n* laca para el cabello
**hairy** (*hê*^ö-ri) *adj* cabelludo
**half**¹ (haaf) *adj* medio
**half**² (haaf) *n* (pl halves) mitad *f*
**half time** (haaf-*taim*) *n* descanso *m*
**halfway** (haaf-^u*ei*) *adv* a mitad de camino
**halibut** (*hæ*-li-böt) *n* (pl ~) halibut *m*
**hall** (hool) *n* vestíbulo *m*; sala *f*
**halt** (hoolt) *v* pararse
**halve** (haav) *v* partir por la mitad
**ham** (hæm) *n* jamón *m*
**hamlet** (*hæm*-löt) *n* aldea *f*
**hammer** (*hæ*-mö) *n* martillo *m*
**hammock** (*hæ*-mök) *n* hamaca *f*
**hamper** (*hæm*-pö) *n* cesto *m*
**hand** (hænd) *n* mano *f*; *v* alargar; ~ **cream** crema para las manos
**handbag** (*hænd*-bægh) *n* bolso *m*
**handbook** (*hænd*-buk) *n* manual *m*
**handbrake** (*hænd*-breik) *n* freno de mano
**handcuffs** (*hænd*-kafss) *pl* esposas *fpl*
**handful** (*hænd*-ful) *n* puñado *m*
**handicap** (*hæn*-di-kæp) *n* desventaja *f*
**handicapped** (*hæn*-di-kæpt) *n* minusválido *m*
**handicraft** (*hæn*-di-kraaft) *n* trabajo manual; artesanía *f*
**handkerchief** (*hæng*-kö-chif) *n* pañuelo *m*
**handle** (*hæn*-döl) *n* mango *m*; *v* manejar; tratar
**hand-made** (hænd-*meid*) *adj* hecho a mano
**handshake** (*hænd*-ʃeik) *n* apretón de manos
**handsome** (*hæn*-ssöm) *adj* guapo
**handwork** (*hænd*-^uöök) *n* obra hecha a mano
**handwriting** (*hænd*-rai-ting) *n* escritura *f*
**handy** (*hæn*-di) *adj* manejable
***hang** (hæng) *v* *colgar
**hanger** (*hæng*-ö) *n* percha *f*
**hangover** (*hæng*-ou-vö) *n* resaca *f*
**happen** (*hæ*-pön) *v* suceder, pasar
**happening** (*hæ*-pö-ning) *n* acontecimiento *m*
**happiness** (*hæ*-pi-nöss) *n* felicidad *f*
**happy** (*hæ*-pi) *adj* contento, feliz
**harbo(u)r** (*haa*-bö) *n* puerto *m*
**hard** (haad) *adj* duro; difícil; ~ **disk** disco *m* duro; **hardly** apenas
**hardware** (*haad*-^uê^ö) *n* quincalla *f*; hardware *m*; ~ **store** ferretería *f*
**hare** (hê^ö) *n* liebre *f*
**harm** (haam) *n* perjuicio *m*; mal *m*, daño *m*; *v* perjudicar
**harmful** (*haam*-föl) *adj* perjudicial, dañoso
**harmless** (*haam*-löss) *adj* inocuo; inofensivo
**harmony** (*haa*-mö-ni) *n* armonía *f*
**harp** (haap) *n* arpa *f*
**harpsichord** (*haap*-ssi-kood) *n* clavicémbalo *m*
**harsh** (haaʃ) *adj* áspero; severo; cruel
**harvest** (*haa*-visst) *n* cosecha *f*
**has** (hæs) *v* (pr have)
**haste** (heisst) *n* prisa *f*
**hasten** (*hei*-ssön) *v* apresurarse
**hasty** (*hei*-ssti) *adj* apresurado
**hat** (hæt) *n* sombrero *m*; ~ **rack** percha *f*
**hatch** (hæch) *n* trampa *f*
**hate** (heit) *v* detestar; odiar; *n* odio *m*
**hatred** (*hei*-trid) *n* odio *m*
**haughty** (*hoo*-ti) *adj* altivo
**haul** (hool) *v* arrastrar; transportar
***have** (hæv) *v* *haber, *tener; *hacer; ~ **to** deber
**hawk** (hook) *n* halcón *m*
**hay** (hei) *n* heno *m*; ~ **fever** fiebre del heno
**hazard** (*hæ*-söd) *n* riesgo *m*

**haze** (heis) *n* calina *f*; niebla *f*
**hazelnut** (*hei*-söl-nat) *n* avellana *f*
**hazy** (*hei*-si) *adj* calinoso; brumoso
**he** (hii) *pron* él
**head** (hêd) *n* cabeza *f*; *v* dirigir; ~ **of state** jefe de Estado; ~ **teacher** director *m*, -a *f* de escuela; ~ **waiter** jefe de camareros
**headache** (*hê*-deik) *n* dolor de cabeza
**heading** (*hê*-ding) *n* título *m*
**headlamp** (*hêd*-læmp) *n* fanal *m*
**headland** (*hêd*-lönd) *n* promontorio *m*
**headlight** (*hêd*-lait) *n* faro *m*
**headline** (*hêd*-lain) *n* titular *m*
**headmaster** (hêd-*maa*-sstö) *n* director de escuela
**headmistress** (hêd-*mi*-sströss) *n* directora de escuela
**headquarters** (hêd-*k*$^{u}$*oo*-tös) *pl* cuartel general
**headstrong** (*hêd*-sstrong) *adj* cabezudo
**heal** (hiil) *v* curar
**health** (hêlz) *n* salud *f*; ~ **center** *Am*, ~ **centre** dispensario *m*; ~ **certificate** certificado de salud
**healthy** (*hêl*-zi) *adj* sano
**heap** (hiip) *n* montón *m*
***hear** (hi$^{ö}$) *v* *oír
**hearing** (*hi*$^{ö}$-ring) *n* oído *m*
**heart** (haat) *n* corazón *m*; núcleo *m*; **by** ~ de memoria; ~ **attack** ataque cardíaco
**heartburn** (*haat*-böön) *n* acidez *f*
**hearth** (haaz) *n* fogón *m*
**heartless** (*haat*-löss) *adj* insensible; cruel
**hearty** (*haa*-ti) *adj* cordial
**heat** (hiit) *n* calor *m*; *v* *calentar; **heating pad** almohada eléctrica
**heater** (*hii*-tö) *n* calefactor *m*; **immersion** ~ calentador de inmersión
**heath** (hiiz) *n* brezal *m*
**heathen** (*hii*-ðön) *n* pagano *m*
**heather** (*hê*-ðö) *n* brezo *m*
**heating** (*hii*-ting) *n* calefacción *f*
**heaven** (*hê*-vön) *n* cielo *m*
**heavy** (*hê*-vi) *adj* pesado
**Hebrew** (*hii*-bruu) *n* hebreo *m*
**hedge** (hêdʒ) *n* seto *m*
**hedgehog** (*hêdʒ*-hogh) *n* erizo *m*
**heel** (hiil) *n* talón *m*; tacón *m*
**height** (hait) *n* altura *f*; colmo *m*, apogeo *m*
**heir** (êr) *n* heredero *m*
**heiress** (*ê*-ris) *n* heredera *f*
**helicopter** (*hê*-li-kop-tö) helicóptero *m*
**hell** (hêl) *n* infierno *m*
**hello** (hê-*lou*) hola; ¿sí?, ¿diga?, *Am* ¿alo?; **say** ~ **to** saludar a
**helm** (hêlm) *n* timón *m*
**helmet** (*hêl*-mit) *n* casco *m*
**helmsman** (*hêlms*-mön) *n* timonero *m*
**help** (hêlp) *v* ayudar; *n* ayuda *f*
**helper** (*hêl*-pö) *n* ayudante *m*/*f*
**helpful** (*hêlp*-föl) *adj* útil; atento
**helping** (*hêl*-ping) *n* porción *f*
**hemp** (hêmp) *n* cáñamo *m*
**hen** (hên) *n* gallina *f*
**her** (höö) *pron* la, le; *adj* su
**herb** (hööb) *n* hierba *f*
**herd** (hööd) *n* manada *f*; rebaño *m*
**here** (hi$^{ö}$) *adv* acá; ~ **you are** tenga usted
**hereditary** (hi-*rê*-di-tö-ri) *adj* hereditario
**hernia** (*höö*-ni-ö) *n* hernia *f*
**hero** (*hi*$^{ö}$-rou) *n* (pl ~es) héroe *m*
**heron** (*hê*-rön) *n* garza *f*
**herring** (*hê*-ring) *n* (pl ~, ~s) arenque *m*
**herself** (höö-*ssêlf*) *pron* se; ella misma
**hesitate** (*hê*-si-teit) *v* vacilar
**heterosexual** (hê-tö-rö-*ssêk*-ʃu-öl) *adj* heterosexual

**hiccup** (*hi*-kap) *n* hipo *m*
**hide** (haid) *n* piel *f*; cuero *m*
***hide** (haid) *v* esconder
**hideous** (*hi*-di-öss) *adj* horrible
**hierarchy** (*hai*$^{\ddot{o}}$-raa-ki) *n* jerarquía *f*
**high** (hai) *adj* alto
**highway** (*hai*-$^{u}$ei) *n* carretera *f*; *nAm* autopista *f*
**hijack** (*hai*-dʒæk) *v* secuestrar
**hijacker** (*hai*-dʒæ-kö) *n* secuestrador *m*
**hike** (haik) *v* caminar; ir de excursión a pie
**hill** (hil) *n* colina *f*
**hillside** (*hil*-ssaid) *n* ladera *f*
**hilltop** (*hil*-top) *n* cima *f*
**hilly** (*hi*-li) *adj* montuoso
**him** (him) *pron* le
**himself** (him-*ssêlf*) *pron* se; él mismo
**hinder** (*hin*-dö) *v* *impedir
**hinge** (hindʒ) *n* bisagra *f*
**hint** (hint) *n* pista *f*; consejo *m*; indirecta *f*; rastro *m*
**hip** (hip) *n* cadera *f*
**hire** (hai$^{\ddot{o}}$) *v* alquilar; **for ~** de alquiler; **~ purchase** compra a plazos
**his** (his) *adj* su
**historic** (hi-*ssto*-rik) *adj* histórico
**historical** (hi-*ssto*-ri-köl) *adj* histórico
**history** (*hi*-sstö-ri) *n* historia *f*
**hit** (hit) *n* golpe *m*; éxito *m*
***hit** (hit) *v* pegar; tocar, *acertar
**hitchhike** (*hich*-haik) *v* *hacer autostop
**hitchhiker** (*hich*-hai-kö) *n* autoestopista *m/f*
**hoarse** (hooss) *adj* ronco
**hobby** (*ho*-bi) *n* afición *f*
**hobbyhorse** (*ho*-bi-hooss) *n* comidilla *f*
**hockey** (*ho*-ki) *n* hockey *m*
**hoist** (hoisst) *v* izar
**hold** (hould) *n* presa *f*; dominio *m*; bodega *f*
***hold** (hould) *v* *tener; *retener; **~ on** agarrarse; **~ up** *sostener
**hold-up** (*houl*-dap) *n* atraco *m*
**hole** (houl) *n* bache *m*, agujero *m*; hoyo *m*
**holiday** (*ho*-lö-di) *n* vacaciones *fpl*; **~ camp** colonia veraniega; **~ resort** lugar de descanso; **on ~** de vacaciones
**Holland** (*ho*-lönd) Holanda *f*
**hollow** (*ho*-lou) *adj* hueco; vacío
**holy** (*hou*-li) *adj* santo
**homage** (*ho*-midʒ) *n* homenaje *m*
**home** (houm) *n* casa *f*; hospicio *m*; *adv* en casa, a casa; **at ~** en casa; **~land** *n* patria *f*
**home-made** (houm-*meid*) *adj* casero
**homesickness** (*houm*-ssik-nöss) *n* nostalgia *f*
**homework** (*houm*-$^{u}$öök) deberes *mpl*
**homosexual** (hou-mö-*ssêk*-ʃu-öl) *adj* homosexual
**honest** (*o*-nisst) *adj* honesto; sincero
**honesty** (*o*-ni-ssti) *n* honradez *f*
**honey** (*ha*-ni) *n* miel *f*
**honeymoon** (*ha*-ni-muun) *n* luna de miel
**honk** (hongk) *vAm* tocar la bocina
**hono(u)r** (*o*-nö) *n* honor *m*; *v* honrar, *rendir homenaje
**hono(u)rable** (*o*-nö-rö-böl) *adj* honorable; honesto
**hood** (hud) *n* capucha *f*; *nAm* capó *m*
**hoof** (huuf) *n* casco *m*; pezuña *f*
**hook** (huk) *n* gancho *m*
**hoot** (huut) *v* tocar la bocina
**hooter** (*huu*-tö) *n* bocina *f*
**hoover** (*huu*-vö) *v* pasar el aspirador
**hop**[1] (hop) *v* brincar; *n* salto *m*
**hop**[2] (hop) *n* lúpulo *m*
**hope** (houp) *n* esperanza *f*; *v* esperar
**hopeful** (*houp*-föl) *adj* esperanzado
**hopeless** (*houp*-löss) *adj* desesperado
**horizon** (hö-*rai*-sön) *n* horizonte *m*

**horizontal** (ho-ri-*son*-töl) *adj* horizontal
**horn** (hoon) *n* cuerno *m*; bocina *f*
**horrible** (*ho*-ri-böl) *adj* horrible; terrible, atroz
**horror** (*ho*-rö) *n* espanto *m*, horror *m*
**hors d'œuvre** (oo-*döövr*) *n* entremeses *mpl*
**horse** (hooss) *n* caballo *m*
**horseman** (*hooss*-mön) *n* (pl -men) jinete *m*
**horsepower** (*hooss*-pau$^{ö}$) *n* caballo de vapor
**horserace** (*hooss*-reiss) *n* carrera de caballos
**horseradish** (*hooss*-ræ-diʃ) *n* rábano picante
**horseshoe** (*hooss*-ʃuu) *n* herradura *f*
**horticulture** (*hoo*-ti-kal-chö) *n* horticultura *f*
**hospitable** (*ho*-sspi-tö-böl) *adj* hospitalario
**hospital** (*ho*-sspi-töl) *n* hospital *m*
**hospitality** (ho-sspi-*tæ*-lö-ti) *n* hospitalidad *f*
**host** (housst) *n* anfitrión *m*
**hostage** (*ho*-sstidʒ) *n* rehén *m*
**hostel** (*ho*-sstöl) *n* hospedería *f*
**hostess** (*hou*-sstiss) *n* azafata *f*
**hostile** (*ho*-sstail) *adj* hostil
**hot** (hot) *adj* caliente
**hotel** (hou-*têl*) *n* hotel *m*
**hot-tempered** (hot-*têm*-pöd) *adj* colérico
**hour** (au$^{ö}$) *n* hora *f*
**hourly** (*au$^{ö}$*-li) *adj* a cada hora
**house** (hauss) *n* casa *f*; vivienda *f*; inmueble *m*; ~ **agent** corredor de casas; ~ **block** *Am* manzana de casas; **public** ~ taberna *f*
**houseboat** (*hauss*-bout) *n* casa flotante
**household** (*hauss*-hould) *n* menaje *m*
**housekeeper** (*hauss*-kii-pö) *n* ama de llaves
**housekeeping** (*hauss*-kii-ping) *n* gobierno de la casa
**housemaid** (*hauss*-meid) *n* criada *f*
**housewife** (*hauss*-$^{u}$aif) *n* ama de casa
**housework** (*hauss*-$^{u}$öök) *n* faenas domésticas
**how** (hau) *adv* cómo; qué; ~ **many** cuánto; ~ **much** cuánto
**however** (hau-*ê*-vö) *conj* todavía, sin embargo
**hug** (hagh) *v* abrazar; *n* abrazo *m*
**huge** (hyuudʒ) *adj* enorme; vasto, inmenso
**hum** (ham) *v* tararear
**human** (*hyuu*-mön) *adj* humano; ~ **being** ser humano
**humanity** (hyu-*mæ*-nö-ti) *n* humanidad *f*
**humble** (*ham*-böl) *adj* humilde
**humid** (*hyuu*-mid) *adj* húmedo
**humidity** (hyu-*mi*-dö-ti) *n* humedad *f*
**humorous** (*hyuu*-mö-röss) *adj* chistoso, gracioso, humorístico
**humo(u)r** (*hyuu*-mö) *n* humor *m*
**hundred** (*han*-dröd) *n* ciento
**Hungarian** (hang-*ghê$^{ö}$*-ri-ön) *adj* húngaro
**Hungary** (*hang*-ghö-ri) Hungría *m*
**hunger** (*hang*-ghö) *n* hambre *f*
**hungry** (*hang*-ghri) *adj* hambriento
**hunt** (hant) *v* cazar; *n* caza *f*; ~ **for** buscar
**hunter** (*han*-tö) *n* cazador *m*, -a *f*
**hurricane** (*ha*-ri-kön) *n* huracán *m*; ~ **lamp** lámpara sorda
**hurry** (*ha*-ri) *v* *darse prisa, apresurarse; *n* prisa *f*; **in a** ~ de prisa
***hurt** (hööt) *v* *hacer daño, dañar; ofender
**hurtful** (*hööt*-föl) *adj* perjudicial
**husband** (*has*-bönd) *n* esposo *m*, marido *m*
**hut** (hat) *n* cabaña *f*

**hydrogen** (*hai*-drö-dʒön) *n* hidrógeno *m*
**hygiene** (*hai*-dʒiin) *n* higiene *f*
**hygienic** (hai-*dʒii*-nik) *adj* higiénico
**hymn** (him) *n* himno *m*
**hyphen** (*hai*-fön) *n* guión *m*
**hypocrisy** (hi-*po*-krö-ssi) *n* hipocresía *f*
**hypocrite** (*hi*-pö-krit) *n* hipócrita *m*
**hypocritical** (hi-pö-*kri*-ti-köl) *adj* hipócrita, mojigato
**hysterical** (hi-*sstê*-ri-köl) *adj* histérico

# I

**I** (ai) *pron* yo
**ice** (aiss) *n* hielo *m*; ~ **bag** bolsa de hielo; ~ **cream** helado *m*
**Iceland** (*aiss*-lönd) Islandia *f*
**Icelander** (*aiss*-lön-dö) *n* islandés *m*
**Icelandic** (aiss-*læn*-dik) *adj* islandés
**icon** (*ai*-kon) *n* icono *m*
**idea** (ai-*di*ö) *n* idea *f*; pensamiento *m*; noción *f*, concepto *m*
**ideal** (ai-*di*ö*l*) *adj* ideal; *n* ideal *m*
**identical** (ai-*dên*-ti-köl) *adj* idéntico
**identification** (ai-dên-ti-fi-*kei*-ʃön) *n* identificación *f*
**identify** (ai-*dên*-ti-fai) *v* identificar
**identity** (ai-*dên*-tö-ti) *n* identidad *f*; ~ **card** carnet de identidad
**idiom** (*i*-di-öm) *n* lenguaje *m*; modismo *m*
**idiomatic** (i-di-ö-*mæ*-tik) *adj* idiomático
**idiot** (*i*-di-öt) *n* idiota *m*
**idiotic** (i-di-*o*-tik) *adj* idiota
**idle** (*ai*-döl) *adj* ocioso; vago; vano
**idol** (*ai*-döl) *n* ídolo *m*
**if** (if) *conj* si
**ignition** (igh-*ni*-ʃön) *n* encendido *m*; ~ **coil** bobina del encendido
**ignorant** (*igh*-nö-rönt) *adj* ignorante
**ignore** (igh-*noo*) *v* ignorar
**ill** (il) *adj* enfermo; malo; maligno
**illegal** (i-*lii*-ghöl) *adj* ilegal
**illegible** (i-*lê*-dʒö-böl) *adj* ilegible
**illiterate** (i-*li*-tö-röt) *n* analfabeto *m*
**illness** (*il*-nöss) *n* enfermedad *f*
**illuminate** (i-*luu*-mi-neit) *v* iluminar
**illumination** (i-luu-mi-*nei*-ʃön) *n* iluminación *f*
**illusion** (i-*luu*-ʒön) *n* ilusión *f*
**illustrate** (*i*-lö-sstreit) *v* ilustrar
**illustration** (i-lö-*sstrei*-ʃön) *n* ilustración *f*
**image** (*i*-midʒ) *n* imagen *f*
**imaginary** (i-*mæ*-dʒi-nö-ri) *adj* imaginario
**imagination** (i-mæ-dʒi-*nei*-ʃön) *n* imaginación *f*
**imagine** (i-*mæ*-dʒin) *v* imaginarse; figurarse
**imitate** (*i*-mi-teit) *v* imitar
**imitation** (i-mi-*tei*-ʃön) *n* imitación *f*
**immediate** (i-*mii*-dyöt) *adj* inmediato
**immediately** (i-*mii*-dyöt-li) *adv* inmediatamente, de inmediato
**immense** (i-*mênss*) *adj* inmenso, enorme
**immigrant** (*i*-mi-ghrönt) *n* inmigrante *m*
**immigrate** (*i*-mi-ghreit) *v* inmigrar
**immigration** (i-mi-*ghrei*-ʃön) *n* inmigración *f*
**immodest** (i-*mo*-disst) *adj* inmodesto
**immunity** (i-*myuu*-nö-ti) *n* inmunidad *f*
**immunize** (*i*-myu-nais) *v* inmunizar

**impartial** (im-*paa*-ʃöl) *adj* imparcial
**impassable** (im-*paa*-ssö-böl) *adj* intransitable
**impatient** (im-*pei*-ʃönt) *adj* impaciente
**impede** (im-*piid*) *v* *impedir
**impediment** (im-*pê*-di-mönt) *n* impedimento *m*
**imperfect** (im-*pöö*-fikt) *adj* imperfecto
**imperial** (im-*pi*$^{ö}$-ri-öl) *adj* imperial
**impersonal** (im-*pöö*-ssö-nöl) *adj* impersonal
**impertinence** (im-*pöö*-ti-nönss) *n* impertinencia *f*
**impertinent** (im-*pöö*-ti-nönt) *adj* grosero, descarado, impertinente
**implement**[1] (*im*-pli-mönt) *n* instrumento *m*; herramienta *f*
**implement**[2] (*im*-pli-mênt) *v* efectuar
**implicate** (*im*-pli-keit) *v* implicar
**imply** (im-*plai*) *v* implicar, suponer
**impolite** (im-pö-*lait*) *adj* descortés
**import**[1] (im-*poot*) *v* importar
**import**[2] (*im*-poot) *n* importación *f*; **~ duty** impuestos de importación
**importance** (im-*poo*-tönss) *n* importancia *f*
**important** (im-*poo*-tönt) *adj* importante
**importer** (im-*poo*-tö) *n* importador *m*
**imposing** (im-*pou*-sing) *adj* imponente
**impossible** (im-*po*-ssö-böl) *adj* imposible
**impotence** (*im*-pö-tönss) *n* impotencia *f*
**impotent** (*im*-pö-tönt) *adj* impotente
**impress** (im-*prêss*) *v* impresionar
**impression** (im-*prê*-ʃön) *n* impresión *f*
**impressive** (im-*prê*-ssiv) *adj* impresionante
**imprison** (im-*pri*-sön) *v* encarcelar
**imprisonment** (im-*pri*-sön-mönt) *n* encarcelamiento *m*
**improbable** (im-*pro*-bö-böl) *adj* improbable
**improper** (im-*pro*-pö) *adj* impropio
**improve** (im-*pruuv*) *v* mejorar
**improvement** (im-*pruuv*-mönt) *n* mejora *f*
**improvise** (*im*-prö-vais) *v* improvisar
**impudent** (*im*-pyu-dönt) *adj* impudente
**impulse** (*im*-palss) *n* impulso *m*; estímulo *m*
**impulsive** (im-*pal*-ssiv) *adj* impulsivo
**in** (in) *prep* en; dentro de; *adv* adentro
**inaccessible** (i-næk-*ssê*-ssö-böl) *adj* inaccesible
**inaccurate** (i-*næ*-kyu-röt) *adj* inexacto
**inadequate** (i-*næ*-di-k$^{u}$öt) *adj* inadecuado
**incapable** (ing-*kei*-pö-böl) *adj* incapaz
**incense** (*in*-ssênss) *n* incienso *m*
**inch** (inch) *n* pulgada *f*
**incident** (*in*-ssi-dönt) *n* incidente *m*
**incidental** (in-ssi-*dên*-töl) *adj* imprevisto
**incite** (in-*ssait*) *v* incitar
**inclination** (ing-kli-*nei*-ʃön) *n* inclinación *f*
**incline** (ing-*klain*) *n* inclinación *f*
**inclined** (ing-*klaind*) *adj* dispuesto, inclinado; ***be ~ to** *v* inclinarse
**include** (ing-*kluud*) *v* *incluir
**inclusive** (ing-*kluu*-ssiv) *adj* incluso
**income** (*ing*-köm) *n* ingresos *mpl*; **~ tax** impuesto sobre los ingresos
**incompetent** (ing-*kom*-pö-tönt) *adj* incompetente
**incomplete** (in-köm-*pliit*) *adj* incompleto
**inconceivable** (ing-kön-*ssii*-vö-böl) *adj* inconcebible
**inconspicuous** (ing-kön-*sspi*-kyu-

öss) *adj* discreto
**inconvenience** (ing-kön-*vii*-nyönss) *n* incomodidad *f*, inconveniencia *f*
**inconvenient** (ing-kön-*vii*-nyönt) *adj* inoportuno; molesto
**incorrect** (ing-kö-*rêkt*) *adj* inexacto, incorrecto
**increase**[1] (ing-*kriiss*) *v* aumentar; incrementar, *acrecentarse
**increase**[2] (*ing*-kriiss) *n* aumento *m*
**incredible** (ing-*krê*-dö-böl) *adj* increíble
**incurable** (ing-*kyu*$^{ö}$-rö-böl) *adj* incurable
**indecent** (in-*dii*-ssönt) *adj* indecente
**indeed** (in-*diid*) *adv* en efecto
**indefinite** (in-*dê*-fi-nit) *adj* indefinido
**indemnity** (in-*dêm*-nö-ti) *n* indemnización *f*
**independence** (in-di-*pên*-dönss) *n* independencia *f*
**independent** (in-di-*pên*-dönt) *adj* independiente; autónomo
**index** (*in*-dêkss) *n* índice *m*; ~ **finger** índice *m*
**India** (*in*-di-ö) India *f*
**Indian** (*in*-di-ön) *adj* indio; *n* indio *m*
**indicate** (*in*-di-keit) *v* señalar, indicar
**indication** (in-di-*kei*-ʃön) *n* señal *f*, indicación *f*
**indicator** (*in*-di-kei-tö) *n* indicador *m*
**indifferent** (in-*di*-fö-rönt) *adj* indiferente
**indigestion** (in-di-*dʒêss*-chön) *n* indigestión *f*
**indignation** (in-digh-*nei*-ʃön) *n* indignación *f*
**indirect** (in-di-*rêkt*) *adj* indirecto
**individual** (in-di-*vi*-dʒu-öl) *adj* aparte, individual; *n* individuo *m*
**Indonesia** (in-dö-*nii*-si-ö) Indonesia *f*
**Indonesian** (in-dö-*nii*-si-ön) *adj* indonesio
**indoor** (*in*-doo) *adj* interior
**indoors** (in-*doos*) *adv* en casa
**indulge** (in-*daldʒ*) *v* consentir a
**industrial** (in-*da*-sstri-öl) *adj* industrial; ~ **area** zona industrial
**industrious** (in-*da*-sstri-öss) *adj* aplicado
**industry** (*in*-dö-sstri) *n* industria *f*
**inedible** (i-*nê*-di-böl) *adj* incomible
**inefficient** (i-ni-*fi*-ʃönt) *adj* ineficiente
**inevitable** (i-*nê*-vi-tö-böl) *adj* inevitable
**inexpensive** (i-nik-*sspên*-ssiv) *adj* barato
**inexperienced** (i-nik-*sspi*$^{ö}$-ri-önsst) *adj* inexperto
**infant** (*in*-fönt) *n* criatura *f*
**infantry** (*in*-fön-tri) *n* infantería *f*
**infect** (in-*fêkt*) *v* infectar
**infection** (in-*fêk*-ʃön) *n* infección *f*
**infectious** (in-*fêk*-ʃöss) *adj* contagioso
**infer** (in-*föö*) *v* *deducir
**inferior** (in-*fi*$^{ö}$-ri-ö) *adj* inferior
**infinite** (*in*-fi-nöt) *adj* infinito
**infinitive** (in-*fi*-ni-tiv) *n* infinitivo *m*
**inflammable** (in-*flæ*-mö-böl) *adj* inflamable
**inflammation** (in-flö-*mei*-ʃön) *n* inflamación *f*
**inflatable** (in-*flei*-tö-böl) *adj* inflable
**inflate** (in-*fleit*) *v* hinchar
**inflation** (in-*flei*-ʃön) *n* inflación *f*
**inflict** (in-*flikt*) *v* infligir
**influence** (*in*-flu-önss) *n* influencia *f*; *v* *influir
**influential** (in-flu-*ên*-ʃöl) *adj* influyente
**influenza** (in-flu-*ên*-sö) *n* gripe *f*
**inform** (in-*foom*) *v* informar; comunicar
**informal** (in-*foo*-möl) *adj* informal
**information** (in-fö-*mei*-ʃön) *n* información *f*; informes *mpl*, comunicado *m*; ~ **bureau** oficina de informaciones

**infra-red** (in-frö-*rêd*) *adj* infrarrojo
**infrequent** (in-*frii*-kᵘönt) *adj* infrecuente
**ingredient** (ing-*ghrii*-di-önt) *n* ingrediente *m*
**inhabit** (in-*hæ*-bit) *v* habitar
**inhabitable** (in-*hæ*-bi-tö-böl) *adj* habitable
**inhabitant** (in-*hæ*-bi-tönt) *n* habitante *m*
**inhale** (in-*heil*) *v* inhalar
**inherit** (in-*hê*-rit) *v* heredar
**inheritance** (in-*hê*-ri-tönss) *n* herencia *f*
**inhibit** (in-*hi*-bit) *v* impedir; inhibir, cohibir
**initial** (i-*ni*-ʃöl) *adj* inicial; *n* inicial *f*; *v* rubricar
**initiate** (i-*ni*-ʃyeit) *v* iniciar
**initiative** (i-*ni*-ʃö-tiv) *n* iniciativa *f*
**inject** (in-*dʒêkt*) *v* inyectar
**injection** (in-*dʒêk*-ʃön) *n* inyección *f*
**injure** (*in*-dʒö) *v* *herir; ofender
**injury** (*in*-dʒö-ri) *n* herida *f*; lesión *f*
**injustice** (in-*dʒa*-sstiss) *n* injusticia *f*
**ink** (ingk) *n* tinta *f*
**inlet** (*in*-lêt) *n* ensenada *f*
**inn** (in) *n* posada *f*; parador *m*
**inner** (*i*-nö) *adj* interior; ~ **tube** cámara de aire
**innocence** (*i*-nö-ssönss) *n* inocencia *f*
**innocent** (*i*-nö-ssönt) *adj* inocente
**inoculate** (i-*no*-kyu-leit) *v* vacunar
**inoculation** (i-no-kyu-*lei*-ʃön) *n* inoculación *f*
**inquire** (ing-*kᵘaiᵒ̈*) *v* informarse, *pedir informes
**inquiry** (ing-*kᵘaiᵒ̈*-ri) *n* pregunta *f*, indagación *f*; encuesta *f*; ~ **office** oficina de informaciones
**inquisitive** (ing-*kᵘi*-sö-tiv) *adj* curioso
**insane** (in-*ssein*) *adj* loco
**inscription** (in-*sskrip*-ʃön) *n* inscripción *f*
**insect** (*in*-ssêkt) *n* insecto *m*; ~ **repellent** insectífugo *m*
**insecticide** (in-*ssêk*-ti-ssaid) *n* insecticida *m*
**insensitive** (in-*ssên*-ssö-tiv) *adj* insensible
**insert** (in-*ssööt*) *v* insertar
**inside** (in-*ssaid*) *n* interior *m*; *adj* interior; *adv* adentro; dentro; *prep* en, dentro de; ~ **out** al revés; **insides** entrañas *fpl*
**insight** (*in*-ssait) *n* entendimiento *m*; perspicacia *f*
**insignificant** (in-ssigh-*ni*-fi-könt) *adj* insignificante; irrelevante; baladí
**insist** (in-*ssisst*) *v* insistir; persistir
**insolence** (*in*-ssö-lönss) *n* insolencia *f*
**insolent** (*in*-ssö-lönt) *adj* insolente
**insomnia** (in-*ssom*-ni-ö) *n* insomnio *m*
**inspect** (in-*sspêkt*) *v* inspeccionar
**inspection** (in-*sspêk*-ʃön) *n* inspección *f*; control *m*
**inspector** (in-*sspêk*-tö) *n* inspector *m*, -a *f*; revisor *m*, -a *f*
**inspire** (in-*sspaiᵒ̈*) *v* inspirar
**install** (in-*sstool*) *v* instalar
**installation** (in-sstö-*lei*-ʃön) *n* instalación *f*
**instal(l)ment** (in-*sstǫol*-mönt) *n* plazo *m*; ~ **plan** compra a plazos
**instance** (*in*-sstönss) *n* ejemplo *m*; caso *m*; **for** ~ por ejemplo
**instant** (*in*-sstönt) *n* instante *m*
**instantly** (*in*-sstönt-li) *adv* instantáneamente, inmediatamente, al instante
**instead of** (in-*sstêd* ov) en lugar de; en vez de
**instinct** (*in*-sstingkt) *n* instinto *m*
**institute** (*in*-ssti-tyuut) *n* instituto *m*; institución *f*; *v* *instituir
**institution** (in-ssti-*tyuu*-ʃön) *n* instituto *m*, institución *f*

**instruct** (in-*sstrakt*) *v* *instruir
**instruction** (in-*sstrak*-ʃön) *n* instrucción *f*
**instructive** (in-*sstrak*-tiv) *adj* instructivo
**instructor** (in-*sstrak*-tö) *n* instructor *m*, -a *f*
**instrument** (*in*-sstru-mönt) *n* instrumento *m*; **musical ~** instrumento músico
**insufficient** (in-ssö-*fi*-ʃönt) *adj* insuficiente
**insulate** (*in*-ssyu-leit) *v* aislar
**insulation** (in-ssyu-*lei*-ʃön) *n* aislamiento *m*
**insulator** (*in*-ssyu-lei-tö) *n* aislador *m*
**insult**[1] (in-*ssalt*) *v* insultar
**insult**[2] (*in*-ssalt) *n* insulto *m*
**insurance** (in-ʃ*u*ᵒ-rönss) *n* seguro *m*; **~ policy** póliza de seguro
**insure** (in-ʃ*u*ᵒ) *v* asegurar
**intact** (in-*tækt*) *adj* intacto
**integrate** (*in*-ti-greit) *v* integrar
**intellect** (*in*-tö-lêkt) *n* intelecto *m*
**intellectual** (in-tö-*lêk*-chu-öl) *adj* intelectual
**intelligence** (in-*tê*-li-dʒönss) *n* inteligencia *f*
**intelligent** (in-*tê*-li-dʒönt) *adj* inteligente
**intend** (in-*tênd*) *v* intentar, *tener la intención de
**intense** (in-*tênss*) *adj* intenso
**intensify** (in-*tên*-si-fai) *v* intensificar; intensificarse
**intention** (in-*tên*-ʃön) *n* intención *f*
**intentional** (in-*tên*-ʃö-nöl) *adj* intencional
**intercourse** (*in*-tö-kooss) *n* trato *m*; comercio *m*; coito *m*
**interest** (*in*-trösst) *n* interés *m*; rédito *m*; *v* interesar; **interested** *adj* interesado
**interesting** (*in*-trö-ssting) *adj* interesante
**interfere** (in-tö-*fi*ᵒ) *v* interferir; **~ with** mezclarse en
**interference** (in-tö-*fi*ᵒ-rönss) *n* interferencia *f*
**interim** (*in*-tö-rim) *n* ínterin *m*
**interior** (in-*ti*ᵒ-ri-ö) *n* interior *m*
**interlude** (*in*-tö-luud) *n* intermedio *m*
**intermediary** (in-tö-*mii*-dyö-ri) *n* intermediario *m*
**intermission** (in-tö-*mi*-ʃön) *n* entreacto *m*
**internal** (in-*töö*-nöl) *adj* interno
**international** (in-tö-*næ*-ʃö-nöl) *adj* internacional
**Internet** (in-*töö*-nöl) Internet *f*; **on the Internet** en Internet
**interpret** (in-*töö*-prit) *v* interpretar
**interpreter** (in-*töö*-pri-tö) *n* intérprete *m*
**interrogate** (in-*tê*-rö-gheit) *v* interrogar
**interrogation** (in-tê-rö-*ghei*-ʃön) *n* interrogatorio *m*
**interrogative** (in-tö-*ro*-ghö-tiv) *adj* interrogativo
**interrupt** (in-tö-*rapt*) *v* interrumpir
**interruption** (in-tö-*rap*-ʃön) *n* interrupción *f*
**intersection** (in-tö-*ssêk*-ʃön) *n* intersección *f*
**interval** (*in*-tö-völ) *n* intervalo *m*
**intervene** (in-tö-*viin*) *v* *intervenir
**interview** (*in*-tö-vyuu) *n* entrevista *f*
**intestine** (in-*tê*-sstin) *n* intestino *m*
**intimate** (*in*-ti-möt) *adj* íntimo
**into** (*in*-tu) *prep* dentro de
**intolerable** (in-*to*-lö-rö-böl) *adj* insoportable; inaguantable
**intoxicated** (in-*tok*-ssi-kei-tid) *adj* borracho
**intrigue** (in-*triigh*) *n* intriga *f*
**introduce** (in-trö-*dyuuss*) *v* presentar; *introducir

**introduction** (in-trö-*dak*-ʃön) *n* presentación *f*; introducción *f*
**invade** (in-*veid*) *v* invadir
**invalid**$^{1}$ (*in*-vö-liid) *n* inválido *m*; *adj* inválido
**invalid**$^{2}$ (in-*væ*-lid) *adj* nulo
**invasion** (in-*vei*-ʒön) *n* irrupción *f*, invasión *f*
**invent** (in-*vênt*) *v* inventar
**invention** (in-*vên*-ʃön) *n* invención *f*
**inventive** (in-*vên*-tiv) *adj* inventivo
**inventor** (in-*vên*-tö) *n* inventor *m*
**inventory** (*in*-vön-tri) *n* inventario *m*
**invert** (in-*vööt*) *v* *invertir
**invest** (in-*vêsst*) *v* *invertir
**investigate** (in-*vê*-ssti-gheit) *v* investigar
**investigation** (in-vê-ssti-*ghei*-ʃön) *n* investigación *f*
**investment** (in-*vêsst*-mönt) *n* inversión *f*
**investor** (in-*vê*-sstö) *n* inversionista *m*
**invisible** (in-*vi*-sö-böl) *adj* invisible
**invitation** (in-vi-*tei*-ʃön) *n* invitación *f*
**invite** (in-*vait*) *v* invitar, convidar
**invoice** (*in*-voiss) *n* factura *f*
**involve** (in-*volv*) *v* *envolver; implicar
**involved** implicado; complicado
**inwards** (*in*-$^{u}$öds) *adv* hacia adentro
**iodine** (*ai*-ö-diin) *n* yodo *m*
**Iran** (i-*raan*) Irán *m*
**Iranian** (i-*rei*-ni-ön) *adj* iraní
**Iraq** (i-*raak*) Irak *m*
**Iraqi** (i-*raa*-ki) *adj* iraquí
**Ireland** (*ai*$^{ö}$-lönd) Irlanda *f*
**Irish** (*ai*$^{ö}$-riʃ) *adj* irlandés
**Irishman** (*ai*$^{ö}$-riʃ-mön) *n* (pl -men) irlandés *m*
**iron** (*ai*-ön) *n* hierro *m*; plancha *f*; de hierro; *v* planchar
**ironical** (ai-*ro*-ni-köl) *adj* irónico
**irony** (*ai*$^{ö}$-rö-ni) *n* ironía *f*
**irregular** (i-*rê*-ghyu-lö) *adj* irregular
**irreparable** (i-*rê*-pö-rö-böl) *adj* irreparable
**irrevocable** (i-*rê*-vö-kö-böl) *adj* irrevocable
**irritable** (*i*-ri-tö-böl) *adj* irritable
**irritate** (*i*-ri-teit) *v* irritar
**is** (is) *v* (pr be)
**island** (*ai*-lönd) *n* isla *f*
**isolate** (*ai*-ssö-leit) *v* aislar
**isolation** (ai-ssö-*lei*-ʃön) *n* aislamiento *m*
**Israel** (*is*-reil) Israel *m*
**Israeli** (is-*rei*-li) *adj* israelí
**issue** (*i*-ʃuu) *v* *distribuir; *n* emisión *f*, tirada *f*, edición *f*; cuestión *f*, punto *m*; consecuencia *f*, resultado *m*, conclusión *f*, término *m*; salida *f*
**it** (it) *pron* lo; **its** *adj* su
**itself** (it-*ssêlf*) *pron* se; **by ~** aislado, solo
**Italian** (i-*tæl*-yön) *adj* italiano
**Italy** (*i*-tö-li) Italia *f*
**itch** (ich) *n* picazón *f*; prurito *m*; *v* picar
**item** (*ai*-töm) *n* ítem *m*; punto *m*
**itinerary** (ai-*ti*-nö-rö-ri) *n* itinerario *m*
**ivory** (*ai*-vö-ri) *n* marfil *m*
**ivy** (*ai*-vi) *n* hiedra *f*

# J

**jack** (dʒæk) *n* gato *m*
**jacket** (*dʒæ*-kit) *n* americana *f*, chaqueta *f*; sobrecubierta *f*; saco *mMe*
**jade** (dʒeid) *n* jade *m*
**jail** (dʒeil) *n* cárcel *f*
**jam** (dʒæm) *n* mermelada *f*; congestión *f*
**janitor** (*dʒæ*-ni-tö) *n* conserje *m*
**January** (*dʒæ*-nyu-ö-ri) enero
**Japan** (dʒö-*pæn*) Japón *m*
**Japanese** (dʒæ-pö-*niis*) *adj* japonés
**jar** (dʒaa) *n* jarra *f*
**jaundice** (*dʒoon*-diss) *n* ictericia *f*
**jaw** (dʒoo) *n* mandíbula *f*
**jealous** (*dʒê*-löss) *adj* celoso
**jealousy** (*dʒê*-lö-ssi) *n* celos
**jeans** (dʒiins) *pl* vaqueros *mpl*
**jelly** (*dʒê*-li) *n* jalea *f*
**jellyfish** (*dʒê*-li-fiʃ) *n* medusa *f*
**jersey** (*dʒöö*-si) *n* jersey *m*
**jet** (dʒêt) *n* chorro *m*; avión a reacción
**jetty** (*dʒê*-ti) *n* muelle *m*
**Jew** (dʒuu) *n* judío *m*, -a *f*
**jewel** (*dʒuu*-öl) *n* joya *f*
**jewel(l)er** (*dʒuu*-ö-lö) *n* joyero *m*, -a *f*
**jewellery,** *Am* **jewelry** (*dʒuu*-öl-ri) *n* joyería *f*
**Jewish** (*dʒuu*-iʃ) *adj* judío
**job** (dʒob) *n* tarea *f*; puesto *m*, empleo *m*
**jobless** (*dʒob*-löss) *adj* desempleado, *Span* parado
**jockey** (*dʒo*-ki) *n* jockey *m*
**join** (dʒoin) *v* juntar; unirse a, asociarse a; ensamblar, reunir
**joint** (dʒoint) *n* articulación *f*; soldadura *f*; *adj* unido, en común
**jointly** (*dʒoint*-li) *adv* juntamente
**joke** (dʒouk) *n* broma *f*
**jolly** (*dʒo*-li) *adj* jovial
**Jordan** (*dʒoo*-dön) Jordania *f*
**Jordanian** (dʒoo-*dei*-ni-ön) *adj* jordano
**journal** (*dʒöö*-nöl) *n* diaro *m*; periódico *m*; revista *f*
**journalism** (*dʒöö*-nö-li-söm) *n* periodismo *m*
**journalist** (*dʒöö*-nö-lisst) *n* periodista *m/f*
**journey** (*dʒöö*-ni) *n* viaje *m*
**joy** (dʒoi) *n* alegría *f*, júbilo *m*
**joyful** (*dʒoi*-föl) *adj* alegre, jubiloso
**jubilee** (*dʒuu*-bi-lii) *n* aniversario *m*
**judge** (dʒadʒ) *n* juez *m/f*; *v* juzgar
**judgment** (*dʒadʒ*-mönt) *n* juicio *m*
**jug** (dʒagh) *n* cántaro *m*
**juggernaut** (*dʒagh*-ö-noot) *n* camión grande *m*
**juice** (dʒuuss) *n* zumo *m*; jugo *m*
**juicy** (*dʒuu*-ssi) *adj* zumoso; jugoso
**July** (dʒu-*lai*) julio
**jump** (dʒamp) *v* saltar; *n* salto *m*
**jumper** (*dʒam*-pö) *n* jersey *m*; *Am* vestido sin mangas
**junction** (*dʒangk*-ʃön) *n* encrucijada *f*; empalme *m*
**June** (dʒuun) junio
**jungle** (*dʒang*-ghöl) *n* selva *f*, jungla *f*
**junior** (*dʒuu*-nyö) *adj* menor; ~ **school** escuela primaria
**junk** (dʒangk) *n* cachivache *m*
**jury** (*dʒuö*-ri) *n* jurado *m*
**just** (dʒasst) *adj* justo; recto; merecido; *adv* apenas; exactamente; solamente
**justice** (*dʒa*-sstiss) *n* derecho *m*; justicia *f*
**justify** (*dʒass*-ti-fai) *v* justificar
**juvenile** (*dʒuu*-vö-nail) *adj* juvenil

# K

**kangaroo** (kæng-ghö-*ruu*) *n* canguro *m*
**keel** (kiil) *n* quilla *f*
**keen** (kiin) *adj* entusiasta; agudo
***keep** (kiip) *v* *tener; guardar; continuar; ~ **away from** *mantenerse alejado de; ~ **off** no tocar; ~ **on** continuar; ~ **quiet** *estarse quieto; ~ **up** perseverar; ~ **up with** *seguir el paso
**kennel** (*kê*-nöl) *n* perrera *f*; perrera *m*
**Kenya** (*kê*-nyö) Kenya *m*
**kerosene** (*kê*-rö-ssiin) *n* petróleo lampante
**kettle** (*kê*-töl) *n* olla *f*
**key** (kii) *n* llave *f*
**keyboard** (*kii*-bood) teclado *m*
**keyhole** (*kii*-houl) *n* ojo de la cerradura
**khaki** (*kaa*-ki) *n* caqui *m*
**kick** (kik) *v* patear; *n* patada *f*
**kickoff** (ki-*kof*) *n* saque inicial
**kid** (kid) *n* niño *m*, chico *m*; cabritilla *f*; *v* bromearse
**kidney** (*kid*-ni) *n* riñón *m*
**kill** (kil) *v* matar
**kilogram** (*ki*-lö-ghræm) *n* kilogramo *m*
**kilometer** *Am*, **kilometre** (*ki*-lö-mii-tö) *n* kilómetro *m*
**kind** (kaind) *adj* amable, bondadoso; bueno; *n* género *m*
**kindergarten** (*kin*-dö-ghaa-tön) *n* escuela de párvulos, jardín de infancia
**king** (king) *n* rey *m*
**kingdom** (*king*-döm) *n* reino *m*
**kiosk** (*kii*-ossk) *n* quiosco *m*
**kiss** (kiss) *n* beso *m*; *v* besar
**kit** (kit) *n* avíos *mpl*
**kitchen** (*ki*-chin) *n* cocina *f*; ~ **garden** huerto *m*; ~ **towel** *Am* paño de cocina
**Kleenex**® (*klii*-nêkss) *n* pañuelo de papel
**knapsack** (*næp*-ssæk) *n* mochila *f*
**knave** (neiv) *n* sota *f*
**knee** (nii) *n* rodilla *f*
**kneecap** (*nii*-kæp) *n* rótula *f*
***kneel** (niil) *v* arrodillarse
**knew** (nyuu) *v* (p know)
**knife** (naif) *n* (pl knives) cuchillo *m*
**knight** (nait) *n* caballero *m*
***knit** (nit) *v* *hacer punto
**knob** (nob) *n* botón *m*; bulto *m*
**knock** (nok) *v* golpear; llamar (a la puerta); *n* golpe *m*; llamada *f* (a la puerta); ~ **against** chocar contra; ~ **down** derribar
**knot** (not) *n* nudo *m*; *v* anudar
***know** (nou) *v* *saber, *conocer
**knowledge** (*no*-lidʒ) *n* conocimiento *m*
**knuckle** (*na*-köl) *n* nudillo *m*

# L

**label** (*lei*-böl) *n* rótulo *m*; etiqueta *f*; *v* rotular
**laboratory** (lö-*bo*-rö-tö-ri) *n* laboratorio *m*
**labo(u)r** (*lei*-bö) *n* trabajo *m*, labor *f*; dolores *mpl*; *v* ajetrearse, bregar; **labor permit** *Am* permiso de trabajo
**labo(u)rer** (*lei*-bö-rö) *n* obrero *m*

**labo(u)r-saving** (*lei*-bö-ssei-ving) *adj* economizador de trabajo
**labyrinth** (*læ*-bö-rinz) *n* laberinto *m*
**lace** (leiss) *n* encaje *m*, puntilla *f*; cordón *m*
**lack** (læk) *n* falta *f*; *v* *carecer
**lacquer** (*læ*-kö) *n* laca *f*
**lad** (læd) *n* joven *m*, muchacho *m*
**ladder** (*læ*-dö) *n* escalera de mano
**lady** (*lei*-di) *n* señora *f*; **ladies' room** lavabos para señoras
**lagoon** (lö-*ghuun*) *n* laguna *f*
**lake** (leik) *n* lago *m*
**lamb** (læm) *n* cordero *m*
**lame** (leim) *adj* cojo
**lamentable** (*læ*-mön-tö-böl) *adj* lamentable
**lamp** (læmp) *n* lámpara *f*
**lamppost** (*læmp*-pousst) *n* poste de farol
**lampshade** (*læmp*-ʃeid) *n* pantalla *f*
**land** (lænd) *n* país *m*, tierra *f*; *v* aterrizar; desembarcar
**landlady** (*lænd*-lei-di) *n* proprietaria *m*, dueña *f*, patrona *f*
**landlord** (*lænd*-lood) *n* propietario *m*, dueño *m*; patrón *m*
**landmark** (*lænd*-maak) *n* punto de referencia; mojón *m*
**landscape** (*lænd*-sskeip) *n* paisaje *m*
**lane** (lein) *n* callejón *m*; pista *f*
**language** (*læng*-gh$^{u}$idʒ) *n* lengua *f*; ~ **laboratory** laboratorio de lenguas
**lantern** (*læn*-tön) *n* linterna *f*
**lap** (*læp*) *n* regazo *m*; falta *f*; *v* traslapar(se)
**lapel** (lö-*pêl*) *n* solapa *f*
**larder** (*laa*-dö) *n* despensa *f*
**large** (laadʒ) *adj* grande; espacioso; **largely** *adv* en gran parte, principalmente
**lark** (laak) *n* alondra *f*
**laryngitis** (læ-rin-*dʒai*-tiss) *n* laringitis *f*
**last** (laasst) *adj* último; precedente; *v* durar; **at** ~ al fin; al final
**lasting** (*laa*-ssting) *adj* duradero
**latchkey** (*læch*-kii) *n* llave de la casa
**late** (leit) *adj* tardío; retrasado
**lately** (*leit*-li) *adv* últimamente, recientemente
**lather** (*laa*-ðö) *n* espuma *f*
**Latin America** (*læ*-tin ö-*mê*-ri-kö) América Latina
**Latin-American** (læ-tin-ö-*mê*-ri-kön) *adj* latinoamericano
**latitude** (*læ*-ti-tyuud) *n* latitud *f*
**laugh** (laaf) *v* *reír; *n* risa *f*; carcajada *f*
**laughter** (*laaf*-tö) *n* risa *f*; risas *fpl*
**launch** (loonch) *v* lanzar; *n* buque a motor
**launching** (*loon*-ching) *n* botadura *f*
**launderette** (loon-dö-*rêt*) *n* lavandería de autoservicio
**laundry** (*loon*-dri) *n* lavandería *f*; ropa sucia
**lavatory** (*læ*-vö-tö-ri) *n* lavabo *m*; aseos *mpl*
**lavish** (*læ*-viʃ) *adj* pródigo; profuso
**law** (loo) *n* ley *f*; derecho *m*; ~ **court** tribunal *m*
**lawful** (*loo*-föl) *adj* lícito
**lawn** (loon) *n* césped *m*
**lawsuit** (*loo*-ssuut) *n* proceso *m*, causa *f*
**lawyer** (*loo*-yö) *n* abogado *m*; jurista *m*
**laxative** (*læk*-ssö-tiv) *n* laxante *m*
***lay** (lei) *v* colocar, *poner; ~ **bricks** mampostear
**layer** (lei$^{ö}$) *n* capa *f*
**layman** (*lei*-mön) *n* lego *m*; profano *m*
**lazy** (*lei*-si) *adj* perezoso
**lead**[1] (liid) *n* ventaja *f*; dirección *f*; traílla *f*
**lead**[2] (lêd) *n* plomo *m*
***lead** (liid) *v* *conducir
**leader** (*lii*-dö) *n* jefe *m*, líder *m*

**leadership** (*lii*-dö-ʃip) *n* dirección *f*
**leading** (*lii*-ding) *adj* dominante, principal
**leaf** (liif) *n* (pl leaves) hoja *f*
**league** (liigh) *n* liga *f*
**leak** (liik) *v* gotear; *n* goteo *m*
**leaky** (*lii*-ki) *adj* agujerado
**lean** (liin) *adj* magro
***lean** (liin) *v* apoyarse
**leap** (liip) *n* salto *m*
***leap** (liip) *v* saltar
**leap year** (*liip*-yi$^{ö}$) *n* año bisiesto
***learn** (löön) *v* aprender
**learner** (*löö*-nö) *n* principiante *m*
**lease** (liiss) *n* contrato de arrendamiento; arrendamiento *m*; *v* *arrendar, alquilar
**leash** (liiʃ) *n* correa *f*
**least** (liisst) *adj* mínimo, menos; **at ~** por lo menos
**leather** (*lê*-ðö) *n* cuero *m*
**leave** (liiv) *n* licencia *f*; permiso *m*
***leave** (liiv) *v* partir, dejar; salir de; **~ out** omitir
**Lebanese** (lê-bö-*niis*) *adj* libanés
**Lebanon** (*lê*-bö-nön) Líbano *m*
**lecture** (*lêk*-chö) *n* curso *m*, conferencia *f*
**left**[1] (lêft) *adj* izquierdo
**left**[2] (lêft) *v* (p, pp leave)
**left-hand** (*lêft*-hænd) *adj* izquierdo, de izquierda
**left-handed** (lêft-*hæn*-did) *adj* zurdo
**leg** (lêgh) *n* pata *f*, pierna *f*
**legacy** (*lê*-ghö-ssi) *n* herencia *f*
**legal** (*lii*-ghöl) *adj* legítimo, legal; jurídico
**legalization** (lii-ghö-lai-*sei*-ʃön) *n* legalización *f*
**legation** (li-*ghei*-ʃön) *n* legación *f*
**legible** (*lê*-dʒi-böl) *adj* legible
**legitimate** (li-*dʒi*-ti-möt) *adj* legítimo
**leisure** (*lê*-ʒö) *n* ocio *m*; tiempo *m* libre
**lemon** (*lê*-mön) *n* limón *m*
**lemonade** (lê-mö-*neid*) *n* limonada *f*
***lend** (lênd) *v* prestar
**length** (lêngz) *n* longitud *f*
**lengthen** (*lêng*-zön) *v* alargar
**lengthways** (*lêngz*-$^{u}$eis) *adv* longitudinalmente
**lens** (lêns) *n* lente *m/f*; **telephoto ~** teleobjetivo *m*; **zoom ~** lente de foco regulable
**leprosy** (*lê*-prö-ssi) *n* lepra *f*
**less** (lêss) *adv* menos
**lessen** (*lê*-ssön) *v* *disminuir
**lesson** (*lê*-ssön) *n* lección *f*
***let** (lêt) *v* dejar; permitir; alquilar; **~ down** decepcionar
**letter** (*lê*-tö) *n* carta *f*; letra *f*; **~ of credit** carta de crédito; **~ of recommendation** carta de recomendación; **~ opener** *Am* abrecartas *m*
**letterbox** (*lê*-tö-bokss) *n* buzón *m*
**lettuce** (*lê*-tiss) *n* lechuga *f*
**level** (*lê*-völ) *adj* igual; plano, llano; *n* nivel *m*; *v* igualar, nivelar; **~ crossing** paso a nivel
**lever** (*lii*-vö) *n* palanca *f*
**Levis** (*lii*-vais) *pl* jeans *mpl*
**liability** (lai-ö-*bi*-lö-ti) *n* responsabilidad *f*
**liable** (*lai*-ö-böl) *adj* responsable; **~ to** sujeto a
**liar** (lair) mentiroso *m*, -a *f*
**liberal** (*li*-bö-röl) *adj* liberal; generoso, dadivoso
**liberation** (li-bö-*rei*-ʃön) *n* liberación *f*
**Liberia** (lai-*bi*$^{ö}$-ri-ö) Liberia *f*
**Liberian** (lai-*bi*$^{ö}$-ri-ön) *adj* liberiano
**liberty** (*li*-bö-ti) *n* libertad *f*
**library** (*lai*-brö-ri) *n* biblioteca *f*
**licence** (*lai*-ssönss) *n* licencia *f*; permiso *m*; **driving ~** permiso de conducir
**license** (*lai*-ssönss) *v* autorizar; *nAm*

licencia *f*; permiso *m*; ~ **number** (número de) matrícula; ~ **plate** (placa de) matrícula
**lick** (lik) *v* lamer
**lid** (lid) *n* tapa *f*
**lie** (lai) *v* *mentir; *n* mentira *f*
***lie** (lai) *v* *yacer; ~ **down** *tenderse
**life** (laif) *n* (pl lives) vida *f*; ~ **insurance** seguro de vida
**lifebelt** (*laif*-bêlt) *n* chaleco salvavidas
**lifetime** (*laif*-taim) *n* vida *f*
**lift** (lift) *v* levantar; *n* ascensor *m*; elevador *mMe*
**light** (lait) *n* luz *f*; *adj* ligero; pálido; ~ **bulb** bombilla *f*
***light** (lait) *v* *encender
**lighter** (*lai*-tö) *n* encendedor *m*
**lighthouse** (*lait*-hauss) *n* faro *m*
**lighting** (*lai*-ting) *n* alumbrado *m*
**lightning** (*lait*-ning) *n* relámpago *m*
**like** (laik) *v* *querer; gustar; *adj* semejante; *conj* como
**likely** (*lai*-kli) *adj* probable
**like-minded** (laik-*main*-did) *adj* unánime
**likewise** (*laik*-ᵘais) *adv* así también, asimismo
**lily** (*li*-li) *n* azucena *f*
**limb** (lim) *n* miembro *m*
**lime** (laim) *n* cal *f*; tilo *m*; lima *f*
**limetree** (*laim*-trii) *n* tilo *m*
**limit** (*li*-mit) *n* límite *m*; *v* limitar
**limp** (limp) *v* cojear; *adj* inerte
**line** (lain) *n* renglón *m*; raya *f*; cordón *m*; línea *f*; cola *f*
**linen** (*li*-nin) *n* lino *m*; ropa blanca
**liner** (*lai*-nö) *n* vapor de línea
**lingerie** (*long̅*-ʒö-rii) *n* ropa interior de mujer
**lining** (*lai*-ning) *n* forro *m*
**link** (lingk) *v* enlazar; *n* enlace *m*; eslabón *m*
**lion** (*lai*-ön) *n* león *m*
**lip** (lip) *n* labio *m*
**lipstick** (*lip*-sstik) *n* lápiz labial
**liqueur** (li-*kyu*ᵒ̈) *n* licor *m*
**liquid** (*li*-kᵘid) *adj* líquido; *n* líquido *m*
**liquor** (*li*-kö) *n* bebidas alcohólicas; ~ **store** *Am* almacén de licores
**liquorice** (*li*-kö-riss) *n* regaliz *m*
**list** (lisst) *n* lista *f*; *v* inscribir
**listen** (*li*-ssön) *v* escuchar
**listener** (*liss*-nö) *n* oyente *m*
**literary** (*li*-trö-ri) *adj* literario
**literature** (*li*-trö-chö) *n* literatura *f*
**liter** *Am*, **litre** (*lii*-tö) *n* litro *m*
**litter** (*li*-tö) *n* desperdicio *m*; trastos *mpl*; lechigada *f*
**little** (*li*-töl) *adj* pequeño; poco
**live**[1] (liv) *v* vivir
**live**[2] (laiv) *adj* vivo
**livelihood** (*laiv*-li-hud) *n* sustento *m*
**lively** (*laiv*-li) *adj* animado
**liver** (*li*-vö) *n* hígado *m*
**living** (*li*-ving) *adj* vivo; *n* vida *f*; **standard of** ~ estándar *m* de vida; ~ **room** *n* sala de estar
**lizard** (*li*-zörd) lagarto *m*
**load** (loud) *n* carga *f*; fardo *m*; *v* cargar
**loaf** (louf) *n* (pl loaves) barra *f* (de pan)
**loan** (loun) *n* préstamo *m*
**lobby** (*lo*-bi) *n* vestíbulo *m*
**lobster** (*lob*-sstö) *n* langosta *f*
**local** (*lou*-köl) *adj* local; ~ **call** llamada local; ~ **train** tren de cercanías
**locality** (lou-*kæ*-lö-ti) *n* localidad *f*
**locate** (lou-*keit*) *v* localizar
**location** (lou-*kei*-ʃön) *n* colocación *f*; localidad *f*
**lock** (lok) *v* *cerrar con llave; *n* cerradura *f*; esclusa *f*; ~ **up** guardar con llave
**locker** (*lo*-kö) *n* taquilla *f*
**locomotive** (lou-kö-*mou*-tiv) *n* locomotora *f*
**lodge** (lodʒ) *v* alojar; *n* apeadero de caza; posada *f*

**lodger** (*lo*-dʒö) *n* huésped *m*
**lodgings** (*lo*-dʒings) *pl* alojamiento *m*
**log** (logh) *n* madero *m*; tronco *m*
**logic** (*lo*-dʒik) *n* lógica *f*
**logical** (*lo*-dʒi-köl) *adj* lógico
**lonely** (*loun*-li) *adj* solitario; aislado
**long** (long) *adj* largo; ~ **for** anhelar; **no longer** ya no
**longing** (*long*-ing) *n* anhelo *m*
**longitude** (*lon*-dʒi-tyuud) *n* longitud *f*
**look** (luk) *v* mirar; *parecer, *tener aires de; *n* ojeada *f*, mirada *f*; aspecto *m*; ~ **after** ocuparse de, cuidar de; ~ **at** mirar; ~ **for** buscar; ~ **out** prestar atención, *tener cuidado; ~ **up** buscar
**looking-glass** (*lu*-king-ghlaass) *n* espejo *m*
**loop** (luup) *n* lazo *m*; presilla *f*
**loose** (luuss) *adj* suelto
**loosen** (*luu*-ssön) *v* *soltar
**lord** (lood) *n* lord *m*; señor *m*
**lorry** (*lo*-ri) *n* camión *m*
***lose** (luus) *v* *perder
**loser** (*luu*-sö) perdedor *m*, -a *f*; fracasado *m*, -a *f*
**loss** (loss) *n* pérdida *f*
**lost** (losst) *adj* perdido; desaparecido; ~ **and found** objetos perdidos; ~ **property office** oficina de objetos perdidos
**lot** (lot) *n* lote *m*; suerte *f*, destino *m*; masa *f*, cantidad *f*; parcela *f*; **a** ~ mucho(s)
**lotion** (*lou*-ʃön) *n* loción *f*; **aftershave** ~ loción para después de afeitarse
**lottery** (*lo*-tö-ri) *n* lotería *f*
**loud** (laud) *adj* alto; ruidoso; fuerte
**loudspeaker** (laud-*sspii*-kö) *n* altavoz *m*
**lounge** (laundʒ) *n* salón *m*
**louse** (lauss) *n* (pl lice) piojo *m*
**love** (lav) *v* amar; *n* amor *m*; **in** ~ enamorado
**lovely** (*lav*-li) *adj* encantador; bonito
**lover** (*la*-vö) *n* amante *m*/*f*
**love story** (*lav*-sstoo-ri) *n* historia de amor
**low** (lou) *adj* bajo; profundo; deprimido; ~ **tide** bajamar *f*
**lower** (*lou*-ö) *v* bajar; rebajar; arriar; *adj* inferior
**lowlands** (*lou*-lönds) *pl* tierra baja
**loyal** (*loi*-öl) *adj* leal
**lubricate** (*luu*-bri-keit) *v* lubrificar, lubricar
**lubrication** (luu-bri-*kei*-ʃön) *n* lubricación *f*; ~ **oil** aceite lubricante; ~ **system** sistema de lubricación
**luck** (lak) *n* éxito *m*, suerte *f*; azar *m*
**lucky** (*la*-ki) *adj* afortunado; dichoso; ~ **charm** talismán *m*
**ludicrous** (*luu*-di-kröss) *adj* ridículo, grotesco
**luggage** (*la*-ghidʒ) *n* equipaje *m*; **hand** ~ equipaje de mano; **left** ~ **office** consigna *f*; ~ **rack** portabagajes *m*, rejilla *f*; ~ **van** furgón de equipajes
**lukewarm** (*luuk*-$^{u}$oom) *adj* tibio
**lumbago** (lam-*bei*-ghou) *n* lumbago *m*
**luminous** (*luu*-mi-nöss) *adj* luminoso
**lump** (lamp) *n* nudo *m*, grumo *m*, terrón *m*; chichón *m*; ~ **of sugar** terrón de azúcar; ~ **sum** suma global
**lumpy** (*lam*-pi) *adj* apelmazado; deforme; desproporcionado
**lunacy** (*luu*-nö-ssi) *n* locura *f*
**lunatic** (*luu*-nö-tik) *adj* lunático; *n* alienado *m*
**lunch** (lanch) *n* almuerzo *m*
**luncheon** (*lan*-chön) *n* almuerzo *m*
**lung** (lang) *n* pulmón *m*
**lust** (lasst) *n* lujuria *f*; concupiscencia *f*
**luxurious** (lagh-*ʒu*$^{ö}$-ri-öss) *adj* lujoso
**luxury** (*lak*-ʃö-ri) *n* lujo *m*

# M

**machine** (mö-*ʃiin*) *n* aparato *m*, máquina *f*
**machinery** (mö-*ʃii*-nö-ri) *n* maquinaria *f*; mecanismo *m*
**mackerel** (*mæ*-kröl) *n* (pl ~) escombro *m*
**mackintosh** (*mæ*-kin-toʃ) *n* impermeable *m*
**mad** (mæd) *adj* loco; rabioso; furioso
**madam** (*mæ*-döm) *n* señora *f*
**madness** (*mæd*-nöss) *n* locura *f*
**magazine** (mæ-ghö-*siin*) *n* revista *f*
**magic** (*mæ*-dʒik) *n* magia *f*; *adj* mágico
**magician** (mö-*dʒi*-ʃön) *n* mago *m*, prestidigitador *m*
**magistrate** (*mæ*-dʒi-sstreit) *n* magistrado *m*
**magnetic** (mægh-*nê*-tik) *adj* magnético
**magneto** (mægh-*nii*-tou) *n* (pl ~s) magneto *m*
**magnificent** (mægh-*ni*-fi-ssönt) *adj* magnífico; grandioso, espléndido
**magnify** (*mægh*-ni-fai) *v* aumentar; magnificar
**magpie** (*mægh*-pai) *n* urraca *f*
**maid** (meid) *n* criada *f*; sirvienta *f*
**maiden name** (*mei*-dön neim) apellido de soltera
**mail** (meil) *n* correo *m*; *v* enviar por correo
**mailbox** (*meil*-bokss) *nAm* buzón *m*
**main** (mein) *adj* principal; mayor; ~ **deck** puente superior; ~ **line** línea principal; ~ **road** camino principal; ~ **street** calle mayor
**mainland** (*mein*-lönd) *n* tierra firme
**mainly** (*mein*-li) *adv* principalmente
**mains** (meins) *pl* conducción principal
**maintain** (mein-*tein*) *v* *mantener
**maintenance** (*mein*-tö-nönss) *n* mantenimiento *m*
**maize** (meis) *n* maíz *m*
**major** (*mei*-dʒö) *adj* grande; mayor; *n* mayor *m*
**majority** (mö-*dʒo*-rö-ti) *n* mayoría *f*
***make** (meik) *v* *hacer; ganar; *conseguir; ~ **do with** arreglarse con; ~ **good** compensar; ~ **up** redactar
**make-up** (*mei*-kap) *n* maquillaje *m*
**malaria** (mö-*lê*ö-ri-ö) *n* malaria *f*
**Malay** (mö-*lei*) *n* malayo *m*
**Malaysia** (mö-*lei*-si-ö) Malasia *f*
**Malaysian** (mö-*lei*-si-ön) *adj* malayo
**male** (meil) *adj* macho
**malicious** (mö-*li*-ʃöss) *adj* malicioso
**malignant** (mö-*ligh*-nönt) *adj* maligno
**mallet** (*mæ*-lit) *n* mazo *m*
**malnutrition** (mæl-nyu-*tri*-ʃön) *n* desnutrición *f*
**mammal** (*mæ*-möl) *n* mamífero *m*
**mammoth** (*mæ*-möz) *n* mamut *m*
**man** (mæn) *n* (pl men) hombre *m*; **men's room** lavabos para caballeros
**manage** (*mæ*-nidʒ) *v* administrar; *tener éxito
**manageable** (*mæ*-ni-dʒö-böl) *adj* manejable
**management** (*mæ*-nidʒ-mönt) *n* manejo *m*; gestión *f*
**manager** (*mæ*-ni-dʒö) *n* jefe *m*, director *m*, -a *f*
**mandarin** (*mæn*-dö-rin) *n* mandarina *f*
**mandate** (*mæn*-deit) *n* mandato *m*
**manger** (*mein*-dʒö) *n* pesebre *m*
**manicure** (*mæ*-ni-kyuö) *n* manicura *f*; *v* *hacer la manicura
**manipulate** (mæ-*ni*-pyö-leit) *v* *person, bones* manipular
**mankind** (mæn-*kaind*) *n* humanidad *f*
**mannequin** (*mæ*-nö-kin) *n* maniquí *m*
**manner** (*mæ*-nö) *n* modo *m*, manera *f*;

**manners** *pl* modales *mpl*
**manor house** (*mæ*-nö-hauss) *n* casa señorial
**mansion** (*mæn*-ʃön) *n* mansión *f*
**manual** (*mæ*-nyu-öl) *adj* manual
**manufacture** (mæ-nyu-*fæk*-chö) *v* fabricar
**manufacturer** (mæ-nyu-*fæk*-chö-rö) *n* fabricante *m*
**manure** (mö-*nyu*ö) *n* estiércol *m*, abono *m*
**manuscript** (*mæ*-nyu-sskript) *n* manuscrito *m*
**many** (*mê*-ni) *adj* muchos
**map** (mæp) *n* carta *f*; mapa *m*; plano *m*
**maple** (*mei*-pöl) *n* arce *m*
**marble** (*maa*-böl) *n* mármol *m*; canica *f*
**March** (maach) marzo
**march** (maach) *v* marchar; *n* marcha *f*
**mare** (mêö) *n* yegua *f*
**margarine** (maa-dʒö-*riin*) *n* margarina *f*
**margin** (*maa*-dʒin) *n* margen *m*
**marine** (mæ-*riin*) *adj* marino; *m* marine *m/f*
**maritime** (*mæ*-ri-taim) *adj* marítimo
**mark** (maak) *v* marcar; caracterizar; *n* marca *f*; nota *f*; blanco *m*
**market** (*maa*-kit) *n* mercado *m*
**marketplace** (*maa*-kit-pleiss) *n* plaza de mercado
**marmalade** (*maa*-mö-leid) *n* confitura *f*
**marriage** (*mæ*-ridʒ) *n* matrimonio *m*
**marrow** (*mæ*-rou) *n* médula *f*
**marry** (*mæ*-ri) *v* casarse; **married** *adj* casado; **married couple** cónyuges *mpl*
**marsh** (maaʃ) *n* pantano *m*
**martyr** (*maa*-tö) *n* mártir *m*
**marvel** (*maa*-völ) *n* maravilla *f*; *v* maravillarse
**marvellous** (*maa*-vö-löss) *adj* maravilloso
**mascara** (mæ-*sskaa*-rö) *n* rímel *m*
**masculine** (*mæ*-sskyu-lin) *adj* masculino
**mash** (mæʃ) *v* machacar
**mask** (maassk) *n* máscara *f*
**Mass** (mæss) *n* misa *f*
**mass** (mæss) *n* masa *f*; ~ **production** producción en serie
**massage** (*mæ*-ssaaʒ) *n* masaje *m*; *v* *dar masaje
**masseur** (mæ-*ssöö*) *n* masajista *m*
**massive** (*mæ*-ssiv) *adj* macizo
**mast** (maasst) *n* mástil *m*
**master** (*maa*-sstö) *n* maestro *m*; patrón *m*; profesor *m*; *v* dominar
**masterpiece** (*maa*-sstö-piiss) *n* obra maestra
**mat** (mæt) *n* estera *f*; *adj* mate, apagado
**match** (mæch) *n* cerilla *f*; partido *m*; cerillo *mMe*; *v* *hacer juego con
**matchbox** (*mæch*-bokss) *n* caja de cerillas
**material** (mö-*ti*ö-ri-öl) *n* material *m*; tejido *m*; *adj* material
**mathematical** (mæ-zö-*mæ*-ti-köl) *adj* matemático
**mathematics** (mæ-zö-*mæ*-tikss) *n* matemáticas *fpl*
**matrimony** (*mæ*-tri-mö-ni) *n* matrimonio *m*
**matter** (*mæ*-tö) *n* materia *f*; asunto *m*, cuestión *f*; *v* *tener importancia; **as a ~ of fact** efectivamente, en realidad
**matter-of-fact** (mæ-tö-röv-*fækt*) *adj* desapasionado; práctico
**mattress** (*mæ*-tröss) *n* colchón *m*
**mature** (mö-*tyu*ö) *adj* maduro
**maturity** (mö-*tyu*ö-rö-ti) *n* madurez *f*
**mauve** (mouv) *adj* malva
**May** (mei) mayo
***may** (mei) *v* *poder
**maybe** (*mei*-bii) *adv* quizás

**mayor** (mê$^{ö}$) *n* alcalde *m*
**maze** (meis) *n* laberinto *m*
**me** (mii) *pron* me
**meadow** (*mê*-dou) *n* prado *m*
**meal** (miil) *n* comida *f*
**mean** (miin) *adj* mezquino; *n* promedio *m*
***mean** (miin) *v* significar; *querer decir
**meaning** (*mii*-ning) *n* significado *m*
**meaningless** (*mii*-ning-löss) *adj* sin sentido
**means** (miins) *n* medio *m*; **by no ~** en ningún caso, de ningún modo
**meantime: in the ~** (in ðö *miin*-taim) entretanto
**meanwhile** (*miin*-$^{u}$ail) *adv* entretanto
**measles** (*mii*-söls) *n* sarampión *m*
**measure** (*mê*-ʒö) *v* *medir; *n* medida *f*
**meat** (miit) *n* carne *f*
**mechanic** (mi-*kæ*-nik) *n* mecánico *m*
**mechanical** (mi-*kæ*-ni-köl) *adj* mecánico
**mechanism** (*mê*-kö-ni-söm) *n* mecanismo *m*
**medal** (*mê*-döl) *n* medalla *f*
**media** (*mii*-diö) *npl*: **the ~** los medios de comunicación
**mediaeval** (mê-di-*ii*-völ) *adj* medieval
**mediate** (*mii*-di-eit) *v* mediar
**mediator** (*mii*-di-ei-tö) *n* mediador *m*
**medical** (*mê*-di-köl) *adj* médico
**medicine** (*mêd*-ssin) *n* medicamento *m*; medicina *f*
**meditate** (*mê*-di-teit) *v* meditar
**Mediterranean** (mê-di-tö-*rei*-ni-ön) Mediterráneo
**medium** (*mii*-di-öm) *adj* mediano, medio
***meet** (miit) *v* *encontrarse con
**meeting** (*mii*-ting) *n* asamblea *f*, reunión *f*; encuentro *m*
**meeting place** (*mii*-ting-pleiss) *n* lugar de reunión
**melancholy** (*mê*-löng-kö-li) *n* melancolía *f*
**mellow** (*mê*-lou) *adj* suave
**melodrama** (*mê*-lö-draa-mö) *n* melodrama *m*
**melody** (*mê*-lö-di) *n* melodía *f*
**melon** (*mê*-lön) *n* melón *m*
**melt** (mêlt) *v* fundir
**member** (*mêm*-bö) *n* miembro *m*; **Member of Parliament** diputado *m*
**membership** (*mêm*-bö-ʃip) *n* afiliación *f*
**memo** (*mê*-mou) *n* (pl ~s) apunte *m*
**memorable** (*mê*-mö-rö-böl) *adj* memorable
**memorial** (mö-*moo*-ri-öl) *n* monumento *m*
**memorize** (*mê*-mö-rais) *v* aprenderse de memoria
**memory** (*mê*-mö-ri) *n* memoria *f*; recuerdo *m*
**mend** (mênd) *v* reparar, *remendar
**menstruation** (mên-sstru-*ei*-ʃön) *n* menstruación *f*
**mental** (*mên*-töl) *adj* mental
**mention** (*mên*-ʃön) *v* nombrar, mencionar; *n* mención *f*
**menu** (*mê*-nyuu) *n* menú *m*
**merchandise** (*möö*-chön-dais) *n* mercancía *f*
**merchant** (*möö*-chönt) *n* comerciante *m*
**merciful** (*möö*-ssi-föl) *adj* misericordioso
**mercury** (*möö*-kyu-ri) *n* mercurio *m*
**mercy** (*möö*-ssi) *n* misericordia *f*, clemencia *f*
**mere** (mi$^{ö}$) *adj* puro; mero
**merely** (*mi*$^{ö}$-li) *adv* solamente
**merge** (mööd3) *v* juntarse, unirse; fusionarse
**merger** (*möö*-d3ö) *n* fusión *f*
**merit** (*mê*-rit) *v* *merecer; *n* mérito *m*

**merry** (*mê*-ri) *adj* alegre; feliz
**merry-go-round** (*mê*-ri-ghou-raund) *n* tiovivo *m*, caballitos *mpl*
**mesh** (mêʃ) *n* malla *f*
**mess** (mêss) *n* desorden *m*; confusión *f*; ~ **up** estropear
**message** (*mê*-ssidʒ) *n* mensaje *m*
**messenger** (*mê*-ssin-dʒö) *n* mensajero *m*
**metal** (*mê*-töl) *n* metal *m*; metálico
**meter** (*mii*-tö) *n* contador *m*; *nAm* metro *m*
**method** (*mê*-zöd) *n* método *m*; orden *m*
**methodical** (mö-*zo*-di-köl) *adj* metódico
**metre** (*mii*-tö) *n* metro *m*
**Mexican** (*mêk*-ssi-kön) *adj* mejicano; *n* mejicano *m*
**Mexico** (*mêk*-ssi-kou) Méjico *m*
**mice** (mais) *n* (pl mouse)
**microphone** (*mai*-krö-foun) *n* micrófono *m*
**midday** (*mid*-dei) *n* mediodía *m*
**middle** (*mi*-döl) *n* medio *m*; *adj* medio; **Middle Ages** Edad Media; ~ **class** clase media; **middle-class** *adj* de la clase media
**midnight** (*mid*-nait) *n* medianoche *f*
**midst** (midsst) *n* medio *m*
**midsummer** (*mid*-ssa-mö) *n* pleno verano
**midwife** (*mid*-ᵘaif) *n* (pl -wives) comadrona *f*
**might** (mait) *n* fuerza *f*; poder *m*
***might** (mait) *v* *poder
**mighty** (*mai*-ti) *adj* fuerte; poderoso
**migraine** (*mi*-ghrein) *n* migraña *f*; jaqueca *f*
**mild** (maild) *adj* suave; templado; manso
**mildew** (*mil*-dyu) *n* moho *m*
**mile** (mail) *n* milla *f*
**mileage** (*mai*-lidʒ) *n* millaje *m*
**milepost** (*mail*-pousst) *n* cipo *m*
**milestone** (*mail*-sstoun) *n* piedra miliar
**milieu** (*mii*-lyöö) *n* ambiente *m*; mundo circundante
**military** (*mi*-li-tö-ri) *adj* militar; ~ **force** fuerzas armadas
**milk** (milk) *n* leche *f*
**milkman** (*milk*-mön) *n* (pl -men) lechero *m*
**milkshake** (*milk*-ʃeik) *n* batido de leche
**milky** (*mil*-ki) *adj* lechoso
**mill** (mil) *n* molino *m*; fábrica *f*
**miller** (*mi*-lö) *n* molinero *m*
**million** (*mil*-yön) *n* millón *m*
**millionaire** (mil-yö-*nê*ᵒ̈) *n* millonario *m*, -a *f*
**mince** (minss) *v* picar
**mind** (maind) *n* mente *f*; *v* *hacer objeción a; fijarse en, *tener cuidado con
**mine** (main) *n* mina *f*
**miner** (*mai*-nö) *n* minero *m*
**mineral** (*mi*-nö-röl) *n* mineral *m*; ~ **water** agua mineral
**mingle** (*ming*-göl) *v of sounds, smells* mezclarse; *at party* alternar
**miniature** (*min*-yö-chö) *n* miniatura *f*
**minimum** (*mi*-ni-möm) *n* mínimum *m*
**mining** (*mai*-ning) *n* minería *f*
**minister** (*mi*-ni-sstö) *n* ministro *m*; clérigo *m*; **Prime Minister** Presidente de Consejo de ministros
**ministry** (*mi*-ni-sstri) *n* ministerio *m*
**mink** (mingk) *n* visón *m*
**minor** (*mai*-nö) *adj* pequeño, escaso, menor; secundario; *n* menor de edad
**minority** (mai-*no*-rö-ti) *n* minoría *f*
**mint** (mint) *n* menta *f*
**minus** (*mai*-nöss) *prep* menos
**minute**[1] (*mi*-nit) *n* minuto *m*; **minutes** actas
**minute**[2] (mai-*nyuut*) *adj* menudo

**miracle** (*mi*-rö-köl) *n* milagro *m*
**miraculous** (mi-*ræ*-kyu-löss) *adj* milagroso
**mirror** (*mi*-rö) *n* espejo *m*
**misbehave** (miss-bi-*heiv*) *v* portarse mal
**miscarriage** (miss-*kæ*-ridʒ) *n* aborto *m*
**miscellaneous** (mi-ssö-*lei*-ni-öss) *adj* misceláneo
**mischief** (*miss*-chif) *n* diabluras *fpl*; mal *m*, daño *m*, malicia *f*
**mischievous** (*miss*-chi-vöss) *adj* travieso
**miserable** (*mi*-sö-rö-böl) *adj* desdichado; triste; abatido
**misery** (*mi*-sö-ri) *n* tristeza *f*; necesidad *f*
**misfortune** (miss-*foo*-chên) *n* desgracia *f*; contratiempo *m*, infortunio *m*
**mishap** (*miss*-hæp) contratiempo *m*
***mislay** (miss-*lei*) *v* extraviar
**misplaced** (miss-*pleisst*) *adj* inoportuno; fuera de lugar
**mispronounce** (miss-prö-*naunss*) *v* pronunciar mal
**miss**[1] (miss) señorita *f*
**miss**[2] (miss) *v* *perder; echar de menos
**missing** (*mi*-ssing) *adj* que falta; ~ **person** desaparecido *m*
**mist** (misst) *n* niebla *f*
**mistake** (mi-*ssteik*) *n* error *m*, equivocación *f*
***mistake** (mi-*ssteik*) *v* confundir
**mistaken** (mi-*sstei*-kön) *adj* equivocado; ***be** ~ equivocarse
**mister** (*mi*-sstö) señor *m*
**mistress** (*mi*-sströss) *n* señora *f*; dueña *f*; querida *f*
**mistrust** (miss-*trasst*) *v* desconfiar de
**misty** (*mi*-ssti) *adj* nebuloso
***misunderstand** (mi-ssan-dö-*sstænd*) *v* comprender mal
**misunderstanding** (mi-ssan-dö-*sstæn*-ding) *n* equivocación *f*
**misuse** (miss-*yuuss*) *n* abuso *m*
**mittens** (*mi*-töns) *pl* guantes *mpl*
**mix** (mikss) *v* mezclar; ~ **with** alternar con
**mixed** (miksst) *adj* mezclado
**mixer** (*mik*-ssö) *n* batidora *f*
**mixture** (*mikss*-chö) *n* mezcla *f*
**moan** (moun) *v* *gemir
**moat** (mout) *n* foso *m*
**mobile** (*mou*-bail) *adj* móvil; ~ **phone** teléfono *m* móvil
**mock** (mok) *v* burlarse de
**mockery** (*mo*-kö-ri) *n* burla *f*
**model** (*mo*-döl) *n* modelo *m*/*f*; patrón *m*; *v* modelar
**modem** (*mou*-dêm) módem *m*
**moderate** (*mo*-dö-röt) *adj* moderado
**modern** (*mo*-dön) *adj* moderno
**modest** (*mo*-disst) *adj* modesto
**modesty** (*mo*-di-ssti) *n* modestia *f*
**modify** (*mo*-di-fai) *v* modificar
**moist** (moisst) *adj* húmedo
**moisten** (*moi*-ssön) *v* *humedecer
**moisture** (*moiss*-chö) *n* humedad *f*; **moisturizing cream** crema hidratante
**molar** (*mou*-lö) *n* muela *f*
**moment** (*mou*-mönt) *n* momento *m*
**momentary** (*mou*-mön-tö-ri) *adj* momentáneo
**monarch** (*mo*-nök) *n* monarca *m*
**monarchy** (*mo*-nö-ki) *n* monarquía *f*
**monastery** (*mo*-nö-sstri) *n* monasterio *m*
**Monday** (*man*-di) lunes *m*
**monetary** (*ma*-ni-tö-ri) *adj* monetario; ~ **unit** unidad monetaria
**money** (*ma*-ni) *n* dinero *m*; ~ **exchange** oficina de cambio; ~ **order** giro *m* postal
**monk** (mangk) *n* monje *m*

**monkey** (*mang*-ki) *n* mono *m*
**monologue** (*mo*-no-logh) *n* monólogo *m*
**monopoly** (mö-*no*-pö-li) *n* monopolio *m*
**monotonous** (mö-*no*-tö-nöss) *adj* monótono
**month** (manz) *n* mes *m*
**monthly** (*manz*-li) *adj* mensual; ~ **magazine** revista mensual
**monument** (*mo*-nyu-mönt) *n* monumento *m*
**mood** (muud) *n* humor *m*; disposición *f*
**moon** (muun) *n* luna *f*
**moonlight** (*muun*-lait) *n* luz de la luna
**moor** (mu$^{ö}$) *n* brezal *m*, turbera *f*
**moose** (muuss) *n* (pl ~, ~s) alce *m*
**moped** (*mou*-pêd) *n* bicimotor *m*
**moral** (*mo*-röl) *n* moraleja *f*; *adj* moral; virtuoso; **morals** moralidad *f*; ética *f*
**morality** (mö-*ræ*-lö-ti) *n* moralidad *f*
**more** (moo) *adj* más; **once** ~ otra vez
**moreover** (moo-*rou*-vö) *adv* además
**morning** (*moo*-ning) *n* mañana *f*; ~ **paper** diario matutino
**Moroccan** (mö-*ro*-kön) *adj* marroquí
**Morocco** (mö-*ro*-kou) Marruecos *m*
**morphia** (*moo*-fi-ö) *n* morfina *f*
**morphine** (*moo*-fiin) *n* morfina *f*
**morsel** (*moo*-ssöl) *n* trozo *m*; bocado *m*
**mortal** (*moo*-töl) *adj* fatal, mortal
**mortgage** (*moo*-ghidʒ) *n* hipoteca *f*
**mosaic** (mö-*sei*-ik) *n* mosaico *m*
**mosque** (mossk) *n* mezquita *f*
**mosquito** (mö-*sskii*-tou) *n* (pl ~es) mosquito *m*; ~ **net** mosquitero *m*
**moss** (moss) *n* musgo *m*
**most** (mousst) *adj* el más; **at** ~ a lo sumo, como máximo; ~ **of all** sobre todo
**mostly** (*mousst*-li) *adv* generalmente
**motel** (mou-*têl*) *n* motel *m*
**moth** (moz) *n* polilla *f*
**mother** (*ma*-ðö) *n* madre *f*; ~ **tongue** lengua materna
**mother-in-law** (*ma*-ðö-rin-loo) *n* (pl mothers-) suegra *f*
**mother of pearl** (ma-ðö-röv-*pööl*) *n* nácar *m*
**motion** (*mou*-ʃön) *n* movimiento *m*; moción *f*
**motivate** (*mou*-ti-veit) *v* motivar
**motive** (*mou*-tiv) *n* motivo *m*
**motor** (*mou*-tö) *n* motor *m*; *v* *ir en coche; **starter** ~ motor de arranque
**motorbike** (*mou*-tö-baik) *nAm* motocicleta *f*
**motorboat** (*mou*-tö-bout) *n* bote a motor
**motorcar** (*mou*-tö-kaa) *n* automóvil *m*
**motorcycle** (*mou*-tö-ssai-köl) *n* motocicleta *f*
**motoring** (*mou*-tö-ring) *n* automovilismo *m*
**motorist** (*mou*-tö-risst) *n* automovilista *m*
**motorway** (*mou*-tö-$^{u}$ei) *n* autopista *f*
**motto** (*mo*-tou) *n* (pl ~es, ~s) lema *f*
**mo(u)ldy** (*moul*-di) *adj* enmohecido
**mound** (maund) *n* montículo *m*
**mount** (maunt) *v* montar; *n* monte *m*
**mountain** (*maun*-tin) *n* montaña *f*; ~ **pass** paso *m*; ~ **range** cordillera *f*
**mountaineering** (maun-ti-*ni*$^{ö}$-ring) *n* montañismo *m*
**mountainous** (*maun*-ti-nöss) *adj* montañoso
**mourning** (*moo*-ning) *n* luto *m*
**mouse** (mauss) *n* (pl mice) ratón *m*
**moustache** (mö-*sstaaʃ*) *n* bigote *m*
**mouth** (mauz) *n* boca *f*; hocico *m*; desembocadura *f*
**mouthwash** (*mauz*-$^{u}$oʃ) *n* enjuague bucal

**movable** (*muu*-vö-böl) *adj* movible
**move** (muuv) *v* *mover; trasladar; mudarse; *conmover; *n* jugada *f*, paso *m*; mudanza *f*
**movement** (*muuv*-mönt) *n* movimiento *m*
**movie** (*muu*-vi) *n* película *f*; **the ~s** el cine
**much** (mach) *adj* mucho; **as ~** tanto
**muck** (mak) *n* suciedad *f*
**mud** (mad) *n* lodo *m*
**muddle** (*ma*-döl) *n* dédalo *m*, embrollo *m*; *v* embrollar
**muddy** (*ma*-di) *adj* lodoso
**mug** (magh) *n* vaso *m*, taza *f*
**mule** (myuul) *n* mulo *m*; mula *f*
**multiplication** (mal-ti-pli-*kei*-ʃön) *n* multiplicación *f*
**multiply** (*mal*-ti-plai) *v* multiplicar
**mumps** (mampss) *n* paperas *fpl*
**municipal** (myuu-*ni*-ssi-pöl) *adj* municipal
**municipality** (myuu-ni-ssi-*pæ*-lö-ti) *n* municipalidad *f*
**murder** (*möö*-dö) *n* asesinato *m*; *v* asesinar
**murderer** (*möö*-dö-rö) *n* asesino *m*, -a *f*
**muscle** (*ma*-ssöl) *n* músculo *m*
**muscular** (*ma*-sskyu-lö) *adj* musculoso
**museum** (myuu-*sii*-öm) *n* museo *m*
**mushroom** (*maʃ*-ruum) *n* seta *f*; hongo *m*
**music** (*myuu*-sik) *n* música *f*; **~ academy** conservatorio *m*; **~ hall** teatro de variedades
**musical** (*myuu*-si-köl) *adj* musical; *n* comedia musical
**musician** (myuu-*si*-ʃön) *n* músico *m*, -a *f*
**mussel** (*ma*-ssöl) *n* mejillón *m*
***must** (masst) *v* *tener que
**mustard** (*ma*-sstöd) *n* mostaza *f*
**mute** (myuut) *adj* mudo
**mutiny** (*myuu*-ti-ni) *n* amotinamiento *m*
**mutton** (*ma*-tön) *n* carnero *m*
**mutual** (*myuu*-chu-öl) *adj* mutuo, recíproco
**my** (mai) *adj* mi
**myself** (mai-*ssêlf*) *pron* me; yo mismo
**mysterious** (mi-*ssti*$^{ö}$-ri-öss) *adj* misterioso
**mystery** (*mi*-sstö-ri) *n* enigma *m*, misterio *m*
**myth** (miz) *n* mito *m*

# N

**nail** (neil) *n* uña *f*; clavo *m*
**nailbrush** (*neil*-braʃ) *n* cepillo para las uñas
**nail file** (*neil*-fail) *n* lima para las uñas
**nail polish** (*neil*-po-liʃ) *n* laca de uñas
**nail scissors** (*neil*-ssi-sös) *pl* tijeras para las uñas
**naïve** (naa-*iiv*) *adj* ingenuo
**naked** (*nei*-kid) *adj* desnudo
**name** (neim) *n* nombre *m*; *v* nombrar; **in the ~ of** en nombre de
**namely** (*neim*-li) *adv* a saber
**nap** (næp) *n* siesta *f*
**napkin** (*næp*-kin) *n* servilleta *f*
**nappy** (*næ*-pi) *n* pañal *m*
**narcosis** (naa-*kou*-ssiss) *n* (pl -ses) narcosis *f*
**narcotic** (naa-*ko*-tik) *n* narcótico *m*

**narration** (nö-*rei*-ʃön) *n* narración *f*
**narrow** (*næ*-rou) *adj* angosto, estrecho
**narrow-minded** (næ-rou-*main*-did) *adj* intolerante
**nasty** (*naa*-ssti) *adj* antipático, desagradable; repulsivo; sucio
**nation** (*nei*-ʃön) *n* nación *f*; pueblo *m*
**national** (*næ*-ʃö-nöl) *adj* nacional; del Estado; ~ **anthem** himno nacional; ~ **dress** traje del país; ~ **park** parque nacional
**nationality** (næ-ʃö-*næ*-lö-ti) *n* nacionalidad *f*
**nationalize** (*næ*-ʃö-nö-lais) *v* nacionalizar
**native** (*nei*-tiv) *n* nativo *m*, -a *f*; indígena *m*; *adj* nativo; ~ **country** patria *f*, país natal; ~ **language** lengua materna
**natural** (*næ*-chö-röl) *adj* natural; innato
**naturally** (*næ*-chö-rö-li) *adv* naturalmente, por supuesto
**nature** (*nei*-chö) *n* naturaleza *f*; natural *m*
**naughty** (*noo*-ti) *adj* travieso
**nausea** (*noo*-ssi-ö) *n* náusea *f*
**naval** (*nei*-völ) *adj* naval
**navel** (*nei*-völ) *n* ombligo *m*
**navigable** (*næ*-vi-ghö-böl) *adj* navegable
**navigate** (*næ*-vi-gheit) *v* navegar
**navigation** (næ-vi-*ghei*-ʃön) *n* navegación *f*
**navy** (*nei*-vi) *n* marina *f*
**near** (niö) *prep* cerca de; *adj* cercano
**nearby** (*niö*-bai) *adj* cercano; próximo
**nearly** (*niö*-li) *adv* casi, de cerca; por poco
**neat** (niit) *adj* pulcro; bien arreglado; puro
**necessary** (*nê*-ssö-ssö-ri) *adj* necesario
**necessity** (nö-*ssê*-ssö-ti) *n* necesidad *f*
**neck** (nêk) *n* cuello *m*; **nape of the** ~ nuca *f*
**necklace** (*nêk*-löss)*n* collar *m*
**necktie** (*nêk*-tai) *n* corbata *f*
**need** (niid) *v* deber, necesitar; *n* necesidad *f*; ~ **to** deber
**needle** (*nii*-döl) *n* aguja *f*
**needlework** (*nii*-döl-uöök) *n* labor de aguja
**negative** (*nê*-ghö-tiv) *adj* negativo; *n* negativo *m*
**neglect** (ni-*ghlêkt*) *v* descuidar; no cumplir; olvidar; *n* negligencia *f*; abandono *m*
**neglectful** (ni-*ghlêkt*-föl) *adj* negligente
**negligee** (*nê*-ghli-ʒei) *n* bata suelta
**negotiate** (ni-*ghou*-ʃi-eit) *v* negociar
**negotiation** (ni-ghou-ʃi-*ei*-ʃön) *n* negociación *f*
**neighbo(u)r** (*nei*-bö) *n* vecino *m*, -a *f*
**neighbo(u)rhood** (*nei*-bö-hud) *n* vecindad *f*
**neighbo(u)ring** (*nei*-bö-ring) *adj* contiguo, vecino
**neither** (*nai*-ðö) *pron* ninguno de los dos; **neither … nor** ni … ni
**neon** (*nii*-on) *n* neón *m*
**nephew** (*nê*-fyuu) *n* sobrino *m*
**nerve** (nööv) *n* nervio *m*; valor *m*; descaro *m*
**nervous** (*nöö*-vöss) *adj* nervioso
**nest** (nêsst) *n* nido *m*
**net** (nêt) *n* red *f*; *adj* neto
**Netherlands** (*nê*-ðö-lönds): **the** ~ Países Bajos *mpl*
**network** (*nêt*-uöök) *n* red *f*
**neuralgia** (nyuö-*ræl*-dʒö) *n* neuralgia *f*
**neurosis** (nyuö-*rou*-ssiss) *n* neurosis *f*
**neuter** (*nyuu*-tö) *adj* neutro
**neutral** (*nyuu*-tröl) *adj* neutral
**never** (*nê*-vö) *adv* nunca
**nevertheless** (nê-vö-ðö-*lêss*) *adv* no obstante

**new** (nyuu) *adj* nuevo; **New Year** año nuevo
**news** (nyuus) *n* noticiario *m*, noticia *f*; noticias *fpl*
**newsagent** (*nyuu*-sei-dʒönt) *n* vendedor de periódicos
**newspaper** (*nyuus*-pei-pö) *n* diario *m*; periódico *m*
**newsreel** (*nyuus*-riil) *n* noticiario *m*
**newsstand** (*nyuus*-sstænd) *n* quiosco de periódicos
**New Zealand** (nyuu *sii*-lönd) Nueva Zelanda
**next** (nêksst) *adj* próximo; siguiente; **~ to** junto a
**next-door** (nêksst-*doo*) *adv* al lado
**nice** (naiss) *adj* agradable, bonito, ameno; rico; simpático
**nickel** (*ni*-köl) *n* níquel *m*
**nickname** (*nik*-neim) *n* mote *m*
**nicotine** (*ni*-kö-tiin) *n* nicotina *f*
**niece** (niiss) *n* sobrina *f*
**Nigeria** (nai-*dʒi*ᵒ-ri-ö) Nigeria *f*
**Nigerian** (nai-*dʒi*ᵒ-ri-ön) *adj* nigeriano
**night** (nait) *n* noche *f*; **by ~** de noche; **~ cream** crema de noche; **~ flight** vuelo nocturno; **~ rate** tarifa nocturna; **~ train** tren nocturno
**nightclub** (*nait*-klab) *n* cabaret *m*
**nightdress** (*nait*-drêss) *n* camisón *m*
**nightingale** (*nai*-ting-gheil) *n* ruiseñor *m*
**nightly** (*nait*-li) *adj* nocturno
**nightmare** (*nait*-mær) pesadilla *f*
**nil** (nil) nada
**nine** (nain) *num* nueve
**nineteen** (nain-*tiin*) *num* diecinueve
**nineteenth** (nain-*tiinz*) *num* decimonono
**ninety** (*nain*-ti) *num* noventa
**ninth** (nainz) *num* noveno
**nitrogen** (*nai*-trö-dʒön) *n* nitrógeno *m*
**no** (nou) no; *adj* ninguno; **~ one** nadie
**nobility** (nou-*bi*-lö-ti) *n* nobleza *f*
**noble** (*nou*-böl) *adj* noble
**nobody** (*nou*-bo-di) *pron* nadie
**nod** (nod) *n* cabeceo *m*; *v* cabecear
**noise** (nois) *n* ruido *m*; alboroto *m*
**noisy** (*noi*-si) *adj* ruidoso
**nominal** (*no*-mi-nöl) *adj* nominal
**nominate** (*no*-mi-neit) *v* nombrar
**nomination** (no-mi-*nei*-ʃön) *n* nominación *f*, nombramiento *m*
**none** (nan) *pron* ninguno
**nonsense** (*non*-ssönss) *n* tontería *f*
**noon** (nuun) *n* mediodía *m*
**nor** (noor) *conj* ni; **nor do I** yo tampoco, ni yo
**normal** (*noo*-möl) *adj* normal
**north** (nooz) *n* norte *m*; *adj* septentrional; **North Pole** polo norte
**north-east** (nooz-*iisst*) *n* nordeste *m*
**northerly** (*noo*-ðö-li) *adj* del norte
**northern** (*noo*-ðön) *adj* norteño
**north-west** (nooz-ᵘ*êsst*) *n* noroeste *m*
**Norway** (*noo*-ᵘei)Noruega *f*
**Norwegian** (noo-ᵘ*ii*-dʒön) *adj* noruego
**nose** (nous) *n* nariz *f*
**nosebleed** (*nous*-bliid) *n* hemorragia nasal
**nostril** (*no*-sstril) *n* ventana de la nariz
**nosy** (*nou*-si) *adj colloquial* entrometido
**not** (not) *adv* no
**notary** (*nou*-tö-ri) *n* notario *m*
**note** (nout) *n* apunte *m*, esquela *f*; nota *f*; tono *m*; *v* notar; observar, *comprobar
**notebook** (*nout*-buk) *n* libreta de apuntes; cuaderno *m*; ordenador portátil, *L.Am.* computadora portátil
**noted** (*nou*-tid) *adj* afamado, conocido
**notepaper** (*nout*-pei-pö) *n* papel de escribir, papel para cartas
**nothing** (*na*-zing) *n* nada *f*, nada
**notice** (*nou*-tiss) *v* observar, notar,

*advertir; *ver; *n* aviso *m*, noticia *f*; atención *f*
**noticeable** (*nou*-ti-ssö-böl) *adj* perceptible; notable
**notify** (*nou*-ti-fai) *v* notificar
**notion** (*nou*-ʃön) *n* noción *f*; opinión *f*
**notorious** (nou-*too*-ri-öss) *adj* de mala fama
**nougat** (*nuu*-ghaa) *n* turrón *m*
**nought** (noot) *n* cero *m*
**noun** (naun) *n* nombre *m*, substantivo *m*
**nourishing** (*na*-ri-ʃing) *adj* nutritivo
**novel** (*no*-völ) *n* novela *f*
**novelist** (*no*-vö-lisst) *n* novelista *m/f*
**November** (nou-*vêm*-bö) noviembre
**now** (nau) *adv* ahora; actualmente; ~ **and then** de vez en cuando
**nowadays** (*nau*-ö-deis) *adv* hoy en día
**nowhere** (*nou*-$^{u}$ê$^{ö}$) *adv* en ninguna parte
**nozzle** (*no*-söl) *n* tobera *f*
**nuance** (nyuu-*angss*) *n* matiz *m*
**nuclear** (*nyuu*-kli-ö) *adj* nuclear; ~ **energy** energía nuclear
**nucleus** (*nyuu*-kli-öss) *n* núcleo *m*
**nude** (nyuud)*adj* desnudo; *n* desnudo *m*
**nuisance** (*nyuu*-ssönss) *n* molestia *f*
**numb** (nam) *adj* entumecido; aterido
**number** (*nam*-bö) *n* número *m*; cifra *f*; cantidad *f*
**numeral** (*nyuu*-mö-röl) *n* numeral *m*
**numerous** (*nyuu*-mö-röss) *adj* numeroso
**nun** (nan) *n* monja *f*
**nunnery** (*na*-nö-ri) *n* convento *m*
**nurse** (nööss)*n* enfermero *m*, -a *f*; niñera *f*; *v* *atender a; amamantar
**nursery** (*nöö*-ssö-ri) *n* cuarto de niños; guardería *f*; vivero *m*
**nut** (nat) *n* nuez *f*; tuerca *f*
**nutcrackers** (*nat*-kræ-kös) *pl* cascanueces *m*
**nutmeg** (*nat*-mêgh) *n* nuez moscada
**nutritious** (nyuu-*tri*-ʃöss) *adj* nutritivo
**nutshell** (*nat*-ʃêl) *n* cáscara de nuez
**nylon** (*nai*-lon) *n* nilón *m*

# O

**oak** (ouk) *n* roble *m*
**oar** (oo) *n* remo *m*
**oasis** (ou-*ei*-ssiss) *n* (pl oases) oasis *f*
**oath** (ouz) *n* juramento *m*
**oats** (outss) *pl* avena *f*
**obedience** (ö-*bii*-di-önss) *n* obediencia *f*
**obedient** (ö-*bii*-di-önt) *adj* obediente
**obesity** (ö-*bii*-ssi-ti) *n* obesidad *f*
**obey** (ö-*bei*) *v* *obedecer
**object**[1] (*ob*-dʒikt) *n* objeto *m*
**object**[2] (öb-*dʒêkt*) *v* objetar; ~ **to** *oponerse a
**objection** (öb-*dʒêk*-ʃön)*n* objeción *f*
**objective** (öb-*dʒêk*-tiv) *adj* objetivo; *n* objetivo *m*
**obligatory** (ö-*bli*-ghö-tö-ri) *adj* obligatorio
**oblige** (ö-*blaidʒ*) *v* obligar; ***be obliged to** *estar obligado a; *tener que
**obliging** (ö-*blai*-dʒing) *adj* atento; servicial
**oblong** (*ob*-long) *adj* oblongo; *n* rectángulo *m*
**obscene** (öb-*ssiin*) *adj* obsceno
**obscure** (öb-*sskyu*$^{ö}$) *adj* obscuro, misterioso, oscuro

**observation** (ob-sö-*vei*-ʃön) *n* observación *f*
**observatory** (öb-*söö*-vö-tri) *n* observatorio *m*
**observe** (öb-*söőv*) *v* observar
**obsession** (öb-*ssê*-ʃön) *n* obsesión *f*
**obstacle** (*ob*-sstö-köl) *n* obstáculo *m*
**obstinate** (*ob*-ssti-nöt) *adj* obstinado; pertinaz
**obtain** (öb-*tein*) *v* *conseguir, *obtener
**obtainable** (öb-*tei*-nö-böl) *adj* adquirible
**obvious** (*ob*-vi-öss) *adj* obvio
**occasion** (ö-*kei*-ʒön) *n* ocasión *f*; motivo *m*
**occasionally** (ö-*kei*-ʒö-nö-li) *adv* de vez en cuando, ocasionalmente
**occupant** (*o*-kyu-pönt) *n* ocupante *m*
**occupation** (o-kyu-*pei*-ʃön) *n* ocupación *f*; empleo *m*; profesión *f*
**occupy** (*o*-kyu-pai) *v* ocupar
**occur** (ö-*köö*) *v* suceder, ocurrir, *acontecer
**occurrence** (ö-*ka*-rönss) *n* acontecimiento *m*
**ocean** (*ou*-ʃön)*n* océano *m*
**October** (ok-*tou*-bö) octubre
**octopus** (*ok*-tö-pöss) *n* pulpo *m*
**oculist** (*o*-kyu-lisst) *n* oculista *m/f*
**odd**(od) *adj* raro; impar
**odo(u)r** (*ou*-dö) *n* olor *m*
**of** (ov, öv) *prep* de
**off** (of) *adv* fuera; *prep* de
**offence** (ö-*fênss*) *n* falta *f*; ofensa *f*, escándalo *m*
**offend** (ö-*fênd*) *v* ofender; transgredir
**offense** (ö-*fênss*) *nAm* falta *f*; ofensa *f*, escándalo *m*
**offensive** (ö-*fên*-ssiv) *adj* ofensivo; insultante; *n* ofensivo *m*
**offer** (*o*-fö) *v* *ofrecer; presentar; *n* oferta *f*
**office** (*o*-fiss) *n* oficina *f*; despacho *m*; cargo *m*; ~ **hours** horas de oficina
**officer** (*o*-fi-ssö) *n* oficial *m*
**official** (ö-*fi*-ʃöl) *adj* oficial
**off-licence** (*of*-lai-ssönss) *n* almacén de licores
**often** (*o*-fön) *adv* a menudo, frecuentemente
**oil** (oil) *n* aceite *m*; petróleo *m*; **fuel** ~ combustible líquido; ~ **filter** filtro del aceite; ~ **painting** pintura al óleo; ~ **pressure** presión del aceite; ~ **refinery** refinería de petróleo; ~ **well** pozo de petróleo
**oily** (*oi*-li) *adj* aceitoso
**ointment** (*oint*-mönt) *n* ungüento *m*
**okay!** (ou-*kei*) ¡de acuerdo!
**old** (ould) *adj* viejo; ~ **age** vejez *f*
**old-fashioned** (ould-*fæ*-ʃönd) *adj* anticuado; pasado de moda
**olive** (*o*-liv) *n* aceituna *f*; ~ **oil** aceite de oliva
**omelette** (*om*-löt) *n* tortilla *f*
**ominous** (*o*-mi-nöss) *adj* siniestro; de mal agüero
**omit** (ö-*mit*) *v* omitir
**omnipotent** (om-*ni*-pö-tönt) *adj* omnipotente
**on** (on) *prep* sobre; encima de; acerca de
**once** (ᵘanss) *adv* una vez; antes; **at** ~ en seguida; ~ **more** otra vez
**oncoming** (*on*-ka-ming) *adj* venidero; que viene
**one** (ᵘan) *num* uno; *pron* uno
**oneself** (ᵘan-*ssêlf*) *pron* uno mismo
**onion** (*a*-nyön) *n* cebolla *f*
**only** (*oun*-li) *adj* solo; *adv* sólo, solamente; *conj* pero
**onwards** (*on*-ᵘöds) *adv* adelante
**onyx** (*o*-nikss) *n* ónix *m*
**opal** (*ou*-pöl) *n* ópalo *m*
**open** (*ou*-pön) *v* abrir; *adj* abierto; sincero
**opening** (*ou*-pö-ning) *n* abertura *f*

**opera** (*o*-pö-rö) *n* ópera *f*; ~ **house** teatro de la ópera
**operate** (*o*-pö-reit) *v* operar, funcionar
**operation** (o-pö-*rei*-ʃön) *n* funcionamiento *m*; operación *f*
**operator** (*o*-pö-rei-tö) *n* operador *m*, -a *f*; operario *m*, -a *f*
**operetta** (o-pö-*rê*-tö) *n* opereta *f*; zarzuela *f*
**opinion** (ö-*pi*-nyön) *n* parecer *m*, opinión *f*
**opponent** (ö-*pou*-nönt) *n* contrincante *m/f*; adversario *m*, -a *f*
**opportunity** (o-pö-*tyuu*-nö-ti) *n* oportunidad *f*
**oppose** (ö-*pous*) *v* *oponerse
**opposite** (*o*-pö-sit) *prep* enfrente de; *adj* contrario, opuesto
**opposition** (o-pö-*si*-ʃön)*n* oposición *f*
**oppress** (ö-*prêss*)*v* oprimir
**optician** (op-*ti*-ʃön) *n* óptico *m*, -a *f*
**optimism** (*op*-ti-mi-söm) *n* optimismo *m*
**optimist** (*op*-ti-misst) *n* optimista *m/f*
**optimistic** (op-ti-*mi*-sstik) *adj* optimista
**optional** (*op*-ʃö-nöl) *adj* opcional
**or** (oo) *conj* o
**oral** (*oo*-röl) *adj* oral
**orange** (*o*-rindʒ) *n* naranja *f*; *adj* de color naranja
**orbit** (*oo*-bit) *n* órbita *f*; *v* girar alrededor de; **send into** ~ poner en órbita
**orchard** (*oo*-chöd) *n* vergel *m*
**orchestra** (*oo*-ki-sströ) *n* orquesta *f*; ~ **seat** *Am* butaca *f*
**order** (*oo*-dö) *v* ordenar; *pedir; *n* orden *m*; orden *f*, mandato *m*; pedido *m*; **in** ~ en regla; **in** ~ **to** para; **made to** ~ hecho a la medida; **out of** ~ averiado; **postal** ~ giro postal
**order form** (*oo*-dö-foom) *n* hoja de pedido
**ordinary** (*oo*-dön-ri) *adj* común, ordinario
**ore** (oo) *n* mineral *m*
**organ** (*oo*-ghön) *n* órgano *m*
**organic** (oo-*ghæ*-nik) *adj* orgánico
**organization** (oo-ghö-nai-*sei*-ʃön) *n* organización *f*
**organize** (*oo*-ghö-nais) *v* organizar
**Orient** (*oo*-ri-önt) *n* oriente *m*
**oriental** (oo-ri-*ên*-töl) *adj* oriental
**orientate** (*oo*-ri-ön-teit) *v* orientarse
**origin** (*o*-ri-dʒin) *n* origen *m*; descendencia *f*, procedencia *f*
**original** (ö-*ri*-dʒi-nöl) *adj* auténtico, original
**originally** (ö-*ri*-dʒi-nö-li) *adv* originalmente
**orlon** (*oo*-lon) *n* orlón *m*
**ornament** (*oo*-nö-mönt) *n* adorno *m*
**ornamental** (oo-nö-*mên*-töl) *adj* ornamental
**orphan** (*oo*-fön) *n* huérfano *m*
**orthodox** (*oo*-zö-dokss) *adj* ortodoxo
**ostrich** (*o*-sstrich) *n* avestruz *m*
**other** (*a*-ðö) *adj* otro
**otherwise** (*a*-ðö-$^{u}$ais) *conj* si no; *adv* de otra manera
***ought to** (oot) *v/aux* *tener que; **he/they** ~ **know** debe/deben saberlo; **you** ~ **have done it** deberías haberlo hecho
**ounce** (auns) onza *f*
**our** (au$^{ö}$) *adj* nuestro
**ours** (au$^{ö}$s) *pron* el nuestro, la nuestra; **a friend of** ~ un amigo nuestro
**ourselves** (au$^{ö}$-*ssêlvs*)*pron* nos; nosotros mismos
**out** (aut) *adv* fuera; afuera; de fuera; apagado; al descubierto; ~ **of** fuera de
**outbreak** (*aut*-breik) *n* explosión *f*
**outburst** (*aut*-böösst) *n* arrebato *m*, arranque *m*
**outcome** (*aut*-kam) *n* resultado *m*

***outdo** (aut-*duu*) *v* superar
**outdoors** (aut-*doos*) *adv* afuera; al aire libre
**outer** (*au*-tö) *adj* exterior, externo
**outfit** (*aut*-fit) *n* equipo *m*; conjunto *m*
**outing** (*au*-ting) excursión *f*
**outline** (*aut*-lain) *n* contorno *m*; *v* bosquejar
**outlook** (*aut*-luk) *n* previsión *f*; punto de vista; perspectiva *f*
**output** (*aut*-put) *n* producción *f*
**outside** (aut-*ssaid*) *adv* afuera; *prep* fuera de; *n* exterior *m*
**outsize** (*aut*-ssais) *n* tamaño extra grande
**outskirts** (*aut*-ssköötss) *pl* afueras *fpl*
**outstanding** (aut-*sstæn*-ding) *adj* eminente, destacado; pendiente
**outward** (*aut*-ᵘöd) *adj* externo
**outwards** (*aut*-ᵘöds) *adv* hacia afuera
**oval** (*ou*-völ) *adj* ovalado
**oven** (*a*-vön) *n* horno *m*; **microwave ~** horno de microonda
**over** (*ou*-vö) *prep* sobre; encima de; durante; por; *adv* encima; **~ here** acá; **~ there** allá; **to be ~** estar terminado
**overall** (*ou*-vö-rool) *adj* por lo general; en conjunto
**overalls** (*ou*-vö-rools) *pl* mono *m*; overol *mMe*
**overcast** (*ou*-vö-kaasst) *adj* anublado
**overcoat** (*ou*-vö-kout) *n* abrigo *m*
***overcome** (ou-vö-*kam*) *v* vencer
***overdo** (ou-vö-*duu*) *v* exagerar; recocer, cocinar demasiado; **you're overdoing things** te estás excediendo
**overdue** (ou-vö-*dyuu*) *adj* retrasado
**overdraft** (*ou*-vö-draaft) *n* descubierto *m*
***overdraw** (ou-vö-*droo*) *v* dejar al descubierto
**overgrown** (ou-vö-*ghroun*) *adj* cubierto de verdor
**overhaul** (ou-vö-*hool*) *v* revisar
**overhead** (ou-vö-*hêd*) *adv* en alto, de arriba; *n* gastos generales
**overlook** (ou-vö-*luk*) *v* pasar por alto
**overnight** (ou-vö-*nait*) *adv* de noche
**overseas** (ou-vö-*ssiis*) *adj* ultramar
**oversight** (*ou*-vö-ssait) *n* descuido *m*
***oversleep** (ou-vö-*ssliip*) *v* quedarse dormido
**overstrung** (ou-vö-*sstrang*) *adj* sobreexcitado; muy tenso
***overtake** (ou-vö-*teik*)*v* alcanzar; adelantar; **no overtaking** prohibido adelantar
**over-tired** (ou-vö-*taiᵒd*) *adj* agobiado; muy fatigado
**overture** (*ou*-vö-chö) *n* obertura *f*
**overweight** (*ou*-vö-ᵘeit) *n* sobrepeso *m*
**overwhelm** (ou-vö-*ᵘêlm*) *v* *desconcertar, subyugar; abrumar
**overwork** (ou-vö-*ᵘöök*) *v* trabajar demasiado
**owe** (ou) *v* deber; **owing to** a causa de, debido a
**owl** (aul) *n* buho *m*
**own** (oun) *v* *poseer; *adj* propio
**owner** (*ou*-nö) *n* propietario *m*, -a *f*
**ox** (okss) *n* (pl oxen) buey *m*
**oxygen** (*ok*-ssi-dʒön)*n* oxígeno *m*
**oyster** (*oi*-sstö) *n* ostra *f*
**ozone** (*ou*-soun) *n* ozono *m*

# P

**pace** (peiss) *n* paso *m*; ritmo *m*
**Pacific Ocean** (pö-*ssi*-fik *ou*-ʃön) Océano Pacífico
**pacifism** (*pæ*-ssi-fi-söm) *n* pacifismo *m*
**pacifist** (*pæ*-ssi-fisst) *n* pacifista *m*
**pack** (pæk) *v* embalar; **~ up** empaquetar
**package** (*pæ*-kidʒ) *n* paquete *m*
**packet** (*pæ*-kit) *n* paquete *m* pequeño
**packing** (*pæ*-king) *n* embalaje *m*
**pact** (pækt) *n* pacto *m*
**pad** (pæd) *n* almohadilla *f*; bloc *m*
**paddle** (*pæ*-döl) *n* remo *m*
**padlock** (*pæd*-lok) *n* candado *m*
**pagan** (*pei*-ghön) *adj* pagano; *n* pagano *m*
**page** (peidʒ) *n* página *f*
**pageboy** (*peidʒ*-boi) *n* paje *m*
**pail** (peil) *n* balde *m*
**pain** (pein) *n* dolor *m*; **pains** pena *f*
**painful** (*pein*-föl) *adj* doloroso
**painkiller** (*pein*-ki-lö) *n* analgésico *m*
**painless** (*pein*-löss) *adj* sin dolor
**paint** (peint) *n* pintura *f*; *v* pintar
**paintbox** (*peint*-bokss) *n* caja de colores
**paintbrush** (*peint*-braʃ) *n* pincel *m*
**painter** (*pein*-tö) *n* pintor *m*, -a *f*
**painting** (*pein*-ting) *n* pintura *f*
**pair** (pêö) *n* par *m*
**Pakistan** (paa-ki-*sstaan*) Paquistán *m*
**Pakistani** (paa-ki-*sstaa*-ni) *adj* paquistaní
**pal** (pæl) *n colloquial* amigo *m*, -a *f*; colega *m/f*
**palace** (*pæ*-löss) *n* palacio *m*
**pale** (peil) *adj* pálido
**palm** (paam) *n* palma *f*
**palpable** (*pæl*-pö-böl) *adj* palpable
**palpitation** (pæl-pi-*tei*-ʃön) *n* palpitación *f*
**pan** (pæn) *n* cazuela *f*; **frying ~** sartén *f*
**pancake** (*pæn*-keik) *n* crepe *m*, *L.Am.* panqueque *m*
**pane** (pein) *n* cristal *m*
**panel** (*pæ*-nöl) *n* panel *m*, entrepaño *m*; tablero *m*
**panel(l)ing** (*pæ*-nö-ling) *n* enmaderado *m*
**panic** (*pæ*-nik) *n* pánico *m*
**pant** (pænt) *v* jadear
**panties** (*pæn*-tis) *pl* braga *f*
**pants** (pæntss) *pl* calzoncillos *mpl*; *plAm* pantalones *mpl*
**pant suit** (*pænt*-ssuut) *n* traje pantalón
**panty hose** (*pæn*-ti-hous) *n* media panty
**paper** (*pei*-pö) *n* papel *m*; periódico *m*; de papel; **carbon ~** papel carbón; **~ bag** bolsa de papel; **~ knife** abrecartas *m*; **~ napkin** servilleta de papel; **typing ~** papel para mecanografiar; **wrapping ~** papel de envolver
**paperback** (*pei*-pö-bæk) *n* libro de bolsillo
**parade** (pö-*reid*) *n* parada *f*, desfile *m*
**paradise** (*pæ*-rö-dais) *n* paraíso *m*
**paraffin** (*pæ*-rö-fin) *n* parafina *f*
**paragraph** (*pæ*-rö-ghraaf)*n* párrafo *m*
**parakeet** (*pæ*-rö-kiit) *n* perico *m*
**parallel** (*pæ*-rö-lêl) *adj* paralelo; *n* paralelo *m*
**paralyse** *Am*, **paralyze** (*pæ*-rö-lais) *v* paralizar
**parcel** (*paa*-ssöl) *n* paquete *m*
**pardon** (*paa*-dön)*n* perdón *m*; indulto *m*
**parent** (*pêö*-rönt) *n* padre *m*; madre *f*; **parents** *pl* padres *mpl*
**parents-in-law** (*pêö*-röntss-in-loo) *pl* padres políticos
**parish** (*pæ*-riʃ) *n* parroquia *f*

**park** (paak) *n* parque *m*; *v* estacionar
**parking** (*paa*-king) *n* aparcamiento *m*; **no ~** prohibido estacionarse; **~ fee** derechos de estacionamiento; **~ light** luz de estacionamiento; **~ lot** *Am* estacionamiento *m*; **~ meter** parquímetro *m*; **~ zone** zona de aparcamiento
**parliament** (*paa*-lö-mönt) *n* parlamento *m*
**parliamentary** (paa-lö-*mên*-tö-ri) *adj* parlamentario
**parrot** (*pæ*-röt) *n* loro *m*; papagayo *m*
**parsley** (*paa*-ssli) *n* perejil *m*
**parson** (*paa*-ssön) *n* pastor *m*
**parsonage** (*paa*-ssö-nidʒ) *n* curato *m*
**part** (paat) *n* parte *f*; pieza *f*; *v* separar; **spare ~** recambio *m*
**partial** (*paa*-ʃöl) *adj* parcial
**participant** (paa-*ti*-ssi-pönt) *n* participante *m/f*
**participate** (paa-*ti*-ssi-peit) *v* participar
**particular** (pö-*ti*-kyu-lö) *adj* especial, particular; exigente; **in ~** en particular
**parting** (*paa*-ting) *n* despedida *f*; raya *f*
**partition** (paa-*ti*-ʃön) *n* tabique *m*
**partly** (*paat*-li) *adv* en parte
**partner** (*paat*-nö) *n* pareja *f*; socio *m*, -a *f*; compañero *m*, -a *f*
**partridge** (*paa*-tridʒ) *n* perdiz *f*
**party** (*paa*-ti) *n* partido *m*; guateque *m*, fiesta *f*; grupo *m*
**pass** (paass) *v* transcurrir, pasar; *aprobar; **~ by** pasar de largo; **~ through** *atravesar
**passage** (*pæ*-ssidʒ) *n* pasaje *m*; travesía *f*; trozo *m*
**passenger** (*pæ*-ssön-dʒö) *n* pasajero *m*, -a *f*; **~ train** tren de pasajeros
**passer-by** (paa-ssö-*bai*) *n* transeúnte *m*
**passion** (*pæ*-ʃön) *n* pasión *f*; cólera *f*
**passionate** (*pæ*-ʃö-nöt) *adj* apasionado
**passive** (*pæ*-ssiv) *adj* pasivo
**passport** (*paass*-poot) *n* pasaporte *m*; **~ control** inspección de pasaportes; **~ photograph** fotografía de pasaporte
**password** (*paass*-ᵘööd) *n* santo y seña; contraseña de acceso
**past** (paasst) *n* pasado *m*; *adj* pasado; transcurrido; *prep* a lo largo de, más allá de
**paste** (peisst) *n* pasta *f*; *v* pegar
**pastime** (*paass*-taim) *n* pasatiempo *m*
**pastry** (*pei*-sstri) *n* pasteles *mpl*; **~ shop** pastelería *f*
**pasture** (*paass*-chö) *n* prado *m*
**pasty** (*pei*-ssti) *adj* pálido
**patch** (pæch) *v* *remendar
**patent** (*pei*-tönt) *n* patente *f*
**path** (paaz) *n* senda *f*; sendero *m*
**patience** (*pei*-ʃönss) *n* paciencia *f*
**patient** (*pei*-ʃönt) *adj* paciente; *n* paciente *m/f*
**patriot** (*pei*-tri-öt) *n* patriota *m/f*
**patrol** (pö-*troul*) *n* patrulla *f*; *v* patrullar; vigilar
**pattern** (*pæ*-tön) *n* modelo *m*; dibujo *m*; patrón *m*
**pause** (poos) *n* pausa *f*; *v* *hacer una pausa
**pave** (peiv) *v* pavimentar
**pavement** (*peiv*-mönt) *n* acera *f*; pavimento *m*
**pavilion** (pö-*vil*-yön) *n* pabellón *m*
**paw** (poo) *n* pata *f*
**pawn** (poon) *v* empeñar; *n* peón *m*
**pawnbroker** (*poon*-brou-kö) *n* prestamista *m*
**pay** (pei) *n* salario *m*, sueldo *m*
***pay** (pei) *v* pagar; *rendir; **~ attention to** prestar atención a; **~ desk** caja *f*; **~ off** amortizar; **~ on account** pagar a plazos; **~ phone** teléfono público; **paying** rentable

**payee** (pei-*ii*) *n* favorecido *m*, -a *f*
**payment** (*pei*-mönt) *n* pago *m*
**PC** (pii-*ssii*)*n* PC *m*, ordenador *m* personal, computadora *f* personal; *adj* políticamente correcto
**pea** (pii)*n* guisante *m*
**peace** (piiss) *n* paz *f*
**peaceful** (*piiss*-föl) *adj* tranquilo
**peach** (piich) *n* melocotón *m*
**peacock** (*pii*-kok) *n* pavo *m*
**peak** (piik)*n* pico *m*; cumbre *f*; ~ **hours** horas punta; ~ **season** apogeo de la temporada
**peanut** (*pii*-nat)*n* cacahuete *m*; cacahuate *mMe*
**pear** (pêö) *n* pera *f*
**pearl** (pööl) *n* perla *f*
**peasant** (*pê*-sönt) *n* campesino *m*
**pebble** (*pê*-böl) *n* guijarro *m*
**peculiar** (pi-*kyuul*-yö) *adj* extraño; especial, peculiar
**peculiarity** (pi-kyuu-li-æ-rö-ti) *n* particularidad *f*
**pedal** (*pê*-döl) *n* pedal *m*
**pedestrian** (pi-*dê*-sstri-ön) *n* peatón *m*; **no pedestrians** prohibido para los peatones; ~ **crossing** cruce para peatones
**peel** (piil) *v* pelar; *n* piel *f*
**peep** (piip) *v* espiar
**peg** (pêgh) *n* percha *f*
**pelican** (*pê*-li-kön)*n* pelícano *m*
**pelvis** (*pêl*-viss) *n* pelvis *m*
**pen** (pên) *n* pluma *f*
**penalty** (*pê*-nöl-ti) *n* pena *f*; castigo *m*; ~ **kick** penalty *m*
**pencil** (*pên*-ssöl) *n* lápiz *m*; ~ **sharpener** sacapuntas *m*
**pendant** (*pên*-dönt) *n* pendiente *m*
**penetrate** (*pê*-ni-treit) *v* penetrar
**penguin** (*pêng*-ghuin) *n* pingüino *m*
**penicillin** (pê-ni-*ssi*-lin) *n* penicilina *f*
**peninsula** (pö-*nin*-ssyu-lö) *n* península *f*
**penknife** (*pên*-naif) *n* (pl -knives) cortaplumas *m*
**penny** (*pê*-ni) *n* penique *m*
**pension**[1] (*pang*-ssi-ong) *n* pensión *f*
**pension**[2] (*pên*-ʃön)*n* pensión *f*
**people** (*pii*-pöl) *pl* gente *f*; *n* pueblo *m*
**pepper** (*pê*-pö) *n* pimienta *f*
**peppermint** (*pê*-pö-mint) *n* menta *f*
**per** (pö) *prep* por; **per** ~ al año, por año
**perceive** (pö-*ssiiv*) *v* percibir
**percent** (pö-*ssênt*) *n* por ciento
**percentage** (pö-*ssên*-tidʒ) *n* porcentaje *m*
**perceptible** (pö-*ssêp*-ti-böl) *adj* perceptible
**perception** (pö-*ssêp*-ʃön) *n* percepción *f*
**perch** (pööch) (pl ~) perca *f*
**percolator** (*pöö*-kö-lei-tö) *n* cafetera filtradora
**perfect** (*pöö*-fikt) *adj* perfecto
**perfection** (pö-*fêk*-ʃön) *n* perfección *f*
**perform** (pö-*foom*) *v* ejecutar, desempeñar
**performance** (pö-*foo*-mönss) *n* representación *f*
**perfume** (*pöö*-fyuum) *n* perfume *m*
**perhaps** (pö-*hæpss*) *adv* quizás
**peril** (*pê*-ril) *n* peligro *m*; riesgo *m*
**perilous** (*pê*-ri-löss) *adj* peligroso
**period** (*piö*-ri-öd) *n* época *f*, período *m*; punto *m*
**periodical** (piö-ri-*o*-di-köl) *n* periódico *m*; *adj* periódico
**perish** (*pê*-riʃ) *v* *perecer
**perishable** (*pê*-ri-ʃö-böl) *adj* perecedero
**perjury** (*pöö*-dʒö-ri) *n* perjurio *m*
**perm** (pööm) *n* permanente *f*; *v* hacer la permanente; **she had her hair permed** se hizo la permanente
**permanent** (*pöö*-mö-nönt) *adj* duradero, permanente; estable, fijo;

~ **press** planchado permanente; ~ **wave** ondulación permanente
**permission** (pö-*mi*-ʃön) *n* permiso *m*, autorización *f*; licencia *f*
**permit**[1] (pö-*mit*) *v* permitir
**permit**[2] (*pöö*-mit) *n* permiso *m*
**peroxide** (pö-*rok*-ssaid) *n* peróxido *m*
**perpendicular** (pöö-pön-*di*-kyu-lö) *adj* perpendicular
**Persian** (*pöö*-ʃön) *adj* persa
**person** (*pöö*-ssön) *n* persona *f*; **per** ~ por persona
**personal** (*pöö*-ssö-nöl) *adj* personal
**personality** (pöö-ssö-*næ*-lö-ti) *n* personalidad *f*
**personnel** (pöö-ssö-*nêl*) *n* personal *m*
**perspective** (pö-*sspêk*-tiv) *n* perspectiva *f*
**perspiration** (pöö-sspö-*rei*-ʃön) *n* transpiración *f*, sudor *m*
**perspire** (pö-*sspai*[ö]) *v* transpirar, sudar
**persuade** (pö-*ss*[u]*eid*) *v* persuadir; convencer
**persuasion** (pö-*ss*[u]*ei*-ʒön) *n* convicción *f*
**pessimism** (*pê*-ssi-mi-söm) *n* pesimismo *m*
**pessimist** (*pê*-ssi-misst) *n* pesimista *m/f*
**pessimistic** (pê-ssi-*mi*-sstik) *adj* pesimista
**pet** (pêt) *n* animal doméstico; cariño *m*; favorito
**petal** (*pê*-töl) *n* pétalo *m*
**petition** (pi-*ti*-ʃön) *n* petición *f*
**petrol** (*pê*-tröl) *n* gasolina *f*; **unleaded** ~ gasolina sin plomo; ~ **pump** bomba de gasolina; ~ **station** puesto de gasolina; ~ **tank** depósito de gasolina
**petroleum** (pi-*trou*-li-öm) *n* petróleo *m*
**petty** (*pê*-ti) *adj* pequeño, fútil, insignificante; ~ **cash** calderilla *f*
**pewit** (*pii*-[u]it) *n* avefría *f*
**pewter** (*pyuu*-tö) *n* estaño *m*
**phantom** (*fæn*-töm) *n* fantasma *m*
**pharmacy** (*faa*-mö-ssi) *n* farmacia *f*; droguería *f*
**pheasant** (*fê*-sönt) *n* faisán *m*
**Philippine** (*fi*-li-pain) *adj* filipino
**Philippines** (*fi*-li-piins) *pl* Filipinas *fpl*
**philosopher** (fi-*lo*-ssö-fö) *n* filósofo *m*, -a *f*
**philosophy** (fi-*lo*-ssö-fi) *n* filosofía *f*
**phone** (foun) *n* teléfono *m*; *v* llamar por teléfono, telefonear; ~ **card** tarjeta *f* telefónica
**phonetic** (fö-*nê*-tik) *adj* fonético
**photo** (*fou*-tou) *n* (pl ~s) foto *f*
**photocopy** (*fou*-tö-ko-pi) *n* fotocopia *f*; *v* fotocopiar
**photograph** (*fou*-tö-ghraaf) *n* fotografía *f*; *v* fotografiar
**photographer** (fö-*to*-ghrö-fö) *n* fotógrafo *m*
**photography** (fö-*to*-ghrö-fi) *n* fotografía *f*
**phrase** (freis) *n* frase *f*; ~ **book** manual de conversación
**physical** (*fi*-si-köl) *adj* físico
**physician** (fi-*si*-ʃön) *n* médico *m*, -a *f*
**physicist** (*fi*-si-ssisst) *n* físico *m*
**physics** (*fi*-sikss) *n* física *f*
**physiology** (fi-si-*o*-lö-dʒi) *n* fisiología *f*
**pianist** (*pii*-ö-nisst) *n* pianista *m*
**piano** (pi-*æ*-nou) *n* piano *m*; **grand** ~ piano de cola
**pie** (pai) *n* pastel *m*
**pick** (pik) *v* recoger; escoger; *n* elección *f*; ~ **up** recoger; *ir a buscar; **pick-up van** camioneta de reparto
**pickles** (*pi*-köls) *pl* encurtidos *mpl*
**picnic** (*pik*-nik) *n* picnic *m*; merienda en el campo; *v* *hacer un día de campo
**picture** (*pik*-chö) *n* cuadro *m*;

ilustración *f*, grabado *m*; imagen *f*; ~ **postcard** tarjeta postal ilustrada
**picturesque** (pik-chö-*rêssk*) *adj* pintoresco
**piece** (piiss) *n* fragmento *m*, pedazo *m*
**pier** (pi^ö^) *n* muelle *m*
**pierce** (pi^ö^ss) *v* punzar
**pig** (pigh) *n* cerdo *m*
**pigeon** (*pi*-dʒön) *n* paloma *f*
**pig-headed** (pigh-*hê*-did) *adj* testarudo
**piglet** (*pigh*-löt) *n* cochinillo *m*
**pigskin** (*pigh*-sskin) *n* piel de cerdo
**pike** (paik)(pl ~) lucio *m*
**pile** (pail) *n* montón *m*; *v* amontonar; **piles** *pl* hemorroides *fpl*
**pilgrim** (*pil*-ghrim) *n* peregrino *m*
**pilgrimage** (*pil*-ghri-midʒ) *n* peregrinación *f*
**pill** (pil) *n* píldora *f*
**pillar** (*pi*-lö) *n* columna *f*, pilar *m*
**pillarbox** (*pi*-lö-bokss) *n* buzón *m*
**pillow** (*pi*-lou) *n* almohadón *m*, almohada *f*
**pillowcase** (*pi*-lou-keiss) *n* funda de almohada
**pilot** (*pai*-löt) *n* piloto *m*; práctico *m*
**pimple** (*pim*-pöl) *n* grano *m*
**pin** (pin) *n* alfiler *m*; *v* sujetar; prender; enclavijar; **bobby** ~ *Am* horquilla *f*
**pincers** (*pin*-ssös) *pl* tenazas *fpl*
**pinch** (pinch) *v* pellizcar; *n* pellizco *m*; aprieto *m*
**pineapple** (*pai*-næ-pöl) *n* piña *f*
**ping-pong** (*ping*-pong) *n* tenis de mesa
**pink** (pingk) *adj* rosado
**pint** (paint) *n* pinta *f*, (medida equivalente a 0,473 litros en Estados Unidos o a 0,568 litros en Gran Bretaña)
**pioneer** (pai-ö-*ni*^ö^) *n* pionero *m*
**pious** (*pai*-öss) *adj* pío
**pip** (pip) *n* pepita *f*
**pipe** (paip) *n* pipa *f*; conducto *m*; ~ **cleaner** limpiapipas *m*; ~ **tobacco** tabaco de pipa
**pipeline** (*paip*-lain) *n* oleoducto *m*; gasoducto *m*; **in the** ~ en trámite
**pirate** (*pai*^ö^-röt) *n* pirata *m*
**pistol** (*pi*-sstöl) *n* pistola *f*
**piston** (*pi*-sstön) *n* pistón *m*; ~ **ring** aro de émbolo
**pit** (pit) *n* hoyo *m*; mina *f*
**pitcher** (*pi*-chö) *n* cántaro *m*
**pity** (*pi*-ti) *n* piedad *f*; *v* *tener piedad de, compadecerse de; **what a pity!** ¡qué lástima!
**placard** (*plæ*-kaad) *n* cartel *m*
**place** (pleiss) *n* lugar *m*; *v* *poner, colocar; ~ **of birth** lugar de nacimiento; ***take** ~ *tener lugar
**plague** (pleigh) *n* plaga *f*
**plaice** (pleiss) (pl ~) platija *f*
**plain** (plein) *adj* claro; corriente, sencillo; *n* llano *m*
**plan** (plæn) *n* plan *m*; plano *m*; *v* planear
**plane** (plein) *adj* plano; *n* avión *m*; ~ **crash** accidente aéreo
**planet** (*plæ*-nit) *n* planeta *m*
**planetarium** (plæ-ni-*tê*^ö^-ri-öm) *n* planetario *m*
**plank** (plængk) *n* tablón *m*
**plant** (plaant) *n* planta *f*; instalación *f*; *v* plantar
**plantation** (plæn-*tei*-ʃön) *n* plantación *f*
**plaster** (*plaa*-sstö) *n* estuco *m*, yeso *m*; esparadrapo *m*
**plastic** (*plæ*-sstik) *adj* de plástico; *n* plástico *m*; ~ **bag** bolsa *f* de plástico
**plate** (pleit) *n* plato *m*; chapa *f*
**plateau** (*plæ*-tou) *n* (pl ~x, ~s) meseta *f*
**platform** (*plæt*-foom) *n* andén *m*; ~ **ticket** billete de andén
**platinum** (*plæ*-ti-nöm) *n* platino *m*

**play** (plei) *v* *jugar; tocar; *n* juego *m*; obra de teatro; **one-act ~** pieza en un acto; **~ truant** *hacer novillos
**player** (pleiᵒ) *n* jugador *m*
**playground** (*plei*-ghraund) *n* patio de recreo
**playing card** (*plei*-ing-kaad) *n* naipe *m*
**playwright** (*plei*-rait) *n* dramaturgo *m*
**plea** (plii) *n* argumento *m*; súplica *f*; defensa *f*
**plead** (pliid) *v* suplicar; defender
**pleasant** (*plê*-sönt) *adj* agradable, simpático
**please** (pliis) por favor; *v* *placer; **pleased** contento; **pleasing** agradable
**pleasure** (*plê*-ʒö) *n* placer *m*, diversión *f*
**plentiful** (*plên*-ti-föl) *adj* abundante
**plenty** (*plên*-ti) *n* abundancia *f*; **~ of** muchos; bastante
**pliers** (plaiᵒs) *pl* alicates *mpl*
**plimsolls** (*plim*-ssöls) *pl* zapatos de gimnasia
**plot** (plot) *n* complot *m*; trama *f*; parcela *f*
**plough** (plau) *n* arado *m*; *v* arar
**plucky** (*pla*-ki) *adj* valiente; animoso
**plug** (plagh) *n* enchufe *m*; **~ in** enchufar
**plum** (plam) *n* ciruela *f*
**plumber** (*pla*-mö) *n* fontanero *m*
**plump** (plamp) *adj* regordete
**plural** (*pluᵒ*-röl) *n* plural *m*
**plus** (plass) *prep* más
**pneumatic** (nyuu-*mæ*-tik) *adj* neumático
**pneumonia** (nyuu-*mou*-ni-ö) *n* neumonía *f*
**poach** (pouch) *v* cazar en vedado
**pocket** (*po*-kit) *n* bolsillo *m*
**pocketknife** (*po*-kit-naif) *n* (pl -knives) navaja *f*
**poem** (*pou*-im) *n* poema *m*
**poet** (*pou*-it) *n* poeta *m*
**poetry** (*pou*-i-tri) *n* poesía *f*
**point** (point) *n* punto *m*; punta *f*; *v* señalar con el dedo; **~ of view** punto de vista; **~ out** apuntar
**pointed** (*poin*-tid) *adj* puntiagudo
**poison** (*poi*-sön) *n* veneno *m*; *v* envenenar
**poisonous** (*poi*-sö-nöss) *adj* venenoso
**Poland** (*pou*-lönd) Polonia *f*
**Pole** (poul) *n* polaco *m*
**pole** (poul) *n* palo *m*; polo *m*; pértiga *f*
**police** (pö-*liiss*) *pl* policía *f*; **~ station** comisaría *f*
**policeman** (pö-*liiss*-mön) *n* (pl -men) agente de policía, guardia *m*
**policy** (*po*-li-ssi) *n* política *f*; póliza *f*
**polio** (*pou*-li-ou) *n* polio *f*, poliomielitis *f*
**Polish** (*pou*-liʃ) *adj* polaco
**polish** (*po*-liʃ) *v* pulir
**polite** (pö-*lait*) *adj* cortés
**political** (pö-*li*-ti-köl) *adj* político
**politician** (po-li-*ti*-ʃön) *n* político *m*
**politics** (*po*-li-tikss) *n* política *f*
**poll** (poul) *n* encuesta *f*, sondeo *m*; *v* sondear; **the polls** las elecciones; **go to the polls** acudir a las urnas
**pollute** (pö-*luut*) *v* contaminar
**pollution** (pö-*luu*-ʃön) *n* contaminación *f*, polución *f*
**pond** (pond) *n* estanque *m*
**pony** (*pou*-ni) *n* caballito *m*; jaca *f*; poni *m*
**pool¹** (puul) *n* piscina *f*, *L.Am.* pileta *f*, *Me* alberca *f*; charco *m*
**pool²** (puul) *n* fondo común; *v* juntar
**poor** (puᵒ) *adj* pobre; mediocre
**pope** (poup) *n* Papa *m*
**pop music** (pop *myuu*-sik) música pop
**poppy** (*po*-pi) *n* amapola *f*;

adormidera *f*
**popular** (*po*-pyu-lö) *adj* popular
**population** (po-pyu-*lei*-ʃön) *n* población *f*
**populous** (*po*-pyu-löss) *adj* populoso
**porcelain** (*poo*-ssö-lin) *n* porcelana *f*
**porcupine** (*poo*-kyu-pain) *n* puerco espín
**pork** (pook) *n* carne de cerdo
**port** (poot) *n* puerto *m*; babor *m*
**portable** (*poo*-tö-böl) *adj* portátil
**porter** (*poo*-tö) *n* mozo *m*; portero *m*
**porthole** (*poot*-houl) *n* portilla *f*
**portion** (*poo*-ʃön) *n* porción *f*
**portrait** (*poo*-trit) *n* retrato *m*
**Portugal** (*poo*-tyu-ghöl) Portugal *m*
**Portuguese** (poo-tyu-*ghiis*) *adj* portugués
**posh** (poʃ) *adj colloquial* elegante; pijo
**position** (pö-*si*-ʃön) *n* posición *f*; actitud *f*; puesto *m*
**positive** (*po*-sö-tiv) *adj* positivo; *n* positiva *f*
**possess** (pö-*sêss*) *v* *poseer; **possessed** *adj* poseído
**possession** (pö-*sê*-ʃön) *n* posesión *f*; **possessions** bienes *mpl*
**possibility** (po-ssö-*bi*-lö-ti) *n* posibilidad *f*
**possible** (*po*-ssö-böl) *adj* posible; eventual
**post** (pousst) *n* poste *m*; puesto *m*; correo *m*; *v* echar al correo; ~ **office** (oficina de) correos
**postage** (*pou*-sstidʒ) *n* franqueo *m*; ~ **paid** franco; ~ **stamp** sello de correos; timbre *mMe*
**postcard** (*pousst*-kaad) *n* tarjeta postal
**poster** (*pou*-sstö) *n* cartel *m*
**poste restante** (pousst rê-*sstangt*) lista de correos
**postman** (*pousst*-mön) *n* (pl -men) cartero *m*
**post-paid** (pousst-*peid*) *adj* franco
**postpone** (pö-*sspoun*) *v* aplazar
**pot** (pot) *n* olla *f*; maceta *f*
**potato** (pö-*tei*-tou) *n* (pl ~es) patata *f*; papa *fMe*
**pottery** (*po*-tö-ri) *n* cerámica *f*; loza *f*
**pouch** (pauch) *n* bolsa *f*; morral *m*
**poulterer** (*poul*-tö-rö) *n* pollero *m*
**poultry** (*poul*-tri) *n* aves de corral
**pound** (paund) *n* libra *f*
**pour** (poo) *v* *verter
**poverty** (*po*-vö-ti) *n* pobreza *f*
**powder** (*pau*-dö) *n* polvo *m*; *v* emplvarse; ~ **compact** polvera *f*; **talc** ~ talco *m*
**power** (pauö) *n* fuerza *f*, energía *f*; poder *m*; potencia *f*; ~ **station** central eléctrica
**powered by** impulsado por
**powerful** (*pauö*-föl) *adj* poderoso; fuerte
**powerless** (*pauö*-löss) *adj* impotente
**practical** (*præk*-ti-köl) *adj* práctico
**practically** (*præk*-ti-kli) *adv* prácticamente
**practice** (*præk*-tiss) *n* práctica *f*
**practise** (*præk*-tiss) *v* practicar; ensayarse
**praise** (preis) *v* alabar; *n* elogio *m*
**pram** (præm) *n* cochecillo de niño
**prawn** (proon) *n* gamba *f*
**pray** (prei) *v* orar
**prayer** (prêö) *n* oración *f*
**preach** (priich) *v* predicar
**precarious** (pri-*kêö*-ri-öss) *adj* precario
**precaution** (pri-*koo*-ʃön) *n* precaución *f*
**precede** (pri-*ssiid*) *v* preceder
**preceding** (pri-*ssii*-ding) *adj* precedente
**precious** (*prê*-ʃöss) *adj* precioso; querido

**precipice** (*prê*-ssi-piss) *n* precipicio *m*
**precipitation** (pri-ssi-pi-*tei*-ʃön) *n* precipitación *f*
**precise** (pri-*ssaiss*) *adj* preciso, exacto; meticuloso
**predecessor** (*prii*-di-ssê-ssö) *n* predecesor *m*
**predict** (pri-*dikt*) *v* *predecir
**prefer** (pri-*föö*) *v* *preferir
**preferable** (*prê*-fö-rö-böl) *adj* preferible
**preference** (*prê*-fö-rönss) *n* preferencia *f*
**prefix** (*prii*-fikss) *n* prefijo *m*
**pregnant** (*prêgh*-nönt) *adj* encinta, embarazada
**prejudice** (*prê*-dʒö-diss) *n* prejuicio *m*
**preliminary** (pri-*li*-mi-nö-ri) *adj* preliminar
**premature** (*prê*-mö-chu$^{ö}$) *adj* prematuro
**premier** (*prêm*-i$^{ö}$) *n* jefe de gobierno
**premises** (*prê*-mi-ssis) *pl* finca *f*
**premium** (*prii*-mi-öm) *n* prima *f*
**prepaid** (prii-*peid*) *adj* pagado por adelantado
**preparation** (prê-pö-*rei*-ʃön) *n* preparación *f*
**prepare** (pri-*pê*$^{ö}$) *v* preparar
**preposition** (prê-pö-*si*-ʃön) *n* preposición *f*
**prescribe** (pri-*sskraib*) *v* prescribir
**prescription** (pri-*sskrip*-ʃön) *n* prescripción *f*
**presence** (*prê*-sönss) *n* presencia *f*
**present**[1] (*prê*-sönt) *n* regalo *m*, presente *m*; *adj* actual; presente
**present**[2] (pri-*sênt*) *v* presentar
**presently** (*prê*-sönt-li) *adv* en seguida, dentro de poco
**preservation** (prê-sö-*vei*-ʃön) *n* conservación *f*
**preserve** (pri-*sööv*) *v* preservar; conservar
**president** (*prê*-si-dönt) *n* presidente *m*
**press** (prêss) *n* prensa *f*; *v* empujar, *apretar; planchar; ~ **agency** agencia de prensa; ~ **conference** conferencia de prensa
**pressing** (*prê*-ssing) *adj* urgente
**pressure** (*prê*-ʃö) *n* presión *f*; tensión *f*; **atmospheric** ~ presión atmosférica
**prestige** (prê-*sstiiʒ*) *n* prestigio *m*
**presumable** (pri-*syuu*-mö-böl) *adj* presumible
**presume** (pri-*syuum*) *v* suponer
**presumptuous** (pri-*samp*-ʃöss) *adj* presuntuoso; presumido
**pretence** (pri-*tênss*) *n* pretexto *m*
**pretend** (pri-*tênd*) *v* fingir
**pretext** (*prii*-têksst) *n* pretexto *m*
**pretty** (*pri*-ti) *adj* bonito; *adv* bastante
**prevent** (pri-*vênt*) *v* *impedir; *prevenir
**preventive** (pri-*vên*-tiv) *adj* preventivo
**preview** (*prii*-vyuu) *n* preestreno *m*; *v* hacer la presentación previa de
**previous** (*prii*-vi-öss) *adj* precedente, anterior, previo
**pre-war** (prii-$^{u}$*oo*) *adj* de la preguerra
**price** (praiss) *n* precio *m*; *v* fijar el precio
**priceless** (*praiss*-löss) *adj* inapreciable
**price list** (*praiss*-lisst) *n* lista de precios
**prick** (prik) *v* pinchar
**pride** (praid) *n* orgullo *m*
**priest** (priisst) *n* cura *m*
**primary** (*prai*-mö-ri) *adj* primario; primero, primordial; elemental
**prince** (prinss) *n* príncipe *m*
**princess** (prin-*ssêss*) *n* princesa *f*
**principal** (*prin*-ssö-pöl) *adj* principal; *n* principal *m*/*f*; director *m*, -a *f*
**principle** (*prin*-ssö-pöl) *n* principio *m*

**print** (print) *v* *imprimir; *n* positiva *f*; grabado *m*; **printed matter** impreso *m*
**printer** (*prin*-tö) *n* impresor *m*; impresora *f*; imprenta *f*
**printout** (*print*-aut) *n* copia *f* impresa
**prior** (prai[ö]) *adj* anterior
**priority** (prai-*o*-rö-ti) *n* prioridad *f*
**prison** (*pri*-sön) *n* prisión *f*
**prisoner** (*pri*-sö-nö) *n* preso *m*, prisionero *m*; **~ of war** prisionero de guerra
**privacy** (*prai*-vö-ssi) *n* intimidad *f*, vida privada
**private** (*prai*-vit) *adj* particular, privado; personal
**privilege** (*pri*-vi-lidʒ) *n* privilegio *m*
**prize** (prais) *n* premio *m*; recompensa *f*
**probable** (*pro*-bö-böl) *adj* probable
**probably** (*pro*-bö-bli) *adv* probablemente
**problem** (*pro*-blöm) *n* problema *m*
**procedure** (prö-*ssii*-dʒö) *n* procedimiento *m*
**proceed** (prö-*ssiid*) *v* *proseguir; proceder
**process** (*prou*-ssêss) *n* procedimiento *m*, proceso *m*
**procession** (prö-*ssê*-ʃön) *n* procesión *f*, comitiva *f*
**proclaim** (prö-*kleim*) *v* proclamar
**produce**[1] (prö-*dyuuss*) *v* *producir
**produce**[2] (*prod*-yuuss) *n* producto *m*
**producer** (prö-*dyuu*-ssö) *n* productor *m*
**product** (*pro*-dakt) *n* producto *m*
**production** (prö-*dak*-ʃön) *n* producción *f*
**profession** (prö-*fê*-ʃön) *n* profesión *f*
**professional** (prö-*fê*-ʃö-nöl) *adj* profesional
**professor** (prö-*fê*-ssö) *n* profesor *m*, -a *f*
**profit** (*pro*-fit) *n* beneficio *m*, ganancia *f*; ventaja *f*; *v* aprovechar
**profitable** (*pro*-fi-tö-böl) *adj* provechoso
**profound** (prö-*faund*) *adj* profundo
**program(me)** (*prou*-ghræm) *n* programa *m*
**progress**[1] (*prou*-ghrêss) *n* progreso *m*
**progress**[2] (prö-*ghrêss*) *v* progresar
**progressive** (prö-*ghrê*-ssiv) *adj* progresista; progresivo
**prohibit** (prö-*hi*-bit) *v* prohibir
**prohibition** (prou-i-*bi*-ʃön) *n* prohibición *f*
**prohibitive** (prö-*hi*-bi-tiv) *adj* exorbitante
**project** (*pro*-dʒêkt) *n* plan *m*, proyecto *m*
**promenade** (pro-mö-*naad*) *n* paseo *m*
**promise** (*pro*-miss) *n* promesa *f*; *v* prometer
**promote** (prö-*mout*) *v* *promover
**promotion** (prö-*mou*-ʃön) *n* promoción *f*
**prompt** (prompt) *adj* inmediato, pronto
**pronoun** (*prou*-naun) *n* pronombre *m*
**pronounce** (prö-*naunss*) *v* pronunciar
**pronunciation** (prö-nan-ssi-*ei*-ʃön) *n* pronunciación *f*
**proof** (pruuf) *n* prueba *f*
**propaganda** (pro-pö-*ghæn*-dö) *n* propaganda *f*
**propel** (prö-*pêl*) *v* propulsar
**propeller** (prö-*pê*-lö) *n* hélice *f*
**proper** (*pro*-pö) *adj* justo; debido, conveniente, apropiado
**property** (*pro*-pö-ti) *n* propiedad *f*; bienes *mpl*; cualidad *f*
**prophet** (*pro*-fit) *n* profeta *m*
**proportion** (prö-*poo*-ʃön) *n* proporción *f*
**proportional** (prö-*poo*-ʃö-nöl) *adj* proporcional
**proposal** (prö-*pou*-söl) *n* propuesta *f*

**propose** (prö-*pous*) *v* *proponer
**proposition** (pro-pö-*si*-ʃön) *n* propuesta *f*
**proprietor** (prö-*prai*-ö-tö) *n* propietario *m*, -a *f*
**prospect** (*pro*-sspêkt) *n* perspectiva *f*
**prospectus** (prö-*sspêk*-töss) *n* prospecto *m*
**prosperity** (pro-*sspê*-rö-ti) *n* prosperidad *f*
**prosperous** (*pro*-sspö-röss) *adj* próspero
**prostitute** (*pro*-ssti-tyuut) *n* prostituta *f*
**protect** (prö-*têkt*) *v* proteger
**protection** (prö-*têk*-ʃön) *n* protección *f*
**protein** (*prou*-tiin) *n* proteína *f*
**protest**[1] (*prou*-têsst) *n* protesta *f*
**protest**[2] (prö-*têsst*) *v* protestar
**Protestant** (*pro*-ti-sstönt) *adj* protestante
**proud** (praud) *adj* orgulloso
**prove** (pruuv) *v* *demostrar, *comprobar; resultar
**proverb** (*pro*-vööb) *n* proverbio *m*
**provide** (prö-*vaid*) *v* *proveer; **provided that** con tal que
**province** (*pro*-vinss) *n* provincia *f*
**provincial** (prö-*vin*-ʃöl) *adj* provincial
**provisional** (prö-*vi*-ʒö-nöl) *adj* provisional
**provisions** (prö-*vi*-ʒöns) *pl* provisiones *fpl*
**prune** (pruun) *n* ciruela pasa
**psychiatrist** (ssai-*kai*-ö-trisst) *n* psiquiatra *m*
**psychic** (*ssai*-kik) *adj* psíquico
**psychoanalyst** (ssai-kou-*æ*-nö-lisst) *n* psicoanalista *m*
**psychological** (ssai-ko-*lo*-dʒi-köl) *adj* psicológico
**psychologist** (ssai-*ko*-lö-dʒisst) *n* psicólogo *m*
**psychology** (ssai-*ko*-lö-dʒi) *n* psicología *f*
**pub** (pab) *n* bar *m*; taberna *f*
**public** (*pa*-blik) *adj* público; general; *n* público *m*; ~ **garden** jardín público; ~ **house** taberna *f*
**publication** (pa-bli-*kei*-ʃön) *n* publicación *f*
**publicity** (pa-*bli*-ssö-ti) *n* publicidad *f*
**publish** (*pa*-bliʃ) *v* publicar
**publisher** (*pa*-bli-ʃö) *n* editor *m*, -a *f*
**puddle** (*pa*-döl) *n* charco *m*
**pull** (pul) *v* tirar; ~ **out** arrancar; ~ **up** pararse
**pulley** (*pu*-li) *n* (pl ~s) polea *f*
**Pullman** (*pul*-mön) *n* coche Pullman
**pullover** (*pu*-lou-vö) *n* jersey *m*; pulóver *m*
**pulpit** (*pul*-pit) *n* púlpito *m*
**pulse** (palss) *n* pulso *m*
**pump** (pamp) *n* bomba *f*; *v* bombear
**pun** (pan) *n* juego *m* de palabras
**punch** (panch) *v* *dar puñetazos; *n* puñetazo *m*
**punctual** (*pangk*-chu-öl) *adj* puntual
**puncture** (*pangk*-chö) *n* pinchazo *m*
**punctured** (*pangk*-chöd) *adj* pinchado
**punish** (*pa*-niʃ) *v* castigar
**punishment** (*pa*-niʃ-mönt) *n* castigo *m*
**pupil**[1] (*pyuu*-pöl) *n* alumno *m*, -a *f*
**pupil**[2] (*pyuu*-pöl) *n* pupila *f*
**puppet show** (*pa*-pit-ʃou) *n* teatro de títeres
**purchase** (*pöö*-chöss) *v* comprar; *n* compra *f*; ~ **price** precio de compra; ~ **tax** impuesto sobre la venta
**purchaser** (*pöö*-chö-ssö) *n* comprador *m*, -a *f*
**pure** (pyu$^{ö}$) *adj* casto, puro
**purple** (*pöö*-pöl) *adj* purpúreo, morado
**purpose** (*pöö*-pöss) *n* propósito *m*, fin

*m*, intención *f*; **on ~** intencionado
**purse** (pööss) *n* bolsa *f*, monedero *m*
**pursue** (pö-*ssyuu*) *v* *perseguir
**pus** (pass) *n* pus *f*
**push** (puʃ) *n* empujón *m*; *v* empujar
**push button** (*puʃ*-ba-tön) *n* pulsador *m*
***put** (put) *v* colocar, *poner; meter; plantear; **~ away** guardar; **~ off** aplazar; **~ on** *ponerse; **~ out** apagar
**puzzle** (*pa*-söl) *n* rompecabezas *m*; enigma *m*; *v* confundir; **jigsaw ~** rompecabezas *m*
**puzzling** (*pas*-ling) *adj* incomprensible; misterioso
**pyjamas** (pö-*dʒaa*-mös) *pl* pijama *m*

# Q

**quadrangle** (k$^{u}$od-*ræng-göl*) *n* cuadrángulo *m*; patio *m*
**quail** (k$^{u}$eil) *n* (pl ~, ~s) codorniz *f*
**quaint** (k$^{u}$eint) *adj* curioso; anticuado
**qualification** (k$^{u}$o-li-fi-*kei*-ʃön) *n* aptitud *f*; reserva *f*, restricción *f*
**qualified** (*k$^{u}$o*-li-faid) *adj* calificado; competente
**qualify** (*k$^{u}$o*-li-fai) *v* *ser capaz de, *ser apto para
**quality** (*k$^{u}$o*-lö-ti) *n* calidad *f*; característica *f*
**quantity** (*k$^{u}$on*-tö-ti) *n* cantidad *f*; número *m*
**quarantine** (*k$^{u}$o*-rön-tiin) *n* cuarentena *f*
**quarrel** (*k$^{u}$o*-röl) *v* disputar, *reñir; *n* disputa *f*
**quarry** (*k$^{u}$o*-ri) *n* cantera *f*; presa *f*
**quarter** (*k$^{u}$oo*-tö) *n* cuarto *m*; trimestre *m*; barrio *m*; **~ of an hour** cuarto de hora
**quarterly** (*k$^{u}$oo*-tö-li) *adj* trimestral
**quay** (kii) *n* muelle *m*
**queen** (k$^{u}$iin) *n* reina *f*
**queer** (k$^{u}$i$^{ö}$) *adj* singular, extraño
**query** (*k$^{u}$i$^{ö}$*-ri) *n* pregunta *f*; *v* indagar; *poner en duda
**question** (*k$^{u}$êss*-chön) *n* pregunta *f*; cuestión *f*, problema *m*; *v* interrogar; *poner en duda; **~ mark** signo de interrogación
**queue** (kyuu) *n* cola *f*; *v* *hacer cola
**quick** (k$^{u}$ik) *adj* rápido; ágil
**quick-tempered** (k$^{u}$ik-*têm*-pöd) *adj* irascible; irritable
**quiet** (*k$^{u}$ai*-öt) *adj* quieto, tranquilo; *n* silencio *m*, paz *f*
**quilt** (k$^{u}$ilt) *n* edredón *m*
**quit** (k$^{u}$it) *v* cesar; dejar; abandonar
**quite** (k$^{u}$ait) *adv* enteramente, completamente; bastante; muy
**quiz** (k$^{u}$is) *n* (pl ~zes) concurso *m*
**quota** (*k$^{u}$ou*-tö) *n* cuota *f*
**quotation** (k$^{u}$ou-*tei*-ʃön) *n* cita *f*; **~ marks** comillas *fpl*
**quote** (k$^{u}$out) *v* citar

# R

**rabbit** (*ræ*-bit) *n* conejo *m*
**rabies** (*rei*-bis) *n* rabia *f*
**race** (reiss) *n* carrera *f*; raza *f*
**racecourse** (*reiss*-kooss) *n* pista para carreras, hipódromo *m*
**racehorse** (*reiss*-hooss) *n* caballo de carrera
**racetrack** (*reiss*-træk) *n* pista para carreras
**racial** (*rei*-ʃöl) *adj* racial
**racket** (*ræ*-kit) *n* raqueta *f*; alboroto *m*
**radiator** (*rei*-di-ei-tö) *n* radiador *m*
**radical** (*ræ*-di-köl) *adj* radical
**radio** (*rei*-di-ou) *n* radio *f*
**radish** (*ræ*-diʃ) *n* rábano *m*
**radius** (*rei*-di-öss) *n* (pl radii) radio *m*
**raft** (raaft) *n* balsa *f*
**rag** (rægh) *n* trapo *m*
**rage** (reidʒ) *n* furor *m*, rabia *f*; *v* rabiar
**raid** (reid) *n* irrupción *f*
**rail** (reil) *n* barandilla *f*, barrera *f*
**railing** (*rei*-ling) *n* barandilla *f*
**railroad** (*reil*-roud) *nAm* vía del tren, ferrocarril *m*
**railway** (*reil*-ᵘei) *n* ferrocarril *m*
**rain** (rein) *n* lluvia *f*; *v* *llover
**rainbow** (*rein*-bou) *n* arco iris
**raincoat** (*rein*-kout) *n* impermeable *m*
**rainproof** (*rein*-pruuf) *adj* impermeable
**rainy** (*rei*-ni) *adj* lluvioso
**raise** (reis) *v* alzar; aumentar; educar, cultivar, criar; recaudar; *nAm* aumento de sueldo
**raisin** (*rei*-sön) *n* pasa *f*
**rake** (reik) *n* rastrillo *m*
**rally** (*ræ*-li) *n* reunión *f*
**ramp** (ræmp) *n* rampa *f*
**ramshackle** (*ræm*-ʃæ-köl) *adj* destartalado
**rancid** (*ræn*-ssid) *adj* rancio
**rang** (ræng) *v* (p ring)
**range** (reindʒ) *n* extensión *f*; alcance *m*; **mountain** ~ sierra cordillera; ~ **finder** telémetro *m*
**rank** (rængk) *n* rango *m*; fila *f*
**ransom** (*ræn*-ssöm) *n* rescate *m*
**rape** (reip) *v* violar
**rapid** (*ræ*-pid) *adj* rápido
**rapids** (*ræ*-pids) *pl* rápidos de río
**rare** (rêᵒ) *adj* raro
**rarely** (*rêᵒ*-li) *adv* raras veces
**rascal** (*raa*-ssköl) *n* pícaro *m*, pillo *m*
**rash** (ræʃ) *n* erupción *f*; *adj* precipitado, imprudente
**raspberry** (*raas*-bö-ri) *n* frambuesa *f*
**rat** (ræt) *n* rata *f*
**rate** (reit) *n* precio *m*, tarifa *f*; velocidad *f*; **at any** ~ de todos modos, en todo caso; ~ **of exchange** cambio *m*
**rather** (*raa*-ðö) *adv* bastante; más bien, algo
**ration** (*ræ*-ʃön) *n* ración *f*
**rattan** (ræ-*tæn*) *n* rota *f*
**raven** (*rei*-vön) *n* cuervo *m*
**raw** (roo) *adj* crudo; ~ **material** materia prima
**ray** (rei) *n* rayo *m*
**rayon** (*rei*-on) *n* rayón *m*
**razor** (*rei*-sö) *n* máquina de afeitar; ~ **blade** hoja de afeitar
**reach** (riich) *v* alcanzar; *n* alcance *m*
**react** (ri-*ækt*) *v* reaccionar
**reaction** (ri-*æk*-ʃön) *n* reacción *f*
***read** (riid) *v* *leer
**reader** (*rii*-dö) lector *m*, -a *f*
**reading** (*rii*-ding) *n* lectura *f*; ~ **lamp** lámpara para lectura; ~ **room** sala de lectura
**ready** (*rê*-di) *adj* preparado, listo
**ready-made** (rê-di-*meid*) *adj* confeccionado; hecho
**real** (riᵒl) *adj* verdadero

**reality** (ri-æ-lö-ti) *n* realidad *f*
**realizable** (*ri*$^{ö}$-lai-sö-böl) *adj* realizable
**realize** (*ri*$^{ö}$-lais) *v* *reconocer; realizar
**really** (*ri*$^{ö}$-li) *adv* verdaderamente, en realidad; de veras
**rear** (ri$^{ö}$) *n* parte posterior; *v* criar
**rear light** (ri$^{ö}$-*lait*) *n* luz trasera
**reason** (*rii*-sön) *n* causa *f*, razón *f*; sentido *m*; *v* razonar
**reasonable** (*rii*-sö-nö-böl) *adj* razonable
**reassure** (rii-ö-*ʃu*$^{ö}$) *v* tranquilizar
**rebate** (*rii*-beit) *n* reducción *f*, rebaja *f*
**rebellion** (ri-*bêl*-yön) *n* sublevación *f*, rebelión *f*
**recall** (ri-*kool*) *v* *acordarse; llamar; revocar
**receipt** (ri-*ssiit*) *n* recibo *m*
**receive** (ri-*ssiiv*) *v* recibir
**receiver** (ri-*ssii*-vö) *n* receptor *m*
**recent** (*rii*-ssönt) *adj* reciente
**recently** (*rii*-ssönt-li) *adv* recientemente
**reception** (ri-*ssêp*-ʃön) *n* recepción *f*; acogida *f*; ~ **desk** recepción
**receptionist** (ri-*ssêp*-ʃö-nisst) *n* recepcionista *m/f*
**recession** (ri-*ssê*-ʃön) *n* retroceso *m*; recesión *f*
**recipe** (*rê*-ssi-pi) *n* receta *f*
**recital** (ri-*ssai*-töl) *n* recital *m*
**reckon** (*rê*-kön) *v* calcular; considerar; *creer
**recognition** (rê-kögh-*ni*-ʃön) *n* reconocimiento *m*
**recognize** (*rê*-kögh-nais) *v* *reconocer
**recollect** (rê-kö-*lêkt*) *v* *acordarse
**recommence** (rii-kö-*mênss*) *v* *recomenzar
**recommend** (rê-kö-*mênd*) *v* *recomendar; aconsejar
**recommendation** (rê-kö-mên-*dei*-ʃön) *n* recomendación *f*
**reconciliation** (rê-kön-ssi-li-*ei*-ʃön) *n* reconciliación *f*
**record**[1] (*rê*-kood) *n* disco *m*; récord *m*; registro *m*; partida *f*; ~ **player** tocadiscos *m*
**record**[2] (ri-*kood*) *v* registrar; grabar
**recorder** (ri-*koo*-dö) *n* registrador *m*; flauta *f* dulce
**recording** (ri-*koo*-ding) *n* grabación *f*
**recover** (ri-*ka*-vö) *v* recuperar; *restablecerse, curarse
**recovery** (ri-*ka*-vö-ri) *n* curación *f*, restablecimiento *m*
**recreation** (rê-kri-*ei*-ʃön) *n* recreación *f*, recreo *m*; ~ **center** *Am*, ~ **centre** centro de recreo; ~ **ground** terreno de recreo público
**recruit** (ri-*kruut*) *n* recluta *m/f*
**rectangle** (*rêk*-tæng-ghöl) *n* rectángulo *m*
**rectangular** (rêk-*tæng*-ghyu-lö) *adj* rectangular
**rector** (*rêk*-tö) *n* pastor *m*, rector *m*
**rectory** (*rêk*-tö-ri) *n* rectoría *f*
**rectum** (*rêk*-töm) *n* intestino recto
**recyclable** (ri-*ssai*-klö-böl) *adj* reciclable
**recycle** (ri-*ssai*-köl) *v* reciclar
**red** (rêd) *adj* rojo
**redeem** (ri-*diim*) *v* redimir
**reduce** (ri-*dyuuss*) *v* *reducir, *disminuir, rebajar
**reduction** (ri-*dak*-ʃön) *n* rebaja *f*, reducción *f*
**redundant** (ri-*dan*-dönt) *adj* superfluo
**reed** (riid) *n* junquillo *m*
**reef** (riif) *n* arrecife *m*
**refer** (ri-*föö*) *v*: ~ **to** remitir a
**reference** (*rêf*-rönss) *n* referencia *f*; relación *f*; **with ~ to** con respecto a
**referee** (rê-fö-*rii*) árbitro *m*, -a *f*; persona que pueda dar referencias
**refill** (*rii*-fil) *n* repuesto *m*; recambio *m*
**refinery** (ri-*fai*-nö-ri) *n* refinería *f*

**reflect** (ri-*flêkt*) *v* reflejar
**reflection** (ri-*flêk*-ʃön) *n* reflejo *m*; imagen reflejada
**refresh** (ri-*frêʃ*) *v* refrescar
**refreshment** (ri-*frêʃ*-mönt) *n* refresco *m*
**refrigerator** (ri-*fri*-dʒö-rei-tö) *n* refrigerador *m*
**refugee** (rê-fyuu-*ʒii*) *n* refugiado *m*, -a *f*
**refund**[1] (ri-*fand*) *v* reintegrar
**refund**[2] (*rii*-fand) *n* reintegro *m*
**refusal** (ri-*fyuu*-söl) *n* negativa *f*
**refuse**[1] (ri-*fyuus*) *v* rehusar
**refuse**[2] (*rê*-fyuuss) *n* desecho *m*
**regard** (ri-*ghaad*) *v* considerar; *n* respeto *m*; **with ~ to** en cuanto a
**regarding** (ri-*ghaa*-ding) *prep* relativo a, tocante a; respecto a
**regatta** (ri-*ghæ*-tö) *n* regata *f*
**régime** (rei-*ʒiim*) *n* régimen *m*
**region** (*rii*-dʒön) *n* región *f*; comarca *f*
**regional** (*rii*-dʒö-nöl) *adj* regional
**register** (*rê*-dʒi-sstö) *v* inscribirse; certificar; **registered letter** carta certificada
**registration** (rê-dʒi-*sstrei*-ʃön) *n* inscripción *f*; **~ form** formulario de matriculación; **~ number** matrícula *f*; **~ plate** placa *f*
**regret** (ri-*ghrêt*) *v* *sentir; *n* arrepentimiento *m*
**regular** (*rê*-ghyu-lö) *adj* regular; corriente, normal
**regulate** (*rê*-ghyu-leit) *v* regular
**regulation** (rê-ghyu-*lei*-ʃön) *n* reglamento *m*, regulación *f*; regla *f*
**rehabilitation** (rii-hö-bi-li-*tei*-ʃön) *n* rehabilitación *f*
**rehearsal** (ri-*höö*-ssöl) *n* ensayo *m*
**rehearse** (ri-*hööss*) *v* ensayar
**reign** (rein) *n* reinado *m*; *v* *gobernar
**reimburse** (rii-im-*bööss*) *v* reembolsar
**reindeer** (*rein*-diö) *n* (pl ~) reno *m*
**reject** (ri-*dʒêkt*) *v* rehusar, rechazar; *reprobar
**relate** (ri-*leit*) *v* *contar
**related** (ri-*lei*-tid) *adj* emparentado
**relation** (ri-*lei*-ʃön) *n* relación *f*; pariente *m*; **relationship** relación *f*
**relative** (*rê*-lö-tiv) *n* pariente *m*; *adj* relativo
**relax** (ri-*lækss*) *v* descansar
**relaxation** (ri-læk-*ssei*-ʃön) *n* relajación *f*
**reliable** (ri-*lai*-ö-böl) *adj* fiable, fidedigno
**relic** (*rê*-lik) *n* reliquia *f*
**relief** (ri-*liif*) *n* alivio *m*; ayuda *f*; relieve *m*
**relieve** (ri-*liiv*) *v* aliviar
**religion** (ri-*li*-dʒön) *n* religión *f*
**religious** (ri-*li*-dʒöss) *adj* religioso
**rely on** (ri-*lai*) *contar con
**remain** (ri-*mein*) *v* quedarse; quedar; sobrar
**remainder** (ri-*mein*-dö) *n* resto *m*
**remaining** (ri-*mei*-ning) *adj* demás, restante
**remark** (ri-*maak*) *n* observación *f*; *v* *hacer una observación
**remarkable** (ri-*maa*-kö-böl) *adj* notable
**remedy** (*rê*-mö-di) *n* remedio *m*
**remember** (ri-*mêm*-bö) *v* *acordarse
**remembrance** (ri-*mêm*-brönss) *n* recuerdo *m*
**remind** (ri-*maind*) *v* *recordar
**remit** (ri-*mit*) *v* remitir
**remittance** (ri-*mi*-tönss) *n* remesa *f*
**remnant** (*rêm*-nönt) *n* resto *m*, residuo *m*, remanente *m*
**remote** (ri-*mout*) *adj* remoto, lejano
**removal** (ri-*muu*-völ) *n* remoción *f*
**remove** (ri-*muuv*) *v* *remover
**remunerate** (ri-*myuu*-nö-reit) *v* remunerar

**remuneration** (ri-myuu-nö-*rei*-ʃön) *n* remuneración *f*
**renew** (ri-*nyuu*) *v* *renovar; alargar
**rent** (rênt) *v* alquilar; *n* alquiler *m*
**repair** (ri-*pê^ö*) *v* arreglar, reparar; *n* reparación *f*
**reparation** (rê-pö-*rei*-ʃön) *n* reparación *f*
***repay** (ri-*pei*) *v* reintegrar
**repayment** (ri-*pei*-mönt) *n* reintegro *m*
**repeat** (ri-*piit*) *v* *repetir
**repellent** (ri-*pê*-lönt) *adj* repugnante, repelente
**repentance** (ri-*pên*-tönss) *n* arrepentimiento *m*
**repertory** (*rê*-pö-tö-ri) *n* repertorio *m*
**repetition** (rê-pö-*ti*-ʃön) *n* repetición *f*
**replace** (ri-*pleiss*) *v* reemplazar
**reply** (ri-*plai*) *v* responder; *n* respuesta *f*; **in ~** en contestación
**report** (ri-*poot*) *v* relatar; informar; presentarse; *n* relato *m*, informe *m*
**reporter** (ri-*poo*-tö) *n* reportero *m*, -a *f*
**represent** (rê-pri-*sênt*) *v* representar
**representation** (rê-pri-sên-*tei*-ʃön) *n* representación *f*
**representative** (rê-pri-*sên*-tö-tiv) *adj* representativo
**reprimand** (*rê*-pri-maand) *v* reprender
**reproach** (ri-*prouch*) *n* reproche *m*; *v* reprochar
**reproduce** (rii-prö-*dyuuss*) *v* *reproducir
**reproduction** (rii-prö-*dak*-ʃön) *n* reproducción *f*
**reptile** (*rêp*-tail) *n* reptil *m*
**republic** (ri-*pa*-blik) *n* república *f*
**republican** (ri-*pa*-bli-kön) *adj* republicano
**repulsive** (ri-*pal*-ssiv) *adj* repulsivo
**reputation** (rê-pyu-*tei*-ʃön) *n* reputación *f*; renombre *m*
**request** (ri-*k^uêsst*) *n* ruego *m*; demanda *f*; *v* solicitar; pedir
**require** (ri-*k^uai^ö*) *v* *requerir
**requirement** (ri-*k^uai^ö*-mönt) *n* requerimiento *m*
**requisite** (*rê*-k^ui-sit) *adj* necesario
**rescue** (*rê*-sskyuu) *v* rescatar; *n* rescate *m*
**research** (ri-*ssööch*) *n* investigación *f*
**resemblance** (ri-*sêm*-blönss) *n* semejanza *f*
**resemble** (ri-*sêm*-böl) *v* asemejarse
**resent** (ri-*sênt*) *v* *resentirse por
**reservation** (rê-sö-*vei*-ʃön) *n* reservación *f*
**reserve** (ri-*söö*v) *v* reservar; *n* reserva *f*
**reserved** (ri-*söövd*) *adj* reservado
**reservoir** (*rê*-sö-v^uaa) *n* embalse *m*
**reside** (ri-*said*) *v* residir
**residence** (*rê*-si-dönss) *n* residencia *f*; **~ permit** permiso de residencia
**resident** (*rê*-si-dönt) *n* residente *m/f*; *adj* residente; interno
**resign** (ri-*sain*) *v* resignar
**resignation** (rê-sigh-*nei*-ʃön) *n* resignación *f*
**resin** (*rê*-sin) *n* resina *f*
**resist** (ri-*sisst*) *v* resistir
**resistance** (ri-*si*-sstönss) *n* resistencia *f*
**resolute** (*rê*-sö-luut) *adj* resuelto, decidido
**respect** (ri-*sspêkt*) *n* respeto *m*; estimación *f*, reverencia *f*; *v* respetar
**respectable** (ri-*sspêk*-tö-böl) *adj* respetable
**respectful** (ri-*sspêkt*-föl) *adj* respetuoso
**respective** (ri-*sspêk*-tiv) *adj* respectivo
**respiration** (rê-sspö-*rei*-ʃön) *n* respiración *f*
**respite** (*rê*-sspait) *n* respiro *m*

**responsibility** (ri-sspon-ssö-*bi*-lö-ti) *n* responsabilidad *f*
**responsible** (ri-*sspon*-ssö-böl) *adj* responsable
**rest** (rêsst) *n* descanso *m*; resto *m*; *v* *hacer reposo, descansar; ~ **home** residencia de ancianos; ~ **room** aseo, servicios
**restaurant** (*rê*-sstö-rong) *n* restaurante *m*
**restful** (*rêsst*-föl) *adj* reposado
**restless** (*rêsst*-löss) *adj* inquieto
**restrain** (ri-*sstrein*) *v* *contener, *impedir
**restriction** (ri-*sstrik*-ʃön) *n* restricción *f*
**result** (ri-*salt*) *n* resultado *m*; consecuencia *f*; *v* resultar
**resume** (ri-*syuum*) *v* reemprender
**résumé** (*rê*-syu-mei) *n* resumen *m*; *Am* currículum vitae
**retail** (*rii*-teil) *v* vender al detalle; ~ **trade** comercio al por menor
**retailer** (*rii*-tei-lö) *n* comerciante al por menor, minorista *m/f*; revendedor *m*, -a *f*
**retina** (*rê*-ti-nö) *n* retina *f*
**retire** (ri-*taiö*) *v* jubilarse; retirar; **retired** jubilado; **retirement** jubilación *f*
**return** (ri-*töön*) *v* *volver; *n* regreso *m*; vuelta *f*; devolución *f*; ~ **flight** vuelo de regreso; ~ **ticket** billete de ida y vuelta
**reunite** (rii-yuu-*nait*) *v* reunir
**reveal** (ri-*viil*) *v* *manifestar, revelar
**revelation** (rê-vö-*lei*-ʃön) *n* revelación *f*
**revenge** (ri-*vêndʒ*) *n* venganza *f*
**revenue** (*rê*-vö-nyuu) *n* ingresos *mpl*, renta *f*
**reverse** (ri-*vööss*) *n* contrario *m*; reverso *m*; marcha atrás; revés *m*; *adj* inverso; *v* *dar marcha atrás
**review** (ri-*vyuu*) *n* reseña *f*; revista *f*
**revise** (ri-*vais*) *v* revisar
**revision** (ri-*vi*-ʒön) *n* revisión *f*
**revival** (ri-*vai*-völ) *n* recuperación *f*
**revolt** (ri-*voult*) *v* sublevarse; *n* rebelión *f*, revuelta *f*
**revolting** (ri-*voul*-ting) *adj* repugnante, chocante, repelente
**revolution** (rê-vö-*luu*-ʃön) *n* revolución *f*
**revolutionary** (rê-vö-*luu*-ʃö-nö-ri) *adj* revolucionario
**revolver** (ri-*vol*-vö) *n* revólver *m*
**revue** (ri-*vyuu*) *n* revista *f*
**reward** (ri-*uood*) *n* recompensa *f*; *v* recompensar
**rheumatism** (*ruu*-mö-ti-söm) *n* reumatismo *m*
**rhinoceros** (rai-*no*-ssö-röss) *n* (pl ~, ~es) rinoceronte *m*
**rhubarb** (*ruu*-baab) *n* ruibarbo *m*
**rhyme** (raim) *n* rima *f*
**rhythm** (*ri*-ðöm) *n* ritmo *m*
**rib** (rib) *n* costilla *f*
**ribbon** (*ri*-bön) *n* cinta *f*
**rice** (raiss) *n* arroz *m*
**rich** (rich) *adj* rico
**riches** (*ri*-chis) *pl* riqueza *f*
**rid** (rid): **get ~ of** deshacerse de
**riddle** (*ri*-döl) *n* adivinanza *f*
**ride** (raid) *n* paseo *m*
***ride** (raid) *v* *ir en coche; montar
**rider** (*rai*-dö) *n* jinete *m*
**ridge** (ridʒ) *n* cresta *f*; lomo *m*
**ridicule** (*ri*-di-kyuul) *v* ridiculizar
**ridiculous** (ri-*di*-kyu-löss) *adj* ridículo
**riding** (*rai*-ding) *n* equitación *f*; ~ **school** picadero *m*; escuela de equitación
**rifle** (*rai*-föl) *v* rifle *m*
**right** (rait) *n* derecho *m*; *adj* correcto; derecho; justo; **all right!** ¡de acuerdo!; ***be ~** *tener razón; **~ now** ahora mismo; **~ of way** prioridad de

paso
**righteous** (*rai*-chöss) *adj* justo; recto; honrado
**right-hand** (*rait*-hænd) *adj* derecho
**rightly** (*rait*-li) *adv* justamente
**rim** (rim) *n* llanta *f*; borde *m*
**ring** (ring) *n* anillo *m*; círculo *m*; pista *f*
***ring** (ring) *v* *sonar; ~ **up** llamar por teléfono
**rinse** (rinss) *v* enjuagar; *n* enjuague *m*
**riot** (*rai*-öt) *n* motín *m*
**rip** (rip) *v* rasgar
**ripe** (raip) *adj* maduro
**rise** (rais) *n* aumento de sueldo, aumento *m*; levantamiento *m*; subida *f*; nacimiento *m*
***rise** (rais) *v* levantarse; subir
**rising** (*rai*-sing) *n* levantamiento *m*
**risk** (rissk) *n* riesgo *m*; peligro *m*; *v* arriesgar
**risky** (*ri*-sski) *adj* arriesgado
**rival** (*rai*-völ) *n* rival *m/f*; competidor *m*, -a *f*; *v* rivalizar
**rivalry** (*rai*-völ-ri) *n* rivalidad *f*; competencia *f*
**river** (*ri*-vö) *n* río *m*; ~ **bank** ribera *f*
**riverside** (*ri*-vö-ssaid) *n* ribera *f*
**roach** (rouch) *n* (pl ~) escarcho *m*
**road** (roud) *n* calle *f*, camino *m*; ~ **fork** *n* bifurcación *f*; ~ **map** mapa de carreteras; ~ **system** red de carreteras; ~ **up** cerrado por obras
**roadhouse** (*roud*-hauss) *n* albergue *m* de carretera
**roadside** (*roud*-ssaid) *n* borde del camino
**roam** (roum) *v* vagar; recorrer
**roar** (roo) *v* mugir, rugir; *n* rugido *m*, retumbo *m*
**roast** (rousst) *v* asar, asar en parrilla
**rob** (rob) *v* robar
**robber** (*ro*-bö) *n* ladrón *m*
**robbery** (*ro*-bö-ri) *n* robo *m*
**robe** (roub) *n* manto *m*, túnica *f*
**robin** (*ro*-bin) *n* petirrojo *m*
**robust** (rou-*basst*) *adj* robusto
**rock** (rok) *n* roca *f*; *v* mecer
**rocket** (*ro*-kit) *n* cohete *m*
**rocky** (*ro*-ki) *adj* rocoso
**rod** (rod) *n* barra *f*
**roe** (rou) *n* huevos de los peces, hueva *f*
**role** (roul) *n* papel *m*
**roll** (roul) *v* *rodar; *n* rollo *m*; panecillo *m*
**roller-skating** (*rou*-lö-sskei-ting) *n* patinaje de ruedas
**Roman Catholic** (*rou*-mön *kæ*-zö-lik) católico
**romance** (rö-*mænss*) *n* amorío *m*
**romantic** (rö-*mæn*-tik) *adj* romántico
**roof** (ruuf) *n* techo *m*; **thatched ~** techo de paja
**room** (ruum) *n* habitación *f*; espacio *m*, sitio *m*; ~ **and board** pensión completa; ~ **service** servicio de habitación; ~ **temperature** temperatura ambiente
**roomy** (*ruu*-mi) *adj* espacioso
**root** (ruut) *n* raíz *f*
**rope** (roup) *n* soga *f*
**rosary** (*rou*-sö-ri) *n* rosario *m*
**rose** (rous) *n* rosa *f*; *adj* rosa
**rotten** (*ro*-tön) *adj* podrido
**rouge** (ruuʒ) *n* colorete *m*
**rough** (raf) *adj* áspero
**roulette** (ruu-*lêt*) *n* ruleta *f*
**round** (raund) *adj* redondo; *prep* alrededor de, en torno de; *n* vuelta *f*; ~ **trip** *Am* ida y vuelta
**roundabout** (*raun*-dö-baut) *n* glorieta *f*
**rounded** (*raun*-did) *adj* redondeado
**route** (ruut) *n* ruta *f*
**routine** (ruu-*tiin*) *n* rutina *f*
**row**[1] (rou) *n* fila *f*; *v* remar
**row**[2] (rau) *n* bronca *f*
**rowdy** (*rau*-di) *adj* alborotador

**row(ing) boat** (*rou*-ing-bout) *n* bote *m*
**royal** (*roi*-öl) *adj* real
**rub** (rab) *v* frotar
**rubber** (*ra*-bö) *n* caucho *m*; goma de borrar; hule *mMe*; ~ **band** elástico *m*
**rubbish** (*ra*-biʃ) *n* basura *f*; habladuría *f*, tontería *f*; **talk** ~ *decir tonterías
**rubbish bin** (*ra*-biʃ-bin) *n* cubo de la basura
**ruby** (*ruu*-bi) *n* rubí *m*
**rucksack** (*rak*-ssæk) *n* mochila *f*
**rudder** (*ra*-dö) *n* timón *m*
**rude** (ruud) *adj* grosero
**rug** (ragh) *n* alfombrilla *f*
**ruin** (*ruu*-in) *v* arruinar; *n* ruina *f*
**rule** (ruul) *n* regla *f*; régimen *m*, gobierno *m*, dominio *m*; *v* *gobernar, *regir; **as a** ~ generalmente, por regla general
**ruler** (*ruu*-lö) *n* monarca *m*, gobernante *m*; regla *f*
**Rumania** (ruu-*mei*-ni-ö) Rumania *f*
**Rumanian** (ruu-*mei*-ni-ön) *adj* rumano
**rumo(u)r** (*ruu*-mö) *n* rumor *m*
***run** (ran) *v* correr; dirigir; funcionar; fluir; ~ **into** *encontrarse con
**runaway** (*ra*-nö-ᵘei) *n* fugitivo *m*
**rung** (ran) *v* (pp ring)
**runner** (*ra*-nö) corredor *m*, -a *f*
**runway** (*ran*-ᵘei) *n* pista de despegue; pista de aterrizaje
**rural** (*ru*ᵒ-röl) *adj* rural
**ruse** (ruus) *n* astucia *f*
**rush** (raʃ) *v* precipitarse; ir de prisa; *n* junco *m*; ~ **hour** hora punta
**Russia** (*ra*-ʃö) Rusia *f*
**Russian** (*ra*-ʃön) *adj* ruso
**rust** (rasst) *n* herrumbre *f*
**rustic** (*ra*-sstik) *adj* rústico
**rusty** (*ra*-ssti) *adj* oxidado

# S

**sack** (ssæk) *n* saco *m*
**sacred** (*ssei*-krid) *adj* sagrado
**sacrifice** (*ssæ*-kri-faiss) *n* sacrificio *m*; *v* sacrificar
**sacrilege** (*ssæ*-kri-lidʒ) *n* sacrilegio *m*
**sad** (ssæd) *adj* triste; afligido, melancólico
**saddle** (*ssæ*-döl) *n* silla *f* de montar
**sadness** (*ssæd*-nöss) *n* tristeza *f*
**safe** (sseif) *adj* seguro; ileso; *n* caja fuerte
**safety** (*sseif*-ti) *n* seguridad *f*; ~ **belt** cinturón de seguridad; ~ **pin** imperdible *m*
**sail** (sseil) *v* navegar; *n* vela *f*
**sail(ing) boat** (*ssei*-ling-bout) *n* velero *m*
**sailor** (*ssei*-lö) *n* marinero *m*
**saint** (sseint) *n* santo *m*
**salad** (*ssæ*-löd) *n* ensalada *f*; ~ **dressing** aderezo para ensalada
**salary** (*ssæ*-lö-ri) *n* sueldo *m*
**sale** (sseil) *n* venta *f*; **clearance** ~ liquidación *f*; **for** ~ de venta; **sales** rebajas *fpl*
**saleable** (*ssei*-lö-böl) *adj* vendible
**salesgirl** (*sseils*-ghööl) *n* vendedora *f*
**salesman** (*sseils*-mön) *n* (pl -men) vendedor *m*
**salmon** (*ssæ*-mön) *n* (pl ~) salmón *m*
**salon** (*ssæ*-long) *n* salón *m*
**saloon** (ssö-*luun*) *n* bar *m*; cantina *fMe*
**salt** (ssoolt) *n* sal *f*; ~ **cellar,** *Am* ~

**shaker** salero *m*
**salty** (*ssool*-ti) *adj* salado
**salute** (ssö-*luut*) *v* saludar
**salve** (ssaav) *n* ungüento *m*
**same** (sseim) *adj* mismo; idéntico
**sample** (*ssaam*-pöl) *n* muestra *f*
**sanatorium** (ssæ-nö-*too*-ri-öm) *n* (pl ~s, -ria) sanatorio *m*
**sand** (ssænd) *n* arena *f*
**sandal** (*ssæn*-döl) *n* sandalia *f*
**sandpaper** (*ssænd*-pei-pö) *n* papel de lija
**sandwich** (*ssæn*-$^{u}$idʒ) *n* bocadillo *m*; sandwich *m*
**sandy** (*ssæn*-di) *adj* arenoso
**sanitary** (*ssæ*-ni-tö-ri) *adj* sanitario; **~ napkin** *Am*, **~ towel** paño higiénico, compresa
**sapphire** (*ssæ*-fai$^{ö}$) *n* zafiro *m*
**sardine** (ssaa-*diin*) *n* sardina *f*
**satchel** (*ssæ*-chöl) *n* cartapacio *m*; bolso *m*
**satellite** (*ssæ*-tö-lait) *n* satélite *m*
**satin** (*ssæ*-tin) *n* raso *m*
**satisfaction** (ssæ-tiss-*fæk*-ʃön) *n* satisfacción *f*
**satisfactory** (ssæ-tiss-*fæk*-tö-ri) *adj* satisfactorio; suficiente
**satisfy** (*ssæ*-tiss-fai) *v* *satisfacer
**Saturday** (*ssæ*-tö-di) sábado *m*
**sauce** (ssooss) *n* salsa *f*
**saucepan** (*ssooss*-pön) *n* cacerola *f*
**saucer** (*ssoo*-ssö) *n* platillo *m*
**Saudi Arabia** (ssau-di-ö-*rei*-bi-ö) Arabia Saudí
**Saudi Arabian** (ssau-di-ö-*rei*-bi-ön) *adj* saudí
**sauna** (*ssoo*-nö) *n* sauna *f*
**sausage** (*sso*-ssidʒ) *n* salchicha *f*
**savage** (*ssæ*-vidʒ) *adj* salvaje
**save** (sseiv) *v* salvar; ahorrar
**savings** (*ssei*-vings) *pl* ahorros *mpl*; **~ bank** caja de ahorros
**savio(u)r** (*ssei*-vyö) *n* salvador *m*
**savo(u)ry** (*ssei*-vö-ri) *adj* sabroso; picante
**saw**$^{1}$ (ssoo) *v* (p see)
**saw**$^{2}$ (ssoo) *n* sierra *f*
**sawdust** (*ssoo*-dasst) *n* serrín *m*
**sawmill** (*ssoo*-mil) *n* serrería de maderas
***say** (ssei) *v* *decir
**scaffolding** (*sskæ*-föl-ding) *n* andamio *m*
**scale** (sskeil) *n* escala *f*; escala musical; escama *f*; **scales** *pl* balanza *f*, báscula *f*
**scandal** (*sskæn*-döl) *n* escándalo *m*
**Scandinavia** (sskæn-di-*nei*-vi-ö) Escandinavia *f*
**Scandinavian** (sskæn-di-*nei*-vi-ön) *adj* escandinavo
**scapegoat** (*sskeip*-ghout) *n* cabeza de turco
**scar** (sskaa) *n* cicatriz *f*
**scarce** (sskê$^{ö}$ss) *adj* escaso
**scarcely** (*sskê*$^{ö}$-ssli) *adv* apenas
**scarcity** (*sskê*$^{ö}$-ssö-ti) *n* escasez *f*
**scare** (sskê$^{ö}$) *v* asustar; *n* susto *m*
**scarf** (sskaaf) *n* (pl ~s, scarves) bufanda *f*
**scarlet** (*sskaa*-löt) *adj* escarlata
**scary** (*sskê*$^{ö}$-ri) *adj* alarmante; asustadizo
**scatter** (*sskæ*-tö) *v* esparcir
**scene** (ssiin) *n* escena *f*
**scenery** (*ssii*-nö-ri) *n* paisaje *m*
**scenic** (*ssii*-nik) *adj* pintoresco
**scent** (ssênt) *n* perfume *m*; olor *m*
**schedule** (*ʃê*-dyuul) *n* horario *m*
**scheme** (sskiim) *n* esquema *m*; proyecto *m*
**scholar** (*ssko*-lö) *n* erudito *m*, -a *f*; alumno *m*, -a *f*
**scholarship** (*ssko*-lö-ʃip) *n* beca *f*
**school** (sskuul) *n* escuela *f*
**schoolboy** (*sskuul*-boi) *n* alumno *m*; colegial *m*

**schoolgirl** (*sskuul*-ghööl) *n* alumna *f*; colegiala *f*
**schoolmaster** (*sskuul*-maa-sstö) *n* maestro *m*
**schoolteacher** (*sskuul*-tii-chö) *n* maestro *m*, -a *f*
**science** (*ssai*-önss) *n* ciencia *f*
**scientific** (ssai-ön-*ti*-fik) *adj* científico
**scientist** (*ssai*-ön-tisst) *n* científico *m*, -a *f*
**scissors** (*ssi*-sös) *pl* tijeras *fpl*
**scold** (sskould) *v* reprender; regañar
**scooter** (*sskuu*-tö) *n* motoneta *f*; patín *m*
**score** (sskoo) *n* tanteo *m*; partitura *f*; *v* marcar un gol; tantear
**scorn** (sskoon) *n* escarnio *m*, desprecio *m*; *v* despreciar
**Scot** (sskot) *n* escocés *m*
**Scotch** (sskoch) *adj* escocés; **scotch tape** cinta adhesiva
**Scotland** (*sskot*-lönd) Escocia *f*
**Scotsman** (*sskots*-mön) escocés *m*
**Scotswoman** (*sskots*-ᵘu-mön) escocesa *f*
**Scottish** (*ssko*-tiʃ) *adj* escocés
**scout** (sskaut) *n* explorador *m*
**scrap** (sskræp) *n* pedazo *m*
**scrapbook** (*sskræp*-buk) *n* álbum *m*
**scrape** (sskreip) *v* raspar
**scratch** (sskræch) *v* *hacer raeduras, rascar; *n* raedura *f*, rasguño *m*
**scream** (sskriim) *v* gritar, chillar; *n* grito *m*, chillido *m*
**screen** (sskriin) *n* pantalla *f*
**screw** (sskruu) *n* tornillo *m*; *v* atornillar
**screwdriver** (*sskruu*-drai-vö) *n* destornillador *m*
**scrub** (sskrab) *v* *fregar; *n* matorral *m*
**sculptor** (*sskalp*-tö) *n* escultor *m*, -a *f*
**sculpture** (*sskalp*-chö) *n* escultura *f*
**sea** (ssii) *n* mar *m*; ~ **urchin** erizo de mar; ~ **water** agua de mar
**seabird** (*ssii*-bööd) *n* ave marina
**seacoast** (*ssii*-kousst) *n* litoral *m*
**seafood** (*ssii*-fuud) *n* marisco(s) *m(pl)*
**seagull** (*ssii*-ghal) *n* gaviota *f*
**seal** (ssiil) *n* sello *m*; foca *f*
**seam** (ssiim) *n* costura *f*
**seaman** (*ssii*-mön) *n* (pl -men) marino *m*
**seamless** (*ssiim*-löss) *adj* sin costura
**seaport** (*ssii*-poot) *n* puerto de mar
**search** (ssööch) *v* buscar; cachear; *n* búsqueda *f*
**searchlight** (*ssööch*-lait) *n* reflector *m*
**seascape** (*ssii*-sskeip) *n* marina *f*
**seashell** (*ssii*-ʃêl) *n* concha *f*
**seashore** (*ssii*-ʃoo) *n* orilla del mar
**seasick** (*ssii*-ssik) *adj* mareado
**seasickness** (*ssii*-ssik-nöss) *n* mareo *m*
**seaside** (*ssii*-ssaid) *n* orilla del mar; ~ **resort** playa de veraneo
**season** (*ssii*-sön) *n* temporada *f*, estación *f*; **high** ~ temporada alta; **low** ~ temporada baja; **off** ~ fuera de temporada
**season ticket** (*ssii*-sön-ti-kit) *n* tarjeta de temporada
**seat** (ssiit) *n* asiento *m*; sitio *m*, localidad *f*; sede *f*; ~ **belt** cinturón de seguridad
**second** (*ssê*-könd) *num* segundo; *n* segundo *m*; instante *m*
**secondary** (*ssê*-kön-dö-ri) *adj* secundario; ~ **school** escuela secundaria
**second-hand** (ssê-könd-*hænd*) *adj* de segunda mano
**secret** (*ssii*-kröt) *n* secreto *m*; *adj* secreto
**secretary** (*ssê*-krö-tri) *n* secretaria *f*; secretario *m*
**section** (*ssêk*-ʃön) *n* sección *f*; división *f*, departamento *m*
**secure** (ssi-*kyu*ᵒ) *adj* seguro; firme; *v*

asegurar; conseguir
**security** (ssi-*kyu*$^{ö}$-rö-ti) *n* seguridad *f*; fianza *f*
**sedative** (*ssê*-dö-tiv) *n* calmante *m*
**seduce** (ssi-*dyuuss*) *v* *seducir
***see** (ssii) *v* *ver; comprender, *darse cuenta; ~ **to** *atender a
**seed** (ssiid) *n* semilla *f*
***seek** (ssiik) *v* buscar
**seem** (ssiim) *v* *parecer
**seen** (ssiin) *v* (pp see)
**seesaw** (*ssii*-ssoo) *n* columpio *m*
**seize** (ssiis) *v* agarrar; prender
**seldom** (*ssêl*-döm) *adv* pocas veces, rara vez
**select** (ssi-*lêkt*) *v* seleccionar, *elegir; *adj* seleccionado, selecto
**selection** (ssi-*lêk*-ʃön) *n* elección *f*, selección *f*
**self** (ssêlf) (pl selves) ego *m*; **my other** ~ mi otro yo
**self-centered** *Am*, **self-centred** (ssêlf-*ssên*-töd) *adj* egocéntrico
**self-employed** (ssêl-fim-*ploid*) *adj* que trabaja por cuenta propia
**self-evident** (ssêl-*fê*-vi-dönt) *adj* evidente por sí mismo
**self-government** (ssêlf-*gha*-vö-mönt) *n* autonomía *f*
**selfish** (*ssêl*-fiʃ) *adj* egoísta
**selfishness** (*ssêl*-fiʃ-nöss) *n* egoísmo *m*
**self-service** (ssêlf-*ssöö*-viss) *n* autoservicio *m*
***sell** (ssêl) *v* vender
**semblance** (*ssêm*-blönss) *n* apariencia *f*
**semi-** (*ssê*-mi) semi-
**semicircle** (*ssê*-mi-ssöö-köl) *n* semicírculo *m*
**semicolon** (ssê-mi-*kou*-lön) *n* punto y coma
**senate** (*ssê*-nöt) *n* senado *m*
**senator** (*ssê*-nö-tö) *n* senador *m*
***send** (ssênd) *v* enviar, mandar; ~ **back** *devolver; ~ **for** mandar a buscar; ~ **off** despachar
**sender** (*ssên*-dö) *n* remitente *m/f*
**senile** (*ssii*-nail) *adj* senil
**senior** (*ssiin*-yö) *adj* mayor; superior; ~ **citizen** persona de la tercera edad
**sensation** (ssên-*ssei*-ʃön) *n* sensación *f*
**sensational** (ssên-*ssei*-ʃö-nöl) *adj* sensacional
**sense** (ssênss) *n* sentido *m*; juicio *m*, razón *f*; *v* *sentir; ~ **of humo(u)r** sentido del humor
**senseless** (*ssênss*-löss) *adj* insensato; sin sentido
**sensible** (*ssên*-ssö-böl) *adj* sensato; razonable; práctico
**sensitive** (*ssên*-ssi-tiv) *adj* sensible
**sentence** (*ssên*-tönss) *n* frase *f*; sentencia *f*; *v* sentenciar
**sentimental** (ssên-ti-*mên*-töl) *adj* sentimental
**separate**$^{1}$ (*ssê*-pö-reit) *v* separar
**separate**$^{2}$ (*ssê*-pö-röt) *adj* separado
**separately** (*ssê*-pö-röt-li) *adv* por separado
**September** (ssêp-*têm*-bö) septiembre
**septic** (*ssêp*-tik) *adj* séptico; ***become** ~ infectarse
**sequel** (*ssii*-k$^{u}$öl) *n* continuación *f*
**sequence** (*ssii*-k$^{u}$önss) *n* sucesión *f*; serie *f*
**serene** (ssö-*riin*) *adj* sereno; claro
**serial** (*ssi*$^{ö}$-ri-öl) *n* novela por entregas
**series** (*ssi*$^{ö}$-riis) *n* (pl ~) serie *f*
**serious** (*ssi*$^{ö}$-ri-öss) *adj* serio
**seriousness** (*ssi*$^{ö}$-ri-öss-nöss) *n* seriedad *f*
**sermon** (*ssöö*-mön) *n* sermón *m*
**serum** (*ssi*$^{ö}$-röm) *n* suero *m*
**servant** (*ssöö*-vönt) *n* criado *m*
**serve** (ssööv) *v* *servir
**service** (*ssöö*-viss) *n* servicio *m*; ~

**charge** servicio *m*; ~ **station** puesto de gasolina
**serviette** (ssöö-vi-*êt*) *n* servilleta *f*
**session** (*ssê*-ʃön) *n* sesión *f*
**set** (ssêt) *n* juego *m*, grupo *m*
***set** (ssêt) *v* *poner; colocar; montar; fijar; ~ **menu** cubierto a precio fijo; ~ **out** partir; ~ **up** establecer
**setting** (*ssê*-ting) *n* escena *f*; ~ **lotion** fijador *m*
**settle** (*ssê*-töl) *v* arreglar; ~ **down** arraigarse
**settlement** (*ssê*-töl-mönt) *n* acuerdo *m*, arreglo *m*, convenio *m*
**seven** (*ssê*-vön) *num* siete
**seventeen** (ssê-vön-*tiin*) *num* diecisiete
**seventeenth** (ssê-vön-*tiinz*) *num* decimoséptimo
**seventh** (*ssê*-vönz) *num* séptimo
**seventy** (*ssê*-vön-ti) *num* setenta
**several** (*ssê*-vö-röl) *adj* varios
**severe** (ssi-*viᵒ̈*) *adj* severo; grave; duro
**sew** (ssou) *v* coser; ~ **up** *hacer una sutura
**sewer** (*ssuu*-ö) *n* desagüe *m*
**sewing machine** (*ssou*-ing-mö-ʃiin) *n* máquina de coser
**sex** (ssêkss) *n* sexo *m*; sexualidad *f*
**sexual** (*ssêk*-ʃu-öl) *adj* sexual
**sexuality** (ssêk-ʃu-*æ*-lö-ti) *n* sexualidad *f*
**shade** (ʃeid) *n* sombra *f*; tono *m*
**shadow** (*ʃæ*-dou) *n* sombra *f*
**shady** (*ʃei*-di) *adj* sombreado
***shake** (ʃeik) *v* sacudir
**shaky** (*ʃei*-ki) *adj* vacilante
***shall** (ʃæl) *v* *tener que
**shallow** (*ʃæ*-lou) *adj* poco profundo; superficial
**shame** (ʃeim) *n* vergüenza *f*; deshonra *f*; **shame!** ¡qué vergüenza!
**shampoo** (ʃæm-*puu*) *n* champú *m*
**shamrock** (*ʃæm*-rok) *n* trébol *m*
**shape** (ʃeip) *n* forma *f*; *v* formar
**share** (ʃêᵒ̈) *v* compartir; *n* parte *f*; acción *f*
**shark** (ʃaak) *n* tiburón *m*
**sharp** (ʃaap) *adj* afilado
**sharpen** (*ʃaa*-pön) *v* afilar
**shave** (ʃeiv) *v* rasurarse, afeitarse
**shaver** (*ʃei*-vö) *n* máquina de afeitar
**shaving brush** (*ʃei*-ving-braʃ) *n* brocha de afeitar
**shaving cream** (*ʃei*-ving-kriim) *n* crema de afeitar
**shaving soap** (*ʃei*-ving-ssoup) *n* jabón de afeitar
**shawl** (ʃool) *n* chal *m*
**she** (ʃii) *pron* ella
**shed** (ʃêd) *n* cobertizo *m*
***shed** (ʃêd) *v* derramar; esparcir
**sheep** (ʃiip) *n* (pl ~) oveja *f*
**sheer** (ʃiᵒ̈) *adj* absoluto, puro; fino, traslúcido
**sheet** (ʃiit) *n* sábana *f*; hoja *f*; chapa *f*
**shelf** (ʃêlf) *n* (pl shelves) estante *m*
**shell** (ʃêl) *n* concha *f*; cáscara *f*
**shellfish** (*ʃêl*-fiʃ) *n* marisco *m*
**shelter** (*ʃêl*-tö) *n* refugio *m*; *v* abrigar
**shepherd** (*ʃê*-pöd) *n* pastor *m*
**shift** (ʃift) *n* turno *m*
***shine** (ʃain) *v* *relucir; brillar, *resplandecer
**ship** (ʃip) *n* buque *m*; *v* transportar; **shipping line** línea de navegación
**shipowner** (*ʃi*-pou-nö) *n* armador *m*
**shipyard** (*ʃip*-yaad) *n* astillero *m*
**shirt** (ʃööt) *n* camisa *f*
**shiver** (*ʃi*-vö) *v* *temblar, tiritar; *n* escalofrío *m*
**shock** (ʃok) *n* choque *m*; *v* chocar; ~ **absorber** amortiguador *m*
**shocking** (*ʃo*-king) *adj* chocante
**shoe** (ʃuu) *n* zapato *m*; **gym shoes** zapatos de gimnasia; ~ **polish** betún *m*; grasa *fMe*; ~ **shop** zapatería *f*
**shoelace** (*ʃuu*-leiss) *n* cordón *m*

**shoemaker** (ʃ*uu*-mei-kö) *n* zapatero *m*
**shook** (ʃuk) *v* (p shake)
***shoot** (ʃuut) *v* tirar
**shop** (ʃop) *n* tienda *f*; *v* *ir de compras; **~ assistant** dependiente *m*, -a
**shopping** (ʃ*o*-ping) compra *f*; **do one's ~** hacer la compra; **~ bag** saco de compras; **~ centre, ~ mall** centro comercial
**shopkeeper** (ʃ*op*-kii-pö) *n* tendero *m*, -a *f*
**shopwindow** (ʃop-*ᵘin*-dou) *n* escaparate *m*
**shore** (ʃoo) *n* ribera *f*, orilla *f*
**short** (ʃoot) *adj* corto; bajo; **~ circuit** cortocircuito *m*
**shortage** (ʃ*oo*-tidʒ) *n* carencia *f*, escasez *f*
**shorten** (ʃ*oo*-tön) *v* acortar
**shorthand** (ʃ*oot*-hænd) *n* taquigrafía *f*
**shortly** (ʃ*oot*-li) *adv* pronto, próximamente
**shorts** (ʃootss) *pl* pantalones cortos, pantalones de gimnasia; *plAm* calzoncillos *mpl*
**short-sighted** (ʃoot-*ssai*-tid) *adj* miope
**shot** (ʃot) *n* disparo *m*; inyección *f*; secuencia *f*
***should** (ʃud) *v* *tener que
**shoulder** (ʃ*oul*-dö) *n* hombro *m*
**shout** (ʃaut) *v* gritar; *n* grito *m*
**shovel** (ʃ*a*-völ) *n* pala *f*
**show** (ʃou) *n* representación *f*, espectáculo *m*; exposición *f*
***show** (ʃou) *v* *mostrar; enseñar; *demostrar
**showcase** (ʃ*ou*-keiss) *n* vitrina *f*
**shower** (ʃauᵒ) *n* ducha *f*; aguacero *m*
**showroom** (ʃ*ou*-ruum) *n* sala de exposición; salón de demostraciones
**shriek** (ʃriik) *v* chillar; *n* chillido *m*
**shrimp** (ʃrimp) *n* camarón *m*
**shrine** (ʃrain) *n* santuario *m*
***shrink** (ʃringk) *v* encogerse
**shrinkproof** (ʃ*ringk*-pruuf) *adj* no encoge
**shrub** (ʃrab) *n* arbusto *m*
**shudder** (ʃ*a*-dö) *n* estremecimiento *m*
**shuffle** (ʃ*a*-föl) *v* barajar
***shut** (ʃat) *v* *cerrar; **~ in** *encerrar
**shutter** (ʃ*a*-tö) *n* persiana *f*
**shy** (ʃai) *adj* esquivo, tímido
**shyness** (ʃ*ai*-nöss) *n* timidez *f*
**Siamese** (ssai-ö-*miis*) *adj* siamés
**sick** (ssik) *adj* enfermo; que tiene náuseas
**sickness** (*ssik*-nöss) *n* enfermedad *f*; náusea *f*
**side** (ssaid) *n* lado *m*; partido *m*; **one-sided** *adj* unilateral
**sideburns** (*ssaid*-bööns) *pl* patillas *fpl*
**sidelight** (*ssaid*-lait) *n* luz lateral
**side street** (*ssaid*-sstriit) *n* calle lateral
**sidewalk** (*ssaid*-ᵘook) *nAm* acera *f*
**sideways** (*ssaid*-ᵘeis) *adv* lateralmente
**siege** (ssiidʒ) *n* sitio *m*
**sieve** (ssiv) *n* tamiz *m*; *v* tamizar
**sift** (ssift) *v* tamizar
**sight** (ssait) *n* vista *f*; aspecto *m*; curiosidad *f*
**sightseeing** (*ssait*-sii-ying) *n*: **go ~** hacer turismo
**sign** (ssain) *n* signo *m*, señal *f*; gesto *m*, seña *f*; *v* suscribir, firmar
**signal** (*ssigh*-nöl) *n* señal *f*; *v* *hacer señales
**signature** (*ssigh*-nö-chö) *n* firma *f*
**significant** (ssigh-*ni*-fi-könt) *adj* significativo
**signpost** (*ssain*-pousst) *n* poste de indicador
**silence** (*ssai*-lönss) *n* silencio *m*; *v* acallar
**silencer** (*ssai*-lön-ssö) *n* silenciador *m*

**silent** (*ssai*-lönt) *adj* callado; ***be ~** callarse
**silk** (ssilk) *n* seda *f*
**silly** (*ssi*-li) *adj* necio, bobo
**silver** (*ssil*-vö) *n* plata *f*; de plata
**silversmith** (*ssil*-vö-ssmiz) *n* platero *m*
**silverware** (*ssil*-vö-ᵘêᵒ) *n* plata labrada
**similar** (*ssi*-mi-lö) *adj* similar
**similarity** (ssi-mi-*læ*-rö-ti) *n* semejanza *f*
**simple** (*ssim*-pöl) *adj* ingenuo, simple; ordinario
**simply** (*ssim*-pli) *adv* simplemente
**simulate** (*ssi*-myu-leit) *v* simular
**simultaneous** (ssi-möl-*tei*-ni-öss) *adj* simultáneo
**sin** (ssin) *n* pecado *m*
**since** (ssinss) *prep* desde; *adv* desde entonces; *conj* desde que; puesto que
**sincere** (ssin-*ssiᵒ*) *adj* sincero; **Yours sincerely** atentamente
**sinew** (*ssi*-nyuu) *n* tendón *m*
***sing** (ssing) *v* cantar
**singer** (*ssing*-ö) *n* cantante *m/f*
**single** (*ssing*-ghöl) *adj* solo; soltero
**singular** (*ssing*-ghyu-lö) *n* singular *m*; *adj* singular
**sinister** (*ssi*-ni-sstö) *adj* siniestro
**sink** (ssingk) *n* fregadero *m*
***sink** (ssingk) *v* hundirse; disminuir
**sip** (ssip) *n* sorbo *m*
**sir** (ssöö) señor *m*
**siren** (*ssaiᵒ*-rön) *n* sirena *f*
**sister** (*ssi*-sstö) *n* hermana *f*
**sister-in-law** (*ssi*-sstö-rin-loo) *n* (pl sisters-) cuñada *f*
***sit** (ssit) *v* *estar sentado; **~ down** *sentarse
**site** (ssait) *n* sitio *m*
**sitting room** (*ssi*-ting-ruum) *n* sala de estar
**situated** (*ssi*-chu-ei-tid) *adj* situado
**situation** (ssi-chu-*ei*-ʃön) *n* situación *f*; ubicación *f*
**six** (ssikss) *num* seis
**sixteen** (ssikss-*tiin*) *num* dieciséis
**sixteenth** (ssikss-*tiinz*) *num* decimosexto
**sixth** (ssikssz) *num* sexto
**sixty** (*ssikss*-ti) *num* sesenta
**size** (ssais) *n* tamaño *m*, número *m*; dimensión *f*; formato *m*
**skate** (sskeit) *v* patinar; *n* patín *m*
**skating** (*sskei*-ting) *n* patinaje *m*
**skating rink** (*sskei*-ting-ringk) *n* pista de patinaje
**skeleton** (*sskê*-li-tön) *n* esqueleto *m*
**sketch** (sskêch) *n* dibujo *m*, bosquejo *m*; *v* dibujar, bosquejar
**ski¹** (sskii) *v* esquiar
**ski²** (sskii) *n* (pl ~, ~s) esquí *m*; **~ boots** botas de esquí; **~ pants** pantalones de esquí; **~ sticks** bastones de esquí
**skid** (sskid) *v* patinar
**skier** (*sskii*-ö) *n* esquiador *m*
**skiing** (*sskii*-ing) *n* esquí *m*
**ski jump** (*sskii*-dʒamp) *n* salto de esquí
**skil(l)ful** (*sskil*-föl) *adj* hábil, diestro
**ski lift** (*sskii*-lift) *n* telesilla *m*
**skill** (sskil) *n* habilidad *f*
**skilled** (sskild) *adj* hábil; especializado
**skin** (sskin) *n* piel *f*; cutis *m*; cáscara *f*; **~ cream** crema para la piel
**skip** (sskip) *v* saltar; brincar
**skirt** (sskööt) *n* falda *f*
**skull** (sskal) *n* cráneo *m*; calavera *f*
**sky** (sskai) *n* cielo *m*
**skyscraper** (*sskai*-sskrei-pö) *n* rascacielos *m*
**slack** (sslæk) *adj* flojo
**slacks** (sslækss) *pl* pantalones *mpl*
**slam** (sslæm) *v* *dar un portazo
**slander** (*sslaan*-dö) *n* calumnia *f*
**slang** (sslaang) argot *m*, jerga *f*

**slant** (sslaant) *v* inclinarse
**slanting** (*sslaan*-ting) *adj* oblicuo, pendiente, inclinado
**slap** (sslæp) *v* pegar; abofetear; *n* bofetada *f*
**slate** (ssleit) *n* pizarra *f*
**slave** (ssleiv) *n* esclavo *m*
**sledge** (sslêdʒ) Am sled *n* trineo *m*
**sleep** (ssliip) *n* sueño *m*
***sleep** (ssliip) *v* *dormir
**sleeping bag** (*sslii*-ping-bægh) *n* saco de dormir
**sleeping car** (*sslii*-ping-kaa) *n* coche cama
**sleeping pill** (*sslii*-ping-pil) *n* somnífero *m*
**sleepless** (*ssliip*-löss) *adj* desvelado
**sleepy** (*sslii*-pi) *adj* soñoliento
**sleeve** (ssliiv) *n* manga *f*; funda *f*
**sleigh** (sslei) *n* trineo *m*
**slender** (*sslên*-dö) *adj* esbelto; delgado
**slice** (sslaiss) *n* tajada *f*
**slide** (sslaid) *n* desliz *m*; tobogán *m*; diapositiva *f*
***slide** (sslaid) *v* deslizarse
**slight** (sslait) *adj* ligero; leve
**slim** (sslim) *adj* esbelto; *v* adelgazar
**slip** (sslip) *v* deslizarse, resbalar; *n* desliz *m*; combinación *f*; fondo *mMe*
**slipper** (*ssli*-pö) *n* zapatilla *f*
**slippery** (*ssli*-pö-ri) *adj* resbaladizo
**slogan** (*sslou*-ghön) *n* lema *m*, slogan *m*
**slope** (ssloup) *n* pendiente *f*; *v* inclinarse
**sloping** (*sslou*-ping) *adj* inclinado
**sloppy** (*sslo*-pi) *adj* chapucero
**slot** (sslot) *n* ranura *f*; **~ machine** máquina tragamonedas
**slovenly** (*ssla*-vön-li) *adj* descuidado
**slow** (sslou) *adj* lerdo, lento; **~ down** desacelerar, *ir más despacio; frenar
**sluice** (ssluuss) *n* compuerta *f*
**slum** (sslam) *n* barrio bajo
**slump** (sslamp) *n* baja *f*
**slush** (sslaʃ) *n* aguanieve *f*
**sly** (sslai) *adj* astuto
**smack** (ssmæk) *v* pegar (con la mano); *n* palmada *f*
**small** (ssmool) *adj* pequeño; menudo
**smallpox** (*ssmool*-pokss) *n* viruelas *fpl*
**smart** (ssmaat) *adj* inteligente, listo; elegante
**smash** (ssmæʃ) *n* estruendo *m*; choque *m*; smash *m*, mate *m*; *v* acer pedazos, acer añicos; romperse
**smell** (ssmêl) *n* olor *m*; olfato *m*
***smell** (ssmêl) *v* *oler
**smelly** (*ssmê*-li) *adj* que huele mal
**smile** (ssmail) *v* sonreír; *n* sonrisa *f*
**smith** (ssmiz) *n* herrero *m*
**smog** (ssmog) *n* niebla *f* tóxica
**smoke** (ssmouk) *v* fumar; *n* humo *m*; **no smoking** prohibido fumar
**smoker** (*ssmou*-kö) *n* fumador *m*; compartimento para fumadores
**smoking compartment** (*ssmou*-king-köm-paat-mönt) *n* compartimento para fumadores
**smooth** (ssmuuð) *adj* llano, liso; suave
**smuggle** (*ssma*-ghöl) *v* contrabandear
**snack** (ssnæk) *n* tentempié *m*; **~ bar** cafetería *f*
**snail** (ssneil) *n* caracol *m*
**snake** (ssneik) *n* culebra *f*
**snapshot** (*ssnæp*-ʃot) *n* instantánea *f*
**sneakers** (*ssnii*-kös) *plAm* zapatos de gimnasia
**sneeze** (ssniis) *v* estornudar
**sniper** (*ssnai*-pö) *n* francotirador *m*
**snooty** (*ssnuu*-ti) *adj* arrogante
**snore** (ssnoo) *v* roncar
**snorkel** (*ssnoo*-köl) *n* esnórquel *m*
**snout** (ssnaut) *n* hocico *m*
**snow** (ssnou) *n* nieve *f*; *v* *nevar
**snowstorm** (*ssnou*-sstoom) *n* nevasca

*f*
**snowy** (*ssnou*-i) *adj* nevoso; cubierto de nieve
**so** (ssou) *conj* por tanto; *adv* así; a tal grado, tan; **and ~ on** etcétera; **~ far** hasta ahora; **~ that** así que, a fin de
**soak** (ssouk) *v* empapar, remojar
**soap** (ssoup) *n* jabón *m*; **~ powder** jabón en polvo
**sober** (*ssou*-bö) *adj* sobrio; ponderado
**so-called** (ssou-*koold*) *adj* así llamado; supuesto
**soccer** (*sso*-kö) *n* fútbol *m*; **~ team** equipo *m*
**social** (*ssou*-ʃöl) *adj* social
**socialism** (*ssou*-ʃö-li-söm) *n* socialismo *m*
**socialist** (*ssou*-ʃö-lisst) *adj* socialista; *n* socialista *m*
**society** (ssö-*ssai*-ö-ti) *n* sociedad *f*; asociación *f*; compañía *f*
**sock** (ssok) *n* calcetín *m*
**socket** (*sso*-kit) *n* casquillo *m*; sóquet *mMe*
**soda water** (*ssou*-dö-ᵘoo-tö) *n* gaseosa *f*
**sofa** (*ssou*-fö) *n* sofá *m*
**soft** (ssoft) *adj* blando; **~ drink** bebida no alcohólica
**soften** (*sso*-fön) *v* ablandar
**software** (*ssoft*-ᵘêᵒ) software *m*
**soil** (ssoil) *n* suelo *m*; tierra *f*; *v* ensuciar
**soiled** (ssoild) *adj* manchado
**sold** (ssould) *v* (p, pp sell); **~ out** agotado
**soldier** (*ssoul*-dʒö) *n* militar *m*, soldado *m*
**sole¹** (ssoul) *adj* único
**sole²** (ssoul) *n* suela *f*; lenguado *m*
**solely** (*ssoul*-li) *adv* exclusivamente
**solemn** (*sso*-löm) *adj* solemne
**solicitor** (ssö-*li*-ssi-tö) *n* procurador *m*, -a *f*, abogado *m*, -a *f*
**solid** (*sso*-lid) *adj* robusto, sólido; macizo; *n* sólido *m*
**soluble** (*sso*-lyu-böl) *adj* soluble
**solution** (ssö-*luu*-ʃön) *n* solución *f*
**solve** (ssolv) *v* *resolver
**somber** *Am*, **sombre** (*ssom*-bö) *adj* sombrío
**some** (ssam) *adj* algunos, unos; *pron* algunos, unos; un poco; **~ day** uno u otro día; **~ more** algo más; **~ time** alguna vez
**somebody** (*ssam*-bö-di) *pron* alguien
**somehow** (*ssam*-hau) *adv* de un modo u otro
**someone** (*ssam*-ᵘan) *pron* alguien
**something** (*ssam*-zing) *pron* algo
**sometimes** (*ssam*-taims) *adv* a veces
**somewhat** (*ssam*-ᵘot) *adv* algo
**somewhere** (*ssam*-ᵘêᵒ) *adv* en alguna parte
**son** (ssan) *n* hijo *m*
**song** (ssong) *n* canción *f*
**son-in-law** (*ssa*-nin-loo) *n* (pl sons-) yerno *m*
**soon** (ssuun) *adv* rápidamente, pronto, en breve; **as ~ as** tan pronto como
**sooner** (*ssuu*-nö) *adv* más bien
**sore** (ssoo) *adj* doloroso; *n* llaga *f*; úlcera *f*; **~ throat** dolor de garganta
**sorrow** (*sso*-rou) *n* tristeza *f*, sufrimiento *m*, pena *f*
**sorry** (*sso*-ri) *adj* apenado; **sorry!** ¡dispense usted!, ¡disculpe!, ¡perdón!
**sort** (ssoot) *v* clasificar, *disponer; *n* clase *f*; **all sorts of** toda clase de
**soul** (ssoul) *n* alma *f*
**sound** (ssaund) *n* sonido *m*; *v* *sonar, *resonar; *adj* bueno
**soundproof** (*ssaund*-pruuf) *adj* insonorizado
**soup** (ssuup) *n* sopa *f*
**sour** (ssauᵒ) *adj* agrio
**source** (ssooss) *n* fuente *f*

**south** (ssauz) *n* sur *m*; **South Pole** polo sur
**South Africa** (ssauz æ-fri-kö) África del Sur
**southeast** (ssauz-*iisst*) *n* sudeste *m*
**southerly** (*ssa*-ðö-li) *adj* meridional
**southern** (*ssa*-ðön) *adj* meridional
**southwest** (ssauz-*ᵘêsst*) *n* sudoeste *m*
**souvenir** (*ssuu*-vö-niᵒ) *n* recuerdo *m*
**sovereign** (*ssov*-rin) *n* soberano *m*
***sow** (ssou) *v* *sembrar
**soy** (ssoi) *n* soja *f*
**spa** (sspaa) *n* balneario *m*
**space** (sspeiss) *n* espacio *m*; distancia *f*; *v* espaciar; ~ **shuttle** transbordador espacial
**spacious** (*sspei*-ʃöss) *adj* espacioso
**spade** (sspeid) *n* azada *f*, pala *f*
**Spain** (sspein) España *f*
**Spaniard** (*sspæ*-nyöd) *n* español *m*, -a *f*
**Spanish** (*sspæ*-niʃ) *adj* español
**spanking** (*sspæng*-king) *n* zurra *f*
**spanner** (*sspæ*-nö) *n* llave inglesa
**spare** (sspêᵒ) *adj* de reserva, disponible; *v* pasarse sin; ~ **part** pieza de repuesto; ~ **room** cuarto para huéspedes; ~ **time** tiempo libre; ~ **tire** *Am*, ~ **tyre** neumático de repuesto; ~ **wheel** rueda de repuesto
**sparing** (*sspêᵒ*-ing) *adj* escaso; económico
**spark** (sspaak) *n* chispa *f*
**spark(ing) plug** (*sspaa*-king-plagh) *n* bujía *f*
**sparkling** (*sspaa*-kling) *adj* centelleante; espumante
**sparrow** (*sspæ*-rou) *n* gorrión *m*
***speak** (sspiik) *v* hablar
**spear** (sspiᵒ) *n* lanza *f*
**special** (*sspê*-ʃöl) *adj* especial; ~ **delivery** por expreso
**specialist** (*sspê*-ʃö-lisst) *n* especialista *m/f*
**speciality** (sspê-ʃi-*æ*-lö-ti) *n* especialidad *f*
**specialize** (*sspê*-ʃö-lais) *v* especializarse
**specially** (*sspê*-ʃö-li) *adv* en particular
**species** (*sspii*-ʃiis) *n* (pl ~) especie *f*
**specific** (sspö-*ssi*-fik) *adj* específico
**specimen** (*sspê*-ssi-mön) *n* espécimen *m*; muestra *f*
**speck** (sspêk) *n* mancha *f*
**spectacle** (*sspêk*-tö-köl) *n* espectáculo *m*; **spectacles** anteojos *mpl*, gafas *fpl*
**spectator** (sspêk-*tei*-tö) *n* espectador *m*
**speculate** (*sspê*-kyu-leit) *v* especular
**speech** (sspiich) *n* habla *f*; discurso *m*; lenguaje *m*
**speechless** (*sspiich*-löss) *adj* atónito
**speed** (sspiid) *n* velocidad *f*; rapidez *f*, prisa *f*; **cruising** ~ velocidad de cruce; ~ **limit** límite de velocidad
***speed** (sspiid) *v* *dar prisa; correr demasiado
**speeding** (*sspii*-ding) *n* exceso de velocidad
**speedometer** (sspii-*do*-mi-tö) *n* velocímetro *m*
**spell** (sspêl) *n* encanto *m*
***spell** (sspêl) *v* deletrear
**spelling** (*sspê*-ling) *n* deletreo *m*
***spend** (sspênd) *v* gastar; pasar
**sphere** (ssfiᵒ) *n* esfera *f*
**spice** (sspaiss) *n* especia *f*
**spiced** (sspaisst) *adj* condimentado
**spicy** (*sspai*-ssi) *adj* picante
**spider** (*sspai*-dö) *n* araña *f*; **spider's web** telaraña *f*
***spill** (sspil) *v* *verter
***spin** (sspin) *v* hilar; *hacer girar
**spinach** (*sspi*-nidʒ) *n* espinacas *fpl*
**spine** (sspain) *n* espinazo *m*
**spinster** (*sspin*-sstö) *n* solterona *f*
**spire** (sspaiᵒ) *n* aguja *f*

**spirit** (*sspi*-rit) *n* espíritu *m*; ánimo *m*; humor *m*; **spirits** bebidas espirituosas; moral *f*; ~ **stove** calentador de alcohol
**spiritual** (*sspi*-ri-chu-öl) *adj* espiritual
**spit** (sspit) *n* esputo *m*, saliva *f*; espetón *m*
***spit** (sspit) *v* escupir
**spite: in ~ of** (in sspait ov) a pesar de
**spiteful** (*sspait*-föl) *adj* malévolo
**splash** (ssplæʃ) *v* salpicar
**splendid** (*ssplên*-did) *adj* magnífico, espléndido
**splendo(u)r** (*ssplên*-dö) *n* esplendor *m*
**splint** (ssplint) *n* tablilla *f*
**splinter** (*ssplin*-tö) *n* astilla *f*
***split** (ssplit) *v* *hender
***spoil** (sspoil) *v* echar a perder; mimar
**spoke**[1] (sspouk) *v* (p speak)
**spoke**[2] (sspouk) *n* radio *m*
**sponge** (sspandʒ) *n* esponja *f*
**spook** (sspuuk) *n* fantasma *m*
**spool** (sspuul) *n* bobina *f*
**spoon** (sspuun) *n* cuchara *f*
**spoonful** (*sspuun*-ful) *n* cucharada *f*
**sport** (sspoot) *n* deporte *m*
**sports car** (*sspootss*-kaa) *n* coche de carreras
**sports jacket** (*sspootss*-dʒæ-kit) *n* chaqueta de deporte
**sportsman** (*sspootss*-mön) *n* (pl -men) deportista *m*
**sportswoman** (*sspootss*-$^{u}$u-mön) *n* (pl -women) deportista *f*
**sportswear** (*sspootss*-$^{u}$ê$^{ö}$) *n* conjunto de deporte
**spot** (sspot) *n* mancha *f*; lugar *m*, puesto *m*
**spotless** (*sspot*-löss) *adj* inmaculado
**spotlight** (*sspot*-lait) *n* foco *m*, proyector *m*
**spotted** (*sspo*-tid) *adj* moteado; manchado
**spout** (sspaut) *n* chorro *m*; pico *m*; conducto *m*
**sprain** (ssprein) *v* *torcerse; *n* torcedura *f*
**spray** (ssprei) *n* rociada *f*; spray *m*; aerosol *m*; *v* rociar; echar spray (a)
***spread** (ssprêd) *v* *extender
**spring** (sspring) *n* primavera *f*; muelle *m*; manantial *m*
**springtime** (*sspring*-taim) *n* primavera *f*
**sprouts** (ssprautss) *pl* col de Bruselas
**spy** (sspai) *n* espía *m*
**squadron** (*ssk$^{u}$o*-drön) *n* escuadrilla *f*
**square** (ssk$^{u}$ê$^{ö}$) *adj* cuadrado; *n* cuadrado *m*; plaza *f*
**squash** (ssk$^{u}$oʃ) *n* zumo *m*; *Am* calabacín
**squeeze** (ssk$^{u}$iis) *n* apretón *m*; *v* apretar; exprimir
**squirrel** (*ssk$^{u}$i*-röl) *n* ardilla *f*
**squirt** (ssk$^{u}$ööt) *n* chorretada *f*
**stable** (*sstei*-böl) *adj* estable; *n* establo *m*
**stack** (sstæk) *n* montón *m*
**stadium** (*sstei*-di-öm) *n* estadio *m*
**staff** (sstaaf) *n* personal *m*; palo *m*; vara *f*
**stage** (ssteidʒ) *n* escenario *m*; fase *f*; etapa *f*
**stain** (sstein) *v* manchar; *n* mancha *f*; **stained glass** vidrio de color; ~ **remover** quitamanchas *m*
**stainless** (*sstein*-löss) *adj* inmaculado; ~ **steel** acero inoxidable
**staircase** (*sstê$^{ö}$*-keiss) *n* escalera *f*
**stairs** (sstê$^{ö}$s) *pl* escalera *f*
**stale** (ssteil) *adj* viejo, viciado, rancio
**stall** (sstool) *n* puesto *m*; butaca *f*
**stamp** (sstæmp) *n* sello *m*; *v* sellar; patear; *n* estampilla *fMe*; ~ **machine** máquina expendedora de sellos
**stand** (sstænd) *n* puesto *m*; tribuna *f*
***stand** (sstænd) *v* *estar de pie

**standard** (*sstæn*-död) *n* norma *f*; normal; ~ **of living** nivel de vida
**stanza** (*sstæn*-sö) *n* estrofa *f*
**staple** (*sstei*-pöl) *n* grapa *f*
**star** (sstaa) *n* estrella *f*
**starboard** (*sstaa*-böd) *n* estribor *m*
**stare** (sstê$^{ö}$) *v* mirar fijamente
**starling** (*sstaa*-ling) *n* estornino *m*
**start** (sstaat) *v* *empezar; *n* comienzo *m*
**starting point** (*sstaa*-ting-point) *n* punto de partida
**state** (ssteit) *n* Estado *m*; estado *m*; *v* declarar; **the States** Estados Unidos
**statement** (*ssteit*-mönt) *n* declaración *f*
**statesman** (*ssteitss*-mön) *n* (pl -men) estadista *m*
**station** (*sstei*-ʃön) *n* estación *f*; puesto *m*
**stationary** (*sstei*-ʃö-nö-ri) *adj* estacionario
**stationer's** (*sstei*-ʃö-nös) *n* papelería *f*
**stationery** (*sstei*-ʃö-nö-ri) *n* papelería *f*
**statistics** (sstö-*ti*-sstikss) *pl* estadística *f*
**statue** (*sstæ*-chuu) *n* estatua *f*
**stay** (sstei) *v* quedarse; hospedarse; *n* estancia *f*
**steadfast** (*sstêd*-faasst) *adj* constante
**steady** (*sstê*-di) *adj* firme
**steak** (ssteik) *n* biftec *m*
***steal** (sstiil) *v* hurtar; robar
**steam** (sstiim) *n* vapor *m*
**steamer** (*sstii*-mö) *n* vapor *m*
**steel** (sstiil) *n* acero *m*
**steep** (sstiip) *adj* empinado
**steeple** (*sstii*-pöl) *n* campanario *m*
**steer** (sstii$^{ö}$) *v* dirigir; conducir; *L.Am.* manejar; gobernar; navigar
**steering column** (*ssti*$^{ö}$-ring-ko-löm) *n* columna del volante
**steering wheel** (*ssti*$^{ö}$-ring-$^{u}$iil) *n* volante *m*
**steersman** (*ssti*$^{ö}$*s*-mön) *n* (pl -men) timonel *m*
**stem** (sstêm) *n* tallo *m*; caña *f*
**step** (sstêp) *n* paso *m*; peldaño *m*; *v* pisar
**stepchild** (*sstêp*-chaild) *n* (pl -children) hijastro(a) *m*/*f*
**stepfather** (*sstêp*-faa-ðö) *n* padrastro *m*
**stepmother** (*sstêp*-ma-ðö) *n* madrastra *f*
**stereo** (*ssti*-ri-ou) *n* equipo *m* de música
**sterile** (*sstê*-rail) *adj* estéril
**sterilize** (*sstê*-ri-lais) *v* esterilizar
**steward** (*sstyuu*-öd) *n* mayordomo *m*; camarero *m*
**stewardess** (*sstyuu*-ö-dêss) *n* azafata *f*
**stick** (sstik) *n* palo *m*
***stick** (sstik) *v* pegar; clavar; fijar
**sticky** (*ssti*-ki) *adj* pegajoso
**stiff** (sstif) *adj* tieso; rígido
**still** (sstil) *adv* todavía; sin embargo; *adj* quieto
**stimulant** (*ssti*-myu-lönt) *n* estimulante *m*
**stimulate** (*ssti*-myu-leit) *v* estimular
**sting** (ssting) *n* picadura *f*
***sting** (ssting) *v* picar
**stingy** (*sstin*-dʒi) *adj* mezquino
***stink** (sstingk) *v* apestar
**stipulate** (*ssti*-pyu-leit) *v* estipular
**stipulation** (ssti-pyu-*lei*-ʃön) *n* estipulación *f*
**stir** (sstöö) *v* *mover; *revolver
**stitch** (sstich) *n* punto *m*, punzada *f*; sutura *f*
**stock** (sstok) *n* existencias *fpl*; *v* *tener en existencia; ~ **exchange** bolsa de valores, bolsa *f*; ~ **market** bolsa *f*; **stocks and shares** acciones *fpl*
**stocking** (*ssto*-king) *n* media *f*
**stole**[1] (sstoul) *v* (p steal)

**stole**[2] (sstoul) *n* estola *f*
**stomach** (*ssta*-mök) *n* estómago *m*
**stomachache** (*ssta*-mö-keik) *n* dolor de estómago
**stone** (sstoun) *n* piedra *f*; hueso *m*; **pumice ~** piedra pómez
**stood** (sstud) *v* (p, pp stand)
**stop** (sstop) *v* cesar; dejar de; *n* parada *f*; **stop!** ¡alto!
**stopper** (*ssto*-pö) *n* tapón *m*
**storage** (*sstoo*-ridʒ) *n* almacenaje *m*
**store** (sstoo) *n* tienda *f*; almacén *m*; *v* almacenar
**storehouse** (*sstoo*-hauss) *n* almacén *m*
**stor(e)y** (*sstoo*-ri) *n* piso *m*
**stork** (sstook) *n* cigüeña *f*
**storm** (sstoom) *n* tormenta *f*
**stormy** (*sstoo*-mi) *adj* tempestuoso
**story** (*sstoo*-ri) *n* cuento *m*
**stout** (sstaut) *adj* gordo, corpulento
**stove** (sstouv) *n* estufa *f*; cocina *f*
**straight** (sstreit) *adj* derecho; honesto; *adv* directamente; **~ ahead** todo seguido; **~ away** directamente, en seguida; **~ on** todo seguido
**strain** (sstrein) *n* esfuerzo *m*; tensión *f*; *v* *forzar; filtrar
**strainer** (*sstrei*-nö) *n* escurridor *m*
**strange** (sstreindʒ) *adj* extraño; raro
**stranger** (*sstrein*-dʒö) *n* extranjero *m*, -a *f*; forastero *m*, -a *f*; desconocido *m*, -a *f*
**strangle** (*sstræng*-ghöl) *v* estrangular
**strap** (sstræp) *n* correa *f*
**straw** (sstroo) *n* paja *f*
**strawberry** (*sstroo*-bö-ri) *n* fresa *f*
**stream** (sstriim) *n* arroyo *m*; corriente *f*; *v* *fluir
**street** (sstriit) *n* calle *f*
**streetcar** (*sstriit*-kaa) *nAm* tranvía *m*
**strength** (sstrêngz) *n* fuerza *f*, vigor *m*
**stress** (sstrêss) *n* esfuerzo *m*; énfasis *m*; *v* acentuar
**stretch** (sstrêch) *v* estirar; *n* trecho *m*
**strict** (sstrikt) *adj* estricto; severo
**strife** (sstraif) *n* lucha *f*
**strike** (sstraik) *n* huelga *f*
***strike** (sstraik) *v* golpear; atacar; impresionar; *estar en huelga; arriar
**striking** (*sstrai*-king) *adj* impresionante, notable, vistoso
**string** (sstring) *n* cordel *m*; cuerda *f*
**strip** (sstrip) *n* faja *f*
**stripe** (sstraip) *n* raya *f*
**striped** (sstraipt) *adj* rayado
**stroke** (sstrouk) *n* ataque *m*; golpe *m*
**stroll** (sstroul) *v* pasear; *n* paseo *m*
**strong** (sstrong) *adj* fuerte
**stronghold** (*sstrong*-hould) *n* plaza fuerte
**structure** (*sstrak*-chö) *n* estructura *f*
**struggle** (*sstra*-ghöl) *n* combate *m*, lucha *f*; *v* luchar
**stub** (sstab) *n* talón *m*
**stubborn** (*ssta*-bön) *adj* testarudo
**student** (*sstyuu*-dönt) *n* estudiante *m*; estudiante *f*
**study** (*ssta*-di) *v* estudiar; *n* estudio *m*; despacho *m*
**stuff** (sstaf) *n* substancia *f*; cachivache *m*
**stuffed** (sstaft) *adj* rellenado; **stuffed animal** muñeco de peluche
**stuffing** (*ssta*-fing) *n* relleno *m*
**stuffy** (*ssta*-fi) *adj* sofocante
**stumble** (*sstam*-böl) *v* *tropezarse
**stung** (sstang) *v* (p, pp sting)
**stupid** (*sstyuu*-pid) *adj* estúpido
**style** (sstail) *n* estilo *m*; **stylish** elegante
**subject**[1] (*ssab*-dʒikt) *n* sujeto *m*; súbdito *m*; **~ to** sujeto a
**subject**[2] (ssöb-*dʒêkt*) *v* someter
**submarine** (ssab-mö-*riin*) submarino *m*
**submit** (ssöb-*mit*) *v* someterse
**subordinate** (ssö-*boo*-di-nöt) *adj*

subalterno; subordinado
**subscriber** (ssöb-*sskrai*-bö) *n* abonado *m*, -a *f*; suscriptor *m*, -a *f*
**subscription** (ssöb-*sskrip*-ʃön) *n* abono *f*
**subsequent** (*ssab*-ssi-k$^{u}$önt) *adj* posterior
**subsidy** (*ssab*-ssi-di) *n* subsidio *m*
**substance** (*ssab*-sstönss) *n* sustancia *f*
**substantial** (ssöb-*sstæn*-ʃöl) *adj* material; real; sustancial
**substitute** (*ssab*-ssti-tyuut) *v* *sustituir; *n* sustituto *m*, -a *f*
**subtitle** (*ssab*-tai-töl) *n* subtítulo *m*
**subtle** (*ssa*-töl) *adj* sutil
**subtract** (ssöb-*trækt*) *v* restar
**suburb** (*ssa*-bööb) *n* suburbio *m*
**suburban** (ssö-*böö*-bön) *adj* suburbano
**subway** (*ssab*-$^{u}$ei) *nAm* metro *m*
**succeed** (ssök-*ssiid*) *v* *tener éxito; suceder
**success** (ssök-*ssêss*) *n* éxito *m*
**successful** (ssök-*ssêss*-föl) *adj* exitoso
**succumb** (ssö-*kam*) *v* sucumbir
**such** (ssach) *adj* tal; *adv* tan; **~ as** tal como
**suck** (ssak) *v* chupar
**sudden** (*ssa*-dön) *adj* súbito
**suddenly** (*ssa*-dön-li) *adv* repentinamente
**suede** (ss$^{u}$eid) *n* gamuza *f*
**suffer** (*ssa*-fö) *v* sufrir
**suffering** (*ssa*-fö-ring) *n* sufrimiento *m*
**suffice** (ssö-*faiss*) *v* bastar
**sufficient** (ssö-*fi*-ʃönt) *adj* suficiente, bastante
**suffrage** (*ssa*-fridʒ) *n* derecho electoral, sufragio *m*
**sugar** (*ʃu*-ghö) *n* azúcar *m/f*
**suggest** (ssö-*dʒêsst*) *v* *sugerir
**suggestion** (ssö-*dʒêss*-chön) *n* sugestión *f*
**suicide** (*ssuu*-i-ssaid) *n* suicidio *m*
**suit** (ssuut) *v* *convenir; adaptar; *ir bien; *n* traje *m*
**suitable** (*ssuu*-tö-böl) *adj* apropiado, apto
**suitcase** (*ssuut*-keiss) *n* maleta *f*
**suite** (ss$^{u}$iit) *n* apartamento *m*
**sum** (ssam) *n* suma *f*
**summary** (*ssa*-mö-ri) *n* resumen *m*, sumario *m*
**summer** (*ssa*-mö) *n* verano *m*; **~ time** horario de verano
**summit** (*ssa*-mit) *n* cima *f*
**sun** (ssan) *n* sol *m*
**sunbathe** (*ssan*-beið) *v* tomar el sol
**sunburn** (*ssan*-böön) *n* quemadura del sol
**Sunday** (*ssan*-di) domingo *m*
**sunglasses** (*ssan*-ghlaa-ssis) *pl* gafas de sol
**sunlight** (*ssan*-lait) *n* luz del sol
**sunny** (*ssa*-ni) *adj* soleado
**sunrise** (*ssan*-rais) *n* amanecer *m*
**sunset** (*ssan*-ssêt) *n* ocaso *m*
**sunshade** (*ssan*-ʃeid) *n* quitasol *m*
**sunshine** (*ssan*-ʃain) *n* sol *m*
**sunstroke** (*ssan*-sstrouk) *n* insolación *f*
**suntan oil** (*ssan*-tæn-oil) aceite bronceador
**super** (*ssuu*-pö) *adj colloquial* genial, estupendo ; *n* portero *m*, -a *f*
**superb** (ssu-*pööb*) *adj* grandioso, soberbio
**superficial** (ssuu-pö-*fi*-ʃöl) *adj* superficial
**superfluous** (ssu-*pöö*-flu-öss) *adj* superfluo
**superior** (ssu-*pi*$^{ö}$-ri-ö) *adj* mejor, mayor, superior
**superlative** (ssu-*pöö*-lö-tiv) *adj* superlativo; *n* superlativo *m*
**supermarket** (*ssuu*-pö-maa-kit) *n* supermercado *m*

**superstition** (ssuu-pö-*ssti*-ʃön) *n* superstición *f*
**supervise** (*ssuu*-pö-vais) *v* supervisar
**supervision** (ssuu-pö-*vi*-ʒön) *n* supervisión *f*
**supervisor** (*ssuu*-pö-vai-sö) *n* supervisor *m*, -a *f*
**supper** (*ssa*-pö) *n* cena *f*
**supple** (*ssa*-pöl) *adj* flexible, ágil
**supplement** (*ssa*-pli-mönt) *n* suplemento *m*
**supply** (ssö-*plai*) *n* abastecimiento *m*, suministro *m*; existencias *fpl*; oferta *f*; *v* suministrar
**support** (ssö-*poot*) *v* apoyar, *sostener, soportar; *n* apoyo *m*; **~ hose** medias elásticas
**supporter** (ssö-*poo*-tö) *n* aficionado *m*, -a *f*; partidario *m*, -a *f*; seguidor *m*, -a *f*
**suppose** (ssö-*pous*) *v* *suponer; **supposing that** dado que
**suppository** (ssö-*po*-si-tö-ri) *n* supositorio *m*
**suppress** (ssö-*prêss*) *v* reprimir
**surcharge** (*ssöö*-chaadʒ) *n* sobretasa *f*
**sure** (ʃu$^{ö}$) *adj* seguro
**surely** (*ʃu$^{ö}$*-li) *adv* seguramente
**surface** (*ssöö*-fiss) *n* superficie *f*
**surfboard** (*ssööf*-bood) *n* tabla para surf
**surgeon** (*ssöö*-dʒön) *n* cirujano *m*; **veterinary ~** veterinario *m*
**surgery** (*ssöö*-dʒö-ri) *n* operación *f*; consultorio *m*
**surname** (*ssöö*-neim) *n* apellido *m*
**surplus** (*ssöö*-plöss) *n* sobra *f*
**surprise** (ssö-*prais*) *n* sorpresa *f*; *v* sorprender; extrañar
**surrender** (ssö-*rên*-dö) *v* *rendirse; *n* rendición *f*
**surround** (ssö-*raund*) *v* rodear, cercar
**surrounding** (ssö-*raun*-ding) *adj* circundante
**surroundings** (ssö-*raun*-dings) *pl* alrededores *mpl*
**survey** (*ssöö*-vei) *n* resumen *m*; encuesta *f*
**survival** (ssö-*vai*-völ) *n* supervivencia *f*
**survive** (ssö-*vaiv*) *v* sobrevivir
**suspect**[1] (ssö-*sspêkt*) *v* sospechar
**suspect**[2] (*ssa*-sspêkt) *n* persona sospechosa
**suspend** (ssö-*sspênd*) *v* suspender
**suspenders** (ssö-*sspên*-dös) *plAm* tirantes *mpl*
**suspension** (ssö-*sspên*-ʃön) *n* suspensión *f*; **~ bridge** puente colgante
**suspicion** (ssö-*sspi*-ʃön) *n* sospecha *f*; suspicacia *f*, desconfianza *f*
**suspicious** (ssö-*sspi*-ʃöss) *adj* sospechoso; suspicaz, desconfiado
**sustain** (ssö-*sstein*) *v* soportar
**Swahili** (ss$^{u}$ö-*hii*-li) *n* suahili *m*
**swallow** (*ss$^{u}$o*-lou) *v* tragar; *n* golondrina *f*
**swam** (ss$^{u}$æm) *v* (p swim)
**swamp** (ss$^{u}$omp) *n* marisma *f*
**swan** (ss$^{u}$on) *n* cisne *m*
**swap** (ss$^{u}$op) *v* *trocar
***swear** (ss$^{u}$ê$^{ö}$) *v* jurar
**sweat** (ss$^{u}$êt) *n* sudor *m*; *v* sudar
**sweater** (*ss$^{u}$ê*-tö) *n* suéter *m*
**Swede** (ss$^{u}$iid) *n* sueco *m*
**Sweden** (*ss$^{u}$ii*-dön) Suecia *f*
**Swedish** (*ss$^{u}$ii*-diʃ) *adj* sueco
***sweep** (ss$^{u}$iip) *v* barrer
**sweet** (ss$^{u}$iit) *adj* dulce; lindo; *n* caramelo *m*; dulce *m*
**sweeten** (*ss$^{u}$ii*-tön) *v* endulzar
**sweetheart** (*ss$^{u}$iit*-haat) *n* amor *m*, querida *f*
**sweetshop** (*ss$^{u}$iit*-ʃop) *n* confitería *f*
**swell** (ss$^{u}$êl) *adj* estupendo
***swell** (ss$^{u}$êl) *v* hincharse
**swelling** (*ss$^{u}$ê*-ling) *n* hinchazón *f*

**swift** (ss$^{u}$ift) *adj* veloz
***swim** (ss$^{u}$im) *v* nadar
**swimmer** (*ss$^{u}$i*-mö) *n* nadador *m*, -a *f*
**swimming** (*ss$^{u}$i*-ming) *n* natación *f*; ~ **pool** piscina *f*
**swim(ming) trunks** (*ss$^{u}$i*-ming-trangkss) *n* calzón de baño, bañador
**swimsuit** (*ss$^{u}$im*-ssuut) *n* traje de baño
**swindle** (*ss$^{u}$in*-döl) *v* estafar; *n* estafa *f*
**swindler** (*ss$^{u}$in*-dlö) *n* estafador *m*, -a *f*
**swing** (ss$^{u}$ing) *n* columpio *m*
***swing** (ss$^{u}$ing) *v* oscilar; columpiarse
**Swiss** (ss$^{u}$iss) *adj* suizo
**switch** (ss$^{u}$ich) *n* interruptor *m*; *v* cambiar; ~ **off** apagar; ~ **on** *encender
**switchboard** (*ss$^{u}$ich*-bood) *n* cuadro de distribución
**Switzerland** (*ss$^{u}$it*-ssö-lönd) Suiza *f*
**sword** (ssood) *n* espada *f*
**swum** (ss$^{u}$am) *v* (pp swim)
**syllable** (*ssi*-lö-böl) *n* sílaba *f*
**symbol** (*ssim*-böl) *n* símbolo *m*
**sympathetic** (ssim-pö-*zê*-tik) *adj* cordial, compasivo
**sympathy** (*ssim*-pö-zi) *n* simpatía *f*; compasión *f*
**symphony** (*ssim*-fö-ni) *n* sinfonía *f*
**symptom** (*ssim*-töm) *n* síntoma *m*
**synagogue** (*ssi*-nö-ghogh) *n* sinagoga *f*
**synonym** (*ssi*-nö-nim) *n* sinónimo *m*
**synthetic** (ssin-*zê*-tik) *adj* sintético
**Syria** (*ssi*-ri-ö) Siria *f*
**Syrian** (*ssi*-ri-ön) *adj* sirio
**syringe** (ssi-*rindʒ*) *n* jeringa *f*
**syrup** (*ssi*-röp) *n* jarabe *m*
**system** (*ssi*-sstöm) *n* sistema *m*; **decimal** ~ sistema decimal
**systematic** (ssi-sstö-*mæ*-tik) *adj* sistemático

# T

**table** (*tei*-böl) *n* mesa *f*; tabla *f*; ~ **of contents** índice *m*; ~ **tennis** tenis de mesa
**tablecloth** (*tei*-böl-kloz) *n* mantel *m*
**tablespoon** (*tei*-böl-sspuun) *n* cuchara *f*
**tablet** (*tæ*-blit) *n* pastilla *f*
**taboo** (tö-*buu*) *n* tabú *m*
**tactics** (*tæk*-tikss) *pl* táctica *f*
**tag** (tægh) *n* cabo *m*; etiqueta *f*
**tail** (teil) *n* cola *f*; rabo *m*
**taillight** (*teil*-lait) *n* farol trasero
**tailor** (*tei*-lö) *n* sastre *m*
**tailor-made** (*tei*-lö-meid) *adj* hecho a la medida
***take** (teik) *v* coger; tomar; llevar; comprender, *entender; ~ **away** quitar; llevarse; ~ **off** despegar; ~ **out** sacar; ~ **over** encargarse de; ~ **place** *tener lugar; ~ **up** ocupar
**take-off** (*tei*-kof) *n* despegue *m*
**tale** (teil) *n* cuento *m*
**talent** (*tæ*-lönt) *n* talento *m*
**talented** (*tæ*-lön-tid) *adj* talentoso
**talk** (took) *v* hablar; *n* conversación *f*
**talkative** (*too*-kö-tiv) *adj* locuaz
**tall** (tool) *adj* alto
**tame** (teim) *adj* manso, domesticado; *v* domesticar
**tampon** (*tæm*-pön) *n* tapón *m*; tampón *m*
**tangerine** (tæn-dʒö-*riin*) *n* mandarina *f*
**tangible** (*tæn*-dʒi-böl) *adj* tangible;

palpable
**tank** (tængk) *n* tanque *m*; depósito *m*
**tanker** (*tæng*-kö) *n* petrolero *m*
**tanned** (tænd) *adj* bronceado
**tap** (tæp) *n* grifo *m*; golpecito *m*; *v* golpear
**tape** (teip) *n* cinta *f*; **adhesive ~** cinta adhesiva; esparadrapo *m*
**tape recorder** (*teip*-ri-koo-dö) *n* magnetófono *m*
**tar** (taa) *n* brea *f*; alquitrán *m*
**target** (*taa*-ghit) *n* objetivo *m*, blanco *m*
**tariff** (*tæ*-rif) *n* arancel *m*; tarifa *f*
**task** (taassk) *n* tarea *f*
**taste** (teisst) *n* gusto *m*; *v* *saber a; *probar
**tasteless** (*teisst*-löss) *adj* insípido
**tasty** (*tei*-ssti) *adj* rico, sabroso
**taught** (toot) *v* (p, pp teach)
**tavern** (*tæ*-vön) *n* taberna *f*
**tax** (tækss) *n* impuesto *m*; *v* *imponer contribuciones
**taxation** (tæk-*ssei*-ʃön) *n* impuesto *m*
**tax-free** (*tækss*-frii) *adj* libre de impuestos
**taxi** (*tæk*-ssi) *n* taxi *m*; **~ driver** taxista *m/f*; **~ rank** parada de taxis; **~ stand** *Am* parada de taxis
**taximeter** (*tæk*-ssi-mii-tö) *n* taxímetro *m*
**tea** (tii) *n* té *m*; merienda *f*
***teach** (tiich) *v* enseñar
**teacher** (*tii*-chö) *n* profesor *m*, -a *f*, maestro *m*, -a *f*; institutor *m*
**teachings** (*tii*-chings) *pl* enseñanza *f*
**tea cloth** (*tii*-kloz) *n* trapo de cocina
**teacup** (*tii*-kap) *n* taza de té
**team** (tiim) *n* equipo *m*
**teapot** (*tii*-pot) *n* tetera *f*
**tear**[1] (tiö) *n* lágrima *f*
**tear**[2] (têö) *n* rasgón *m*; ***tear** *v* desgarrar
**tearjerker** (*tiö*-dʒöö-kö) *n* obra lacrimosa
**tease** (tiis) *v* tomar el pelo
**tea set** (*tii*-ssêt) *n* juego de té
**tea-shop** (*tii*-ʃop) *n* salón de té
**teaspoon** (*tii*-sspuun) *n* cucharilla *f*
**teaspoonful** (*tii*-sspuun-ful) *n* cucharadita *f*
**technical** (*têk*-ni-köl) *adj* técnico
**technician** (têk-*ni*-ʃön) *n* técnico *m*
**technique** (têk-*niik*) *n* técnica *f*
**technological** (têk-nö-*lo*-dʒi-köl) *adj* tecnológico
**technology** (têk-*no*-lö-dʒi) *n* tecnología *f*
**teenager** (*tii*-nei-dʒö) *n* adolescente *m/f*
**teetotaller** (tii-*tou*-tö-lö) *n* abstemio *m*
**telepathy** (ti-*lê*-pö-zi) *n* telepatía *f*
**telephone** (*tê*-li-foun) *n* teléfono *m*; **~ book** *Am* listín telefónico, guía telefónica; **~ booth** cabina telefónica; **~ call** llamada telefónica; **~ directory** guía telefónica, listín telefónico; directorio telefónico *Me*; **~ exchange** central telefónica
**television** (*tê*-li-vi-ʒön) *n* televisión *f*; **~ set** televisor *m*; **cable ~** televisión por cable; **satellite ~** televisión por satélite
**telex** (*tê*-lêkss) *n* télex *m*
***tell** (têl) *v* *decir; *contar
**temper** (*têm*-pö) *n* humor *m*; disposición *f*
**temperature** (*têm*-prö-chö) *n* temperatura *f*
**tempest** (*têm*-pisst) *n* tempestad *f*
**temple** (*têm*-pöl) *n* templo *m*; sien *f*
**temporary** (*têm*-pö-rö-ri) *adj* provisional, temporal
**tempt** (têmpt) *v* *tentar
**temptation** (têmp-*tei*-ʃön) *n* tentación *f*
**ten** (tên) *num* diez

**tenant** (*tê*-nönt) *n* inquilino *m*
**tend** (tênd) *v* *tender a; cuidar de; ~ **to** *tender a
**tendency** (*tên*-dön-ssi) *n* inclinación *f*, tendencia *f*
**tender** (*tên*-dö) *adj* tierno, delicado
**tendon** (*tên*-dön) *n* tendón *m*
**tennis** (*tê*-niss) *n* tenis *m*; ~ **court** campo de tenis, cancha *f*; ~ **shoes** zapatos de tenis
**tense** (tênss) *adj* tenso; tieso; *n* tiempo *m*
**tension** (*tên*-ʃön) *n* tensión *m*
**tent** (tênt) *n* tienda *f* de campaña
**tenth** (tênz) *num* décimo
**tepid** (*tê*-pid) *adj* tibio
**term** (tööm) *n* término *m*; período *m*, plazo *m*; condición *f*
**terminal** (*töö*-mi-nöl) *n* estación terminal; *adj* mortal
**terrace** (*tê*-röss) *n* terraza *f*
**terrain** (tê-*rein*) *n* terreno *m*
**terrible** (*tê*-ri-böl) *adj* tremendo, terrible, pésimo
**terrific** (tö-*ri*-fik) *adj* fantástico; estupendo
**terrify** (*tê*-ri-fai) *v* aterrorizar; **terrifying** aterrador
**territory** (*tê*-ri-tö-ri) *n* territorio *m*
**terror** (*tê*-rö) *n* terror *m*
**terrorism** (*tê*-rö-ri-söm) *n* terrorismo *m*, terror *m*
**terrorist** (*tê*-rö-risst) *n* terrorista *m/f*
**test** (têsst) *n* prueba *f*, ensayo *m*; *v* *probar, ensayar
**testify** (*tê*-ssti-fai) *v* testimoniar
**text** (têksst) *n* texto *m*
**textbook** (*têkss*-buk) *n* libro de texto
**textile** (*têk*-sstail) *n* textil *m*
**texture** (*têkss*-chö) *n* textura *f*
**Thai** (tai) *adj* tailandés
**Thailand** (*tai*-lænd) Tailandia *f*
**than** (ðæn) *conj* que
**thank** (zængk) *v* *agradecer; ~ **you** gracias
**thankful** (*zængk*-föl) *adj* agradecido
**that** (ðæt) *adj* aquel, ese; *pron* aquél, eso; que; *conj* que
**thaw** (zoo) *v* descongelarse; *n* deshielo *m*
**the** (ðö, ði) *art* el *art*; **the … the** cuanto más … más
**theater** *Am*, **theatre** (*ziᵒ*-tö) *n* teatro *m*
**theft** (zêft) *n* robo *m*; hurto *m*
**their** (ðêᵒ) *adj* su
**them** (ðêm) *pron* les
**theme** (ziim) *n* tema *m*, sujeto *m*
**themselves** (ðöm-*ssêlvs*) *pron* se; ellos mismos
**then** (ðên) *adv* entonces; después; en tal caso
**theology** (zi-*o*-lö-dʒi) *n* teología *f*
**theoretical** (ziᵒ-*rê*-ti-köl) *adj* teórico
**theory** (*ziᵒ*-ri) *n* teoría *f*
**therapy** (*zê*-rö-pi) *n* terapia *f*
**there** (ðêᵒ) *adv* allí; hacia allá
**therefore** (*ðêᵒ*-foo) *conj* por lo tanto
**thermometer** (zö-*mo*-mi-tö) *n* termómetro *m*
**thermostat** (*zöö*-mö-sstæt) *n* termostato *m*
**these** (ðiis) *adj* éstos
**thesis** (*zii*-ssiss) *n* (pl theses) tesis *f*
**they** (ðei) *pron* ellos
**thick** (zik) *adj* espeso; denso
**thicken** (*zi*-kön) *v* espesar
**thickness** (*zik*-nöss) *n* espesor *m*
**thief** (ziif) *n* (pl thieves) ladrón *m*, ladrona *f*
**thigh** (zai) *n* muslo *m*
**thimble** (*zim*-böl) *n* dedal *m*
**thin** (zin) *adj* delgado; flaco
**thing** (zing) *n* cosa *f*
***think** (zingk) *v* *pensar; reflexionar; ~ **of** *pensar en; *recordar; ~ **over** considerar
**third** (zööd) *num* tercero

**thirst** (zöösst) *n* sed *f*
**thirsty** (*zöö*-ssti) *adj* sediento
**thirteen** (zöö-*tiin*) *num* trece
**thirteenth** (zöö-*tiinz*) *num* treceno
**thirtieth** (*zöö*-ti-öz) *num* treintavo
**thirty** (*zöö*-ti) *num* treinta
**this** (ðiss) *adj* este, esto; *pron* éste
**thistle** (*zi*-ssöl) *n* cardo *m*
**thorn** (zoon) *n* espina *f*
**thorough** (*za*-rö) *adj* minucioso
**thoroughfare** (*za*-rö-fê$^{ö}$) *n* ruta principal, arteria principal
**those** (ðous) *adj* aquellos; *pron* aquéllos
**though** (ðou) *conj* si bien, aunque; *adv* sin embargo
**thought**[1] (zoot) *v* (p, pp think)
**thought**[2] (zoot) *n* pensamiento *m*
**thoughtful** (*zoot*-föl) *adj* pensativo; atento
**thousand** (*zau*-sönd) *num* mil
**thread** (zrêd) *n* hilo *m*; *v* enhebrar
**threadbare** (*zrêd*-bê$^{ö}$) *adj* gastado
**threat** (zrêt) *n* amenaza *f*
**threaten** (*zrê*-tön) *v* amenazar
**threatening** amenazador
**three** (zrii) *num* tres
**three-quarter** (zrii-*k$^{u}$oo*-tö) *adj* tres cuartos
**threshold** (*zrê*-ʃould) *n* umbral *m*
**threw** (zruu) *v* (p throw)
**thrifty** (*zrif*-ti) *adj* económico
**throat** (zrout) *n* garganta *f*
**throne** (zroun) *n* trono *m*
**through** (zruu) *prep* a través de
**throughout** (zruu-*aut*) *adv* por todas partes
**throw** (zrou) *n* lanzamiento *m*
***throw** (zrou) *v* tirar, arrojar
**thrush** (zraʃ) *n* tordo *m*
**thumb** (zam) *n* pulgar *m*
**thumbtack** (*zam*-tæk) *nAm* chinche *f*
**thump** (zamp) *v* golpear; aporrear
**thunder** (*zan*-dö) *n* trueno *m*; *v* *tronar
**thunderstorm** (*zan*-dö-sstoom) *n* tronada *f*
**thundery** (*zan*-dö-ri) *adj* tormentoso
**Thursday** (*zöös*-di) jueves *m*
**thus** (ðass) *adv* así; por consiguiente
**thyme** (taim) *n* tomillo *m*
**tick** (tik) *n* señal *f*; ~ **off** señalar; fastidiar
**ticket** (*ti*-kit) *n* billete *m*; multa *f*; boleto *mMe*; ~ **collector** revisor *m*; ~ **office** taquilla *f*
**tickle** (*ti*-köl) *v* cosquillear
**tide** (taid) *n* marea *f*; **high** ~ pleamar *f*; **low** ~ bajamar *f*
**tidy** (*tai*-di) *adj* arreglado; limpio, aseado; ~ **up** arreglar
**tie** (tai) *v* anudar, atar; *n* corbata *f*
**tiger** (*tai*-ghö) *n* tigre *m*
**tight** (tait) *adj* estrecho; angosto, apretado; *adv* fuertemente
**tighten** (*tai*-tön) *v* estrechar, *apretar; estrecharse
**tights** (taitss) *pl* traje de malla
**tile** (tail) *n* azulejo *m*; teja *f*
**till** (til) *prep* hasta; *conj* hasta que
**timber** (*tim*-bö) *n* madera de construcción
**time** (taim) *n* tiempo *m*; vez *f*; hora *f*; época *f*; **all the** ~ continuamente; **in** ~ a tiempo; ~ **of arrival** hora de llegada; ~ **of departure** hora de salida
**time-saving** (*taim*-ssei-ving) *adj* que economiza tiempo
**timetable** (*taim*-tei-böl) *n* horario *m*
**timid** (*ti*-mid) *adj* tímido
**timidity** (ti-*mi*-dö-ti) *n* timidez *f*
**tin** (tin) *n* estaño *m*; lata *f*; ~ **opener** abrelatas *m*; **tinned food** conservas *fpl*
**tinfoil** (*tin*-foil) *n* papel de estaño
**tiny** (*tai*-ni) *adj* menudo
**tip** (tip) *n* punta *f*; propina *f*
**tire**[1] (tai$^{ö}$) *n* neumático *m*; llanta *fMe*

**tire**$^{2}$ (tai$^{ö}$) *v* cansar
**tired** (tai$^{ö}$d) *adj* cansado; **~ of** harto de
**tissue** (*ti*-ʃuu) *n* tejido *m*; pañuelo de papel
**title** (*tai*-töl) *n* título *m*
**to** (tuu) *prep* hasta; a, para, en, hacia
**toad** (toud) *n* sapo *m*
**toadstool** (*toud*-sstuul) *n* hongo *m* venenoso
**toast** (tousst) *n* pan tostado; brindis *m*
**tobacco** (tö-*bæ*-kou) *n* (pl ~s) tabaco *m*; **~ pouch** petaca *f*
**tobacconist** (tö-*bæ*-kö-nisst) *n* estanquero *m*; **tobacconist's** estanco *m*
**today** (tö-*dei*) *adv* hoy
**toddler** (*tod*-lö) *n* niño que empieza a andar
**toe** (tou) *n* dedo del pie
**toffee** (*to*-fi) *n* caramelo *m*
**together** (tö-*ghê*-ðö) *adv* juntos
**toilet** (*toi*-löt) *n* retrete *m*; **~ case** neceser *m*; **~ paper** papel higiénico
**toiletry** (*toi*-lö-tri) *n* artículos de tocador
**token** (*tou*-kön) *n* señal *f*; prueba *f*; ficha *f*
**told** (tould) *v* (p, pp tell)
**tolerable** (*to*-lö-rö-böl) *adj* tolerable
**toll** (toul) *n* peaje *m*
**tomato** (tö-*maa*-tou) *n* (pl ~es) tomate *m*; jitomate *mMe*
**tomb** (tuum) *n* tumba *f*
**tombstone** (*tuum*-sstoun) *n* lápida *f*
**tomorrow** (tö-*mo*-rou) *adv* mañana
**ton** (tan) *n* tonelada *f*
**tone** (toun) *n* tono *m*; timbre *m*
**tongs** (tongs) *pl* tenazas *f*
**tongue** (tang) *n* lengua *f*
**tonic** (*to*-nik) *n* tónico *m*
**tonight** (tö-*nait*) *adv* esta noche
**tonsilitis** (ton-ssö-*lai*-tiss) *n* amigdalitis *f*
**tonsils** (*ton*-ssöls) *pl* amígdalas *fpl*
**too** (tuu) *adv* demasiado; también
**took** (tuk) *v* (p take)
**tool** (tuul) *n* herramienta *f*; **~ kit** bolsa de herramientas
**tooth** (tuuz) *n* (pl teeth) diente *m*
**toothache** (*tuu*-zeik) *n* dolor de muelas
**toothbrush** (*tuuz*-braʃ) *n* cepillo de dientes
**toothpaste** (*tuuz*-peisst) *n* pasta dentífrica
**toothpick** (*tuuz*-pik) *n* palillo *m*
**toothpowder** (*tuuz*-pau-dö) *n* polvo para los dientes
**top** (top) *n* cima *f*; cumbre *f*; tapa *f*; **on ~ of** encima de; **~ side** parte superior
**topic** (*to*-pik) *n* asunto *m*; tema *m*
**topical** (*to*-pi-köl) *adj* actual
**torch** (tooch) *n* antorcha *f*; linterna *f*
**torment**$^{1}$ (too-*mênt*) *v* atormentar
**torment**$^{2}$ (*too*-mênt) *n* tormento *m*
**torture** (*too*-chö) *n* tortura *f*; *v* torturar
**toss** (toss) *v* lanzar al aire; sacudir
**tot** (tot) *n* niño pequeño
**total** (*tou*-töl) *adj* total; completo, absoluto; *n* total *m*
**totalitarian** (tou-tæ-li-*tê*$^{ö}$-ri-ön) *adj* totalitario
**touch** (tach) *v* tocar; *concernir; *n* contacto *m*, toque *m*; tacto *m*
**touching** (*ta*-ching) *adj* conmovedor
**tough** (taf) *adj* duro
**tour** (tu$^{ö}$) *n* excursión *f*; viaje *m*; *v* viajar por; recorrer
**tourism** (*tu*$^{ö}$-ri-söm) *n* turismo *m*
**tourist** (*tu*$^{ö}$-risst) *n* turista *m/f*; **~ class** clase turista; **~ office** oficina de tourismo
**tournament** (*tu*$^{ö}$-nö-mönt) *n* torneo *m*
**tow** (tou) *v* remolcar
**towards** (tö-$^{u}$*oods*) *prep* hacia; para con
**towel** (tau$^{ö}$l) *n* toalla *f*
**towel(l)ing** (*tau*$^{ö}$-ling) *n* tela para

toallas
**tower** (tau$^{ö}$) *n* torre *f*
**town** (taun) *n* ciudad *f*; **~ center** *Am*, **~ centre** centro de la ciudad; **~ hall** ayuntamiento *m*
**townspeople** (*tauns*-pii-pöl) *pl* ciudadanos *mpl*
**toxic** (*tok*-ssik) *adj* tóxico
**toy** (toi) *n* juguete *m*
**toyshop** (*toi*-ʃop) *n* juguetería *f*
**trace** (treiss) *n* huella *f*; *v* rastrear
**track** (træk) *n* vía *f*; pista *f*
**tractor** (*træk*-tö) *n* tractor *m*
**trade** (treid) *n* comercio *m*; oficio *m*; *v* comerciar
**trademark** (*treid*-maak) *n* marca de fábrica
**trader** (*trei*-dö) *n* comerciante *m*
**tradesman** (*treids*-mön) *n* (pl -men) tendero *m*
**trade union** (treid-*yuu*-nyön) *n* sindicato *m*
**tradition** (trö-*di*-ʃön) *n* tradición *f*
**traditional** (trö-*di*-ʃö-nöl) *adj* tradicional
**traffic** (*træ*-fik) *n* tránsito *m*; **~ jam** embotellamiento *m*; **~ light** semáforo *m*
**trafficator** (*træ*-fi-kei-tö) *n* indicador *m*
**tragedy** (*træ*-dʒö-di) *n* tragedia *f*
**tragic** (*træ*-dʒik) *adj* trágico
**trail** (treil) *n* rastro *m*, sendero *m*
**trailer** (*trei*-lö) *n* remolque *m*; *nAm* caravana *f*
**train** (trein) *n* tren *m*; *v* amaestrar, entrenar; **local ~** tren de cercanías; **through ~** tren directo; **~ ferry** transbordador de trenes
**trainee** (trei-*nii*) aprendiz *m*, -a *f*
**trainer** (*trei*-nö) entrenador *m*, -a *f*; adiestrador *m*, -a *f*
**training** (*trei*-ning) *n* entrenamiento *m*
**trait** (treit) *n* rasgo *m*
**traitor** (*trei*-tö) *n* traidor *m*
**tram** (træm) *n* tranvía *m*
**tramp** (træmp) *n* vagabundo *m*; *v* vagabundear
**tranquil** (*træng*-k$^{u}$il) *adj* tranquilo
**tranquillizer** (*træng*-k$^{u}$i-lai-sö) *n* calmante *m*
**transaction** (træn-*sæk*-ʃön) *n* transacción *f*
**transatlantic** (træn-söt-*læn*-tik) *adj* transatlántico
**transfer** (trænss-*föö*) *v* *transferir
**transform** (trænss-*foom*) *v* transformar
**transformer** (trænss-*foo*-mö) *n* transformador *m*
**transition** (træn-*ssi*-ʃön) *n* transición *f*
**translate** (trænss-*leit*) *v* *traducir
**translation** (trænss-*lei*-ʃön) *n* traducción *f*
**translator** (trænss-*lei*-tö) *n* traductor *m*, **-a** *f*
**transmission** (træns-*mi*-ʃön) *n* transmisión *f*
**transmit** (træns-*mit*) *v* transmitir
**transmitter** (træns-*mi*-tö) *n* emisor *m*
**transparent** (træn-*sspê*$^{ö}$-rönt) *adj* transparente
**transport**[1] (*træn*-sspoot) *n* transporte *m*
**transport**[2] (træn-*sspoot*) *v* transportar
**transportation** (træn-sspoo-*tei*-ʃön) *n* transporte *m*
**trap** (træp) *n* trampa *f*
**trash** (træʃ) *n* basura *f*
**travel** (*træ*-völ) *v* viajar; **~ agency** agencia de viajes; **~ agent** agente de viajes; **~ agency** agencia de viajes; **~ insurance** seguro de viaje; **travel(l)ing expenses** gastos de viaje
**travel(l)er** (*træ*-vö-lö) *n* viajero *m*, -a *f*; **traveler's check** *Am*, **traveller's cheque** cheque de viajero

**tray** (trei) *n* bandeja *f*; charola *fMe*
**treason** (*trii*-sön) *n* traición *f*
**treasure** (*trê*-ʒö) *n* tesoro *m*
**treasurer** (*trê*-ʒö-rö) *n* tesorero *m*
**treasury** (*trê*-ʒö-ri) *n* Tesorería *f*
**treat** (triit) *v* tratar; convidar
**treatment** (*triit*-mönt) *n* tratamiento *m*
**treaty** (*trii*-ti) *n* tratado *m*
**tree** (trii) *n* árbol *m*
**tremble** (*trêm*-böl) *v* *temblar; vibrar
**tremendous** (tri-*mên*-döss) *adj* tremendo
**trendy** (*trên*-di) *adj* de moda; moderno
**trespass** (*trêss*-pöss) *v* infringir
**trespasser** (*trêss*-pö-ssö) *n* intruso *m*
**trial** (trai$^{ö}$l) *n* proceso *m*; prueba *f*
**triangle** (*trai*-æng-ghöl) *n* triángulo *m*
**triangular** (trai-*æng*-ghyu-lö) *adj* triangular
**tribe** (traib) *n* tribu *m*
**tributary** (*tri*-byu-tö-ri) *n* afluente *m*
**tribute** (*tri*-byuut) *n* homenaje *m*; tributo *m*
**trick** (trik) *n* truco *m*; trampa *f*; estafa *f*
**trigger** (*tri*-ghö) *n* gatillo *m*
**trim** (trim) *v* recortar; cortar; podar
**trip** (trip) *n* viaje *m*
**triumph** (*trai*-ömf) *n* triunfo *m*; *v* triunfar
**triumphant** (trai-*am*-fönt) *adj* triunfante
**troops** (truupss) *pl* tropas *fpl*
**tropical** (*tro*-pi-köl) *adj* tropical
**tropics** (*tro*-pikss) *pl* trópicos *mpl*
**trouble** (*tra*-böl) *n* preocupación *f*, molestia *f*; aprieto *m*; *v* molestar; inquietar
**troublesome** (*tra*-böl-ssöm) *adj* molesto
**trousers** (*trau*-sös) *pl* pantalones *mpl*
**trout** (traut) *n* (pl ~) trucha *f*
**truck** (trak) *nAm* camión *m*
**true** (truu) *adj* verdadero; real, auténtico; leal, fiel
**trumpet** (*tram*-pit) *n* trompeta *f*
**trunk** (trangk) *n* baúl *m*; tronco *m*; *nAm* portaequipajes *m*; **trunks** *pl* bañador *m*
**trust** (trasst) *v* confiar en; *n* confianza *f*
**trustworthy** (*trasst*-$^{u}$öö-ði) *adj* confiable
**truth** (truuz) *n* verdad *f*
**truthful** (*truuz*-föl) *adj* verídico
**try** (trai) *v* intentar; *esforzarse; *n* tentativa *f*; **~ on** *probarse
**tube** (tyuub) *n* tubo *m*
**tuberculosis** (tyuu-böö-kyu-*lou*-ssiss) *n* tuberculosis *f*
**Tuesday** (*tyuus*-di) martes *m*
**tug** (tagh) *v* remolcar; *n* remolcador *m*; estirón *m*
**tuition** (tyuu-*i*-ʃön) *n* enseñanza *f*; *Am* cuota *f* de enseñanza
**tulip** (*tyuu*-lip) *n* tulipán *m*
**tumbler** (*tam*-blö) *n* vaso *m*
**tumo(u)r** (*tyuu*-mö) *n* tumor *m*
**tuna** (*tyuu*-nö) *n* (pl ~, ~s) atún *m*
**tune** (tyuun) *n* tonada *f*; **~ in** sintonizar
**tuneful** (*tyuun*-föl) *adj* melodioso
**tunic** (*tyuu*-nik) *n* túnica *f*
**Tunisia** (tyuu-*ni*-si-ö) Túnez *m*
**Tunisian** (tyuu-*ni*-si-ön) *adj* tunecino
**tunnel** (*ta*-nöl) *n* túnel *m*
**turbine** (*töö*-bain) *n* turbina *f*
**turbojet** (töö-bou-*dʒêt*) *n* avión turborreactor
**Turk** (töök) *n* turco *m*
**Turkey** (*töö*-ki) Turquía *f*
**turkey** (*töö*-ki) *n* pavo *m*
**Turkish** (*töö*-kiʃ) *adj* turco; **~ bath** baño turco
**turn** (tööm) *v* girar; *volver; *n* cambio *m*, vuelta *f*; curva *f*; turno *m*; **~ back** *volver; **~ down** rechazar; **~ into** *convertirse en; **~ off** *cerrar; **~ on** *encender; abrir; **~ over** *volver; ~

**round** *volver; *volverse
**turning** (*töö*-ning) *n* vuelta *f*; ~ **point** punto decisivo
**turnover** (*töö*-nou-vö) *n* volumen de transacciones; ~ **tax** impuesto sobre la venta
**turnpike** (*töön*-paik) *nAm* autopista de peaje
**turpentine** (*töö*-pön-tain) *n* trementina *f*
**turtle** (*töö*-töl) *n* tortuga *f*
**tutor** (*tyuu*-tö) *n* maestro particular; tutor *m*, -a *f*; profesor *m*, -a *f* particular
**tuxedo** (tak-*ssii*-dou) *nAm* (pl ~s, ~es) smoking *m*
**TV** (tii-*vii*) televisión *f*; **on TV** en la televisión
**tweed** (t$^{u}$iid) *n* paño *m* de lana
**tweezers** (*t$^{u}$ii*-sös) *pl* pinzas *fpl*
**twelfth** (t$^{u}$êlfz) *num* duodécimo
**twelve** (t$^{u}$êlv) *num* doce
**twentieth** (*t$^{u}$ên*-ti-öz) *num* vigésimo
**twenty** (*t$^{u}$ên*-ti) *num* veinte
**twice** (t$^{u}$aiss) *adv* dos veces
**twig** (t$^{u}$igh) *n* ramita *f*
**twilight** (*t$^{u}$ai*-lait) *n* crepúsculo *m*
**twine** (t$^{u}$ain) *n* trenza *f*
**twins** (t$^{u}$ins) *pl* gemelos *mpl*; **twin beds** camas gemelas
**twist** (t$^{u}$isst) *v* *torcer; *n* torsión *f*
**two** (tuu) *num* dos
**two-piece** (tuu-*piiss*) *adj* de dos piezas
**type** (taip) *v* escribir a máquina, mecanografiar; *n* tipo *m*
**typewriter** (*taip*-rai-tö) *n* máquina de escribir
**typhoid** (*tai*-foid) *n* tifus *m*
**typical** (*ti*-pi-köl) *adj* característico, típico
**typist** (*tai*-pisst) *n* dactilógrafa *f*
**tyrant** (*tai$^{ö}$*-rönt) *n* tirano *m*, -a *f*
**tire** *Am*, **tyre** (tai$^{ö}$) *n* neumático *m*; ~ **pressure** presión del neumático

# U

**ugly** (*a*-ghli) *adj* feo
**ulcer** (*al*-ssö) *n* úlcera *f*
**ultimate** (*al*-ti-möt) *adj* último
**ultraviolet** (al-trö-*vai$^{ö}$*-löt) *adj* ultravioleta
**umbrella** (am-*brê*-lö) *n* paraguas *m*
**umpire** (*am*-pai$^{ö}$) *n* árbitro *m*
**unable** (a-*nei*-böl) *adj* incapaz
**unacceptable** (a-nök-*ssêp*-tö-böl) *adj* inaceptable
**unaccountable** (a-nö-*kaun*-tö-böl) *adj* inexplicable
**unaccustomed** (a-nö-*ka*-sstömd) *adj* desacostumbrado
**unanimous** (yuu-*næ*-ni-möss) *adj* unánime
**unanswered** (a-*naan*-ssöd) *adj* sin contestación
**unauthorized** (a-*noo*-zö-raisd) *adj* desautorizado
**unavoidable** (a-nö-*voi*-dö-böl) *adj* inevitable
**unaware** (a-nö-*$^{u}$ê$^{ö}$*) *adj* inconsciente; **be ~ of** ignorar
**unbearable** (an-*bê$^{ö}$*-rö-böl) *adj* insoportable
**unbreakable** (an-*brei*-kö-böl) *adj* irrompible
**unbroken** (an-*brou*-kön) *adj* intacto
**unbutton** (an-*ba*-tön) *v* desabotonar
**uncertain** (an-*ssöö*-tön) *adj* incierto
**uncle** (*ang*-köl) *n* tío *m*

**unclean** (an-*kliin*) *adj* sucio
**uncomfortable** (an-*kam*-fö-tö-böl) *adj* incómodo; molesto
**uncommon** (an-*ko*-mön) *adj* insólito, raro
**unconditional** (an-kön-*di*-ʃö-nöl) *adj* incondicional
**unconscious** (an-*kon*-ʃöss) *adj* inconsciente
**uncork** (an-*kook*) *v* descorchar
**uncover** (an-*ka*-vö) *v* destapar
**uncultivated** (an-*kal*-ti-vei-tid) *adj* inculto; yermo
**under** (*an*-dö) *prep* debajo de, bajo
**undercurrent** (*an*-dö-ka-rönt) *n* tendencia *f* oculta; corriente *f* submarina
**underestimate** (an-dö-*rê*-ssti-meit) *v* subestimar
**underground** (*an*-dö-ghraund) *adj* subterráneo; *n* metro *m*
**underline** (an-dö-*lain*) *v* subrayar
**underneath** (an-dö-*niiz*) *adv* debajo; por debajo
**undershirt** (*an*-dö-ʃööt) *n* camiseta *f*
***understand** (an-dö-*sstænd*) *v* comprender
**understanding** (an-dö-*sstæn*-ding) *n* comprensión *m*
**understatement** (an-dö-*ssteit*-mönt) *n*: **that's an ~** ¡y te quedas corto!
***undertake** (an-dö-*teik*) *v* emprender
**undertaking** (an-dö-*tei*-king) *n* empresa *f*
**underwater** (*an*-dö-ᵘoo-tö) *adj* subacuático
**underwear** (*an*-dö-ᵘêö) *n* ropa interior
**undesirable** (an-di-*saiö*-rö-böl) *adj* indeseable
***undo** (an-*duu*) *v* desatar
**undoubtedly** (an-*dau*-tid-li) *adv* sin duda
**undress** (an-*drêss*) *v* desnudarse
**unearned** (a-*nööñd*) *adj* inmerecido
**uneasy** (a-*nii*-si) *adj* inquieto; inseguro; intranquilo
**uneducated** (a-*nê*-dyu-kei-tid) *adj* inculto
**unemployed** (a-nim-*ploid*) *adj* parado; sin empleo
**unemployment** (a-nim-*ploi*-mönt) *n* paro *m*; desempleo *m*
**unequal** (a-*nii*-kᵘöl) *adj* desigual
**uneven** (a-*nii*-vön) *adj* desigual; irregular
**unexpected** (a-nik-*sspêk*-tid) *adj* imprevisto, inesperado
**unfair** (an-*fêö*) *adj* ímprobo, injusto
**unfaithful** (an-*feiz*-föl) *adj* infiel
**unfamiliar** (an-fö-*mil*-yö) *adj* desconocido
**unfasten** (an-*faa*-ssön) *v* desatar
**unfavo(u)rable** (an-*fei*-vö-rö-böl) *adj* desfavorable
**unfit** (an-*fit*) *adj* inadecuado
**unfold** (an-*fould*) *v* *desplegar
**unfortunate** (an-*foo*-chö-nöt) *adj* desafortunado
**unfortunately** (an-*foo*-chö-nöt-li) *adv* por desgracia, desgraciadamente
**unfriendly** (an-*frênd*-li) *adj* poco amistoso
**ungrateful** (an-*ghreit*-föl) *adj* ingrato
**unhappy** (an-*hæ*-pi) *adj* desdichado
**unhealthy** (an-*hêl*-zi) *adj* enfermizo; insalubre
**unhurt** (an-*hööt*) *adj* ileso
**uniform** (*yuu*-ni-foom) *n* uniforme *m*; *adj* uniforme
**unimportant** (a-nim-*poo*-tönt) *adj* insignificante
**uninhabitable** (a-nin-*hæ*-bi-tö-böl) *adj* inhabitable
**uninhabited** (a-nin-*hæ*-bi-tid) *adj* inhabitado
**unintentional** (a-nin-*tên*-ʃö-nöl) *adj* no intencional
**union** (*yuu*-nyön) *n* unión *f*; liga *f*,

confederación *f*; sindicato *m*
**unique** (yuu-*niik*) *adj* único
**unit** (*yuu*-nit) *n* unidad *f*
**unite** (yuu-*nait*) *v* unir; **united** unido
**United States** (yuu-*nai*-tid ssteitss) Estados Unidos
**unity** (*yuu*-nö-ti) *n* unidad *f*
**universal** (yuu-ni-*vöö*-ssöl) *adj* general, universal
**universe** (*yuu*-ni-vööss) *n* universo *m*
**university** (yuu-ni-*vöö*-ssö-ti) *n* universidad *f*
**unjust** (an-*dʒasst*) *adj* injusto
**unkind** (an-*kaind*) *adj* desagradable, arisco
**unknown** (an-*noun*) *adj* desconocido
**unlawful** (an-*loo*-föl) *adj* ilegal
**unlearn** (an-*löön*) *v* desacostumbrar
**unless** (ön-*lêss*) *conj* a menos que; a no ser que
**unlike** (an-*laik*) *adj* diferente
**unlikely** (an-*lai*-kli) *adj* improbable
**unlimited** (an-*li*-mi-tid) *adj* ilimitado
**unload** (an-*loud*) *v* descargar
**unlock** (an-*lok*) *v* abrir con llave
**unlucky** (an-*la*-ki) *adj* desafortunado
**unnecessary** (an-*nê*-ssö-ssö-ri) *adj* innecesario
**unoccupied** (a-*no*-kyu-paid) *adj* desocupado; vacante
**unofficial** (a-nö-*fi*-ʃöl) *adj* no oficial
**unpack** (an-*pæk*) *v* desempaquetar; deshacer las maletas
**unpleasant** (an-*plê*-sönt) *adj* desagradable; antipático
**unpopular** (an-*po*-pyu-lö) *adj* impopular
**unprotected** (an-prö-*têk*-tid) *adj* indefenso
**unqualified** (an-*k*ᵘ*o*-li-faid) *adj* incompetente
**unreal** (an-*ri*ᵒ*l*) *adj* irreal
**unreasonable** (an-*rii*-sö-nö-böl) *adj* irrazonable
**unreliable** (an-ri-*lai*-ö-böl) *adj* no confiable
**unrest** (an-*rêsst*) *n* disturbio *m*; inquietud *f*
**unsafe** (an-*sseif*) *adj* inseguro
**unsatisfactory** (an-ssæ-tiss-*fæk*-tö-ri) *adj* insatisfactorio
**unscrew** (an-*sskruu*) *v* destornillar
**unselfish** (an-*ssêl*-fiʃ) *adj* desinteresado
**unskilled** (an-*sskild*) *adj* inexperto; no especializado; no cualificado
**unsound** (an-*ssaund*) *adj* defectuoso; erróneo
**unstable** (an-*sstei*-böl) *adj* inestable
**unsteady** (an-*sstê*-di) *adj* poco firme, inestable
**unsuccessful** (an-ssök-*ssêss*-föl) *adj* fracasado
**unsuitable** (an-*ssuu*-tö-böl) *adj* inadecuado
**unsurpassed** (an-ssö-*paasst*) *adj* sin igual
**untidy** (an-*tai*-di) *adj* desaliñado; desordenado
**untie** (an-*tai*) *v* desatar
**until** (ön-*til*) *prep* hasta
**untrue** (an-*truu*) *adj* falso
**untrustworthy** (an-*trasst*-ᵘöö-ði) *adj* indigno de confianza
**unusual** (an-*yuu*-ʒu-öl) *adj* inusitado, insólito
**unwell** (an-ᵘ*êl*) *adj* indispuesto
**unwilling** (an-ᵘ*i*-ling) *adj* desinclinado
**unwise** (an-ᵘ*ais*) *adj* imprudente
**unwrap** (an-*ræp*) *v* *desenvolver
**up** (ap) *adv* hacia arriba, arriba
**upholster** (ap-*houl*-sstö) *v* tapizar
**upkeep** (*ap*-kiip) *n* manutención *f*
**uplands** (*ap*-lönds) *pl* altiplano *m*; meseta *f*
**upon** (ö-*pon*) *prep* sobre
**upper** (*a*-pö) *adj* superior; más alto
**upright** (*ap*-rait) *adj* derecho; *adv* de

pie
**upset** (ap-*ssêt*) *v* trastornar; volcar; perturbar; *adj* trastornado; perturbado
**upside down** (ap-ssaid-*daun*) *adv* al revés
**upstairs** (ap-*sstêös*) *adv* arriba
**upstream** (ap-*sstriim*) *adv* río arriba
**upwards** (*ap*-uöds) *adv* hacia arriba
**urban** (*öö*-bön) *adj* urbano
**urge** (öödʒ) *v* estimular; *n* impulso *m*
**urgency** (*öö*-dʒön-ssi) *n* urgencia *f*
**urgent** (*öö*-dʒönt) *adj* urgente
**urine** (*yuö*-rin) *n* orina *f*
**Uruguay** (*yuö*-rö-ghuai) Uruguay *m*
**Uruguayan** (yuö-rö-*ghuai*-ön) *adj* uruguayo
**us** (ass) *pron* nosotros
**usable** (*yuu*-sö-böl) *adj* utilizable
**usage** (*yuu*-sidʒ) *n* uso *m*
**use**[1] (yuus) *v* usar; ***be used to** *estar acostumbrado a; **~ up** consumir
**use**[2] (yuuss) *n* uso *m*; utilidad *f*; ***be of ~** *servir
**useful** (*yuuss*-föl) *adj* útil
**useless** (*yuuss*-löss) *adj* inútil
**user** (*yuu*-sö) *n* usuario *m*
**usher** (*a*-ʃö) *n* acomodador *m*
**usherette** (a-ʃö-*rêt*) *n* acomodadora *f*
**usual** (*yuu*-ʒu-öl) *adj* usual
**usually** (*yuu*-ʒu-ö-li) *adv* habitualmente
**utensil** (yuu-*tên*-ssöl) *n* herramienta *f*, utensilio *m*
**utility** (yuu-*ti*-lö-ti) *n* utilidad *f*
**utilize** (*yuu*-ti-lais) *v* utilizar
**utmost** (*at*-mousst) *adj* extremo; último
**utter** (*a*-tö) *adj* completo, total; *v* emitir; pronunciar; proferir

# V

**vacancy** (*vei*-kön-ssi) *n* vacante *f*
**vacant** (*vei*-könt) *adj* vacante
**vacate** (vö-*keit*) *v* vaciar
**vacation** (vö-*kei*-ʃön) *n* vacaciones *fpl*
**vaccinate** (*væk*-ssi-neit) *v* vacunar
**vaccination** (væk-ssi-*nei*-ʃön) *n* vacunación *f*
**vacuum** (*væ*-kyu-öm) *n* vacío *m*; **~ cleaner** aspiradora *f*; **~ flask** termo *m*
**vague** (veigh) *adj* vago
**vain** (vein) *adj* vanidoso; vano; **in ~** inútilmente, en vano
**valet** (*væ*-lit) *n* ayuda de cámara
**valid** (*væ*-lid) *adj* vigente
**valley** (*væ*-li) *n* valle *m*
**valuable** (*væ*-lyu-böl) *adj* valioso; **valuables** *pl* objetos de valor
**value** (*væ*-lyuu) *n* valor *m*; *v* valuar
**valve** (vælv) *n* válvula *f*
**van** (væn) *n* camioneta *f*
**vanilla** (vö-*ni*-lö) *n* vainilla *f*
**vanish** (*væ*-niʃ) *v* *desaparecer
**vapo(u)r** (*vei*-pö) *n* vapor *m*
**variable** (*vêö*-ri-ö-böl) *adj* variable
**variation** (vêö-ri-*ei*-ʃön) *n* variación *f*; cambio *m*
**varied** (*vêö*-rid) *adj* variado
**variety** (vö-*rai*-ö-ti) *n* variedad *f*; **~ show** espectáculo de variedades; **~ theater** *Am*, **~ theatre** teatro de variedades
**various** (*vêö*-ri-öss) *adj* varios
**varnish** (*vaa*-niʃ) *n* barniz *m*; *v* barnizar
**vary** (*vêö*-ri) *v* variar; cambiar; *diferir
**vase** (vaas) *n* vaso *m*

**vaseline** (*væ*-ssö-liin) *n* vaselina *f*
**vast** (vaasst) *adj* vasto
**vault** (voolt) *n* bóveda *f*; caja de caudales
**veal** (viil) *n* carne de ternera
**vegetable** (*vê*-dʒö-tö-böl) *n* legumbre *f*
**vegetarian** (vê-dʒi-*têö*-ri-ön) *n* vegetariano *m*, -a *f*
**vegetation** (vê-dʒi-*tei*-ʃön) *n* vegetación *f*
**vehicle** (*vii*-ö-köl) *n* vehículo *m*
**veil** (veil) *n* velo *m*
**vein** (vein) *n* vena *f*; **varicose ~** varice *f*
**velvet** (*vêl*-vit) *n* terciopelo *m*
**velveteen** (vêl-vi-*tiin*) *n* pana *f*
**venerable** (*vê*-nö-rö-böl) *adj* venerable
**venereal disease** (vi-*niö*-ri-öl di-*siis*) enfermedad venérea
**Venezuela** (vê-ni-*sueі*-lö) Venezuela *f*
**Venezuelan** (vê-ni-*suei*-lön) *adj* venezolano
**ventilate** (*vên*-ti-leit) *v* ventilar; airear
**ventilation** (vên-ti-*lei*-ʃön) *n* ventilación *f*; aireo *m*
**ventilator** (*vên*-ti-lei-tö) *n* ventilador *m*
**venture** (*vên*-chö) *v* arriesgar
**veranda** (vö-*ræn*-dö) *n* veranda *f*; terraza *f*
**verb** (vööb) *n* verbo *m*
**verbal** (*vöö*-böl) *adj* verbal
**verdict** (*vöö*-dikt) *n* sentencia *f*, veredicto *m*; fallo *m*
**verge** (vöödʒ) *n* borde *m*; margen *m*; **on the ~ of** al borde de
**verify** (*vê*-ri-fai) *v* verificar
**verse** (vööss) *n* verso *m*
**version** (*vöö*-ʃön) *n* versión *f*
**versus** (*vöö*-ssöss) *prep* contra
**vertical** (*vöö*-ti-köl) *adj* vertical
**very** (*vê*-ri) *adv* mucho, muy; *adj* preciso, verdadero; extremo
**vessel** (*vê*-ssöl) *n* embarcación *f*, buque *m*; vasija *f*
**vest** (vêsst) *n* camiseta *f*; *nAm* chaleco *m*
**veterinary surgeon** (*vê*-tri-nö-ri *ssöö*-dʒön) veterinario *m*, -a *f*
**via** (vaiö) *prep* por
**viaduct** (*vaiö*-dakt) *n* viaducto *m*
**vibrate** (vai-*breit*) *v* vibrar
**vibration** (vai-*brei*-ʃön) *n* vibración *f*
**vicar** (*vi*-kö) *n* vicario *m*
**vicarage** (*vi*-kö-ridʒ) *n* casa del párroco
**vice president** (vaiss-*prê*-si-dönt) *n* vicepresidente *m*
**vicinity** (vi-*ssi*-nö-ti) *n* vecindad *f*
**vicious** (*vi*-ʃöss) *adj* vicioso
**victim** (*vik*-tim) *n* víctima *f*
**victory** (*vik*-tö-ri) *n* victoria *f*
**video** (*vi*-di-ou) *n* vídeo *m*; *v* grabar en vídeo; **~ camera** videocámara; **~ cassette** videocassette; **~ game** videojuego; **~ recorder** videograbadora
**view** (vyuu) *n* vista *f*; parecer *m*, opinión *f*; *v* mirar; contemplar; considerar
**vigilant** (*vi*-dʒi-lönt) *adj* vigilante
**villa** (*vi*-lö) *n* villa *f* ; chalet *m*
**village** (*vi*-lidʒ) *n* pueblo *m*
**villain** (*vi*-lön) *n* malvado *m*
**vinegar** (*vi*-ni-ghö) *n* vinagre *m*
**vineyard** (*vin*-yöd) *n* viña *f*
**vintage** (*vin*-tidʒ) *n* vendimia *f*
**violation** (vaiö-*lei*-ʃön) *n* violación *f*
**violence** (*vaiö*-lönss) *n* violencia *f*
**violent** (*vaiö*-lönt) *adj* violento; impetuoso
**violet** (*vaiö*-löt) *n* violeta *f*; *adj* morado
**violin** (vaiö-*lin*) *n* violín *m*
**VIP** (vii-ai-*pii*) *n* (= **very important person**) VIP *m*
**virgin** (*vöö*-dʒin) *n* virgen *f*

**virtue** (*vöö*-chuu) *n* virtud *f*
**visa** (*vii*-sö) *n* visado *m*
**visibility** (vi-sö-*bi*-lö-ti) *n* visibilidad *f*
**visible** (*vi*-sö-böl) *adj* visible
**vision** (*vi*-ʒön) *n* visión *f*
**visit** (*vi*-sit) *v* visitar; *n* visita *f*; **visiting hours** horas de visita
**visitor** (*vi*-si-tö) *n* visitante *m/f*
**vital** (*vai*-töl) *adj* esencial
**vitamin** (*vi*-tö-min) *n* vitamina *f*
**vivid** (*vi*-vid) *adj* vivo
**vocabulary** (vö-*kæ*-byu-lö-ri) *n* vocabulario *m*; glosario *m*
**vocal** (*vou*-köl) *adj* vocal
**vocalist** (*vou*-kö-lisst) *n* vocalista *m*
**voice** (voiss) *n* voz *f*
**void** (void) *adj* vacío
**volcano** (vol-*kei*-nou) *n* (pl ~es, ~s) volcán *m*
**volt** (voult) *n* voltio *m*
**voltage** (*voul*-tidʒ) *n* voltaje *m*
**volume** (*vo*-lyum) *n* volumen *m*; tomo *m*
**voluntary** (*vo*-lön-tö-ri) *adj* voluntario
**volunteer** (vo-lön-*ti*[ö]) *n* voluntario *m*
**vomit** (*vo*-mit) *v* vomitar
**vote** (vout) *v* votar; *n* voto *m*; votación *f*
**voter** (*vou*-tö) votante *m/f*
**voucher** (*vau*-chö) *n* recibo *m*, comprobante *m*
**vow** (vau) *n* voto *m*, juramento *m*; *v* prestar juramento
**vowel** (vau[ö]l) *n* vocal *f*
**voyage** (*voi*-idʒ) *n* viaje *m*
**vulgar** (*val*-ghö) *adj* vulgar; popular, ordinario
**vulnerable** (*val*-nö-rö-böl) *adj* vulnerable
**vulture** (*val*-chö) *n* buitre *m*

# W

**wade** ([u]eid) *v* vadear
**wafer** ([u]*ei*-fö) *n* oblea *f*
**waffle** ([u]*o*-föl) *n* barquillo *m*
**wages** ([u]*ei*-dʒis) *pl* salario *m*; sueldo *m*
**wag(g)on** ([u]*æ*-ghön) *n* vagón *m*
**waist** ([u]eisst) *n* cintura *f*
**waistcoat** ([u]*eiss*-kout) *n* chaleco *m*
**wait** ([u]eit) *v* esperar; ~ **on** *servir
**waiter** ([u]*ei*-tö) *n* camarero *m*; mesero *mMe*
**waiting** *n* espera *f*; ~ **list** lista de espera; ~ **room** sala de espera
**waitress** ([u]*ei*-triss) *n* camarera *f*; mesera *fMe*
***wake** ([u]eik) *v* *despertar; ~ **up** *despertarse
**walk** ([u]ook) *v* *andar; pasear; *n* paseo *m*; caminata *f*; **walking** a pie
**walker** ([u]*oo*-kö) *n* paseante *m*
**walking stick** ([u]*oo*-king-sstik) *n* bastón *m*
**wall** ([u]ool) *n* muro *m*; pared *f*
**wallet** ([u]*o*-lit) *n* cartera *f*; monedero *m*
**wallpaper** ([u]*ool*-pei-pö) *n* papel pintado
**walnut** ([u]*ool*-nat) *n* nogal *m*
**waltz** ([u]oolss) *n* vals *m*
**wander** ([u]*on*-dö) *v* vagar, *errar
**want** ([u]ont) *v* *querer; desear; *n* necesidad *f*; carencia *f*, falta *f*
**war** ([u]oo) *n* guerra *f*
**warden** ([u]*oo*-dön) *n* guardián *m*
**wardrobe** ([u]*oo*-droub) *n* guardarropa

*m*, vestuario *m*
**warehouse** (*ᵘê*^ö^-hauss) *n* almacén *m*
**wares** (ᵘê^ö^s) *pl* mercancías *fpl*
**warm** (ᵘoom) *adj* caliente; *v* *calentar
**warmth** (ᵘoomz) *n* calor *m*
**warn** (ᵘoon) *v* *advertir
**warning** (*ᵘoo*-ning) *n* advertencia *f*
**wary** (*ᵘê*^ö^-ri) *adj* prudente; cauteloso
**was** (ᵘos) *v* (p be)
**wash** (ᵘoʃ) *v* lavar; **~ and wear** no precisa plancha; **~ up** *fregar
**washable** (*ᵘo*-ʃö-böl) *adj* lavable
**washbasin** (*ᵘo*ʃ-bei-ssön) *n* palangana *f*
**washing** (*ᵘo*-ʃing) *n* lavado *m*; ropa sucia; **~ machine** lavadora *f*; **~ powder** jabón en polvo
**washroom** (*ᵘo*ʃ-ruum) *nAm* lavabo *m*
**wasp** (ᵘossp) *n* avispa *f*
**waste** (ᵘeisst) *v* *perder; despilfarrar; malgastar; *n* despilfaro *m*; basura *f*; *adj* baldío; desechado, inútil
**wasteful** (*ᵘeisst*-föl) *adj* derrochador
**wastepaper basket** (ᵘeisst-*pei*-pö-baa-sskit) *n* cesto para papeles
**watch** (ᵘoch) *v* mirar, observar; vigilar; *n* reloj *m*; **~ for** acechar; **~ out** *tener cuidado
**watchmaker** (*ᵘoch*-mei-kö) *n* relojero *m*, -a *f*
**watchstrap** (*ᵘoch*-sstræp) *n* correa de reloj
**water** (*ᵘoo*-tö) *n* agua *f*; **iced ~** agua helada; **running ~** agua corriente; **~ pump** bomba de agua; **~ ski** esquí acuático; **~ softener** ablandador *m*
**watercolo(u)r** (*ᵘoo*-tö-ka-lö) *n* acuarela *f*
**watercress** (*ᵘoo*-tö-krêss) *n* berro *m*
**waterfall** (*ᵘoo*-tö-fool) *n* cascada *f*
**watermelon** (*ᵘoo*-tö-mê-lön) *n* sandía *f*
**waterproof** (*ᵘoo*-tö-pruuf) *adj* impermeable
**waterway** (*ᵘoo*-tö-ᵘei) *n* vía navegable
**watt** (ᵘot) *n* vatio *m*
**wave** (ᵘeiv) *n* ondulación *f*, ola *f*; *v* *hacer señales
**wavelength** (*ᵘeiv*-lêngz) *n* longitud de onda
**wavy** (*ᵘei*-vi) *adj* ondulado
**wax** (ᵘækss) *n* cera *f*
**waxworks** (*ᵘækss*-ᵘöökss) *pl* museo de figuras de cera
**way** (ᵘei) *n* manera *f*; camino *m*; lado *m*, dirección *f*; distancia *f*; **any ~** de todos modos; **by the ~** a propósito; **one-way traffic** dirección única; **out of the ~** apartado; **the other ~ round** al revés; **~ back** vuelta *f*; **~ in** entrada *f*; **~ out** salida *f*
**wayside** (*ᵘei*-ssaid) *n* borde del camino
**we** (ᵘii) *pron* nosotros
**weak** (ᵘiik) *adj* débil; flojo
**weakness** (*ᵘiik*-nöss) *n* debilidad *f*
**wealth** (ᵘêlz) *n* riqueza *f*
**wealthy** (*ᵘêl*-zi) *adj* rico
**weapon** (*ᵘê*-pön) *n* arma *f*
***wear** (ᵘê^ö^) *v* llevar; **~ out** gastar
**weary** (*ᵘi*^ö^-ri) *adj* cansado; abatido
**weather** (*ᵘê*-ðö) *n* tiempo *m*; **~ forecast** boletín meteorológico
***weave** (ᵘiiv) *v* tejer
**weaver** (*ᵘii*-vö) *n* tejedor *m*, -a *f*
**web** (ᵘêb) *n* tela *f*; **the Web** la Web
**wedding** (*ᵘê*-ding) *n* matrimonio *m*, boda *f*; **~ ring** anillo de boda
**wedge** (ᵘêdʒ) *n* cuña *f*
**Wednesday** (*ᵘêns*-di) miércoles *m*
**weed** (ᵘiid) *n* mala hierba
**week** (ᵘiik) *n* semana *f*
**weekday** (*ᵘiik*-dei) *n* día laborable
**weekend** (*ᵘii*-kênd) *n* fin de semana
**weekly** (*ᵘii*-kli) *adj* semanal
***weep** (ᵘiip) *v* llorar
**weigh** (ᵘei) *v* pesar
**weighing machine** (*ᵘei*-ing-mö-ʃiin)

*n* báscula *f*
**weight** (ᵘeit) *n* peso *m*
**welcome** (*ᵘêl*-köm) *adj* bienvenido; *n* bienvenida *f*; *v* *dar la bienvenida
**weld** (ᵘêld) *v* *soldar
**welfare** (*ᵘêl*-fêᵒ) *n* bienestar *m*
**well**[1] (ᵘêl) *adv* bien; *adj* sano; **as ~** también; **as ~ as** así como; **well!** ¡bueno!
**well**[2] (ᵘêl) *n* pozo *m*
**well-founded** (ᵘêl-*faun*-did) *adj* fundamentado
**well-known** (*ᵘêl*-noun) *adj* notorio
**well-to-do** (ᵘêl-tö-*duu*) *adj* acomodado
**went** (ᵘênt) *v* (p go)
**were** (ᵘöö) *v* (p be)
**west** (ᵘêsst) *n* occidente *m*, oeste *m*
**westerly** (*ᵘê*-sstö-li) *adj* occidental
**western** (*ᵘê*-sstön) *adj* occidental
**wet** (ᵘêt) *adj* mojado; húmedo
**whale** (ᵘeil) *n* ballena *f*
**wharf** (ᵘoof) *n* (pl ~s, wharves) muelle *m*
**what** (ᵘot) *pron* qué; lo que; **~ for** para que
**whatever** (ᵘo-*tê*-vö) *pron* cualquier cosa que
**wheat** (ᵘiit) *n* trigo *m*
**wheel** (ᵘiil) *n* rueda *f*
**wheelbarrow** (*ᵘiil*-bæ-rou) *n* carretilla *f*
**wheelchair** (*ᵘiil*-chêᵒ) *n* silla de ruedas
**when** (ᵘên) *adv* cuándo; *conj* cuando
**whenever** (ᵘê-*nê*-vö) *conj* cuando quiera que
**where** (ᵘêᵒ) *adv* dónde; *conj* donde
**wherever** (ᵘêᵒ-*rê*-vö) *conj* dondequiera que
**whether** (*ᵘê*-ðö) *conj* si; **whether … or** si … o
**which** (ᵘich) *pron* lo que, lo cual, la cual; cuál?
**whichever** (ᵘi-*chê*-vö) *adj* cualquiera
**while** (ᵘail) *conj* mientras; *n* rato *m*
**whilst** (ᵘailsst) *conj* mientras
**whim** (ᵘim) *n* antojo *m*, capricho *m*
**whip** (ᵘip) *n* azote *m*; látigo *m*; *v* azotar; batir
**whiskers** (*ᵘi*-sskös) *pl* patillas *fpl*
**whisper** (*ᵘi*-sspö) *v* susurrar; *n* susurro *m*
**whistle** (*ᵘi*-ssöl) *v* silbar; *n* silbato *m*
**white** (ᵘait) *adj* blanco
**whiting** (*ᵘai*-ting) *n* (pl ~) merluza *f*
**Whitsun** (*ᵘit*-ssön) Pentecostés *m*
**who** (huu) *pron* quien; que
**whoever** (huu-*ê*-vö) *pron* quienquiera
**whole** (houl) *adj* completo, entero; intacto; *n* total *m*
**wholesale** (*houl*-sseil) *n* venta al por mayor; **~ dealer** mayorista *m*
**wholesome** (*houl*-ssöm) *adj* salubre
**wholly** (*houl*-li) *adv* totalmente
**whom** (huum) *pron* a quien(es)
**whore** (hoo) *n* puta *f*
**whose** (huus) *pron* cuyo; de quien(es)
**why** (ᵘai) *adv* por qué; para qué
**wicked** (*ᵘi*-kid) *adj* malvado
**wide** (ᵘaid) *adj* vasto, ancho
**widen** (*ᵘai*-dön) *v* ensanchar
**widow** (*ᵘi*-dou) *n* viuda *f*
**widower** (*ᵘi*-dou-ö) *n* viudo *m*
**width** (ᵘidz) *n* anchura *f*
**wife** (ᵘaif) *n* (pl wives) esposa *f*, mujer *f*
**wig** (ᵘigh) *n* peluca *f*
**wild** (ᵘaild) *adj* salvaje; feroz
**will** (ᵘil) *n* voluntad *f*; testamento *m*
***will** (ᵘil) *v* *querer
**willing** (*ᵘi*-ling) *adj* dispuesto
**willingly** (*ᵘi*-ling-li) *adv* gustosamente
**willpower** (*ᵘil*-pauᵒ) *n* fuerza de voluntad
***win** (ᵘin) *v* vencer
**wind** (ᵘind) *n* viento *m*
***wind** (ᵘaind) *v* serpentear; *dar cuerda, enrollar

**winding** (*ᵘain*-ding) *adj* tortuoso
**windmill** (*ᵘind*-mil) *n* molino de viento
**window** (*ᵘin*-dou) *n* ventana *f*
**windowsill** (*ᵘin*-dou-ssil) *n* antepecho *m*
**windscreen** (*ᵘind*-sskriin) *n* parabrisas *m*; ~ **wiper** limpiaparabrisas *m*
**windshield** (*ᵘind*-ʃiild) *nAm* parabrisas *m*
**windy** (*ᵘin*-di) *adj* ventoso
**wine** (ᵘain) *n* vino *m*; ~ **cellar** cueva *f*; ~ **list** carta de vinos; ~ **merchant** vinatero *m*
**wing** (ᵘing) *n* ala *f*
**winkle** (*ᵘing*-köl) *n* caracol marino
**winner** (*ᵘi*-nö) *n* vencedor *m*
**winning** (*ᵘi*-ning) *adj* ganador; **winnings** *pl* ganancias *fpl*
**winter** (*ᵘin*-tö) *n* invierno *m*; ~ **sports** deportes de invierno
**wipe** (ᵘaip) *v* enjugar
**wire** (ᵘaiᵒ) *n* alambre *m*; telegrama *m*
**wireless** (ᵘaiᵒ-löss) *adj* inalámbrico
**wisdom** (*ᵘis*-döm) *n* sabiduría *f*; juicio *m*
**wise** (ᵘais) *adj* sabio; juicioso
**wish** (ᵘiʃ) *v* desear; *n* deseo *m*
**wit** (ᵘit) ingenio *m*; ingenioso *m*, -a *f*; **be at one's wits' end** estar desesperado; **be scared out of one's wits** estar aterrorizado
**witch** (ᵘich) *n* bruja *f*
**with** (ᵘið) *prep* con; de
***withdraw** (ᵘið-*droo*) *v* retirar
**within** (ᵘi-ð*in*) *prep* dentro de; *adv* de dentro
**without** (ᵘi-ð*aut*) *prep* sin
**wit** (uit) *n* ingenio *m*
**witness** (*ᵘit*-nöss) *n* testigo *m*
**witty** (*ᵘi*-ti) *adj* ingenioso, chistoso
**wolf** (ᵘulf) *n* (pl wolves) lobo *m*
**woman** (*ᵘu*-mön) *n* (pl women) mujer *f*
**womb** (ᵘuum) *n* matriz *f*
**won** (ᵘan) *v* (p, pp win)
**wonder** (*ᵘan*-dö) *n* milagro *m*; asombro *m*; *v* preguntarse
**wonderful** (*ᵘan*-dö-föl) *adj* estupendo, maravilloso; delicioso
**wood** (ᵘud) *n* madera *f*; bosque *m*
**wooded** (*ᵘu*-did) *adj* selvoso
**wooden** (*ᵘu*-dön) *adj* de madera; ~ **shoe** zueco *m*
**woodland** (*ᵘud*-lönd) *n* arbolado *m*
**wool** (ᵘul) *n* lana *f*; **darning** ~ hilo de zurcir
**wool(l)en** (*ᵘu*-lön) *adj* de lana
**word** (ᵘööd) *n* palabra *f*
**wore** (ᵘoo) *v* (p wear)
**work** (ᵘöök) *n* obra *f*; trabajo *m*; *v* trabajar; funcionar; **working day** día de trabajo; ~ **of art** obra de arte; ~ **permit** permiso de trabajo
**worker** (*ᵘöö*-kö) *n* obrero *m*
**working** (*ᵘöö*-king) *n* funcionamiento *m*
**workman** (*ᵘöök*-mön) *n* (pl -men) obrero *m*
**works** (ᵘöökss) *pl* fábrica *f*
**workshop** (*ᵘöök*-ʃop) *n* taller *m*
**world** (ᵘööld) *n* mundo *m*; ~ **war** guerra mundial
**world-famous** (ᵘööld-*fei*-möss) *adj* de fama mundial
**world-wide** (*ᵘööld*-ᵘaid) *adj* mundial
**worm** (ᵘööm) *n* gusano *m*
**worn** (ᵘoon) *adj* (pp wear) gastado
**worn-out** (ᵘoon-*aut*) *adj* gastado; estropeado
**worried** (*ᵘa*-rid) *adj* inquieto; preocupado
**worry** (*ᵘa*-ri) *v* inquietarse; *n* preocupación *f*, inquietud *f*
**worse** (ᵘööss) *adj* peor; *adv* peor
**worship** (*ᵘöö*-ʃip) *v* venerar; adorar; *n* culto *m*; adoración *f*
**worst** (ᵘöösst) *adj* pésimo; *adv* peor

**worth** (ᵘööz) *n* valor *m*; mérito *m*; ***be ~** *valer; ***be worth-while** *valer la pena
**worthless** (*ᵘööz*-löss) *adj* sin valor
**worthy of** (*ᵘöö*-ði öv) digno de
**would** (ᵘud) *v* (p will) *soler
**wound¹** (ᵘuund) *n* herida *f*; *v* ofender, *herir
**wound²** (ᵘaund) *v* (p, pp wind)
**wrap** (ræp) *v* *envolver
**wreck** (rêk) *n* pecio *m*; *v* *destruir
**wrench** (rênch) *n* llave *f* inglesa; tirón *m*; *v* dislocar
**wrinkle** (*ring*-köl) *n* arruga *f*
**wrist** (risst) *n* muñeca *f*
**wristwatch** (*risst*-ᵘoch) *n* reloj de pulsera
***write** (rait) *v* escribir; **in writing** por escrito; **~ down** anotar
**writer** (*rai*-tö) *n* escritor *m*
**writing pad** (*rai*-ting-pæd) *n* bloc *m*
**writing paper** (*rai*-ting-pei-pö) *n* papel de escribir
**written** (*ri*-tön) *adj* (pp write) por escrito
**wrong** (rong) *adj* impropio, erróneo; *n* mal *m*; *v* agraviar; ***be ~** no *tener razón
**wrote** (rout) *v* (p write)

# X

**Xmas** (*kriss*-möss) Navidad *f*
**X-ray** (*êkss*-rei) *n* radiografía *f*; *v* radiografiar

# Y

**yacht** (yot) *n* yate *m*
**yacht club** (*yot*-klab) *n* club de yates
**yachting** (*yo*-ting) *n* deporte de vela
**yard** (yaad) *n* patio *m*; jardín *m*; corral *m*
**yarn** (yaan) *n* hilo *m*
**yawn** (yoon) *v* bostezar
**year** (yiᵒ) *n* año *m*
**yearly** (*yiᵒ*-li) *adj* anual
**yeast** (yiisst) *n* levadura *f*
**yell** (yêl) *v* gritar; *n* grito *m*
**yellow** (*yê*-lou) *adj* amarillo
**yes** (yêss) sí
**yesterday** (*yê*-sstö-di) *adv* ayer
**yet** (yêt) *adv* aun; *conj* pero, sin embargo
**yield** (yiild) *v* producir; ceder; *n* rendimiento *m*; cosecha *f*
**yoke** (youk) *n* yugo *m*
**yolk** (youk) *n* yema *f*
**you** (yuu) *pron* tú; a ti; usted; a usted; vosotros; os; ustedes
**young** (yang) *adj* joven
**your** (yoo) *adj* de usted; tu; vuestro, tuyos
**yours** (yoos) *pron* el tuyo, la tuya, *L.Am.* el suyo, la suya; *pl* el vuestro, la vuestra; **a friend of yours** un amigo tuyo/suyo/vuestro; **yours ...** un saludo

**yourself** (yoo-*ssêlf*) *pron* te; tú mismo; usted mismo
**yourselves** (yoo-*ssêlvs*) *pron* se; vosotros mismos; ustedes mismos
**youth** (yuuz) *n* juventud *f*

# Z

**zap** (sæp) *v colloquial* borrar; liquidar; golpear; enviar
**zeal** (siil) *n* celo *m*; ardor *m*
**zealous** (*sê*-löss) *adj* celoso; fervoroso
**zebra** (*sii*-brö) *n* cebra *f*
**zenith** (*sê*-niz) *n* cenit *m*; apogeo *m*
**zero** (*si*ö-rou) *n* (pl ~s) cero *m*
**zest** (sêsst) *n* energía *f*; entusiasmo *m*
**zinc** (singk) *n* cinc *m*
**zip** (sip) *n* cremallera *f*; ~ **code** *Am* código postal
**zipper** (*si*-pö) *nAm* cremallera *f*
**zodiac** (*sou*-di-æk) *n* zodíaco *m*
**zone** (soun) *n* zona *f*; región *f*
**zoo** (suu) *n* (pl ~s) jardín zoológico
**zoology** (sou-*o*-lö-dʒi) *n* zoología *f*

# Léxico gastronómico

## Comidas

**almond** almendra
**anchovy** anchoa
**angel food cake** pastel confeccionado con clara de huevo
**angels on horseback** ostras envueltas en tocino, asadas y servidas en pan tostado
**appetizer** entremés
**apple** manzana
~ **charlotte** pastel de compota de manzanas y pan rallado
~ **dumpling** bola de masa hervida de manzanas
~ **pie** pastel de manzanas
~ **sauce** puré de manzanas
**apricot** albaricoque
**Arbroath smoky** róbalo ahumado
**artichoke** alcachofa
**asparagus** espárrago
~ **tip** punta de espárrago
**aspic** (en) gelatina
**assorted** variado
**aubergine** berenjena
**avocado (pear)** aguacate
**bacon** tocino
~ **and eggs** huevos con tocino
**bagel** panecillo en forma de corona
**baked** al horno
~ **Alaska** helado cubierto con merengue, dorado en el horno; se sirve flameado como postre
~ **beans** judías blancas en salsa de tomates
~ **potato** patata sin pelar cocida al horno
**Bakewell tart** pastel de almendras con mermelada de frambuesas
**baloney** especie de mortadela
**banana** plátano
~ **split** dos mitades de plátano servidas con helado y nueces, rociadas con almíbar o crema de chocolate
**barbecue** 1) carne picada de ternera en una salsa a base de tomates, servida en un panecillo 2) comida al aire libre
~ **sauce** salsa de tomates muy picante
**barbecued** asado a la parrilla con carbón de leña
**basil** albahaca
**bass** lubina (pescado)
**bean** judía, haba, fríjol
**beef** carne de vaca, carne de res
~ **olive** rollo de carne de ternera
~ **Stroganoff** bistec asado con fideos y crema ágria
**beefburger** bistec de carne picada, asado y a veces servido en un panecillo
**beet, beetroot** remolacha
**bilberry** arándano
**bill** cuenta
~ **of fare** lista de platos
**biscuit** 1) galleta (GB) 2) panecillo (US)
**black pudding** morcilla
**blackberry** zarzamora
**blackcurrant** grosella negra
**bloater** arenque salado, ahumado
**blood sausage** morcilla
**blueberry** arándano
**boiled** hervido
**Bologna (sausage)** especie de mortadela
**bone** hueso
**boned** deshuesado
**Boston baked beans** judías blancas con tocino y melaza

**Boston cream pie** torta rellena de nata en capas superpuestas, cubierta de chocolate
**brains** sesos
**braised** asado
**bramble pudding** pudín de zarzamoras (a menudo con manzanas)
**braunschweiger** salchichón de hígado ahumado
**bread** pan
**breaded** empanado
**breakfast** desayuno
**bream** brema (pescado)
**breast** pecho, pechuga
**brisket** pecho
**broad bean** haba
**broth** caldo
**brown Betty** especie de compota de manzanas, con especias y cubierta de pan rallado
**brunch** comida que reemplaza el desayuno y el almuerzo
**brussels sprout** col de Bruselas
**bubble and squeak** patatas y coles picadas que se fríen, mezcladas a veces con trozos de carne de ternera (especie de tortilla)
**bun** 1) panecillo dulce confeccionado con frutas secas 2) especie de panecillo (US)
**butter** mantequilla
**buttered** con mantequilla
**cabbage** col, repollo
**Caesar salad** ensalada verde con ajo, anchoas, cuscurro y queso rallado
**cake** pastel, torta
**cakes** galletas, pastelillos
**calf** ternera
**Canadian bacon** lomo de cerdo ahumado que se corta en lonchas finas
**cantaloupe** melón
**caper** alcaparra
**capercaillie, capercailzie** urogallo grande
**caramel** caramelo
**carp** carpa
**carrot** zanahoria
**cashew** anacardo
**casserole** cacerola
**catfish** siluro (pescado)
**catsup** salsa de tomate
**cauliflower** coliflor
**celery** apio
**cereal** cereal
**hot ~** gachas
**chateaubriand** solomillo de ternera
**check** cuenta
**Cheddar (cheese)** queso de textura firme y de sabor ligeramente ácido
**cheese** queso
**~ board** bandeja de quesos
**~ cake** pastel de queso doble crema, ligeramente azucarado
**cheeseburger** bistec de carne picada, asado con una loncha de queso, servido en un panecillo
**chef's salad** ensalada de jamón, pollo, huevos cocidos, tomates, lechuga y queso
**cherry** cereza
**chestnut** castaña
**chicken** pollo
**chicory** 1) endibia (GB) 2) escarola, achicoria (US)
**chili pepper** chile, ají
**chips** 1) patatas fritas (GB) 2) chips (US)
**chitt(er)lings** tripas de cerdo
**chive** cebolleta
**choice** elección, surtido
**chop** costilla
**~ suey** plato hecho con carne picada de cerdo o de pollo, arroz y legumbres
**chopped** picado
**chowder** sopa espesa a base de

mariscos
**Christmas pudding** pudín inglés hecho con frutas secas, a veces flameado, muy nutritivo y que se sirve en Navidad
**chutney** condimento indio muy sazonado, con sabor agridulce
**cinnamon** canela
**clam** almeja
**club sandwich** bocadillo doble con tocino, pollo, tomates, lechuga y mayonesa
**cobbler** compota de frutas cubierta con una capa de pasta
**cock-a-leekie soup** sopa de pollo y puerros
**coconut** coco
**cod** bacalao
**Colchester oyster** ostra inglesa muy afamada
**cold cuts/meat** fiambres
**coleslaw** ensalada de col
**compote** compota
**condiment** condimento
**cooked** cocido
**cookie** galleta
**corn** 1) trigo (GB) 2) maíz (US) **~ on the cob** mazorca de maíz
**cornflakes** copos de maíz
**corned beef** carne de ternera sazonada
**cottage cheese** requesón
**cottage pie** carne picada que se cuece con cebollas y se cubre con puré de patatas
**course** plato
**cover charge** precio del cubierto
**crab** cangrejo de mar
**cracker** galletita salada
**cranberry** arándano agrio
**~ sauce** mermelada de arándanos agrios
**crawfish, crayfish** 1) cangrejo de río 2) langosta (GB) 3) langostino (US)
**cream** 1) nata 2) crema (sopa) 3) crema (postre)
**~ cheese** queso doble crema
**~ puff** pastelillo con nata
**creamed potatoes** patatas cortadas en forma de dados en salsa blanca
**creole** plato muy condimentado con tomates, pimientos y cebollas; suele servirse con arroz blanco
**cress** berro
**crisps** patatas a la inglesa, chips
**croquette** croqueta
**crumpet** especie de panecillo redondo, asado y untado de mantequilla
**cucumber** pepino
**Cumberland ham** jamón ahumado, muy conocido
**Cumberland sauce** jalea de grosellas sazonada de vino, jugo de naranja y especias
**cupcake** pastelillo, hojaldre
**cured** salado y ahumado
**currant** 1) pasa de Corinto 2) grosella
**curried** con curry
**custard** 1) crema 2) flan
**cutlet** 1) chuleta 2) escalope 3) fina lonja de carne
**dab** lenguado
**Danish pastry** pastelillos hojaldrados
**date** dátil
**Derby cheese** queso blando picante, de color amarillo claro
**dessert** postre
**devilled** con aliño muy fuerte
**devil's food cake** torta de chocolate muy nutritiva
**devils on horseback** ciruelas pasas cocidas en vino tinto, rellenas de almendras y anchoas, envueltas en tocino, asadas y servidas en una tostada
**Devonshire cream** crema doble muy espesa

**diced** cortado en daditos
**diet food** alimento dietético
**dill** eneldo
**dinner** cena
**dish** plato
**donut, doughnut** buñuelo en forma de anillo, rosquilla
**double cream** doble crema, nata
**Dover sole** lenguado de Dover, muy afamado
**dressing** 1) salsa para ensalada 2) relleno para aves (US)
**Dublin Bay prawn** langostino
**duck** pato
**duckling** anadón
**dumpling** albóndiga de pasta
**Dutch apple pie** tarta de manzanas, cubierta con una capa de azúcar negra y mantequilla
**éclair** pastelillo relleno de crema de chocolate o de café
**eel** anguila
**egg** huevo
  **Benedict** ~ con jamón o tocino y salsa holandesa
  **boiled** ~ pasado por agua
  **fried** ~ frito
  **hard-boiled** ~ duro
  **poached** ~ escalfado
  **salad** ~ con cebolla, apio, mayonesa y mostaza
  **scrambled** ~ revuelto
  **soft-boiled** ~ poco pasado por agua
**eggplant** berenjena
**endive** 1) escarola, achicoria (GB) 2) endibia (US)
**entrecôte** solomo de ternera
**entrée** 1) entrada (GB) 2) plato principal (US)
**fennel** hinojo
**fig** higo
**filet mignon** solomillo
**fillet** filete de carne o de pescado
**finnan haddock** róbalo ahumado
**fish** pescado
  ~ **and chips** filetes de pescado y patatas fritas
  ~ **cake** albóndigas, galleta de pescado y patatas
**flan** tarta de frutas
**flapjack** hojuela espesa
**flounder** fleso (pescado)
**forcemeat** relleno, picadillo
**fowl** ave
**frankfurter** salchicha de Francfort
**French bean** judía verde
**French bread** pan francés
**French dressing** 1) vinagreta (GB) 2) salsa cremosa de ensalada con salsa de tomates (US)
**french fries** patatas fritas
**French toast** rebanada de pan, mojada en huevos batidos, frita en una sartén y servida con mermelada o azúcar
**fresh** fresco
**fried** frito, asado
**fritter** buñuelo
**frogs' legs** ancas de rana
**frosting** capa de azúcar garrapiñado
**fruit** fruta
**fry** fritura
**galantine** trozos de carne y picadillo cocidos en gelatina
**game** caza
**gammon** jamón ahumado
**garfish** anguila de mar
**garlic** ajo
**garnish** aderezo
**gherkin** pepinillo
**giblets** menudillos de ave
**ginger** jengibre
**gingerbread** pastel hecho con melaza y especias
**goose** ganso
  ~**berry** grosella espinosa
**grape** uva
  ~**fruit** pomelo, toronja

**grated** rallado
**gravy** jugo de carne, salsa
**grayling** pescado de la familia del salmón
**green bean** judía verde
**green pepper** pimiento verde
**green salad** ensalada verde
**greens** verduras
**grilled** asado a la parrilla
**grilse** salmón joven
**grouse** urogallo
**gumbo** 1) legumbre de origen africano 2) plato criollo a base de okra, con carne o pescado y tomates
**haddock** róbalo
**haggis** panza de cordero rellena de copos de avena
**hake** merluza
**half** mitad, semi
**ham** jamón
 **~ and eggs** huevos con jamón
**hamburger** hamburguesa
**hare** liebre
**haricot bean** alubia blanca
**hash** 1) carne picada 2) picadillo de carne de ternera cubierto con patatas y legumbres
**hash brown potatoes** patatas ralladas fritas
**hazelnut** avellana
**heart** corazón
**herb** hierba aromática
**herring** arenque
**home-made** de confección casera
**hominy grits** crema espesa de harina de maíz, especie de polenta
**honey** miel
 **~dew melon** tipo de melón cuya carne es de color verde amarillento
**hors-d'œuvre** entremeses
**horse-radish** rábano picante
**hot** 1) caliente 2) con especias
 **~ cross bun** bollito con pasas (que se come durante la Cuaresma)
 **~ dog** salchicha caliente en un panecillo
**huckleberry** especie de arándano
**hush puppy** buñuelo a base de harina de maíz
**ice-cream** helado
**iced** helado
**icing** capa de azúcar garrapiñado
**Idaho baked potato** patata sin pelar cocida al horno
**Irish stew** guisado de cordero con cebollas y patatas
**Italian dressing** vinagreta
**jam** confitura
**jellied** en gelatina
**Jell-O** postre a la gelatina
**jelly** gelatina o jalea de frutas
**Jerusalem artichoke** aguaturma
**John Dory** especie de dorada
**jugged hare** estofado de liebre
**juice** jugo, zumo
**juniper berry** baya de enebro
**junket** leche cuajada azucarada
**kale** cob rizada
**kedgeree** migajas de pescado aderezadas con arroz, huevos y mantequilla
**ketchup** salsa de tomates
**kidney** riñón
**kipper** arenque ahumado
**lamb** cordero
**Lancashire hot pot** guisado de chuletas y riñones de cordero, con patatas y cebollas
**larded** mechado
**lean** magro
**leek** puerro
**leg** pierna, muslo, corvejón
**lemon** limón
 **~ sole** especie de platija
**lentil** lenteja
**lettuce** lechuga, ensalada verde
**lima bean** haba grande
**lime** lima (limón verde)

**liver** hígado
**loaf** pan, hogaza
**lobster** bogavante
**loin** lomo
**Long Island duck** pato de Long Island, muy afamado
**low-calorie** pobre en calorías
**lox** salmón ahumado
**lunch** almuerzo
**macaroni** macarrones
~ **and cheese** macarrones al horno con queso
**macaroon** macarrón (almendrado)
**mackerel** caballa
**maize** maíz
**mandarin** mandarina
**maple syrup** jarabe de arce
**marinade** escabeche
**marinated** en escabeche
**marjoram** mejorana
**marmalade** mermelada de naranja u otros sabores
**marrow** tuétano
~ **bone** hueso con tuétano
**marshmallow** dulce de malvavisco
**marzipan** mazapán
**mashed potatoes** puré de patatas
**mayonnaise** mayonesa
**meal** comida
**meat** carne
~**ball** albóndiga de carne
~ **loaf** carne picada preparada en forma de un pan y que se cuece al horno
**medium** (**done**) a punto
**melted** derretido
**Melton Mowbray pie** especie de empanada de carne
**menu** lista de platos
**meringue** merengue
**milk** leche
**mince** picadillo
~ **pie** tarta de frutas confitadas cortadas en daditos, con manzanas y especias (con o sin carne)
**minced** picado
~ **meat** carne picada
**mint** menta
**mixed** mezclado, surtido
~ **grill** brocheta de carne
**molasses** melaza
**morel** morilla
**mousse** postre de nata aromatizada
**muffin** mollete; tarta pequeña (US)
**mulberry** mora
**mullet** mújol (pescado)
**mulligatawny soup** sopa de pollo muy picante de origen indio
**mushroom** champiñón
**muskmelon** tipo de melón
**mussel** mejillón
**mustard** mostaza
**mutton** carnero
**noodle** tallarín
**nut** nuez
**oatmeal** (**porrdige**) gachas de avena
**oil** aceite
**okra** fruto del gumbo utilizado generalmente para espesar las sopas y guisados
**olive** aceituna
**omelet** tortilla
**onion** cebolla
**orange** naranja
**ox tongue** lengua de buey
**oxtail** cola de buey (sopa)
**oyster** ostra
**pancake** hojuela espesa, torta de sartén
**paprika** pimiento
**Parmesan** (**cheese**) queso parmesano
**parsley** perejil
**parsnip** chirivía
**partridge** perdiz
**pastry** pastel, pastelillo
**pasty** empanadilla de carne
**pea** guisante
**peach** melocotón

**peanut** cacahuete, maní
~ **butter** manteca de cacahuete
**pear** pera
**pearl barley** cebada perlada
**pepper** pimienta
**peppermint** menta
**perch** perca
**persimmon** caqui
**pheasant** faisán
**pickerel** lucio pequeño (pescado)
**pickle** 1) legumbre o fruta en vinagre 2) pepinillo (US)
**pickled** conservado en salmuera o vinagre
**pie** torta a menudo cubierta con una capa de pasta, rellena de carne, legumbres, frutas o crema inglesa
**pig** cerdo
**pigeon** pichón
**pike** lucio
**pineapple** piña
**plaice** platija, acedía
**plain** natural
**plate** plato
**plum** ciruela, ciruela pasa
~ **pudding** pudín inglés hecho con frutas secas, a veces flameado, muy nutritivo y que se sirve en Navidad
**poached** escalfado
**popcorn** palomitas de maíz
**popover** panecillo esponjoso cocido en el horno
**pork** cerdo
**porridge** gachas
**porterhouse steak** lonja espesa de solomillo de res
**pot roast** carne de ternera asada y legumbres
**potato** patata, papa
~ **chips** 1) patatas fritas (GB) 2) chips (US)
~ **in its jacket** patata sin pelar
**potted shrimps** mantequilla sazonada, derretida y enfriada, servida con camarones
**poultry** ave de corral
**prawn** camarón grande
**prune** ciruela seca
**ptarmigan** perdiz blanca
**pudding** pudín blando o consistente hecho con harina, relleno de carne, pescado, legumbres o frutas
**pumpernickel** pan hecho con harina gruesa de centeno
**pumpkin** calabaza
~ **pie** pastel de calabaza con canela y nuez moscada
**quail** codorniz
**quince** membrillo
**rabbit** conejo
**radish** rábano
**rainbow trout** trucha arco iris
**raisin** pasa
**rare** poco hecho
**raspberry** frambuesa
**raw** crudo
**red mullet** salmonete
**red (sweet) pepper** pimiento morrón
**redcurrant** grosella roja
**relish** condimento hecho con trocitos de legumbres y vinagre
**rhubarb** ruibarbo
**rib (of beef)** costilla (de ternera)
**rib-eye steak** solomillo
**rice** arroz
**rissole** croqueta de pescado o carne
**river trout** trucha de río
**roast(ed)** asado
**Rock Cornish hen** pollo tomatero
**roe** huevos de pescado
**roll** panecillo
**rollmop herring** filete de arenque escabechado con vino blanco, enrollado con un pepinillo en medio
**round steak** filete de pierna de ternera
**Rubens sandwich** carne de ternera en pan tostado, con col fermentada,

queso suizo y salsa para ensalada; se sirve caliente
**rump steak** filete de lomo de ternera
**rusk** rebanadas tostadas de pan de molde
**rye bread** pan de centeno
**saddle** cuarto trasero
**saffron** azafrán
**sage** salvia
**salad** ensalada
~ **bar** surtido de ensaladas
~ **cream** salsa cremosa para ensalada, ligeramente azucarada
~ **dressing** salsa para ensalada
**salmon** salmón
~ **trout** trucha asalmonada
**salt(ed)** sal(ado)
**sandwich** bocadillo, emparedado
**sardine** sardina
**sauce** salsa
**sauerkraut** col fermentada
**sausage** salchicha
**sauté(ed)** salteado
**scallop** 1) venera 2) escalope de ternera
**scampi** langostino
**scone** panecillo tierno hecho con harina de avena o cebada
**Scotch broth** caldo a base de carne de carnero o de buey y legumbres
**Scotch woodcock** pan tostado con huevos revueltos y crema de anchoas
**sea bass** róbalo, lubina
**sea kale** col marina
**seafood** mariscos y peces marinos
**(in) season** (en su) época (estación del año)
**seasoning** condimento, sazón
**service** servicio
~ **charge** importe que se paga por el servicio
~ **(not) included** servicio (no) incluido
**set menu** menú fijo
**shad** alosa, sábalo
**shallot** chalote
**shellfish** marisco
**sherbet** sorbete
**shoulder** espalda
**shredded wheat** hojuelas de trigo en croquetas (se sirven en el desayuno)
**shrimp** camarón, gamba
**silverside (of beef)** codillo (de ternera)
**sirloin steak** bistec del solomillo
**skewer** brocheta
**slice** loncha, rodaja
**sliced** cortado en lonchas
**sloppy Joe** carne picada de ternera con una salsa picante de tomates, se sirve en un panecillo
**smelt** eperlano
**smoked** ahumado
**snack** comida ligera
**sole** lenguado
**soup** sopa, crema
**sour** agrio
**soused herring** arenque conservado en vinagre y especias
**spaghetti** espaguetis
~ **and meatballs** con albóndigas
**spare rib** costilla de cerdo casi descarnada
**spice** especia
**spinach** espinaca
**spiny lobster** langosta
**(on a) spit** (en un) espetón
**sponge cake** bizcocho ligero y esponjoso
**sprat** arenque pequeño, sardineta
**squash** calabaza
**starter** entrada
**steak and kidney pie** empanada de carne de ternera y riñones
**steamed** cocido al vapor
**stew** guisado
**Stilton (cheese)** queso inglés afamado (blanco o con mohos

azules)
**strawberry** fresa
**string bean** judía verde
**stuffed** relleno
**stuffing** (el) relleno
**suck(l)ing pig** lechón
**sugar** azúcar
**sugarless** sin azúcar
**sundae** copa de helado con frutas, nueces, nata batida y a veces jarabe
**supper** comida ligera de la noche, cena
**swede** naba de Suecia
**sweet** 1) dulce 2) postre
~ **corn** maíz blanco
~ **potato** batata
**sweetbread** lechecillas
**Swiss cheese** queso suizo (Emmenthal)
**Swiss roll** bizcocho enrollado y relleno de mermelada
**Swiss steak** lonja de ternera asada con legumbres y especias
**T-bone steak** bistec y filete de ternera separados por un hueso en forma de T
**table d'hôte** menú fijo
**tangerine** especie de mandarina
**tarragon** estragón
**tart** tarta de frutas
**tenderloin** filete de carne
**Thousand Island dressing** salsa para ensalada, sazonada, hecha de mayonesa y pimientos
**thyme** tomillo
**toad-in-the-hole** carne de ternera (o salchicha) cubierta de pasta y cocida al horno
**toast** pan tostado, tostada
**toasted** tostado
~ **cheese** pan tostado con queso derretido
**tomato** tomate
**tongue** lengua
**tournedos** bistec espeso del filete (ternera)
**treacle** melaza
**trifle** pastel con jerez o aguardiente, hecho con almendras, mermelada y crema batida o natillas y crema de vainilla
**tripe** tripas, callos
**trout** trucha
**truffle** trufa
**tuna, tunny** atún
**turbot** rodaballo, rombo
**turkey** pavo
**turnip** nabo
**turnover** pastelillo relleno de compota o mermelada
**turtle** tortuga
**underdone** poco hecho
**vanilla** vainilla
**veal** ternera
~ **bird** pulpeta de ternera
**vegetable** legumbre
~ **marrow** calabacín
**venison** caza, corzo
**vichyssoise** sopa fría preparada con puerros, patatas y crema
**vinegar** vinagre
**Virginia baked ham** jamón cocido al horno, adornado con clavos de especia, rebanadas de piña y cerezas; se le baña con el jugo de las frutas
**vol-au-vent** pastel de hojaldre relleno de salsa con crema, trozos de carne y champiñones
**wafer** barquillo
**waffle** especie de barquillo caliente
**Waldorf salad** ensalada de apio, manzanas, nueces y mayonesa
**walnut** nuez
**water ice** sorbete
**watercress** berro de agua
**watermelon** sandía
**well-done** bastante hecho
**Welsh rabbit/rarebit** queso derretido

sobre una tostada
**whelk** buccino (molusco)
**whipped cream** nata batida
**whitebait** boquerón
**Wiener schnitzel** escalope de ternera empanado
**wine list** lista de vinos
**woodcock** becada
**Worcestershire sauce** condimento líquido picante a base de vinagre, soja y ajo
**yam** camote
**yoghurt** yogur
**York ham** jamón de York (ahumado)
**Yorkshire pudding** especie de pasta de hojuelas que se sirve con el rosbif
**zucchini** calabacín
**zwieback** rebanadas tostadas de pan de molde

## Bebidas

**ale** cerveza negra, ligeramente azucarada, fermentada a elevada temperatura
**bitter ~** negra, amarga y más bien pesada
**brown ~** negra de botella, ligeramente azucarada
**light ~** dorada de botella
**mild ~** negra de barril, bastante fuerte
**pale ~** dorada de botella
**angostura** esencia aromática amarga que se añade a los cócteles
**applejack** aguardiente de manzanas
**Athol Brose** bebida escocesa hecha con whisky, miel, agua y a veces copos de avena
**Bacardi cocktail** cóctel de ron con ginebra, jarabe de granadina y jugo de limón
**barley water** bebida refrescante a base de cebada y aromatizada con limón
**barley wine** cerveza negra muy alcoholizada
**beer** cerveza
**bottled ~** de botella
**draft, draught ~** de barril
**bitters** aperitivos y digestivos a base de raíces, corteza o hierbas
**black velvet** champán mezclado con stout (acompaña con frecuencia las ostras)
**bloody Mary** vodka, jugo de tomate y especias
**bourbon** whisky americano, a base de maíz
**brandy** 1) denominación genérica de los aguardientes de uvas y otras frutas 2) coñac
**~ Alexander** mezcla de aguardiente, crema de cacao y nata
**British wines** vino fermentado en Gran Bretaña, fabricado a base de uvas o jugo de uvas importados
**cherry brandy** licor de cerezas
**cider** sidra
**~ cup** mezcla de sidra, especias, azúcar y hielo
**claret** vino tinto de Burdeos
**cobbler** long drink helado a base de frutas, al que se añade vino o licor
**coffee** café
**~ with cream** con nata
**black ~** solo
**caffeine-free ~** descafeinado

**white ~** con leche, cortado
**cordial** licor estimulante y digestivo
**cream** nata
**cup** bebida refrescante a base de vino helado, sifón, un espirituoso y adornada con una raja de naranja, de limón o de pepino
**daiquiri** cóctel de ron con jugo de limón y de piña
**double** doble porción
**Drambuie** licor a base de whisky y miel
**dry martini** 1) vermú seco (GB) 2) cóctel de ginebra con algo de vermú seco (US)
**eggnog** bebida de ron u otro licor fuerte con yemas de huevos batidas y azúcar
**gin** ginebra
**gin and it** mezcla de ginebra y vermú italiano
**gin-fizz** mezcla de ginebra, jugo de limón, sifón y azúcar
**ginger ale** bebida sin alcohol, perfumada con extracto de jengibre
**ginger beer** bebida ligeramente alcohólica, a base de jengibre y azúcar
**grasshopper** mezcla de crema de menta, crema de cacao y nata
**Guinness (stout)** cerveza negra, con gusto muy pronunciado y algo dulce, con mucha malta y lúpulo
**half pint** aproximadamente 3 decilitros
**highball** whisky o aguardiente diluido con agua, soda o ginger ale
**iced** helado
**Irish coffee** café con azúcar y whisky irlandés, cubierto con nata batida (Chantilly)
**Irish Mist** licor irlandés a base de whisky y miel
**Irish whiskey** whisky irlandés menos áspero que el whisky escocés (scotch); además de cebada contiene centeno, avena y trigo
**juice** jugo, zumo
**lager** cerveza dorada ligera
**lemon squash** zumo de limón
**lemonade** limonada
**lime juice** zumo de lima (limón verde)
**liqueur** licor, poscafé
**liquor** aguardiente
**long drink** licor diluido en agua o tónica y servido con cubitos de hielo
**madeira** vino de Madera
**Manhattan** whisky americano, vermú y angostura
**milk** leche
**~ shake** batido
**mineral water** agua mineral
**mulled wine** vino caliente con especias
**neat** bebida pura, sola, sin hielo y sin agua
**old-fashioned** whisky, angostura, cerezas con marrasquino y azúcar
**on the rocks** con cubitos de hielo
**Ovaltine** Ovomaltina
**Pimm's cup(s)** bebida alcohólica compuesta por alguno de los siguientes licores; se mezcla con zumo de fruta y algunas veces con agua de Seltz
**~ No. 1** a base de ginebra
**~ No. 2** a base de whisky
**~ No. 3** a base de ron
**~ No. 4** a base de aguardiente
**pink champagne** champán rosado
**pink lady** mezcla de clara de huevo, Calvados, zumo de limón, jarabe de granadina y ginebra
**pint** aproximadamente 6 decilitros
**port (wine)** (vino de) Oporto
**porter** cerveza negra y amarga
**punch** ponche
**quart** 1,14 litro (US 0,95 litro)

**root beer** bebida edulcorada efervescente, aromatizada con hierbas y raíces
**rum** ron
**rye (whiskey)** whisky de centeno, más pesado y más áspero que el bourbon
**scotch (whisky)** whisky escocés, mezcla de whisky de trigo y de whisky de cebada
**screwdriver** vodka y zumo de naranja
**shandy** bitter ale mezclada con zumo de limón o con una ginger beer
**sherry** jerez
**short drink** todo licor no diluido, puro
**shot** dosis de cualquier licor espirituoso
**sloe gin-fizz** licor de endrina con sifón y zumo de limón
**soda water** agua gaseosa
**soft drink** bebida sin alcohol
**spirits** aguardientes
**stinger** coñac y crema de menta
**stout** cerveza negra con mucho lúpulo y alcohol
**straight** alcohol que se bebe seco, sin mezcla
**tea** té
**toddy** ponche hecho de ron, agua, limón y azúcar
**Tom Collins** ginebra, zumo de limón, sifón y azúcar
**tonic (water)** (agua) tónica, agua gaseosa, a base de quinina
**vermouth** vermú
**water** agua
**whisky sour** whisky, zumo de limón, azúcar y sifón
**wine** vino
  **dessert ~** de postre
  **dry ~** seco
  **red ~** tinto
  **rosé ~** clarete, rosado
  **sparkling ~** espumoso
  **sweet ~** dulce (de postre)
  **white ~** blanco

# Mini-gramática

## El artículo

El artículo determinado (el, la, los, las) tiene una sola forma: *the*.

| | |
|---|---|
| **the room, the rooms** | el cuarto, los cuartos |
| **the end of the month** | el fin del mes |

El artículo indeterminado (un, una, unos, unas) tiene dos formas: *a* se usa cuando precede a sonidos consonantes; *an* antes de sonidos vocales.

**a coat** un abrigo **an umbrella** un paraguas **an hour** una hora

## Plurales

El plural de la mayor parte de los nombres se forma añadiendo -(*e*)*s* al singular. Según el sonido final del singular, el plural se pronuncia -*ss* o -*s* o -*is* (que forma una sílaba extra).

**cup — cups** (taza — tazas) **dress — dresses** (vestido — vestidos)

Los plurales siguientes son irregulares:

| | |
|---|---|
| **man — men** (hombre/s) | **foot — feet** (pie/s) |
| **woman — women** (mujer/es) | **tooth — teeth** (diente/s) |
| **child — children** (niño/s) | **mouse — mice** (ratón/ratones) |

## El posesivo

1. Si el poseedor es una persona: los nombres en singular y los plurales que no terminan en -*s* añaden *'s*.

| | |
|---|---|
| **the boy's room** | el cuarto del muchacho |
| **the children's clothes** | los vestidos de los niños |

Los nombres terminados en -*s* (incluyendo la mayoría de los plurales), añaden solamente el apóstrofe (').

| | |
|---|---|
| **the boys' room** | el cuarto de los muchachos |

2. Si el poseedor no es una persona: se emplea la preposición *of*.

| | |
|---|---|
| **the key of the door** | la llave de la puerta |

## Adjetivos

Los adjetivos preceden normalmente al nombre.

| | |
|---|---|
| **a large brown suitcase** | una maleta marrón grande |

El comparativo y el superlativo de los adjetivos se pueden formar de dos maneras:

1. Los adjetivos monosílabos y muchos adjetivos bisílabos añaden -(*e*)*r* y -(*e*)*st*.

**small** (pequeño) – **smaller** – **smallest**
**busy** (ocupado) – **busier** – **busiest**

2. Los adjetivos de tres sílabas o más y algunos adjetivos de dos sílabas (los que terminan en *-ful* o *-less*, por ejemplo) no sufren inflexión y forman los comparativos y superlativos con las palabras *more* y *most*.

**expensive** (caro) – **more expensive** – **most expensive**
**careful** (cuidadoso) – **more careful** – **most careful**

Nótense los siguientes comparativos irregulares:

**good** (bueno) – **better** – **best**
**bad** (malo) – **worse** – **worst**
**little** (poco) – **less** – **least**
**much/many** (mucho) – **more** – **most**

## Pronombres

| | | Sujeto | Objeto (dir./indir.) | Posesivo 1 | 2 |
|---|---|---|---|---|---|
| Singular | | | | | |
| 1.ª persona | | **I** | **me** | **my** | **mine** |
| 2.ª persona | | **you** | **you** | **your** | **yours** |
| 3.ª persona | (m) | **he** | **him** | **his** | **his** |
| | (f) | **she** | **her** | **her** | **hers** |
| | (n) | **it** | **it** | **its** | – |
| Plural | | | | | |
| 1.ª persona | | **we** | **us** | **our** | **ours** |
| 2.ª persona | | **you** | **you** | **your** | **yours** |
| 3.ª persona | | **they** | **they** | **their** | **theirs** |

*Nota*: en inglés *you* es tanto singular como plural. No existe la distinción como en español entre «tú» y «usted».
El caso acusativo se usa también para el complemento indirecto y antes de las preposiciones.

| | |
|---|---|
| **Give it to me.** | Dámelo. |
| **He came with us.** | Él vino con nosotros. |

La forma 1 del posesivo se usa antes del nombre, la forma 2 se usa sola.

| | |
|---|---|
| **Where's my key?** | ¿Dónde está mi llave? |
| **That's not mine.** | Esa no es mía. |

## Verbos

La misma forma que el infinitivo para todas las personas excepto la 3.ª persona del singular, ésta se forma añadiendo -(*e*)*s* al infinitivo.

| | **to love**<br>amar | **to come**<br>venir | **to go**<br>ir |
|---|---|---|---|
| **I** | **love** | **come** | **go** |
| **you** | **love** | **come** | **go** |
| **he/she** | **loves** | **comes** | **goes** |
| **we** | **love** | **come** | **go** |
| **they** | **love** | **come** | **go** |

Los negativos se forman empleando el verbo auxiliar *do*/*does* + *not* + infinitivo.

**We do not (don't) like this hotel.** No nos gusta este hotel.
**She does not (doesn't) smoke.** Ella no fuma.

Los interrogativos se forman empleando el verbo auxiliar *do* + pronombre + infinitivo.

**Do you like it?** ¿Te gusta?
**Does he live here?** ¿Vive aquí?

### Verbos irregulares

En la siguiente lista damos los verbos irregulares ingleses. Los verbos compuestos o los que llevan un prefijo se conjugan como los verbos simples, por ej.: *mistake* y *overdrive* se conjugan como *take* y *drive*.

| *Infinitivo* | *Pret. indefinido* | *Participio pasado* | |
|---|---|---|---|
| **arise** | arose | arisen | *levantarse* |
| **awake** | awoke | awoken | *despertarse* |
| **be** | was | been | *ser, estar* |
| **bear** | bore | borne | *soportar* |
| **beat** | beat | beaten | *batir* |
| **become** | became | become | *llegar a ser* |
| **begin** | began | begun | *comenzar* |
| **bend** | bent | bent | *doblar* |
| **bet** | bet | bet | *apostar* |
| **bid** | bade/bid | bidden/bid | *pedir* |
| **bind** | bound | bound | *atar* |
| **bite** | bit | bitten | *morder* |
| **bleed** | bled | bled | *sangrar* |

| | | | |
|---|---|---|---|
| **blow** | blew | blown | *soplar* |
| **break** | broke | broken | *romper* |
| **breed** | bred | bred | *criar* |
| **bring** | brought | brought | *traer* |
| **build** | built | built | *construir* |
| **burn** | burnt/burned | burnt/burned | *quemar* |
| **burst** | burst | burst | *reventar* |
| **buy** | bought | bought | *comprar* |
| **can*** | could | — | *poder* |
| **cast** | cast | cast | *arrojar* |
| **catch** | caught | caught | *coger* |
| **choose** | chose | chosen | *escoger* |
| **cling** | clung | clung | *adherirse* |
| **clothe** | clothed/clad | clothed/clad | *vestir* |
| **come** | came | come | *venir* |
| **cost** | cost | cost | *costar* |
| **creep** | crept | crept | *arrastrar* |
| **cut** | cut | cut | *cortar* |
| **deal** | dealt | dealt | *distribuir* |
| **dig** | dug | dug | *cavar* |
| **do (he does)** | did | done | *hacer* |
| **draw** | drew | drawn | *dibujar* |
| **dream** | dreamt/dreamed | dreamt/dreamed | *soñar* |
| **drink** | drank | drunk | *beber* |
| **drive** | drove | driven | *conducir* |
| **dwell** | dwelt | dwelt | *habitar* |
| **eat** | ate | eaten | *comer* |
| **fall** | fell | fallen | *caer* |
| **feed** | fed | fed | *alimentar* |
| **feel** | felt | felt | *sentir* |
| **fight** | fought | fought | *luchar* |
| **find** | found | found | *encontrar* |
| **flee** | fled | fled | *huir* |
| **fling** | flung | flung | *lanzar* |
| **fly** | flew | flown | *volar* |
| **forsake** | forsook | forsaken | *renunciar* |
| **freeze** | froze | frozen | *helar* |
| **get** | got | got | *obtener* |
| **give** | gave | given | *dar* |
| **go** | went | gone | *ir* |
| **grind** | ground | ground | *moler* |
| **grow** | grew | grown | *crecer* |

* presente de indicativo

| | | | |
|---|---|---|---|
| **hang** | hung | hung | *colgar* |
| **have** | had | had | *tener* |
| **hear** | heard | heard | *oír* |
| **hew** | hewed | hewed/hewn | *cortar* |
| **hide** | hid | hidden | *esconder* |
| **hit** | hit | hit | *golpear* |
| **hold** | held | held | *sostener* |
| **hurt** | hurt | hurt | *herir* |
| **keep** | kept | kept | *guardar* |
| **kneel** | knelt | knelt | *arrodillarse* |
| **knit** | knitted/knit | knitted/knit | *juntar* |
| **know** | knew | known | *saber* |
| **lay** | laid | laid | *acostar* |
| **lead** | led | led | *dirigir* |
| **lean** | leant/leaned | leant/leaned | *apoyarse* |
| **leap** | leapt/leaped | leapt/leaped | *saltar* |
| **learn** | learnt/learned | learnt/learned | *aprender* |
| **leave** | left | left | *marcharse* |
| **lend** | lent | lent | *prestar* |
| **let** | let | let | *permitir* |
| **lie** | lay | lain | *acostarse* |
| **light** | lit/lighted | lit/lighted | *encender* |
| **lose** | lost | lost | *perder* |
| **make** | made | made | *hacer* |
| **may*** | might | — | *poder* |
| **mean** | meant | meant | *significar* |
| **meet** | met | met | *encontrar* (*personas*) |
| **mow** | mowed | mowed/mown | *segar* |
| **must*** | — | — | *tener que* |
| **ought (to)*** | — | — | *deber* |
| **pay** | paid | paid | *pagar* |
| **put** | put | put | *poner* |
| **read** | read | read | *leer* |
| **rid** | rid | rid | *desembarazar* |
| **ride** | rode | ridden | *cabalgar* |
| **ring** | rang | rung | *sonar* |
| **rise** | rose | risen | *ascender* |
| **run** | ran | run | *correr* |
| **saw** | sawed | sawn | *aserrar* |
| **say** | said | said | *decir* |
| **see** | saw | seen | *ver* |
| **seek** | sought | sought | *buscar* |

* presente de indicativo

| | | | |
|---|---|---|---|
| **sell** | sold | sold | *vender* |
| **send** | sent | sent | *enviar* |
| **set** | set | set | *poner* |
| **sew** | sewed | sewed/sewn | *coser* |
| **shake** | shook | shaken | *agitar* |
| **shall*** | should | — | *deber* |
| **shed** | shed | shed | *desprenderse* |
| **shine** | shone | shone | *brillar* |
| **shoot** | shot | shot | *tirar* |
| **show** | showed | shown | *mostrar* |
| **shrink** | shrank | shrunk | *encogerse* |
| **shut** | shut | shut | *cerrar* |
| **sing** | sang | sung | *cantar* |
| **sink** | sank | sunk | *hundir* |
| **sit** | sat | sat | *sentarse* |
| **sleep** | slept | slept | *dormir* |
| **slide** | slid | slid | *resbalar* |
| **sling** | slung | slung | *lanzar* |
| **slink** | slunk | slunk | *escabullirse* |
| **slit** | slit | slit | *rajar* |
| **smell** | smelled/smelt | smelled/smelt | *oler* |
| **sow** | sowed | sown/sowed | *sembrar* |
| **speak** | spoke | spoken | *hablar* |
| **speed** | sped/speeded | sped/speeded | *apresurarse* |
| **spell** | spelt/spelled | spelt/spelled | *deletrear* |
| **spend** | spent | spent | *gastar* |
| **spill** | spilt/spilled | spilt/spilled | *derramar* |
| **spin** | spun | spun | *girar* |
| **spit** | spat | spat | *escupir* |
| **split** | split | split | *rajar* |
| **spoil** | spoilt/spoiled | spoilt/spoiled | *estropear* |
| **spread** | spread | spread | *extender* |
| **spring** | sprang | sprung | *saltar* |
| **stand** | stood | stood | *estar de pie* |
| **steal** | stole | stolen | *robar* |
| **stick** | stuck | stuck | *hundir* |
| **sting** | stung | stung | *picar* |
| **stink** | stank/stunk | stunk | *apestar* |
| **strew** | strewed | strewed/strewn | *esparcir* |
| **stride** | strode | stridden | *andar a pasos largos* |
| **strike** | struck | struck/stricken | *golpear* |
| **string** | strung | strung | *atar* |

* presente de indicativo

| | | | |
|---|---|---|---|
| **strive** | strove | striven | *esforzarse* |
| **swear** | swore | sworn | *jurar* |
| **sweep** | swept | swept | *barrer* |
| **swell** | swelled | swollen | *hinchar* |
| **swim** | swam | swum | *nadar* |
| **swing** | swung | swung | *balancearse* |
| **take** | took | taken | *tomar* |
| **teach** | taught | taught | *enseñar* |
| **tear** | tore | torn | *desgarrar* |
| **tell** | told | told | *decir* |
| **think** | thought | thought | *pensar* |
| **throw** | threw | thrown | *arrojar* |
| **thrust** | thrust | thrust | *impeler* |
| **tread** | trod | trodden | *pisotear* |
| **wake** | woke/waked | woken/waked | *despertar* |
| **wear** | wore | worn | *llevar puesto* |
| **weave** | wove | woven | *tejer* |
| **weep** | wept | wept | *llorar* |
| **will*** | would | – | *querer* |
| **win** | won | won | *ganar* |
| **wind** | wound | wound | *enrollar* |
| **wring** | wrung | wrung | *torcer* |
| **write** | wrote | written | *escribir* |

* presente de indicativo

# Abreviaturas inglesas

| | | |
|---|---|---|
| **AA** | *Automobile Association* | Asociación Automovilística |
| **AAA** | *American Automobile Association* | Asociación Automovilística de los Estados Unidos |
| **ABC** | *American Broadcasting Company* | Sociedad Privada de Radiodifusión y Televisión (EE.UU.) |
| **A.D.** | *anno Domini* | año de Cristo |
| **Am.** | *America; American* | América; americano |
| **a.m.** | *ante meridiem (before noon)* | de la mañana (de 00.00 a 12.00 h.) |
| **Amtrak** | *American railroad corporation* | Sociedad Privada de Compañías de Ferrocarriles Americanos |
| **AT & T** | *American Telephone and Telegraph Company* | Compañía Americana de Teléfonos y Telégrafos |
| **Ave.** | *avenue* | avenida |
| **BBC** | *British Broadcasting Corporation* | Sociedad Británica de Radiodifusión y Televisión |
| **B.C.** | *before Christ* | antes de Cristo |
| **bldg.** | *building* | edificio |
| **Blvd.** | *boulevard* | bulevar |
| **B.R.** | *British Rail* | Ferrocarriles Británicos |
| **Brit.** | *Britain; British* | Gran Bretaña; británico |
| **Bros.** | *brothers* | hermanos |
| **¢** | *cent* | 1/100 de dólar |
| **Can.** | *Canada; Canadian* | Canadá; canadiense |
| **CBS** | *Columbia Broadcasting System* | Sociedad Privada de Radiodifusión y Televisión (EE.UU.) |
| **CID** | *Criminal Investigation Department* | Oficina de Investigación Criminal |
| **CNR** | *Canadian National Railway* | Ferrocarriles Canadienses |
| **c/o** | *(in) care of* | al cuidado de |
| **Co.** | *company* | compañía |
| **Corp.** | *corporation* | compañía |
| **CPR** | *Canadian Pacific Railways* | Compañía Privada de Ferrocarriles Canadienses |
| **D.C.** | *District of Columbia* | Distrito de Columbia (Washington, D.C.) |
| **DDS** | *Doctor of Dental Science* | Dentista |
| **dept.** | *department* | departamento, división administrativa |
| **EEC** | *European Economic Community* | Comunidad Económica Europea |
| **e.g.** | *for instance* | por ejemplo, verbigracia |
| **Eng.** | *England; English* | Inglaterra; inglés |
| **excl.** | *excluding; exclusive* | no incluido |

| | | |
|---|---|---|
| **ft.** | *foot/feet* | pie/pies (medida: 30,5 cm.) |
| **GB** | *Great Britain* | Gran Bretaña |
| **H.E.** | *His/Her Excellency; His Eminence* | Su Excelencia; Su Eminencia |
| **H.H.** | *His Holiness* | Su Santidad |
| **H.M.** | *His/Her Majesty* | Su Majestad |
| **H.M.S.** | *Her Majesty's ship* | navío de guerra británico |
| **hp** | *horsepower* | caballos de vapor |
| **Hwy** | *highway* | carretera principal |
| **i.e.** | *that is to say* | a saber, es decir |
| **in.** | *inch* | pulgada (medida: 2,54 cm.) |
| **Inc.** | *incorporated* | Sociedad Anónima |
| **incl.** | *including, inclusive* | incluido |
| **£** | *pound sterling* | libra esterlina |
| **L.A.** | *Los Angeles* | Los Angeles |
| **Ltd.** | *limited* | Sociedad Anónima |
| **M.D.** | *Doctor of Medicine* | médico |
| **M.P.** | *Member of Parliament* | Miembro del Parlamento |
| **mph** | *miles per hour* | millas por hora |
| **Mr.** | *Mister* | Señor |
| **Mrs.** | *Missis* | Señora |
| **Ms.** | *Missis/Miss* | Señora/Señorita |
| **nat.** | *national* | nacional |
| **NBC** | *National Broadcasting Company* | Sociedad Privada de Radiodifusión y Televisión (EE.UU.) |
| **No.** | *number* | número |
| **N.Y.C.** | *New York City* | Ciudad de Nueva York |
| **O.B.E.** | *Officer (of the Order) of the British Empire* | Caballero de la Orden del Imperio Británico |
| **p.** | *page; penny/pence* | página; 1/100 de libra |
| **p.a.** | *per annum* | por año |
| **Ph.D.** | *Doctor of Philosophy* | Doctor en Filosofía |
| **p.m.** | *post meridiem (after noon)* | de la tarde/noche (de 12.00 a 24.00 h.) |
| **PO** | *Post Office* | Oficina de Correos |
| **POO** | *post office order* | giro postal |
| **pop.** | *population* | población |
| **P.T.O.** | *please turn over* | vuelva la página, por favor |
| **RAC** | *Royal Automobile Club* | Real Club Autómovil (Gran Bretaña) |
| **RCMP** | *Royal Canadian Mounted Police* | Policía Montada de Canadá |
| **Rd.** | *road* | carretera |
| **ref.** | *reference* | referencia |

| | | |
|---|---|---|
| **Rev.** | *reverend* | Reverendo (pastor de la Iglesia Anglicana) |
| **RFD** | *rural free delivery* | distribución del correo en el campo |
| **RR** | *railroad* | ferrocarril |
| **RSVP** | *please reply* | se ruega contestación |
| **$** | *dollar* | dólar |
| **Soc.** | *society* | sociedad |
| **St.** | *saint; street* | santo(a); calle |
| **STD** | *Subscriber Trunk Dialling* | teléfono automático |
| **UN** | *United Nations* | Organización de las Naciones Unidas |
| **UPS** | *United Parcel Service* | Compañía Privada de Expedición de Paquetes (EE.UU.) |
| **US** | *United States* | Estados Unidos de América |
| **USS** | *United States Ship* | navío de guerra (EE.UU.) |
| **VAT** | *value added tax* | tasa al valor añadido |
| **VIP** | *very important person* | persona importante que beneficia de ventajas particulares |
| **Xmas** | *Christmas* | Navidad |
| **yd.** | *yard* | yarda (medida: 91,44 cm.) |
| **YMCA** | *Young Men's Christian Association* | Asociación Cristiana de Muchachos |
| **YWCA** | *Young Women's Christian Association* | Asociación Cristiana de Muchachas |
| **ZIP** | *ZIP code* | número de distrito postal |

# Numerales

## Cardinales

| | |
|---|---|
| 0 | zero |
| 1 | one |
| 2 | two |
| 3 | three |
| 4 | four |
| 5 | five |
| 6 | six |
| 7 | seven |
| 8 | eight |
| 9 | nine |
| 10 | ten |
| 11 | eleven |
| 12 | twelve |
| 13 | thirteen |
| 14 | fourteen |
| 15 | fifteen |
| 16 | sixteen |
| 17 | seventeen |
| 18 | eighteen |
| 19 | nineteen |
| 20 | twenty |
| 21 | twenty-one |
| 22 | twenty-two |
| 23 | twenty-three |
| 24 | twenty-four |
| 25 | twenty-five |
| 30 | thirty |
| 40 | forty |
| 50 | fifty |
| 60 | sixty |
| 70 | seventy |
| 80 | eighty |
| 90 | ninety |
| 100 | a/one hundred |
| 230 | two hundred and thirty |
| 500 | five hundred |
| 1,000 | a/one thousand |
| 10,000 | ten thousand |
| 100,000 | a/one hundred thousand |
| 1,000,000 | a/one million |

## Ordinales

| | |
|---|---|
| 1st | first |
| 2nd | second |
| 3rd | third |
| 4th | fourth |
| 5th | fifth |
| 6th | sixth |
| 7th | seventh |
| 8th | eighth |
| 9th | ninth |
| 10th | tenth |
| 11th | eleventh |
| 12th | twelfth |
| 13th | thirteenth |
| 14th | fourteenth |
| 15th | fifteenth |
| 16th | sixteenth |
| 17th | seventeenth |
| 18th | eighteenth |
| 19th | nineteenth |
| 20th | twentieth |
| 21st | twenty-first |
| 22nd | twenty-second |
| 23rd | twenty-third |
| 24th | twenty-fourth |
| 25th | twenty-fifth |
| 26th | twenty-sixth |
| 27th | twenty-seventh |
| 28th | twenty-eighth |
| 29th | twenty-ninth |
| 30th | thirtieth |
| 40th | fortieth |
| 50th | fiftieth |
| 60th | sixtieth |
| 70th | seventieth |
| 80th | eightieth |
| 90th | ninetieth |
| 100th | hundredth |
| 230th | two hundred and thirtieth |
| 500th | five hundredth |
| 1,000th | thousandth |

## La hora

Los británicos y los americanos utilizan el sistema de 12 horas. La abreviatura *a.m.* (*ante meridiem*) designa las horas anteriores al mediodía, *p.m.* (*post meridiem*) las de la tarde o de la noche. Sin embargo, en Gran Bretaña existe la tendencia, cada vez más acentuada, a indicar los horarios como en el continente.

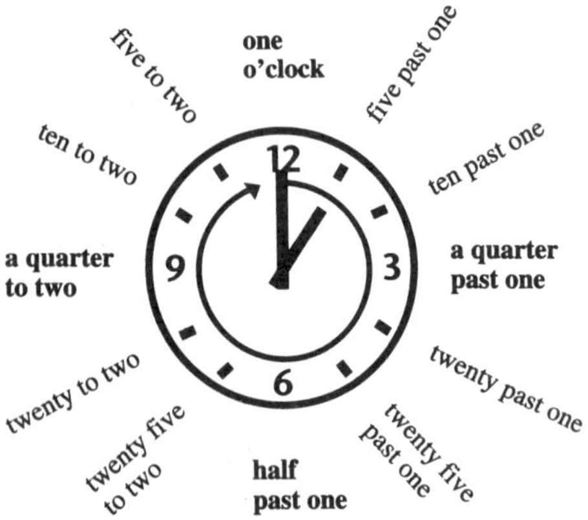


| | |
|---|---|
| *I'll come at seven a.m.* | Vendré a las 7 de la mañana. |
| *I'll come at two p.m.* | Vendré a las 2 de la tarde. |
| *I'll come at eight p.m.* | Vendré a las 8 de la noche. |

### Los días de la semana

| | | | |
|---|---|---|---|
| *Sunday* | domingo | *Thursday* | jueves |
| *Monday* | lunes | *Friday* | viernes |
| *Tuesday* | martes | *Saturday* | sábado |
| *Wednesday* | miércoles | | |

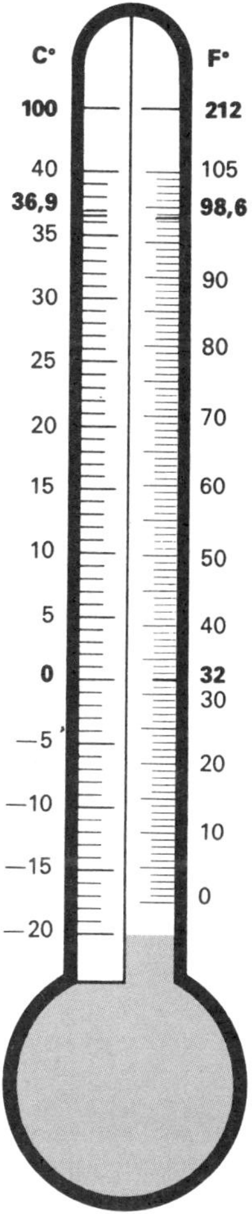


# Conversion tables/ Tablas de conversión

## Metres and Feet

The figure in the middle stands for both metres and feet, e.g. 1 metre = 3.281 ft. and 1 foot = 0.30 m.

## Metros y pies

Los números de la columna del centro son válidos tanto para los metros, como para los pies, p.ej.: 1 metro = 3,281 pies, 1 pie = 0,30 metros.

| Metres/Metros | | Feet/Pies |
|---|---|---|
| 0.30 | **1** | 3.281 |
| 0.61 | **2** | 6.563 |
| 0.91 | **3** | 9.843 |
| 1.22 | **4** | 13.124 |
| 1.52 | **5** | 16.403 |
| 1.83 | **6** | 19.686 |
| 2.13 | **7** | 22.967 |
| 2.44 | **8** | 26.248 |
| 2.74 | **9** | 29.529 |
| 3.05 | **10** | 32.810 |
| 3.66 | **12** | 39.372 |
| 4.27 | **14** | 45.934 |
| 6.10 | **20** | 65.620 |
| 7.62 | **25** | 82.023 |
| 15.24 | **50** | 164.046 |
| 22.86 | **75** | 246.069 |
| 30.48 | **100** | 328.092 |

## Temperature

To convert Centigrade to Fahrenheit, multiply by 1.8 and add 32.
To convert Fahrenheit to Centigrade, subtract 32 from Fahrenheit and divide by 1.8.

## Temperatura

Para convertir de grados Celsius a Fahrenheit, se multiplica la cantidad de grados Celsius por 1,8 y luego se añade 32.
Para convertir de Fahrenheit a Celsius, se resta 32 y luego se divide por 1,8.